Roster of Ohio Soldiers in the War of 1812

Adjutant General of Ohio

HERITAGE BOOKS
2007

HERITAGE BOOKS
AN IMPRINT OF HERITAGE BOOKS, INC.

Books, CDs, and more—Worldwide

For our listing of thousands of titles see our website
at
www.HeritageBooks.com

A Facsimile Reprint
Published 2007 by
HERITAGE BOOKS, INC.
Publishing Division
65 East Main Street
Westminster, Maryland 21157-5026

Copyright © 1995 Heritage Books

— Publisher's Notice —
In reprints such as this, it is often not possible to remove blemishes from the original. We feel the contents of this book warrant its reissue despite these blemishes and hope you will agree and read it with pleasure.

International Standard Book Number: 978-0-7884-0198-5

surname is shown as "Pimcions" or he on page 53 who is identified as James "Durmp."

All that said, we are most fortunate to have this fine source, and of the more than 25,000 names appearing here, most are spelled in one of the more common variations familiar to family researchers of those lines. As to those names not so recognizable, we are challenged and must strive to translate them. Their children and grandchildren moved on to settle and populate the early west, all of the states, and even Alaska and Hawaii. The faceless names found here are the ancestors of hundreds of thousands of Americans, and, but for this listing, the memories of many are lost to all time.

Paul Drake, J.D.
March, 1995

All photographs, including front cover, courtesy of
George and Mary Ann Jones Thomas of Radnor, Ohio.

ROSTER

OF

OHIO SOLDIERS

IN THE

WAR of 1812

Published Under Authority of Law by
THE ADJUTANT GENERAL OF OHIO.
1916.

(House Bill No. 572.)

AN ACT

Authorizing the publication and distribution of a roster of Ohio soldiers in the war with Spain.

Be it enacted by the General Assembly of the State of Ohio:

Section 1. That the governor, secretary of state and adjutant general be, and they are, hereby authorized to secure the publication, in book form, of a complete roster of all Ohio soldiers who entered the volunteer service of the United States in the war with Spain and in the war of 1812; said publication to contain the main items of the record of each officer and soldier, as shown by the rolls in the adjutant general's office, and in the war department at Washington.

They shall begin such work as soon as practicable and continue the same until the roster is completed, the preparation, to be under the direction of the adjutant general, and the printing and binding to be under the direction of the supervisor of public printing.

For the preparation, printing and binding of such roster, of which not more than 10,000 copies shall be printed, there is hereby appropriated, out of any money in the state treasury to the credit of the general revenue fund, not otherwise appropriated, the sum of fifteen thousand dollars, or so much thereof as may be necessary for the purpose.

Section 2. The distribution of said volumes shall be under the direction of the adjutant general and shall be as follows:

To each member of the general assembly, ten copies.

To the adjutant general, for distribution to the adjutants general of each state and territory, and proper officials of the Ware Department at Washington, D. C., seventy copies.

To each state officer of Ohio (elective or appointive), to be kept as a part of the official records of his office, one copy.

To the state library, fifty copies for exchanges, and ten copies to be retained permanently therein.

To each incorporated public library of the state, one copy.

To each county recorder, to be by him kept in his office, and transferred to his successor as other public records, one copy.

The remainder of said copies after such distribution shall be placed on sale by the adjutant general, at a price not exceeding $1.00 per volume. He shall keep a record of such sales, and shall, at the end of each quarter of the fiscal year, pay into the state treasury the sum received, until all of said volumes are sold, unless otherwise directed by the general assembly; provided that he shall not sell more than one copy of each of said volumes to the same person.

CHARLES D. CONOVER,
Speaker of the House of Representatives.

C. J. HOWARD,
President pro tem. of the Senate.

Passed May 19, 1915.
Approved May 25, 1915.
FRANK B. WILLIS, Governor.

Press of The Edward T. Miller Co., Columbus, Ohio.

INTRODUCTION

It takes but a few hours for the beginning family researcher to come to the realization that over the years virtually all surnames, even the simplest ones (and many given names, as well) have been spelled in a wide variety of ways. The causes of those variations are several.

During the early years of the midwest of today, wherein was to be found Ohio (it gained statehood in 1803), except for small communities wherein groups of farmers or small merchant immigrants retained the religion, languages and customs of their homelands, the dominant language--that spoken by the majority of the settlers and required by the legal and taxing systems--was English. So it was that those who could read and write that language (often only barely so) did the pronunciation, spelling, writing, and frequently the communication for those who did not so speak and write.

Even then, since the newcomers could pronounce but not spell their names, spelling was very often phonetic. Were that not enough to bring wide variety, spelling was not very important to those busy ancestors, and references to a dictionary (only the Englishman, Samuel Johnson, had written one of quality) were almost unknown, especially on the outer edges of settlement.

In order to learn something of the new language and customs, and to have some additional income (small as it usually was), many of the early male foreign-speaking migrants to the frontier--especially the unmarried of those groups--went "soldiering." Free public education being quite unknown to adult society, the personal contact and camaraderie gained by such military duty very often served to supply just that measure of communication and understanding needed to start a "foreigner" off on his course to citizenship, a highly desired status for almost all.

Those forces were fully at play in Ohio when the War of 1812 began. For the most part, the state had been settled from the south and east by the people of Maryland, Virginia (including the West Virginia of today), and Kentucky, who brought with them their English tongue and institutions. However, Ohio was also witnessing an ever increasing movement of the "Dutch" westward from Pennsylvania and New York, especially young men and their new families.

The anticipation and talk of the war aroused in these settlers, both American and foreign-born, a measure of patriotism, but even more, there was a deep desire to defend their homes and families against what was perceived as a grave danger in the form of movements of hostile Indians from the north and west who, as in earlier years, were thought to have allied themselves with the British. After all, had Colonel Crawford not been burned to death at Upper Sandusky only thirty years earlier, and were there not yet remnants of tribes in and about the northwestern quadrant of that new state, occupying lands that had been reserved to them "forever" by the Greenville Treaty of 1795, just fifteen years before?

So it was that a willing Ohio soldiery was aroused and organized into units, wherein those who commanded and set forth the records almost always spoke and wrote in English (albeit often very poorly) while many of the common soldiers, no matter how accomplished they may have been in their native tongues, could not write or spell in this, their soon to be adopted language.

In addition to these spelling and phonetic variations, there were two problems that were inherent to all record keeping of that day and time. One of these was that the instruments used for creating longhand writings were goose quills--tail feathers with a slot cut in the point end--and were difficult to use with precision, especially when the movement of the writing hand was sharply to the left or right. The other problem was that the ink into which those "pens" were dipped was of a caustic composition that would one day discolor, if not nearly destroy, the paper upon which the records were written.

There was yet one final factor that tended toward unusual spelling, misinterpretations, inaccuracy, and later illegibility in some of the entries to be found here. This transcription from the original handwritten records was not ordered until 1915, one hundred plus years after the records were made, and it is readily apparent that the transcribers were clerks--public servants--and not historians; they were scribes, not genealogists.

So it is that while those of us who have struggled with such as the German Schneyder/Schnider/Snider/Snyder, Beattie/Beaty/Baty, Schaeffer/Shaeffer/Shafer, Schmidt/Smith, and the like, might find that Megrue (p. 19) is readily recognizable as McGrew, Gibruth (p. 103) surely was Galbreath, Gagany (p. 99) was Cagney, Creechbarme (p. 109) was Kreichbaum, Cookns (p. 38) meant Gookins, and Jinkings (p. 122), instead, was Jenkins, what are we to make of "Hesbr" (p. 18), "His" (p. 20), "Keyt" (p. 38), "Martindits" (p. 155), "Rerigh" (p. 126), "Rethn" (p. 13), "Searfus" (p. 32), "Sirk" (p. 90), "Statelu" (p. 16), and, perhaps most mystifying of all, the man on page 27 whose

THE WAR of 1812

Because of war having been declared, President Madison issued instructions to Governor Return Jonathan Meigs of Ohio, on April 6, 1812, to assemble the Militia at Dayton, Ohio, to be drilled and prepared to march to Detroit.

By the end of the month more than the required number of men had been enrolled.

Early in May these troops were fairly equipped and had chosen their Field Officers. The President had commissioned Governor Hull of Michigan, as Brigadier General. General Hull arrived at Dayton, Ohio, on May 25, 1812, and left with his troops, June 1.

According to the records in The Adjutant General's Department at Columbus, Ohio furnished for this war 1759 Officers and 24,521 Enlisted men distributed as follows:

First Regiment Infantry, 108 Companies.
Second Regiment Infantry, 85 Companies.
Third Regiment Infantry, 56 Companies.
Unassigned Infantry, 185 Companies.
Assigned to U. S. Infantry, 5 Companies.
Mounted Infantry, 25 Companies.
Cavalry, 13 Troops.
Artillery, 1 Battery.

ROSTER OF OHIO SOLDIERS IN WAR OF 1812

Page 142. Vol. I.

GENERAL AND FIELD OFFICERS WAR OF 1812-1813.
MAJOR GENERAL ELIJAH WADSWORTH. 4TH DIVISION. OHIO MILITIA.

Rank and Name of Soldier.	Rank and Name of Soldier.	Rank and Name of Soldier.
Maj. Gen. Elijah Wadsworth	Q. M. Gen. Nehemiah King.	Ass't Q. M. Gen. John Austin
Maj. Benjamin Fappeno	Maj. Elisha Whittlesey	Maj. and Insp. G. Pease
Surg. Elijah Coleman	Chaplain, Jonothan Leslie	A. A. G. Josiah M. Brown
P. F. M. Eliphalet Austin	P. W. M. James Hillman	Ass't. W. M. Fred K. Wadsworth
Ass't. F. M. James Kingsbury	Ass't W. M. Israel Robinson	Ass't. P. F. M. Robert Harper
Ass't Q. M. Gen. Lewis Hoyt.	Ass't. Dep. W. M. Jas. Quigley	Ass't. F. M. Wm. Ingersol
F. M. Eliphalet Austin, Jr.	Hosp. —— Oristes K. Hawley	

Page 209 Vol. I.

BRIG. GEN. ROBERT LUCAS. SECOND BRIGADE. OHIO MILITIA.

Brig. Gen. Robert Lucas	Brig. Q. M. Ezra Osborn	Brig. Insp. Wm. Rutledge
Judge Ad. William K. Bond	Maj. P. D. Butler	Capt. Jason B. Curtis

Page 206 Vol. I.

PERSONAL PAYMENTS.

Brig. Gen. Edward W. Tupper	Brig. Gen. John Wingate	Lieut. Col. David Sutton
Maj. Robert Taylor	Maj. Isaiah Ferguson	Maj. Josiah Mott
Brig. Maj. Horace Nye	Maj. George Adams	Maj. Alexander C. Lanier
Maj. Henry Price	Maj. Charles Wolverton	Brig. Q. M. Robert Safford
Brig. Q. M. W. Marshall	Brig. Q. M. James Heaton	Brig. Insp. Horace Nye
Surg. James Wilson	Surg. Reuben Lamb	Q. M. Thomas Thompson
Q. M. Mathew Hewson	Chaplain, Elias Dickens	Capt. William Prince
Capt. R. Westfall	Adjt. E. Hutchinson	Adjt. Alexander Brown
Sergt. Maj. John McCabe	Surg. Mate, William B. Gould	Surg. Mate, Walter Buel
Surg. Mate, James Wilson	Surg. Mate, Able Slaybrook	Surg. Mate, Moses A. Ferris
Drum Maj. James Richardson	Fife Maj. Jacob Stewart	Q. M. Sergt. James Butler
Private, John McDonnell	William Lytle	

Page 207. Vol. I.

Brig. Gen. James Menary	Col. John Ferguson	Col. John McDonald
Col. William Keys	Col. Daniel Collier	Col. James Stewart
Col. Allen Trimble	Col. Jacob Noel	Col. Mills Stephenson
Maj. Benjamin Daniels	Maj. Geo. Edwards	Maj. John Lewis
Capt. Andrew Canell	Ensign Robert Stephens	

Page 208 Vol. I.

Brig. Gen. S. Perkins	Lieut. Col. Wm. W. Cotgreave	Lieut. Col. Thomas Kirkpatrick
Lieut. Col. Mills Stephenson	Maj. R. Beall	Maj. Anthony Pitzer
Maj. E. Whittlesay	Surg. Albron T. Crow	Brig. Q. M. Leyman Austin
Capt. William McConnell	Capt. William S. Drake	Capt. Robert McElwain
Capt. Joseph R. McClure	Capt. William Morrow	Capt. George Yoakin
Chaplain, Joseph Badger	Lieut. Thomas Ewing	Lieut. Jacob Wisecawere
Lieut. William Missner	Ensign John Brown	Surg. Mate, Samuel McKeehan
Surg. Mate, John McCullough	Private, William Morrow	

FIELD OFFICERS, STAFFS NOT GIVEN.

Page 118	Col. A. Butler		Page 193	Col. Campbell
" 87	Col. John T. Edwards		" 156	Col. Samuel Finley
" 16	Col. James McPherson		" 64	Col. A. Root
" 93	Maj. Andrew Byerly		" 78	Maj. William Ward
" 235	Maj. Womeldorf			

GENERAL AND FIELD OFFICERS.
Staffs Not Given.

Vol. 2.

Page 244	Maj. Gen. Wm. H. Harrison
	Brig. Gen. Edmund Munger
Page 4	Brig. Gen. Simon Perkins
" 363	Brig. Gen. John Wingate
" 397	Brig. Gen. Robert Lucas
" 244	Colonel Alexander Ewing
" 132	Colonel John Furgeson, First Regiment.
" 381	Colonel Samuel Findlay, First Regiment.
" 97	Colonel Gano, First Regiment.
" 105	Colonel William Key, First Regiment.
" 119	Colonel James Mills, First Regiment.
" 229	Colonel James Miller, First Regiment.
" 95	Colonel John McDonald, First Regiment.
" 174	Colonel Jacob Noel, First Regiment.
" 111	Lieut. Col. John Riddle, First Regiment.
" 239	Lieut. Col. Feron Holt, First Regiment.
" 394	Lieut. Col. Robert Bay, First Cavalry.
" 244	Major Paul F. Butler.
" 244	Major William Beatty.
" 244	Major James Colwell.
" 244	Major Jerome Holt.
" 244	Major Thomas Moore.
" 211	Major George Adams, First Regiment.
" 113	Major George Edwards, First Regiment.
" 195	Major Jacob Myers, First Regiment.
" 398	Major Samuel Connell, First Cavalry.
" 395	Major Israel Dawson, First Cavalry.

ROSTER OF OHIO SOLDIERS IN WAR OF 1812

Pages 244-245 Vol. 2.

ROLL OF FIELD AND STAFF. WAR OF 1812-1813.
COL. DUNCAN McARTHUR. FIRST REGIMENT. OHIO MILITIA.

Rank and Name of Soldier.
Col. Duncan McArthur
Adjt. Wm. H. Putthorf
Maj. Thomas A. Vanhorne
Q. M. John McDonald
Surg. Samuel Metadow
P. M's. Clk., Q. L. Pleissis
Sergt. Maj. Hugh Wood
Fife Maj. Russell R. Chapman

Rank and Name of Soldier.
Maj. James Denny
Maj. Jeremiah Munson
Q. M. Richard Douglas
Q. M. Sergt. Avery Powers
Surg. Mate, Lincoln Goodale
Drum Maj. Avery Buttles

Rank and Name of Soldier.
Maj. William A. Trimble
Maj. Robert Morrison
Q. M. James Foster
Q. M. Sergt. John Fisher
Pay Master, John McDonald
Sergt. Maj. Thomas Lloyd
Fife Maj. Solomon Fredericks

FIRST REGIMENT OHIO MILITIA. WAR OF 1812-1813.
ROLL OF CAPT. JAMES ALEXANDER'S COMPANY.
(Probably from Jefferson County.)

Page 3. Vol. 2.

Page 31.

Served from August 23 1812 until November 30, 1813.

Capt. James Alexander
Sergt. Samuel Andrews
Sergt. James Tobin
Corp. John Anderson

Lieut. Henry Boyles
Sergt. Alexander Barr
Corp. David Williamson
Corp. James Lyons

Ensign John Myers
Sergt. Martin Saltzman
Corp. Amos West
Corp. Hugh Adams

Privates.
Bay, Joseph
Berry, James
Bennet, William
Call, David
Casselman, David
Duke, William
Groves, Peter
Hytes, George
Johnston, John
Lawrence, James
Laughlin, Nathaniel
Peterson, Peter
Pittinger, Thomas
Saltsman, David.
Sapp, George
Wright, Jacob

Privates.
Alexander, William
Brooks, William
Bennet, Griffith
Call, John
Casselman, William
France, John
Gamble, Henry
Hytes, John
Kinder, Peter
Laughlin, James
Lawrence, William
Prichard, Ziphani
Peterson, William
Swickard, Daniel
Stain, Michael

Privates.
Barr, James D.
Barr, John
Bawers, John
Crawford, Benedict
Culp, Jacob
Grover, Jacob
Householder, George
Hartman, George
Lowery, Alexander
Laughlin, John
Mathers, Levi
Painter, Jacob
Saltsman, Andrews
Swickard, Daniel, Sr
Wells, James

Page 80 Vol. i.

Privates.
Alexander, William
Casselman, William
Johnson, John
Laughlin, Mathew
Peterson, Peter
Peterson, William
Saltman, Daniel
Wright, Jacob

Privates.
Bennett, Griffith
Duke, William
Lawrence, William
Lyons, James
Painter, Jacob
Starn, Michael
Swickard, Daniel, Jr.
Wells, James

Privates.
Bowers, John
Hales, Joel
Laughlin, John
Mathews, Levi
Pitteger, Thomas
Saltman, Andrew
Sapp, George

Page 4. Vol. 2.

LIEUT. COL. JOHN ANDREWS. FIRST REGIMENT. OHIO MILITIA.

Lieut. Col. John Andrews
Maj. George Darrow
Q. M. Jacob Van Hoene
Surg. Mate, Samuel McRickan
Drum Maj. John Hytes

Maj. Thomas Glenn
Maj. Jacob Frederick
Q. M. Sergt. John Patterson
Sergt. Maj. John B. Lowden
Fife Maj. John Neel

Maj. James Campbell
Adjt. Mordecai Bartley
Surg. Thomas Campbell
Drum. Maj. John McClintock
David Kinsey

Page 243. Vol. 2.

COLONEL JOHN DeLONG. FIRST REGIMENT. OHIO MILITIA.

Col. John DeLong
Adjt. Anthony Weyer
Surg. Henry H. Evans
Surg. Mate, Robert Young

Maj. William Crooks
Q. M. John Hanna
Surg. Mate, Thomas Host
Pay Master, Jonothan Carlton

Maj. Wm. Henderson
Q. M. Sergt. James Boy
Surg. Mate, John Harrison

Page 242. Vol. 2.

COLONEL JOHN WILLIAMSON. FIRST REGIMENT. OHIO MILITIA.

Col. John Williamson

Surg. Timothy Burr

Q. M. Sergt. John H. Mifford

Page 243 Vol. 2.

MAJOR JOSEPH JENKINSON. FIRST REGIMENT. OHIO MILITIA.

Maj. Joseph Jenkinson
Q. M. Sergt. Coleman Avery
Fife Maj. Samuel Bonnel

Adjt. John Pursel
Surg. Stephen Woods

Q. M. Joseph Warner
Drum Maj. Alvin Wheeler

ROSTER OF OHIO SOLDIERS IN WAR OF 1812

Page 243 Vol. 2.
COLONEL DAVID SUTTON. FIRST REGIMENT. OHIO MILITIA.

Rank and Name of Soldier.	Rank and Name of Soldier.	Rank and Name of Soldier.
Col. David Sutton	Maj. James Galloway	Pay Master, John H. Smith
Lieut & Clk., John C. McMames.	Surg. Mate, Wm. Greenle	Sergt. Maj. James Reading.

Page 243 Vol. 2.
COLONEL JAMES DENNY. FRST REGIMENT. OHIO MILITIA.

Col. James Denny	Maj. Valentine Keffer	Maj. John Boggs
Adjt. Bartholomew Fryatt	Q. M. Ralph Osborn	Q. M. and Lieut. Joseph Yates
Q. M. Sergt. Samuel Pontius	Surg. Prentice Pork	Pay Master, Ralph Osborn
Sergt. Maj. Joseph Shelby	Sergt. Maj. Thomas Hair	Drum Maj. Charles Swangle

Page 243 Vol. 2.
LIEUT. COL. ALEXANDER ENOS. FIRST REGIMENT. OHIO MILITIA.

Lieut. Col. Alexander Enos	Maj. Samuel Watson	Adjt. Jacob Catterlin
Adjt. John Stilly	Q. M. Samuel Kratzer	Q. M. John Hawn

ROLL OF CAPT. AARON ALLEN'S COMPANY. (County Not Known.)
Pages 5-6-7-23-24-25. Vol. 2.

Served from September 15, 1812 until March 16, 1813.

Capt. Aaron Allen	Lieut. John Vantilburgh	Ensign, William Mills
Sergt. James Clare	Sergt. Richard Shaw	Sergt. John Farquer
Sergt. Thomas Henderson	Corp. Christopher Abel	Corp. Hugh Livingston
Corp. James Johnston	Corp. David Workman	

Privates.

Privates.	Privates.	Privates.
Ault, Phillip	Avery, Samuel	Abel, Benjamin
Ayers, James	Asher, Anthony	Barr, John
Bay, Robert	Burchfield, Frederick	Beemer, Adam
Brown, Nehemiah	Burris, Emery	Brown, William
Barnes, Obediah	Corbit, Lewis	Carter, Ryan
Campbell, Alexander	Close, John	Cann, Alexander
Crofford, Alexander	Carson, John	Carson, Samuel
Caughey, Joseph	Davis, Henry	Degoin, John O.
Durall, Thomas	Doyell, Anthony	Ellison, James
Freet, David	Flecker, Abraham	Fishell, Frederick
Fisher, John	Fivecoat, Michael	George, John
Graden, Thomas	Grim, Martin	Gibson, Joseph
Glodman, Michael	Hardebrook, John	Hill, James
Hardebrook, Jerome	Hukell, James	Haller, Samuel
Haverfield, Joseph	Hill, William	Hoye, John
Haning, Jacob	Harriman, John	Hickory, John
Jinnings, Nathaniel	James, John	Jackman, Thomas
Kean, James	Kerr, Samuel	Logue, John
Lyons, John	Lees, Samuel	Lane, Samuel
Lisle, Jacob	Myers, Emanuel	Moody, John
Myers, Jacob	Mays, James	Malen, Joseph
Montgomery, William	Morehead, James	Myon, Jacob
Miller, Jacob	Main, Samuel	Milter, Jacob
McCloud, William	McNiles, Thomas	McCalley, William
McClintock, William	McClerg, Robert	McClelland, Felix
McCaskey, David	Hitchcock, John	Lyse, Robert
Pugh, Isaac	Palmer, George	Peterson, John
Packman, Thomas	Quin, John	Quillen, Adam
Rutledge, William	Ralston, Robert	Russell, Robert
Richardson, Mathew	Rickey, Daniel	Reynolds, Caleb
Roysell, Job	Ralston, Joseph	Ritter, Benjamin
Ray, James	Shaffer, Phillip	Shawber, Jacob
Stewart, James	Smith, Samuel	Smith, John
Stokes, John	Simmons, Adam	Steven, Daniel
Speed, Allen	Skelton, John	Skelton, William
Sissions, Benjamin	Taylor, John	Thompson, Moses
Shepherd, John	Welsh, Daniel	Willits, John
Wheeler, Nicholas		

ROLL OF CAPT. JACOB GILBERT'S COMPANY.
(Probably from Jefferson County.)
Pages 9-10-29-35-347-348. Vol. 2.

Served from August 25, 1812 until February 28, 1813.

Capt. Jacob Gilbert	Lieut. John Teeters	Ensign Abraham Fox
Ensign Conrad Myers	Sergt. David Shoemaker	Sergt. Samuel Elster
Sergt. Michael Coners	Sergt. Michael Shafer	Corp. Randall Smith
Corp. Peter Miller	Corp. John Eaton	Corp. John Lipley

Privates.	Privates.	Privates.
Alexander, Robert	Adams, William	Blackburn, William
Beacht, George	Barnes, Jacob	Bradfield, Benjamin
Brineman, Richard	Boatman, Henry	Bissilla, Betz
Condon, James	Cook, George	Catt, Phillip
Calihan, William	Clary, James M.	Cahammon, John M.
Estep, George	Engerstem, Henry	Fox, John

Vol. 2.
ROLL OF CAPT. JACOB GILBERT'S COMPANY. (Continued)

Rank and Name of Soldier.   **Rank and Name of Soldier.**   **Rank and Name of Soldier.**

Privates.	Privates.	Privates.
Frederick, John	Feler, Michael	Fisher, Brice
Ford, William	Glass, Mathias	Garringer, David
Hohn, Adam	Hohn, John	Helwick, Nicholas
Hohn, Andrew	Higgins, Samuel	Huffman, Jacob
Haughman, Samuel	Heemthorn, Peter	Hevely, Christopher
Harnish, John	Kennel, Joseph	Kerns, John
Kley, John	Kelley, Alexander	Lower, John
Losure, David	Lane, Samuel	Lawrence, John
Myers, Frederick	Meeker, Michael	Machaman, John
Mall, Henry	Metz, John	Mowen, Jacob
Musser, Michael	Johnston, David	Moore, Ezekiel
Meek, Samuel	Meek, Samuel, Jr.	Meek, John
Meek, John, Jr.	Minton, John	McClung, James
McElroy, John	McClelland, Felix	Preston, John
Painter, James	Palmer, Richard	Pairs, Gainer
Miller, Peter	Routzen, Nathaniel	Randolph, John
Roller, Henry	Rainey, Charles	Rudwill, John
Roller, Joseph	Roach, William	Rock, Henry
Rogers, Thomas	Richey, Isaac	Rough, William
Speaker, Henry	Simons, George	Skidmore, William
Switzer, Jacob	Smith, Henry	Stewart, Hugh
Switzer, George	Schultz, George	Sanor, Michael
Thompson, John	Trasey, James	Wickert, John
Watkins, Benjamin	Watkins, John	Whiteleather, Christian
Wickersham, Joseph	Yoobs, Austin

ROLL OF CAPTAIN JOSEPH HOLMES' COMPANY.
(Probably from Jefferson County.)

Pages 11-12-19-20.

Served from August 23, 1812 until February 28, 1813.

Capt. Joseph Holmes   Lieut. William Thorne   Lieut. John Ramsey
Ensign David Mitchell   Sergt. Francis Popham   Sergt. James Gilmore
Sergt. Alexander Smith   Sergt. John McCully   Corp. Edward Vanhorn
Corp. John Pollock   Corp. Thomas McBride   Corp. Joseph Hagerman
Drummer John McClintick   Drummer James Roff

Privates.	Privates.	Privates.
Arnold, Reason	Arnold, James	Arnold, Samuel
Asher, Anthony	Barcus, William	Brocaw, George
Brotell, John	Barks, William	Belch, James
Brown, James	Brookan, George	Birttel, John
Briggs, David	Carpenter, George	Cahill, Phillip
Chaffin, James	Elliott, Thomas	Elliott, Finley
Edington, Isaac	Ferguson, John	Ferguson, Thomas
Foster, Benjamin	Glass, Thomas	Gilpin, Samuel
Guttery, John A.	Harper, William	Henry, Isaac
Hughes, Joseph	Harriman, John	Hawthorne, John
Kendall, Rhesa	Kelley, Mathew	Kerr, Samuel
Kyle, William	Laning, Jacob	Logan, Richard
Leach, John	Long, James	Minnis, James
Madden, Patrick H.	Miller, Charles M.	Maxwell, Robert
Moore, James	Meek, Jacob	McClay, Benjamin
McElroy, George	McCullough, James	McMillan, Charles
McDonald, Thomas	McClery, Benjamin	McClintock, William
McClintock, John	McFadden, Thomas	Osborn, Jacob
Osler, Jacob	Parks, John	Porter, Hugh
Potts, David	Robertson, Charles	Ross, Richard
Robbins, Johnston	Robertson, John	Ross, James
Roach, Jeremiah	Roach, Ebenezer	Reels, Isaac S.
Smith, Charles	Scholes, John	Sankey, James
Snider, Henry	Strall, Joseph	Sullivan, George
Stevens, David	Tipton, Luke	Tipton, William
Tipton, Jonothan	Van Bibben, Isaac	White, Joseph
West, Jonothan	Yealdhall, Edwin

ROLL OF CAPT. WILLIAM FOULK'S COMPANY.
(Probably from Jefferson County.)

Pages 12-14-21-22-345-346.

Served from August 25, 1812 until February 28, 1813.

Capt. William Foulks   Lieut. John Burkdale   Ensign Robert Ramsey
Ensign Jacob Crouse   Sergt. John Hester   Sergt. John Cannon
Sergt. John Huston   Sergt. John Chaney   Sergt. Henry Fisher
Sergt. John Charing   Corp. Alexander Armstrong   Corp. James Swin
Corp. Addison McKinnon   Corp. Rudolph Brandaberry   Corp. Andrew Armstrong
Corp. James Anderson   Fifer Daniel McConkey

ROLL OF CAPT. WILLIAM FOULK'S COMPANY. (Continued)

Rank and Name of Soldier.

Privates.

Bowman, Christian
Black, John
Cripps, John
Caughey, James
Crevan, John
Davis, William
Fisher, Henry
Grimm, George
Huston, Samuel
Hunter, George
Iddings, William
Lyon, Joseph
Melone, David
Marsh, Henry
Martin, Henry
McCready, William
McLaughlin, John
McMillen, James
McIntosh, Angus
McKee, Alexander
McConikey, Daniel
Phillips, William
Poe, Thomas
Randolph, James
Riley, Mathew
Rees, John
Saint, John
Swim, James
Smoot, William
Welch, Lewis
Zear, Anthony

Rank and Name of Soldier.

Privates.

Brandaberry, Jacob
Brady, William
Crowl, Henry
Credmer, John
Cox, Thomas
Fish, Richard
Grou, Henry
Grace, Henry
Hartman, Solomon
Heddings, William
Jones, Abraham
Leslie, Joseph
Marshall, John
Maxwell, Robert
Miller, Henry
McCombs, Jacob
McMillen, Alexander
McKee, James
McCoy, Daniel
McKee, Daniel
Ogle, Hercules
Poe, William
Quinn, Daniel
Reed, Elias
Robinson, Aaron
Spacht, John
Sheehan, William
Spearth, John
Whitmore, John
Walker, Peter

Rank and Name of Soldier.

Privates.

Burback, Arthur
Cross, James
Cramer, John
Crouch, Henry
Davis, Abednego
Frederick, Samuel
Gribner, George
Gruner, George
Hull, Samuel
Henderson, James
Kees, John
Match, Henry
Muce, Jacob
March, Samuel
Moore, George
McLaughlin, Ephraim
McCoy, David
McKee, John
McKay, Daniel
McIntosh, Anguish
Perry, James
Perry, John
Randolph, William
Ritter, Jacob
Ritchie, Isaac
Smith, Jabez
Smith, Lewis
Smith, Jesse
Way, Eli
Year, Armstrong

Pages 15-16-41-42-17.

ROLL OF CAPT. THOMAS LATTA'S COMPANY.
(Probably from Jefferson County.)

Served from September 15, 1812 until March 21, 1813.

Capt. Thomas Latta
Ensign William Prichard
Sergt. Alexander Patterson
Sergt. John Haughey
Corp. Cornelius Peterson
Corp. Mathew Palmer

Lieut. John Buck
Sergt. George Browers
Sergt. Isaac Wolms
Corp. William Betz

Lieut. Hugh Christy
Sergt. George Brown
Sergt. George Emaling
Sergt. Richard Brown
Corp. James Holes

Privates.

Argo, Jeremiah
Adams, Thomas
Bulger, Michael
Burk, Moses
Brown, John
Beamer, Adam
Bair, David
Brockar, John
Bamhill, William
Camp, Henry
Dick, John
Derry, William
Ellison, David
Ferguson, James
Gibson, William
Graham, Jesse
Glosson, John
Hanlon, Allen
Henry, George
Hayes, Richard
Holmes, Isaac
Johnston, Henry
Kyt, William
Lindreyd, Charles
Lemasten, Isaac
Meeks, Jacob
Murray, Patrick
Mills, Eli
McColley, Robert
McCullough, David
McClelland, William
McFall, Barnet
Patterson, Robert
Potts, Joshua
Pinckney, Adam
Revenaugh, Samuel

Privates.

Agler, William
Adams, John
Bell, William
Browner, Samuel
Browern, Samuel
Boils, Richard
Beamer, Adam, Jr.
Brockar, William
Cook, James
Chase, Patrick
Dickey, James
Dickey, John
Ferguson, John
Franas, James
Gilliland, William
Green, Ebenezer
Gutshall, Henry
Henry, Henry
Hull, Joseph
Hunter, John
Heath, Solomon
Kelley, Jonothan
Lauthers, Alexander
Lisle, Robert
Miser, John
Montier, Robert
Morrison, James
Maxwell, William
McDonald, John
McFadden, Thomas
McCleary, John
Odbert, John
Potts, John
Prichard, John
Robb, William
Revenaugh, John

Privates.

Allbaugh, Solomon
Allbaugh, George
Bell, Adam
Bailiss, William
Buckley, John
Baird, Andrew
Barnes, John
Bratell, John
Ceasson, John
Dick, Robert
Devore, James
Druchmiller, Frederick
Fisher, Thomas
Fulton, John
Greenlee, Alexander
Guttery, Samuel
Hanley, William
Hicks, James
Hirth, Holmes
Hanenau, David
Jeffey, James
Kelley, William
Loury, John
Leather, Alexander
Marshall, Thomas
Messer, Boyd
Moore, William
McConnell, Joseph
McColin, James
McRankey, William
McGonigre, Thomas
Pool, Conrad
Palmer, Ephraim
Pipenger, Peter
Rippey, Joseph
Russell, Robert

ROSTER OF OHIO SOLDIERS IN WAR OF 1812

ROLL OF CAPT. THOMAS LATTA'S COMPANY. (Continued)

Rank and Name of Soldier.

Privates.

Right, Joseph
Rolleur, Johnston
Ruly, John
Swamby, Daniel
Snider, Adam
Scott, Thomas
Simmons, Jacob
Sheebr, Nicholas
Solomon, Samuel
Thompson, Isaac
Thompson, John
Updegraft, James
Vaughn, Richard
Willsby, Robert
Worley, Thomas
Wallace, John

Rank and Name of Soldier.

Privates.

Rouse, Benjamin
Reed, John
Sewison, Benjamin
Swam, Hezekiah
Saimmons, Cornelius
Stevens, David
Spiker, Isaac
Smith, John
Simmons, Adam
Truckmiller, Frederick
Tipton, John
Vaughn, John
Vaughn, Jonothan
Woistell, William
White, William

Rank and Name of Soldier.

Privates.

Riddel, John
Ragison, Jacob
Spiken, Phillip
Smith, Nathaniel
Scott, John
Sullivan, George
Strain, Robert
Stover, Samuel
Smith, Andrew
Tharp, William
Turnipseed, John
Vubs, Isaac
Williby, Frederick
Welday, Jacob
Wilkins, Archibold

Pages 27-28-51-52. Vol. 2.

ROLL OF CAPT. DAVID PECK'S COMPANY.
(From Either Harrison or Jefferson County.)

Served from August 25, 1812, until February 28, 1813.

Capt. David Peck
Sergt. John Stoaks
Sergt. Jesse Harnum
Corp. James Miller

Lieut. Joseph Davis
Sergt. Daniel Higgins
Corp. John Vaughn
Corp. Wm. McConkey

Ensign Jacob Shaffer
Sergt. Dudley Smith
Corp. James Davis

Privates.

Albert, John
Barnes, Obediah
Burchfield, Charles
Christy, George
Crawford, Alexander
Degar, Peter
Dewall, Thomas N.
Fisher, Samuel
Gutshall, Henry
Gibson, Joseph
Hosben, Michael
Lisle, Robert
Morrison, William
Miller, Isaac
McCombs, John
McKinner, Samuel
Quillen, Joshua
Pumphrey, Zachariah
Raynolds, Caleb
Ross, William
Simmons, Adam
Smith, Andrew
Taylor, Henry
Thompson, Robert
Titus, Timothy

Privates.

Armstrong, Archibold
Bennet, Thomas
Busy, Joshua
Chrys, George
Dowden, John N.
Devore, Abraham
Dickey, William
Fisher, Ephraim
Gutshall, George
Huffman, John
Johnston, Peter
Lisle, William
Meach, Ephraim
Miller, Jacob
McIntire, Archibold
McCleary, Robert
Quillen, Adam
Richards, Jacob
Rolston, Joseph
Smith, Robert
Spiker, Jacob
Smith, John
Tipton, John
Tharp, William
Woods, Josiah

Privates.

Ayers, James
Beard, James
Chambers, James
Conn, Alexander
Derry, William
Devore, James
Dickey, James
Fisher, John
Gordon, George
Hunter, John
Lyons, John
Morrison, Joseph
Mann, Samuel
Montgomery, Abel
McKinsea, Nathaniel
McAdams, William
Quillen, John
Ruley, John
Ritter, Benjamin
Shepherd, John
Scholes, John
Spiker, Isaac
Tingley, Benjamin
Toppe, Abraham

Pages 33-34. Vol. 2.

ROLL OF CAPT. WiLLIAM STOAKES COMPANY.
(Probably from Harrison County.)

Served from August 21, 1812 until February 28, 1813.

Capt. William Stoakes
Sergt. John Elrod
Sergt. William Bashford
Corp. Isaac Bail
Drummer, Thomas Bay

Lieut. Thomas Orr
Sergt. John Paramore
Corp. Benjamin Dean
Corp. John Palmer

Ensign John Cantwell
Sergt. David Hinzy or Kinzan
Corp. William Crothers
Fifer, Samuel Solomon

Privates.

Andrews, John
Bruce, Thomas
Barnes, John
Brokaw, John
Cowthers (or Carothers),
Conaway, John
Emry, George
Fulton, John
Hamilton, John
Hartshorn, Spry
Johnson, James
Kizen, Jacob
Martin, James
McCatchen, Samuel
McClary, John

Privates.

Archbod, Patrick
Baker, John
Beamer, Adam
Belknap, Horace
Geo. Cupp, John
Conaway, Michael
Eckley, George
Fletcher, Archibald
Hull, John
Hail, Andrew
Joseph, Michael
Lutz, Henry
Moore, James
McEntire, Stephen
Nixon, William

Privates.

Benett, Benjamin
Darnett, George
Brokaw, William
Clifford, James
Chambers, William
Davidson, Joshua
Emery, Abraham
Guttery, Samuel
Hull, Jesse
Johnston, Daniel
Jack, Edward
Moore, William
Muntier, Robert
McGonegal, Thomas
Peterson, Hugh

ROLL OF CAPT. WILLIAM STOAKES' COMPANY. (Continued)

Rank and Name of Soldier.
Privates.
Pittinger, Peter
Reed, John Sr.
Rider, Jacob
Spidel, Joseph
Stuse (or Steer), Jacob
Strain, Robert
Updegraft, James
West, Robert
West, Joshua
White, William

Rank and Name of Soldier.
Privates.
Patterson, John
Reed, John Jr.
Rickey, John
Spidy (or Speedy), William
Simmons, Jacob
Throckmorton, Thomas
Updegraft, Jesse
Wallace, John
Whitaker, Obed
Welch, John

Rank and Name of Soldier.
Privates.
Porter, Samuel A.
Riley, James
Reed, Samuel
Sanderlin, Thomas
Skeels, Nicholas
Tranen, James
Wallace, James
Wingfield, Elijah
Walker, John
Welkin, Archibald

Pages 35-36.

ROLL OF CAPT. ALLEN SCROGGS' COMPANY.
(Probably from Jefferson County.)
Served from September 21, 1812 until November 30, 1812.

Capt. Allen Scroggs
Sergt. William Wilkin
Sergt. William Robertson
Corp. John Connaway

Lieut. John Ramsey
Sergt. William Dunlap
Corp. Samuel Avery
Corp. John Wallace

Ensign John Caldwell
Sergt. William Holson
Corp. Joseph Haverfield

Privates.
Abbott, Benjamin
Baricklow, Fanington
Brokan, William
Cann, James F.
Foster, Benjamin
Heinary, Abraham
Hill, William
Gray, Ebenezer
Findley, David
Mintier, Robert
McCormack, John
McKain, William
Pittinger, Peter
Reed, John
Reed, Samuel
Scholes, John
Thompson, Moses
Yielhall, Edward

Privates.
Bebout, Peter
Beamer, Adam
Belknap, Horace
Fletcher, Archibald
Fivecoats, Michael
Hitchcock, John
Jack, Edward
Laurence, Duber
Lees, Samuel
Myers, Jacob
McGonigle, Thomas
McCally, William
Porter, Samuel A.
Robertson, Charles
Robb, Moses
Smith, Samuel
Welch, John

Privates.
Brokan, John
Buris, Homeny
Connaway, Michael
Francis, James
Gladmore, Michael
Holly, Samuel
Johnson, Henry
Dewalt, John
Moffit, James
McClary, John
McFadden, Thomas
Parson, Charles
Pessy, Stephen
Reed, John Jr.
Shale, Nicholas
Tenet, Charles
Wilkins, Archibald

Pages 43-44. Vol. 2

ROLL OF CAPT. DAVID LISTS' COMPANY. (From Franklin County.)
Served from July 28, 1813 until September 6, 1813.

Capt. David List
Sergt. Henry Grim
Sergt. David Hostetter
Corp. Daniel Swaggert

Lieut. Peter Bawsher
Sergt. Henry Spiker
Corp. George List
Corp. John Clark

Ensign Daniel Puncher
Sergt. Dunovan Reed
Corp. Phillip, Sanfoss
Musician, Jacob Grove

Privates.
Bowsher, Jacob
Bawm, Jacob
Burney, Thomas
Clark, Alphus
Dresbach, Samuel
Greenoh, James
Hedges, Benjamin
Harmon, George
Justice, Jesse
Kintzel, Samuel
Miller, Stephen
Overmieir, John
Stover, Christopher
Smith, Phillip
Till, John
Walton, John
Wize, Henry

Privates.
Bell, Joseph
Black, William
Bowsher, Henry
Coons, John
Finck, Solomon
Greenoh, Jacob
Harmon, Jacob
Hiser, William
Johnston, Robert
List, Phillip
Martin, William
Row, Peter
Smith, Elisha
Salarts, John
Uartz, Christian
Weaver, Jacob

Privates.
Betser, Peter
Bawsher, Anthony
Bowsher, John
Curtz, Hector
Grim, George
Harman, Samuel
Hossman, George
Harpster, Peter
Kile, William
Lloyd, John
Neff, Adam
Spelman, Thomas
Swigart, John
Puntius, Conrad
Vandorm, William
Winlin, William

Pages 45-46-47.

ROLL OF CAPT. GEORGE GIBSON'S COMPANY. (County Unknown.)
Served from July 28, 1813 until September 6, 1813 and from August 23, 1814 until January 11, 1815.

Capt. George Gibson
Ensign David Coon
Sergt. John Stephens
Sergt. John Armstrong
Corp. Thomas Barton
Corp. John Smith
Corp. Leeds William

Lieut. Archibald Campbell
Ensign Henry Goetlery
Sergt. Andrew Reed
Sergt. James McCalister
Corp. John Hawthorn
Corp. Thomas Richardson
Drummer, Jacob Chion

Lieut. Mathew Littleton
Sergt. Mathew Mitchell
Sergt. Jacon Hawman
Sergt. George Watson
Corp. Isaac Rinear
Corp. Richard Bradley
Fifer, Thomas Littleton

ROLL OF CAPT. GEORGE GIBSON'S COMPANY. (Continued)

Rank and Name of Soldier.

Privates.

Adams, John
Brown, Samuel
Benjamin, William
Carpenter, George
Crumb, Thomas
Decker, Joseph
Davidson, John
Edwards, John
George, Henry
Huffhinds, William
Hoover, Jacob
Hetsel, Daniel
Heaston, Martin
Jones, Abel
Long, John
Muller, Benjamin
Morris, Richard
Menshall, Thomas
McCoy, John
Neadstay, John
Ritter, John
Ridenour, George
Ritchy, Andrew
Saul, John
Sweet, Stephen
Stutts, Jacob
Wolff, Mathias
Wood, Benjamin

Pages 53-54. Vol. 2.

Rank and Name of Soldier.

Privates.

Anderson, James
Bowen, William
Campbell, Hugh
Coon, George
Crossley, Henry
Decker, Luke
Ellis, Thomas
Fuller, Alexander
Groom, William
Huffhinds, Jacob
Hussetter, Jacob
Haverlow, William
Iggs, Daniel
King, Joshua
Leck, John
Martin, David
Mann, Reuben P.
McCartney, Duke
McArthur, Duncan
Purcell, John
Ridenour, David
Ridenour, John
Stephens, Ebenezer
Swaggart, Daniel
Smith, John
Teagarden, William
Waggoner, John
Wolf, Phillip

Rank and Name of Soldier.

Privates.

Argo, Abraham
Burton, Boswell
Cutler, James
Culbertson, Samuel
Culbertson, Robert
DeWitt, Robert
Elder, Thomas
Francisco, Joseph
Groom, Jobe
Huff, John
Harrison, James
Hamilton, James
Gerome, William
Kerr, James
Laverty, John
Machin, Thomas
Mason, James
McFadden, William
McCohn, Archibald
Rodes, Peter
Roberts, Thomas
Rogers, Philemon
Smith, Jacob
Scoomover, Abraham
Simpson, Richard
Tivel, John
Wood, Robert
Young, Phillip

ROLL OF CAPTAIN JOHN ALEXANDER'S COMPANY.
(Probably Harrison or Jefferson County.)

Served from Sept. 21, 1812, until Dec. 8, 1812, and from July 29, 1813, until Aug. 22, 1813.

Capt. John Alexander
Ensign David Jackson
Sergt. Robert Blackford
Sergt. Robert Stayton
Corp. William M. Coy
Corp. Charles Lunay
Fifer, John Neel

Privates.

Ayers, James
Burkis, Richard
Buckley, John
Brown, Samuel
Christ, George
Fisher, Darius
Frame, James
Greenlee, Alexander
Lisle, Robert Sr.
Mann, John
Meek, Jacob
Parker, Justus
Reynolds, Caleb
Russel, Robert
Scott, John
Shiveley, William
Smith, Nathaniel
Welday, James

Pages 55-56.

Lieut. Hugh Christy
Sergt. George Ermabringer
Sergt. Hugh McGee
Sergt. Robert Kennedy
Corp. Joseph Washburn
Corp. Thomas Mantial
Fifer, Rodman Gardner

Privates.

Adams, Thomas
Barnes, Obadiah
Browner, Samuel
Boland, William
Deval, Thomas
Fisher, Ephraim
Ferguson, James
Harland, Michael
Lisle, Robert Jr.
Miller, James
McCollan, James
Quillin, Adam
Revenaugh, John
Riddle, John
Simpson, James
Scott, Thomas
Tipton, John
White, Joseph

Lieut. Angus McCoy
Sergt. John Linch
Sergt. Stephen Paugburn
Sergt. Robert Miller
Corp. Jeremiah Ango
Corp. William Ross

Privates.

Adams, John
Bailey, William
Brown, John
Crawford, Alexander
Ellison, David
Fisher, John
Gamble, William
Lowery, John
Lacock, Moses
Mansfield, Samuel
McCulloch, David
Reed, Mathew
Revenaugh, Samuel
Ross, Henry
Simmons, Cornelius
Smith, John
Worstell, William

ROLL OF CAPTAIN MARTIN SHUEY'S COMPANY.
(Probably Montgomery County.)

Served from August 25, 1814, until February 26, 1815.

Capt. Martin Shuey
Sergt. Robert McKee
Sergt. Levi Williams
Corp. David Lamm
Drummer, John Lypcap

Privates.

Antonides, Vincen
Boal, John
Baker, Bruget
Camler, David
Depriest, Charles
Frakes, Nathan
Grubb, Daniel

Lieut. Christopher Sranfe
Sergt. Lewis Sranfe
Corp. D. McCord
Corp. Robert Meper

Privates.

Basche, John
Barker, Joseph
Chivilier, Charles
Cavin, George N.
Ensey, Dennis
Gable, Daniel
Hurley, Connell

Ensign George Sranfe
Sergt. John Confer
Corp. Jeremiah Bateman
Corp. Alvin Richison

Privates.

Bodder, John
Battrick, William
Curry, Josiah
Davidson, Abraham
Fields, Reuben
Glenn, Thomas
Heaton, Joseph

ROLL OF CAPT. MARTIN SHUEY'E COMPANY. (Continued)

Rank and Name of Soldier.
Privates.
Harshman, Jacob
Kelsey, Isaac
Moorman, Pleastent
Perry, Joseph
Ryan, Cornelius
Thomas, Alexander
Wilson, John

Rank and Name of Soldier.
Privates.
Harshman, Henry
Martin, Moses
McLong, James
Peck, John
Sanders, Arnsey
Townsley, Samuel
Williams, James

Rank and Name of Soldier.
Privates.
Harten, Frederick
Murphey, John
Nason, Daniel
Ridler, Abraham
Smith, Spencer
Wilson, Francis
Yazel, Jacob

Pages 57-58.   Vol. 2.

ROLL OF CAPTAIN ASA HINCKLES' COMPANY.
(Probably Butler County.)

Served from Aug. 11, 1812, until Nov. 30, 1812, and from Jan. 1 until Feb. 15, 1813.

Capt. Asa Hinckle
Sergt. Thomas Richey
Sergt. Joseph McNight
Corp. Lewis Drake

Lieut. Benaiah Ayres
Sergt. James Burns
Corp. John Ferris
Corp. Daniel Hunter

Ensign James Cummins
Sergt. Calvan Tipman
Corp. Garnit Swallow
Musician, William H. Wilcox

Privates.
Brexcunt, David
Brown, David
Cosbey, Thomas
Danford, William
Haney, George
Hinckle, Henry
Larne, Moses
Meland, James
Mathers, James
McClellan, William
Nichols, Prosper
Redingban, Frederick
Redenbaugh, Jeremiah
Runion, Isaac
Redenbaugh, Phillip
Stirlen, James
Thornhill, William

Privates.
Boys, Ezekial
Beard, Samuel
Chirington
Denman, Nathaniel
Hinckle, John
Hinckle, John
Line, Joseph
Morris, Daniel
Murdock, William
Moncrief, Caleb
Pierson, Lewis
Riker, William
Riker, Thomas
Rickey, John
Riker, Jacob
Sampson, John
White, Benjamin

Privates.
Bonnel, Lewis
Clark, John
Cosbey, Samuel
Graham, Isaac
Hinckle, Ziba
Kennedy, David
Morse, John
Murdock, John
McClelland
Nichols, Lenester
Redenbaugh, John
Rian, Martin
Redenbaugh, George
Redenbaugh, Adam
Sipe, Charles
Thompson, Joseph

Page 59.

ROLL OF CAPTAIN MATTHIAS CORWIN'S COMPANY.
(Probably Butler County.)

Served from August 11 until November 30, 1812, and from January 5 until February 11, 1813.

Capt. Matthias Corwin
Sergt. Jeremiah Smith

Lieut. Nathaniel McLean

Ensign John Ruser

Privates.
Adams, John
Bishop, David W.
Dunlary, Howard
Lenawred, John
Neville, David
Runion, Absalom
Richardson, Elijah
Seward, John
Townsend, Benjamin
Wooters, Richard

Privates.
Bell, Simion
Birdrall, Henry
Eddy, John
Maish, William
Phillips, William
Ross, Joseph
Reding, James
Sinnard, Thoman
Voorhis, Jacob
Wolf, Michael

Privates.
Bartleson, Andrew
Cruters, Ezekial
Jones, Henry C.
McWhorten, Tyler
Rush, Abraham
Reeder, Micaiah
Skinner, David
Timothy, Millard
Wiles, James

Pages 61-62.

ROLL OF CAPTAIN JOSEPH W. ROSS' COMPANY.
(Probably Ross County.)

Served from September 1, 1813, until March 1, 1814.

Capt. Joseph Ross
Sergt. Elnathan Barlow
Sergt. John Donnly
Corp. William Winnison
Musician, Colemuel, Green

Lieut. James Mullin
Sergt. James Robertson
Sergt. James Brown
Corp. Calvin Danes
Musician, Benjamin Martin

Ensign Zeptha Danes
Sergt. Frost Levi
Corp. James Gohan
Corp. Samuel Firestone

Privates.
Arbute, Abraham
Brand, Adam
Childers, Mosley
Cornett, John
Crouch, Joseph
Dust, David
Fulton, Loammi
Gibson, John
Hall, Samuel
Holden, John
Kikabiaugh, Reuben
Longbrake, Daniel

Privates.
Bolabob, Abraham
Brooks, Isaac
Collison, William
Cremeens, Moses
Crouse, Jacob
Eckert, John
Ganer, Jacob
Gibson, George
Hanna, John
Humphrey, James
Long, William Sr.
Mansfield, John

Privates.
Bolabob, John
Burman, Frederick
Cornett, Abraham
Cremeens, Isaac
Denny, William
Fisher, Benjamin
Gibson, James
Griffith, Abraham
Hertand, Joseph
Huntcrock, Henry
Long, William Jr.
Martin, James

Vol. 2.
ROLL OF CAPTAIN JOSEPH W. ROSS' COMPANY. (Continued)

Rank and Name of Soldier.

Privates.

Mayse, Archibald
Morris, Elijah
McKee, Samuel
Parde, Richard
Prince, William
Purdy, William
Row, Phillip
Sumter, Richard
Waugh, Gory
Whitelock, James

Rank and Name of Soldier.

Privates.

Mathews, Nathan
Mayer, David
McKee, John
Phelps, Roswell
Price, John
Reeves, William
Royston, John
Thompson, Calvin
Webb, Hanley
Williams, Solomon

Rank and Name of Soldier.

Privates.

Miller, John
McDonald, David
Oversteel, John
Picket, Samuel
Price, Joseph
Rice, James
Stockwell, William
Vandemark, John
West, William
Wisely, John

Pages 63-64-65-66.

ROLL OF CAPTAIN JACOB SHINGLEDECKER'S COMPANY.
(From Greene County.)

Served August 24 until December 31, 1812.

Capt. Jacob Shingledecker
Sergt. John Todd
Sergt. Thomas Cottrell
Corp. Oliver Crawford
Corp. James Downey

Lieut. Samuel Butts
Sergt. Jacob Truby
Corp. John Wiland
Corp. John Davis
Trumpeter, William Burrows

Ensign William Yates
Sergt. Daniel Peterbaugh or Butterbaugh
Corp. Alexander Forbens

Privates.

Aley, John
Burres, William
Beal, Jonothan
Chambers, Adam
Cremwell, Samuel
Folck, George
Gray, Abraham
Hyers, Anthony
Keigler, Samuel
Kirkwood, William
Low, William
Miner, William
Messer, Henry
Nave, Jacob
Rue, Jacob
Shingledecker, Abraham
Stewart, Aaron
Tingley, John A.
Vogle, Peter
Wilson, William

Privates.

Ankeney, Henry
Beal, George
Buker, Peter
Chambers, William
Coster, Henry
Fogle, Peter
Hoover, John
Holverstat, John
Kisor, Richard
Longstreth, Andrew
Livingston, Andrew
Minniear, William
McCormack, James
Ritter, Jacob
Rubart, Enos
Shingledecker, John
Steward, Moses
Trubee, John
Wilson, Michael
Westfall, Jonothan

Privates.

Barkard, John
Beal, Aaron
Bochert, John
Crawford, Oliver
Eli, John
Gray, Henry
Haddix, Nimrod
Hollinger, Daniel
Kooglar, Samuel
Lee, John
Morningstar, George
May, George
Nelson, John
Ritter, John
Rethn, Jacob
Sipe, William
Smith, Jacob
Steward, Andrew
Wyland, John
Wilson, Jeremiah

Pages 67-68.

ROLL OF CAPTAIN WILLIAM STEPHENSON'S COMPANY.
(Probably Belmont County.)

Vol. 2.

Served from September 3, 1813, until March 20, 1814.

Capt. William Stephenson
Sergt. James Quigley
Sergt. Robert Yost
Corp. Thomas Holmes
Musician, James Tuttle

Lieut. Daniel Berry
Sergt. Hugh Brady
Corp. William McCormack
Corp. William McCraghill

Ensign John Bell
Sergt. John Hardesty
Corp. James Logan
Musician, James H. Ball

Privates.

Brem, Benjamin
Barton, William
Bright, Nicholas
Boneham, Aaron
Caruthers, Christopher
Engle, Michael
Floyd, Aaron
Grimes, John
Heske, Samuel
Harriman, David
Kinkead, Joseph
Mitchell, Peter
Maring, Phineas
McPherson, Daniel
McFadden, Charles
Price, Phineas
Parrish, Joseph
Payques, John
Rammage, William
Swark, John
Snelling, Aquilla
Stewart, Samuel
Taylor, James
Wagoner, John

Privates.

Bun, George
Bramhall, William
Burney, John B.
Bundy, Joseph
Clifford, William
Elliott, Thomas
Farnon, Alpheus
Gilham, Thomas
Homdel, Richard
Irwin, John
Lyons, John
Mitchell, John
Murdock, Joseph
McConnell, James
Nichols, Eli
Parcels, Richard
Perry, William
Pitman, William
Robinson, Samuel
Stewart, Edie
Stilwell, Obediah
Stewart, John
Truex, Abraham
Yerian, John

Privates.

Burk, Thomas
Brooke, Benjamin
Boy, John
Coss, George
Decker, Simon
Forrest, Gabriel
Findley, William
Henry, Joseph
Henry, Francis
Irwin, George
Lloyd, James
Maring, Peter
Murphy, William
McPherson, John
Naufossen, George
Park, William
Pyatt, Thomas
Reed, Jeremiah
Rush, James
Snidiker, Nicholas
Smith, Williams
Stypman, Stephen
Warren, Daniel
Zarbit, John

Pages 69-70.

ROLL OF CAPTAIN JOHN WILEY'S COMPANY.
(County Unknown.)
Served from August 30, 1813, until February 28, 1814.

Rank and Name of Soldier.	Rank and Name of Soldier.	Rank and Name of Soldier.
Capt. John Wiley	Lieut. David Hunter	Ensign Ephraim Bilderback
Sergt. William Rice	Sergt. John Barks	Sergt. John Wanwey
Sergt. James Hunter	Corp. John Westenbaegar	Corp. Elijah Atha
Corp. William Ingmand	Corp. Jacob Barler	Corp. William Wolf

Privates.

Allen, Whiting	Allspaugh, John	Allen, Judiah
Allspaugh, Henry	Bay, James	Bailes, James
Brukebill, Peter	Bailer, Samuel	Bernhart, Peter
Bernhart, Jacob	Beary, Abraham	Clarton, John
Cox, John	Curtis, Jonothan	Caves, Nath
Cline, Andrew	Deafenbaugh, Adam	England, William
Gessell, William	Greer, William	Hutton, Isaac
Hedges, Joseph	Huffman, Julius	Hedges, Peter
Horne, Christian	Hedges, Josiah	Howard, Joseph
Ingman, Henry	Kigar, George	Kinnard, James
Kigar, Peter	Kraniac, James	Kamele, Michael
Kinser, Peter	Kirk, George	Lockhart, William M.
Linzee, William	Lane, Dutton	Murray, William
Miller, Abraham	Mackrell, Samuel	Miller, Emanuel
Miller, Phillip	McCormack, Moses	McFerston, Alexander
Newman, Henry	Ponenmyer, Samuel	Potter, Nathaniel
Peterson, John	Pinkstath, Frederick	Peaugh, George
Radon, George	Rogers, James	Reynolds, Caleb
Shope, William	Shoemaker, William	Striper, Warner
Shode, James	Smith, John, Sr.	Smith, John, Jr.
Swiles, John	Sheaffer, Peter	Thompson, Andrew
Tolbert, John	Trout, Jacob	Vandermart, John
Walters, Christopher	White, Jeremiah	Young, William
Young, Robert		

Pages 71-72 Vol. 2.

ROLL OF CAPT. JACOB CATTERLINE'S COMPANY. (County Unknown)
Served from Sept. 1, 1813 until March 1, 1814.

Capt. Jacob Catterline	Lieut. James Hooper	Ensign Jared Bonn
Sergt. Henry Smith	Sergt. Thomas Warner	Sergt. Edwin Croose
Sergt. Daniel Ponce	Corp. George Norris	Corp. Henry Hannah
Corp. William Mast	Corp. Jesse Cloud	Fifer, George Hallinger
Drummer, Nathan Bonn		

Privates.

Boyle, James	Baker, Christian	Browning, Leonard
Bury, Elijah	Black, George	Clayton, John
Cooley, Edward	Copeland, Caleb	Copeland, William
Clayton, Joseph	Fulk, Nicholas	Found, William
Fate, George	Foster, George	Huffman, Henry
Helser, John	Hall, William	Johnston, John
Johnston, Luke	Kirkland, John	Lamb, Jacob
Lewis, John	Murphy, Benjamin	Mannon, Jacob
Miksell, Adam	Primmer, Adam	Phillips, John
Pelly, Moses	Ridenhour, John	Ridenhour Jacob
Ridenhour, Luderick	Reed, John	Roberts, Jonothan
Ruffner, Jacob	Rightley, Coonrod	Stally, George
Smith, Christian	Smith, Joseph	Smith, Andrew
Stephenson, Edward	Sartman, Henry	Torbet, William
Vanalla, John	Wagoner, John	Wallard, Henry

Pages 75-76

ROLL OF CAPT. JOHN THORNLEY'S COMPANY.
(Probably from Washington County.)
Served from January 6, until March 6, 1814.

Capt. John Thornley or Thorniley	Lieut. David Merchant or Meredith	Ensign, Elisha Chapman
Sergt. St. Clear Kelley	Sergt. Lemanuel Cooper	Sergt. Thomas Ady
Sergt. Daniel McClain	Corp. William Henkins	Corp. Solomon Tise
Corp. William Smith	Fifer, David Cox	Corp. David Alpha
Drummer, William Magee		

Privates.

Archer, John	Andrews, Jerid	Baichet, Jonah
Bell, John	Borth, Daniel	Banthan, Perry G.
Bird, William	Beamer, Henry	Barkey, Samuel
Brown, Jesse	Bennett, Joel	Corbet, Robert
Clark, William	Cline, George	Crouch, Samuel
Chapman, Simeon	Creig, John	Chapman, Hezekiah
Connet, John	Connet, Abraham	Darling, Jonothan
Davidson, Mathew	Edward, David	Emerson, Luke

ROSTER OF OHIO SOLDIERS IN WAR OF 1812   15

ROLL OF CAPT. JOHN THORNLEY'S CO.—(Continued)

Rank and Name of Soldier.

Privates.
Fugate, Jeremiah
Grose, John
Harris, George
Keiser, John
Lamb, Benjamin
McCleain, Andrew
Petty, Pressley
Ramsey, Samuel
Skipton, John
Sills, Jonothan
Tipton, Solomon
Willis, Richard

Rank and Name of Soldier.

Privates.
Ferguson, Abner
Hill, Thomas
Hepsen, Benjamin
Kidd, William
Marshall, Thomas
Newel, Thomas
Ramsey, William
Row, Nicholas
Saltingstall, John
Stanley, Francis
Vulgenoit, Jacob
Walker, William

Rank and Name of Soldier.

Privates.
Fost, Ephraim
Hartley, Thomas
Jolley, William
Lynn, John
Millford, Joseph
Oglesby, James
Ramsey, John
Riley, James
Smith, John
Tison, Zephamiah
Vaughan, Alexander

Pages 77-78

ROLL OF CAPT. WILLIAM WILSON'S COMPANY. (County Unknown.)

Served from August 1, until September 9, 1812.

Capt. William Wilson
Sergt. Jacob Marris
Sergt. John Day

Lieut. John Robinson
Sergt. William Forgason

Ensign, John Philbey
Sergt. George Ritchey

Privates.
Ashiraft, Jonothan
Chambers, Joseph
Davis, William
Fox, John
Haidesty, Samuel
Hawker, Christian
Helms, Daniel
Mariaty, John
Moore, Henry
Rowell, Moses
Richey, Gideon
Sebring, Rudolph
Smith, Silas
Tharp, William
Winters, James
Wilson, George
Wheeler, John
Zane, Joel

Privates.
Binter, Jacob
Chambers, Mathew
Ewing, Edmond
Graves, Benjamin
Hawkins, William
Hensley, John
Latimore, Jesse
Mathews, Noah
Moore, David
Ripe, John
Slaughter, Elias
Stradley, Ayers
Taylor, William
Tharp, John
Wagoner, Daniel
Welch, James
Wells, John

Privates.
Baughman, Henry
Conn, Thomas
Fletcher, Spinier
Greenfield, John
Hadesty, Urich
Hayman, Abijah
Lane, Samuel
Mathews, Thomas
Pryer, Frederick
Rodwick, Lewis
Stoner, John
Starkey, John
Thompson, William
Vanwikle, Paul
Wagoner, Joseph
Welch, John
Young, Ephraim

Pages 79-80

ROLL OF CAPT. ABNER BARRETT'S COMPANY.
(Probably from Champaign County.)

Served from August 21, until October 21, 1812 and from January 1, until February 21, 1813.

Capt. Abner Barrett
Sergt. Wanet Owen
Sergt. Daniel Weal
Corp. Stephen Runyon
Fifer, John Swisher

Lieut. William Chenoweth
Sergt. Thomas Green
Corp. Daniel Helmick
Corp. William Runyon

Ensign, John Owen
Sergt. Jesse Frankelberger
Corp. James Walker
Drummer, John Rupe

Privates.
Brousman, Nicodemus
Blue, William
Blue, William
Carbert, Thomas
Coterel, Hiram
Curl, Jeremiah
Flood, Francis
Graften, James
Gran, William
Huffman, Abraham
Helmick, Daniel
Leeper, James
Mayfield, Emanuel
Merchant, Joseph
Menice, John
Nicles, Ninion
Peno, Jacob
Rodes, William
Rodes, Conway
Sargent, Enock
Sprey, Lodman
Stanford, E.
Standford, Elijah
Weever, Aaron
Yutsler, Jacob

Privates.
Bay, Robert
Bouseman, John
Bay, Hugh
Clark, Abraham
Cosan, Thomas
Dawson, William
Frerwods, John
Gilmore, John
Hendrix, John
Hashparger, Christian
Kelley, John
Littell, David
Morris, John
Moody, David
McKinney, Edward
Nunengan, William
Reed, James
Russell, James
Shepard, William
Stanley, Thomas
Swisher, Jacob
Storm, Henry
Templin, James
West, Stake

Privates.
Beatty, William
Bishop, Aquilla
Coon, Barnabus
Cowan, Miles
Conkel, Michal
Frerwode, John
Gilpin, Elias
Green, William
Hoge, James
Hobson, John
Kizer, Joseph
Lonsdale, Thomas
Mathews, George
Monmar, William
Neville, James
Pettled, Horatio
Rector, William
Rees, Jeremiah
Sweet, Joshua
Stanley, William
Sibart, George
Scribner, Aaron
Waltz, Edward
Wells, Joseph

Pages 81-82   Vol. 2.

ROLL OF CAPT. MARTIN ARMSTRONG'S COMPANY. (County Unknown)

Served from August 22, 1812 until February 22, 1813.

Rank and Name of Soldier.	Rank and Name of Soldier.	Rank and Name of Soldier.
Capt. Martin Armstrong	Lieut. James Bryan	Ensign, Andrew McKew
Sergt. Hartley Melone	Sergt. Adam Cell	Sergt. Robert Brown
Sergt. Andrew Kelley	Corp. George Boots	Corp. Phillip Waldren
Corp. William Odle	Corp. Caleb Odle	Drummer, Jesse Howe

Privates.	Privates.	Privates.
Alexander, Joseph	Brown, Nimrod	Bell, John
Boots, Martin	Bagby, Thomas	Cating, Edward
Carpenter, Jesse	Camble, Jonothan	Doll, Daniel
Fryar, Benjamin	Doll, Abraham	Gilmore, Andrew
Garrison, Asbe	Hanks, John	Hanks, Joseph
Kelley, James	Kelley, John, Sr.	Kelley, John, Jr.
Kelley, William	Kelley, Andrew	Kelley, Alexander
Jacobs, Samuel	Linton, Lawson	Linton, Zecharia
Loury, Samuel	Lockard, James	Lockard, Joseph
Malone, Richard	Miller, Isaac	Miller, Robert
McClintock, Alexander	McClintock, Joseph	McClintock, John
Pearce, James	Queen, John	Reynolds, Anthony
Ross, John	Smith, James	Smith, Samuel
Seymore, Solomon	Smith, David	Salts, John
Van Embaugh, Abraham	Williams, John	Windpan, Frederick
Zeigler, George		

Pages 83-84

ROLL OF CAPT. JOHN SPENCER'S COMPANY.
(Probably from Ross County.)

Served from June 1, 1812 until May 31, 1813.

Capt. John Spencer	Lieut. Robert Davidson	Ensign, Andrew Ellison
Sergt. James Gibson	Sergt. Samuel Smith	Sergt. James Seymour
Sergt. Joseph Statelu	Corp. Thomas Hughs	Corp. Joseph Cunningham
Corp. Samuel Murphy	Corp. Elias Hughs	

Privates.	Privates.	Privates.
Barrack, John	Bernard, Jacob	Bernard, Mathew
Bevard, Jacob	Cunningham, William	Casey, Archibald
Casey, Jonothan	Chadwick, James	Cadwick, David
Drum, John	Devour, Enos	Drum, Thomas
Davis, Moses	Davis, Thomas	Evans, John
Evans, Joshua	Farn, John	Furry, John
Harris, John	Hall, John	Harris, Joshua
Jones, Thomas	Johnston, John	Kimannon, ———
Little, Jacob	Myers, Henry	Mutherbaugh, John
Mepenger, David	Marfoot, Samuel	McCawn, Robert
Pickering, Jacob	Parr, William	Paris, John
Roe, William	Steward, Andrew	Scott, James
Smith, Archibald	Spelman, Spencer	Smith, James
Shaddock, John	Walker, William	Wright, Joseph
Young, William		

Pages 85-86

ROLL OF CAPT. DANIEL CONNER'S COMPANY.
(Probably from Belmont County.)

Served from January 13, until March 17, 1814.

Capt. Daniel Conner	Lieut. Thomas Dunn	Ensign, Alfred Weeden
Sergt. Thomas Henry	Sergt. Absalom Waddell	Sergt. James Edwards
Sergt. Henry Van Fossen	Sergt. Eli Nichols	Corp. William Clifford
Corp. William West	Corp. David Milar	Corp. Samuel Perkins
Fifer, Isaac Midkiff	Drummer, Peter Hanson	

Privates.	Privates.	Privates.
Boyd, John	Bonehan, Aaron	Bundy, Joseph
Clark, James	Conklin, David	DeWitt, John
Decker, Simion	Findley, William	Ferrier, John
Grove, Barnet	Gassway, Robert	Harrington, Charles
Hart, John	Harper, Francis	Holmes, Samuel
Howel, Daniel	Honnel, Richard	Hupp, Phillip
Heaney, John	Joyques, John	Lanham, Elisha
Lloyd, James	Lonner, Thomas	Murphy, Westley
Murphey, William	Medley, Joseph	McFadden, Charles
Perkins, John	Pitman, Elias	Pitman, William
Pyatte, Thomas	Read, Jeremiah	Simmons, Thomas
Stellar, Mathias	Stella, Henry	Smith, Nichols
Stewart, John	Silvis, John	Scott, James
Shipman, Stephen	Truax, Abraham	Vanfossen, George
Waddle, James	Ware, Robert	Wagoner, John
West Enos	Yerlan, George	

Pages 87-88 Vol. 2.

ROLL OF CAPT. JOEL COLLIN'S COMPANY.
(Probably from Butler County.)

Served from August 11, 1812 until February, 1813.

Rank and Name of Soldier.
Capt. Joel Collins
Sergt. Jeremiah Gard
Sergt. John Price
Corp. George Sutton
Drummer, Henry Thompson

Rank and Name of Soldier.
Lieut. Ephraim Gard
Sergt. David Sutton
Corp. Zechariah Parish
Corp. Jacob Gard

Rank and Name of Soldier.
Ensign, John Hall
Sergt. Joseph Haines
Corp. Joseph Douglas
Fifer, Hays Taylor

Privates.
Anderson, James
Broadbury, James
Boys, George
Carper, John
DeCamp, William
Gray, Robert
Garver, Peter
Howard, Thomas
Jones, Henry
Lintner, Andrew
Martin, James
Mansfield, John
McMaken, Joseph
Owens, Silas
Pilson, Robert
Rutledge, Isaac
Scott, Richard
Stephen, Thomas
Smiley, John
Smith, Andrew
Sackett, John
Steele, Samuel
Stonebrake, John
Thompson, Samuel
Wilson, Thomas
Wickart, Joseph

Privates.
Bone, John
Brown, John
Casker, James
Crane, William
Dilleoe, Vincent
Gower, Jacob
Gard, Moses
Hyder, John
Kirkpatrick, George
Malone, John
Malone, Samuel
McManus, William
McNeal, James
Pine, Benjamin
Rainy, William
Scott, John E.
Sinnors, John
Smith, William
Smiley, James
Salmon, Jacob
Sullivan, William
Simpson, Samuel
Tigard, George
Taylor, Robert
Watson, Isaac
Wilever, Joseph

Privates.
Broadbury, Simeon
Beeler, George
Carr, James
Deneen, John
Dickard, Jacob
Gates, Jacob
Heath, William
Isaacs, John
Kerr, Jacob
Mosteller, Christopher
Megongle, Phillip
McKinstry, John
Newkirk, Robinson
Price, Joseph
Rinehart, Jacob
Stell, Alexander
Stark, Archibald
Smith, David
Shields, John
Stephens, Samuel
Sullivan, Patrick
Sutton, William
Tigard, William
Watson, Eber
Woodfin, Nicholas
Woods, Andrew

Pages 89-90

ROLL OF CAPT. GEORGE RICHARDSON'S COMPANY. (County Unknown.)

Served from August 31, until December 1, 1813.

Capt. George Richardson
Sergt. Edward Jackson
Sergt. Samuel Waters
Corp. John Huchinson

Lieut. John Ward
Sergt. Samuel Bay
Corp. Thomas Jackson
Corp. Abraham Cherryholmey

Ensign, John Kline
Sergt. Samuel Linton
Corp. Joseph Steins
Drummer, George Rummel

Privates.
Ashton, William
Baker, John
Bay, James
Bumtrager, John
Collins, Elijah
Croy, Mathew
Everhart, Frederick
Garnet, Francis
Hall, Hamilton
Hosack, William
Hoy, Samuel
Jennings, Bailess
Kellar, Martin
Miller, John
Marling, John
McMullin, Joseph
Price, Christopher
Robb, Joshua
Reamer, Adam
Smith, Thomas
Seaton, Robert
Trumble, John
Zeiglar, Phillip

Privates.
Allen, Jacob M.
Biddinger, Henry
Bryan, William
Casebear, Samuel
Cherry, William
DeLong, James
Fuller, Joseph
Gibson, George
Hall, Samuel
Hedges, Aaron
Harper, William
Koon, George
Ldman, John
Miller, Henry
Milslagel, Andrew
Neal, Joseph
Phillips, Enoch
Reeves, Joshua
Shaneman, Henry
Shepard, William
Sherick, Everett
Waller, Lewis

Privates.
Burges, Samuel
Bates, John
Burris, John
Clumm, John
Collis, David
DuWitt, Paul
Frederick, Peter
Hall, Joseph
Hughs, Jacob
Hedges, Israel
Howe, Jacob
Krutzer, Henry
Mizer, George
Moorehead, James
Moorehead, William
Oldham, James
Roop, Jacob
Reamer, John
Seward, William
Smith, Jacob
Thompson, Michael
Waller, John

Pages 91-92-93-94.

ROLL OF CAPT. JOHN JONES' COMPANY.
(Probably from Highland County.)

Served from May 1, 1812 until May 1, 1813.

Capt. John Jones
Sergt. John Fisher
Sergt. Elijah C. Wilkerson
Corp. John Campbell
Corp. Walker Baldwin
Fifer, Samuel Stephenson

Lieut. James Patterson
Sergt. James McConnel
Sergt. Thomas Smith
Corp. James Strain
Corp. Robert Strain

Ensign, Thomas Rogers
Sergt. Jacob Baker
Corp. Chalfin Robert
Corp. James Stanbury
Drummer, William Bunten

ROLL OF CAPT. JOHN JONES' COMPANY. (Continued)

Rank and Name of Soldier.

Privates.
- Belser, Micajah
- Braidy, Harrison
- Baldwin, Walton
- Countryman, Henry
- Gall, George
- Hastings, Henry
- Harper, Alexander
- Jonikin, Noah
- Lynch, John
- Miller, Peter
- Newman, Howard
- Plott, William
- Roads, George
- Reed, Rezin
- Stanberry, James
- Slaughter, Moses
- Swisher, Abraham
- Ward, Samuel

Rank and Name of Soldier.

Privates.
- Baker, Jacob
- Bell, George
- Coons, William R.
- Earls, David
- Hathaway, David
- Hart, Silas
- Harvey, Beacher
- Leaverton, John
- Little, Alexander
- McConnel, James
- Nicely, David
- Reader, Charles
- Roades, Phillip
- Ramsey, John L.
- Strain, Robert
- Swadley, Jacob
- Therman, John
- Williams, Mathew

Rank and Name of Soldier.

Privates.
- Bunten, William
- Bell, John
- Childers, Joseph
- Earls, Isaac
- Hastings, George
- Hartman, Jacob
- Jonikin, Eli
- Leaverton, James
- Leaverton, Thomas
- Nelson, Charles
- Patchel, John
- Rosebrough, John
- Rees, Owen
- Rubb or Ruble, Owen
- Shoemaker, Simeon
- Still, Samuel
- Thornton, Samuel

Page 95.

ROLL OF CAPT. HENRY MALLON'S COMPANY.
(Probably from Ross County.)

Served from July 28, until August 16, 1813.

- Capt. Henry Mallon
- Sergt. Christopher Popejoy
- Sergt. Edward Briant
- Corp. John Briant

- Lieut. Solomon Bonner
- Sergt. Martin Patterson
- Corp. Aaron Orahood
- Corp. William McCartney

- Ensign, Charles Wells
- Sergt. William Popejoy
- Corp. John Hoddy

Privates.
- Briggs, Samuel
- Briant, Jonothan
- Christian, Leathlin
- Crowley, Joseph
- Criminie, Jacob
- Day, Overton
- Huffman, Leonard
- McCartney, Duke
- Stookey, Daniel
- Stookey, Jacob
- Toohinder, Thomas
- Woolf, Jonothan

Privates.
- Boyd, Francis
- Bowers, Michael
- Christie, Joel
- Clark, James
- Carr, Martin
- Fennemore, John
- Huffman, Joseph
- McCoy, John
- Strader, Christopher
- Stingley, Leonard
- Wells, Squire
- Whetstone, Abraham

Privates.
- Boots, Jacob
- Bennet, Isaac
- Clouser, John
- Clark, Robert
- Day, Martin
- Gregg, William
- Monroe, Lemule
- McCartney, John
- Strader, Michael
- Shaw, Giddeon
- Wonsoy, Daniel

Pages 97-98.

ROLL OF CAPT. WILLIAM HUMPHREY'S COMPANY. (County Unknown.)

Served from April, 1812 until ——————.

- Capt. William Humphrey
- Sergt. Andrew Robbe
- Sergt. Mathias Dean
- Corp. Josiah Bradway

- Lieut. Peter Deardorf
- Sergt. Wright Elliott
- Corp. Hezekiah Cartwright
- Corp. John Flemming

- Ensign Robert Sweeney
- Sergt. James Thirby
- Corp. John Young

Privates.
- Anderson, John
- Cummins, John
- Fisher, David
- Garrison, John
- Garrison, David
- Hight, Abraham
- Hamilton, Elias
- Kindespeker, Jacob
- Lee, John
- Mullen, John
- Nicholson, Andrew
- Rees, Boon
- Thomas, David
- Venard, John

Privates.
- Blake, Nathan
- Fitzgerel, Asen
- Garwood, William
- Garrison, Jeremiah
- Garrison, Hezekiah
- Hand, Benjamin
- Hyde, Samuel
- Long, William D.
- Murphy, Benjamin
- Martin, John
- Patten, William
- Spencer, James
- Stanbrough, Nehemiah
- Warts, John

Privates.
- Branstetter, Andrew
- Fisher, Jacob
- Garrison, Benjamin
- Garrison, Persons
- Harris, James
- Hesbr, Jacob
- Holcombe, Asen
- Lasey, John
- Monroe, Charles
- Marley, William
- Reaglen, Wright
- Seward, John
- Treland, William
- Wright, George

Page 99.

ROLL OF CAPT. WILLIAM SUMNER'S COMPANY.
(Probably from Fairfield County.)

Served from July 31, until September 6, 1813.

- Capt. William Sumner
- Sergt. John Bly
- Sergt. Archibald Carnian
- Corp. Asa Hubble

- Lieut. William Martin
- Sergt. Isaac Painter
- Corp. Mathew Wolford
- Corp. Ira Bing

- Lieut. Sostehenese McCabe
- Sergt. Daniel Brumback
- Corp. George Lafery
- Musician, Richard Thompson

ROLL OF CAPT. WILLIAM SUMMER'S COMPANY. (Continued)

Rank and Name of Soldier.

Privates.
Arendt, Peter
Bretz, Conrad
Cagy, Jacob
Giger, Martin
Hutchinson, James
Little, George
McCabe, Ezra
Polly, Jacob
Sechrist, Peter
Thompson, William
Weaver, Christian
Watson, Richard

Privates.
Bryan, William
Bretz, John
Frieze, Peter
Hershberger, David
Hammond, Michael
Musser, Muly
Oiler, George
Reed, John
Senior, Jacob
Tricker, John
Wolf, Henry

Privates.
Bush, Martin
Brown, Joseph
Goss, Jacob
Harod, James
Lamb, William
Myers, Jacob
Phelps, Hezekiah
Swartz, Frederick
Spitler, Warner
Winter, Abraham
Watson, James

Pages 101-102.

ROLL OF CAPT. WILLIAM McMAIN'S (or McMean's) COMPANY.
(From Clermont or Butler Counties.)
Served from August 11, 1812 until February 11, 1813.

Capt. William McMain (or Mean)
Sergt. Archibald Clinton
Sergt. John Coteral
Corp. Enoch McMaines

Mc-Lieut. Paul Rush
Sergt. Joseph Cotteral
Sergt. Isaac Elston
Corp. Edwin Hughs

Ensign Robert Orn
Sergt. Henry Stroman
Corp. Joseph Hutchinson
Corp. James Mullin

Privates.
Abat, Jeremiah
Barber, Daniel
Clark, William
Crawford, Charles
Davison, William
Durham, Silas
Easton, William
Farden, Christopher
Fisher, Samuel
Hughes, Isaac
Hutchinson, Joseph
Long, Frank
Lenning, David
Megrue, Charles
Malot, Peter
McCollum, James
Price, Jeremiah
Pobst, Frederick
Sinnard, Abraham
Shields, David
Wakeland, Charles

Privates.
Brown, John
Cotrell, William
Cummins, John
Crawford, Clark
Daniels, William
Eastwood, Joseph
Elston, William
Flagle, Valentine
Gilmon, Daniel
Hughes, James
Jones, James
Long, Jacob
Lenet, Adam
Megrue, Paul
Motsiner, Felix
McDonnough, Samuel
Parks, James
Reeves, Alexander
Stewart, Hall
Webster, John
Wableton, John

Privates.
Briding, Thomas
Cramer, David
Cambo, Thomas
Dougherty, David
Davis, Thomas
Eacret, William
Frazer, David
Finlong, Lewis
Gost, Jacob
Huddleston, James
Jones, Thomas
Lenning, Nicholas
Lining, Gabriel
Merrit, Isaac
McMains, Benjamin
Notruge, Felix
Porter, Victor
Ramsey, George
Stronie, Collen
Wikkel, James

Pages 103-104.

ROLL OF CAPT. ROBERT HAYES' COMPANY. (County Unknown.)
Served from April 27, 1812 until ————.

Capt. Robert Hayes
Sergt. Bryan Williams
Sergt. Samuel S. Jack
Corp. John Robinson

Lieut. Samuel Pope
Sergt. Michael Brown
Corp. Joseph McEdwards
Corp. Seth St. John

Ensign John Sheet
Sergt. John Ross
Corp. Isaac Heaton

Privates.
Brenney, John
Baker, Clark
Camron, John
Estel, William L.
Graham, Levi
Huthoe, John
Hutchinson, James
Hoole, James
Jester, Eli
Leoman, Christopher
Manning, Daniel
McDaniel, William
McCristy, Jesse
Rochefiter, Samuel
Stiles, Henry
Snooke, Martin
Smoot, Dixon
Thatcher, Elijah
Tuttle, Isaiah
Trump, Andrew
Voorhis, Jeremiah
Weain, Adam

Privates.
Bowers, David
Caslet, Alexander
Disberry, James
Farmer, Michael
Goodpasture, Jesse
Hayes, John
Hercules, William
Jack, James
Jennings, David
Martin, William
Mosbry, John
McCollister, Hugh
Powell, Jacob
Roberts, Aaron
Snuff, John
Sharohan, John
Stearns, Jabez
Trimble, Moses
Trimble, James
Turman, John
Wear, Robert
Waters, Richard

Privates.
Bowen, John
Calril, Alexander
Dill, John
Frourdale, Samuel
Hamilton, Jacob
Hardy, James
Hoges, William
Jeffries, George
Kitchel, James L.
Miller, John
Macy, Seth
McCullister, John
Rhynearson, Miller
Shaw, Archibald
Sutton, John
Stiles, John A.
Samson, Jehiel
Tutler, John
Trudle, George
Vanskike, David
Wallace, William
Wear, Elisha

Pages 105-106. Vol. 2.
ROLL OF CAPT. JAMES ODELL'S COMPANY. (County Unknown.)

Served from July 29, until September 8, 1813.

Rank and Name of Soldier.
Capt. James Odell
Sergt. John McCombs
Sergt. Joseph Smalley
Corp. William Johnson

Privates.

Brown, Nathan
Barngroover, David
Bell, Andrew
Collins, Isaac
Galaspy, Thomas
Hough,, Ashford
McGee, John
Prather, Thomas
Roberts, James
Smally, Isaac
Strain, John C.
Thermon, James
Wilkin, John
Whitley, Thomas

Rank and Name of Soldier.
Lieut. David Johnson
Sergt. Thomas Grover
Corp. Thomas McStrain
Corp. John Bereman

Privates.

Bigley, Peter
Barngroover, John
Bonar, Joseph
Chapman, David
His, James
Hamilton, Alexander
McNeeley, George
Pettijohn, Abraham
Smith, Archibald
Strain, John H.
Strain, John
Thermon, David
Walker, Elijah
White, Joseph

Rank and Name of Soldier.
Ensign James Rogers
Sergt. James B. Strain
Corp. James McCollon

Privates.

Brower, David
Brown, Charles
Chapman, John
Chapman, Aschel
Henderson, Joseph
McGee, Thomas
Nays, Thomas
Ross, John
Smally, Thomas
Small, Jacob
Therman, Talbot
White, William
Whitley, John

Pages 107-108.
ROLL OF CAPT. ROBERT MORRISON'S COMPANY.
(Probably from Belmont County.)

Served from July 29, until September 8, 1813.

Capt. Robert Morrison
Sergt. Robert Findlay
Sergt. Alexander Baldridge
Corp. William Smith
Fifer, David Smith

Privates.

Alexander, Benjamin
Burnett, Lewis
Bisship, Peter
Bailey, James
Clark, John
Cross, William
Eyler, Joseph
Findley, Samuel
Gordon, James
Mailatt, George
Mehafey, Andrew
McNeal, John
Morris, John
Parker, Silvenes
Ramsey, William
Smith, John
Thompson, Robert
Washburn, ----------
Wright, Stephen
Young, Thomas

Lieut. Thomas Wason
Sergt. Robert Young
Corp. James Winter
Corp. Alexander Liget

Privates.

Alexander, Gabriel
Bair, George
Brown, John
Caskey, James
Coppel, Daniel
Cross, Richard
Eginton, Joseph
Foster, John
Kruzen, Thomas
Mehafey, John
McNeal, James
McColpen, Robert
Nelson, James
Patton, William
Rodgers, William
Sargent, James
Wilson, Robert
Wright, Joseph
Williamson, James

Ensign David Young
Sergt. Abraham Thomas
Corp. John McClure
Drummer, William Hamilton

Privates.

Alexander, James
Bovel, John
Bilbee, John
Craig, Robert
Crust, Henry
Edginton, George
Findley, William
Gleze, Nathan
Liget, William
Mintire, George
McNeal, Joseph
McColgan, William
Odell, Thomas
Patton, Nathaniel
Reed, Nathaniel
Smittel, David
Wilkes, John
Wright, William
Young, James

Pages 109-110-111-112.
ROLL OF CAPT. LUTHER LEONARD'S COMPANY.
(Probably from Butler County.)

Served from August 11, until November 30, 1812, and from July 5, until July 23, 1814.

Capt. Luther Leonard
Ensign William Mitchell
Sergt. Jonothan Harris
Sergt. Burgan Miller
Corp. William Robinson
Corp. Mathias Roosa

Privates.

Bolser, John H.
Boraff, Michael
Broadwell, Elliott
Bowman, John
Bowman, George W.
Cochran Joseph
Christ, Abraham
Cummings, John D.
Card, Abraham
Doughty, John
Everhart, Frederick
Edwards, Thomas
Finney, Thomas

Lieut. Clarkson Price
Sergt. William Cochran
Sergt. John Mellen
Sergt. Samuel McKee
Corp. John Moore
Corp. Benjamin Danford

Privates.

Bolner, John
Bolsel, John C.
Black, Mathias
Bradwell, David
Byfield, Horatio
Cochran, Richard
Cummings, William
Canter, Shaffield
Cochran, Thomas
Dunlap, Josiah
Edwards, Noah
Edwards, John
Frazer, John

Lieut. Nathaniel Terwillegar
Sergt. John Terwillegar
Sergt. Henry Miller
Corp. James Mitchell
Corp. John Hetzer

Privates.

Bolser, Henry
Borau, Jesse
Burns, John
Bowerly, Tapin
Cochran, John
Cochran, Samuel
Cummings, Peter W.
Christ, Joseph
Cochran, Nathaniel
Elliott, Simon
Evans, Jeremiah
Flinn, Jacob
Fitzwater, Samuel

Vol. 2.

ROLL OF CAPT. LUTHER LEONARD'S COMPANY. (Continued)

Rank and Name of Soldier.	Rank and Name of Soldier.	Rank and Name of Soldier.
Privates.	**Privates.**	**Privates.**
Gomly, Thomas	Griffin, Wilson	Gambriel, Travis
Ganard, Will	Harris, Amos	Harris, William
Husler, or Hustin, George	Haggerty, John H.	Hoover, Michael
Jones, Evan	Jones, Oliver	James, William
Kitchel, Moses	Kerns, Daniel	Kerns, Jacob
Kerns, Joseph	Jones, William	Little, David
Landon, William	Lions, Henry	Landon, John
Mulin, Mathew	Morrison, William	Mondor, Jacob
Madaris, William	Mathews, Abraham	McCain, Robert
McCown, John	McGee, Joseph	McCohn, Thomas
Nash, John	Porter, Thomas	Patterson, Moses
Price, Peter	Perry, William	Price, Clarkson
Roosa, Jacob	Rude, James	Roosa, Abraham
Ramsey, John	Reeder, Reuben	Ramsey, Robert
Slaughter, Jeremiah	Snyder, John	Shaffer, Joseph
Snyder, William	Skinner, Joseph M.	Seaman, Abraham
Smith, Abraham	Smith, James	Taselman, John
Thompson, Aaron	Thompson, Caleb	Thompson, Joshua
Tunttiger, Mathew	Voorhees, Jacob N.	Waggoner, Joseph
Willer, John	Whitside, William	Whiteride, James
Whiteman, Robert	Whitcomb, John	Ward, Squier
Ward, Silas	Wortman, John	Whitsell, William

Pages 113-114.

ROLL OF CAPT. ABRAHAM SHEPHERD'S COMPANY.
(Probably from Ross County.)

Served from September 2, until October 2, 1812 and from July 29, until August 22, 1813.

Capt. Abraham Shepherd	Lieut. Robert Wright	Ensign Samuel Evans
Sergt. Silas Thomas	Sergt. Robert Moore	Sergt. Samuel Buth
Sergt. Samuel Mathers	Sergt. Terry Womacks	Sergt. William Reynolds
Sergt. Joseph Bratten	Corp. David Reynolds	Corp. James Blaze
Corp. William McCelgin	Corp. Huston Martin	Corp. William Colgan
Fifer, George Reynolds	Drummer, William Reynolds	

Privates.	Privates.	Privates.
Cary, Isaac	Carter, Thomas	Edwards, John
Graham, David	Grant, William	Glendaning, William
Hatfield, John	Howland, John	Hewitt, Jacob
Jorden, Samuel	Kinkaid, Samuel	Kratzer, Jacob
Kirkpatrick, Charles	Kanet, Samuel	Kinnett, James
Kinnett, Thomas	Letters, Jacob	Morrow, Robert
Myers, William	Martin, Hutson	Mathers, Samuel
McKilkrick, William	Nilson, or Wilson, James	Nilson or Wilson, John
Newland, James	Pettijohn, Isaac	Reynolds, Oliver
Reynolds, Stephen	Robbins, Vinien	Sillman, John
Snedakerger, Warren	Seller, Michael	Shaw, Anthony
Snedaker, Ganett	Wright, Samuel	Wyckoff, Asher
Wilson, Josiah		

Page 115.

ROLL OF CAPT. ROBERT WEST'S COMPANY.
(Probably from Ross County.)

Served from July 30, until August 23, 1813.

Capt. Robert West	Lieut. Joseph Daniel	Sergt. Samuel Jacobs
Sergt. William Reid	Sergt. William Baggeass	Sergt. John McNown
Fifer, Samuel Wilson	Drummer, Benjamin Perry	

Privates.	Privates.	Privates.
Anderson, William	Corn, Joseph	Gilbert, William
Griffith, Benjamin	Housh, John, Jr.	Hodges, Nathaniel
Hayman, Wilson	Lang, John	Lowill, James
Laney, Samuel	Scott, Robert J.	

Page 117.

ROLL OF LIEUT. DANIEL COE'S COMPANY.
(Probably from Adams County.)

Served from July 30, until August 29, 1813.

Lieut. Daniel Coe	Sergt. William Newell	Sergt. Mathew Gentree
Ensign, Robert Stevers	Corp. Jorn Purdon	

Privates.	Privates.	Privates.
Ballard, Lyman	Crusan, Israel	Fisher, John
Kingan, William	Moore, William	Newell, Thomas
Sames, Stephen	Woods, James	

ROLL OF CAPT. ELIJAH MARTIN'S COMPANY.
(Probably from Brown County.)

Served from February 1, until August 12, 1813.

Rank and Name of Soldier.	Rank and Name of Soldier.	Rank and Name of Soldier.
Capt. Elijah Martin	Lieut. Jacob Jacobs	Lieut. Zechariah Riggs
Ensign, Joseph Stewart	Sergt. David Flaugher	Sergt. Henry Hawk
Sergt. William Yates	Sergt. Archibald Parker	Sergt. William Dixon
Sergt. James Higgins	Corp. Richard Brown	Corp. John Hawk
Corp. Henry Haldesty	Musician, Jeremiah Martin	

Privates.

Brown, William	Cochran, Jacob	Cooper, John
Creed, Mathew	Churin, Thomas R.	Dixon, William
Dixon, David	Dixon, John	Davis, Henson
Douglas, Samuel	Dougherty, Samuel	Flauglar, David
Flaugher, Henry	Flaugher, Jacob	Fisher, George
Forbus, William	Findley, James	Gibson, Thomas
Godfrey, James	Gotliffe, John S.	Higgins, James
Hawk, Phillip	Hughes, William	Jones, William
Leachman, Thomas	Linn, John	Lathen, James
Middlesworth, James	Middletown, Thomas	McFerron, David
Newell, Robert	Parker, Archibald	Panmire, Ellis
Panner, James	Panner, William	Page, David
Riley, Benjamin	Stewart, Joseph	Savage, John
Staton, Hill	Stephens, Samuel D.	Sharp, Isaac
	Wallace, William	

ROLL OF LIEUT. BARNET RISTEIN'S COMPANY.
(Probably from Ross County.)

Served from July 29, until August 22, 1813.

Ensign John Coppel	Sergt. Icabod Howland	Sergt. Elijah Hendrickson

Privates.

Acton, Phillip	Askrin, David	Brooks, Mason
Bayn, Samuel	Cox, Thomas	Howland, Isatis
Husband, John	Harbaugh, Phillip	Huey, Samuel
Hughs, Joseph	Johnston, Robert	Liginbotham, John
Montgomery, David	Mahaffey, John	Moore, Samuel
Moore, Thomas	Mahaffey, William	Rittenger, William
Sparkes, James	Shaw, Samuel	Shilton, William
Sargent, James	Wilson, Samuel	

ROLL OF LIEUT. FRANCIS CUNNINGHAM'S COMPANY. (County Unknown.)

Served from July 5, until July 23, 1814.

Lieut. Francis Cunningham	Ensign, Titus Everhart	Sergt. Martin Robinson
Sergt. Thomas Biggs	Sergt. Abner Hibber	Corp. James Buckles
Corp. Samuel Pearson	Corp. Thomas Baning	Drummer, Howell, Campbell
Fifer, Daniel Crane		

Privates.

Buckles, William	Brewer, Charles	Carman, Joshua
Case, John	Cochran, Robert	Day, Peter
Ensby, Christopher	Freed, John	Gullifer, Stephen
Goode, Burwell	Jones, Joshua	Lucas, Francis
Moore, Hugh	McKinsey, Nehemiah	McKewn, John
Pierson, Barton	Reagan, Wright	Wilson, David
Wilson, George	Whickear, Luke	Wilson, Isaiah
Waldorf, Isaac	Wilson, Gabriel	Williams, William
Whickear, Asa	Wright, Stephen	

ROLL OF CAPT. NICHOLAS MURRAY'S COMPANY.
(From Jefferson County.)

Served from August 25, until December 25, 1812.

Capt. Nicholas Murray	Lieut. Nathaniel Windryer, or Wintringer	Ensign, John Camell
Sergt. Phillip Fulton		Sergt. Joseph Batchlor
Sergt. James Kernahan	Sergt. George Beatty	Corp. James Patten
Corp. Kames Hakill		

Privates.

Anderson, David	Ashby, Abel	Bayley, Joshua
Brown, George	Blackburn, John	Bow, Curtis
Collins, John	Carrel, James	Carlisle, James
Cummins, Robert	Carter, Bryan	Evans, Richard
Erwin, Robert	Fowler, James	Gillis, James B.
Henderson, James	Hunt, George	Murray, Charles
McPake, Thomas	McClelland, William	Niblack, John
Parker, John	Reder, George	Richards, Samuel
Steel, Josiah	Snyder, Jacob	Thompson, Lewis
Williams, Samuel	Worstell, Joseph	

ROSTER OF OHIO SOLDIERS IN WAR OF 1812

Pages 129-130.   Vol. 2.

ROLL OF CAPTAIN WILLIAM DUNLAP'S COMPANY.
(Probably from Highland County.)
Served from July 29, until September 8, 1913.

Rank and Name of Soldier.
Capt. William Dunlap
Sergt. Stephen Parker
Sergt. Timothy Shirely
Corp. James Henland
Corp. George Davidson

Privates.
Austain, Nelson
Beasley, Jepther
Carr, John
Carr, James
Cartmill, John
Finley, Reisten
Games, John W.
Hock, John
Hineman, John
Howard, Abner
Jacobs, William
Lewis, George
Masters, Vaschel
Martin, John
McCoy, John
Parker, Christopher
Snyder, Daniel
Shelton, John
Strain, Thomas

Rank and Name of Soldier.
Lieut. Daniel Coe
Sergt. Thomas Bayne
Sergt. Benjamin Cutler
Corp. Abraham McDaniel
Corp. John Readman

Privates.
Beard, John
Bayne, John
Carter, John
Cavet, James
Dickins, Thomas
Fetters, Daniel
Hopkins, Robert
Hathaway, Aaron
Hanover, Isaac
Henany, James
King, James
Lang, Elijah
Mather, William
McKinney, Hezekiah
Neal, Samuel
Race, Moses
Sutherland, Ebenezer
Shepherd, John
Woods, James
Wright, Samuel

Rank and Name of Soldier.
Ensign Henry Bayne
Sergt. Ebenezer David
Sergt. Arthur O'Hara
Corp. John Meyars

Privates.
Bayne, William
Cummings, Anthony
Cumberland, Thomas
Canady, James
Dryden, Thomas
Fisher, Jacob
Hopkins, John
Hall, Joseph
Highes, William
Jacoby, William
Little, Thomas
Long, Benjamin
Moore, Levi
McClean, John
Potter, Barnabus
Rewes, Daniel
Smith, Isaac
Salisbury, Thomas
Wallace, Edward

Pages 131-132.

ROLL OF CAPT. JOHN H. LINDSEY'S COMPANY.
(Probably from Scioto County.)
Served from July 28, until August 28, 1813.

Capt. John H. Lindsey
Sergt. Robert B. Scott
Sergt. James Thompson
Corp. John Bennet

Privates.
Bachus, Michael
Benson, Joseph
Bennet, Benjamin
Culp, Cornelius
Dilawter, Isaac
Keys, John
Lindsey, Peter
McKenney, Theodore
Nelson, Jonothan R.
Priest, Richard
Shunkweiler, Daniel
Shope, William
Sikes, Edwin
Thompson, Robert
Utt, Henry

Lieut. Jesse Marshall
Sergt. John Higgins
Corp. Allen Moore
Corp. William Moore

Privates.
Biber, John Van
Bowen, John
Barkelov, Edward
Craig, William
Dilawter, Lawrence
Kneff, George
Marshall, Samuel
McDowell, James
Perry, Samuel
Snyder, Andrew
Shope, John
Sikes, Levi
Shoupe, John
Utt, John
Wilson, Alexander

Ensign, William Rollins
Sergt. William Plumb
Corp. David Crull

Privates.
Biber, Jacob Van
Bowen, William
Collins, Martin
Day, Ezekial
Holland, Francis
Lindsey, William
McDowe" William
Nelson, Ralph
Pyles, Absalom
Shunkweiler, Simon
Snedecor, John
Stroufver, John
Traxler, William
Utt, Jacob

Pages 133-134.

ROLL OF CAPT. ISAAC MONNETT'S COMPANY. (From Ross County.)
Served from July 28, until September 6, 1813.

Capt. Isaac Monnett
Sergt. Thomas Reid
Sergt. Jacob Plummer
Corp. Humphrey Mounts

Privates.
Andersin, Griffith
Brown, Henry
Caldwell, Alexander
Dresbach, Benjamin
Davis, Albar C.
Dunn, Henry
Ferrin, Daniel
Goodenough, Solomon
Higgins, Lemuel
Holverstott, Jacob
Ingham, Isaiah
Justine, Jesse
Mullott, John
Miller, John
Patten, Thomas
Reedy, John
Spong, John
Strosser, Henry
Van Blarecon, Samuel

Lieut. Samuel Jones
Sergt. Adam Bawhan
Corp. Jonas Markel
Corp. John Wilson

Privates.
Biaccus, Joseph
Caldwell, William
Clayton, William
Depbach, Henry
Dunn, Peter
Doty, John M.
Frye, George
Hinton, Thomas
Haynes, Frederick
Henry, James
Jones, Henry
Knife, Peter
Moses, Jacob
Morris, Jeremiah
Ross, Solomon
Strosser, Peter
Stutterbach, John
Throgmorton, John
Weider, Henry
Warline, Samuel

Ensign, Thomas Armstrong
Sergt. Ellis Minshal
Corp. Samuel Federolph

Privates.
Bowsher, William
Cade, Robert
Campbell, Hiram
Dunn, Christian
Dyser, Stephen
Exline, Edward
Glover, William
Hedington, John
Heinly, Jacob
Harper, John
Jones, Davis
Moss, Joseph
Myers, Jacob
Niece, Andrew
Reedy, Michael
Straw, Solomon
Signer, George
Throgmorton, Peter
White, Jeremiah

Page 135. Vol. 2.
ROLL OF CAPT. JOHN A. COLLINS' COMPANY. (County Unknown.)

Served from July 31, until August 14, 1813.

Rank and Name of Soldier.
Capt. John A. Collins
Sergt. John McCrorg
Sergt. Abraham Hiestand
Corp. William Kennard

Privates.
Arendt, Peter
Bretz, John
Hufford, Daniel
Hutchinson, James
Mawyers, Jacob
Smith, William
Swarts, Frederick
Wolf, Henry

Rank and Name of Soldier.
Lieut. Ellison Martin
Sergt. John Trusner
Corp. John Cook
Corp. Moses Thompson

Privates.
Brown, David
Collins, John
Hunsbach, Conrad
Lariner, John
Phelph, Hezekiah
Stephenson, Elijah
Thompson, William

Rank and Name of Soldier.
Ensign, John McClung
Sergt. John Shaw
Corp. Christian Hiestand
Drummer, David Thompson

Privates.
Bretz, Conrad
Freeze, Peter
Herod, James
Martin, James
Shaw, Andrew
Shesler, John
Wills, Samuel

Page 136.
ROLL OF CAPT. JONOTHAN BABB'S COMPANY. (County Unknown.)

Served from July 31, until August 14, 1813.

Capt. Jonothan Babb
Sergt. Jacob Maines
Corp. Isaiah Buck
Fifer, William Lashly

Privates.
Alexander, James
Hardin, James
McGehron, John
Staimates, Peter

Lieut. Thomas Hammond
Sergt. Jacob Collins
Corp. John Smith

Privates.
Breome, George
Jackson, George
Reynolds, Levi
Shiner, Daniel

Ensign, George Frunk
Sergt. Jacob Trout
Drummer, John Finke

Privates.
Brandt, John
Jarvis, William
Reed, William
Trout, John

Page 137.
ROLL OF CAPT. JOHN DAVIDSON'S COMPANY.
(Probably from Adams County.)

Served from July 28, until September 8, 1813.

Capt. John Davidson
Ensign, Absalom Kirkpatrick
Ensign, James Campbell
Corp. Jacob Sebret
Fifer, Andrew Burns

Privates.
Beard, Samuel
Campbell, William
Drenan, David
Featherkille, Andrew
Izzard, Eli
Kirkpatrick, Samuel
Montgomery, Adam
Moore, Michael
Pelson, Francis
Pyke, William
Robbins, Thomas
Tucker, Levin
Williamson, Timothy, Sr.

Lieut. Andrew McIntire
Corp. James McIntire
Corp. James Stockwell
Corp. John Wallis
Wagoner, John Hayes

Privates.
Campbell, George
Cain, Stephen
Elliott, Andrew
Fenton, Samuel
Kemp, Richard
Kirkpatrick, James
Murphy, Robert
McIntire, William
Paris, William
Robbins, John
Smith, John
Vanpelt, John
White, John

Ensign, Robert Glasgon
Ensign, Edward Scott
Corp, Hugh Montgomery
Drummer, Jacob Storms

Privates.
Cain, Jesse
Dryden, William
Elliott, Robert Jr.
Goody, John
Kirkpatrick, George
Lockart, Moses
Marshall, David
McCheney, Alexander
Penniwit, Mark
Redman, William
Simons, Jacob
Williamson, Timothy, Jr.
Whaley, John

Page 139.
ROLL OF CAPT. ROBERT RUSSELL'S COMPANY. (County Unknown.)

Served from July 28, until September 8, 1813.

Capt. Robert Russell
Sergt. Joseph Westbrook
Sergt. William Riggs
Corp. Robert Conn

Privates.
Adams, Henry H.
Black, James
Colvin, George
Fethers, Charles
Henderson, Thomas
Kilpatrick, John
McClaren, James
Nash, Thomas
Russell, Alexander
Stickler, John
Smith, William
Thompson, Hugh
Washborn, Abraham

Lieut. Samuel Davidson
Sergt. Simion Smith
Corp. Daniel Cline
Corp. Mathew Kincaid

Privates.
Akins, William
Brikan, Absalom
Eaton, Thomas R.
Fetters, Michael
Hughes, Samuel
Leech, James
Nixon, William
Pennewit, Tavender
Riggs, James
Stout, Josiah
Storer, William
Thatcher, Joseph
Young, George

Ensign, John Harris
Sergt. James Hayslip
Corp. Joseph McGlone

Privates.
Anderson, John
Cannon, John
Foster, Samuel
Hutson, William
Keyon, Daniel
Leech, John
Oldrid, John
Pollard, Robert
Scott, Moses
Stethern, William
Tucker, Kelley
Wood, Joseph

Page 141 Vol. 2.

ROLL OF CAPT. WATSON DOUGLAS' COMPANY.
(Probably from Ross County.)
Served from July 29, until August 26, 1813.

Rank and Name of Soldier.	Rank and Name of Soldier.	Rank and Name of Soldier.
Capt. Watson Douglas	Sergt. Gavin Mitchell	Sergt. Alexander Morrow
Corp. Robert Morrow		Corp. Edward Bian
Privates.	**Privates.**	**Privates.**
Bell, Joseph	Bell, Josiah D.	Ballard, Thomas
Coffey, John	Clevenger, Titus	Combs, Joeb
Duval, Samuel	Eray, Nathan	Eisley, Aaron
Elwood, William	Elwood, Henry	Elwood, Robert
Elwood, George	Garret, William	Hughey, William
Hickson, Joseph	Johnston, Andrew	Johnston, James
Leverton, Daniel	Lloyd, Charles	Morrow, William
McVilan, Thomas	Minor, Rufus	Patten, James
Patten, William	Strain, Thomas	Strain, David
Strain, John R.	Thornton, John	Thurman, Thomas
Thurman, Daniel	Wright, William	Wright, James
	West, Herman K.	

Page 143.

ROLL OF LIEUT. JOSEPH DRYDEN'S COMPANY.
(Probably from Ross County.)
Served from July 29, until August 26, 1813.

Lieut. Joseph Dryden	Sergt. John Worson	Sergt. Newton Doggett
Corp. Robert Patterson		
Privates.	**Privates.**	**Privates.**
Adair, Hugh	Benjamin, John	Beason, Benjamin
Chaney, Nathan	Creed, D. C.	Creed, James
Creek, James	Creek, Jacob	Gamer, Reuben
Jolly, William	Joslin, William	Murfin, William
Nelson, Charles	Robbins, Thomas	Shinn, George
Tomlin, Terry	Troupe, Jacob	Vanzant, James

Page 145.

ROLL OF CAPT. ROBERT KERR'S COMPANY.
(Probably from Adams County.)
Served from July 28, until September 8, 1813.

Capt. Robert Kerr	Lieut. William Wickoff	Ensign James Davis
Sergt. Samuel Burkett	Sergt. Benjamin Kennels	Sergt. Turmin Moore
Sergt. Mathew Williams	Corp. Samuel McClure	Corp. Jacob Hempleman
Corp. William Newman	Corp. Nathaniel Newman	Fifer, John Copas
Privates.	**Privates.**	**Privates.**
Allen, Liman	Brewer, Charles	Buzzard, Henry
Copas, Thomas	Cane, Cornelius	Collier, Daniel
Dilworth, William	DeCamps, David	Engle, Thomas
Ellison, George	Fry, Henry	Freeland, Aaron
Freeland, Isaac	Grooms, John	Helterbrand, Solomon
Helmer, George	Jack, Andrew	Jack, James
Jones, Mathew	King, Patrick	Kerr, Samuel
Moore, Henry	Moore, Aaron	Murphy, Asa
Mitchell, George	McCoy, James	McColum, Isaac
McDermit, David	McCall, James	Osman, Jabus
Peterson, Thomas	Pile, Henry	Rodgers, John
Roebuck, Aaron	Stuce, Henry	Shewmaker, Solomon
Storey, William	Waggoner, Adam	Williams, Joseph
	Young, William	

Pages 147-148.

ROLL OF CAPT. WILLIAM KEY'S COMPANY.
(Probably from Ross County.)
Served from April 27, until June 30, 1812.

Capt. William Keys	Lieut. Andrew Lindsay	Ensign Isaac N. Riley
Sergt. James Foster	Sergt. Adam R. Keys	Sergt. Obed Harrison
Sergt. John Irwin	Corp. Henry Doyle	Corp. Henry Wisthay
Corp. Richard Cavett	Corp. Moses Morgan	Musician, George Grover
Privates.	**Privates.**	**Privates.**
Bachan, John	Byers, Isaac	Blane, William
Chonay, Ralph	Cavett, Richard	Connor, John
Dalsen, Peter	Davidson, Thomas	Dexan, Caleb
England, Titus	England, Joseph	Emberry, Abner Van
Fry, Jacob	Grant, John H.	Greenman, Jeremiah
Graytes, Nathaniel	Garrett, Edward	Galbraith, William
Hutchinson, Robert	Housmond, George	Hurd, Samuel
Harrison, Elisha	Hoover, Henry	Heath, William
Jones, Thomas	Jordan, Isaac	Kerns, Felix
Layton, William	Lloyd, Thomas	Lake, Jonothan
Maron, Thomas	Minshall, Edward	Moffett, Nath
McCrady, William	McArthur, Duncan	McCollister, Clement
Otter, Robert	Sands, Joseph	Sponge, Henry
Smith, Peter	Sinn, Jacob	White, Robert
Winder, James	Wilson, Robert	Wall, Jeptha

Pages 149-150. Vol. 2.

ROLL OF CAPT. HENRY ULNEY'S COMPANY. (County Unknown.)

Served From April 27, until June 30, 1812.

Rank and Name of Soldier.	Rank and Name of Soldier.	Rank and Name of Soldier.
Capt. Henry Ulney	Lieut. Peter Frederick	Ensign Henry Frederick
Sergt. John G. Caldwell	Sergt. John Roberts	Sergt. John Crouch
Sergt. William Evans	Corp. Henry Coza	Corp. Henry Roberts
Corp. Henry Bun	Corp. Jacob Gray	

Privates.

Bitzer, Jacob	Brown, John	Bawn, John
Bush, Joseph	Bitzer, William	Bunn, David
Cox, James	Cozad, Joe	Cozad, Daniel
Caldwell, William	Clark, Thomas	Campbell, Thomas
Claypool, Jacob	Cannor, Aaron	DeHaven, John
DeHaven, Abraham	DeHaven, Harman	Dysart, Joseph
Dillon, William	Elder, Thomas	Exline, Edward
Elder, James	Ferguson, John	Finnemore, John
Frederick, Solomon	Fugate, Samuel	Gump, William
Hurt, Clement	Hays, John	Jenkins, James
James, Samuel	Johnston, William	Kempt, John
King, Garret	Lynes, William	Miller, Jesse
Maden, Alfred	McKanna, Hugh	McCall, Samuel
Nelson, John	Ritten, Henry	Ruse, Jeremiah
Richardson, Jonothan	Simes, William	Shruh Garnett
Steel, Samuel	Tidd, Moses	Teets, Lawrence
Vanhoot, Thomas	Wolf, Henry	Waggoner, John
	Webster, John	

Pages 151-152.

ROLL OF CAPT. DAVID RUPE'S (or Roop) COMPANY.
(Probably from Scioto County.)

Served from April 27, until September 30, 1812.

Capt. David Rupe or Roop	Lieut. Thomas Arnold	Ensign Richard McDugal
Sergt. Benjamin Rankins	Sergt. James Cochran	Sergt. William Coberly
Sergt. Meshach Plowman	Corp. Beasan Faily	Corp. John Carey
Corp. Thomas Bevins	Corp. Daniel Rardin	Drummer, Enos Mustard

Privates.

Brewer, Richard	Collins, Thomas	Clark, John
Carey, William	Darlington, Abisha	Dover, James
Deve, William	Feuit, Gabriel	Glaze, John
Glaze, Pachart	Glaze, Andrew	Groninger, John
Groninger, Abraham	Hollan, James Mill	Harris, William
Leforgah, John	Moore, John	Mustard, Joseph
Moholen, Charles	McDougal, George	McDougal, Joseph
Noel, John Sr.	Noel, John Jr.	Noel, Daniel
Noel, Peter Sr.	Noel, Peter Jr.	Noel, Abraham
Noel, Jacob	Noel, Phillip	Nicols, Joseph
Nicholas, Noel	Rinely, Henry	Randan, John
Randan, James	Smith, John	Shelpman, Spicer
Smith, Isaac	Steward, Paul	Smith, John
Stewart, Paul	Willcoxen, Walta	Wilcoxen, Levin
Williamson Francis	Wright, William	Wilcoxen, George
	Wilcoxen, Thomas	

Pages 153-154.

ROLL OF CAPT. JOSIAH LOCKHART'S COMPANY. (County Unknown.)

Served from May 4 until July 4, 1812.

Capt. Josiah Lockhart	Lieut. Edward Wade	Lieut. John Woods
Ensign William Robbins	Sergt. William Adams	Sergt. James Bradfield
Sergt. John Bryan	Sergt. John Higgenbotham	Corp. Jacob Copple
Corp. James Peaseley	Corp. Fountain Pemberton	Corp. John Downing
Corp. Enoch Laycock	Fifer, John Grimmings	

Privates.

Aldrid, John	Adams, David	Bonner, Reuben
Booncutter, Martin	Borcin, John	Berry, Joseph
Bergis, James	Baughman, John	Burcaw, Peter
Cartmile, John	Conn, Joshua	Crawford, George
Collier, Thomas	Cameron, Angus	Earley, George
Greenley, William	Groomer, Abraham	Horsberry, John
Hemphill, John	Hayes, John	Highbans, William
Jones, Benjamin	Jennings, John	Kultz, John
Lucas, James	Laycock, William	Lane, Elias, Jr.
Lockhart, Robert	Laycock, Moses	Losh, Charles
Laycock, Levi	Moore, Samuel	Murphy, William
Miller, James	Murphy, Asa	Malory, Lamon
Moore, Corp. Samuel	McElroy, James	McKinney, George
McCollester, Samuel	McCollester, John	Osman, Zodoc
Odell, John W.	Parker, Hiram	Page, David
Pitty, John	Pucket, Redmond	Robinson, Richard
Redmond, William	Reed, John	Robinson, William
Soms, Nehemiah	Segert, Thomas	Stephenson, James
Stivers, Samuel H.	Sharp, Hugh	Stephenson, William
Stanbury, John	Spiers, William	Thomas, William
Underwood, Benjamin	Washburn, John	Williams, Benjamin
Wright, John	Ellis, Samuel, Drummer	

ROSTER OF OHIO SOLDIERS IN WAR OF 1812

Pages 155-156. Vol. 2.

ROLL OF CAPT. SAMUEL SPANGLER'S COMPANY. (County Unknown.)

Served from July 31, 1813, until January 1, 1815.

Rank and Name of Soldier.	Rank and Name of Soldier.	Rank and Name of Soldier.
Capt. Samuel Spangler	Ensign Samuel Nigh	Lieut. Daniel Lethers
Sergt. George Nigh	Sergt. Daniel Peters	Sergt. Jacob Hoke
Sergt. David Campbell	Corp. Jacob Peters	Corp. Zephamah Dixon
Corp. James Decker	Corp. John Henry	Corp. Henry Christy
Corp. Peter Good	Sergt. George Delshaver	Sergt. John Christie
Musician, Adam Nigh	Musician, Michael Kisner	

Privates.	Privates.	Privates.
Allen, Aaron	Allen, Moses	Antricks, Frederick
Barr, Thomas	Bloo, Frederick	Bruner, Jacob
Beul, Joseph	Baumgardner, John	Brine, George
Baumgardner, Henry	Bruner, Jacob	Bresslee, Jacob
Brian, Caleb	Bobbenmyer, John	Conrad, John
Clayton, Henry	Detzler, Daniel	Ditto, John
DeLong, Isaac	Dilshaver, Henry	Duke, Joseph
Decker, James	Everman, John	Farrell, Noah
Fassnaught, Jacob	Hialt, Hezekiah	Hyett, William
Hoffman, Frederick	Heighey, Nathan	Harnel, George
Huffer, Isaac	Huffer, Henry	Hunter, Thomas
Hiland, Edward	Kunp, Jacob	Miller, Bush
Mooney, Jacob	Neff, Jacob	Neff, John
Neff, George	Nigh, John	Owen, James
Pimcions, Peter	Peters, Daniel	Riggan, John
Road, Daniel	Ridenour, George	Ridenour, Michael
Ridenour, John	Stall, Alexander	Sholenberger, Jonas
Shaw, Alexander	Stall, Isaac	Shoop, John
Vandey, Jacob	Wheeler, Thomas	Wiand, Frederick
Walbt, George	Weshamer, Frederick	

Pages 157-158.

ROLL OF CAPT. JAMES CRITTEN'S COMPANY.
(Probably from Licking County.)

Served from July 30 until August 16, 1813.

Capt. James Critten	Lieut. Jeremiah Johnson	Ensign William Evans
Sergt. Jacob Stult	Sergt. John Levenston	Sergt. James Cunningham
Sergt. James Ward	Corp. Jacob Hahn	Corp. Samuel Murfoot
Corp. Adam Stultz	Corp. James Canel	

Privates.	Privates.	Privates.
Baker, Ephraim	Boucher, John	Baker, Joseph
Bawick, William	Carlisle, John	Coccion, Jeremiah
Channel, Joseph	Cool, Isaac	Denman, William
Denman, Hathaway	Dunn, Benjamin	DeWeese, Get
Doty, William	Duke, Levi	Elliott, Alexander
Gladman, Thomas	Gilmore, John	Green, William
Gibson, James	Harding, Abraham	Harris, Isaac
Hoover, Eli	Hoover, Sam	Harris, Joshua
Livingston, Tobias	Little, Shubel	Moody, John
Montgomery, William	Nicholas, Joseph	Nicholas, John
Robe, William	Simpson, Isaac	Suthard, Francis
Shadwick, James	Shepard, James	Simpson, William
Silers, William	Wells, Osmond	Whealer, Samuel
Wilson, Benjamin		

Pages 159-160.

ROLL OF CAPT. PETER LAMB'S COMPANY. (County Unknown.)

Served from July 31 until August 4, 1813, and from August 31, 1813, until March 4, 1814

Capt. Peter Lamb	Lieut. Thomas McMachten	Lieut. William Wagner
Ensign William Hill	Sergt. Jobe Baker	Sergt. David Geiger
Sergt. Abraham Miller	Sergt. Henry Baker	Sergt. Hugh Mills
Sergt. Abraham Rean	Sergt. Lemuel Steel	Sergt. Frederick Stonebring
Corp. Daniel Baker	Corp. Samuel Trovinger	Corp. Samuel Baker
Corp. George McNames	Corp. Henry Bratz	Corp. Michael Spiedle
Corp. William M. Moore	Corp. Benjamin William	Drummer, John Beaver
Fifer, Isaac Becker		

Privates.	Privates.	Privates.
Brombach, Daniel	Ashbaugh, John	Ashbaugh, Frederick
Bryan, William	Brown, Joseph	Baldin, James
Brookhart, Henry	Borrow, Joseph	Bellaire, John
Cugy, Jacob	Croffad, Robert	Conner, Abraham
Disherty, Joseph	Dupret, John B.	Duplete, Lanis
Farmer, William	Fouler, Miles	Fitzgerald, Henry
Funk, Daniel	Geiger, Jacob	Geiger, Martin
Gaster, John	Hite, Samuel	Hite, Joseph
Hill, Jonothan	Hoover, Joseph	Hashbarger, David
Hammon, Michael	Hall, Daniel	Lamb, William
Lemmon, Adam	Lampher, Hynser	Lambright, John

ROLL OF CAPT. PETER LAMB'S COMPANY. (Continued)

Rank and Name of Soldier.

Privates.

Mires, Jacob
Murphy, David
Mackeral, John
Nolen, Samuel
Reed, John
Roods, Benjamin
Reynolds, Ephraim
Siple, Frederick
Stupe, William
Troovinger, Samuel
Watson, Richard

Rank and Name of Soldier.

Privates.

Morehart, Christian
Mason, Thomas
McNaghten, James
Poling, Samuel
Rely, Jacob
Reynolds, Thomas
Rudloph, Henry
Sturgeon, Robert
Signar, George
Wagg, Phillip
Winters, Abraham

Rank and Name of Soldier.

Privates.

Mock, Daniel
Murray, John
McCrary, Solomon
Reed, Stephen
Roods, William
Reynolds, Dickerson
Raredon, Smith, John C.
Springer, Henry
Soledy, Frederick
Watson, James
Young, John

Page 161.
ROLL OF CAPT. ABRAHAM MYERS' COMPANY. (County Unknown.)
Served from July 31, until August 15, 1813.

Capt. Abraham Myers
Sergt. John Ridenour
Sergt. Thomas Shelby
Corp. William Hunter

Privates.

Benheimer, John
Bressler, Jacob
Bressler, Valentine
Ehuman, John
Hufferd, Isaac
Kessler, Samuel
Ridenour, George

Lieut. John List
Sergt. Eli Barker
Corp. John Roberts
Corp. Joseph England

Privates.

Bohenmoyer, George
Bohenmoyer, John
Barr, John
Hunter, Robert
Hufferd, Henry
Morris, James
Weaver, Jacob

Ensign Jacon Gardner
Sergt. John Tarrance
Corp. Thomas Smith

Privates.

Bryan, Caleb
Brandhever, Adam
Bohenmoyer, Samuel
Hyland, Edward
Hunter, Thomas
Ridenour, Michael

Page 162.
ROLL OF LIEUT. JOHN HAMBERGER'S COMPANY. (County Unknown.)
Served from July 31, until August 31, 1813.

Lieut. John Hamberger
Sergt. Jacob Wetmer
Corp. John Boyer
Corp. Benjamin Ausbach

Privates.

Becker, John
Fisher, John
Huffman, Henry
King, David
Parr, Richard

Ensign John Spohn
Sergt. Christian Ausbauch
Corp. Jacob Christ
Drummer, John Ausbauch

Privates.

Dorenhour, John
Fisher, Michael
Johnston, John
Lessler, George
Spohn, Jacob

Sergt. John Crull
Sergt. Leonard Hartz
Corp. James Anderson
Fifer, Jonothan Zootman

Privates.

Fisher, Adam
Hullenberger, Peter
King, Christian
Miller, Lewis
Zignen, George

Pages 163-164.
ROLL OF CAPT. DANIEL LIDEY'S COMPANY. (County Unknown.)
Served from July 31, until September 6, 1813.

Capt. Daniel Lidey
Sergt. George Overmire
Sergt. Jacob Pence
Corp. John Heck
Drummer, Michael Dittoe

Privates.

Alexander, James
Auspach, Michaael
Brent, John
Blatner, Conrad
Clines, Moses
Fisher, John
Haritz, John
Huffman, Henry
Jackson, George
King, Christian
McCormick, James
Petty, John
Runkle, John
Sauft, Henry
Epies, Philip
Voland, William

Lieut. John Humberger
Sergt. John Harris
Corp. John Miller
Corp. Adam Householder

Privates.

Alsbach, Bastion
Auspach, Benjamin
Brame, George
Beard, Bennet
Denny, George
Hairact, Jacob
Hulstar, John
Heintz, Leonard
Kemft, Jacob
Loeffer, George
McCormick, John
Parr, Richard
Spohn, Daniel
Strobe, John N.
Stoltz, Samuel
Vanderman, George
Wilson, Joseph

Ensign Jacob Rankle
Sergt. Henry Strong
Corp. James Vanatta
Fifer, Peter Dittoe

Privates.

Auspach, Adam
Bowman, Henry
Boyer, John
Beard, Samuel
Fisher, Adam
Hardin, Thomas
Horden, James
Henderson, James
Kitzmiller, William
Miller, Henry
Petty, Moses
Plumer, George
Steir, Jacob
Stoltz, Henry
Shirer, Daniel
Vanattate, Aaron

Page 165.
ROLL OF CAPT. GEORGE HOSIER'S COMPANY. (County Unknown.)
Served from July 31, until August 14, 1813.

Capt. George Hosier
Sergt. John Miller
Corp. John Claus

Lieut. Jacob Overmier
Sergt. John Fisher
Corp. James Baley

Ensign, Aaron Vansatta
Sergt. George Blatner
Drummer, William Boen

Vol. 2.
ROLL OF CAPT. GEORGE HOSIER'S COMPANY. (Continued)

Rank and Name of Soldier.

Privates.
Alspach, Daniel
Baugher, John
Fuller, Henry
Nieason, John
Thrash, Michael

Rank and Name of Soldier.

Privates.
Antrink, Jacob
Black, John
Knoyer, Samuel
Orwig, Henry

Rank and Name of Soldier.

Privates.
Bonslater, William
Edging, Asa
Miller, Conrad
Rader, Jacob

Page 166.
ROLL OF CAPT. JOHN HARRISON'S COMPANY. (County Unknown.)
Served from July 31, until August 14, 1813.

Capt. John Harrison
Sergt. Robinson Fletcher
Sergt. Benjamin Allen
Corp. James Harrison
Drummer, Christian Graybill

Lieut. Dathan Lane
Sergt. Thomas Ashy
Corp. Joshua Cole
Corp. Thomas Burrows

Ensign Peter Huber
Sergt. Reuben Williams
Corp. Christian Morehart
Fifer, Rudolph Death

Privates.
Brooks, Joseph
Bear, George
Falkner, Martin
Huber, Philip
Long, Thomas
Myers, John
McFarland, Walter
Whitehouse, Jacob

Privates.
Brooks, James
Davis, Nathan
Growel, George
Holder, Daniel
Long, John
Menser, John
Russle, Jacob
Wotring, Abraham

Privates.
Burman, Henry
Dibert, John
Hood, Robert
Keizer, Jacob
Morehart, Jacob
Miller, Daniel
Vandemark, Daniel

Pages 167-168.
ROLL OF CAPT. SAMUEL DUNNAVAN'S COMPANY. (County Unknown.)
Served from July 31, until September 5, 1813.

Capt. Samuel Dunnavan
Sergt. Samuel Stewart
Sergt. Hiram P. Rose
Corp. James McGinley

Lieut. Josiah Graves
Sergt. Wothy Pratt
Corp. Stephen Hinthorn
Drummer, James Olive

Ensign Noble Root
Sergt. Joseph Linnet
Corp. Amos Carpenter
Fifer, Jesse Larne

Privates.
Abraham, James
Benner, Daniel
Barlow, Abraham
Cornell, Abraham
Crouch, Reason
Campbell, James
Drake, David
Evans, Robert
Farmer, Elias
Gray, William
Haydon, William
Hunter, Samuel
James, Henry
Kelley, Leonard
Mallory, Ira
Payn, John
Pugh, Samuel
Riley, Jacob
Stephenson, Asa
Scott, Robert
Winchit, Silas
Willias, David

Privates.
Abbot, Elisha
Benner, Peter
Bort, E. Jesse
Carpenter, Samuel
Cramer, John
Donnelly, Felix
Davis, Samuel
Elliott, Cornelius
Ginnings, Benjamin
Garrit, Markus A.
Harris, Jonah
Inscho, John
Jones, Erasmus
Moore, Lucius
McLain, John
Pratt, John
Robinson, Martin
Rigely, Bazeled
Scott, James
Thomas, John
Wright, Abraham
Wesh, William

Privates.
Bowman, Jacob
Baumont, Isaiah
Cooley, Hosea
Cargey, John
Critchet, Mathew N.
Davis, John
Evans, George
Frye, Jacob
Goodrich, Stephen
Harris, Samuel
Hayes, William
Johnston, David
Jamison, Joseph
Moats, David
McKitterick, James
Pugh, Cran
Robinson, Joel
Stephens, Justus
Smith, Charles
Twig, Charles
Williamson, John

Pages 169-170.
ROLL OF CAPT. JOHN BARTHOLOMEW'S COMPANY. (County Unknown.)
Served from July 31, until September 5, 1813.

Capt. John Bartholomew
Lieut. George Hull
Sergt. James Cunningham
Sergt. George Gregar
Corp. Samuel Morphey
Corp. Joshua Brown

Lieut. Jeremiah Johnson
Sergt. Abraham Bennet
Sergt. James Ward
Corp. William Sain
Corp. Levi Duke

Ensign Samuel Hull
Sergt. Peter Card
Sergt. Hannah Fory
Corp. George Hull
Corp. Henry Trout

Privates.
Allberry, Thomas
Burn, Daniel
Brown, James
Critten, James
Coffman, Peter
Clark, William
Elliott, Samuel
Farmer, Samuel
*Green, William
Green, Michael

Privates.
Baker, Joseph
Beam, Benjamin
Brown, Jacob
Cool, Isaac
Chapman, William
Debott, William
Elliott, Alexander
Fiddler, John
Green, John
Galor, Jacob

Privates.
Baker, Ephraim
Beam, John
Courssen, John
Coklo, Jeremiah
Claybough, William
Dixon, John
Evans, John H.
Farmer, Isaac
Gilmore, John
Haines, Isaac

Vol. 2.
ROLL OF CAPT. JOHN BARTHOLOMEW'S COMPANY. (Continued)

Rank and Name of Soldier.
Privates.
Hunter, John
Harris, Isaac
Harris, William
Haniel, James
Hamil, Thomas
Johnston, William
Livingston, Peter
Lipengeit, Ephraim
Parr, John
Pogne, Samuel
Stotts, Daniel
Sellers, William
Wayman, James
Wilkins, Samuel

Rank and Name of Soldier.
Privates.
Hull, Uriah
Hoover, Eli
Howel, David
Herbeit, James
Hunter, Adam
Johnston, Henry
Luke, Redmond
Marbed, John
Parr, Thomas
Roads, John
Simpson, William
Sprag, David
Wheeler, Samuel
Young, John

Rank and Name of Soldier.
Privates.
Harris, John
Hoover, Samuel
Haines, Joseph
Horn, William
Iler, John
Kneff, George
Lake, Willis
Orr, Robert
Pickering, Jacob
Sutton, John
Shepher, James
Siglar, Peter
Winegaide, Adam

Pages 171-172.

ROLL OF CAPT. JOHN CHONNER'S COMPANY. (County Unknown.)
Served from July 31, until August 14, 1813.

Capt. John Chonner
Sergt. George Willis
Sergt. Joseph Wells
Corp. John Mays
Musician, James Olive

Lieut. James Holmes
Sergt. Samuel Jameson
Corp. John Moone
Corp. Ben Farmer

Ensign Aaron Brown
Sergt. William Holmes
Corp. Cornelius Lane
Musician, Jesse Larne

Privates.
Bush, George
Camble, James
Dickson, William
Engliss, John
Forsyth, Thomas
Gavit, Markus A.
Huston, Andrew
Hunter, Robert
Jones, Arasmus
McKitrick, James
Page, Jeremiah
Smith, Charles
Thompson, John
Williamson, John

Privates.
Black, John
Critten, Gabriel
Elliott, Cornelius
Frye, Jacob
Forsyth, William
Green, John
Hunter, Samuel
Helphrey, John
Jamison, Joseph
McCown, John
Ridgle,y Razaleel
Scott, Robert
Trump, Jacob
Welch, William

Privates.
Barlow, Abraham
Dickson, Samuel
Evans, Joseph
Farmer, Elias
Green, Ezekial
Hase, William
Hunter, George
Iles, Frederick
Jones, Lemuel
Pew, Samuel
Scott, James
Sully, Leonard
Williams, David
Young, William

Pages 173-174.

ROLL OF CAPT. BARTHOLOMEW FRYATT'S COMPANY. (County Unknown.)
Served from April 27, until June 30, 1812.

Capt. Bartholomew Fryatt
Sergt. Thomas Spillman
Sergt. James Burns
Corp. James Salsbury

Lieut. R. Douglas
Sergt. Hugh Woods
Corp. Enos Strawn
Corp. James Lindsey

Ensign David Killey
Sergt. Mark Cook
Corp. William Black

Privates.
Buck, John
Bleekman, Nathan
Denny, William
Elias, Jonothan
Hopkins, Robert
Hostleton, Joseph
Johnston, John
Knight, William
Mouser, Thomas
Nevel, Robert
Shenfelt, William
Sliger, David
Sullavan, William

Privates.
Bouse, Michael
Cooder, Jonothan
Downing, Timothy
Edwards, William
Hillary, Joseph
Harvey, Golwell
Jones, William
Milton, Rendal
McFardin, William
Perry, Ebenezer
Strese, Phillip
Salyard, John
Trimble, Abner
Wilson, Daniel

Privates.
Brown, Henry
Cook, Thomas
Denam, John
Gold, William
Hobaugh, Andrew
Hunt, George
James, John
Marbel, David
McChine, David
Reed, Joshua
Strauss, Joseph
Shaverdecker, Jacob
Wildbahn, George

Page 174.

ROLL OF LIEUT. DAVID STORER'S COMPANY.
(Probably from Scioto County.)
Served from July 28, until August 28, 1813.

Lieut. David Storer
Sergt. Adam Logen
Corp. Isaac Wooley

Ensign James Hutton
Sergt. James Smith

Sergt. Peter Lewis
Corp. William Hower

Privates.
Andrews, James
Cooper, Samuel
Grimes, Consider
Hamilton, Reuben
Salsbury, William
Wright, Isaac

Privates.
Bondle, Enoch
Dean, William
Grubb, Joseph
McLaughlin, Bonman
Smith, John

Privates.
Cowper, John
Green, Bun
Hutton, Charles P.
Nichols, David
Wood, Daniel

ROSTER OF OHIO SOLDIERS IN WAR OF 1812

Page 175. Vol. 2.

ROLL OF CAPT. HUGH ROGERS' COMPANY.
(Probably from Highland County.)
Served from July 28, until August 26, 1813.

Rank and Name of Soldier.	Rank and Name of Soldier.	Rank and Name of Soldier.
Capt. Hugh Rogers	Lieut. John Evans	Ensign Eli Blunt
Sergt. Roland Rogers	Sergt. Hugh Hill	Sergt. Pearce Evans
Sergt. M. D. Swearengen	Corp. Joseph Chaney	Corp. Isaac Evans
Privates.	**Privates.**	**Privates.**
Blount, Andrew	Calvin, Thomas	Davidson, Joseph
Davidson, Thomas	Evans, Dan	Evans, Amos
Ferguson, John	Frederick, George	Hinton, Evan
Hinton, William	Hinton, Benjamin	Headman, John
Houghman, Isaac	Houghman, Moses	Hare, William
Hunter, Thomas	Rouse, Henry	Stillman, William
Stafford, James	Savage, James	Shaver, Andrew
Swartz, Sebastian	Wright, William	Wilkinson, William
Wilken, Philip	Wilkin, Benjamin	Walter, John

Pages 177-178.

ROLL OF CAPT. JAMES PATTERSON'S COMPANY.
(Probably from Highland County.)
Served from July 28, until September 8, 1813.

Capt. James Patterson	Lieut. Oliver Harris	Ensign Jacob Moury
Sergt. Samuel Boyd	Sergt. John Shefer	Sergt. George Caley
Sergt. William Thompson	Corp. David McConnel	Corp. John Gosselt
Corp. Jacob Shafer	Corp. Ozwell Ayers	
Privates.	**Privates.**	**Privates.**
Berryman, Thomas	Blunt, Solomon	Boyd, James
Barr, Thomas	Barnes, John	Chailes, Andrew
Calvin, James	Davidson, David	Dill, Thomas
Eakins, John	Emry, John	Flinn, Joshua
Flinn, John	Gasset, Moses	Harvey, Samuel
Giblen, John	Hatter, Andrew	Gribby, Frederick
Hicks, Nathan	Hair, Stephenson	Hiltebrand, Philip
Hair, William	Houghan, John	Kingery, David
Layman, David	Lear, Andrew	Malcolm, Joseph
Midsker, David	Midsker, Isaac	Mathews, Peter
Murrey, John	McNeal, Archibald	McLaughlin, John
Pittenger, Isaac	Patten, Robert	Patterson, Joseph
Ray, William	Roush, George	Rush, James
Richards, Augustus	Richards, William	Swartz, Henry
Smithson, George	Smith, George Jr.	Sanderson, George
Vanmater, Pierce	Walter, Gaudin	

Page 179.

ROLL OF CAPT. SAMUEL LYBRAND'S COMPANY.
(Probably from Franklin County.)
Served from July 28, until September 6, 1813.

Capt. Samuel Lybrand	Lieut. Cornelius Casey	Ensign Philip Wheitzell
Sergt. Jacob O. Lutz	Sergt. Jacob H. Lutz	Sergt. Noble Roberts
Sergt. Isaiah Willetts	Corp. Robert Field	Corp. Jesse Willets
Corp. Jacob Whitesell		
Privates.	**Privates.**	**Privates.**
Busbey, John	Culp, Sebastian	Culp, Peter
Dunkel, John	Fogler, John	Fogler, Henry
Grundy, Abraham	Heller, George	Judey, Simon
Justice, Griffith	Kline, Henry	Koons, Peter
Myers, John	Marts, Peter	Markel, Abraham
Palmer, Jesse	Richeldaifer, Henry	Shisler, John
Stump, Joel	Whitzell, George	Willits, Isaac
Willits, James	Willits, William	Wildban, George
Zearing, Peter		

Pages 181-182.

ROLL OF CAPT. HUGH CRAIGHTON'S COMPANY. (County Unknown.)
Served from July 28, until September 6, 1813, and part served until 1816.

Capt. Hugh Craighton	Lieut. Edward Larkin	Ensign George Deal
Sergt. George Louther	Sergt. George A. Gordon	Sergt. Amos Barr
Sergt. Charles McDonald	Corp. John Laverty	Corp. Felix Miller
Corp. Jacob L. Levi	Corp. Charles Winims	
Privates.	**Privates.**	**Privates.**
Altman, Adam	Brown, Joshua	Brown, Elisha
Brown, Bryan	Barnhart, Simon	Baker, Philip
Bartley, Jacob	Bennet, John	Broton, James
Cloar, John	Clark, Elias	Clark, Robert
Cherry, Burris	Coonrad, John C.	Coonrad, John, Jr.

ROLL OF CAPT. HUGH CRAIGHTON'S COMPANY. (Continued.)

Rank and Name of Soldier.

Privates.
- Cherry, John
- Collins, William K.
- Early, William
- Gordon, George A.
- Hott, Adam
- Holmes, James
- Hor, Jacob
- Kimble, Jacob
- Louther, George
- Menterly, Amos
- Palmer, Purmeal
- Rinkin, William
- Stimmel, Daniel
- VanVickel, Daniel
- Wilson, James

Privates.
- Cramer, William
- Donelson, Moses
- Ellis, John
- Hall, Joshua
- Hoover, Thomas
- Hudson, Thomas
- Kile, William
- Kimble, Jonothan
- Laverty, James
- McDaniel, Charles
- Rolston, Benjamin
- Searfas, John
- Thompson, Thomas
- Williamson, Abraham
- Winis, Charley

Privates.
- Cherry, Jesse
- Davies, Samuel
- French, John
- Hott, Jacob
- Hoover, Christian
- Heifkin, George
- Kile, Enoch
- Kinsel, John
- Miller, Felix
- McCandless, John
- Rowl, William
- Smith, John
- Thomas, John
- Wilson, John

Pages 183-184.

ROLL OF CAPT. ADAM BERRY'S COMPANY. (County Unknown.)

Served from July 28, until September 6, 1813.

- Capt. Adam Berry
- Sergt. Parker Lee
- Sergt. Absalom Adams
- Corp. Richard Hobbs
- Fifer, George Spangler

- Lieut. John Pain
- Sergt. Adam Zering
- Corp. Jacob Smith
- Corp. Jacob Zering

- Ensign John Harnan
- Sergt. Jacob Mathias
- Corp. Jacob Repner
- Drummer, Jacob Spangler

Privates.
- Allison, Jesse
- Bear, Peter
- Cashner, Martin
- Diam, Henry
- Fields, Jonothan
- Hinton, Michael
- Lonbach, Henry
- Moore, James
- Miller, George
- Mounts, Ornphrey
- March, George
- North, James
- Penty, George
- Raybourn, Hugh
- Simmons, Erterling
- Veail, John
- Veoge, Abraham
- Willetts, James
- Worline, Jacob
- Weiser, Frederick

Privates.
- Boyer, Stephen
- Black, Charles
- Cashner, George
- Fowler, Samuel
- Grimm, John
- Hollory, Jeremiah
- Lim, James
- Marts, Abraham
- Mathews, John
- Myers, John
- Moon, James
- Odle, Stephen
- Provatt, Thomas
- Reickeldarfer, John
- Stall, Hugh
- Veail, Thomas
- Vohs, William
- Whetsel, Abraham
- Whisler, John

Privates.
- Boyer, George
- Beventon, Charles
- Deal, Adam
- Filson, Reuben
- Hillary, John
- Johnston, Henry
- Lois, William
- Monnett, Osborn
- Mosh, Peter
- Mandy, John
- McBroom, Robert
- Pontius, George
- Peters, Jacob
- Saylor, Michael
- Throgmorton, Elijah
- Veliogall, Jacob
- Witmoer, John
- Whetsel, John
- Wescot, Isaac

Pages 185-186.

ROLL OF CAPT. LEVI PINNEY'S COMPANY. (County Unknown.)

Served from May 1, until December 12, 1812.

- Capt. Levi Pinney
- Sergt. Peter Barker
- Sergt. William Noteman
- Corp. William Johnson
- Drummer, Charles Crosby

- Lieut. John Moore
- Sergt. David Douglas
- Corp. Henry Skeels
- Corp. Henry W. Judy

- Ensign John Gwinne
- Sergt. William Elliott
- Corp. John McNutt
- Fifer, Roswell Chapman

Privates.
- Adair, Samuel
- Blair, John
- Beardsley, Hyman
- Boyard, Joseph
- Douglas, George
- Downing, John
- Edson, Luther
- Frazer, Alexander
- Hoskins, Jeremiah
- Hedges, Obed
- Lane, Samuel
- Lyne, Lewis
- McHenry, Alexander
- Marckel, Ezra
- Osterhout, William
- Russell, Thomas
- Ragan, William
- Tucker, Frederick
- Tullis, Jonothan
- Zimmerman, Henry

Privates.
- Bennet, Elijah
- Bradley, William
- Ballard, James
- Brading, James
- Downing, Josiah
- Denny, John
- Ewing, Samuel
- Gatewood, Philip
- Harriman, David
- Ice, George
- Love, Henry
- McNutt, Samuel
- McLane, Jacob
- Marckel, Samuel
- Osterhout, Gideon
- Strain, William
- Springer, Shadrach
- Todd, Robert
- White, James

Privates.
- Bennet, Henry
- Bradley, Hiram
- Brown, James
- Champ, Nathaniel
- Davies, William
- Denny, David
- Frye, Jacob
- Hughey, James
- Hedges, Davis
- Jelland, David
- Lewin, John
- McConnell, William
- McCanless, John
- Noiswenter, Fred
- Pierce, Asahel
- Simkins, Thomas
- Stevenson, Zechariah
- Whitford, John B.
- Wolf, Charles

Pages 187-188. Vol. 2.

ROLL OF CAPT. CHRISTIAN BROTHERLAN'S COMPANY. (County Unknown.)
Served from July 28, until September 6, 1813.

Rank and Name of Soldier.
Capt. Christian Brotherlan
Sergt. Thomas Ing
Sergt. Titus Hubbert
Corp. William Bilsland
Musician, George Rager

Privates.
Badkin, George
Coberley, James
Cutright, Samuel
Davis, Robert
Evans, John
Hopkins, Archibald
Hoss, Jacob
Hobough, Solomon
Kingery, Stephen
Loofbarrow, Ebenezer
Morris, Benjamin
Pollard, John
Reed, James
Verdon, Alinson
Warner, John
Watson, David

Rank and Name of Soldier.
Lieut. Jacob Willenmeyer
Sergt. John Fultz
Corp. Samuel Watkins
Corp. Jacob Hasleton

Privates.
Cline, Jacob
Coberley, William
Carr, Richard
Davis, William H.
Fortner, John
Hopkins, James
Hill, William
Johnson, David
Loofbarrow, Benjamin
Messick, George
Morris, Isaac
Richter, George
Trey, Jacob
Will, David
Warner, Robert
Watson, Abraham

Rank and Name of Soldier.
Ensign, William Clune
Sergt. John Tryback
Corp. William Black
Musician, Andrew Fultz

Privates.
Cutrite, William
Coberley, Jobe
Dickson, George N.
Evans, Jonah
Graham, James
Hoss, John
Harris, David
Kingery, David
Loofbarrow, Nathan
Messer, Joseph
McFarland, John
Richardson, John
Thompson, John
Wright, John
Wingett, William
Waggoner, Daniel

Pages 189-190.

ROLL OF CAPT. ROBERT REID'S COMPANY.
(Probably from Delaware County.)
Served from July 28, until Sept. 6, 1813.

Capt. Robert Reid
Lieut. George Teagarden
Sergt. James Tollman
Sergt. Isaac Hoffhines
Corp. John Reid
Sergt. ———— Missamore

Privates.
Anderson, John
Butlinger, George
Brinker, George
Bishop, William
Bennet, Henry
Cuttler, Enos
Coonrad, Henry
Champ, John
Edwards, William
Gibson, James
Hardesty, Richard
Hatten, Charles
Kuikendall, John
Lofer, John
Miller, Joseph
Meet, Bazel
Nigh, Jacob
Punches, George
Swisher, Abraham
Shoup, Jacob
Turner, Daniel

Lieut. John Hedges
Sergt. Joshua Hedges
Corp. John Childs
Corp. Isaiah Bell
Sergt. James Reid

Privates.
Bell, Abner
Butlinger, John
Briner, John
Brown, William
Cole, Joshua
Clark, William
Cup, Phillip
Columber, Richard
Fridley, Lewis
Hagerman, Thomas
Hughes, Jesse
King, Trueman
Henry, Enoch
Lape, John
Moore, Elijah
McLane, Zechariah
Nigh, Spencer
Paul, Zechariah
Smith, Henry
Sockrider, John
Writter, Henry

Ensign, John Cole
Sergt. Henry Bennet
Corp. Benjamin Smith
Sergt. James Lallern
Sergt. John Winterstein

Privates.
Burton, Bazel
Bell, James
Burgett, Jacob
Brown, Samuel
Champ, William
Cock, David
Cuttler, Jonothan
Cupt, Conrad
Gothrop, Richard
Hayes, Luther
Hiland, John
Kilwell, James
Kuikendall, George
Miller, Peter
Morris, Jacob
Noys, John
Punches, Peter
Swisher, John
Stultz, Henry
Teagarden, Jacob

Pages 191-192.

ROLL OF CAPT. JOHN LUCAS' COMPANY.
(Scioto County.)
Served from April 27, until September 30, 1812.

Capt. John Lucas
Sergt. William Baird
Sergt. Richard Hammell
Corp. Robert Givens

Privates.
Andrews, James
Bennet, James
Bonser, Joseph
Cadow, Claudious
Davis, Levi
Gee, Joseph
Hotzenbecklar, Henry
Johnson, John
Love, William
Miller, James
Offner, John
Runnelds, William
Sampson, Violet
Vaser, Peter
Williams, Nathan

Lieut. Dennis Murphy
Sergt. Jeremiah Downing
Sergt. William Clerk
Corp. Richard McAuley

Privates.
Benson, Joseph,
Barber, Samuel
Brient, Isaac
Cochrain, James
Emmins, William
George, John
Houset, Samuel
Lawson, John
Lucas, Robert
Magill, James
Powell, Charles
Stanely, James
Tomlinson, Jesse
Vanriñort, ————

Ensign, Joseph Barber
Sergt. Robert Darlington
Corp. William Nice
Corp. Noah Davis

Privates.
Burk, John
Bennet, Joshua
Clark, William
Downing, John
Emmet, Johnston
Gilleland, Samuel
Johnson, William
Lamkins, Prosper
Moore, Thomas
Moore, John
Rook, John
Samples, David
Travis, Abraham
Vontorer, George

ROLL OF ENSIGN WILLIAM CLOSSON'S COMPANY.
(Probably from Ross County.)

Served from July 28, until August 16, 1813.

Rank and Name of Soldier.	Rank and Name of Soldier.	Rank and Name of Soldier.
Ensign, William Closson	Sergt. Richard Hoddy	Sergt. William Stachel
Sergt. George Mark	Sergt. Curtis Jones	
Privates.	**Privates.**	**Privates.**
Crabb, Daniel	Clifton, George	Crabb, Roswell
Cory, Stephen	Camun, John	Cochran, William
Evans, James	Fluharty, William	Haggert, William
Moses, Thomas	McNeal, John	McIna, James
Morris, John	Roseboom, Andrew	Roseboom, Garret
Russell, Pire	Shepherd, John	Shepherd, David
Sisk, John	Vanderwolt, Samuel	

ROLL OF CAPT. JOHN GRAY'S COMPANY.
(Probably from Ross County.)

Served from August 30, until October 9, 1812.

Capt. John Gray	Lieut. Michael Ginsel	Ensign, Warford Bonhan
Sergt. William Stockton	Sergt. John Patterson	Sergt. Joseph Reader
Sergt. Amos Reader	Corp. John Edmiston	Corp. David Taylor
Corp. John Santee	Corp. William Black	
Privates.	**Privates.**	**Privates.**
Bragg, John	Berry, Stephen	Crawford, Alexander
Caldwell, John	Dunlap, John	Dunlap, Robert
Ewing, Samuel	Gardner, Samuel	Gaul, Jacob
Hartley, Joseph	Hartley, Thomas	Hartley, John
Irwin, William	King, John	Kent, Peter
Murphy, William	Maloney, Isaac	McKenzie, John
McClure, William	Prickett, John	Taylor, John
Truber, Joseph	Tuthill, James	Turrell, John
Warnoch, William	Wilson, Nathaniel	

ROLL OF CAPT. GEORGE BRIANT'S COMPANY.
(Probably from Ross County.)

Served from July 28, until August 21, 1813.

Capt. George O. Briant	Lieut. Joseph O. Briant	Ensign, John Stouten
Sergt. James Davis	Sergt. Lawrence Grove	Sergt. John Bartan
Sergt. John Hendershot	Corp. Providence Williams	Corp. John Leeth
Corp. Charles O. Briant	Corp. Benjamin Bromley	Drummer, James Latin
Privates.	**Privates.**	**Privates.**
Boviker, John	Briant, Enoch O.	Briant, Peter O.
Beckman, William	Beckman, Abraham	Briant, Elijah O.
Briant, James O.	Beckman, Christian	Beckman, Aaron
Clay, William	Elliott, Burgess	Foster, Lawrence
Fernan, Philip	Groves, Michael	Gardiner, Thomas
Groves, George	Grover, Frederick	Irons, James
Irons, Thomas	Johnston, John	Kincaid, William
Lowman, Joseph	Long, John	Lane, James
Lowman, Michael	Layton, Asher	Layton, Elias
Mustard, George	Marquis, Isaac	McCoy, James
McFarland, Garrison	McBride, William	Powelson, Cornelius
Pitlers, Josiah	Price, Robert	Parkerson, William
Parker, William	Strattan, Charles	Skouten, Samuel
Wheaton, Humphrey	Wyckoff, Isaac	Williams, George

ROLL OF CAPT. NICHOLAS CUNNINGHAM'S COMPANY. (County Unknown.)

Served from April 27, until October 27, 1812.

Capt. Nicholas Cunningham	Lieut. John Harness	Ensign, Henry Flesher
Sergt. Eccleston Smith	Sergt. William McDonald	Sergt. William Loveless
Sergt. Thomas Chill	Corp. William McCarrol	Corp. Andrew Hayes
Corp. John Bailey	Corp. Benjamin Rogers	Musician, Ebenezer Mattox
Fifer, Alston Phillips		
Privates.	**Privates.**	**Privates.**
Berkolur, Tiberius	Becket, Bider	Black, Charles
Clover, Joshua	Clifford, George	Corwin, Oliver
Clevenger, William	Carsey, Randolph	Cisna, Stephen
Clifton, Philip	Donemire, Daniel	Davis, James
Everts, Ebenezer	Familiar, John	Fanata, Samuel
Layton, George	Miller, Adam	Martin, John
Martin, Tubman	Mablise, Joshua	McCallister, James
McCall, Montgomery	Neley, Nicholas	Powers, Jacob
Powers, Joseph	Pain, Adam	Roof, Samuel
Rankin, John M.	Stuthard, John	Saunders, Benjamin
Thomas, Jeremiah	Thompson, David	Thompson, John
Vanveal, Aaron	Venson, Thomas	Wilson, James
William Bazel	Williams, Samuel	White, William
Williams, Joseph	Williams, John	Wats, Henkson
Wilcock, David	Webb, William	Willcocks, Jonothan
Young, Solomon	Young, Jacob	

ROSTER OF OHIO SOLDIERS IN WAR OF 1812   35

Page 199.   Vol. 2.

ROLL OF CAPT. DAVID ELLIOTT'S COMPANY.
(Probably from Ross County.)
Served from July 28, until August 17, 1813.

Rank and Name of Soldier.
Capt. David Elliott
Sergt. William Ross
Sergt. John Williams
Corp. Charles Mahan
Corp. Solomon Clover

Privates.
Bishop, David
Cochran, Andrew
Files, Robert
Hopkins, William
Lewis, John
Myers, John
McCracken, Isaac
Powell, Emery
Sadler, William
Teeter, George

Rank and Name of Soldier.
Lieut. John Allemang
Sergt. Phillip Hare
Sergt. John Lewis
Corp. Nathan Rotan
Drummer, Daniel Johnstown

Privates.
Bishop, Frederick
Cover, Christian
Grub, Jacob
Hoskinson, John
Long, John
Moots, Charles
Newland, Jacob
Rambo, Michael
Shoemaker, David
Turner, James

Rank and Name of Soldier.
Ensign, Jacob Hare
Sergt. Henry Long
Sergt. Jacob Myers
Corp. William Johnson
Fifer, Frederick Recob

Privates.
Cochran, Hugh
Cove, Henry
Grub, Daniel
Kerr, George
Michel, Frederick
Myers, Jacob
Platter, Henry
Stagner, Peter
Strwy, Peter
Williams, John

Page 200.

ROLL OF LIEUT. JORDAN MANNING'S COMPANY.
(Probably from Clinton County.)
Served from November 28, 1814, until April 10, 1815.

Lieut. Jordan Manning
Sergt. Thomas Jett
Musician, John Pickens

Privates.
Allison, Charles
Brooks, Thomas
Conner, Adam
Howe, Baizille
McMahan, William
Seward, Samuel
Tate, George

Ensign, John Hill
Corp. Richard Dowler

Privates.
Brandeberry, Frederick
Butler, James
Davidson, Murray
Hewitt, Aaron
Phillips, Jesse
Phelps, Hiram
Wallace, John

Sergt. Benjamin Harber
Corp. William Cook

Privates.
Brooks, William
Chaplin, Francis R.
Gardner, Daniel
Kidd, Isaac
Signer, George
Terry, Samuel
Weese, John

Page 201.

ROLL OF ENSIGN AMAZIAH MORGAN'S COMPANY.
(Ross County.)
Served from July 28, until August 9, 1813.

Ensign, Amaziah Morgan
Sergt. Levi Wells
Corp. Adam Gilfillan

Privates.
Black, Abraham
Dill, Robert
Freshour, Abraham
Slater, James
Woolcut, Johnson

Sergt. David Campbell
Sergt. Righ Ford
Corp. Peter Clover

Privates.
Baigle, Henry
Devorss, Daniel
Farley, Joseph
Slater, Jeremiah

Sergt. Robert Darling
Corp. James Irwin
Corp. Valentine Knight

Privates.
Devorss, John
Devorss, Joseph
Ladd, Ellson
Slater, John

Pages 203-204.

ROLL OF CAPT. JAMES JEFFRIES' COMPANY. (County Unknown.)
Served from August 29, until September 9, 1812.

Capt. James Jeffries

Privates.
Armstrong, James
Beard, Benjamin
Baird, James
Bush, Jacob
Croy, Benjamin
Crooks, Jacob
Cussack, Andrew
Dile, Burton
Edgell, Moses
Ellison, Thomas
Flowers, Joseph
Graper, George
Gooden, Samuel
Hanner, George
Hammell, Charles
Hendrick, John
Longwell, James
Mills, Samuel
Petite, Thomas
Ryder, Adam
Richmond, Joseph
Skinner, George
Shaw, John
Smith, Jesse
Tonner, David
Wallace, James C.

Capt. Samuel Baird

Privates.
Bateson, Samuel
Burgess, Joseph
Ball, James
Carroll, Thomas
Curick, Daniel
Clayhold, Joseph H.
Dusinberry, John
Dile, John P.
Evans, John
Ferson, Robert
Gooden, Moses
Gibson, Thomas
Howler, John
Harrington, John
Hammell, Mathias
Kreizer, George
Mills, Joseph
Phillips, John
Petite, Samuel
Robarm, Charles
Rum, John
Stakeley, David
Stapers, William
Turner, William
Tool, Benjamin

Ensign, John Day

Privates.
Bonny, Nathaniel
Brown, Joshua
Betchman, Joseph
Carroll, David
Cowden, John
Chandler, Daniel
Decaver, Levi
Edgell, Asa
Embrick, John
Foreacre, John
Good, Jacob
German, Moses
Hull, John
Hamilton, Samuel
Hartsell, John
Knox, Tillman
Martin, Joseph
Parker, Benyan
Pierce, Nicholas
Russell, Richard
Rees, Michael
Sniff, Martin
Sample, Benjamin
Throcrt, James
Walls, Eli

Pages 205-206. Vol. 2.

ROLL OF CAPT. AMMI MALTBIE'S COMPANY. (County Unknown.)

Served from August 25, until September 29, 1812.

Rank and Name of Soldier.
Capt. Ammi Maltbie
Sergt. John Gowdy
Sergt. John B. Burrel
Corp. James Webb
Bugler, Thomas Morgan

Privates.
Anderson, James
Barrett, Phillip
Beakes, William
Bussel, Samuel
Clark, William
Hale, John
Jolly, John
Lawrence, William
Marshall, John
Mock, Daniel
Morgan, Jonothan
Owens, James
Sanders, Faris
Starett, Joseph
Torrence, William
Vance, Joseph
Whicker, Mathew

Rank and Name of Soldier.
Lieut. Benjamin Haines
Sergt. Samuel Larne
Corp. Henry Bist
Corp. Henry Buckles

Privates.
Anderson, John
Bird, Andrew
Burney, James
Buckles, David
Elam, John
Honk, John
Kennedy, James
Lamme, William
Morgan, George
Martin, Ezekial
Owens, Jonothan
Porter, James
Starett, Robert
Stips, Isaac
Towell, John
Williams, John
Williams, Remembrance
Gillian, Andrew

Rank and Name of Soldier.
Ensign, John Buckles
Sergt. Joshua Carraman
Corp. Robert McConnell
Fifer, John Nocks

Privates.
Anderson, Mason
Bell, David
Bane, James
Carprass, Adam
Gillian, Jesse
Innman, John
King, William
Lamme, David
Miller, Augustus
Murphy, John
Owens, George
Snodgrass, James
Sutton, Robert
Stephens, John
Vance, John
Williams, Garrett
Wolcott, John H.

Page 207.

ROLL OF CAPT. WILLIAM McCONNELL'S COMPANY. (County Unknown.)

Served from August 29, until Sept. 9, 1812.

Capt. William McConnell
Sergt. John Handle
Sergt. Phillip Baker

Privates.
Ayers, William
Bower, John
Boggs, James
Cooksey, Josiah
Echbury, John
Hart, David
Hunter, David
Kinney, William
Moon, John
McConnell, Joseph
Starker, Jacob
Spurgin, William
Vainum, John
Walters, Benjamin

Lieut. Jacob Wisecarver
Sergt. Samuel Walters or Wat-tens.

Privates.
Bower, Jacob
Border, George
Banit, Hauson
Caphart, Anthony
Darmer, Daniel
Hover, Jacob
Harden, William
Kinney, Thomas
Mann, Daniel
Paton, Robert
Starker, George
Vernam, Joseph
Walters, Jacob

Ensign, John Brown
Sergt. Robert Willson

Privates.
Boggs, Robert
Bell, John
Culbertson, Robert
Durogen, Wanen
Darmer, Jacob
Hocks, Robert
Zardem, John
Moon, Robert
Muchlin, Henry
Robinson, David
Stout, Jacob
Vernam, Samuel
Walters, John

Pages 209-210.

ROLL OF CAPT. LLEWELLYN PIERCE'S COMPANY. (County Unknown.)

Served from Aug. 29, until September 9, 181

Capt. Llewellyn Pierce
Sergt. Samuel Scott
Sergt. Sanford Ramsey

Privates.
Ayers, Lewis
Briggs, James
Culver, Levi
Culbertson, Samuel W.
Campbell, Archibald
Deckie, Moses
Dickson, Joseph
Green, Samuel
Green, John
Gardner, William
Hover, Jacob
Hamilton, Alexander
Herron, Nathaniel
Jett, Daniel
Murphy, William
Moore, James
McDonald, Joseph
Narman, Isaac
Norris, William
Raney, Jacob
Spangler, Henry
Shilling, Amos
Tomtiz, Frederick
Tulk, James
William, Joseph

Lieut. Stephen Reeves
Sergt. John Messer

Privates.
Armstrong, James
Bell, William
Christ, Daniel
Culver, Phillip
Crane, Evan
Devalt, Isaac
Ecleberry, William
Gardner, Robert
Graham, George
Granger, Ebenezer
Herron, David
Hardesty, Abraham
James, David
Lehugh, Spencer
Mitchell, Mathew
Monroe, Robert
McLean, Alexander
Norris, Moses
Phillis, John
Roof, Peter
Sawyer, Porter
Smeltzer, Valentine
Tucker, Alexander
Watson, James
Yoder, Henry

Ensign, George Crandalls
Sergt. Solomon Devedaugh

Privates.
Allen, Thomas
Bliss, Samuel
Collins, Samuel
Chambers, Manlove
Celix, David
Dickson, Thomas
Forrest, James
Green, Isaac
Geer, John
Gibbon, George
Harris, John
Hoover, William
Joseph, William
Linn, James
Merwin, Simion
McDonald, John
McCutcheon, James
Newman, George
Risoner, Solomon
Ruck, John
Spangler, Jacob
Stover, Henry
Taylor, John
Woodward, Willis

ROSTER OF OHIO SOLDIERS IN WAR OF 1812

ROLL OF CAPT. MICHAEL GUNCKEL'S COMPANY. (County Unknown.)

Served from August 23, 1812 until February 22, 1813.

Rank and Name of Soldier.
Capt. Michael Gunckel
Sergt. Felix Gunckel
Sergt. John Shideler
Corp. William Wirick
Drummer, Henry Zeller

Privates.
Brewer, John
Foust, Phillip
Gushwa, Peter
Gephart, George
Istry, Daniel
Kirker, Jacob
Loye, Jacob
Micksell, David
Nutts, George
Stump, John
Ungren, Daniel

Rank and Name of Soldier.
Lieut. John Protzman
Sergt. Peter Shefer
Corp. Phillip Hartzel
Corp. George Wolf

Privates.
Chest, Jacob
Foust, Andrew
Gephart, Philip
Gebhart, Philip
Katterman, Michael
Karn, George
Leslie, Daniel
Miller, Moses
Pickle, George
Sonab, John
Wirick, David

Rank and Name of Soldier.
Ensign, Jacob Suzart
Sergt. Henry Smith
Corp. Jacob Mullenowe
Fifer, George Boyer

Privates.
Emerick, Christopher
Gunckel, Daniel
Gephart, John
Istry, Conrad
Kester, George
Kaug, Phillip
Moyer, John
Meyers, David
Reagel, John
Trion, Peter
Zeller, John

Pages 213-214.

ROLL OF CAPT. WILLIAM S. DRAKE'S COMPANY. (County Unknown.)

Served from February 14, until August 14, 1813.

Capt. William S. Drake
Sergt. William Blane
Sergt. John Martin
Corp. Jacob B. Tucker

Privates.
Anderson, Ezekial
Blaugher, Jacob
Cherry, Abraham
Ewing, William
Groves, Thomas
Hurst, Henry
Kensor, Adam
Martin, Joseph
Meeker, Aaron
Plummer, Banach
Simmons, John
Stagle, Jacob J.
Sherwood, Lewis
Williams, Lewis
Winsed, Joseph

Lieut. Robert McGowan
Sergt. Nicholas McCally
Corp. Jacob Cline
Corp. Samuel Monohan

Privates.
Adams, Johnson
Bowman, William
Carrel, Samuel
Francis, Rezin
Gard, Job
Johon, Thomas
Lampheir, Pierce
Mathew, C. Joseph
Parmester, Erastus
Rose, Cornelius
Simpson, Richard
Shoat, Story
Thompson, John
Weeks, Daniel
Young, Samuel

Ensign, John Mark
Sergt. Lausing Lewis
Corp. Newman Mitchel

Privates.
Berry, Conrad
Bishop, William
DeWitt, Barnet
Grant, William
Hays, Raymond
Isahart, Jacob
Moss, John
Mitchel, Robert
Parish, Ira
Rush, Francis
Shaw, John
Simmons, Thomas
Totten, John
William Richard

Pages 215-216.

ROLL OF CAPT. DANIEL HEATON'S COMPANY. (County Unknown.)

Served from March 27, until September 26, 1813.

Capt. Daniel Heaton
Sergt. John Davis
Sergt. Edward Hokmer
Corp. William Payn
Fifer, John Johnson

Privates.
Andrews, Adam
Allen, Jacob
Burnes, Thomas
Cornelison, Marsh
Flowers, James
Fitsort, Abraham
Huffman, Jacob
Johnson, Gideon
Moyer, Jacob
Mills, Joseph
Patten, Isaac
Russell, Jesse
Smith, Jacob
Shaffer, Abraham
Timmards, George
Wesling, Jacob

Lieut. James Sherard
Sergt. John Andrew
Corp. Solomon Symonds
Corp. Phillip Ray

Privates.
Ashby, Milton
Ble, John
Comhwast, John
Digby, John
Flowers, Aaron
Gilkey, Robert
Hougham, Jonothan
Kepshart, John
Moore, Phillip
Morris, William
Patten, Isaac, Jr.
Ray, Andrew
Sherard, Samuel
Southard, George
Thompson, William
Welch, Benjamin
Whitacre, John

Ensign Lewis Moore
Sergt. Samuel Schenck
Corp. John Clark
Drummer, John Flower

Privates.
Athel, Furgeson
Baker, William
Cornelison, John
Davis, Daniel
Flowers, Andrew
Gee, William
Hardisty, Daniel
Long, Stephen
Morris, John
Mires, Jacob
Reson, Bailey
Symonds, John
Smith, William
Sunderland, Cornelius
Templar, James
Woodruff, Israel

Pages 217-218.

ROLL OF CAPT. NATHAN HATFIELD'S COMPANY. (County Unknown.)

Served from March 20, until September 19, 1813.

Capt. Nathan Hatfield
Sergt. Stephen Cobley
Sergt. Alonzo Applegate
Corp. Robert Welsh

Lieut. Charles Johnson
Sergt. Benjamin Sutton
Corp. Henry Riggs
Corp. Abraham Miley

Ensign, Andrew McMahon
Sergt. James Gordon
Corp. Robert Hawkins

ROLL OF CAPT. NATHAN HATFIELD'S COMPANY. (Continued)

Rank and Name of Soldier.	Rank and Name of Soldier.	Rank and Name of Soldier.
Privates.	**Privates.**	**Privates.**
Askin, Thomas	Abbott, Elisha	Birtsill, Josiah
Burnett, Abel	Brown, Joshua	Brude, Daniel
Bridger, Benjamin	Bennett, Samuel	Black, David W.
Clark, Joseph	Clark, Daniel	Coleman, James
Coleman, Charles	Cailey, James S.	Coon, Levi
Dunseth, Samuel	Denike, Samuel	Gray, George
Ganard, John	Griffin, Joseph	Herrin, William
Hunsiker, Waite	Henley, Cornelius	Hahan, Samuel
Hawkins, Rexin	Hawkins, Cardil	Hathorn, John
Hawkins, William	Hawkins, Joseph	Heron, Daniel
Ketchum, Richard	Lindsey, Elijah	Miley, Abraham
Morrison, Alexander	Mathews, Joseph	Martin, William
McMahon, Hugh	McLaughlin, William	McAdams, Thomas
Reed, Martin	Scamehorn, Amos	Silvers, Enoch
Spencer, Ezra	Vail, Isaac	Wells, William
Welch, Thomas	Woodruff, Hezekiah	Wilson, James

Pages 219-220.

ROLL OF CAPT. THOMAS SETON'S COMPANY. (County Unknown.)
Served from February 5, until Aug. 12, 1813.

Capt. Thomas Seton	Lieut. William Ogden	Ensign, John Tweed
Sergt. Lewis Keyt	Sergt. Thomas Scott	Sergt. Joshua Gordan
Sergt. Phillip P. Byron	Corp. Samuel Tatman	Corp. Rezin Tevis
Corp. William Taylor	Corp. William Holmes	Musician Jeremiah Smith
Privates.	**Privates.**	**Privates.**
Abraham, Joseph	Blue, David	Bruse, Frederick
Byrn, Lawrence	Cookns, Jacob	Conley, Rhiza
Debrubar, Jacob	Debruber, John	Foncher, William
Flora, James	Fisher, David	Graham, John
Goodin, James	Holmes, William, Sr.	Jones, George
Knight, James	Kenton, Simon	Lippencock, Morgan
Moore, William	Martin, Edmund	Morris, Randolph
Mahala, John	McCoy, Duncan	McConnel, John
McEvain, David	Perry, William	Ray, Isaac
Riley, Alexsis	Swim, Jacob	Skidmore, Ralph
Shenkle, Jacob	Smith, Benton	Simmerman, Frederick
Smith, Jeremiah	Woodruff, William	Watson, Jacob
Wharton, Henry	Wilson, John	Wright, George
	Younger, William	

Page 221.

ROLL OF CAPT. THEOPHILUS SIMONTON'S COMPANY. (County Unknown.)
Served from March 23, until October 1, 1813.

Capt. Theophilus Simonton	Lieut. William Hopkins	Ensign, William Spence
Sergt. Abraham Hany	Sergt. Thomas Clark	Sergt. James Johnson
Sergt. Samuel Coburn	Corp. Hugh McCullough	Corp. James Kelley
Corp. Samuel B. Walker	Corp. William Burton	
Privates.	**Privates.**	**Privates.**
Anderson, Samuel	Bannon, Michael	Bigam, John
Bigam, Alexander	Briant, John	Briant, William
Brown, Stacey	Coburn, William	Crawford, Thomas
Entel, Valentine	Fargner, Charles	Gillis, John
Hill, James	Hart, James	Livingston, David
McCollister, Alexander	McCollister, James	Orr, William
Patten, William	Riggs, Amos	Snyder, Arnold
Shields, Robert	Swank, Daniel	Snell, Henry
Simonton, Alexander	Thompson, Roden	Vanderwort, Jonah
Vanderwort, Paul	Vanderwort, John	Vernon, Joseph
Wilson, Sylvester	Wilkinson, Moses	Work, Alexander
	Wasson, Theophilus	

Page 222.

ROLL OF CAPT. DAVID E. HENDRICK'S COMPANY. (County Unknown.)
Served from May 1, until Nov. 18, 1813.

Capt. David E. Hendricks	Capt. Richard L. Leason	Ensign, Mathew Harbison
Sergt. Conrad Bonbrake	Sergt. Samuel Truax	Sergt. Samuel Parker
Sergt. John Truax	Corp. Whitesel Dan	Corp. Jonothan Harris
Corp. John Larsh	Drummer, Absalom Starr	Fifer, Adam Whitesell
Privates.	**Privates.**	**Privates.**
Bonebrake, Adam	Bristow, Henry	Bristow, Payton
Bonebrake, Peter	Carr, Samuel	Dooley, Silas
Duggin, Henry	Hand, Chas.	Harbison, John
Kincaid, John	Llewellan, Thomas	Larsh, Lewis
Moon, James	Moore, John	Marks, John
McDonald, Hugh	McClung, James	McCalla, James C.
McCormick, William	McClung, Mathew	Patterson, John
Potterf, Jacob	Potterf, John	Potterf, Joseph
Rimion, Robert	Singer, Thomas	Sarsh, John
Starr, John	Strader, Daniel	Stuart, Chas.
Truax, Nathan	Wolf, Andrew	Wirgent, Chas.
Worshen, Daniel	White, James	Wade, John

Pages 223-224. Vol. 2.

ROLL OF CAPT. DANIEL HOSBROOK'S COMPANY. (County Unknown.)

Served from February 5, until August 12, 1813.

Rank and Name of Soldier.	Rank and Name of Soldier.	Rank and Name of Soldier.
Capt. Daniel Hosbrook	Lieut. Joseph Davis	Ensign. William Shilling
Sergt. David R. VanWinkle	Sergt. Baxter Broadwell	Sergt. Jacob Bradbury
Sergt. Lawrence Swing	Corp. Robert Erwin	Corp. Isaac Covalt
Corp. William Johnson	Corp. William Patterson	Drummer, Lewis Bailey
Fifer, Robert Ross		

Privates.

Abbott, Joseph	Bailey, James	Burris, John
Barton, Joseph	Bridges, Elisha	Bennett, Leonard
Bowman, George	Campbell, James	Clark, Jonothan
Curry, John	Crank, John G.	Carter, John
Couch, Isaiah	Daniel, Isaac	Dougherty, James
Dowden, Thomas	Edinger, Boyd	Farmer, Fred
Fleek, John	Flora. Thomas	Gaston, William
Goldalhy, William	Gillman, Ichabod W.	Grey, Runey
Hamilton, John	Irwin, John	Jenkins, Henry
Ketchum, Jeremiah	Job, Archibald R.	Knott, John
Landor, John	Linning, Joseph	Laird, David
Landon, John	Lovel, John	Muney, Charles
Mathews, G. W.	McNeilly, Robert	McMullin, Loe
Neely, John	Neville, William	Pine, William
Plicard, Henry	Patterson, Thomas	Sedgwick, George
Shederly, Henry	Strickland, Mark	Skinner, Caleb
South, Peter	Shinn, Joab	Trukle, Henry
Thompson, James	Tibeighein, Leo	Tomley. Amos
Wooley, Joseph	Weir, James	Westerfteld, Peter
Wright, Zephamiah	White, Forman	Warbington, James
Winner, John	Woodworth, Daniel	

Pages 225-226.

ROLL OF CAPT. MATTHIAS ENGLE'S COMPANY. (County Unknown.)

Served from February 6, until August 5, 1813.

Capt. Matthias Engle	Lieut. Henry Henson	Ensign, Jacob Culp
Sergt. Elisha Harrison	Sergt. Henry Hathaw	Sergt. Jacob Sin
Sergt. Noah Clark	Corp. William Betts	Corp. Charles Cook
Corp. Anderson Hunter	Corp. Robert Cladwell	Musician Zechariah Hart.
Musician, George Painter		

Privates.

Applegate, Charles	Bennett, George	Burtle, John
Blocksom. Moses	Brown, Henry	Byers, Isaac
Bryant, Isaac	Basculoe, Isaac	Butler, John
Bradshaw, Robert	Beach, John	Bouron, Alexander
Casey, John	Callihan, Samuel	Cane, Charles
Dolby, John	Daily, John	Dollerhide, John
Enlit, Thomas	Frederick, Henry	Free, Adam
Gilbreath, William	Gay, George	Goodin, Thomas
Gaston, Thomas	Huws, William	Humes, John
Hitchins, George	Harr. David	Jacobs, Jacob
Johnson, John	Keller, Jacob	Morrison, Samuel
Moore, William	Melone, John	Moore, William I.
Norlam, James	Poffinberger, John	Power, William
Reynolds, John	Ragger, John	Robinson, William G.
Shewald, Isaiah	Stotts, Jacob	Swegart, Daniel
Shingler, John	SeWill, John	Smith, Archibald
Stewart, James	Thomas, Jesse	Wolf, Thomas
Willis, John	Widner, David	

Pages 227-228.

ROLL OF CAPT. VAN M. HENRY'S COMPANY. (County Unknown.)

Served from February 5, until August 4, 1813.

Capt. Van M. Henry	Lieut. William Thomas	Ensign Jonothan Markland
Ensign ————-, Goodwin	Sergt. Thomas D. Wheelan	Sergt. Justice Gibbs
Sergt. Conrad Plow	Sergt. Gad Waggonner	Corp. James Armstrong
Corp. Chas. Stephens	Corp. Richard L. Campbell	Corp. Samuel Dodson

Privates.

Arnold, William	Davis, James	Burnett, Daniel
Boyer, Sweden	Chaisman, Henry	Cox, Benjamin B.
Campbell, William F.	Davis, Thomas	Freedly, John
Ford, William	Fenton, Jacob	Frazer, Samuel
Frasier, David	Frost, John	Herrin, Beverly
Harcourt, Enoch	Howard, Phillip	Hartman, Joseph
Ingersol, Joseph	Ireland, Moses	Jacobs, John
Longfellow, Thomas	Lancaster, John F.	Marshall, James
Miller, Frederick	Mitchel, William	Millholland, William
DuMont, Peter	Marshall, William	Menel, Adam
Mizner, Jacob	Norris, Caleb	Nugin, Thomas
Olendorf, Frederick	Plow, Phillip	Posy, Armsted

Pages 227-228.   Vol. 2.

ROLL OF CAPT. VAN M. HENRY'S COMPANY. (Continued.)

Rank and Name of Soldier.

Privates.
Richardson, Jacob
Sargent, John
Shupe, Daniel
Scogin, Eli
Torrence, John C.
Veach, John

Rank and Name of Soldier.

Privates.
Risner, John
Stout, Thomas T.
Stewart, Charles
Tollar, Asa
Taylor, Cornelius
Willey, George
Wallis, Aaron

Rank and Name of Soldier.

Privates.
Stout, Andrew S.
Smith, William
Sherwin, William
Teaboult, Uriah
Taylor, Henry
Wilkinson, Joel T.
Walden, James

Pages 229-230.

ROLL OF CAPT. JOHN HAMILTON'S COMPANY.
(From Ross or Butler County.)
Served from February 6, until August 6, 1813. Part of company served until 1816.

Capt. John Hamilton
Sergt. John Haynes
Sergt. Eli Davis
Corp. John Cain

Privates.
Anthony, Mark
Bailey, John
Craig, John
Cain, Robert
Dickey, James
Fraser, Joseph
Flemming, Samuel
Hunter, John
Immick, John
Kiger, Christopher
Miller, Jacob
Potts, William
Russell, Geo.
Stone, Benjamin
Scuder, Stephen
Vansickle, Robert
Vinage, David
Weir, Thomas

Lieut. William Sheafor
Sergt. Adam Stonebaker
Corp. Nicholas Bailey
Corp. John Porter

Privates.
Abbott, Joseph
Brosure, Peter
Clark, Daniel
Colby, Samuel
Denney, Joseph
Feaster, John
Gregory, Thomas
Heaton, James
Jordon, Robert
Linder, Stephen
McCloskey, John
Park, Arthur
Squire, David
Shuckman, John
Thomas, Henry
Vansickle, Evert
Winn, Benjamin
Wells, John

Ensign James Harper
Sergt. Benjamin Barry
Corp. John Miller
Drummer, Mark Briny

Privates.
Baker, Daniel
Briam, Joshua
Chambers, Samuel
Carlisle, James
Emerson, Winthrop
Flemming, Alexander
Galloway, Enoch
Huffman, Abraham
Johnson, Thomas
Martin, John
Price, William
Pierce, John
Stine, Christian
Spencer, Thomas
Thompson, John
Vansickle, Robert, Sr.
Winn, James
Winn, Warner

Pages 231-232.

ROLL OF CAPT. PATRICK SHAW'S COMPANY. (County Unknown.)
Served from February 8, until August 6, 1813.

Capt. Patrick Shaw
Sergt. Byrim William
Sergt. Joseph Dill
Corp. James Kennedy
Musician, John Tuttle

Privates.
Abbott, James
Burns, Thomas
Coleman, Philip
Dunaham, Edward
Harris, Samuel
Irwin, James
King, Alexander
Moore, Irvin
McCristey, John
Perro, George
Stanton, John
Skearnes, Jabez
Spencer, Thomas W.
Terry, Daniel
White, Robert

Lieut. Jacob Vance
Sergt. Richard Camplin
Corp. James Kitchel
Corp. William Laren

Privates.
Briney, Frederick
Cummin, James
Cartwright, Levan W.
Drake, Peter
Hibbs, Ezer
Jester, Eli
Murphy, Nathaniel
Martin, William
Newport, Train
Rynearson, John
Sutton, James
Spirling, Jesse
Tapin, John
Thompson, Thomas
Wallace, Thomas

Ensign William Dill
Sergt. Peter Keenin
Corp. John Wiley
Musician, Daniel Fister

Privates.
Bailey, Thomas Z.
Cowan, William
Drake, Joseph
Fordice, James
Hunter, Nicholas
Little, William
Moore, William
McCain, William
Osborn, Barzels
Robertson, David
Snook, Jacob
Sutton, John
Tullis, Michael
Weer, Elisha
Weeks, James

Page 233.

ROLL OF CAPT. WILLIAM B. FORDYCE'S COMPANY. (County Unknown.)
Served from September 4, 1812, until March 15, 1814.

Capt. William B. Fordyce
Sergt. David Bennet
Corp. Ausboum Cooper
Corp. Cornelius Voorhins
Musician, Samuel Shannon

Privates.
Archer, Chas. or Jack
Biggs, William
Bone or Bowen, Thomas
Coughlin, Jacob
Deane, Aaron
Gard, Joab
Hardin, Samuel
Sampson, John

Ensign Jonas Baldwin
Sergt. David Newport
Corp. William Cummins
Corp. Ulm Stranbaugh
Musician, John York

Privates.
Ballard, Isaac
Burr, Peter
Claspell, Joseph
Clebinger, David
Danhan, David
Gard, Daniel
Person, Enoch
Wilson, Joseph

Sergt. Larkins Reynolds
Sergt. James Shepler
Corp. Thomas Moorhead
Musician, Aaron Brown

Privates.
Bates, William
Bush, Abraham
Cast, Ezekial
Deane, Uriah
Garrison, Emanuel
Hathaway, Daniel
Rogan, Elijah
Wright, Samuel

Pages 235-236. Vol. 2.

ROLL OF CAPT. THOMAS SHANNON'S COMPANY. (County Unknown.)

Served from January 13, until March 17, 1814.

Rank and Name of Soldier.	Rank and Name of Soldier.	Rank and Name of Soldier.
Capt. Thomas Shannon	Lieut. Thomas Henderson	Ensign Robert Grier
Sergt. Thomas Grier	Sergt. Thomas Dougher	Sergt. Samuel Marlow
Sergt. James Boler	Corp. John Douglas	Corp. Robert Stewart
Corp. John Dillon	Corp. Christopher Craten	
Privates.	**Privates.**	**Privates.**
Ager, William	Adindel, Cornelius	Blaylock, Richard
Barton, Benjamin	Barrett, John	Bates, Humphrey
Brevard, Charles	Brevard, William	Barnes, Ebenezer
Brill, George	Brill, Henry	Coffield, James
Craton, Andrew	Doherty, Andrew	Douglas, William
Devore, John	Devore, Henry	Erwin, James
Ford Hugh	Floyd, Aaron	Forest, Archibald
Gilliland, John	Grier, Thomas, Sr.	Harris, George
Hall, James	Holmes, Henry	Henry, Francis
Hutchinson, James	Hager, Jacob	Jenkins, Jacob
Kinkead, Joseph	Linly, William	Muizel, John
Masters, Robert	Moore, James	McMillen, Joseph
Newben, Abraham	Pully, Samuel	Roof, Daniel
Rogers, Joseph	Stewart, Samuel	Scoggans, John
Smith, James	Thorp, Job	Thompson, William
Vance, James	Vamoy, Joseph	Wherry, James
Wilson, William	Wilson, Samuel	Watkins, Thomas
	Williams, William	

Pages 237-238.

ROLL OF CAPT. JOHN HOWELL'S COMPANY.
(From Belmont County.)

Served from September 3, 1813, until January 3 and March 16, 1814.

Capt. John Howell	Lieut. Jacob Moore	Ensign Mathew Howell
James Brown	Sergt. Gilbert McCoy	Sertg. James Westlake
Sergt. Robert Millawy	Sergt. Robert Hathaway	Sergt. Isaiah Shepherd
Corp. Richard McElhiney	Corp. John Arick	Corp. John Shepard
Corp. Moses DeLong	Drummer, Phines Shephard	Fifer, Joseph Reed
Privates.	**Privates.**	**Privates.**
Ault, Johann	Ault, Jacob, Sr.	Alban, Geo.
Aurs, Reuben	Brown, James	Bonor James
Belville, James	Boker, Jacob	Carpenter, David
Carpenter, Joseph	Carpenter, John	Cobman, Samuel
Crow, John	Dinford, William	Dunfield, Joseph
Devall, John	Ferier, John	Grimes, Arthir
Hubbs, Isaac	Hartley, David	Joy, John
King, Robert	Henthorn, Adam	Kitz, Joseph
Kitz, Henry	Limley, George	Latimore, Thomas
Lashley, Caleb	Miller, Francis	Miers, George
Moore, Samuel	Miller, Frederick	Moose, John
McGaughey, William	McElhiny, Richard	Noble, Alexander
Petman, Elias	Pound, Joseph	Price, Nathan
Ross, Enoch	Ruble, Isaac	Ross, Robinson
Rutter, Peter	Rutter, Jonothan	Reed, John
Smith, John	Shipman, Mathias	Sprags, John
Shepherd, John	Sutton, William	Walters, David
Silvers, John	Ward, Moses	Vaneter, Mordical
Workman, Abraham	Wiley, Joseph	Yoke, Samuel

Pages 239-240.

ROLL OF CAPT. WILLIAM VAN CLEVE'S COMPANY. (County Unknown.)

Served from May 21, until July 24, 1812.

Capt. William Van Cleve	Lieut. James Barnett	Ensign David Steele
Sergt. James Wilson	Sergt. Joseph Kemp	Sergt. Isaac Westfall
Sergt. Nicholas Stephens	Corp. William McCleary	Corp. William Westfall
Corp. William Burnes	Corp. Lewis Davis	Corp. Henry King
Fifer, Peter Musselman		
Privates.	**Privates.**	**Privates.**
Archer, Zechariah	Alten, Jeremiah	Brown, Joseph
Butt, Henry	Butler, Thomas	Baltimore, Philip
Berryhill, James	Barlon, William A.	Cox, Abraham
Carney, Lott	Cline, Abraham	Consolver, Jacob
Codington, Isaac	Dean, Adam	Enoch, John
Ellzroth, John	Harvey, Abraham	Harmon, Solomon
Harrit, Robert	Hamon, William	Ingenon, Benjamin
Isenogel, Abraham	John, Thomas	Johnston, Elisha
Kyle, John	Leachman, John	Law, William
Miller, Conkling	Miller, Charles	Miller, Jacob
Miller, Isaac	McLain, James	McCun, John
McGrew, Archibald	McCune, Alexander	McClane, John
Neff, Lewis	Neff, Abraham	Poncott, Edward
Patterson, Samuel R.	Reed, John	Rose, Benjamin
Richardson, Abram	Sathren, John	Scott, Benjamin

ROLL OF CAPT. WILLIAM VAN CLEVE'S COMPANY (Continued).

Rank and Name of Soldier.
Privates.
Slagle, John
Speare, Peter
Vanasdol, William
Woodman, John

Rank and Name of Soldier.
Privates.
Swartwood, Abraham
Shepherd, Thomas
Witters, Jacob
Wolf, Conrad

Rank and Name of Soldier.
Privates.
Snodgrass, William
Tennet, Alexander
Wolf, John
Westfall, John

Pages 241-242.

ROLL OF CAPT. JACOB BOERSTLER'S COMPANY.
(From Clermont County.)

Served from April 24, until May 23, 1812.

Capt. Jacob Boerstler
Sergt. Daniel Campbell
Sergt. Chas. Waites
Corp. John Hankins

Lieut. Thomas Kain
Sergt. Edward Brown
Corp. John Conroy
Corp. Jaspar Shopwell

Ensign Thomas Foster
Sergt. Hally Raper
Corp. Samuel Raper

Privates.
Arthurs, Abner
Berry, Michael E.
Colthard, James
Davis, William
Davis, John
Fite, John W.
Gould, Daniel
Harris, Hiram
Last, John
Maloot, Sam R.
McMillan, Geo.
Oakman, John
Smith, Peter
Tuble, Cornelius
Waidlaw, Hugh
Williams, Thomas

Privates.
Brunk, Joseph
Chambers, James
Colthard, Isaac
Davis, Lewis
Digbee, William
Frazer, John
Hunt, Thomas
Kenton, Simon
Little, Jonothan
McCollun, Daniel
Neff, Geo.
Reed, John
Stephens, Walker
Wood, Joseph
Waidlaw, William
Walker, John D.

Privates.
Buchanan, John
Compton, William
Denham, James
Dennis, Richard
Fite, John
Gibson, Arch
Hunt, Geo.
Little, Joel
Martin, Joseph
McHarm, James
Naylor, John
Smalwood, Richard
Tollia, Farro Jones
Waits, Peter
Waits, Reuben

Page 389. Vol. 2.

ROLL OF FIELD AND STAFF, WAR OF 1812-1813.

COLONEL JAMES FINDLAY, SECOND REGIMENT, OHIO MILITIA.

Rank and Name of Soldier.
Col. James Findlay
Pay Master & Q. M. Clk., P.Q. M. Sergt. Math. S. Spencer
T. Schenck
Surg. Mate, Edward Y. Kemper

Rank and Name of Soldier.
Maj. Thomas B. Vanhorn
Musician, Enoch Jackman

Rank and Name of Soldier.
Pay Master & Q. M. Thos. Dugan
Sergt. Maj. Allison C. Looker

Page 389. Vol. 2.

COLONEL JAMES RENICK, SECOND REGIMENT, OHIO MILITIA.

Col. James Renick
Adjt. James R. Hulse
Q. M. Sergt. Jonothan Renick
Fife Maj. Moses Abderson

Maj. Aaron Strong
Q. M. Daniel Hoofman
Surg. Mate, Thomas Shieves

Maj. Joseph Campbell
Q. M. William Gibson
Sergt. Maj. John Stephenson

Page 239. Vol. 2.

COLONEL WILLIAM W. COTGREAVE, SECOND REGIMENT, OHIO MILITIA.

Col. William Cotgreave
Q. M., E. J. Hoover
Surg. Mate, Sylvanus Suly

Maj. Jacob Roller
Q. M. Sergt. John Frank
Pay Master, W. Morrow

Adjt. David Bell
Surg. J. B. Harmon
Sergt. Maj. L. F. Leavitt

Page 389. Vol. 2.

COLONEL ROBERT SAFFORD, SECOND REGIMENT, OHIO MILITIA.

Col. Robert Safford
Adjt. Hugh Rogers
Surg. Leonard Jewitt
Sergt. Maj. Stephen Reynolds

Maj. Nehemiah Beasley
Q. M. John Roadamour
Surg. Mate William Beebe
Drum Maj. Benjamin Mills

Maj. Jeheil Linsey
Q. M. Sergt. Caleb McDaniel
Pay Master Horace Nye
Fife Maj. Jacob Walters

Page 390. Vol. 2.

MAJOR STEPHEN MASON, SECOND REGIMENT, OHIO MILITIA.

Maj. Stephen Mason
Q. M. Rufus Edwards
Surg. Joseph DeWolf
Fife Maj. Philo Hall

Maj. Thaddeus Andrews
Q. M. Charles Curtis
Pay Master Hiram Roundy

Adjt. Erastus Skinner
Q. M. Sergt. William Kennedy
Sergt. Maj. Arthur Anderson

Page 390. Vol. 2.
COLONEL JOHN HINDMAN, SECOND REGIMENT, OHIO MILITIA.

Rank and Name of Soldier.	Rank and Name of Soldier.	Rank and Name of Soldier.
Col. John Hindman	Maj. Peter Musser	Maj. Jacob Frederick
Adjt. Jacob Musser	Adjt. John Care	Q. M. John Taggart
Q. M. James Alexander	Q. M. Sergt. James Alexander	Q. M. Sergt. Robert Alexander
Pay Master David Clendenin	Surg. John Menary	Surg. Mate John McKeehan
Sergt. Maj. James Blackburn	Sergt. Maj. Stephen Miller	Drum Maj. Sylvanus Burk
Fife Maj. Stephen Palmer		

Page 390. Vol. 2.
MAJOR GEORGE DARROW, ODD BATTALION, OHIO MILITIA.

Maj. George Darrow	Adjt. Benjamin Whedom	Q. M. Ebenezer Sheldon, Jr.
Q. M. Sergt. John Cochran	Q. M. Pt. George Pease	Surg. Moses Thompson
Surg. Mate Jonothan Metcalf	Pay Master Samuel King	Clerk Joseph Darrow
For. M. Stephen Butler	Drum Maj. Josiah Starr	Fife Maj. James Darrow
Sergt. Maj. James Robinson		

FIELD OFFICERS, STAFFS NOT GIVEN.

Page 259.	Col. Daniel Collins, 2nd Regt.	Page 1. Lt. Col. Henry Zumalt, 2nd Regt.
Page 73.	Col. John Dougherty, 2nd Regt.	Page 367. Maj. Anthony Pitzer, 2nd Regt.
Page 312.	Col. John Mann, 2nd Regt.	Page 361. Maj. Henry Price, 2nd Regt.
Page 382.	Col. Allen Trimble, 2nd Regt.	Page 287. Maj. John Willetts, 2nd Regt.

SECOND REGIMENT, OHIO MILITIA, WAR OF 1812-1813.
ROLL OF CAPT. JOSEPH CARPENTER'S COMPANY
(Probably from Hamilton Co.)
Pages 1, 2, 375, 376, 377, 378. Vol. 2.

Served from January 4, until March 17, 1814.

Capt. John Carpenter	Lieut. William. L. Stake	Ensign Benjamin Loder
Sergt. William Preston	Sergt. Jacob Fomble	Sergt. John Swain
Sergt. William F. Smith	Corp. Ashur Ploolley	Corp. James McAulley
Corp. William Johnson	Corp. David Seisco	Musician, Nimrod Troutwine

Privates.

Auter, Thomas	Arthurs, Samuel	Brown, Titus
Babbet, Calvin	Bowman, John	Batchelder, Jonothan
Collard, Isaac	Cole, Robert	Clark, Robert
Cogswell, William	Collard, Nathaniel	Cormac, Lewis
Dove, John	Edwin, John	Edwards, Thomas
Gillis, William	Gamble, James	Green, Moses
Gatton, Jeremiah	Hamill, Christopher	Hill, John
Hinckley, Abner	Hathaway, Abner	Johnson, William
Johnson, William	Johnson, Caleb	Johnson, James
Laughlin, Brownson	Lord, Joseph	Love, William
Lyon, Moses	Millholland, William	Miller, Moses
Miller, David H.	May, James	McIntof, Emanuel
McVay, William	McNeall, James	Morton, John
Nichols, William	Neavis, Daniel	Pixley, William
Patterson, Martin	Reagin, Rezin	Russell, Rowley
Rodgers, Seever	Somen, Thomas	Smith, Ebenezer
Sutton, Amos	Smith, Joel	Spooner, Reed
Simmins, Richard	Thornly, Enoch	Tucker, James
Wood, David	Woodruff, David	Wilson, William
White, Alexander	Wright, John Sr.	Wright, John Jr.
Williams, Joshua	Wykoff, Jacob	Wilson, James
Warden, Jesse	Williams, Nathaniel	

Pages 73, 257.
ROLL OF CAPT. ARTHUR LAYTON'S CO. (Probaably from Champaign Co.)

Served from December 11, 1812, until January 11, 1813.

Capt. Arthur Layton	Lieut. Nathaniel Williams	Ensign Elias Baker
Sergt. John Layton	Sergt. John John	Sergt. Aaron Werner
Sergt. Adam Howel	Corp. William Layton	Corp. Philip Mower
Fifer, John Husted		

Privates.

Albin, Gabriel	Albin, Samuel	Crites, Conrad
Gregory, Joshua	Hicks, William	Hughel, Richard
Husted, Moses	Husted, Solomon	Husted, Isaac
Husted, Samuel	Hulbert, Isaac	Jones, Gabriel
Kelley, John	Lawman, Joseph	Minich, Michael
McKinley, James	McDonough, Edward	Ray, Lewis
Reed, Benjamin	Reifer, Joseph	Rankin, James
Smith, Henry	Tunderburg, Jacob	Williams, Thomas
Wood, Thomas	Wallace, Reuben	Wood, James

44 ROSTER OF OHIO SOLDIERS IN WAR OF 1812

Pages 251-252. Vol. 2.

ROLL OF CAPT. JOHN JONES' COMPANY.
(Probably from Ross and Highland Counties.)
Served from July 29, until September 8, 1813.

Rank and Name of Soldier.
Capt. John Jones
Sergt. John Robbins
Sergt. Henry Anderson
Corp. Frederick Dueknall

Privates.

Anderson, Balaam
Brackney, Eli
Baldwin, Richard
Charweater, Thomas
Collins, James
Garret, Charles
Hunt, Ira
Johnson, Simeon
Johnson, James
Milligan, James
Moore, Elijah
Perkins, Andrew
Richardson, Samuel
Shukey, Christian
Thornberry, Abel
Wright, John, Sr.
Wever, Stephen

Rank and Name of Soldier.
Lieut. Alexander Morrow
Sergt. Robert Duncan
Corp. Richard P. Johnson
Corp. Thomas Coffey

Privates.

Adams, David
Bronce, Frederick
Byles, Thomas
Currey, Nathaniel
Caps, James
Grad, James
Hicks, Moses
Jones, Thomas
Leaverton, Wilson
Miller, Isaac
Morris, John
Potter, George
Stewart, William
Sharp, Henry
Wilson, Benjamin
Wright, John Jr.

Rank and Name of Soldier.
Ensign Samuel Kilgore
Sergt. John King
Corp. Jeremiah Lane

Privates.

Bell, Charles
Benton, Moses
Cupps, William
Caw, Nathaniel
Chaney, Gabriel
Hutsenpeller, John
Hoten, James
Johnson, Larkin
Kingery, Benjamin
Mathews, Ira
McMillen, William N.
Reece, Hiram
Spence, Robert
Trop, Henry
Wright, James
Wright, Samuel

Pages 253-254.

ROLL OF CAPT. NEHEMIAH GREGORY'S COMPANY (County Unknown.)
Served from January 1, until February 21, 1813.

Capt. Nehemiah Gregory
Sergt. David Vaughan
Sergt. David Walt
Corp. Thaddius Crippen

Privates.

Boils, John
Bowers, William
Cross, Israel
Caplin, Cyrus
Driggs, George
Fulton, Samuel
Hoskenson, Joshua
Hecox, Jeptha
Hilliard, James
Haney, James
Kimes, Abraham
Polk, Alpheus
Reynolds, Samuel H.
Stroud, Joel
Stewart, Charles
Smith, Jonas
Wood, Joshua, Jr.
Waterman, Asher

Lieut. James Crippen
Sergt. Israel Wood
Corp. Barnet Brice
Corp. William Williams

Privates.

Beeb, Peter
Bowman, Jabez
Chadwick, Thomas
Davis, Bial
Field, Simons
Foster Ira
Gibbs, James
Hewitt, John
Haney, David
Husey Jarvis
McKinstry, John
Rowell, Daniel
Ross, Henry
Still, William
Sloan, John
Stanby, John
Weckham, John

Ensign William McKinstry
Sergt. William Starr
Corp. David Shideles

Privates.

Boils, Martin
Cullison, Thomas
Coe, John
Dains, Calvin
Feltch, Joel
Gibbs, Almond
Hanning, Moses
Hanning, Aaron
Hatch, Ebenezer
Jones, Jared
Paull, Ebenezer
Reeves, Reuben
Rice, Jonas
Stewart, Andrew
Sage, Joel
Varner, John
Weir, James

Page 256.

ROLL OF CAPT. THOMAS WISBEY'S CO. (Probably from Highland Co.)
Served from July 29, until August 19, 1813.

Capt. Thomas Wisbey
Sergt. Isaac Collins
Corp. Andrew Badgley

Privates.

Boatman, George
Chapman, Isaac
Gibler, Daniel
Lantz, John
Sloan, James

Lieut. Nathaniel Campbell
Sergt. Thomas McCoy

Privates.

Bell, Andrew
Chapman, Asabel
Gossett, John
Ross, St. Clair
Super, Henry

Ensign Jacob Moury
Corp. Samuel W. Finley

Privates.

Coffman, Phillip
Duncan, Amos
Lantz, Heary
Ross, Isaiah
Stoot, Jacob

Page 255.

ROLL OF CAPT. JEHIEL GREGORY, JR.'S CO. (County Unknown).
Served from August 9, until February 19, 1812.

Capt. Jehiel Gregory
Sergt. James Crippen
Sergt. William Starr
Corp. Peter Beeb
Drummer Jarvis Haley

Lieut. Nehemiah Gregory
Sergt. Isaac Wood
Corp. Barnet Bour
Corp. William Williams

Ensign William McKintry
Sergt. Abel Stedman
Corp. David Shidler
Fifer, Jacob Waters

ROLL OF CAPT. JEHIEL GREGORY, JR.'S CO. (Continued)

Rank and Name of Soldier.

Privates.
- Bechs, William
- Coe, John
- Frost, Joseph
- Griffin, Thaddeus
- Hatch, Ebenezer
- Haney, Moses
- Jones, Jerret
- Polk, Eber
- Reivs, Reuben
- Slane, John
- Stewart, Charles
- Varner, John
- Watt, David
- Wire, James

Rank and Name of Soldier.

Privates.
- Boyles, Martin
- Davies, Bial
- Fulton, Samuel
- Hilliard, James
- Haney, James
- Hiacon, Jeptha
- Muney, Daniel
- Roso, Henry
- Rice, Jonas
- Stilt, William
- Taylor, John
- Wood, John Jr.
- Wickham, John

Rank and Name of Soldier.

Privates.
- Catlin, Cyrus
- Foster, Hiram
- Gibbs, Abraham
- Haney, David
- Haney, Aaron
- Hines, Abraham
- McKintry, John
- Reynolds, Samuel H.
- Strand, Joel
- Stewart, Andrew
- Vaughn, David
- Wood, John, Sr.
- Watkins, George

Page 258.
ROLL OF ENSIGN WILLIAM LAMMA'S COMPANY (Probably from Clark Co.)
Served from September 18, until October 18, 1813.

- Ensign William Lamma
- Sergt. Thomas Stafford
- Corp. Moses Fuller

Privates.
- Batcher, Joseph
- Cruca, John
- Foagey, Stewart
- Lamma, James
- McPorson, Samuel
- Stafford, George
- Verdier, Adam
- Conner, Jacob

- Sergt. Daniel Hubbell
- Corp. James Black

Privates.
- Brandeburg, Henry
- Chestnut, Joseph
- Howell, Joab
- Long, Brumfield
- Nail, William
- Simes, William
- Wallace, John

- Sergt. Samuel McKinney
- Corp. James Henderson

Privates.
- Black, Andrew
- Fongy, John
- Kelley, Solomon
- Mitchell, Archibald
- Reyburn, James
- Stapleton, William
- Wallace, Moses

Page 259.
ROLL OF LIEUT. ANDREW McINTIRE'S COMPANY (County Unknown).
Served from July 28, until August 22, 1813.

Lieut. Andrew McIntire

Privates.
- Auburn, James
- Burnes, Mathew
- Dryden, Samuel
- Glasgow, Joseph
- Montgomery, Andrew
- McCormick, William
- McWright, William
- Patton, Thomas
- Spurgeon, James

Privates.
- Bayles, Jemiel
- Gavin, John
- Fethercile, Andrew
- Milligen, William
- Mattox, Michael
- McClelland, Thomas
- McWright, James
- Smiley, James
- Shepherd, John

Privates.
- Burnes, James
- Clay, Mathew
- Glasgow, William
- Montgomery, John
- McWright, David
- McCulloch, Alexander
- Noland, James
- Scott, Moses
- Van Pelt, John

Page 260.
ROLL OF CAPT. CHARLES CHESTNUT'S CO. (Probably from Ross County).
Served from July 20, until August 10, 1813.

- Capt. Charles Chestnut
- Sergt. John Lee
- Corp. James Trego

Privates.
- Bird, James
- Groves, John
- Heth, David
- Parks, John
- Rithard, Samuel
- Tuttle, Isaiah

- Lieut. David Ogden
- Sergt. William Worley

Privates.
- Baker, Peter
- Hyde, Nathan
- Lloyd, Morris
- Park, Daniel
- Stinson, Hugh
- Wade, Thomas

- Ensign Peter Clark
- Corp. Samuel Vinson

Privates.
- Gansoy, Samuel
- Gilmore, Robert
- McFarland, John
- Ross, Armstrong
- Summerset, John
- Yokey, John

Pages 261-262.
ROLL OF CAPT. DAVID LYON'S CO. (Probably from Ross County).
Served from July 28, until September 4, 1813.

- Capt. David Lyon
- Ensign William How
- Sergt. George Beshong
- Corp. Joseph Loke
- Drummer, Peter Fisher

Privates.
- Albright, Henry
- Brown, John
- Chinworth, William
- Davis, Remembrance W.

- Lieut. Levi Hodges
- Sergt. John Berry
- Sergt. William Rhea
- Corp. Peter Provott
- Fifer, Henry Rout

Privates.
- Blake, William
- Burk, Robert
- Clemans, Joseph
- Downing, William

- Lieut. Abraham Bennet
- Sergt. John Loke
- Corp. James Tewell
- Corp. James Morrison

Privates.
- Bailey, Stephen
- Burk, William
- Drake, Jordan
- Dougherty, James

ROLL OF CAPT. DAVID LYON'S CO. (Continued)

Rank and Name of Soldier.

Privates.
Foster, Joseph Jr.
Guthrie, George
Hellenbach, William
Higginbotham, William
Kellenger, Jacob
Lewis, Samuel
Mathews, Joseph
Mounts, Asa
McCray, Nathan
Ogg, John
Peters, Thomas
Parsons, Ezekial
Sewell, Joseph
Thorp, Thomas

Rank and Name of Soldier.

Privates.
Foster, William
Higginbotham, James
Howard, Ephraim
Johnston, John
Kellison, John
Lewis, Joseph
Mathews, John
Miller, David
Nolland, William
Ottwell, John
Phillips, Benjamin
Pittenger, James
Sergeant, James
Wright, James

Rank and Name of Soldier.

Privates.
Foster, Isaac
Hampton, Francis
House, John
Johnston, George
Loney, James
Lewis, John
Moore, Edward
McCray, Alexander
Nixon, Allen
Pry, Jacob
Provott, Thomas
Summers, Benjamin
Switzer, Abraham
Williams, John

Pages 263-264-265-266.

ROLL OF CAPT. THOMAS MORGAN'S CO. (From Ross and Scioto Counties).

Served from July 28, until September 9, 1813, and from February 13, until March 18, 1814.

Capt. Thomas Morgan
Ensign John Clemens
Sergt. Samuel Wilson
Sergt. Isaac Johnston
Corp. William Sullivan
Corp. John Thebus

Lieut. James Emerson
Sergt. Nathaniel Barber
Sergt. George Weider
Corp. James Dawson
Corp. Thomas Lasborough
Fifer, John Funk

Ensign James McLain
Sergt. John Barber
Sergt. Job Goslee
Corp. Jesse Martin
Corp. James Furnace
Drummer, Isaac Wheeler

Privates.
Armstrong, Jeremiah
Bell, Benjamin
Brown, William
Bilsley, William
Colegrove, William
Colwell, Thomas
Cochran, Benjamin
Daniels, Samuel
Elza, Nicholas
Ferguson, Eli
Greene, Bunn
Grins, James
Hatticks, Phillip
Hewitt, William
Hobbs, Richard
Kirkendall, Daniel
Justice, Jesse
Louderbach, John
Moore, William
Miller, John, Sr.
Morris, Richard
McCann, Daniel
McCoy, William
McAlister, John
Niece, Andrew
Runcle, George
Salada, David
Wheeler, Isaac

Privates.
Baccus, James
Baty, Alexander
Beyely, R.
Baker, Henry
Crull, John
Coon, Jacob
Dawson, John
Denny, John
Eakin, William
Ferguson, John
Grafton, Ambrose
Hall, John
Hively, Jacob
Howard, Martin
Hughs, James
Knight, William
Lutz, John D.
Louderbach, Peter
Melvin, Jonothan
Miller, John, Jr.
Murray, George
McCann, John
McCullough, John
McDonald, Thomas
Peters, Jacob
Retter, Frederick
Stuckman, Aaron
Watt, James

Privates.
Black, James
Bramble, James
Ballard, Fountain
Berer, Peter
Cutright, William
Cline, Jacob
Duncan, John
Dealle, Adam
Essex, Isaac
Fisher, Frederick
Gilliland, John
Hard, James
Harper, John
Hook, Jacob
Hughs, Nathan
Julin, John
Lawson, Enoch
Louderbach, Conrad
Mathews, James
Monroe, Aaron
Moore, Douglas
McCauly, John
McFarland, John
Niece, George
Richour, Frederick
Starkham, Aaron
Saliady, David
Wolford, Frederick

Pages 267-268.

ROLL OF CAPT. JOHN RUSSELL'S COMPANY (Probably from Ross County).

Served from July 28, until September 9, 1813.

Capt. John Russell
Sergt. William Hadley
Sergt. John McCall
Corp. Walter Meal
Fifer, John Brooks

Lieut. David McMullin
Sergt. Christian Yingling
Corp. John Salisbury
Corp. John Liston

Ensign William Carpenter
Sergt. David Jamison
Corp. Presley Gilliland
Drummer, John Smith

Privates.
Aldwick, Luke
Bell, Isaac
Cross, John
Clark, Cornelius
Conard, John
Fisher, John
Green, Clark
Jones, Isaac
Lewbarger, Peter
Moore, David
Nichlass, William
Russell, James
Spary, Francis
Tawey, George
West, William

Privates.
Abbot, Jeremiah
Bump, Ignatius
Cohall, Edward
Curry, William
Cattim, Samuel
Gilruth, James
Hepler, Jacob
Kimmel, Andrew
Lewis, William
Miller, Abraham
Powell, William
Slaughter, Ezekial
Shute, Richard
Vantine, Samuel

Privates.
Brown, Aaron
Broner, John
Curtis, William
Chemith, Richard
Didmerty, William
Grubb, William
Haley, Andrew
Link, Jacob
Lee, Daniel
Nottingham, Thomas
Reeves, Thomas
Stover, John
Suiter, Hiram
West, Samuel

Pages 269-270.   Vol. 2.

ROLL OF CAPT. JOHN ENTREKIN'S COMPANY (Probably from Ross Co.)

Served from July 28, until September 7, 1813.

Rank and Name of Soldier.	Rank and Name of Soldier.	Rank and Name of Soldier.
Capt. John Entrikin	Lieut. Levi Willoby	Lieut. Jacob Eckleberne
Ensign James McLean	Sergt. John Downs	Sergt. George Ramsey
Sergt. Jacob Cryder	Sergt. David Downs	Sergt. Edward Oldham
Corp. Finney Collumber	Corp. Peter Fortner	Corp. George Linkswiler
Corp. William Ramer	Corp. Samuel McRoberts	

Privates.

Andrew, Ager	Abonather, James	Boakley, Samuel
Barber, Edward	Baker, Peter	Cryder, David
Crooks, Alexander	Chad, George	Downs, James
Dunlap, William	Denson, Samuel	Evans, William
Echeiberger, Stephen	Edmonds, Edmond	Edmonds, Robert
Fulton, William	Gant, John	Gilmore, Robert
Hines, John	Hines, Jacob	Hines, Phillip
Hines, Adam	Hadix, Samuel	Hagley, Isaac
Huse, John	Huston, James	Hutts, Richard
Hyde, Nathan	Immel, Jacob	Immel, Israel
Justice, James	Johnston, Isaac	Little, James
Little, Hugh	Musselman, Benjamin	Mitchell, James
McFarland, Archibald	Overly, Jacob	Overly, David
Painter, John	Parks, Daniel	Rasey, George
Rudesell, Jonas	Severell, William	Sturgeon, Robert
Sidenbender, Henry	Senff, Michael	Spong, Henry
Stinson, Daniel	Summerset, John	Thompson, Wheeler
Tuttle, Isaiah	Walling, John	Wead, Thomas
Wheeland, George	Wheeland, Peter	Wolloughby, Job
Weider, Michael	Winters, John	Yeaky, John

Pages 271-272.

ROLL OF CAPT. JAMES WALLACE'S COMPANY (Probably from Ross Co.)

Served from July 28, until September 7, 1813.

Capt. James Wallace	Lieut. William J. Lee	Ensign, Geo. Stanhope
Sergt. Abraham Miller	Sergt. Edward Caling	Sergt. Andrew Thompson
Sergt. John Kelley	Corp. Frederick Winfaugh	Corp. Hollis Hanson
Corp. Charles Medeira	Corp. Samuel Hanson	Sergt. John Cutright.

Privates.

Argebute, Frederick	Aid, Jacob	Andrew, Thomas
Aters, Thomas	Bunn, Hannan	Baker, John
Bulgar, Elijah	Bour, Adam	Baker, John
Boblits, John	Boots, John	Conner, James, Jr.
Conner, Jesse	Conner, James, Sr.	Carpenter, Elisha
Clark, Thomas	Cox, Thomas	Cutright, Andrew
Cutright, Henry	Dixon, Caleb	Dolahan, Hugh
Dunn, Silas	Ferguson, Isaac	Eseny, Thomas
Evans, Robert	Gaits, John	Franklin, Samuel
Francis, Oliver	Gundey, John	Greene, Joseph
Gundey, Cornelius	Hanson, Benjamin	Gundey, Benjamin
Graves, Lewis	Hieson, Elijah	Hendricks, James
Hushaw, Benjamin	Jones, Henry	Hushaw, John
Irwin, James	Morrison, John	Jones, Zechariah
Kelley, Samuel	Mooney, George	Morrison, James
Morrison, James, Sr.	McClure, James	Meakre, Aaron
Morrison, John	Neff, Cornelius	Nichols, Samuel
Neff, George	Odle, William	Olcott, Josiah
Ortman, John	Rowles, James	Pierce, Burget
Pemberton, William	Russel John	Ray, James
Regan, Richard	Shrickengust, George	Rolbuck, Abner
Salts, Edward	Ulm, John	Smeed, Jesse
Tomlinson, William	Wilkinson, Robert	Wolf, William
Wallace, James	Wallace, Richard	Wilfong, Charles
Wilfong, Christopher		Woolsey, James
Yeakey, Peter		

Pages 273-274.

ROLL OF CAPT. CALEB ODLE'S COMPANY (Probably from Ross County).

Served from Oct. 26, until Nov. 12, 1813. Part of company served from July 28, until Aug. 18, 1813.

Capt. Caleb Odle	Lieut. Arthur McKee	Ensign, Benjamin Brown
Ensign, John Uln	Sergt. James Stephens	Sergt. Henry Wisber
Sergt. James Trego	Sergt. Richard Reagon	Sergt. Marmaduke Earlick
Sergt. Elijah Bulger	Sergt. Benjamin Drummond	Corp. James Alexander
Corp. Thomas Andrews	Corp. Henry Hoover	Corp. John Collumber

Privates.

Alexander, John	Alexander, Joseph	Borrer, Abraham
Borrer, Adam	Barker, Joseph	Bennet, Peter
Brown, William	Bowers, Daniel	Cox, Thomas
Connel, Hiram	Castner, John	Carpenter, Elisha
Downs, David	Denson, Samuel	Dye, Alexander

ROLL OF CAPT. CALEB ODLE'S COMPANY. (Continued)

Rank and Name of Soldier.

Privates.

Cullember, Phenhes
Davis, George
Franklin, John
Gates, John
Graves, William
Hopson, Charles
Harshall, Samuel
Jurdon, William
Lish, Henry
Mackelheny, Robert
McClintock, Adam
Neff, Cornelius
Pealman, Jacob
Ruddick, Jesse
Rains, Isaac
Shagley, Jacob
Smith, Christopher
Tanquary, William
Vangembey, John
Wold, William
Wilson, Benjamin
Webster, Thomas

Elm, Edward
Elsey, Nicholas
Francis, Jonothan
Gender, Samuel V.
Hotticks, Samuel
Hobough, Andrew
Huston, James
Johnston, Joseph
Jones, Henry
Miller, Jacob
McFarland, John
Morris, Benjamin
Roads, John
Read, Enoch
Roules, James
Sidenbender, Henry
Thompson, Wheeler
Tuttle, Isaiah
Welsh, Jacob
Weetard, Peter
Wilkins, Thomas
Yeakey, Peter

Ferguson, Eli
Foy, Jacob
Grove, John
Hines, Phillip
Hatton, James
Johnson, James
Jones, Zechariah
Mussleman, Benjamin
McClintock, John
Neff, George
Orr, Zebulon
Rains, John
Ross, William
Ratcliff, Jesse
Starr, John
Smith, David
Timons, Samuel
Uln, Daniel
Wolf, Isaac
Wilkisson, Solomon
Widner, James

Pages 275-276.

ROLL OF CAPT. SAMUEL JONES' COMPANY (Probably from Ross County).

Served from July 20, until September 7, 1813.

Capt. Samuel L. Jones
Sergt. Daniel Bonner
Sergt. Ebenezer F. Scaman
Sergt. James Johnson
Corp. Samuel McCormick
Corp. James Boyd

Lieut. Jacob Eikelbern
Sergt. Michael Ott
Sergt. Richard Armstrong
Corp. George Horn
Corp. Robert Long

Ensign, William Wallace
Sergt. Frederick Fisher
Sergt. John Mitchell
Corp. Daniel McColister
Corp. John H. Swain

Privates.

Arington, David
Bond, William K.
Cissna, Robert
Dowley, George
Footney, Peter
Flemming, W. W.
Gray, Francis
Hammut, John
Howard, Martin
Lunback, Henry
Looless, Benjamin
Miller, William
McKean, Hugh
Ott, Jacob
Smith, George H.
Scott, James A. P.
Thompson, William
Watson, David

Bell, George
Bowman, Robert
Copes, William
Evans, Job
Fultz, Conrad
Feoru, Jacob
Garret, Joseph
Hoover, Henry
Hunter, John
Lunback, William
Linninger, Fred
Moore, James
Nuner, William
Pickens, John
Shriver, Andrew
Stall, Frederick
Williams, William
Warden, John

Bowers, Price
Bateman, Clement
Douglas, John
England, Joseph
Fimmore, John
Gilmore, William
Higgins, A. N.
Hall, John
Hidrick, Nicholas
Layman, Barnet
Miller, Joseph
McElheny, Robert
Ott, Adam
Pollard, William
Shaver, James
Snyder, Richard
Ward, Elever

Page 277.

ROLL OF CAPT. ANDREW CORRELL'S COMPANY (Probably from Ross Co.)

Served from July 28, until August 20, 1813.

Capt. Andrew Correll
Sergt. Frank Winsough
Corp. George Shagley

Ensign, Benjamin Brown
Sergt. Richard Rogan

Sergt. Thomas McNeal
Corp. James Doren

Privates.

Andrew, Thomas
Baker, Christopher
Cardre, Jacob
Franklin, James
Franklin, Samuel
Hanson, John
Harrison, John
Meakre, Wheeler
Mooney, George
Miller, Alexander
Robinson, William
Tonlinson, William
Vanskoy, Timothy
Wolf, William

Aid, Jacob
Boren, Abraham
Clark, Thomas
Franklin, John
Green, Joseph
Heath, John
Longshore, Mahlon
Miller, Robert
Meakre, Aaron
Odle, Lott
Redfern, John
Tweet, Jesse
Wolf, Samuel
Wood, Joah

Bour, Adam
Boren, Peter
Duncan, Zechariah
France, Oliver
Hickson, Elijah
Harris, Daniel
Lewis, Thomas
Mooney, John
Madary, Charles
Rease, Thomas
Smith, John
Vanskoy, Jonothan
Wolf, Isaac

ROLL OF CAPT. DANIEL McCREERY'S COMPANY (Probably from Ross Co.)

Served from July 29, until September 6, 1813.

Rank and Name of Soldier.
Capt. Daniel McCreery
Sergt. William Hulit
Sergt. Isaac Roads
Corp. Wells Jones

Privates.
Ault, Christian
Brown, Orlando
Bayles, William
Dutton, James
Housman, David
Lucas, Charles
Marshawn, Daniel
Niseley, Samuel
Polland, William
Rhodes, Phillip
Stultz, John
Shaw, Joseph
Swane, Samuel
Troth, Isaac

Rank and Name of Soldier.
Lieut. Isaac Hortman
Sergt. Adam Razier
Corp. John Darby
Corp. Peter Housman

Privates.
Ankerman, John
Baldwin, Daniel
Darby, Stephen
Hatter, Leonard
Jonsojin, Eli
Janiken, Drury
McVay, William
Niuemyor, Jacob
Rhodes, Jacob
Rhodes, John
Smith, Benjamin
Stephens, John
Shields, John
Williams, Thomas

Rank and Name of Soldier.
Ensign, Barton Lucas
Sergt. Thomas Davis
Corp. Christian Housman

Privates.
Bilzer, John
Beason, Jonothan
Darby, Samuel
Housman, George
Lamings, Samuel
Linten, William
McGraw, Hugh
Pudle, Gabriel
Reed, Leonard
Reed, George
Stultz, Peter
Shewmaker, Daniel
Trivet, Joseph
Washburn, James

ROLL OF CAPT. MARTIN ARMSTRONG'S COMPANY (Probably from Ross Co.)

Served from July 28, until August 18, 1813.

Capt. Martin Armstrong
Sergt. Hartley Malone
Corp. William Odle
Corp. Phillip Waldrer

Privates.
Alexander, Joseph
Boots, Martin
Doll, Daniel
Gilmore, Andrew
Kelley, William
Howe, Jesse
Kelley, John, Sr.
Lockhart, Joseph
Malone, Richard
Pierce, Samuel
Reyphole, Anthony
Rhidenour, John
Sell, Adam
Seymour, Solomon

Lieut. James Bryan
Sergt. Edward Caling
Corp. Caleb Odle

Privates.
Bell, John
Boots, John
Doll, Abraham
Hanks, Joseph
Kelley, John, Jr.
Hanks, John
Linton, Lawson
Lockhart, James
McClintock, Joseph
Pierce, Bingett
Ross, John
Smith, James
Sigler, George
Williams, John

Ensign, Andrew McKee
Sergt. Robert Brown
Corp. George Boots

Privates.
Brown, Nimrod
Cogill, Alexander
Fryar, Benjamin
Hendricks, James
Kelley, James
Kelley, Andrew
Linton, Zechariah
Miller, Robert
McClintock, Alexander
Queen, John
Rhidenour, Jacob
Smith, Samuel
Salts, John

ROLL OF CAPT. ISAAC TAYLOR'S COMPANY (Probably from Ross Co.)

Served from July 29, until August 26, 1813.

Capt. Isaac Taylor
Sergt. David Rees

Privates.
Ams, Samuel D.
Beckwer, James
Beason, Benjamin
Cowger, George
Dunham, Samuel
Haller, Jacob
Janegan, Isaac
Kirkpatrick, John
Mannon, Isaac
Powermaster, Henry
Rockhold, John
Stroup, Michael
Tompson, Amos
Wisecoop, Jonas

Lieut John Palmer
Sergt. Edward Hughes

Privates.
Boyd, Jonothan
Burris, Brewster
Countryman, Henry
Coms, John
Davis, Elihu
Hatter, Peter
Kelse, Michael
Lucas, Hugh
Meir, Hugh
Reslinger, John
Rodgers, Aaron
Stewart, Isaac
Troth, Isaac
Wedmore, John
Yorger, Joseph

Ensign, Thomas Wilson
Sergt. Jacob Meyer

Privates.
Burris, Miles
Bates, Hezekiah
Coplinger, William
Cooper, John
Falk, John
Jessup, John
Kellough, George
Lucas, Joshua
Cricket, John
Roads, Jacob
Smith, Zechariah
Troth, William
White, William
Wilson, John

ROLL OF CAPT. EZEKIAL BUNN'S COMPANY (Probably from Ross Co.)

Served from————————.

Capt. Ezekial Bunn
Sergt. John Roberts

Privates.
Bitzer, Anthony
Dozzard, Stephen
James, Samuel
Ritter, Richard
James, Samuel

Lieut. George Frederick
Corp. John Kirk

Privates.
Bunn, James
Dehaven, Abraham
Mitchel, James
Snyder, John

Ensign, John Brown

Privates.
Crouch, James
Hayes, James
Mathias, John
Straw, Solomon

Pages 281-282. Vol. 2.

ROLL OF CAPT. JOHN SPENCER'S COMPANY (County Unknown).

Served from May 5, until May 20, 1813.

Rank and Name of Soldier.
Capt. John Spencer
Ensign, John I. Tullass
Sergt. Thomas Cannon
Corp. John Chonner

Privates.
Abraham, John
Baker, Daniel
Boucher, John
Cunningham, John
Coulter, James
Denman, Hathaway
Gavit, Asa B.
Gilmore, John
Helphrey, John
Hughes, Elias
Insco, John
Kissinger, George
Moody, John
Powell, Samuel
Pence, Isaac
Robinson, Martin
Shedmick, James
Sutton, Jehiel
Vance, Joseph
Wilson, Archibald

Rank and Name of Soldier.
Lieut. James Gibson
Sergt. Morris A. Newman
Sergt. Timothy Spellman
Corp. George McMilles

Privates.
Arnold, Anthony
Brown, Aaron
Coffey, Amos
Cunningham, William
Doughman, James
Davis, Christopher
Green, Michael
Henderson, Titan
Hunter, Robert
Johnston, John, Sr.
Insco, Moses
Kite, Adam
Mathews, Benjamin
Parks, George
Rowe, William
Ridgley, Basil
Scott, Robert
Thrall, James
Ward, James
Ward, Jonas

Rank and Name of Soldier.
Lieut. Elias Hughes
Sergt. James Seymore
Corp. William Blackburn
Corp. Joseph Statelar

Privates.
Baker, Ephraim
Beard, Andrew
Curtis, Hairsmore
Channel, John
Dewees, Jethro
Fulton, Thomas
Gavit, Benjamin
Hoover, Samuel
Hook, John
Johnston, John Jr.
Kirkpatrick, Nathan
Klever, Mathew
McKinley, John
Pegg, Benjamin C.
Robinson, James
Rodgers, Elijah
Stanberry, Job
Vance, Christian
Wheeler, Thomas

Pages 283-284.

ROLL OF CAPT. ISAAC BUTLER'S COMPANY (County Unknown).

Served from August 9, until October 9, 1812.

Capt. Isaac Butler
Sergt. Caleb McDaniel
Sergt. Jehiel McDaniel
Corp. Leonard Hendrick
Drummer, Benjamin Mills

Privates.
Allison, Jesse
Berthe, Lewis
Callison, John
Childers, John
Ellison, Samuel
Frasy, Andrew
Hoislit, John
Knox, Nehemiah
Long, Benjamin
McDaniel, James
Poor, Marton
Rickabaugh, John
Barger, John Moss
Russell, Reuben
Umphreys, Robert
Whitten, Louis
Yates, Samuel

Lieut. John Raydor
Sergt. James Jardin
Corp. William Peth John
Corp. Adam Padse

Privates.
Burel, Francis
Crow, Abraham
Crow, William
Dickeson, John
Ellison, John
Haney, George
Jones, William
Long, Elisha
Lemons, Jacob
McLoud, Collin
Pettijohn, John
Rice, James
Ross, William
Sturgeon, Robert
Waugh, Francis
Ward, Charles

Ensign, Nathan Burrow
Sergt. John K. Holmes
Corp. William Smith
Fifer, Francis Buell

Privates.
Blaze, Peter
Callison, Robert
Corden, Burgess
Brennen, Charles
Farmer, Thomas
Harris, William
Kizer, Henry
Little, George
Miller, Brison
Poor, Alexander
Prose, Daniel
Rickabaugh, Adam
Rickabaugh, John
Scott, Andrew
Waugh, Solomon
Williams, John

Page 285.

ROLL OF CAPT. EBENEZER BENEDICT'S COMPANY (County Unknown.)

Served from August 24, until September 20, 1812.

Capt. Ebenezer Benedict
Sergt. Jesse Alderman
Sergt. Nathaniel Cook
Corp. Linus Tracey
Drummer, Zerah Cook

Privates.
Adgate, John
Boyer, John
Cloe, Samuel
Guild, Jarius
Kline, Philip
Maxwell, Robert
Smith, Daniel
Taylor, Simon
Winter, Alpheus

Lieut. Benjamin White
Sergt. Oliver R. Guild
Corp. Urial Loomis
Corp. Whitney Smith

Privates.
Benedict, Billy
Cook, Christopher
Clark, James H.
Harsh, Jacob
Lyons, John
North, Samuel
Scofield, Edward
Toft, Aaron

Ensign, Sheldon Osborn
Sergt. Caleb Holcomb, Jr.
Corp. Isaac Huff
Fifer, Elijah Daniels

Privates.
Bell, David
Clark, Isaac
Fish, Abner
Johnson, Anson
Mansfield, Mancen
Penny, Levi
Stow, Harvey
Bartholomew, Charley

Page 286. Vol. 2.
ROLL OF CAPT. JOHN CLARK'S COMPANY (Probably from Ross County).
Served from July 28, until August 13, 1813.

Rank and Name of Soldier.
Capt. John Clark
Sergt. John Hill
Sergt. Isachai Pepper
Corp. David Dormin

Privates.
Breddy, James
Coxwell, Leven
Dennis, Putnell
Hamilton, William
Jones, Samuel
Listersen, William
Mickens, John
Simms, Jesse
Timmons, Perry

Rank and Name of Soldier.
Lieut. Armel Holloway
Sergt. Leonard Timons
Corp. Samuel Clark
Corp. Asther Lewis

Privates.
Brown, Zechariah
Collins, Joseph
Dennis, Jonothan
Hardy, David
King, James
Lewis, Jesse
Parker, Charles
Smith, Thomas
Williams, Gamage

Rank and Name of Soldier.
Ensign, Robert Brady
Sergt. Stephen Clark
Corp. Robert Bennis

Privates.
Brady, Benjamin
Dennis, Mathias
Godden, Levi
Hart, Brinkley
Lackey, John
Larrence, Elisha
Ridley, James
Timmons, John W.

Page 290.
ROLL OF CAPT. CLEMENT BROWN'S COMPANY (From Ross County).
Served from July 28, until August 20, 1813.

Capt. Clement Brown
Sergt. Thomas Watson
Sergt. James Timplin
Corp. Nicholas Divault

Privates.
Anderson, William
Brittenham, Aaron
Boyd, Robert
Cochran, James
Hoddy, Robert
Porter, William
Timplin, John

Lieut. Lemuel Dareuth
Sergt. John Brown
Corp. Charles Rollins
Corp. George Hudson

Privates.
Arnold, Samuel
Brittenham, Mathias
Betts, Thomas
Goldsberry, Thomas
Hewitt, William
Timmons, Amarias
Wroten, Henry

Ensign, Arthur McArthur
Sergt. Isaac Timplin
Corp. George Severs
Musician, Noah Downs

Privates.
Betts, John
Brown, Phillip
Clarkson, Major
Hardey, Thomas
McAfferty, John
Timmons, George
Watson, Alexander

Page 287.
ROLL OF CAPT. WILLIAM STOCKTON'S COMPANY (Probably from Ross Co.)
Served from July 28, until August 20, 1813.

Capt. William Stockton
Sergt. John Armstrong
Sergt. Stanley Cook
Corp. John Williams

Privates.
Bradley, Arthur
Baden, Rosel
Cook, James
Dimes, James
Fisher, John
Logue, John
Minear, Phillip
McCollister, Thomas
McAllister, Robert
Richardson, Peter
Robinson, Henry
Shoemaker, Peter

Lieut. Mathias Littleton
Sergt. John Kirkbridge
Corp. William Miskimins
Fifer, Joseph Cox

Privates.
Blissard, John
Cox, John
Carroll, Samuel
Dunlap, James
Hennis, William
Mace, John
Minear, Stephen
McCoy, Dixon
Ogden, John
Rodgers, John
Stockton, William
Thorn, Jacob

Ensign, William Littleton
Sergt. Clement Carroll
Corp. James McCalister
Drummer, James Baltimore

Privates.
Brown, James
Corbet, David
Calhoun, John
Earl, James
Junk, John
Mathias, Samuel
Mitchel, John
McCoy, Alexander
Phelps, William
Richards, William
Short, George
Walker, Charles

Page 288.
ROLL OF LIEUT. ROBERT HARVEY'S COMPANY (Probably from Ross Co.)
Served from July 13, until August 17, 1813.

Lieut. Robert Harvey
Sergt. Richard Berry
Corp. William Dixson

Privates.
Adams, Thomas
Cummings, Joseph
Chappell, George
Furrow, Adam
Gibson, Jacob
Holloway, Thomas
Maughmen, Jacob
Ramsey, Joseph
Strotherd Sephnius
Tootle, Egleston

Ensign, William Holloway
Sergt. James Kirkpatrick
Corp. Alexander Bowman

Privates.
Adams, John
Clifton, John
Crispin, Francis
Furrow, Solomon
Hood, Edward
Jones, Amos
Miller, John
Romine, Amos
Thompson, William
Walker, John

Sergt. Tighlman Willis
Sergt. Lewis Roughton
Corp. Edward Graham

Privates.
Brown, Edward
Corbet, Joseph
Dulgain, William
Green, Moses
Holloway, Isaiah
Long, George
Ramsey, David
Smith, White
Tootle, Thomas

Page 289. Vol. 2.

ROLL OF CAPT. JOHN JACKSON'S COMPANY (From Ross County).

Served from July 28, until August 15, 1813.

Rank and Name of Soldier.	Rank and Name of Soldier.	Rank and Name of Soldier.
Capt. John Jackson	Lieut. Jonothan Crabill	Ensign, Andrew White
Sergt. David T. Hull	Sergt. William Peters	Sergt. Willis Grant
Corp. William Graham	Corp. Joseph James	Drummer, Daniel Jones
Privates.	**Privates.**	**Privates.**
Arnesworth, Abraham	Ater, Abraham	Ater, Thomas
Brown, Joseph	Brown, Thomas	Briggs, Walter
Bowdle, Joseph	Baker, Josiah	Champ, John
Dolbee, Peter	Fisher, William	Flemming, Isaac
Gillaspie, Zach,	Gillaspie, Alexander	King, George
Kindall, Abraham	Keikenedall, Isaac	Mercer, Robert
Mizzick, Nathan	Martin, Benjamin	Nolin, Edward
Ross, Levin	Shanton, Abraham	Shanton, Charles
Tanganary, Abe	Wyer, Obed	Zoops, Adam

Pages 291-292.

ROLL OF CAPT. ALEXANDER ROBINSON'S COMPANY (From Ross County).

Served from July 28, until August 16, 1813.

Capt. Alexander Robinson	Lieut. Enos Pursel	Ensign, Jesse Wiley
Sergt. Thomas Sheilds	Sergt. James B. Johnston	Sergt. Christian Hill
Sergt. James Porter	Corp. Robert Lindsay	Corp. James Ross
Corp. Ephraim Worthington	Corp. Jacob Gooley	
Privates.	**Privates.**	**Privates.**
Brownfield, Robert	Blue, Daniel	Breedlove, David
Clark, Joseph	Davis, James	Dysert, John
Gadberry, James A.	Howard, Nicholas	Haynes, Henry, Sr.
Haynes, Henry, Jr.	Hubbert, Thornton	Hosselton, John
Logue, Samuel	Montgomery, James	McArthur Duncan
McDill, Robert	Nye, Jared	Norris, William
Porter, Peter	Pleasant, Enos	Summerset, Henry
Shepard, Philip	Worthington, John	Wiley, William

Following men were from Pickaway county:
Served from August 30, until October 9, 1812.

Lieut. Asa L. Heath	Ensign, Thomas Hunt	Sergt. Henry Cook
Sergt. Henry Smith	Sergt. Thomas Holloway	Sergt. William Good
Corp. Philip Shentaffer	Corp. Charles Hunt	Corp. Thomas Bootle
Corp. Samuel Atcheson	Corp. Samuel Ater	
Privates.	**Privates.**	**Privates.**
Brown, Edward	Crabb, Thomas	Clark, James
Cooper, Joel	Corkwell, Henry	Clarkson, Major
Dayton, Spencer	Heater, David	Holloway, Abisha
Herstater, Henry	Hust, James	High, Jonothan
Hager, William	King, Isaac	King, James
Kiddy, William	Loury, John	Lynch, Balitha
Lister, William	Laury, John	Linart, Thomas
Manly, Samuel	McArthur, Samuel	McAfferty, William
Norris, Otho	Phebus, Henry	Phebus, George
Renick, Asahel	Renick, Abel	Rickey, Thomas
Radcliffe, Isaac	Freyhart, Henry	Russell, Perry
Salters, John	Toots, Adam	Tumman, William
Ward, Abraham	Young, Hugh	Zeister, Peter

Page 293.

ROLL OF CAPT. GEORGE WOLF'S COMPANY (From Pickaway County).

Served from July 28, until August 26, 1813.

Capt. George Wolf	Lieut. George Steely	Ensign, Jesse Cook
Sergt. Johns Scott	Sergt. Johns Baum	Sergt. Wesley Rush
Sergt. William Cook	Corp. Moses Rush	Corp. Joseph Cravistone
Corp. David Vale	Corp. Josiah Rush	
Privates.	**Privates.**	**Privates.**
Brougher, Conrad	Burnes, Joseph	Baum, Peter
Creigh, Samuel	Chedd, Daniel	Denny, William
Earnest, Michael	Fressman, Hugh	Graham, Robert
Gordon, Alexander	Headley, George	Hiser, William
Julian, John	Lutz, John D.	Lutz, Samuel
Leonard, Abraham	Michael, John	Morehous, Augustine
May, John	Meyguit, John	McClintock, Jeheil
McClintock, William	Nebb, Christian	Neace, George
Rush, Peter	Ross, Jacob B.	Scott, Moses
Shoemake, John	Shoemaker, Jacob	Sharp, George
Torbet, James	Vance, Elisha	Wolf, John

ROSTER OF OHIO SOLDIERS IN WAR OF 1812

Page. 294.   Vol. 2.
ROLL OF CAPT. JACOB RITCHHART'S COMPANY (From Ross County).
Served from July 28, until August 18, 1813.

Capt. Jacob Ritchhart
Sergt. Elisha Emons
Sergt. William Taylor
Corp. Thomas Noland

Lieut. James Hall
Sergt. Henry Wishart
Corp. George Holloway
Corp. David Lilley

Ensign, Andrew Nichols
Sergt. George Clevinger
Corp. William Jewett
Drummer, John Huffman

Privates.
Armon, George
Crossley, John
Ferguson, David
Henderson, Nathaniel
Morris, Samuel
Ritchhart Henry
Shouts, Jacob
Thompson, Oswell

Privates.
Bevers, Michael
Davenport, Abraham
Fulton, Alexander
Loyear, Jacob
Morlana, William
Smith, Aaron
Shirley, Nathan
Thompson, Ignatius

Privates.
Cooper, Joel
Fulton, William
Glascock, Stephen
Lendsey, Abraham
Ritchhart, Abraham
Simpson, John
Thompson, William
Vistel, John

Pages 295-296.
ROLL OF CAPT. ALEXANDER MENARY'S COMPANY (From Ross County).
Served from August 30, until October 12, 1812. Part of Company served from July 28, until September 5, 1813.

Capt. Alexander Menary
Sergt. Ebenezer Petty
Lieut. Enos Pursel

Lieut. Samuel Jenkins,
Sergt. William Wilcox

Ensign, Reuben Pursel
Lieut. William Cochran

Privates.
Acton, William
Bradley, Richard
Earls, Mathew
Johnston, Bazil
Lawyer, Jacob
McElvey, John
Pool, Thomas
Row, James M.
Welch, Joseph

Privates.
Acton, Richard
Brown, Thomas
Funston, Thomas
Jenkins, Alexander
McQuea, Daniel
McDonald, David
Robinson, John
Strain, John M.
Yates, Morris

Privates.
Ashley, Daniel
Coon, Samuel
Goodwin, Levi
Junk, John
McClintock, Alexander
Noble, Thomas
Robinson, Samuel
Severs, George

Following men under Col John McDonald:

Brown, Joseph, Sr.
Baker, Josiah
Dolly, Peter
Fuller, William
Ferguson, David
Hull, David D.
Swanny, John
Simpson, John
Tompson, Abraham

Brown, Joseph, Jr.
Crossley, John
Earls, Mathew, Jr.
Flemin, Isaac
Hill, Christian
Lawyer, Jacob, Jr.
Sherley, Nathan
Smith, Aaron
Tangnary, Abraham

Beavers, Michael
Champ, John
Finnemore, William
Gilaspie, Alexander
Hutson, David
Pursel, Zodock
Shouts, Jacob
Shrokley, Archibald
Teral, John

Page 297.
ROLL OF CAPT. GEORGE YOCUM'S COMPANY (County Unknown).
Served from August 30, until October 9, 1812.

Capt. George Yocum
Sergt. Robert Harley
Sergt. Cornelius Michael
Corp. John Lewis

Lieut. John McArthur
Sergt. Mires
Corp. Francis Tully
Corp. John Ofnear

Ensign, William Arboe
Sergt. James G. Gray
Corp. Jonothan Jones

Privates.
Bishop, Robert
Baigle, Henry
Clover, Solomon
Darlin, Robert
Day, Addison
Harrington, James
Ladd, Ellison
Lloyd, Shadrach
Mustard, George
McElroy, Daniel
O'Brien, Charles
Steen, Moses
Toots, Daniel
Wilson, Thomas
Watts, James

Privates.
Baker, John
Crumhien, James
Campbell, David
Durmp, James
Finley, Joseph
Jefferson, Thomas
Lowman, Joseph
Mayhan, William
Moore, Elisha
McNeal, Archibald
Saddler, William
St. Clair, John
Terret, Daniel
William, Providence
Watts, Leven

Privates.
Baker, James
Clover, Jacob
Copsey, Hezekiah
Devoss, Joseph
Flemming, Robert
Johnston, William
Lank, Elisha
Mark, Michael
McIntire, Samuel
Nowland, John
Slaughter, John
Thirman, Robert
Verdin, Isaac
Wiley, William

Page 298.
ROLL OF CAPT. JOB. RADCLIFF'S COMPANY (County Unknown).
Served from July 26, until August 26, 1813.

Capt. Job Radcliff
Sergt. John Shepard
Sergt. Benjamin Radcliff

Lieut. Jacob Foster
Sergt. Richard Seamore

Ensign, Aaron Seamore
Sergt. John Polsten

Privates.
Argo, John
Coon, George
Jones, James
Morris, Joseph
Messer, Isaac
Pierce, James, Sr.
Rawlings, Nathan
West, Frederick

Privates.
Beckett, Benjamin
Dawitt, Barnett
Johnston, James
Morris, Thomas
McMins, Robert
Polstin, Cornelius
Tipton, Thomas
Williams, Henry, Jr.

Privates.
Clark, Daniel
Galbrith, John
Laverty, James
Miller, James
O'Niel, Johnston
Rawlings, Moses
Vannieter, Abraham

ROLL OF CAPT. JOHN WILSON'S COMPANY (County Unknown).

Served from May 8, until May 29, 1813, and from July 26, until August 26, 1813.

Rank and Name of Soldier.
Capt. John Wilson
Sergt. David Groves
Cor. John Phebus
Corp. Joseph Downing
Musician, Alexander Ross

Privates.
Adder, John
Blair, Michael
Clemons, John
Carpenter, Ira
Cartwal, Samuel
Craft, James
Casto, Abel
Dawson, James
Dawson, Isaac
Graham, James
Hanis, David
Hand, George
Harris, Jonothan
Jimmison, William
Kerr, Samuel
Lafford, Joseph
Morris, Samuel
Martin, John
Oxford, Abel
Pancake, Joseph
Roseberry, John
Saward, Robert
Stewart, Robert
Thompson, John
Vance, Daniel

Rank and Name of Soldier.
Ensign, Elias Brock
Sergt. Michael Bash
Corp. Solomon Crose
Corp. John Scott
Musician, Isaac Hutchison

Privates.
Anderson, Joel
Buck, James
Cherry, Moses
Cubberly, Job
Cubberly, William
Cochern, Cornelius
Carder, George
Dickison, Charles
Downing, Robert
Gregg, William
Hubbard, Titus
Harriman, Charles
Harris, John
Kingsey, Stephen
Kingsey, Michael
Legg, Elijah
Mann, William
Potter, John
Patton, John
Shields, John
Stone, Marshall
Scott, Robert
Troxell, Isaac
Warner, Robert
Wright, James
Warner, John

Rank and Name of Soldier.
Sergt. William Gibson
Sergt. Levi Cantrell
Corp. John C. Davis
Corp. Henry Warner

Privates.
Alkue, Samuel
Brock, William
Cartright, Samuel
Crath, James
Cochran, Thomas
Crawford, George
Downing, Francis
Dennison, James
Foster, Joshua
Gates, Nehemiah
Hobough, Samuel
Hosey, Anderson
Johnston, Abraham
King, John
Knox, Ralph
Moore, Nicholas
Montgomery, Hugh
Powers, Joseph
Rowan, William
Spencer, Thomas
Springer, Thomas
Stockton, David
Watson, Abraham
Watson, David
Wright, Ira

ROLL OF CAPT. ROBERT BRADSHAW'S COMPANY (From Ross County).

Served from July 26, until August 26, 1813.

Capt. Robert Bradshaw
Sergt. John Mitts
Sergt. Sam. R. Davidson
Corp. Adam Metts

Privates.
Abbott, Thomas
Burbridge, James
Baker, Joseph
Caide, Abraham
Dart, David
Gowinge, Joseph
Hayes, Maurice H.
Hornback, Isaac
Lewis, Solomon
Powell, Abel
Reeves, Samuel
Timmons, John
Webb, Robert

Lieut. William Burbridge
Sergt. George Phebus
Corp. John M. Alkire
Corp. Platt, Hull

Privates.
Burbridge, Benjamin
Boggs, Caleb
Beer, William
Crable, John
Dixon, William
Hayes, Jesse
Hayes, Charles
Knoles, Ephraim
Maddox, Lazarus
Phebis, Samuel
Scott, William
Timmons, Peter
Wilson, James
Yates, David

Ensign, Cimon Hornbeck
Sergt. John Phebus
Corp. John Young

Privates.
Baker, Martin
Baker, William
Blue, John
Colstin, Henry
Freeman, Benjamin
Harrison, George
Hayes, Samuel
Knowls, William
McAlister, John
Reeves, Owen T.
Treheran, George
Watson, Levin
Woodsworth, Ezra

ROLL OF LIEUT. CHARLES GILBERT'S COMPANY
(Probably from Portage County).

Served from August 21, until September 4, 1812.

Lieut. Charles Gilbert
Sergt. Truman Gilbert

Privates.
Amasa, Preston
Fisher, John
Hazzard, James
Loury, Chauncey
Smith, Roswell
Tuttle, James

Sergt. Hugh McDaniel
Corp. Gains Smith

Privates.
Boswick, Abnah
Gilbert, Marvin
Jewell, William
Lewis, Joseph
Shank, Nicholas
Trowbridge, Dayton

Sergt. Lyman T. Gilbert
Corp. Zebulon Walker

Privates.
Baldwin, John F.,
Gano, David
Kane, Gabriel
McKelvey, John
Shaw, John

ROLL OF CAPT. ASA BERRAUGH'S COMPANY
(Probably from Portage County).

Served from August 28 until September 24, 1812.

Capt. Asa K. Berraugh
Sergt. Samuel Menson

Privates.
Baker, Joel
Hine, Abel

Lieut. Hezekiah Hime
Drummer, Horace Berraugh

Privates.
Brown, Ephraim
Hine, Lyman

Ensign, Richard E. Gay
Fifer, Greawhood Berraugh

Privates.
Bradley, Benjamin

ROLL OF CAPT. GEORGE SKIDMORE'S CO. (From Franklin County).

Served from August 26, until October 10, 1812.

Rank and Name of Soldier.
Capt. George Skidmore
Sergt. Robert Riley
Sergt. Joseph Skidmore
Corp. John Skinner
Drummer, Ashbaugh

Privates.
Brickle, John
Droddy, John
Fuller, William
Harrington, Daniel
Hearsoff, John
Jones, John
Marsh, Thomas
Morehead, Thomas
Rodgers, John
Step, John
Thomas, Wesley
Winset, Joseph

Rank and Name of Soldier.
Lieut. John Skidmore
Sergt. Thomas Jones
Corp. William Stiarwolt
Corp. Charles Sells

Privates.
Beer, Conrad
Droddy, Aaron
Ford, Frederick
Hamilton, John
Justice, David
Keasnor, Michael
Manning, Elisha
Postler, Job
Shipman, Samuel
Sells, William
Thomas, James
Williams, Lewis

Rank and Name of Soldier.
Ensign, William Marshall
Sergt. John Hickman
Corp. Chester P. Cole
Fifer, Frederick Stirwolt

Privates.
Cooper, Alexander
Flemmin, William
Hickman, Townsend
Hess, Bolser
Johnston, John
Kinser, Adam
Manning, William
Postler, Solomon
Skinner, James
Thomas, Elijah
Vana, Alexander
Waite, George

ROLL OF CAPT. GEORGE WILLIAM'S COMPANY
(Probably from Franklin Co.)

Served from August 26, until October 10, 1812.

Capt. George Williams
Sergt. William Duff
Sergt. Mathew Brown
Corp. John Hoover
Drummer, William McKibben

Privates.
Bennet, Joseph
Clark, Richard
DeWitt, Martin
Hoover, Abraham
Kelsel, Nicholas
Martin, John
McLaughlin, Hiram
Potston, Cornelius
Seymour, Richard
Weatherington, John

Lieut. Jacob Foster
Sergt. John Goldsmith
Corp. William White
Corp. John Stephenson

Privates.
Balenger, Joseph
Carter, Joseph
England, Jacob
Johnston, James
Knis, John
Messer, Isaac
O'Neil, Johnston
Radcliffe, Job
Seeds, John
Williams, John

Ensign, Robert Breckenridge
Sergt. John Carnohan
Corp. Charles O'Neil
Fifer, Thomas Shreves

Privates.
Chinowith, Thomas
Clark, Daniel
Hoffman, Henry
Jones, James
Morris, Joseph
Mathews, Hiram
Parish, Reuben
Romine, Elias
Tanner, Peter

ROLL OF CAPT. TIMOTHY CULVER'S COMPANY
(Probably from Portage Co.)

Served from August 24, until September 4, 1812.

Capt. Timothy Culver
Sergt. William Rogers
Corp. Abel Sabine

Privates.
Cross, Theophilus
Mosher, Henry P.
Sears, Nathan, Jr.
Upson, Freeman

Lieut. Isaac Merriman
Corp. Ephraim Sabin
Drummer, Daniel Ward

Privates.
Goss, John
Savage, Jehiel
Sears, Elias
Ward, Joshua

Sergt. Walter Dickinson
Corp. Oliver C. Dickenson

Privates.
Harris, Joseph
Sears, Elisha
Upson, Arad

ROLL OF CAPT. JOSHUA WOODWARD'S COMPANY
(Probably from Portage County).

Served from August 24, until September 4, 1812.

Capt. Joshua Woodward
Sergt. Almon Babcock

Privates.
Alancon, Baldwin
Crosby, David
King, John
Noble, Quarter
Smith, John B.

Lieut. Linus Curtis
Sergt. Elijah Smith

Privates.
Barnes, George
Cook, James
Knowlton, James
Miller, Jesse
Thompson, Abel

Ensign Anson Beeman

Privates.
Broadway, Ebenezer
Forsburg, Abel
Loomis, Babzemon
Owen, Silas N.
Walfort, Peter

Page 306. Vol. 2.

ROLL OF CAPT. IRA MORSE'S COMPANY (Probably from Portage County.)
Served from August 24, until September 4, 1812.

Rank and Name of Soldier.
Lieut. Ira Morse
Sergt. Jeremiah Jones

Privates.
Baldwin, Moses
Baldwin, Ami
Day, Oratio
Hubbard, Ephraim B.
Hartsell, Abraham
Mott, Ezekial
Quier, John
Taylor, Robert

Rank and Name of Soldier.
Sergt. Hamlet Coe
Corp. Caleb Mattoon

Privates.
Bucksley, Asabel
Carter, James
Granger, Ralph
Hartsell, John
Laughlin, James
Mason, Peter
Strong, William A.
Whittlessey, John H.

Rank and Name of Soldier.
Sergt. Alexander K. Hubbard

Privates.
Baldwin, Allen E.
Chittendon, Almon
Hartzell, William
Hartsell, Peter
Mott, Elijah
Morse, Amos
Sutliff, Jesse

Page 307.

ROLL OF CAPT. FREDERICK CARIS' COMPANY.
(Probably from Portage County.)
Served from August 22, until September 4, 1812.

Capt. Frederick Caris
Sergt. Samuel Coe
Corp. Ariel Case
Fifer, Ashur Guerley

Privates.
Bostwick, Charles H.
Chapman, Chester
Chapman, Beman
McKnight, Robert
Richardson, Mason

Sergt. David Collins
Sergt. Graham Norris
Corp. Lemuel Chapman, Jr.

Privates.
Bostwick, Joseph R.
Elsworth, Colvin
Collins, Daniel L.
Reed, Abraham
Willyard, John

Sergt. Titus Belding
Corp. Samuel B. Spellman
Drummer, Alpheus Andrews

Privates.
Chapman, Ephraim
Heroff, John
Newberry, William
Reed, Timothy

Page 308.

ROLL OF CAPT. HEZEKIAH NOONEY'S COMPANY.
(Probably from Portage County.)
Served from August 24, until September 4, 1812.

Capt. Hezekiah Nooney
Sergt. Seth Harmon
Sergt. Ariel Walden
Corp. Moses McIntosh
Fifer, Joseph Skinner

Privates.
Atwater, Jonothan
Gardner, John
Ladd, Ezekial
Pond, Moses
Russell, William

Lieut. Oliver Snow
Sergt. Gershom Judson
Corp. Henry Blair
Corp. Basil Windsor

Privates.
Bright, Thomas
Judson, Samuel
Leeland, Lyman
Pond, David
Snow, Franklin

Ensign Ella Wilmot
Sergt. Horace Ladd
Corp. Phinas Pond
Drummer Virgil Moore

Privates.
Carlton, Peter
Ladd, Eleazar
Moore, Samuel, Jr.
Ray, Patrick
Terris, Henry B.

Pages 309-371-310.

ROLL OF CAPT. DELANNE MILLS' COMPANY (Probably from Portage Co.)
Served from September 28, until October 12, 1812. From March 7, until September 6, 1814.
From August 24, until September 4, 1812. From February 24, until March 14, 1815.

Capt. Delanne Mills
Lieut. John Redden
Ensign John Brooks
Sergt. Chester Adams
Sergt. George Young
Sergt. John Randall
Sergt. George G. Redden
Corp. David A. Ramsey
Corp. Elisha Hutchinson
Corp. John Spooner
Drummer, Warren Squires

Privates.
Alfred, Oliver
Achison, Benjamin
Blair, Asahel
Bell, John
Castor, John
Dyton, Abraham
Devens, James
Evans, George
Fish, Moses
Gershon, Judson
Higley, Hezekiah
Huston, David
Hill, Jacob
Johnson, Thomas
Lindsey, Richard
Mott, Elijah
McCloud, Francis
Olds, Kingsley
Parker, Elihu
Shaylor, John
Seley, Ephraim H.
Taylor, Oratio
Turner, Samuel
Ward, Daniel
Warner, Chauncey

Lieut. John Caris
Lieut. Thomas Robison
Sergt. Titus Belding
Sergt. Samuel Coe
Sergt. Benjamin Higley
Sergt. John Smith
Sergt. Daniel Sawtell
Corp. Caleb Stow
Corp. Hiram Messenger
Fifer, Freeman Conet

Privates.
Alfred, Levi
Bostwick, Joseph R.
Babcock, Simon
Bell, Samuel
Cole, Lemuel
Donaldson, James
Dixon, James
Ferris, Henry R.
Finlay, John
Gate, Mathew
Hacket, Ephraim
Haley, Ezra
Hanks, John
Jackson, Edward
Mackey, John
Morkier, Thomas
McKinney, James
Pitkin, Orin
Redden, John
Skinner, Joseph
Stratton, John
Thorp, Baralleel
Willyard, John
Wilcox, David
Wilmott, Elisha

Lieut. David Barret
Ensign Asa Trusedale
Sergt. Gershon Norris
Sergt. Oliver Mills
Sergt. John Streator
Sergt. John M. Baldwin
Sergt. Griswold Gillet
Corp. Moses McIntosh
Corp. Lorenzo Holly
Fifer, Oliver Wheeler

Privates.
Artemar, Baker
Bancroft, Randolphus
Bundy, Caleb L.
Cahoon, Joel B.
Carpenter, Lewis
Duck, Samuel
Dundey, John
Fanch, Joseph
Guvoner, John
Granger, Benjamin
Hitchcock, David
Hill, John
Hendrickson, George
Kempton, William
Manly, Martin
Macombo, John
Noble, Quarter
Perry, Hesea
Reed, Jeremiah
Southworth, Joseph
Stanley, Marshall
Terrel, Elijah L.
Windsor, Basil, Jr.
Ward, Elisha

Page 311. Vol. 2.

ROLL OF CAPT. JOSEPH VANCE'S COMPANY (County Unknown).

Served from August 19, until August 29, 1812.

Rank and Name of Soldier.
Capt. Joseph Vance
Sergt. Charles Harrison
Sergt. David Henry
Corp. Frederick Ambrose
Privates.
Custer, Abraham
Clifton, Moses
Egnon, Jesse
McGrew, William
Petty, Solomon
Rigdon, Lewis
Stephens, William
Thomas, Joel
Vance, William

Rank and Name of Soldier.
Lieut. William Ward
Sergt. Zebulon G. Cantrell
Corp. John Taylor
Corp. John Dawson
Privates.
Custer, Isaac
Dowden, Archibald
Gillaspie, Mathew M.
McGrew, Archibald
Richards, Andrew
Rigdon, John
Taber, Bennet, Jr.
Thomas, Ward
Wiley, John

Rank and Name of Soldier.
Ensign Isaac Mynes
Sergt. William H. Tyffe
Corp. William McRoberts
Privates.
Coffen, Henry
Duncan, Joseph
Lewis, Britain
Newcomb, Daniel
Richards, Elijah
Sargent, William
Tharp, Andrew
Turner, Isaac

Page 312.

ROLL OF CAPT. JACOB MANN'S COMPANY (County Unknown).

Served from November 14, 1812, until May 13, 1813.

Capt. Jacob Mann
Corp. John Dye
Privates.
Blue, Uriah
Fallman, Henry
Gissarion, William
Harter, Peter
Scudder, James
Weaver, Peter
Young, Thomas

Ensign John Knight

Privates.
Brown, Abraham
Gregg, Noah
Harter, Benjamin
Kiser, Thomas
Woodburn, Robert
Weaver, John

Sergt. Vincent Dye

Privates.
Cox, Absolom
Goble, Joseph
Haines, John
Levan, John
Winnings, Richard
Williams, Lewis

Page 313.

ROLL OF CAPT. THOMAS RENICK'S COMPANY (From Pickaway County).

Served from July 26, until August 26, 1813.

Capt. Thomas Renick
Sergt. Johnston Hemphill
Sergt. David Marsh
Privates.
Baley, William
Campbell, James
Cuppin, Joseph
Davis, George
Gleeze, Adam
Kearns, Abner
Madden, John
McKinney, Henry
Renick, William
Shreeves, Thomas
Shawbrad, William
Ward, Abraham
Williams, Joseph

Lieut. Asahel Heath
Sergt. Michael Phillip

Privates.
Baley, Robert
Cole, John
Dixson, William
Davis, John
Gaster, Jacob
Linton, William
Marquis, Abraham
Pierce, John
Stiveson, David
Swank, Richard
Shoat, Stoy
Williams, John

Ensign James Halle
Sergt. Edward Conroy

Privates.
Barnes, William
Caster, James
Dixson, Alexander
Fulson, Joshua
Heath, William
Martin, John
Madden, Rowzewed
Pense, John
Swank, William
Short, Stephen
Thomas, David
Williams, Henry

Pages 315-316.

ROLL OF CAPT. JOHN ROBINSON'S COMPANY (Probably from Butler Co.)

Served from July 1, 1812, until April 26, 1813.

Capt. John Robinson
Sergt. Stephen Ball
Sergt. Joseph Nichol
Corp. Robert Reid
Musician, Jonas Smalley
Privates.
Austin, Joseph
Brees, John
Bracken, Joseph
Clark, Barzilla
Davis, Robert
Goble, William
Graham, James
Heaton, John
Hall, Thomas
Loury, Samuel
Lytle, William
Misner, Charles D.
McIntyre, James
Powers, Jonothan
Priddy, Daniel
Reed, William
Reed, Charles
Thomas, Lewis
Vanscoyoe, Jacob
Whittlesey, Duran

Lieut. John Nelson
Sergt. Nicholas Yeager
Corp. Benjamin Virgin
Corp. William Loury

Privates.
Arthur, John
Brackney, John
Carson, John
Clark, David
Finney, John
Gregory, William
Garryson, Jacob
Harlin, Ishmael
Hahn, Joseph
Loury, Fleming
Miller, Samuel
McGouggal, Daniel
Peak, Samuel
Powers, John
Popejoy, Edward
Robby, Isaac
Sisersan, Robert
Thompson, William
Waggamon, Asher
Westfall, Jacob

Ensign Edward Roby
Sergt. Thomas Virgin
Corp. David Hayes
Musician, Ezekial Powers

Privates.
Boggs, James
Barber, Henry
Cullen, Allen
Carnihan, William
Freeman, George
Gregory, James
Graham, Samuel
Hudgall, John
Kountz, Phillip
Landon, David
Murphy, James
McAdams, Thomas
Potts, Jacob
Place, Philip
Popejoy, Nathan
Roby, Abraham
Sproot, David
Virgin, William
Willis, Joseph
Wade, George

Pages 317-318-319. Vol. 2.
ROLL OF CAPT. ROBERT GILCHRIST'S COMPANY (County Unknown).
Served from April 25, until October 26, 1812.

Rank and Name of Soldier.
Capt. Robert Gilchrist
Ensign Samuel Broogher
Sergt. John Shaffer
Sergt. John Bradford
Corp. Archibald Meekle

Privates.
Bayler, John
Broomershine, Jacob
Crider, John
Coffey, John
Cless, John
Fitap, George
Haines, Thomas
Holler, Jacob
Key, Caleb
Kirkpatrick, George
Low, John
Murphy, Aquila
Miller, Jacob
Maxwell, Peter
McNeal, Thomas
Nicholson, William
Roof, P.
Robbe, John
Smith, Gregg
Shaw, Daniel
Scott, William
Tolbert, Oliver
Tigle, George
Whitersell, John
Waggoner, Michael
Winthrop, Emerson
Wagner, Michael
Wright, John

Rank and Name of Soldier.
Lieut. George Minnick
Ensign Samuel Booker
Sergt. Jesse Johnson
Corp. Peter Coblentz
Corp. Thomas Nicholson

Privates.
Baker, Japtha
Bell, John
Carney, Shem
Cross, Israel
Dever, Benjamin
Grimes, Jacob
Hozier, Robert
Ifert, Jacob
Kiser, Aaron
Koue, Jacob
Looks, John
Murphy, John
Miller, George
Minnich, Leonard
McNeal, Daniel
Phillips, George
Rider, James
Ray, Thomas
Sayre, John
Scott, Dunphy
Stoker, Jacob
Taylor, Joseph
VanNott, Joseph
Westfall, Joel
Whitersell, George
Wagamen, Jacob
Withersell, George
Zwerner, Christopher

Rank and Name of Soldier.
Ensign Daniel Shearer
Sergt. Thomas Ray
Sergt. Thomas Patterson
Corp. Austin Webb
Corp. Solomon Cross

Privates.
Beer, John
Boyd, Samuel
Cresswell, James S.
Crowel, Henry
Emerson, W.
Houser, Henry
Hack, Jacob
Jackson, James
Kuhn, Jacob
Lemen, James L.
Laty, John
Meek, Jacob
Mikesel, Peter
McKeel, Daniel
McClary, Thomas
Petticrew, Samuel
Ryan, Joseph
Ream, John
Sheaniks, C.
Shaw, Ludwic
Smith, Nathan
Tinkeys, George
Vail, Samuel
Weaver, Henry
Waggoner, George
Wagner, George
Withersell, John

Pages 320-326.
ROLL OF CAPT. JOHN SHEETS' COMPANY (County Unknown).
Served from April 27, 1812, for one year.

Capt. John Sheets
Sergt. Bryan Williams
Sergt. Samuel S. Jack
Corp. Seth St. John

Privates.
Able, John
Crichor, Henry
Hardy, James
Heaton, Samuel
Hamilton, Jacob
Masey, Seth
Nicholson, Andrew
Stiles, Henry
Trimble, Moses
Weare, Elijah

Lieut. Samuel Pope
Sergt. Michael Bowser
Corp. Joseph M. Edwards
Corp. John Hole

Privates.
Clyne, Ezekial
Estil, William L.
Hayes, John
Hutchinson John
Jennings, David
McDaniel, William
Spencer, Dennis
Shaw, Archibald
Tuttle, Isaiah
Weare, Robert
Vanchorck, David

Lieut. Samuel Miller
Sergt. John Ross
Corp. Isaac Heaton
Musician, John Tuttle

Privates.
Caslet, Alexander
Grimes, Levi
Hart, David
Hamilton, Elias
Munroe, Charles
McCulloch, John
Sterns, Jabez
Thatcher, Elijah
Tearman, John
Wortz, John

Pages 321-322.
ROLL OF CAPT. EPHRAIM BROWN'S COMPANY (County Unknown).
Served from July 2, 1812, until April 24, 1813.

Capt. Ephraim Brown
Sergt. Lyman Crary
Sergt. John Slaybock
Corp. Roswell Hazeltine

Privates.
Auter, Thomas
Babbit, Calvin
Cox, Asa
Dunseth, David Jr.
Furbush, Ephraim
Guthrie, William
Heckweller, Daniel
Jenkinson, John G.
Love, John
Mattox, David A.
Master, David
McCammon, Isaac
Patterson, Martin
Preston, Abijah
Rall, Isaac
Sawyer, Stephen
Swin, Ezer S.
Twaddle, James

Lieut. Robert Guthrie
Sergt. Joseph Cady
Corp. James Risk
Corp. Daniel Jessup

Privates.
Beard, David
Baxter, Thomas
Cooper, Hiram
Danford, Benjamin
Fulton, Abraham T.
Guthrie, John
Johnston, James
Laurance, Azel
Martin, Henry
Matts, Christopher
Miller, John
Newkirk, John
Preston, John
Preston, Joseph
Redenbaugh, James
Shadley, James
Sisco, John
Updegraff, Andrew

Ensign John W. Jones
Sergt. William Gard
Corp. Nathaniel French

Privates.
Brocaw, Henry
Culbages, George
Carle, Stephen
Doty, Zachariah
Gamble, Samuel
Handcock, Daniel
Johnston, Thomas
Ledoi, John
Morton, Washington
Milton, George
McLee, William
Nichols, John
Pasmore, Henry
Pain, Daniel
Riley, Joshua
Steele, John
Tucker, Samuel
Wilkinson, John

Pages 323-324. Vol. 2.

ROLL OF CAPT. JOHN FERRIS' COMPANY (County Unknown).

Served from April 25, until October 25, 1812.

Rank and Name of Soldier.
Capt. John Ferris
Sergt. Samuel Starns
Sergt. James Mundel
Corp. David McLaughlin
Privates.
Andrew, Samuel
Butler, Benjamin
Clark, Caleb
Edwards, James
Fitzgirl, Zadoc
Grayham, George
Humphrey, Robert
Heizer, Lewis
Jones, Philip
Kerr, H.
Manpeny, Thomas
McNeely, Robert
Rettinhouse, E.
Sackwood, William
Smith, Benjamin
Sanburn, John
Whetstone, Reuben
Wilson, Henry

Rank and Name of Soldier.
Lieut. Israel Joslen
Sergt. Adam Weaver
Corp. Theophilus Case
Drummer, John S. Burt
Privates.
Bruner, William
Cunningham, George
Clark, Dennis
Erwin, James
Gentle, John
Hughes, William
Hoover, Daniel
Israel, William
Jennings, Elijah
Langley, John
Mullin, Robert
McKee, Alexander
Redding, Elijah
Seaman, Jaconiah
Sellwood, Henry
Taylor, William
Ware, Thomas
Willis, Samuel
Zimmerman, John

Rank and Name of Soldier.
Ensign Richard Shourd
Sergt. Benjamin Watkins
Corp. William Scudder
Privates.
Bannett, Isaiah
Clark, Jonothan
Deens, Thomas
Fleak, Joseph
Gobin, James L.
Hill, Ezra
Hanet, Thomas
Jones, Isaac
Jones, John
Long, Stephen
Miller, Alexander
Orr, Samuel
Rich, Jacob
Sproul, Hugh
Sheets, Adam
Thompson, John
Wilson, Benjamin
Williamson, S.

Page 325.

ROLL OF CAPT. SAMUEL B. KYLE'S COMPANY. (County Unknown.)

Served from December 1, 1812, until April, 24, 1813.

Capt. Samuel B. Kyle
Sergt. James Fox
Corp. Samuel Ridlen
Privates.
Ashbrook, James
Bates, Amos
Dufer, George
Gardner, William
Gilman, John
Hixson, James
Humphrey, William
Kelley, John
Marsh, Solomon
McCall, John
Pollock, Aaron
Smith, Joshua
Shick, Peter
Templeton, James
White, George

Lieut. Joseph Silley
Sergt. Joseph Gosset
Corp. Richard Benham
Privates.
Arthur, Joseph
Barkdoll, Abraham
Dumford, John
Grey, Amney
Grey, Nathaniel
Horner, William
Hazlett, Robert
Lovel, Timothy
Mack, Dudley
McGill, Stewart
Polsen, Philip
Roman, Jonothan
Shick, Lewis
VanCurin, John
Wilkinson, Thomas B.
Wilson, William

Ensign David Kelly
Sergt. Stephen Ridlen
Corp. John Fisher
Privates.
Bingaman, George
Carvin, Sylvester
Garrison, Jacob
Green, Martin
Hamblen, Benjamin
Harrison, John
Jackman, Bernard
Mallott, David
Meyer, Frederick
Nice, David
Peek, Jacob
Steel, William
Thompson, John
Williamson, Jacob
Wilkinson, Samuel

Pages 327-328-329-330.

ROLL OF CAPT. DAVID SUTTON'S COMPANY.
(Probably from Butler County.)

Served from April 27, until October 27, 1812.

Capt. David Sutton
Sergt. Andrew Robb
Sergt. William Hercules
Corp. John Young
Drummer, John Thompson
Privates.
Anderson, John
Bowers, Reese
Collister, Hugh W.
Dill, John
Garrison, Benjamin
Garrison, David
Hutchinson, James
Jeffries, George
Mullin, John
Moore, William
McCollister, Michael
Rinedson, N.
Snook, Mart
Seward, John
Trump, Andrew
Vingard, John
Warren, Zachariah
Bannon, John
Garrison, Jeremiah
Jester, Eli
McCollister, Hugh
Snuff, Jacob
Thompson, John

Lieut. Robert Sweeney
Sergt. Wright Elliott
Corp. John Shawhan
Corp. John Flaming
Corp. Josiah Bradway
Privates.
Blake, Nathan
Cunningham, Nathaniel
Cahill, Abraham
Fisher, David
Garrison, John
Garrison, Ezekial
Hyde, Samuel
Kitchell, James L.
Martin, John
Martin, William
Powell, Jacob
Stets, John
Smoot, Dixon
Thomas, David
Tindles, J.
Weeks, Job
Wright, George
Fitzgerald, Eson
Holcomb, Asa
Long, William D.
Nearson, Minary
Stiles, John
Vorhis, Jeremiah

Ensign John Vowen
Sergt. D. Bowers
Corp. William DeLong
Fifer, Benjamin Murphy

Privates.
Bunnel, William
Cahill, Alexander
Cummin, J. N.
Fisher, Jacob
Garrison, Person
Goodposter, Isaac
Hester, Jacob
Kindelspeaker, Jacob
Manly, William
Miller, John
Patton, William
Snook, Jacob
Suten, James
Trimble, James
Vorhes, John
Wallach, William

Fisher, James
Hand, Benjamin
Lee, John
Ress, Bown
Tingel, George
Wright, Ragen

Pages 331-332. Vol. 2.
ROLL OF CAPT. SAMUEL STEWART'S COMPANY. (County Unknown.)
Served from April, until October 20, 1812.

Rank and Name of Soldier.	Rank and Name of Soldier.	Rank and Name of Soldier.
Capt. Samuel Stewart	Lieut. Jacob Pentz	Ensign Daniel Jones
Sergt. John Reed	Sergt. Samuel Pollack	Sergt. Samuel Smith
Sergt. Jacob Koogler	Sergt. Elijah Weaver	Sergt. Mathew S. Spencer
Sergt. Evan Stephens	Sergt. William Pringle	Corp. James Barnes
Corp. George Sinkin	Corp. Abner S. Millard	Corp. Elijah Ross
Corp. James Barnes	Drummer, M. Gibson	Fifer, Robert Pringle

Privates.

Albon, George	Busby, John	Botkin, C.
Brown, William	Boyce, Samuel	Butcher, David
Beasley, Isaac	Bacon, George	Cummins, Joseph
Curtis, William	Childers, Henry	Curl, Jeremiah
Cartree, Hiram	Dill, George	Davis, Daniel
Davis, Noah	Daugherty, Thomas	Ennis, Thompson
Ennis, Jeremiah	Hathaway, Wesley	Hixon, Joel
Hardman, Henry	Hall, Moses	Hughey, William
Hughes, John	Hindman, William	Hutchinson, John
Gutridge, William	Gard, Daniel	Jackson, John
Jefferson, James	Kerr, Jesse	Kizer, William
Looker, Allison C.	Long, Daniel	Lufton, John
Millpolland, Hugh	Miller, Adam	Morrison, Michell
Moore, John	Myers, William	McBery, Duncan
McDonald, Daniel	Oliver, John	Perry, Ebenezer
Polen, John	Paxton, James	Porter, Thomas
Perry, Allen	Rhoades, William	Seward, Samuel
Shackly, Clement	Seward, Malen	Smith, Ballard
Sherry, John	Smith, Solomon	Sutton, Jeremiah
Stevens, James	Tarrbutton, Eli	Talor, Peter
Tarbutton, Edward	Thornton, John	Thornton, William
Watson, Joshua	Wolff, John	Williams, William
Williams, Reed	Wilson, Valentine	

Pages 333-334.
ROLL OF CAPT. WILLIAM RAYNOLD'S COMPANY. (County Unknown.)
Served from April 12, 1812, until April 13, 1813.

Capt. William Raynolds	Lieut. Joseph Cairns	Ensign Isaac Van Horne
Sergt. Henry Foore	Sergt. James Nixon	Sergt. John Eagin
Corp. James M. Wood	Corp. William Smith	Corp. Mathias Hollandback
Corp. Samuel Johnstone		

Privates.

Anser, Lloyd	Anser, John	Armstrong, James
Blake, John	Bland, William	Blunt, James
Bland, Thomas	Blake, Nehemiah	Blake, Henry
Barron, William	Cairns, Richard	Colly, Benjamin
Cass, Eyre	Cordray, James	Carhart, William
Craig, William	Coats, John	Cantwell, James
Dowell, John	Dennis, Samuel	Dorrel, Thomas B.
Eddington, Robert	Fickie, Michael	Fickle, George M.
Frye, Isaac	Furthy, Isaac	Gilkinson, Jonothan
Groves, Solomon	Hare, Josiah	Harris, George
Howey, Peter	Hartley, Thomas	Hare, Joseph
Hardesty, George	Jones, William	Jeffers, Jonas
Johnstone, James	Keerns, John	Lackey, Hugh
Lane, Walter	Lawson, Septimus	Loar, John
Lackey, Andrew	Marshall, Thomas	Moore, Peter
Moore, Thomas	Moore, Robert	Mums, John
McFadden, Neal	McNeal, Alexander	McDonald, Stephen
McKinley, Thomas	Pratt, Robert	Peatt, Peter
Pigman, John G.	Pevise, William	Peatt, Stephen
Petitt, Joseph	Parker, Benjamin	Richards, Jacob
Smith, Alexander	Sutton, Joseph	Smith, Benjamin
Shenard, David	Seybring, Robert	Smith, Nathaniel B.
Shadley, Henry	Upp, Upp	Van Sickle, James
Virden, Lacy S.	Welsh, Moses	Watson, James C.
Wassin, James	Winner, John	Williams, Littleton

Pages 337-338.
ROLL OF CAPT. THOMAS McCONNELL'S COMPANY. (County Unknown.)
Served from September 4, until December 31, 1813.

Capt. Thomas McConnell	Lieut. Alexander Hill	Ensign William Fee
Sergt. George Scott	Sergt. Enoch Buchanon	Sergt. Pennel Davis
Sergt. Isaac Sutton	Corp. Joseph Aldridge	Corp. George Fisher
Corp. William C. Goff	Corp. John McCarter	Drummer, John W. Tyler
	Fifer, William Martin	

Privates.

Brundon, Andrew	Bush, Isaac	Brush, Israel
Bradley, William	Butler, John	Cook, Rudolph

Vol. 2.
ROLL OF CAPT. THOMAS McCONNELL'S COMPANY. (Continued)

Rank and Name of Soldier.	Rank and Name of Soldier.	Rank and Name of Soldier.
Privates.	Privates.	Privates.
Cochran, John	Conner, Florence	Cook, William
Cochran, James	Danforth, Eli	Davison, James
Dyal, John	Dye, William	Day, Thomas
Foor, Adam	Foor, John	Griggs, Caleb
Gano, Joseph	Hill, Daniel	Hanna, James Sr.
Hanna, James, Jr.	Henderson, James	Henderson, William
Haynes, Nathan	Higon, Wesley	Hill, William
Johnson, John	Jones, Tarpley	Kindle, Joseph
Kyte, Joel	Kilpatrick, David	Kindle, David
Kirkpatrick, Alexander	Lanham, William	Leusey, Enoch
Lorel, Joseph	Lindsey, John	Lemmont, James
Murray, Daniel	McKinney, Cain	Manahan, Samuel
Martin, John	McCarter, William	Moore, Augustus
McKee, James	Masters, John	Neever, James C.
Ogden, John	Pinnel, Edward	Ralston, James
Richardson, John	Richardson, Lemuel	Sullivan, William
Sargent, Elijah	Stewart, William	Shepherd, Solomon
Shaw, Hugh	Simen, Peter	Springer, John
Shumanion, Samuel R.	Shurran, David	Schooley, Jonothan
Steirs, Andrew	Scott, Trummel	Tyler, Joseph
Tyler, Morris	Welsh, Thomas	Waterfield, Jacob
White, Amos	Woodruff, David	Washburn, Cornelius
Young, Roger		

Pages 339-340.
ROLL OF CAPT. THOMAS FREEMAN'S COMPANY. (County Unknown.)
Served from September 5, 1813, until January 21, 1814.

Capt. Thomas Freeman	Lieut. Joseph Stephens	Sergt. Michael Murray
Ensign Peter Sey	Sergt. James Mills	Sergt. Phillip Place
Sergt. Paul Michael	Sergt. Thomas Monloyne	Corp. Joseph Willis
Corp. Joseph Abbott	Corp. William Street	Corp. George Reprogle
Corp. Samuel Burns	Drummer, Ralph Vorhees	Fifer, Jonothan Potter
Privates.	Privates.	Privates.
Buchanan, James	Bensley, William	Bridge, Ebenezer
Breece, Valentine	Ball, Isaiah	Bant, Silas
Broderick, Nehemiah	Boyland, Nicholas	Bala, Amma
Badene, Clemens	Coalby, Joseph	Caterlin, Joseph
Coldwell, Joseph	Clark, Alexander	Coon, George
Cox, Andrew	Dickey, Samuel	Davis, Robert
Davis, George	Deckey, John H.	Doty, William
Fields, Foster	Fleming, David	Fergesson, Samuel
Foster, Isaac	Fields, James	
Grubbs, George	Hall, James	Hunter, Andrew
Hudgill, John	Kiger, John	Keller, Jonothan
Lewman, William	LaClear, Peter	Logan, Joseph
Missner, Richard	Masterson, William	Maxwell, Samuel
Meredith, Absolom	Morton, James	Miller, Jacob
McEown, James	McNeal, Lazarus	McDowell, Joshua
McKee, Robert	Newcum, Emanuel	Orson, Joseph
Place, Philip	Parsons, David	Reed, John
Reynolds, Jeremiah	Riprogle, Jacob	Reece, William
Robison, John	Shappell, Jacob	Spencer, John
Stine, Daniel	Sutton, Daniel	Spinning, Jonothan
Taylor, Hayse	Taylor, William	VanLeer, Cornelius
VanLeer, Daniel	Watson, Joseph	Wallace, James
Wilson, John Sr.	Wilson, John Jr.	Weaver, George
	Ward, Daniel	

Pages 341-342.
ROLL OF CAPT. JAMES DOWNING'S COMPANY.
(Probably from Jefferson County.)
Served from August 23, until November 30, 1812.

Capt. James Downing	Lieut. Peter Johnson	Ensign Thomas Smith
Sergt. John Forsythe	Sergt. John Barber	Sergt. Michael McGowen
Sergt. Samuel Richards	Corp. Abraham Bair	Corp. Benjamin A. Kinson
Corp. John Warden	Corp. Joseph Balsfore	Fifer, Jesse Ellis
	Drummer, Daniel Smith	
Privates.	Privates.	Privates.
Adam, John	Baindan, Jacob	Buck, John
Baird, John	Bawn, Henry	Bair, David
Barlen, Henry	Baird, John	Baired, Andrew
Crites, William	Chapman, Thomas	Forsythe, Andrew
Funk, Samuel	Fouls, George	Grubb, John
Holts, John	Hawman, Isaac	Henning, Jacob
Hoster, Jacob	Hefner, David	Hartman, David
King, Peter	Knap, Caleb	Kepler, Andrew

ROLL OF CAPT. THOMAS FREEMAN'S COMPANY. (Continued.)

Rank and Name of Soldier.
Privates.
Kinny, Peter
Mettz, Abraham
McKintorpe, John
Patten, Mathew
Price, Benjamin
Rogers, Levi
Stoner, John

Rank and Name of Soldier.
Privates.
Leatherman, Peter
Miles, Eli
Nelson, William
Powell, John
Price, John
Leed, Adam
Shook, David
Stover, Samuel

Rank and Name of Soldier.
Privates.
Mirur, Boyd
McCaughey, Joseph
Neighdick, Samuel
Perkins, James
Richards, Daniel
Strickland, Edward
Smith, Jacob

ROLL OF CAPT. GEORGE STIDGER'S COMPANY.
(Probably from Stark County.)

Served from August 23, 1812, until January 19, 1813.

Capt. George Stidger
Sergt. Daniel McClure
Sergt. William B. Chamberlain
Corp. Jacob Essig

Lieut. Robert Cameron
Sergt. John Miller
Sergt. Christian Flickenger
Corp. Moses Andrews

Ensign Daniel McClure
Sergt. John Shorb
Corp. George Cribs
Bugleman, Thomas Neely

Privates.
Alexander, Ezekial
Black, James
Chisimore, George
Croninger, Benjamin
DeWalt, George
Forber, Daniel
Kroft, John
Livingston, Henry
Moore, James
Rogers, John
Rowland, John
Swigart, Jacob
Stephens, Daniel

Privates.
Andrews, James
Brouse, Philip
Clinger, John
Cresson, Garnett
Elder, John
Gaff, John
Kuntz, John
Monroe, George
McClelland, Samuel
Roose, Abraham
Rice, John
Shisson, John
Short, John

Privates.
Brown, William
Cutthall, John
Carper, John
Duck, Samuel
Essig, Adam
Gaff, Robert
Kirkpatrick, George
Myers, Jacob
Potts, John
Riddle, James
Smith, William
Shields, Thomas
Sheinbarger, John

ROLL OF CAPT. JOSEPH ZIMMERMAN'S COMPANY.
(Probably from Jefferson County.)

Served from August 25, until November 30, 1812.

Capt. Joseph Zimmerman
Sergt. George Estep
Sergt. Christian Krepps
Corp. Ezekiel Moore

Lieut. James Kerr
Sergt. George Schultz
Corp. George Switzer
Corp. Samuel Meck

Ensign Conrad Monzer or Myers
Sergt. William Rough or Pouch
Corp. John Lawrence
Drummer, Byneal Moore

Privates.
Augustine, Henry
Blackburn, William
Cook, George
Ford, William
Gilson, John
Hahan, Andrew
Kelly, Alexander
Meek, Samuel, Jr.
Minton, John
McClary, John
Rogers, Thomas
Shultz, George
Thompson, John

Privates.
Becht, George
Creey, James
Catt, Philip
Faibr, Michael
Hoffman, Jacob
Heckinthorn, Peter
Kemp, Jonothan
Meek, John
Miett, Frederick
Palmer, Richard
Richy, Isaac
Smith, John
Wickersham, Joseph

Privates.
Barnett, Jacob
Callahan, William
Fisher, Brice
Garringer, David
Higgins, Samuel
Kalep, John
Myers, Silas
Meek, John Sr.
McClellan, Felix
Ruck, Henry
Sauer, Michael
Thomas, Robert

ROLL OF CAPT. WILLIAM BLACKBURN'S COMPANY.
(Probably from Columbiana County.)

Served from August 22, until November 30, 1812.

Capt. William Blackburn
Sergt. Stephen Miller
Sergt. Benjamin Hohne
Corp. Daniel Cross

Lieut. Samuel Ferguson
Sergt. William Milnor
Sergt. William Kerr
Corp. Joseph Earle

Ensign George Grimes
Sergt. George Wiseman
Corp. Andrew Gibson

Privates.
Brown, Joseph
Betz, Frederick
Booker, Isaiah
Curls, Charles
Harwood, Eaton
Jump, Henry
Miller, Stephen
Patterson, Joseph
Sheets, George
Twimpseed, John
Woolf, George

Privates.
Britz, George
Bidenger, Joseph
Burnes, George
Grimes, John
Hahn, Caleb
Kutz, Emanuel
Miller, Conrad
Rudinan, Jacob
Soey, Benjamin
Woolf, John
Webb, Richard

Privates.
Branderberry, Conrad
Blake, Price B.
Caughey, Joseph
Gaskill, David
Jumper, Joseph
Moody, Joseph
Palmer, Jesse
Rogers, George
Soey, Samuel
Wolf, Philip

Page 350. Vol. 2.

ROLL OF CAPT. DANIEL HARBAUGH'S COMPANY.
(Probably from Columbiana County.)

Served from August 25, 1812, until February —, 1813.

Rank and Name of Soldier.	Rank and Name of Soldier.	Rank and Name of Soldier.
Capt. Daniel Harbaugh	Lieut. David Scott	Lieut. George Clark
Cornet. Michael Wirtz	Sergt. James Sharp	Sergt. Jonathan Whitacre
Sergt. Mordecai Moore	Sergt. Henry Hepner	Farrier, John Kuntz
	Trumpeter, Daniel L. Smith	
Privates.	**Privates.**	**Privates.**
Allison, Abner	Blackburn, Samuel	Blackburn, John
Campbell, John	Fifer, David	Goble, John
Graham, David	Humbel, James	Hunt, John
Mathews, Jacob	Morris, Morris E.	Meese, Philip
Moore, William	McKinsey, John	Redick, John
Sheehan, Cornelius	Swearinigen Elimeleeh	Wilson, George
Willibey, John	Willibey, Andrew	Watson, James
Zeaner, Jacob		

Pages 351-352.

ROLL OF CAPT. SAMUEL MARTIN'S COMPANY.
(Probably from Greene County.)

Served from August 21, 1813, until February 21, 1814.

Capt. Samuel Martin	Lieut. David Hannah	Ensign Jacob Crouse
Sergt. John Jackson	Sergt. Noah Frederick	Sergt. Robert Corning
Sergt. William Phelps	Corp. Thomas Armstrong	Corp. James Bennet
Corp. Phillip Branaberry	Corp. Benjamin Stephens	Fifer, David M. Casky
	Drummer, Frederick Blaker	
Privates.	**Privates.**	**Privates.**
Anderson, Andrew	Anderson, James	Armstrong, Thomas
Bradfield, Joseph	Bittenger, John	Britton, Archibald
Bell, William	Bishop, Joseph	Basham, Ezekial
Brinker, Peter	Brown, William	Bowlin, Eli
Dougherty, Samuel	Frederick, Thomas	Farmer, Thomas
Fulks, Charles	Fiskel, Fred	Geddes, James
Gilson, David	Gilson, John	Hickman, Nicholas
Helmick, Adam	Harrison, Daniel	Jones, Nicholas
Knight, Robert	Kilton, John S.	Kurtz, John
Lamboon, Josiah	Manning, William	Mann, Philip
Myers, John	Quin, Samuel	Quin, John
Robinson, John	Rossel, Jacob	Robins, John
Stephens, Jacob	Smith, Sampson	Shaw, Jacob
Smaley, John	Tagart, William	Trippy, George
Wollam, Henry	Wollam, Jacob	Welker, William
Willits, John		

Pages 353-354.

ROLL OF CAPT. JOHN RAMSEY'S COMPANY.
(Probably from Columbiana County.)

Served from August 24, until November 30, 1812.

Capt. John Ramsey	Lieut. James Andrews	Ensign Lindsay Cannon
Sergt. Thomas Rosebaugh	Sergt. James Craighead	Sergt. James Ramsey
Corp. John Hunter	Corp. Philip Foult	Corp. Joseph Fife
Fifer, Jacob Grin	Drummer, Peter Shirts	
Privates.	**Privates.**	**Privates.**
Augustine, Henry	Beer, James	Brown, Joseph
Cannon, Thomas	Craig, Robert	Carnes, George
Craig, William	Craig, John	Cambel, John
Daugherty, James	Early, James	Early, David
Fife, James	Fife, Samuel	Fergens, Samuel
Frank, Adam	Forney, John	Forney, Peter
Forney, Adam	Fibe, William	Fegley, Joseph
Goss, Mathias	Gardner, Jacob	Guthrie, William
Graham, John	Hamilton, Jonothan	Hunter, Samuel
Hamilton, William	Hayes, David M.	Hoffman, John
Heck, Jacob	Hamilton, Joseph	Jolley, Samuel
Kees, Russell	Meck, Samuel	Meck, Robert
Meck, William	McLaughlin, Robert	McDonald, Duncan
McLilly, Samuel	McCullough, James	McCredy, William
McLaughlin, William	McCalle, Thomas	Opdyche, Albert
Pollock, Andrew	Paul, Benjamin	Paul, Henry
Paul, William	Po'lock, Thomas	Pierce, William
Robinson, Jonah	Rupperd, Jacob	Sheets, Jacob
Sheets, John	Samcock, Michael	Shook, George
Shivers, Samuel	Thompson, John L.	Ton, Alexander
Vanfresson, Arnold	Watson, James	Wright, Gilbert
Wall, Richard	Whitmore, John	Yeanin, Mathias

ROLL OF CAPT. THOMAS ROWLAND'S COMPANY.
(Probably from Columbiana County.)

Served from July, 1812, until January, 1813.

Capt. Thomas Rowland
Ensign Charles Hoy
Sergt. Samuel Ravers
Corp. Aaron Reese

Lieut. Nathaniel McCracken
Sergt. Thomas R. McKnight
Sergt. James Dyers
Corp. Andre Wesley

Lieut. David Hostetter
Sergt. John Millinger
Corp. Jacob Watson
Corp. Thomas McCracken

Privates.
Byel, James
Buchanan, James
Dull, Aaron
Glenn William
Haley, William
Krupp, Samuel
Mansion, George
McAlister, John
McCann, Peter
Poe, John
Reed, James
Shang, William
Updegraff, John
Willington, Thomas

Privates.
Bates, David
Creighton, John
Fishall, George
Hull, Abner
Hill, Jonothan
Kamp, Samuel
McCulloch, James
McBride, Jeff
McAllister, Walter
Petticord, Oratio
Spidle, John
Thompson, Robert
Wilson, Thomas
Wiley, William
Yarnell, Abraham

Privates.
Boots, Willis
Crane, John
Graham, Daniel
Hunter, John
Keisinger, George
Murray, James
McAlister, James
McLaughlin, Robert
Nool, John
Ritten, Benjamin
Stoner, George
Toppen, Archibald
Wright, Ruel
Yarnell, Alexander

ROLL OF CAPT. JOSEPH CHEWS' COMPANY.
(Probably from Ross County.)

Served from May 8, until May 16, and from July 28, until August 18, 1813.

Capt. Joseph Chews
Sergt. Peter Nichols

Lieut. Hiram Hurdin
Sergt. William Heath

Ensign Abraham Thomas

Privates.
Burnett, William
Barker, Joshua
Groves, William
Johnson, Isaac
Kirkpatrick, Joseph
Rollston, Benjamin
Stinson, Daniel
Smith, Samuel

Privates.
Bennett, John
Clark, William
Grimm, Jacob
Jordon, Isaac
McKinley, John
Richie, David
Stinson, John
Smith, Green N.

Privates.
Brown, Samuel
Grimm, Jonothan
Harrison, Mirajah
Johnston, John
Phillips, James
Richie, William
Shirley, Laurence
Spong, Henry

ROLL OF CAPT. JOSIAH KILBOURN'S COMPANY.
(Probably from Ross County.)

Served from July 28, until August 20, 1813.

Capt. Josiah Kilbourn
Sergt. Phillip Ayubright

Lieut. Jeremiah Cox
Sergt. Joshua Speakman
Corp. Edward McCann

Sergt. James Carter
Corp. Samuel Richardson

Privates.
Barby, Hasel
Dixon, Simon
Huddle, George
Looker, William
Ray, William
Williams, William

Privates.
Barby, Daniel
Day, Thomas
Jordon, William
Pay, John
Ratcliff, John
Wyckoff, William

Privates.
Dixon, Jacob
Francis, Jonothan
Kelly, William
Ruddick, Jesse
Slossen, William
Willfong, David

ROLL OF LIEUT. THOMAS LLOYD'S COMPANY. (County Unknown.)

Served from July 28, until August 10, 1813.

Lieut. Thomas Lloyd
Corp. John Householder

Ensign Robert Robison
Corp. Joseph McKee

Sergt. Samuel Davison

Privates.
Anderson, John
Bramble, James
Delano, Ira
Gibbs, James
Leister, Peter
Riddle, William
Whitecale, Hiram

Privates.
Brown, Edward
Crumpton, John
Daly, E.
Johnson, John
McAllister, Daniel
Romine, Elias
White, Thorley Lee
Gallager, David

Privates.
Brown, Peter
Cook, Samuel
Greenwood, John
Kelley, Jonothan
McKensey, Eli
Witheutt, John
Robison, John H.

ROLL OF CAPT. JAMES TAYLOR'S COMPANY.
(From Ross County.)

Served from August 21, until October 10, 1812.

Capt. James Taylor
Sergt. Henry Cahoon
Sergt. Thomas Wood
Drummer, Abel Honson

Lieut. Abiatha Taylor
Sergt. Amos Cox
Corp. James Kile

Ensign John Gufey
Sergt. Robert Wilson
Fifer, David Taylor

ROLL OF CAPT. JAMES TAYLOR'S COMPANY. (Continued)

Rank and Name of Soldier.
Privates.
Bright, John
Clymer, John
Cramer, George
Hires, Walter
Johnson, Barnabus
Long, John
Pursell, Samuel
Ross, Alexander
Suddick, James
Taylor, John A.
Vencamp, William

Rank and Name of Soldier.
Privates.
Casey, Thomas
Chevergar, William
Creamer, John
Hires, James
King, Phillip
Medford, Charles
Pursell, Jacob
Steveson, George
Swihser, John
Taylor, James A.
Wood, Charles

Rank and Name of Soldier.
Privates.
Chaney, John
Crawford, David
Flemming, Joseph
Hooper, Phillip
Long, Edward
Needles, Cubage
Ross, James
Swaring, William
Taylor, Robert
Vencamp, John
Whitnell, Henry

Page 360.

ROLL OF CAPT. JOSEPH GORTON'S COMPANY.
(Probably from Franklin County.)

Served from August 25, until October 10, 1812.

Capt. Joseph Gorton
Sergt. Mathew Mathews
Drummer, Andrew Corpus

Privates.
Breckenrige, James
Benton, Nathan
Hopper, Robert
Moody, James
Primrose, William
Simmons, John

Privates.
Badger, William
Grubb, Jacob
Instice, John
McNutt, William
Penix, Edward
Webb, Thomas

Privates.
Bailie, Stewart
Gordon, John
John, John
Overdeer, Jacob
Robertson, Francis

Pages 361-362

ROLL OF CAPT. CHARLES HILLIARD'S COMPANY.
(Probably from Miami County.)

Served from Februay 22, until August 21, 1813.

Capt. Charles Hilliard
Sergt. James Frost
Sergt. Samuel Clark
Corp. Lewis Winans
Musician, John Manning

Lieut. John Hill
Sergt. Thomas Ross
Sergt. Benjamin Nogle
Corp. William Ramsey
Corp. William Brown

Ensign John Kiser
Sergt. Thomas Gilbert
Corp. Benjamin B. Winans
Musician, Samuel Haney

Privates.
Anderson, Samuel
Brown, Abraham
Battroll, John
Cary, David
Crawford, James
Foster, Elijah
Hance, Benjamin
Jowles, George
Julin, Isaac
Landry, Simon
Manning, Edward
McReynolds, Robert
Reyonlds, Robert
Weatherhead, John
Whiten, Stephen
Webb, John

Privates.
Blue, Barnabus
Bedler, Calvin
Cox, John
Castle, Ralph
Dunn, Terwin
Favorite, Abraham
Harter, Jacob
Jackson, John
Kimble, Edward
Langley, Benett W.
Miller, David
Pierson, Jacob
Ross, Job
Wilson, Alexander
Wyatt, Andrew
Whitney, Stephen

Privates.
Browning, Abraham
Bayman, Thomas
Cary, Thomas
Castle, Ralph, Sr.
Eller, Adam
Green, James
Ingle, Michael
James, Levi
Krise, Daniel
Livingood, George
Miller, Jacob
Ross, Martin
Studilaker, David
Webb, Joseph B.
Wyatt, John G.
Yontes, George

Pages 363-364.

ROLL OF CAPT. RICHARD SUNDERLAND'S COMPANY. (County Unknown.)

Served from February 16, until August 15, 1813.

Capt. Richard Sunderland
Sergt. William Guy
Corp. William Fryback

Lieut. Asa John
Sergt. John Murphy
Corp. James Wead
Corp. Ephraim Haines

Ensign, John C. Negley
Sergt. Robert Kendall
Corp. James German

Privates.
Ainsworth, John
Buxton, Charles
Coffman, Henry
Cline, Christian
Dawson, John
Ewing, William G.
Guess, Joseph
Harding, Daniel
Holderman, John
Kazee, Randall
Linen, James L.
Littell, Absalom
Middogh, John G.

Privates.
Alhed, Isaac
Barlow, William A.
Codington, Isaac
Croy, David
Duncan, Peter
Greer, Joshua
Hossier, Isaac
Houser, Martin
Isenogle, Abraham
Keggins, Robert
Loveless, Sileness
Loury, James
Martin, William

Privates.
Burgh, William Denning
Bowghman, George
Campbell, John
Dille, Samuel
Elliott, Groseberry
Goode, John
Harding, Richard
Hatfield, Moses
Knee, Philip
Kiser, John
Lumphian, Charles
Michael, Jacob
Miller, John

ROLL OF CAPT. RICHARD SUNDERLAND'S COMPANY. (Continued)

Rank and Name of Soldier.
Privates.
McDonald, Daniel
Perkey, Frederick
Ramsey, Samuel
Swartwood, Abraham
Tennant, Alexander
Vanscoyk, Joseph
Weaver, Peter

Rank and Name of Soldier.
Privates.
Neff, Daniel
Robbins, Thomas
Smith, Adam
Stoner, Jacob
Tolbit, William
Ward, George
Waggner, Michael

Rank and Name of Soldier.
Privates.
Peck, Jacob
Rose, Benjamin
Shantz, Peter
Sproul, Hugh
Vanscoyk, John
Wood, Elijah

Pages 365-366.

ROLL OF CAPT. DANIEL REX'S COMPANY. (County Unknown.)
Served from April 3, until October 3, 1813.

Capt. Daniel Rex
Sergt. David Hendershot
Sergt. Thomas Shiers
Corp. Frederick Michael

Lieut. James Medill
Sergt. William Rash
Corp. John McClarkin
Corp. Benjamin Morphew

Ensign, William Campbell
Sergt. William Ross
Corp. Elijah Allen

Privates.
Allen, John
Alexander, James
Bayne, Samuel
Black, Joseph
Christman, David
Cloyde, James
Easlinger, John
Flick, William
Huffman, Allen
Kelough, William
Knear, Henry
Michael, John
Morphey, Nathan
Owens, Samuel
Price, Daniel
Reed, William
Steel, John K.
Show, John
Sproul, Samuel
Utt, Muchael
Worle, Samuel Jr.

Privates.
Achmand, Alexander
Butler, James
Biggs, Aaron
Bishop, Levin
Caldwell, Jonothan
Dervees, Ezekial
Flemming, James
Heuston, Samuel
Hamilton, Samuel
Kirk, Thomas
Lambert, Courtland
Moore, Alexander
McLarkin, James
Pearson, Thomas
Reid, John
Rooker, William
Stone, William
Smith, Philip
Shull, Philip
Warrell, Attwell
Worle, James, Sr.

Privates.
Adkins, George
Black, Daniel
Boyd, William
Caldwell, Manlove
Crawfort, Jacob
Day, William
Flashman, Peter
Holliday, Samuel
Ireland, James
Knoddle, Jacob
Landers, Samuel
Manlove, George
Nickum, Peter
Payne, Isaac
Russell, Charles
Simonton, John
Shidler, Jacob
Strou, Michael
Tibbs, John
Wickle, Frederick
Williams, Jonothan

Page 367.

ROLL OF CAPT. ROBERT IRWIN'S COMPANY.
(Probably from Belmont County.)
Served from June 1, until August 12, 1813.

Capt. Robert Irwin
Sergt. David Kirkland
Sergt. William Reneson
Corp. John Richardson

Lieut. Thomas Pribble
Sergt. Absalom Dilly
Corp. Solomon James
Corp. William Crothers

Ensign, Thomas McNight
Sergt. Francis Smith
Corp. Samuel Coonts
Drummer, Jacob Castle

Privates.
Barker, Amos
Bruver, John
Boyles, Thomas
Devall, John
Forest, John
Hall, John
Heness, John
Jones, Thomas
Keller, John
Miller, James
Neally, John
Richards, George

Privates.
Bates, Jesse
Billman, Henry
Campbell, James
Ferguson, George
Goomon, William
Hammond, David
Jenkins, John
King, Cornelius
Lattimore, William
McMullen, Samuel
Proudfoot, Alexander
Richards, Daniel

Privates.
Boggs, James
Bryan, Richard
Coss, Daniel
Fleshaman, Jesse
Higgins, William
Hillhouse, John
Johnston, William
King, Samuel
Lorrimy, William
McCoy, Rallston
Richards, James
Stout, Joseph

Page 368.

ROLL OF CAPT. ADAM BINCKLEY'S COMPANY.
(From Perry and Fairfield Counties.)
Served from June 1, until August 12, 1813.

Capt. Adam Binckley
Sergt. William B. Davis
Sergt. Henry M. Davis
Corp. John Henry

Lieut. John Middaugh
Sergt. John Overmire
Corp. Peter King
Corp. John Winner

Ensign, Richard Grabb
Sergt. John Fowler
Corp. John Leidy

Privates.
Amspach, Adam
Acker, George
Bowland, Hugh
Bucket, William
Cock, Jacob

Privates.
Ammach, Abraham
Baker, Henry
Breson, George
Bonesteel, Henry
Deal, David

Privates.
Acklin, Alexander
Bouler, Alexander
Buckson, Thomas
Crosby, Edward
Downhouer, Jacob

ROSTER OF OHIO SOLDIERS IN WAR OF 1812

ROLL OF CAPT. ADAM BINCKLEY'S COMPANY. (Continued)

Rank and Name of Soldier.

Privates.
Dubler, Philip
Grelle, Philip
Hutsman, Jesse
Lancaster, William
Miller, Philip
Rannels, Thomas
Stener, Jacob
Smith, Daniel

Rank and Name of Soldier.

Privates.
Dubler, John
Houty, Christian
Hall, Benjamin
Landfer, Benjamin
Moyer, John
Richard, Samuel
Swinehart, John
Spohn, Adam

Rank and Name of Soldier.

Privates.
Fogt, Michael
Hawk, Solomon
Kinnon, William
Lane, Peter
Notestine, John
Sain, David
Shunk, Henry

Page 369.

ROLL OF CAPT. STEPHEN AIVATT'S COMPANY. (County Unknown.)

Served from March 7, until September 7, 1814.

Capt. Stephen Aivatt
Sergt. Almarin Brooks
Sergt. Oliver Lewis
Corp. Andrew C. Nuerker

Lieut. Asa L. Banning
Sergt. Fillington Moary
Corp. Henry Dennison
Corp. Isaac R. Allen

Ensign, Robert Short
Sergt. Calvin Smith
Corp. Jacob Winas

Privates.
Burnan, Nathaniel
Croft, Jacob
Crooks, Thomas
Dixon, Walter
Goncher, John
Hood, Simon
Johnson, William
King, Samuel
Mackey, John
McCullough, Thomas
Nicholas, William
Rutan, John
Sprague, William
Tamer, Samuel
Weber, Peter

Privates.
Buchanan, Abraham
Chalfint, David
Crawford, Gurron
Elliott, William
Gates, Mathias
Hannah, Isaac
Kincaid, Alexander
Lord, Mathew
McConnel, Elias
McMiller, John
Rolston, Nathaniel
Riche, John
Tend, Roswell
Snider, William

Privates.
Broadwell, Jacob
Crooks, John
Dixon, James
Fannah, Isaac
Gates, John
Johnson, Nathan
Kidd, John
Lightburn, Joseph
McConnel, Mathew
McLinly, William
Robbins, Bowman
Sullivan, William
Thompson, Patrick
Wood, Jonah

Page 370.

ROLL OF CAPT. BARUCH DICKERSON'S COMPANY.
(Probably from Harrison County.)

Served from March 12, until September 12, 1814.

Capt. Baruch Dickerson
Sergt. William Hagerfield
Musician, James Roff

Lieut. John Jamison
Sergt. Charles Holmes
Musician, David Young

Ensign, Samuel Gilmore
Sergt. Laken Wells

Privates.
Browning, Samuel
Carson, John
Foster, Moses
Haverfield, James
Holmes, Samuel
McConkey, James
Parrish, Joseph
Scott, David
Wrist, Nathaniel
Young, George

Privates.
Chambers, Ezekial
Craig, Joseph
Fivecoats, Michael
Hovey, John
Holmes, Elsy
McConkey, Samuel
Richison, John
Steel, Bazallel
Walraven, John

Privates.
Carson, Samuel
Foster, Andrew
Hitchcock, Isaac
Hurless, John
Mechan, Aaron
Nelson, Benjamin
Smith, Francis
Warpenbay, Francis
Welday, Henry

Page 372.

ROLL OF CAPT. ISAAC WARNER'S COMPANY.
(Probably from Columbiana County.)

Served from March 11, until September 11, 1814.

Capt. Isaac Warner
Corp. Michael Musser

Lieut. George Akins
Corp. John Wilkins
Musician, William Altman

Sergt. Reuben Taylor
Corp. Joseph Gastin

Privates.
Bradfield, Benjamin
Cormick, George
Harper, Jacob
McCollister, Jacob
Powell, Michael
Rock, George
Snyder, Stephen
Widick, John
Welker, William

Privates.
Butz, Samuel
Fulk, Johnston
Motinger, George
Piper, Henry
Rogers, John
Switzer, Jacob
Sheets, Christian
Walter, Henry
Wilson, William

Privates.
Babb, Peter
Hahn, Andrew
Morbet, Charles
Pense, Gainer
Ramsey, Charles
Stephens, Peter
Thomas, Michael
Welker, George
Willington, Morgan

Pages 373-374. Vol. 2.

ROLL OF CAPT. WILLIAM ALBAN'S COMPANY. (County Unknown.)

Served from March 12, until September 12, 1814.

Rank and Name of Soldier.	Rank and Name of Soldier.	Rank and Name of Soldier.
Capt. William Alban	Lieut. William Withrow	Ensign, Solomon Gladden
Sergt. Thomas Bolin	Sergt. Thomas B. Roe	Sergt. Joseph Brown
Sergt. William Reed	Corp. George Betz	Corp. John Glenn
Corp. George Shultz	Corp. James Morrison	
Privates.	**Privates.**	**Privates.**
Andrews, Daniel	Anspaugh, Leonard	Brown, William
Bell, Adam	Barr, Samuel	Bruk, Moses
Burgess, Joseph	Barnhill, Samuel	Cole, Ezekial
Cole, Elijah	Caruthers, James	Duke, William
Doman, Jacob	Erick, George	Elliott, Thomas
Fisher, Brice	Frank, John	Freet, George
Farbar, Philip	Gibson, George	Gooden, Abednego
Galbraith, James	Groog, John	Hardenbrooks, Samuel
Hoft, Jacob	Jolly, William	Kyle, Samuel
Miller, John	Metcalf, Mepon	Miller, Phillip
Minay, Patrick	Marshall, William	Martin, James
McCullough, Daniel	Newstetler, Henry	Otis, Ezekial
Patterson, Richard	Patterson, William	Riddle, Samuel
Spangley, Michael	Spielle, John	Shoop, David
Smith, Michael	Stone, Jesse	Swigar, John
Smallwood, Richard	Smith, John	Sullivan, Henry
Taylor, Valentine	Tipton, Luke	Van Horn, Peter
White, Joseph	Wright, Richard	Zimmerman, David

Page 379.

ROLL OF CAPT. THOMAS LEWIS' COMPANY.
(Probably from Adams County.)

Served from July 28, until September 1, 1813.

Capt. Thomas Lewis	Lieut. Samuel Bradford	Ensign, George Sample
Cornet, Isaac Foster	Sergt. Nathan Rogers	Sergt. William Stout
	Sergt. Jacob Shults	
Privates.	**Privates.**	**Privates.**
Baigs, Thomas	Badridge, Samuel	Brigintine, John
Bratton, Jacob	Collins, Elijah	Carr, Daniel
Hanna, William	Little, Thomas	Lockhart, Samuel
Moore, John	Milligin, James	Moore, Aaron
Markland, Jesse	McDermott, John	McHenry, Alexander
McMilligan, J. D.	Paull, James	Pennington, Obediah
Raulston, Robert	Rowland, William	Russell, John, Sr.
Stockard, Thomas	Sanders, Francis	Warner, Peter
	Williamson, Samuel	

Page 380.

ROLL OF LIEUT. JAMES BLACK'S COMPANY. (County Unknown.)

Served from April 15, until October 14, 1813.

Lieut. James Black	Ensign, John T. Ireland	Sergt. John Demoss
Sergt. James Quinn	Corp. William Bennet	Corp. Jabez Bennet
Privates.	**Privates.**	**Privates.**
Banfill, Thomas	Baker, Lewis	Biers, Isaac
Boyd, James	Beasley, Thomas	Cooper, Samuel
Collins, John	Caro, David	DeMoss, William
Davis, William	Fall, Daniel	Gamble, Samuel
Gordon, Charles	Gordon, James	Hoag, Ensebius
Ireland, Samuel	Jones, William	Landers, Daniel
Milner, William	Martin, William	Nickum, Davis
Pilson, Hugh	Pemberton, Joseph	Riley, John
Ringer, Jacob	Scott, Thomas	Shanks, Jacob
Sallee, Samuel	Street, John	Timmons, George
Wilkinson, Charles	Wilson, John	

Page 1. Vol. 1.

SECOND REGIMENT—FIELD, STAFF AND COMPANIES.
ROLL OF FIELD AND STAFF, WAR OF 1812-1813.
COLONEL JAMES STEWART, THIRD REGIMENT, OHIO MILITIA.

Col. James Stewart	Major, Samuel Waddle	Adjt. Joseph Parrott
Q. M., George Allen	Surg. Samuel Baldridge	Surg. Mate, James B. Webster
Pay Master, Wade Loosborough	Q. M. Sergt. Thomas Clark	Sergt. Major, James Carr
Fife Major, Jacob Bushong	Drum Major, Benjamin Davis	

Page. 2. Vol. I.
COL. CHARLES MILLER, THIRD REGIMENT, DRAFTED OHIO MILITIA.

Rank and Name of Soldier.	Rank and Name of Soldier.	Rank and Name of Soldier.
Col. Charles Miller	Major, Abraham Shane	Major, Solomon Bentley
Adjt. Peter Bryans	Q. M. William Marshall	Q. M. Sergt. E. L. Bonham
Q. M., Samuel Taylor	Sergt. Maj., James E. Wells	Surg. James Wilson
Ass't. Surg. Royal N. Powers	Q. M. Sergt., Jacob Clark	

Pages 3-241-440.
COLONEL WILLIAM RAYEN, THIRD REGIMENT, OHIO MILITIA.

Col. William Rayen	Major, George Darrow	Maj. W. W. Colgreave
Maj. Peter Muster	Adjt. James Mackey	Q. M., Arad Way
Pay Master, John E. Woodbridge	Surg. Henry Manning	Surg. Mate, James Hillman
Sergt. Maj., William Ingersol	Sergt. Maj. Stephen Miller	Q. M. Sergt. Lewis Hoyt
Q. M. Sergt. John Srain	Drum Major, William W. Wright	Fife Major, Aaron Collar

Page 4.
COLONEL ROBERT BAY, THIRD REGIMENT, OHIO MILITIA.

Col. Robert Bay	Maj. Peter Cribs	Maj. Thomas Knowls
Surg. Christian Espich	Surg. Mate, Jacob Espich	Q. M., James Cleud
Pay Master, Christian Deardorf	Adjt., Lloyd Talbert	For. M., Henry Laffer

Page 5.
ROLL OF CAPT. CYRUS BEATTY'S COMPANY.
(From Guernsey County.)
Served from October 23, 1812, until February 22, 1813.

Capt. Cyrus Beatty	Lieut. David Burt	Ensign, Nicholas Stoner
Sergt. William Martain	Sergt. Joseph Pollock	Sergt. Samuel Beymer
Sergt. William Van Horn	Corp. John Meek	Corp. Isaac Stiers
Corp. Andrew Anderson	Corp. Elijah Williams	Drummer, Jacob Wirick

Privates.

Addy, Lold	Anderson, William	Conner, John
Cochran, William	Feticuck, Michael	Gibson, William
Hutchins, David	Havens, James	Henderson, John
Johnston, George	Johnston, John	Kirkpatrick, Alexander
Loury, Robert	Meek, Samuel	Martain, John S.
McKee, John	Nance, Samuel C.	Ogle, George
Reasoner, Ganett	Ross, Daniel	Reamey, Robert
Reasoner, William	Reynolds, Joseph	Stiers, Samuel
Shivel, George	Shipley, James	Shipley, John
Shatto, Nicholas	Sparr, James M.	Stanley, Joseph
Turner, William	Talbot, William	Tolbat, Nathaniel
Ward, Joseph	Work, Samuel	Wirick, Michael
Waddle, James	White, Thomas	

Page 6.
ROLL OF CAPT. JAMES WIMP'S COMPANY. (County Unknown.)
Served from September 20, 1812, until February 20, 1813.

Capt. James Wimp	Lieut. James Parker	Ensign, Thomas Rodgers
Sergt. George Hammet	Sergt. Eli Watts	Serjt. George Moore
Sergt. Daniel Swackhamnar	Corp. Robert Frost	Corp. William Richardson
Corp. David Scott	Corp. Henry Weller	

Privates.

Bare, George	Crooks, Anthony	Condron, William
Collins, John	Dill, Solomon	Foraker, Joshua
Gates, Wilson L.	Lefler, John	McBride, Isaac
McElhiney, Patrick	Moore, William	Paret, Allen
Rose, Robert	Rombo, Tobias	Stover, David
Stinson, John	Peargrin, John	Wiseman, Michael
Walls, Benjamin	Wilson, William	

Page 7.
ROLL OF CAPT. ABSALOM MARTIN'S COMPANY.
(From Guernsey or Belmont County.)
Served from August 26, until November 12, 1812.

Capt. Absalom Martin	Lieut. Wyatt Hutchison	Ensign, James Shuman
Sergt. John Broton	Sergt. George Scadan	Sergt. Thomas Mullen
Sergt. William Israel	Corp. Christopher Donouer	Corp. James Edwards
Corp. Edward Davis	Corp. Henry Wolford	Drummer, Thomas DeBatnon
	Fifer, Edward Milner	

Privates.	**Privates.**	**Privates.**
Atkinson, Michael	Brown, David	Bowers, Jonah
Burys, David	Berry, Thomas	Beard, Thomas
Bowers, Joseph	Bell, Joseph	Beard, Moses
Carnes, William	Cogle, Joseph	Carroll, Henry

ROLL OF CAPT. ABSALOM MARTIN'S COMPANY. (Continued)

Privates.

Davis, Henry
Fink, William
Hill, Henry
Launtz, George
Moore, William
McGiffin, William
Pack, Samuel
Reeves, Joshua
Shipley, George
Tetrick, Michael
Warne, Jonothan
Woodbick, John

Delong, Darel
Hart, Jacob
Heage, Aaron
Miller, James
Maple, William
McGiffin, John
Reed, John
Shove, Philip
Salor, John
Tetrick, Richard
Wirick, Andrew
Wanich, Robert
Wirack, Peter

Everett, James
Hanna, William
Lambert, Lewis
Mealman, John
Merrit, Thomas
McWilliams, Phillip
Reed, William
Stites, Jonothan
Tetrick, Jacob
Wilson, David
Wilkins, Thomas
Wanich, James

Page 8.

ROLL OF CAPT. SIMON BEYNER'S COMPANY.
(From Guernsey County.)
Served from August 20, until November 12, 1812.

Capt. Simon Beyner
Sergt. David Slater
Sergt. Robert Ewings
Corp. William Inglehag

Lieut. Stewart Speer
Sergt. George Wine
Corp. Nicholas Bumgavance
Corp. Alexander Barton
Fifer, David Moor

Ensign, Henry Beyner
Sergt. Andrew Dougherty
Corp. William Beyner
Drummer, Frederick Beyner

Privates.

Argo, Morris
Brannan, Thomas
Bates, Ezekial
Clark, Joshua
Dilly, Abraham
Findlay, Collins
Llewellyn, Henry
Larde, James
McConnell, James
Shevel, Samuel
Saterfield, William
Smith, William
Sherman, William
Vanpell, John

Beach, Charles
Barnes, Ford
Chance, William
Doughty, David
Dye, George
Frye, Peter
Lynn, Joseph
Lancing, Robert
Rainey, John
Stephenson, Moses
Smith, Thomas
Sickman, Andrew
Sickman, Pressley
Wright, Moses

Beaham, John
Bates, William
Cook, William
Dilly, Ichabod
Evans, Elisha
Hawkins, James
Levi, Lewis
McGowan, Andrew
Reed, Joseph
Saltsgiver, Frederick
Sickman, John
Stiers, Henry
Thomas, Jacob
William, Nehemiah

Page 9.

ROLL OF CAPT. LEVI ROSE'S COMPANY. (County Unknown.)
Served from June 1, 1812, until June 1, 1813.

Lieut. Sylvanus Mitchell
Sergt. Orin Granger
Corp. Asa B. Gavit
Musician, Justin Thillyer

Capt. Levi Rose
Sergt. John Rees
Corp. Knowles Linnel
Musician, Thomas Spillman

Ensign, Eleazar C. Clemens
Sergt. Timothy Spillman
Corp. Lester Case

Privates.

Alexander, James
Butler, Levent
Clark, Arunna
Ford, Thomas
Gibbons, William B.
Johnston, Hezekiah
Linnell, Benjamin
Martin, John
Owens, Owen
Rees, Theophilus
Spillman, Spencer
Thrall, Colton M.

Avery, George
Clemens, Harry
Cooley, Festus
Gilman, Elias
Gavit, Benjamin F.
Kelley, John
Messenger, David
Messenger, Campbell
Pratt, Calvin
Rose, Ormon
Thompson, William
Thrall, Alexander

Brown, Mahalon
Clark, Rowley
Fox, Elijah
Graves, Clodius L.
Hoskins, Titus S.
Kelley, Hugh
Meed, Seth
Murdock, Dan
Rathbone, Elijah
Shephard, James
Thompson, David
Wells, Joel

Pages 10-11.

ROLL OF CAPT. JOSEPH CAIRNS' COMPANY. (County Unknown.)
Served from December 12, 1812, until April 12, 1813.

Capt. Joseph Cairns
Sergt. Henry Ferris
Sergt. William Smith
Corp. John G. Pigman

Lieut. Isaac VanHorn
Sergt. James Nixon
Corp. Matthias Hollinback
Corp. Richard Cairns
Fifer, Ira Cass

Ensign, John Eason
Sergt. James M. Wood
Corp. Samuel Johnston
Drummer, Henry Blake

Privates.

Armstrong, James
Blunt, James
Blake, Nehemiah
Cacheart, William

Blake, John
Bland, William
Colly, Benjamin
Craig, William

Bland, Thomas
Barren, William
Corberry, James
Coats, John

ROLL OF CAPT. JOSEPH CAIRNS' COMPANY. (Continued)

Rank and Name of Soldier.
Privates.
Cantwell, James
Dennis, Samuel
Fickle, George W.
Futhey, Isaac
Hau, Isaiah
Hare, Joseph
Leckey, Arthur
Lane, Walter
Marshall, Thomas
Moore, Robert
McDonald, Stephen
Pettitt, Joseph
Piatt, Robert
Smith, Alexander
Seabring, Robert
Upp, Francis
Usher, Lloyd
Warson, James

Rank and Name of Soldier.
Privates.
Cares, John
Dowell, John
Fickle, Michael
Groves, Solomon
Harris, George
Johnston, James
Loare, John
Lackey, Hugh
Moore, Petter
McFadden, Neal
McConley, Thomas
Piatt, Stephen
Harvey, Petter
Sutton, Joseph
Shadley, Henry
Verdin, Leary S.
Williams, Littleton
Winner, John

Rank and Name of Soldier.
Privates.
Darrill, Thomas B.
Eddington, Robert
Frey, Isaac
Gilkerson, Jonothan
Hartley, Thomas
Jeffries, James
Lawson, Septemus
Monroe, John
Moore, Thomas
McNeal, Alexander
Parker, Benjamin
Pierce, William
Richards, Jacob
Sherrard, David
Smith, Benjamin
VanWinck, James
Welsh, Moses

Page 12.

ROLL OF CAPT. GEORGE SANDERSON'S COMPANY.
(Fairfield County.)

Served from April 13, 1812, for one year.

Capt. George Sanderson
Sergt. John VanMetre
Sergt. James Larimer
Corp. James White

Lieut. David McCabe
Sergt. John Smith
Corp. Robert Cunningham
Corp. William Wallace

Ensign, Isaac Larrimer
Sergt. Isaac Painter or Winter
Corp. Daniel Hutson or Hudson
Corp. Daniel Huston

Privates.
Baker, Daniel
Coborn, Joseph
Davis, John
Tuchbone, Isaac
Hawwrick, John
Hines, Phillip
Johnston, Jacob
Johnson, Samuel
Mellow, Jacob
Menteenth or Monteith, Jacob
Miller, Daniel
McClung, Lare
Nolan, Samuel
Pyatt, David
Ray, John
Swiler, John
Switer, John
Oborn, Joseph

Privates.
Baker, George
Dagen or Dugan, John
Darnel, Archibald
Falkbone, Jesse
Hiles, Christopher
Huffman, John
Hardy, Thomas
Jenkins, William
Kirby or Kerley, John
Martin, Charles
Martin, Henry
McDonald, William
McClung, William
Nelson, William
Larimer, Robert
Ray, William
Shrimp, George
Smith, David or Daniel
Wright, Spencer
Work, Samuel

Privates.
Collins, John
Darnell, Archibald
Edmind or Edmonds, William
Fitzpatrick, Rees
Highman, John
Hiles, John
Harshman, John
Jenkinson, William
Laefland or Loffland, Joseph
Miller, James
Monteith, Jonas
McIntire, John
Nelson, John
Post, Cornelius
Binbeck or Brubeck, William
Sharp, Henry or Jacob
Short, Thomas
Turly, John
Whitsen or Whetson, Joseph

Page 13.

ROLL OF CAPT. THOMAS COLLIER'S COMPANY.
(Probably from Adams County.)

Served from July 28, until August 21, 1813.

Lieut. Thomas Collier

Sergt. Matthew Jones
Corp. James Killing

Sergt. William Green

Privates.
Anderson, Nathaniel
Collier, Daniel
Daniels, Joseph
McCormick, James
Stuce, Jacob
Thompson, James

Privates.
Black, Zechariah
Chambers, Elijah
Freeland, Jesse
Osmun, John
Shoup, Henry
Wilcoxen, John

Privates.
Burkitt, William
Davis, John
Helterbrand, Daniel
Peterson, Thomas
Trotter, Elijah
Weaver, George

Page 14.

ROLL OF CAPT. JOHN SHARP'S COMPANY.
(Probably from Washington County.)

Served from May 23, 1812, until ---- -.

Capt. John Sharp
Sergt. John H. Simons
Sergt. Otis Reckard
Corp. David Miskgimens

Lieut. William Sawyer
Sergt. Thomas Green
Corp. Joseph Knox
Corp. James Elwell

Ensign, Jacob Trobridge
Sergt. Chester Wilson
Corp. William S. Crain
Musician, Christian B. Smith

ROLL OF CAPT. JOHN SHARP'S COMPANY. (Continued)

Rank and Name of Soldier.
Privates.
Anderson, William
Browning, Balzilla
Bancroft, Samuel
Downing, James
Fox, Joseph
Kelley, Ezra
Langdon, Phillip
McMullen, Samuel
Nixon, Samuel
Skinner, John
Ward, John

Page 15.

Rank and Name of Soldier.
Privates.
Benedick, Alvin
Black, John
Clark, Joseph
Ellis, Hanis
Goldsmith, William
Lynch, William
Mull, Samuel
Nicklow, Jacob
Robertson, John T.
Rogers, Joseph
Williams, David

Rank and Name of Soldier.
Privates.
Beers, Benjamin
Badgly, Benjamin
Dunkin, William
Frazer, Louis
Geary, James
Lyon, Abraham
Murphy, Samuel
Nevels, Jacob
Shingler, John
Tuttle, Jabez
Wall, James

ROLL OF CAPT. JOHN F. MANSFIELD'S COMPANY.
(Probably from Hamilton County.)
Served from May 2, until September 15, 1812.

Capt. John F. Mansfield

Lieut. Stephen McFarland
Sergt. James Chambers

Ensign, Thomas Heckweler

Privates.
Armstrong, John
Cameron, William A.
Englis, Samuel
Gibson, James
Hafrer, Henry
Hatch, William S.
Lawrence, John
Marshall, William
McQuelkin, Samuel
Stephens, Henry
Smith, James
Stephens Blackall
Williamson, John

Pages 16-17.

Privates.
Byers, Israel
Cameron, Robert A.
Everly, Michael
Goodspeed, Gideon
Howell, Stephen
Kautz, Jacob
Madden, Samuel
Moody, Nathaniel
Platt, John H.
Sayre, Elias
Sloo, Thomas, Jr.
Thompson, Erasmus K.
Wallace, Robert
Waring, Henry

Privates.
Crone, John
Ennis, John B.
Gillaspey, Robert
Heighway, John
Harburt, Asher
Lawrence, Thomas
Mann, Isaac
Minshall, Jacob
Rutter, George
Sliezeman, John
Smith, Elias P.
Williams, James
Wade, David

ROLL OF CAPT. BENJAMIN SCHOOLER'S COMPANY.
(Probably from Champaign County.)
Served from February 21, until March 21, 1813.

Capt. Benjamin Schooler
Sergt. Solomon McCulloh
Sergt. Nicholas Stilwell
Corp. William Tinnis

Lieut. John Tulbe
Sergt. Andrew Moore
Corp. Silas McCulloh
Corp. Layton Pollock

Ensign, George McCullough
Sergt. Thomas Dickinson
Corp. Jacob Slagle

Privates.
Asksen, David
Coddington, William
Davis, Turner
Easley, Thomas
Hatfield, Samuel
Moore, George
Moots, Conrad
McDaniel, John
Provolt, John
Shaw, Henry
Schooler, Charles
Terrel, Mathew
Wallace, John

Page 18.

Privates.
Black, Samuel
Dickinson, Joseph
Daniel, Thomas
Henry, James
Jenkins, Jesse
Moore, John
Maggard, Moses
McLane, Charles
Robinson, Samuel
Shaw, James
Tidd, Samuel
Tong, Thomas
Wilkinson, Ashael

Privates.
Cain, Joshua
Dowden, William
Hill, James
Robinson, Thomas
Lewis, Benjamin
Moore, William
Makenson, John
Burdett, Booth
Rutherford, Evan
Schooler, William
Taylor, Henry
Wolverton, Daniel
Zane, Isaac

ROLL OF CAPT. JAMES BROWN'S COMPANY. (County Unknown.)
Served from October 20, 1812, until February 20, 1813

Capt. James Brown
Sergt. Thomas Sells
Sergt. Joseph Hawkins
Corp. William Fuller

Lieut. Amasa Davis
Sergt. Isaac Minshall
Corp. Mathias Spangler
Corp. Samuel Janings

Ensign, Peter Bryan
Sergt. Lewis Steenrod
Corp. Peter Waterson

Privates.
Bane, Daniel
Chilbey, Moses
Chilby, James
Fulk, Joshua
Hammond, Zoeth
Lewis, William
Marshall, Simon
McKee, Thomas
Parker, George
Rainey, John
Parkinson, John
Taylor, Thomas
White, Benjamin

Privates.
Bronkar, Louis
Crawford, Joseph
Cummins, John
Gormor, John
Ingalls, Abraham
Linn, Joseph
Montoney, Isaac
Newton, William
Poke, William
Resener, Benjamin
Swank, George
Cummins, Samuel
Wright, Robert D.

Privates.
Bowman, Daniels
Curtis, Joshua
Dains, Jacob
Hughes, William
Jay, George
Lemon, Stephen
McCulley, Patrick
Owens, Thomas
Pierce, Jonothan
Ross, William
Sawyer, George
Workman, Benjamin

ROSTER OF OHIO SOLDIERS IN WAR OF 1812 73

Page 19. Vol. I.
ROLL OF CAPT. JOSEPH SUTTON'S COMPANY. (County Unknown.)
Served from September 30, 1812, until March 30, 1813.

Rank and Name of Soldier.
Capt. Joseph Sutton
Sergt. John C. Holden
Sergt. David Moore
Corp. Eli Brady

Privates.
Alexander, Henry
Beem, Richard
Conner, Joseph
Carrol, George
Edgol, William
Hull, Samuel
Oakwood, Daniel
Johnston, Robert
Miers, Solomon
McDaniel, William
Moore, Moses
Patter, John
Statloe, John
Wilson, Hyatte

Rank and Name of Soldier.
Lieut. Wilson Holden
Sergt. Thomas Barry
Corp. Mathias Kliever
Corp. Jeremiah Bartholomew

Privates.
Bartholomew, Stephen
Barnes, John
Carson, Benjamin
Damans, Thomas
Fisher, Levin
Herron, Samuel
Hull, George
Livingston, George
Morris, John
McElvey, Samuel
Neff, George
Patter, Hira
Stewart, James
Wilson, Jeremiah

Rank and Name of Soldier.
Ensign, Henry Kliever
Sergt. Jacob Bickell
Corp. Hazle Green

Privates.
Bonham, Elisha L.
Craft, Ridgeway
Conner, John
DeWees, Samuel
Horsey, Henry
Harris, William
Hull, Benjamin
Lianburger, Peter
Motherspaw, Daniel
McCalla, Andrew
Parr, Richard
Rouson, Jonothan
Stotts, Jacob
Wilson, Abraham C.

Page 20.
ROLL OF CAPT. ISAAC EVANS' COMPANY.
(Probably from Coshocton County.)
Served from October 18, 1812, until February 17, 1813.

Capt. Isaac Evans
Sergt. Richard Johnson
Sergt. Thomas Hunt
Corp. Peter Carr

Privates.
Ammon, Jacob
Biggs, James
Cornelius, Isaac
Dorn, Cornelius
Helms, Nicholas
Hahn, George
Adams, Littleton
Nowels, Moses
Snyder, Joseph
Sherard, William
Thompson, Smallwood
Ward, Lewis

Lieut. Joshua Lemert
Sergt. Samuel Gillum
Corp. Barney Cantwell
Waggoner, William Carr

Privates.
Butler, James
Blew, Daniel
Chalney, Samuel
Freeman, Henry
Horton, David
Irven, James
McLane, John
Rickner, Henry
Shotwell, William
Shadley, Daniel
Thompson, Archibald
Ward, Thomas

Ensign, Eli Shryock
Sergt. Silas Smith
Corp. Nathan Devore

Privates.
Baker, Rezin
Cox, Thomas
Cass, John
Gross, John
Hollenback, George
Jeffries, Thomas
McGee, James
Reed, James
Sell, David
Shurtz, George
Parker, Joshua

Page 21.
ROLL OF CAPT. (Jesse or JOHN D. COURTRIGHT'S COMPANY.
(From Fairfield County.)
Served from September 27, 1812, until February 26, 1813,. Part served from October 22, 1812.

Capt. John D. Courtright
Sergt. David Egbert
Sergt. Thomas Pullen
Corp. Pressley Priest

Privates.
Allen, Samuel
Buzzard, David
Buzzard, George
Chaina, John
Gessele, Jacob
Kirk, George Jr.
Long, William
Missmore, John
Proudfoot, John
Doult, James
Silvers, William
Torrance, John
White, William

Lieut. John List
Sergt. Peter Hartsock
Corp. John Smother
Corp. Daniel Escol

Privates.
Bochard, Jacob
Boyles, Thomas
Bradley, John
Chestnut, Elisha
Howitt, Richard
Linback, George
Marshall, John
Paier, John
Punchos, Peter
Shoup, Jacob
Stripes, William
Winterslam, Nicholas
Welshhous, Jacob
Wright, Jeremiah

Ensign, John Glick
Sergt. Isaac Hardin
Corp. John Foust
Fifer, Isaac Stephens

Privates.
Buzzard, William
Burke, Jacob
Carlisle, Bazil
Glick, Solomon
Kirk, George Sr.
Lutz, John
Moore, Peter
Plotner, Daniel
Russell, Jacob
Shawhan, Thomas
Steel, Lemuel
Waite, George
Willits, Elias

Page 22.
ROLL OF CAPT. JOSEPH JOHNSON'S COMPANY. (County Unknown.)
Served from October 18, 1812, until February 18, 1813.

Capt. Joseph Johnson
Sergt. George Gibson
Sergt. James O'Donald
Corp. Jacob Kline

Lieut. John Gard
Sergt. William Henderson
Corp. Jacob Blotzley
Corp. Jesse Foster

Ensign, George Sluthower
Sergt. Lemuel Johnson
Corp. William Hogland
Fifer, David Waggoner

ROLL OF CAPT. JOSEPH JOHNSON'S COMPANY. (Continued)

Rank and Name of Soldier.
Privates.
Armstrong, James
Beymer, John
Baker, George
Cummins, William
Forman, Jacob
Green, Thomas
Hill, William
Griffin, Johnson
Lacey, Thomas S.
Lafferty, Edward
Ray, John
Vanamon, Edward
Weaver, Frederick

Rank and Name of Soldier.
Privates.
Burroughs, John
Bell, Robert
Carson, Samuel
Doty, Arthur
Gibbs, James
Guesbach, Henry
Haversback, Conrad
Johnson, John
Lanman, John
Miller, Jacob
Runk, Michael
Vanande, Aaron
Williams, Thomas

Rank and Name of Soldier.
Privates.
Burroughs, Samuel
Boltzley, John
Carson, John
Eakin, David
Gibbs, William
Hand, Cornelius
Jones, Elijah
Kale, George
Lamb, Lawrence
McGarvey, Alexander
Sodours, Frederick
Williams, Levi
Williams, Benjamin

Page 23.

ROLL OF CAPT. JOSEPH KIRKWOOD'S COMPANY.

Served from October 22, 1812, until February 22, 1813. Part served from December 1, 1812.

Capt. Solomon Bentley
Ensign, Joseph Grimes
Sergt. Hugh Brown
Corp. David Dille
Corp. Israel Day

Capt. Joseph Kirkwood
Sergt. James Kyle
Sergt. John Boyd
Corp. Dennis Forest
Drummer, Evan Rogers

Lieut. George Love
Sergt. Samuel Nixon
Sergt. William McCoy
Corp. Joseph Rankin

Privates.
Duddle, Caleb
Didzler, John
Brill, Michael
Campbell, Dougal
Cluny, Alexander
Fryman, George
Gilliland, Morgan
Grimes, John
Haniman, David
Kyzor, Thomas
Long, Michael
Meek, Samuel
McMahan, Dennis
Russell, John
Shepherd, Isaiah
Tarrier, John
Watson, Robert

Privates.
Dallas, John
Devore, John
Dark, James
Coss, Abraham
Carrington, Nicholas
Gaston, John
Gilliland, Thomas
Herd, William
Irwin, George
Keen, Henry
Lashley, Hezekiah
Marquis, William
Robinson, John
Starr, James
Shannon, John
Thompson, John
Wright, Coleman S.

Privates.
Dillon, Samuel
Davis, Jacob
Coles, Jeremiah
Carpenter, John
Erskine, Thomas
Goosehorn, Leonard
Graham, Thomas
Howell, William
Jaques, John
Long, Adam

Masters, Richard
Ryder, Obed
Shepherd, Arnold
Sturgeon, Reuben
Tuttle, James
Vandine, George

Page 24.

ROLL OF CAPT. CALVIN SHEPARD'S COMPANY. (County Unknown.)

Served from August 9, until October 9, 1812.

Capt. Calvin Shepherd
Sergt. Nathan Newson
Sergt. Joseph Vandenbenen
Corp. David S. Grayum

Lieut. John Roadarmour
Sergt. John Gibson
Corp. Joseph Ganyum
Corp. Solomon Haywood
Fifer, John Rutherford

Ensign, John Boston
Sergt. John Phillips
Corp. Charles Budenot
Drummer, Moses Everett

Privates.
Aleshire, John
Amen, David
Berry, Malachier
Bellar, Elias
Cavin, William
Domly, John
Clifford, John
Entringer, David
Fulton, John
Hubbell, Roland
Graham, Gabriel
Mathews, Thomas
Mannay, James
Martin, James
Ross, Joseph W.
Shaw, John
Sweett, John

Privates.
Aleshire, William
Aleshire, Ephraim
Bailey, Robert
Bray, William
Clark, Samuel
Donaldson, Ebenezer
Durst, Joseph
Ellison, John
Gardner, Joshua
Hill, Jesso
Killen, James
Miller, Martin
McMillin, Joseph
Odell, Isaac
Robinson, Ephraim
Smith, John
Yates, Jacob

Privates.
Atkinson, Wiley
Browbaker, David
Bailey, John
Chitwood, James
Donnolly, Andrew
Denny, William
Entringer, John
Ellison, Joseph
Hubbell, Jesse
Hipkins, Benjamin
Littleton, William
Moreton, John
McCarty, George
Patton, Mathew
Rutherford, Evans
Smith, Constantine
Wadkins, Johnson V.

Page 25.

ROLL OF CAPT. ZADOC MARKLAND'S COMPANY
(Probably from Adams County.)

Served from July 28, until August 28, 1813.

Capt. Zadoc Markland
Corp. Andrew Ellison
Drummer, Charles Olden

Lieut. Thomas Lytle
Sergt. Allen Pucket

Corp. Samuel Naylor
Corp. John Baldwin

ROLL OF CAPT. ZADAC MARKLAND'S COMPANY. (Continued)

Rank and Name of Soldier.

Privates.
Barrett, John
Eastburn, Jesse
Miller, William
Pennecolt, Reuben
Thatcher, Charles

Page 26.

Rank and Name of Soldier.

Privates.
Copaz, Isaiah
John, Thomas
Myers, Abraham
Raider, George
Wasley, Jonothan

Rank and Name of Soldier.

Privates.
Casperson, Tobias
Lovejoy, David
Mellow, Henry
Sutterfield, David
Wood, John

ROLL O F CAPT. PETER WIKOFF'S COMPANY.
(Probably from Adams County.)

Served from July 28, until August 21, 1813.

Capt. Peter Wikoff

Privates.
Antis, John
Cain, Jesse
Moore, John
Smolly, David

Pages 27-76.

Sergt. James Wikoff

Privates.
Boldman, James
Dillion, Isaac
Newman, James
Williams, William

Corp. Lavan Robinston

Privates.
Baker, John
Jones, Andrew
Stephenson, Charles
Young, David

ROLL OF CAPT. EDMUND WADE'S COMPANY. (County Unknown.)

Served from July 28, until August 28, 1813.

Capt. Edmund Wade
Sergt. John Frazier
Corp. Daniel Smith

Privates.
Acton, William
Baldridge, James
Cavin, John
Edgerton, Joshua
Gutridge, Charles
Harper, George
Kirkpatrick, James
Montgomery, Andrew
Maddox, William
McCayne, Thomas
McClenahan, John
McRight, James
Page, David
Roush, John
Tucker, Elwin
Wade, Joseph

Sergt. James Baldwin
Sergt. James Cole
Corp. Robert January

Privates.
Burnes, James
Baird, Robinson
Depue, John
Edginton, Joseph
Glasgow, William
Hayslip, John
Lawrence, Jacob
Montgomery, John
McCormick, Adam
McFadden, Moses
McCulloch, Alexander
McClennahan, John
Patton, Thomas
Shepherd, John
Thompson, James
Wheatley, Walter
Waldron, John

Sergt. Arthur McFarland
Corp. Mathew Campbell

Privates.
Bails, Jemcil
Connell, John R.
Ellison, Robert
Elliott, Robert Sr.
Glasgow, Joseph
Johnston, Elisha
Milligin, William
Mahaffey, John
McLaughlin, John
McCague, William
McClelland, Thomas
Nouelman, Richard
Roe, George
Smiley, James
VanPelt, John
Waldron, Henry

Pages 28-29-436-437-438.

ROLL OF CAPT. CONRAD FLESHER'S COMPANY.
(Probably from Ross County.)

Served from July 28, until September 5, 1813, and from March 12, until April 16, 1814.

Capt. Conrad Flesher
Ensign, John L. Corn
Sergt. Henry Rogers
Sergt. William Hankins
Sergt. Nicholas Young
Corp. Martin Hire
Corp. John Haselton
Corp. William Borland
Musician, Elijah Johnston

Privates.
Ayres, Richard
Blue, Peter
Briant, George
Blair, Thomas
Ballinger, Joseph
Correy, John
Cunningham, Thomas
Cochran, Abraham
Dines, William
Dungelbarger, Frederick
Everett, Samuel
Fennymore, Joseph
Gooley, Jacob
Hinkle, David
Hopkins, James
Hurst, James

Lieut. James Crusan
Ensign, Reuben Pursell
Sergt. Peter Harper
Sergt. Robert Hoddy
Sergt. John Williams
Corp. John Nuland
Corp. Sylvester Root
Fifer, Henry Bevington
Musician, Samuel H. Timmons

Privates.
Anderson, John
Brown, Jacob
Brooks, James
Blue, Jacob
Brant, John
Cain, Richard
Chill, Thomas
Chapman, David
Day, Basil
Decker, James
Eymon, Abraham
Featheringill, George
Goddard, Robert D.
Hill, William
Harper, Cochran
Holloway, Thomas

Lieut. Perceval Adams
Ensign. David Jones
Sergt. Thomas Moore
Sergt. James Carpenter
Corp. John Roebuck
Corp. Samuel Blair
Corp. Robert McElhiny
Drummer, Jeremiah Smith

Privates.
Brunhed, Joseph
Blue, John
Bush, Daniel
Brown, Thomas
Bennet, Darius
Collins, Absalom
Cochran, John
Dickinson, Jacob
Davis, Adam
DeWitt, Martin
Figgins, Edward
Gilbert, Thomas
Hurley, Henry
Hopkins, John
Haggard, William
Hover, George

ROLL OF CAPT. CONRAD FLESHER'S COMPANY (Continued.)

Rank and Name of Soldier.	Rank and Name of Soldier.	Rank and Name of Soldier.
Privates.	**Privates.**	**Privates.**
Humphrey, Lemuel	Hoskins, William	James, Dawson R.
Jones, Amos	Jones, William	King, Isaac
Kerr, John	Kilgore, John	Knight, Orena
King, Charles	Lane, William	Lock, Jesse
Moore, Ezekial	Miller, Henry	Miller, Solomon
Michael, John	Moots, John	Myers, Jacob
Myers, John	Meanaugh, Hugh	Matheny, Nathan
McDonald, Thomas	McCafferty, James	McNeal, Archibald
McCan, Thomas	McGinnis, James	McCafferty, David
McKune, John	Newman, John	Neal, John P.
Olds, Benjamin	Orr, Joseph	Pool, William
Pew, Thomas	Rogers, John	Rosal, James
Roberts, Charles	Rogers, Peleg	Smith, John
Rose, Cornelius	Sidney, Stephen	Simpson, Thomas
Starr, Henry	Skinner, James	Stout, Peter
Stafford, Young	Scoby, William	Stagg, Michael
Sebern, Francis	Stratton, Charles	Smith, Amos
Southard, Hudson	Thompson, James	Timmons, Eli
Thomas, Joseph	Thompson, John	Tuttle, Erastus
Thompson, Edward	Tuller, Orson	Vestal, John
Timons, Henry	Vaughn, Seborn	Warren, Moses
Vaughn, James	Wood, Benjamin	Weeks, William
White, Christopher L.	Wilson, George	Winsett, Joseph
Williams, Amon	Windle, Abraham	Westfall, Joseph
Ward, John	Weeks, John	Wilcox, Edward

Page 30.

ROLL OF LIEUT. JAMES KINSEN'S COMPANY. (County Unknown.)

Served from July 27, until August 16, 1813.

Capt. James Kinsen	Ensign, Phillip Gossard	Sergt. John P. Neal
Sergt. John Hall	Sergt. Thomas Moore	Sergt. William Hawkins
Corp. Francis Waddle	Corp. James Blair	Corp. John Newland
Corp. Jacob Caylor	Musician, Jesse Arnold	
Privates.	**Privates.**	**Privates.**
Ayers, Richard	Burnet, Thomas	Brooks, James
Dunn, James	Downard, James	Foster, Thomas
Feaganz, Edward	Gilbert, Thomas	Hopkins, John
Hopkins, David	Hopkins, James	Jameson, Charles
Moore, Ezekial	Orr, Joseph	Pool, Edward
Rupard, George	Snider, Henry	Snider, Jacob
Thompson, Edward	Wright, David	Wright, John
	Workman, John	

Pages 31-32-33-34.

ROLL OF CAPT. CLARK PARKER'S COMPANY.
(Probably from Geauga County.)

Served from August 22, until October 2, 1812. Part served from December 1, until February 27, 1813.

Capt. Clark Parker	Lieut. Caleb G. Foges	Ensign, Caleb Baldwin
Sergt. William P. Scott	Sergt. Jared Nicholson	Sergt. Theodore Royes
Sergt. Jonothan Russell	Sergt. Stephen Worthington	Sergt. Jonothan Hill
Sergt. Moses Allen	Sergt. Stephen King	Corp. Charles H. Paine
Corp. Ephraim Morrison	Corp. Lewis Smith	Corp. Henry Fitch
Corp. Chester Dean	Drummer, Joseph Burke	Fifer, Avery Button
Privates.	**Privates.**	**Privates.**
Adams, Sebastion	Andrews, Amos	Arnes, Isaac
Abot, Josiah	Arthur, William	Archer, William
Bacon, Dexter	Barker, Samuel	Barker, William
Baker, Noah	Bates, Caleb	Bradby, Selah
Bradley, Gorner	Burdet, Rurand	Burgess, Robert
Buchanan, John	Calhoun, Amos	Chandler, David
Cranny, John	Chase, Daniel	Craw, Henry
Coleman, Jacob	Clapp, Orris	Carlton, Guy
Crocker, Frederick D.	Crossman, Abner	Crawford, William
Craft, Thomas	Crooks, James	Dunn, Elijah
Dillingham, John	Dustman, Jacob	Dennison, David
Eckman, James	Field, Wawing	Fight, Jacob
Fowler, Henry	Frank, Jacob	Gun, Christopher
Goldsmith, Jonothan	Granger, John	Granger, Samuel
Gunn, Elijah	Gilbert, Henry	Gilbert, Samuel
Hayes, Ebenezer	Harvey, Luther	Hooton, John
Hudson, Silas F.	Harper, John R.	Hayes, Seth
Hill, David	Herrington, John	Hamilton, Hugh
Harding, Jacob	Hoel, John	Iles, Jeremiah

Vol. I.
ROLL OF CAPT. CLARK PARKER'S COMPANY. (Continued.)

Rank and Name of Soldier.	Rank and Name of Soldier.	Rank and Name of Soldier.
Privates.	**Privates.**	**Privates.**
Johnson, William	Johnson, Samuel	Jones, Olive
John, Elliott	James, John	Jack, James
Knopp, Christian	Kinney, Manvah	Landon, Henry
Love, William	Leonard William	Love, Samuel
Morley, Isaac	Minor, Phil	Moore, Isaac
Maxum, John	Miller, Theodore	Marlatt, George
Moore, Henry S.	Murphy, John	McMillen, James
McCreary, William	McCombs, Thomas	McCreary, John
McMullin, Charles	McMullen, James	Newton, James
Norton, Simon	Nye, Ebenezer	Olds, Daniel
Olds, James	Pain, Franklin	Prentice, Robert
Parker, Henry	Parsons, Horace	Paris, John
Park, Solomon	Patterson, Richard	Parker, Calvin
Pratt, Harvey	Paxton, John	Peterman, Jacob
Potter, Samuel Y.	McCloud, Francis	Russell, Ralph
Rawlins, James	Rathbone, John	Rusage, James
Russell, Eliakim	Rumage, Thomas	Rose, Robert
Reed, William	Sebastian, Freeman F.	Spencer, Allen
Smith, William	Smith, Francis	Spencer, Allen Sr.
Simons, Adam	Stall, Andrew	Spargo, George
Sell, John	Townsley, John	Thomas, Levi
Turner, Samuel	Turner, Conrad	Moore, Henry T.
Thompson, William	Upton, Benjamin	VanNorman, Joseph
Webster, Elijah	Wood, Benjamin	Wright, Alexander
White, John	White, James	Young, John

Page 35.

ROLL OF CAPT. HORACE FLOWERS' COMPANY. (County Unknown.)

Served from August 24, until August 28, 1812.

Capt. Horace Flowers	Lieut. William Jones	Sergt. Philo Borden
Sergt. Daniel B. Rushnell	Corp. Lewis Bushnell	Corp. Liston Bushnell
Privates.	**Privates.**	**Privates.**
Andrews, Richard	Bates, Liman	Borden, Asahel Jr.
Brockway, Aaron	Bushnell, Alexander	Brockway, Philemon
Brockway, Jesse	Dugan, Thomas	Ellis, William
Fultz, Francis H.	Ganyard, Martin	Hull, John
Hull, George	Hull, John Jr.	Hayes, Listin
Jones, Seldin	Kepnoe, John	McFarland, Thomas
McFarland, Archibald	Phonts, John	Quigle, Michael
Shull, Frederick	Stilwell, Jeremiah	Thompson, Seth
	Woolford, Elijah	

Page 36.

ROLL OF CAPT. CLEMENT TRIFORD'S COMPANY.
(Probably from Fayette County.)

Served from July 26, until August 16, 1812.

Capt. Clement Triford	Lieut. Bazzel Cleavenger	Sergt. David Hayes
Sergt. John Cooper	Corp. John Grubb	Corp. Jacob Pallman
	Drummer, John P. Newman	
Privates.	**Privates.**	**Privates.**
Alexander, David	Blue, John	Blue, Peter
Blue, Jacob	Cradle, John	Compton, George
Gragg, George	Gragg, Reuben	Hayes, William
McDonald, Thomas	McArthur, John	Parker, Nathan
Pool, Thomas	Wilcox, Edward	

Pages 37-38-39-39½

ROLL OF CAPT. JOSHUA T. COTTON'S COMPANY.
(From Trumbull or Mahoning Counties.)

Served from August 26, until November 8, 1812.

Capt. Joshua T. Cotton	Lieut. George Monteith	Lieut. Edmond O. Fanner
Ensign Jacob Irwing	Sergt. John Cotton	Sergt. John Myer
Sergt. George Wintermate	Sergt. Abraham Wintermate	Corp. John Carlton
Corp. Boardman Robins	Corp. John Russell	Corp. George Ounsbury
	Fifer, Daniel Wick	
Privates.	**Privates.**	**Privates.**
Ague, Nathan	Andres, Samuel A.	Boyd, Andrew
Brunsteter, Henry	Bradford, Joel	Bradon, John
Blackman, Simion	Buchanan, Walter	Bradford, William
Brockway, Romant	Craft, Thomas	Crum, Samuel
Carter, Joseph	Calhoun, Samuel	Cummings, Thomas
Cawer, Seneca	Cowden, John	Cummings, Joseph
Curtin, Zenas	Demel, James	Duc, Jacob
Dillon, William	Fisher, Isaac	Foos, Henry

ROLL OF CAPT. JOSUA T. COTTON'S COMPANY. (Continued)

Rank and Name of Soldier.

Privates.

Fankle, William
Goodspeed, Nathaniel
Harvey, Francis
Hamilton, William
Kerr, Robert
Long, Robert
Leach, Abraham
Moore, Sampson
Morris, Archibald
McClellan, David
McMahon, Susan
Irwin, Thomas
Osborn, Joseph
Powers, Jacob
Peny, Levi
Ramage, James
Smith, Daniel
Shatts, Daniel
Veneman, Nicholas
Storm, Michael
Woolcut, Joseph
Whittersbey, Anthony

Rank and Name of Soldier.

Privates.

Gilbert, George
Hayes, John
Hull, Jacob
Henry, Peter
Luts, Daniel
Lyon, Isaac
Moor, John
Maxwell, Robert
Mann, Samuel
McCollom, John
McConnal, Richard
North, Samuel
Parkhurst, Isaac
Prudden, David
Phillip, Kimmel
Swager, Adam
Saxton, John
Smith, George
Stoke, Jacob
Walden, Jonothan
Winans, James
White, John
Zedechai, John

Rank and Name of Soldier.

Privates.

Guy, Mathew
Hover, Abraham
Higgins, Silas
Johnson, Anson
Lyons, John
Leonard, Nicholas
Moore, John, Sr.
Munns, William
McEnery, Thomas
McLaughlin, John
McCreery, William
Osborn, Conrad
Parkhurst, John
Poyens, John
Roll, Benjamin
Shields, William
Simons, Abraham
Steward, Daniel
Thorn, Henry
Wilson, John
White, Samuel
Young, John

Pages 40-41.

ROLL OF CAPT. ICHABOD PLUM'S COMPANY.
(Probably from Delaware County.)

Served from May 4, until May 27, 1813. Part served from July 26, until August 13, 1813.

Capt. Ichabold Plum
Sergt. Thomas Brown
Sergt. David Butler
Corp. Joseph Carrin
Corp. James Carpenter

Lieut. John Milligan
Sergt. Adison Carver
Corp. Joel Taylor
Corp. Gilbert Weeks
Musician, Sylvester Drake

Ensign John Brundage
Sergt. Benjamin Carpenter
Corp. Ezra Olds
Corp. Robert Carpenter

Privates.

Alden, Daniel
Bishop, Elisha
Foust, David
Hull, Nathaniel
Heath, Samuel
Keys, Isaac
Manvil, Eli
Landon, David
Olds, Comfort
Roth, Nathan
Slack, Ralph
Shoemaker, Benjamin
Wyatt, William

Privates.

Armstrong, David
Day, Charles
Fisher, George
Harper, James
Jones, Solomon
Kepler, Samuel
Moles, James
Osterhout, Gideon
Patterson, John
Ridgeway, William
Steward, Solomon
Trindle, James
Welit, Isaac

Privates.

Brown, Ezekiel
Foust, Henry
Gregory, David
Hatch, Nathaniel
Jones, Richard
Main, Eleazar
Munson, Michael
Olds, Benjamin
Patrick, Joseph
Sharp, William
Steudevant, George
Wilson, James

Page 42.

ROLL OF LIEUT. ADDISON GARVER'S COMPANY.
(Probably from Delaware County.)

Served from July 26, until August 13, 1813.

Lieut. Addison Garver

Ensign David Butler

Sergt. Joseph Steward

Privates.

John Leonard
Daniel J. Carpenter
Atkin, Russell
Carpenter, Henry
Helt, George
Longwell, Robert
Phipps, Jacob
Slack, John

Privates.

Crandell Rosecrans
Moses Carpenter
Adams, Johnson
Heaver, William C.
Lewis, John, Jr.
Lewis, Joseph
Rosecrans, John
Stark, James
Young, Andrew

Privates.

Benjamin Patrick
Mathias Nauloon
Carpenter, William
Helt, Michael
Lewis, Chester
Phipps, William
Slack, Ezekial
Taylor, Nathan

Pages 43-44.

ROLL OF CAPT. JOHN FOOS' COMPANY.
(Probably from Delaware County.)

Served from July 26, until August 18, 1813. Part served from September 1, until September 15, 1813.

Capt. John Foos
Sergt. John Davis
Sergt. Robert Perry
Corp. James Carpenter

Lieut. Thomas Driver
Sergt. William Baker
Sergt. Abraham Lookingbell

Ensign Benjamin Warren
Sergt. James Hopkins
Corp. David Shoup

ROLL OF CAPT. JOHN FOOS' COMPANY. (Continued)

Rank and Name of Soldier.

Privates.

Adams, Elijah
Cellar, George
Dilden, Ralph
Foos, William
Gallant, Allen
Hoskins, John
Munroe, Isaac
Fibert, Richard
Pugh, Thomas
Shaw, Samuel
Taylor, Benjamin
Wolf, John
Whiters, Isaac

Rank and Name of Soldier.

Privates.

Cooper, Samuel
Cothren, John
Driver, John
Evins, Edward
Gillies, James
Kyle, Hugh
Marks, David
Roderick, Jacob
Stephens, Reuben
Sloper, Charles
Taylor, Richard
Wison, Frederick
Whittenger, Nicholas

Rank and Name of Soldier.

Privates.

Cellar, John
Davis, David
Delsever, Michael
Gallant, James
Hushow, Phillip
Kepler, Samuel
Mickson, James
Perry, David
Smith, John
Tyler, Samuel
Wright, George
Wilson, John

Page 46.

ROLL OF CAPT. BENJAMIN M. FAIRCHILD'S COMPANY.
(Probably from Delaware County.)

Served from July 26, until August 10, 1813.

Capt. Benjamin Fairchilds
Sergt. Sherman Fairchilds
Sergt. William Hendrichs
Corp. Nathaniel Hatch

Privates.

Andrews, Thomas
Budd, John
Faucher, Samuel
Lock, Jesse
Rogers, Philemon
Schovey, John

Lieut. Gilbert Weeks
Sergt. William Williams
Corp. Barak Weeks
Corp. Lorrin Hills

Privates.

Bennet, James
Budd, William
Hills, Zimri
Plum, Parysek
Robinson, John W.
Smuthers, Christian

Ensign Markus Curtis
Sergt. Daniel Lane
Corp. William Smith

Privates.

Baughman, Adam
Faucher, Henry
Jenkins, David
Pelton, Johnson
Roberts, John
Sebring, Francis

Pages 45-73.

ROLL OF ISRAEL P. CASE'S COMPANY.
(Probably from Franklin County.)

Served from August 24, until October 4, 1812, and from May 4, until May 27, 1813.

Capt. Israel P. Case
Ensign, Timothy Lee
Sergt. Obediah Blakely
Sergt. William Hall
Drummer, Samuel Beach

Privates.

Andrews, Waren
Bristol, Adna
Cochrin, Harper
Case, Henry
Deckron, Daniel
Goodrich, Levi
Morrison, William
Millington, Peter
Palmer, Luther
Twadel, Joseph
Whitford, John B.

Lieut. Cruger Wright
Sergt. George Osborne
Sergt. Charles Thompson
Sergt. Ebenezer Goodrich
Fifer, Jeremiah Boardman

Privates.

Brown, Gilbert
Beech, Samuel
Cochrin, Glass
Clark, Oliver
Denton, Justus
Holmsted, Philo
Morrison, Henry
Parmento, Erastus
Perry, Levi
Vining, William
Wallace, Herman

Lieut. Abiel Case
Sergt. Job W. Case
Sergt. Herman Wheeler
Sergt. Edward Phelps

Privates.

Bisett, William
Bardsley, Ebenezer
Case, Orin
Cooper, Thomas
Goodrich, Bela
Ingham, Abraham
Mitchell, Joseph
Pratt, Lemuel
Rees, Caleb
Wever, John W.
Wilcox, Tracey

Page 47.

ROLL OF CAPT. HENRY SLACK'S COMPANY.
(Probably from Delaware County.)

Served from October 27, until November 19, 1812.

Capt. Henry Slack
Sergt. David Skeels

Privates.

Adams, Samuel
Barker, Joseph
Johnson, Stafford
Marvin, Jesse
Rosecrans, Abraham
Roberts, John
Steudevant, Ira
Show, Jonothan
Welsh, Isaac

Lieut. Samuel Maynard
Sergt. Shearman Fairchild
Sergt. Joel Taylor

Privates.

Brundage, Nathaniel
Cowan, Levi M.
Kyrk, John
Peny, Henry
Roberts, Amar
Rugg, Orn
Swetland, Artemus
James Preston

Ensign, David Butler
Sergt. Ethan Palmer

Privates.

Bishop, Elisha
Foust, John
Lewis, Isaac
Patrick, Benjamin
Rogers, Philemon
Shover, James
Taylor, Nathan
William, Heaver C.

Page 48.

ROLL OF CAPT. SAMUEL MYERS' COMPANY.
(Probably from Fayette County.)
Served from July 26, until August 16, 1813.

Rank and Name of Soldier.	Rank and Name of Soldier.	Rank and Name of Soldier.
Capt. Samuel Myers	Lieut. David Allen	Ensign, John Popejoy
Sergt. Arnold Richards	Sergt. John Harrod	Sergt. James Harvey
Sergt. Solomon Parker	Corp. Shreve Pancoast	Corp. James Davis
Corp. Michael Hawk	Corp. Charles White	Drummer, Armsted Carder
Privates.	**Privates.**	**Privates.**
Allen, Elijah	Allen, James	Busick, George
Campbell, Joseph	Campbell, Runey	Dickison, Isaac
Dickison, Jonothan	Dickison, Jacob	Hinckle, Daniel
Harrod, Samuel	Henderson, James	McGowan, James
McCafferty, James	Page, John	Rozell, James
Smith, John	Stout, William	Stutch, Jesse
Thomas, Joseph	Thompson, James	Westfall, Joseph

Page 49.

ROLL OF CAPT. ROBERT McELWAIN'S COMPANY.
(Probably from Ross County.)
Served from July 16, until August 15, 1813.

Capt. Robert McElwain	Lieut. Jacob Jones	Sergt. William Devlon
Sergt. Aaron Archer	Sergt. John Hayes	Corp. Benjamin Salmon
Corp. John Sowards	Corp. David McElwain	Corp. William Hayes
Privates.	**Privates.**	**Privates.**
Allen, Jeremiah	Biggs, John	Black, William
Bragg, John	Callison, James	Chidester, Elias
Gansel, Michael	Gaskill, John	Gow, Daniel I.
Gilmore, William	Harrison, Joseph	Hannaman, John
Flick, William	Applegate, William	Kent, Penin
LeValley, John	Lee, John	Lafford, Young
Kerr, John	Maxwell, Ephraim	Mowberry, Reuben
McClever, William	Plyman, James	Redden, Mathew
Rankin, John	Reed, William	Reeder, Joseph
Reader, Amos	Rodgers, Benjamin	Runkin, William
Smith, Alexander	Sample, Nathaniel	Taylor, David
Wibright, John	Warwick, James	

Page 50.

ROLL OF CAPT. ADAM KIOUS' COMPANY.
(Probably from Ross County.)
Served from July 28, until August 16, 1813.

Capt. Adam Kious	Lieut. John L. Chorn	Sergt. Samuel Chorn
Sergt. Peter Harper	Sergt. Addison Day	Sergt. Wicks
Corp. Levi Bavington	Corp. Martin Hyer	Corp. Bazil Mysett
	Corp. Daniel Happis	
Privates.	**Privates.**	**Privates.**
Blair, Samuel	Boyd, George	Burnet, David
Brown, Jacob	Bryan, George	Carter, Isaac
Day, Bazel	Dickson, Robert	Finney, Alexander
Hill, Stephen	Hill, William	Mussett, John
McLaughlin, William	Painter, George	Punn, Abraham
Pool, William	Orr, Samuel	Rodgers, Pilique
Seylor, George	Timmons, Eli	Waddle, John
Warren, Humphrey	White, John	Whetston, George

Page 51.

ROLL OF CAPT. THOMAS ROBINSON'S COMPANY. (County Unknown.)
Served from July 28, until August 12, 1813.

Capt. Thomas Robinson	Lieut. Patrick Kerne	Sergt. William C. Scott
Sergt. Risdon McDonald	Sergt. Daniel Honey	Corp. William Holloway
Corp. William Kendal	Drummer, Obediah William	
Privates.	**Privates.**	**Privates.**
Ballinger, Thomas	Bison, Joseph	Carr, Michael
Green, Solomon	Kilgore, John C.	Kellip, John M.
Horney, James	Steady, John	Steady, William
Price, John	Wiley, William	

Page 52.

ROLL OF CAPT. JAMES CROTHER'S COMPANY.
(Probably from Ross County.)
Served from July 27, until August 16, 1813.

Capt. James Crothers	Lieut. Isaac Saunders	Ensign, James Row
Sergt. Richard Davis	Sergt. William Priddy	Sergt. Phillip Olinger
Sergt. William Row	Corp. John Row	Corp. Robert Adams
Corp. David McDonald	Corp. John Draper	

ROLL OF CAPT. JAMES CROTHER'S COMPANY. (Continued)

Rank and Name of Soldier.

Privates.
Arnold, John
Buck, John
Howe, Jacob
Lines, William
Meeny, Hugh
McCoy, Jesse
Tracy, Solomon

Privates.
Babbit, Job
Clark, David
Hand, Lemuel
Garrison, Abner
Moon, William
Pearson, William
Tracey, William
Vaughn, John

Privates.
Barley, William
Gorby, Ebenezer
Knadler, George
Cochran, Barnabus
Mitchell, Jacob
Shroyer, George
Tracey, Wornel

Page 53.

ROLL OF CAPT. PETER COOLEY'S COMPANY.
(Probably from Adams County.)
Served from July 28, until August 28, 1813.

Capt. Peter Cooley
Corp. Thomas Bowman

Sergt. James Heslet
Drummer, John Gillman

Sergt. Nathan Rounsavell

Privates.
Donaldson, Israel
Kimble, Elijah
Riggs, John
Yerden, John

Privates.
Fetters, Charles
Montgomery, Nathaniel
Smith, William

Privates.
Henderson, Thomas
Robb, John
Thomas, Moses

Pages 54-55.

ROLL OF CAPT. JOSHUA FOBES' COMPANY (County Unknown.)
Served from August 24, until November 2, 1812.

Capt. Joshua Fobes
Lieut. Nathaniel Hopkins
Sergt. James W. Foster
Corp. William Clever
Corp. John Burwell
Fifer, Nathan Fobes, Jr.

Lieut. Thaddeus Selby
Ensign, Augustus Smith
Sergt. Jehiel Bidwell
Corp. Jabes Fobes
Corp. Daniel Davis
Drummer, Walter Thorrington

Ensign, Simon Fobes, Jr.
Sergt. Iddo Bailey
Sergt. William Randall
Corp. John Randall
Corp. Justice Fobes

Privates.
Andrews, Marquis
Burnett, Silas
Cone, Lester
Drake, Jesse
Fobes, Justice
Foster, Samuel
Fobes, Elias
Gildersleiver, Bayley
Hulbart, Nathaniel
Hoover, Isaac

Privates.
Ballard, Ezekial
Burnett, Uriel
Coleman, Noah
Daughter, David
Falsone, Noah
Falsone, Moses
Foot, Levi
Fobes, Nathan
Hart, Joseph
Harris, John
Inman, Daniel N.

Privates.
Bidwell, Riverius
Coleman, Nathaniel
Cone, Rabzabon
Duer, John
Folsome, David
Fobes, David
Farrow, Isaac
Hayes, Titus
Hough, Henry
Hannah, Thomas

Pages 56-74.

ROLL OF CAPT. JACOB ULP'S COMPANY (County Unknown.)
Served from August 24, until August 28, 1812.

Capt. Jacob Ulp
Sergt. Henry Hull
Corp. Mathias Swatsweler
Corp. James Thompson

Ensign, Joseph Reeves
Sergt. George Tribey
Corp. David Wheeler
Drummer, William Burnett

Sergt. James Montgomery
Sergt. George Bentley
Corp. Thomas Patton

Privates.
Briggs, John
Burnett, John
Groscost, John
Hughes, John
Kinney, James
Love, Robert
McMarrow, Thomas
Quiggle, Phillip
Swatseller, Martin
Wilson, James

Privates.
Burnett, William, Sr.
Crawford, Alexander
Harson, Robert
Hisley, Daniel
Kerr, Jonothan
Mizner, James
Patrick, John
Rothburn, Amos
Waldorf, Phillip
Yarnal, Job

Privates.
Bradon, John
Cunningham, William
Hughes, James
Huff, Adam
Lake, Constant
Montgomery, Robert
Quiggle, Peter
Strubel, George
White, William
Alderman, Manty

Pages 57-58.

ROLL OF CAPT. JOHN R. REED'S COMPANY (County Unknown.)
Served from August 23, until November 30, 1812, and from January 1, until March, 1813.

Capt. John R. Reed
Sergt. Joseph Kerr
Sergt. Daniel Castle
Corp. Epaphras Lyman
Artificer, Benjamin Hanks

Lieut. Alexander Harper
Sergt. John C. Chase
Corp. David Burrough
Corp. David Doughton
Drummer, William Morrison

Ensign, Samuel Johnson
Sergt. Sebastian Adams
Corp. William Harper
Corp. William Jones
Fifer, David Bartram

ROLL OF CAPT. JOHN REED'S COMPANY. (Continued)

Rank and Name of Soldier.

Privates.
All, Adam
Bartholomew, John
Brown, Samuel
Crosby, Calvin
Chapman, Comfort
Griffin, Sullivan
Gage, John R.
Houghton, Rufus
Hubbard, Manoah
John, Murray
Kent, Elisha
Laughton, Abijah
Morgan, James
Napier, Benjamin A.
Naper, William
Proctor, Jonas
Silverthorn, Thomas
Swift, Philip
Sweet, Peleg, Jr.
Stewart, Ambrose
Shepherd, Marquis
Whetmore, William
Wright, Solomon
Widner, Benjamin
White, Josiah

Rank and Name of Soldier.

Privates.
Beach, Luman
Bartholomew, Joseph
Baldwin, William
Coon, David
Cleveland, Asahel
Gordon, John
Gordon, Thomas
Hanington, Eldad
Healy, Ezra
Joslin, John G.
Lamberton, Amos
Montgomery, John H.
Mann, Warner
Norton, John
Parker, Andrew
Rockwell, Joshua
Strong, Jabez
Spencer, Edward P.
Shepherd, Peletiah
Sweet, Lewis
Tappen, Abraham
Wood, John
Walkly, Jonothan
Wilder, Oliver
Watrous, William
Yates, Benjamin

Rank and Name of Soldier.

Privates.
Bartholomew, Peter
Brooks, James
Curtis, James
Curtis, Jairns G.
Dunbar, Thomas
Gould, John
Hall, Joseph D.
Harmon, Anan
Hitchcock, David
Kent, Batus
Lamont, Robert
Maranvil, Jabez D.
McElvy, James G.
Noyes, Daniel
Pain, Orin F.
Rogers, Phinehas
Spooner, John
Stone, Merit
Strong, Samuel
Strong, Nathan Jr.
Vidite, Jaspar
Wright, John
Widner, John L.
Wallen, Joseph
Whetmore, Collins

Page 59.

ROLL OF LIEUT. ROSWELL FULLER'S COMPANY.
(Probably from Delaware County.)

Served from August 23, until September 24, 1812.

Lieut. Roswell Fuller
Sergt. Martin Pace
Corp. Truman Case

Privates.
Benjamin, Daniel
Davis, Eleazar
Higgins, Josiah
Keys, Talmon
Pierce, Ariel
Skeels, Reuben
Tuller, Roswell, Jr.

Ensign, Joseph Higgins
Sergt. David Buell
Corp. Norman Case
Fifer, John Hardin

Privates.
Carpenter, Alfred
Ely, Peter
Higgins, Ebenezer
Millhiser, Phillip
Powers, Luther
Scribner Elias
Vinning, Elver
Zimmerman, Henry

Sergt. Nathan King
Sergt. Darius Bardsley
Drummer Nathaniel Carpenter

Privates.
Case, Ralph
Gibson, Samuel
Herrick, Septemus
Patton, William
Ryan, Edward
Shaw, Benjamin
Watson, William

Pages 60-61.

ROLL OF CAPT. JOHN SNELBEKER'S COMPANY.
(Probably from Licking County.)

Served from January 30, until March 4, 1815.

Capt. John Snelbeker
Sergt. William Martin
Sergt. Mark Anderson
Corp. Jeremiah Guard

Privates.
Armstrong, James
Barnhart, Jacob
Bowan, Constant
Butler, Joseph
Critz, Andrew
Corbet, Robert
Daine, Asa
Enslow, David
Gibbs, William
Halfhill, Abraham
Jesse, Hutchins
Miller, John
McHenry, Richard
Penticost, James
Rolston, John
Shrayer, Abraham
Torrence, Aaron
Watson, Abraham

Lieut. Jeremiah Doty
Sergt. Thomas Merritt
Corp. Michael B. Miller
Corp. John Belair

Privates.
Arnold, John
Brokes, Jonothan
Ball, Cyrus
Craig, Jonothan
Denney, Daniel
Enos, John
Fussel, William
Gabriel, Reason
Hines, Phillip
Johnson, Samuel
Miller, Michael
Nagal, Andrew
Rees, Thomas, Jr.
Shew, David
Smith, David
Tylers, Isaac
Williams, James
Wolford, Andrew

Ensign, John Dixon
Sergt. Jesse Patterson
Corp. Philip Foreman
Musician, Frederick Beyner

Privates.
Boyd, John
Bloss, Adam
Burge, Henry
Cassman, Joseph
Dennen, William
Engle, John
Green, Thomas
Herron, Phillip
Irwin, George
Kenistrick, Henry
Miers, Jacob
Pardo Richard
Rolins, William
Stout, George
Stockwell, William
Thomas, Cornelius
Whan, John
Wiggins, Robert

ROSTER OF OHIO SOLDIERS IN WAR OF 1812   83

Page 62. Vol. I.
ROLL OF LIEUT. SAMUEL COOPER'S COMPANY.
(Probably from Delaware County.)
Served from August 24, until September 10, 1812.

Rank and Name of Soldier.
Lieut. Samuel Cooper
Privates.
Cooper, John
Davis, David
Evans, Edward
Hoskins, John
Lookingbell, Abraham
Penny, David

Rank and Name of Soldier.
Ensign, David Marks
Sergt. Samuel Harding
Privates.
Driver, John
Davis, John D.
Gallant, Allen
Jones, Richard
Peny, Robert
Shannon, George
Warner, Thomas

Rank and Name of Soldier.
Sergt. Isaac Keys
Privates.
Driver, Thomas
Dunn, Andrew
Gallant, James
Kepler, Samuel
Phillips, John
Scribner, John

Page 63.
ROLL OF CAPT. JOAB NORTON'S COMPANY.
(Probably from Delaware County.)
Served from June 2, until September 19, 1812.

Capt. Joab Norton
Ensign, Jonothan Hatch
Sergt. Erastus Rowe
Corp. Harlock Dunham

Privates.
Aye, Jacob
Cocheran, Harper
Dickey, John
Godfrey, Samuel
Heavilors, Barnett
Leonard, Amos
Monroe, Lemuel F.
Little, William
Root, Azariah, Jr.
Smith, Solomon
Walters, James

Sergt. Ira Carpenter
Sergt. M. McLoeland
Corp. Francis Beebe
Drummer, Jonothan Dunham
Fifer, Silas Denham

Privates.
Brown, John
Crosby, Rhederick
Duncan, James
George, Thomas
Erwin, William
Maker, William
Minter, Valentine
Lemon, David
Price, John
Vox, Rufus

Lieut. John Aye
Sergt. John Depson
Corp. James Miller
Corp. Samuel Scribner

Privates.
Curtis, Asa D.
Conner, Joseph
Diminck, Daniel
Hatch, Nathaniel
Erwin, James
Minter, John, Jr.
McFilly, Thomas
Olds, Benjamin
Rickey, Joseph
Welch, Aurora

Page 64.
ROLL OF CAPT. WILLIAM S. DRAKE'S COMPANY.
(Probably from Delaware County.)
Served from August 24, until September 25, 1812.

Capt. William S. Drake
Privates.
Brundage, Nathaniel
Ely, Peter
Tuboss, Isaac

Ensign Daniel Wyatt
Corp. John Foust
Privates.
Dundleberger, Frederick
Foust, Jacob
Welsh, Isaac

Sergt. Ira Wilcox
Privates.
Dundleberger, Peter
Shaw, Jonothan
Wilcox, Hera

Page 65.
ROLL OF CAPT. JESSE D. JACKSON'S COMPANY. (County Unknown.)
Served from August 23, until September 4, 1812.

Capt. Jesse D. Jackson
Sergt. Erastus Rudd
Sergt. Chauncey Tinker
Corp. Samuel Brown

Privates.
Allen, Merritt
Blackmer, Stephen
Cook, Rosswell
Ferguson, Jonothan
King, Peter, Jr.
Lewis, Jonas
Miranville, Stephen D.
Stuntz, George
Scovill, Linus
Widner, John L.

Lieut. John Rudd, Jr.
Sergt. Samuel Vinton
Corp. Nathan Russell
Drummer, Leonard H. Niles
Fifer, Silas Tinker
Privates.
Brooks, James
Bates, David
Drennen, John
Harrington, Eldad
Leavitt, James
Marainville, Jabez D.
McNear, Thomas
Smith, Chester
Tubbs, Morgan
Withrow, Hugh

Ensign John Brooks
Sergt. Ira Parker
Corp. Daniel Sawtell
Fifer, Horace Pearsons

Privates.
Brooks, Hananiah
Coles, David
Fox, Sinkler
Harring, Samuel
Lewis, Caleb
Moore, John
Noble, Aaron
Spooner, John
Talbot, Daniel
Wooden, Joel

Page 66.
ROLL OF CAPT. WARHAM GRANT'S COMPANY. (County Unknown.)
Served from August 23, until September 4, 1812.

Capt. Warham Grant
Sergt. Daniel Webster
Corp. Nicholas Miller
Privates.
Benjamin, Reuben
Dewey, Rodolphus
Gee, Salmon
Jones, Robert
Peck, Ansel
Smith, Platt

Lieut. Harvey Rockwell
Sergt. Edward B. Spencer
Musician, Martin Huntley
Privates.
Benjamin, Mathew
Ensign, Orrin
Hills, Ira
Peck, Josiah
Strickland, Joshua
Webster, Michael

Sergt. John Shook
Corp. Joseph Miller
Musician, John Gee
Privates.
Asahel, Cleveland
Griggs, Solomon
Huntley, Ezekial
Peck, William
Randall, David
Wrench, William

Page 67. Vol. I.
ROLL OF CAPT JACOB BARTHOLOMEW'S COMPANY. (County Unknown.)
Served from August 23, until September 2, 1812.

Capt. Jacob Bartholomew
Sergt. Lorrin Cowles
Lieut. Benjamin Montgomery

Ensign Uriah Bertram
Sergt. Truman Watkin
Corp. George Hewins

Sergt. Jonothan Hill
Corp. Daniel I. Bartholomew
Fifer, Benjamin Bartholomew

Privates.
Allen, David
Bartholomew, Samuel
Burnum, Enoch
Cowles, Adna
Cook, Stephen
French, Squire B.
Gregory, Daniel
Hartwell, John
Harper, Archibald, Jr.
Heniman, Stephen
Johnson, Otis
Morrison, Strawbridge
Noyes, John
Smith, Stephen A.
Williams, Havel
Wright, Samuel
Ward, Elisha

Privates.
Bartholomew, Abraham
Brown, I. Zadoc
Bartholomew, Isaac
Cowley, Alpheus
Colhoun, Reynolds
Gaylord, Levi, Jr.
Gaylord, Elihu S.
Hale, Jacob
Houghton, Rufus
Jackson, Walter
Kingsley, John
Moore, Henry I.
Parker, Calvin S.
Spencer, Barzilla
Wood, John
Wright, James, Jr.
Webster, Abraham

Privates.
Bartholomew, John B.
Bachman, Ludwick
Cunningham, Cyrus
Cahoon, Reynolds, Jr.
Custin, Benjamin
Gay, Harding
Hewin, William
Harper, William A.
Hill, John
Jones, Billy
Miller, William
Montgomery, Eli
Phelps, Isaac H.
Turney, Daniel
Williams, Joseph
Williams, Samuel
Webster, Norman

Page 68.
ROLL OF CAPT. ROSWELL AUSTIN'S COMPANY. (County Unknown.)
Served from August 23, until September 6, 1812.

Capt. Roswell Austin
Sergt. David J. Stone
Musician, Joseph Cade

Lieut. Aaron Leyon
Sergt. Josiah Atkin
Musician, Obed Didell

Sergt. Edson Phelps
Corp. William Willams

Privates.
Dibble, John, Jr.
Knapp, Elihu
Robbins, Samuel
Rider, Samuel

Privates.
Goff, Benjamin
Lyman, Joshua
Squires, Daniel
Thorp, Alpha

Privates.
Knap, Roswell
Phelps, Stephen K.
Skinner, Ashbel
Wood, Samuel, Jr.

Pages 69-70.
ROLL OF CAPT. CHANCEY BARKER'S COMPANY.
(Probably from Franklin County.)
Served from August 24, until September 15, 1812. Part served from May 4, until May 27, 1813.

Capt. Chancey Barker
Sergt. Eliphalet Barker
Sergt. Silas Barlow
Corp. William Derrickson

Lieut. Samuel Maynard
Sergt. Ethan Palmer
Corp. William Thompson
Corp. Isaac Harrison

Ensign Hector Kilbourn
Sergt. Berkley Comstock
Corp. Abraham Phelps
Musician, Andrews, Noah

Privates.
Allen, Isaac
Crippin, John
Cochrane, Nathaniel
Chapman, Albert
Faulkner, Joshua N.
Hone, Henry
Impson, William
Kirk, John
Maynard, Amos, Jr.
Moore, Simeon, Sr.
Puntney, Aquilla
Smith, John
Skeels, Belias H.
Turbee, Mathias
White, William
Wheeler, Herman

Privates.
Benedict, Asahel
Crippen, Joseph
Case, Orlando
Derickson, John
Glasby, Enos
Hoffman, Jacob
Knight, Oreno
Lee, Asa
Maynard, Moses
McCutchan, Robert
Phelps, Abraham
Sharp, Ganit
Tolland, Thomas
Wilcox, Asa
Willard, Windsor
Yonel, John

Privates.
Brient, Jeremiah
Cooper, John
Crosby, Charles
Fisher, Isaiah
Griswold, Isaac
Hills, James H.
Kilbourn, John
Maxfield, Amos
Mitchell, Newman
Olmsted, Francis
Rugg, Origen
Stanberry, Recompense
Toppin, Zopher
Wilson, Samuel
Weaver, Asa, Jr.

Page 71.
ROLL OF LIEUT. SILAS FLEMING'S COMPANY. (County Unknown.)
Served from August 30, 1812, until February 28, 1813

Lieut. Silas Fleming
Sergt. John Bishop
Drummer, Hugh Smith

Ensign Isaac Sutton
Corp. William Bunch
Fifer, Joseph Smith

Sergt. Charles Johnston
Corp. George Kelley

Privates.
Allen, John
Crowel, Michael
Highly, John
Holdeman, Christian
Ireland, William
LeDruell, John
Melling, Thomas
Purviance, Levi
Railsback, Jacob
Summers John
York, Jeptha

Privates.
Bridge, John
Douglas, Samuel
Hewit, Israel
Hole, Charles
Irwin, Thomas
Lewallen, Thomas
Michael, Jacob
Powell, Hezekiah
Ringen, Jacob
Swisher, William

Privates.
Childer, Thomas
Davis, George
Hudlow, John
Hapner, Abraham
Keaston, Samuel
Lewallen, Phillip
Pain, Isaac
Reesley, Thomas
Summers, James
Tullinger, William

ROSTER OF OHIO SOLDIERS IN WAR OF 1812

Page 72. Vol. I.

ROLL OF CAPT. JOHN FLEMING'S COMPANY. (County Unknown.)

Served from August 23, 1812, until February 22, 1813.

Rank and Name of Soldier.	Rank and Name of Soldier.	Rank and Name of Soldier.
Capt. John Fleming	Lieut. George Richardson	Ensign Henry Mann
Sergt. James W. Maxwell	Sergt. George Hardy	Sergt. William Williman
Sergt. Daniel Knop	Corp. John Morris	Corp. Thomas Morris
Corp. Martin Vance	Corp. Josiah Clawson	
Privates.	**Privates.**	**Privates.**
Alred, Thomas	Allen, John	Atkinson, Ison
Allved, Isaac	Burnes, Barnabus	Boyd, Andrew
Bond, Exum S.	Brown, James	Brown, Nathan
Cristler, Aaron	Caldwell, Joseph W.	Doharty, Edward
Defree, Archibald	Dingman, Daniel V.	Elliott, Ebenezer
Frederick, Christian	Goldsmith, John	Gorman, James
Gearhart, William	Hewitt, David	Hayes, John
Homero, Jacob	Helm, Christian	Ingersom, Benjamin
Gilbert, John	Jones, William	Lindsley, Dennis
Lennox, James	Maundey, Jacob	Marsham, Mathew
Maiers, Jacob	McCoy, Daniel	McComb, Andrew Y.
Nelson, William	Pilson, Hugh	Russel, Charles
Richardson, William	Singer, Thomas	Smith, John
Shackelford, James	Swartword, Abraham	Sumption, Charles
Simpson, Samuel	Studibaker, David	Shackelford, William
Woodward, Jacob	Williams, John	Worle, Samuel, Sr.
	Worle, Samuel, Jr.	

Page 424.

ROLL OF CAPT. GEORGE RICHARDSON'S COMPANY. County Unknown.)

Served from August 29, until October 29, 1812.

Capt. George Richardson	Lieut. Gottfreid Westhofer	Ensign Peter Johnston
Sergt. Jacob Houck	Sergt. William Kemp	Sergt. Robert Sparks
Sergt. Mathias Waggoner	Drummer, Robert Caples	
Privates.	**Privates.**	**Privates.**
Bumtrager, John	Bartlett, Peter	DeLong, Solomon
Davis, Joseph	Davis, David	Everett, Henry
Engle, Levi	Frederick, Peter	Graham, Ebenezer
Griffith, Nathan	Hayes, Samuel	Huston, Michael
Johnson, William	Kinder, John	Knight, Michael
Miller, Henry	Moore, George	Moninger, George
McMullan, David	McDonough, Hugh	Parker, Andrew
Roysher, Daniel	Rebstock, Martin	Sells, Jonothan
Spiker, Phillip	Smith, John	Thompson, Michael
Wycoff, William	Wieland, Peter	Watson, James

Pages 268-269-270-271.

ROLL OF CAPT. JEDEDIAH BURNHAM'S COMPANY. (County Unknown.)

Served from August 24, until November 10, 1812, and from January 1, until February 28, 1813.

Capt. Jedediah Burnham	Lieut. Benjamin Allen	Lieut. Nathaniel Hopkins
Ensign Alexander Mathews	Lieut. Lewis Dill	Ensign Dexter Clinton
Ensign Augustin Smith	Sergt. Aaron Rice	Sergt. James Laughlin
Sergt. Robert Henry	Sergt. Henry Bignel	Sergt. Amzi Webb
Sergt. Gurden Hutchins	Sergt. Iddo Bailey	Sergt. William Randall
Sergt. Justis Fobes	Sergt. William Cleaver	Corp. Daniel Bewen
Corp. Samuel Randall	Corp. Ebenezer Weber	Corp. John L. Cook
Corp. James King	Corp. Michael Rutledge	Corp. Alexander Mathews
Corp. John Burwell	Corp. Samuel Tuthill	
Privates.	**Privates.**	**Privates.**
Adams, Augustus	Allen, Chester	Alexander, Joseph
Anderson, William	Adkinson, Enoch	Andrews, Richard
Alderman, Eber	Alderman, Jonothan	Andrews, Asa
Andrews, Sherman	Brackin, Ezekial	Brakin, David
Buel, Ezra	Burnes, Jacob	Broadwell, Henry
Babcock, Silas	Brainard, Solomon	Barnes, Ebenezer
Burnes, George	Ballard, Ezekial	Brockway, Jesse
Burnham, Joshua	Breden, John	Bates, Dennis
Christy, William	Christy, Andrew	Cossit, Eli
Calvin, Luther	Chapman, Comfort	Carlton, John
Crawford, Alexander	Daly, John	Davis, Walter
Dodge, Samuel	Dickinson, Elisha	Dillon, Asa
Doyle, Anthony	Dillon, Samuel	Ford, Joseph
Ford, Jacob	Ford, Shadrach	Foss, Cotton
Fisher, Benjamin	Folsom, David	Fowler, Chester
Findlay, John	Fobes, Elias	Foot, Levi
Farrow, Isaac	Furgeson, Horace	Folsom, Moses
Giddings, Joshua R.	Giddings, Warren	Goodrich, Gideon
Green, Ebenezer	Galloway, James	Hungerford, Henry
Hutchinson, Daniel	Hill, James	Hough, Henry
Hannah, Thomas	Hill, James, Sr.	Harberson, Robert
Jackson, William	Jones, Silven	Keeler, Ezra

ROLL OF CAPT. JEDTDITH BURNHAM'S COMPANY. (Continued)

Rank and Name of Soldier.   Rank and Name of Soldier.   Rank and Name of Soldier.

Privates.

King, Robert	Kinney, Hutchens	Kerr, William
Kerr, Thomas	Long, Isaac	Leffingwell, William
Lewis, Oliver	Lillie, Hen.y	Lyon, William
Lafferty, William	Langley, John	Lake, Constant
Laughlin, Robert	Mathews, Alexander	Mathews, Thomas, Jr.
Morse, Ansel	Mathews, John	Moses, Azariah
Moses, Eldred	Meeker, Andrew C.	Mapes, Henry, Jr.
Moses, Abner	Moss, Simion	Morey, Hosea
Munson, Calvin	McLaughlin, Patrick	McKey, William
McClerg, David	McFarland, William	Nye, Joshua
Newton, Lemuel	Nelson, Hugh	Noys, Samuel
Ogden, Benjamin	Potter, Thomas	Perkins, Seth
Perkins, Enoch	Patrick, John	Pelton, Harvey
Pelton, Julius	Price, Archibald	Reeve, Jeremiah
Roberts, Thomas	Randall, John	Sutliff, Plumb
Scovill, David	Scott, William	Shull, Frederick
Smith, Joel	Splitstene, Henry	Splitstene, Adam
Scott, William	Scovill, Reuben	Scovill, Ansel
Smith, Amos	Smith, James	Spillhouse, Martin G.
Tidd, Martin	Tidd, Charles	Tuttle, Jonothan
Tuttle, Samuel	Tyrell, Judson	Trusedale, James, Jr.
Taylor, John	Woodworth, Ebenezer	Westbay, James
Woodworth, Divdate	Waid, Robert	Waid, Alexander
Woodworth, Albigence	Wolf, Oratio D.	Wakeman, Silliman
Waldorf, Philip	Wood, John	White, William
Worters, Lester	Yelman, Peter	Fifer, Nicholas Little
Fifer, Nathan Fobes	Drummer, Lemuel Clark	Drummer, Levi Mathews

Page 143, Vol. I.

ROLL OF FIELD AND STAFF, WAR OF 1812-1813.

LIEUT. COL. RICHARD HAYES, ———— REGIMENT, OHIO MILITIA.

Lt. Col. Richard Hayes
Adjt. Sterling G. Bushnell
Q. M. Sergt. Nathaniel Coleman
Sergt. Maj. William Hull

Maj. Zopher Case
Q. M. John Andrews
Surg. Peter Allen
Sergt. Maj. Henry Bignell
Fife Maj. Amos Jones
Drum Maj. Davis Fuller

Maj. Samuel Frazier
Q. M. Clerk Elan Jones
Surg. Mate Erastus Goodwin
Sergt. Maj. Luman Beech

Page 195.

COLONEL LEWIS CASS, ———— REGIMENT, OHIO MILITIA.

Col. Lewis Cass
Surg. Charles Lester
Pay Master Abner Dent
Sergt. Maj. Thomas Foster

Maj. Robert Morrison
Surg. Mate, James Reynolds
Q. M. Elias Gilman
Drum Maj. G. Goodspeed

Maj. Joseph Morrison
Adjt. H Northrop
Q. M. Sergt. James Sharp

Page 202.

LIEUT. COL. NATHAN KING, ———— REGIMENT, OHIO MILITIA.

Lieut. Col. Nathan King
Q. M., I. A. Robinson
Surg. Mate, Elijah Coleman
Fife Maj., Silas Tinker

Maj. Zadoc Thompson
Q. M. Clerk, James A. Harper
Q. M. Sergt. Robert Harper

Adjt. Josiah W. Brown
Surg. Orestes H. Hawley
Drum Maj., David Bertham

Page 203.

LIEUT. COL. MILLS STEPHENSON, ———— REGIMENT, OHIO MILITIA.

Lieut. Col. Mills Stephenson
Adjt. Alexander Bourne
Surg. Mate, John L. McCullough

Maj. Anthony Pitzer
Pay Master Neville Redmon
Q. M. Tingley Sutton
Fife Maj. James K. Caldwell
Sergt. Maj. Isaac Burkellow

Maj. Thomas Moore
Surg. Joseph Keith
Q. M. Sergt. James Finley
Drum Maj. William Smith

Page 242.

COLONEL ROBERT SAFFORD, ———— REGIMENT, OHIO MILITIA.

Col. Robert Safford
Capt. Nehemiah Gregory
Lieut. John Roadamour

Maj. Nathaniel Beasley
Capt. Calvin Shephard
Ensign John Bootom

Maj. Jehiel Gregory
Lieut. John Rader

Page 251.

COLONEL DANIEL COLLIER, ———— REGIMENT, OHIO MILITIA.

Col. Daniel Collier
Q. M. Seth Shoemaker
Sergt. Maj. John Mathews

Maj. Isaac Dawson
Pay Master, James Allen
Q. M. Sergt. John Cavin

Adjt. John Kincade
Surg. Mate Clayton Tiffin
Drum Maj. Jacob Metts

Page 425. Vol. I.

| Rank and Name of Soldier. | Rank and Name of Soldier. | Rank and Name of Soldier. |

LIEUT. COL. JEDEDIAH BEARD, ———— REGIMENT, OHIO MILITIA.

Lieut. Col. Jedediah Beard	Maj. Samuel Jones	Maj. Elezor Hecox
Adjt. Eleazor Patchin	Q. M. Samuel W. Phelps	Pay Master Samuel S. Baldwin
Clerk, Peter Hitchcock	Surg. William Kennedy	Surg. Mate Erastus Goodwin
Fife Maj. David Hill	Q. M. James Strong	Sergt. Maj. Hendrick E. Paine
	Drum Maj. Stephen Bond	

Page 201.

MAJ. SAMUEL CONNELL, ODD BATTALION, OHIO MILITIA.

Maj. Samuel Connell	Adjt. Anthony Wayne	Pay Master Henry H. Evans
	Surg. Henry H. Evans	

Page 294,

MAJ. BENJAMIN DANIELS, ODD BATTALION, OHIO MILITIA.

Maj. Benjamin Daniels	Adjt. William Barnes	Pay Master James Sergeant
Q. M. Joseph I. Martin	Q. M. Sergt. John Stewart	

Page 430,

MAJ. JOSEPH RHODES, ODD BATTALION, OHIO MILITIA.

Maj. Joseph Rhodes	Adjt. Samuel Criswell	Q. M. Lewis Hoyt

Page 315,

MAJ. ALEXANDER C. LANIER, FOURTH DETACHMENT, OHIO MILITIA.

Maj. Alexander C. Lanier	Surg. Mate Walter Buell

Page 75.

THE ROLLS OF THE FOLLOWING COMPANIES DO NOT STATE TO WHICH REGIMENT THEY BELONG.
ROLL OF CAPT. WILLIAMS. (Incomplete.) County Unknown.)

Served from ————————

Capt. Williams   Private, Ballinger, Joseph

Page 77.

ROLL OF CAPT. JARED STRONG'S COMPANY.
(Probably from Ross County.)

Served from July 27, until August 19, 1813.

Capt. Jared Strong	Lieut. Samuel Gallespie	Ensign William How
Sergt. William Givens	Sergt. John Lake	Sergt. David Mitchell
Sergt. Phillip Strather	Corp. Salmon Goodenough	Corp. Alexander Hill
Corp. Joseph Lake	Corp. William Hillenbohker	Drummer, Harris, Perry
	Fifer, James Markey	
Privates.	**Privates.**	**Privates.**
Aldride, Samuel	Burn, Samuel	Baly, Stephen
Black, William	Casdele, Thomas M.	Clemens, Joseph
Elliton, William	Hensete, William	Higginbothom, James
Ogg, John	Phillips, James	Robben, Joseph
Rout, Henry	Skelinge Jacob	Sergant, John
	Watson, Jesse	

Pages 78-79.

ROLL OF CAPT. JAMES MORROW'S COMPANY.
(Probably from Greene County.)

Served from May 10, until May 19, 1813

Capt. James Morrow	Lieut. Christopher Sroupe	Ensign George Townsley
Sergt. Joseph Kyle, Jr.	Sergt. James Colliers	Sergt. Samuel Galloway
Sergt. John McCullough	Corp. George Logan	Corp. Robert Stephenson
Corp. William McCoy	Corp. Arthur McFarland	
Privates.	**Privates.**	**Privates.**
Andrew, James	Andrew, Hugh	Baldwin, David
Barnes, John	Bishop, Solomon	Bull, John
Bull, James	Beatty, William A.	Cannon, Anthony
Confer, George	Chambers, David	Cohagen, John
Currie, William	Dean, Robert	Dermitt, Isaac
Galloway, James N.	Galloway, John	Gant, Robert
Gibson, John	Gibson, Montelion	Gowdy, John
Goldsby, John	Gowdy, Robert	Goldsby, George
Goldsby, Briggs M.	Hivling, John	Ibers, Richard
Jolly, John	Junken, George	Johnston, Arthur
Kendall, John	Moore, Charles	Miller, George
Moore, James	Moodie, Robert	Miller, John
Miller, Daniel	McCarthen, James	McCulley, William
McCulley, James	McCoy, Alexander	McCoy, James
Owings, James	Quinn, Amos	Sparks, Leonard
Stephenson, John	Scott, William	Srouf, David
Sroupe, Lewis	Sterrett, Joseph	Steele, John
Todd, James	Townsley, Thomas	Vancaton, John
Ward, Hervey	Wilson, George	Waltburn, Robert
Woodward, Henry	Winget, Hugh	White, Joseph

Vol. I. Page 81.

ROLL OF CAPT. ISAAC WALKER'S COMPANY. (County Unknown.)

Served from February 10, until April 5, 1813.

Rank and Name of Soldier.	Rank and Name of Soldier.	Rank and Name of Soldier.
Capt. Isaac Walker	Ensign Benjamin Cook	Sergt. Robert Huston
Sergt. Isaac Buchanan	Sergt. Allen Loury	Corp. Robert Watson
	Corp. John Patton	
Privates.	**Privates.**	**Privates.**
Bell, William	Burnett, John	Carter, John
Cross, Nathan	Duncan, John	Deneen, James
Dawson, William	Gerodelle, John	Hany, James
Hyatt, Elisha	Kerr, Nathan	Maxfield, William
Morrison, James	Nye, Joshua	Park, Elijah
Prior, Thomas	Slover, Samuel	Swager, John

Page 82.

ROLL OF CAPT. DANIEL ABEL'S COMPANY. (County Unknown.)

Served from August 24, until August 27, 1812.

Capt. Daniel Abel	Lieut. Elijah Tarnill	Ensign Nathan Webb
Sergt. Abner Fowler	Sergt. George Lilly	Sergt. Ariel Bradley
Sergt. Furzi Webb	Corp. William Deraa	Drummer, John Jackson
Privates.	**Privates.**	**Privates.**
Adams, Augustus	Barnes, Ebenezer	Dickinson, Elisha
Dickerson, Friend	Fisher, Benjamin	Fowler, Chester
Foot, Levi	Fanagh, Isaac	Green, Joseph
Hunt, Ezra	Hungerford, Hervey	Hill, Jared
Jackson, William	Lille, David, Jr.	Lille, Henry
Loury, David	Meeker, Andrew	McKee, William
Nicholson, James	Perkins, Enoch	Perkins, Seth
Silaman, Wakeman	Zeril, Jackson	

Page 83.

ROLL OF CAPT. AMBROSE PALMER'S COMPANY. (County Unknown.)

Served from August 25, until August 28, 1812.

Capt. Ambrose Palmer	Ensign Tensard R. DeWolf	Sergt. Calvin Palmer
Sergt. Samuel Banning	Sergt. Henry Bignol	Sergt. Calvin Smith
Corp. James Bates	Corp. Nathan Chesrey	Corp. Michael Rutledge
Drummer, Stephen Calvin	Fifer, Charles Trunkey	
Privates.	**Privates.**	**Privates.**
Akins, Henry C.	Adkinson, Enoch	Anderson, William
Burnes, Andrew	Brown, William	Brown, James
Calvin, Luther	Case, Ira	DeWolf, Horatio
Gibbs, Isaac	Lewis, Oliver	Linsley, Elan
Langly, John	Moses, Abner	Mowery, Hosea
McClong, David	Scovil, David	Sheldon, Berry
	Yetman, Peter	

Pages 84-85.

ROLL OF CAPT. ASA HUTCHINS' COMPANY. (County Unknown.)

Served from August 24, until November 11, 1812.

Capt. Asa Hutchins	Lieut. William Bartholomew	Ensign Dexter Clinton
Ensign Joseph Reeves	Sergt. Gurden Hutchins	Sergt. Ambrose Hart
Sergt. Silden Scovil, Jr.	Sergt. Aruna Alderman	Sergt. Henry Hull
Corp. Samuel L. Gleason	Corp. Joel Humason	Corp. Lister Bashnell
Corp. Mathias Swatsweller	Corp. Charles Woodruff	Corp. David Wheeler
Privates.	**Privates.**	**Privates.**
Andrews, Asa	Bates, Dennis	Braden, John
Bates, Talcott	Burnett, William	Crawford, Alexander
Crosby, Ezra	Clark, Joseph L.	Clark, Timothy
Clinton, William	Chew, Thomas	Chatfield, William
Alderman, Chauncy	Deming, Phineas	Groscoss, John
Humison, Isaac	Hutchins, Samuel	Heckcox, Chauncy
Hull, John	Hilton, Richard	Hughes, James
Hayes, Lester	Jones, Seldon	Kerr, Thomas
Johnson, Rausen	Kinney, James	Kepner, John
Lowery, Isaac	Lafferty, William	Lowery, Samuel, Jr.
Lewis, Lambert W.	Patrick, John	Smith, James
	Trusdill, James J.	

Page 86.

ROLL OF CAPT. CALEB BALDWIN'S COMPANY. (County Unknown.)

Served from August 23, until September 16, 1812.

Capt. Caleb Baldwin	Ensign Joseph Porter	
Privates.	**Privates.**	**Privates.**
Anderson, James	Burgess, Robert	Beard, John
Barkley, Francis	Cronnan, Abner	Chub, John
Dennison, David	Dustman, Jacob	Dinwiddie, Thomas
Fitch, Henry	Fitch, Andrew	Foulk, Henry
Frank, Jacob	Gilbert, Samuel	Gibson, James
Gilbert, Henry		

ROLL OF CAPT. CALEB BALDWIN'S COMPANY. (Continued.)

Privates.
Hoyls, Nicholas
Love, William
Mears, Joseph
McFall, Malcolm
Peterman, Jacob
Spargo, George S.
Stout, Jonothan
Turner, Samuel
Whitsell, Jacob

Privates.
Hartinger, Jacob
Lowery, Robert
McCreary, John
Ormsby, George
Rose, Robert
Sell, John
Swager, Isaac
Upton, Benjamin
Wilson, Edward

Privates.
Hayden, Samuel
Miller, John
McMullin, John
Onarwert, John
Rose, David
Simon, Adam
State, Andrew
White, James
Willey, Frederick

Pages 87-88.

ROLL OF CAPT. DANIEL DULL'S (Deceased) COMPANY. (County Unknown.)
(This Company was Under the Command of Lieut. Robert Earl.)

Served from August 22, until August 28, 1812, and from January 1, until March 8, 1813.

Capt. Daniel Dull
Sergt. Eber W. Brooks
Sergt. Joseph Allen
Corp. William McKonkey
Fifer, Harmon Deen

Lieut. Robert Earl
Sergt. Benjamin Sutherland
Corp. Levi Patman
Corp. George Shufelton
Drummer, Michael Peltz

Ensign John Shifelton
Sergt. Ira Prescott
Corp. John Allen
Corp. John Colbraith

Privates.
Allen, William
Austin, Calvin
Brown, John
Crooks, Robert
Campbell, Alexander
Cale, Thomas
Dixon, Walter
Earl, Jacob
Fish, Abner
Hutson, Mathew
Hall, William
Harmon, Hiram
Johnson, Abraham
Loveless, Samuel
Marshall, Isaac
McKelvy, William
Norton, Robert
Rook, James
Stillman, John D.
Stanley, Marshall
Snyder, Benjamin
Trescott, Ira
Van Wye, Isaac
Walder, Jonothan
Windle, Francis

Privates.
Alderman, Frederick
Bowen, Lott
Bartholomew, Charles
Carlisle, David
Craige, John
Davison, Benjamin, Jr.
Davidson, William
French, William
Gibson, Samuel
Hill, Alpheus
Hulk, Henry R.
Hickman, Timothy
Kelso, Robert
Lumis, Andrew
More, Joseph
McKenzie, Robert
Porter, Thomas
Rawley, Constant
Storey, Henry
Sacket, Gany
Snyder, William
Turner, Samuel B.
Woodward, John
Winins, Jacob
Young, William

Privates.
Adams, Shubal
Bales, Samuel
Caldwell, John
Custard, Jacob
Cale, William
DeCorsey, Isaac
Earl, Joseph
Freeman, Robert J.
Hemming, Jacob
Hart, Alva
Hampton, John
Hawey, John
Lingo, Joseph
Miller, Jacob
McComb, James
Norton, Michael
Robert, Joseph S.
Reed, Hezekiah
Scott, Joseph
Spoony, Elias
Stow, Chester
Trescott, Russell
Wilson, David
Williams, Benjamin

Page 89.

ROLL OF CAPT. JAMES STONE'S COMPANY. (County Unknown.)

Served from August 23, until September 5, 1812.

Capt. James Stone
Sergt. David Wright
Corp. Roswell Stephens

Lieut. Quintus F. Adkins
Sergt. John Crowell
Drummer, Samuel Knowlton

Ensign Daniel Hall
Corp. Erastus Flower

Privates.
Baily, Benjamin
Griffin, Sullivan
Humprey, Guy
Merrels, Neh
Tuttle, Ara

Privates.
Clieveland, Orison
Hinman, Arad
Knowlton, Stephen
Osborn, Lewis
Walkly, Jonothan
Walkly, Seth

Privates.
Crosby, Calvin
Hall, Joseph
Luman, Beach
Trall, Luman
Walkly, David

Page 90.

ROLL OF CAPT. ALLEN GAYLORD'S COMPANY.
(Probably from Cuyahoga County.)

Served from August 22, until October 24, 1812.

Capt. Allen Gaylord
Sergt. William W. Williams

Lieut. Walter Strong
Drummer, Simon Smith

Ensign, Elijah Nobles
Fifer, Almon Wolcott

Privates.
Abbott, Josiah
Cahoon, Amos
Frazier, Stephen
Hungerford, Asa
King, William, Jr.
Morton, Clark
Rois, Silas

Privates.
Blinn, Richard H.
Comstock, Peter
Gunn, Christopher
Johnson, Samuel
Prentiss, Robert
Porter, Amaziah
White, Charles

Privates.
Chase, Daniel
Ensign, Ira
Gunn, Charles
King, William, Sr.
Prentiss, James
Remington, Justus

ROLL OF CAPT. JAMES THOMPSON'S COMPANY.
(Probably from Geauga County.)
Served from August 22, until August 29, 1812.

Privates.
Capt. James Thompson
Sergt. Lewis Smith
Sergt. Heathman Thomas
Corp. James Heathman

Privates.
Brown, Benoni
Hanchell, Nathan
Russell, Eliakin
White, Holden

Privates.
Lieut. Samuel Hardy
Sergt. Benjamin Wells
Corp. Seth Risley
Corp. Elijah Webster
Fifer, Joseph Young

Privates.
Dustin, John
James, John
Reed, John
Wallace, Robert

Privates.
Ensign John Hopkins
Sergt. Theodorus Miller
Corp. William Thompson
Drummer, John Granger

Privates.
Granger, Samuel
Pomroy, Stephen
Wilcox, Elnathan
Townsley, John

ROLL OF CAPT. NORMAN CANFIELD'S COMPANY.
(Probably from Geauga County.)
Served from August 22, until August 30, 1812.

Capt. Norman Canfield
Sergt. Chandler Pears

Privates.
Bond, Joseph
Hale, Jesse
King, Isaiah
Peare, Menick

Lieut. Allen Humphrey
Sergt. Benjamin Andrews
Corp. Elijah Douglas

Privates.
Elwell, John
Hasher, John R.
Kellog, Aranda
Spencer, Halsey
Spencer, Nathaniel

Ensign Horace Taylor
Corp. Ichabod Pomeroy

Privates.
Elliott, Chester
King, Hosea
King, Nathaniel
Spencer, Allen

ROLL OF ENSIGN PETER HUBER'S COMPANY. (County Unknown.)
Served from October 13, until October 27, 1813.

Ensign Peter Huber
Corp. Joshua Cole

Privates.
Abraham, John
Clark, Oratio
Daubert, John
Greybill, Christopher
Long, Thomas
Morehart, Jacob
McFarland, Walter
Wotring, Abraham

Sergt. Roberson Fletcher
Corp. John Morehart
Corp. Thomas Durris

Privates.
Bush, Martin
Crumley, John
Faulkner, Martin
Harman, Jacob
Long, John
Measomore, John
Sirk, David
Wells, Thomas
Whitehous, James

Sergt. Reuben Williams
Corp. George Harrison

Privates.
Brooks, Joseph
Death, William
Godman, William
Hood, Robert
Miller, Daniel
Measomore, Henry
Vandamark, Daniel
Whitehous, Jacob

ROLL OF CAPT. RICHARD HOOKER'S COMPANY.
(Probably from Franklin and Fairfield Counties.)
Served from May 7, until September 5, 1813.

Capt. Richard Hooker
Sergt. Joseph Hodges
Sergt. George Harrison
Corp. Arthur Stotts

Privates.
Busbee, John
Cline, Andrew
Carlisle, Thomas
Earmman, Frederick
Hamilton, Orange
Highland, Edward
Milton, Isaac
Milison, Barnett
Nye, George
Reat, Hugh
Sowers, John
Wilson, Samuel

Lieut. Valentine Raber
Sergt. Robert Wilson
Corp. Abraham Middlesworth
Corp. Abraham Cole

Privates.
Busbee, George
Cromby, Christ
Delshaver, Jacob
Gessel, John
Harrison, Alexander
Johnston, John
Moore, William
McVay, John
Propeck, Thomas
Stewart, Joseph
Sprader, Jacob
Winders, Daniel

Cornet, James Reed
Sergt. Moses Sowers
Corp. Thomas Duddleson
Trumpeter, Joseph Wright

Privates.
Cameron, Alexander
Cloughburg, Abraham
Delshaver, John
Glick, George
Hayes, Peter
Long, William
Moore, Henry
Nigh, Michael
Ridenhour, Henry
Stotts, Absalom
Shull, Solomon

ROLL OF CAPT. JOHN McCORD'S COMPANY (Probably from Champaign Co.)
Served from September 6, until September 22, 1812.

Capt. John McCord

Privates.
Armstrong, Thomas
Fitzpatrick, John
Lutser, Henry
Powell, Enoch
Patrick, Anthony
Robertson, Isaac
Taber, Robert

Sergt. Joseph Low
Corp. Joseph O. Lemon

Privates.
Byars, David
Ford, Joseph
McCarthy, William
Powell, Elijah
Rhodes, Sandford
Tharp, Jonothan
Viney, John

Sergt. Alexander Allen

Privates.
Evans, Edward
Lemon, Laurence V.
Neally, William
Powell, Timothy
Largent, Abraham
Tharp, Andrew
Whitaker, Josiah

Page 96. Vol. 1.
ROLL OF CAPT. JOHN LINGLE'S COMPANY (Probably from Champaign Co.)
Served from October 15, until November 15, 1812.

Rank and Name of Soldier.
Capt. John Lingle
Sergt. John Crosly
Sergt. William Patten
Corp. William Kirkpatrick

Privates.
Audrick, Christopher
Cleveland, Martin
Goble, Thomas
Harnett, Elijah
Murphy, John
McBeth, William
Reynolds, James
Radish, Nathan
Sparrow, Ferdinand
Walker, George

Rank and Name of Soldier.
Lieut. Cyrus Ward
Sergt. Nicholas Prickett
Corp. Robert Reid
Fifer, John Richards

Privates.
Coventon, Henry
Dougherty, John
Gayne, Charles
Hargadine, William
Meenach, William
Nicholson, James
Rankin, George
Reed, Thomas
Shall, Peter
Wilson, Charles

Rank and Name of Soldier.
Ensign, James Humphreys
Sergt. David Crahill
Corp. George Arbogast
Drummer, Newton Bourroughs

Privates.
Cowen, John
Goble, Daniel
Gamble, Robert
Lewis, John
McBeth, Andrew
Reid, James
Richards, Elijah
Russell, James
Taylor, John

Page 97.
ROLL OF CAPT. JOHN R. LEMMON'S COMPANY
(Probably from Champaign County).
Served from November 12, until December 12, 1812.

Capt. John R. Lemmon
Sergt. Richard Robinson
Corp. Daniel Wren

Privates.
Arbogast, Henry
Botkin, William
Bombgarden, Andrew
Curl, William
Crantrall, Joshua
Dawson, Richard
Hodge, Andrew
Hunter, Jonothan
Lee, James
Marris, William
Runyon, Abraham
Smith, David
Sergant, John
Tuttle, John
Wren, Thomas

Ensign, Joseph Coffey
Sergt. Isaac Elsworth
Corp. Joseph Runyon
Corp. Jacob Elsworth

Privates.
Baldwin, Joshua
Boyer, Samuel
Collins, Joseph
Cartmell, Nathaniel
Dickeson, Joseph
Frost, William
Hunter, John
Hunter, James
Marsh, Malon
McKonkey, Archibald
Roberts, James
Smith, James
Tunks, Thomas
Van Cultz, David
Ward, Richard

Sergt. William Hunt
Sergt. Charles Irwin
Corp. Mathew Shaul

Privates.
Beezly, Isaac
Banes, Oratio
Clemmings, Job
Chance, Samuel
Dawson, James
Graham, David
Hunter, William
Jones, Jonothan
Moss, John
McKinnon, Daniel
Segar, David
Smith, Benjamin
Tunks, Phillip
Van Meter, Solomon

Pages 98-99-100.
ROLL OF CAPT. JOHN R. LEMMON'S COMPANY (Probably from Ross Co.)
Served from January 30, until April 11, 1815.

Capt. John R. Lemmon
Sergt. William Patrick
Sergt. Joshua Williams
Corp. James Tucker

Privates.
Albogast, Silas
Borden, James
Brewer, Jesse
Bane, Oratio
Croy, Jacob
Collison, John
Davis, John
Foust, Abraham
Green, William
Hill, William R.
Huff, Charles
Huston, James
Jamison, Charles
Krein, Adam
Missimore, Henry
McFarland, Daniel
Russell, Robert
Smith, Sherman
Townsley, John
Watson, Lewis
Willis, Hugh
Whitesel John

Lieut. James McArthur
Sergt. Ellis S. Baldwin
Corp. Joshua Spry
Musician, Briton Wright

Privates.
Bagea, Jacob
Buskirk, Lewis D.
Badger, James P.
Crossley, Conrad
Codington, William
Campbell, John
Earl, James
Griffin, Daniel
Goddard, Robert D.
Hird, Thomas
Hood, Edward
Jovin, William
King, William
Lloyd, John
Missimore, John
McHan, William
Stout, Benhon
Shanks, Peter
Tharp, James
Watson, Eli
Wallace, Thomas
Van Amburgh, Abraham

Ensign, David Henderson
Sergt. Phillip Sampson
Corp. John Fitzgerald
Musician, John Clark

Privates.
Bell, Alexander
Borer, Peter
Bulger, Elijah
Collins, Mathias
Clawson, Abraham
Dum, Henry
Fisher, Jonothan
Glass, James
Hickson, Enoch
Haines, Thomas
Hopkins, James
Jones, Robert
Konklin, John
Minor, Moses
McIntosh, William
McCartney, Isaac
Shrofe, David
Tuttle, Simon
Watson, Paschal
Williams, Isaac
Williams, Lewis

Page 101. Vol. I.

ROLL OF CAPT. A. HEMPHILL'S COMPANY (County Unknown).
This Company Under the Comman dof Lieut. Aaron Foster.

Served from July 28, 1813, ——————.

Rank and Name of Soldier.
Lieut. Aaron Foster

Privates.
Connal, William
Fischer, Jacob
Keenor, John
Latta, John
McNeel, Archibald
Ryan, Joshua

Rank and Name of Soldier.
Corp. William Brown

Privates.
Campbell, William
Griffin, Samuel
Little, John
Latta, James
Turnipseed, Christian
Stewart, Archibald
White, Merryman

Rank and Name of Soldier.

Privates.
Eli, William
Given, William
Latta, Moses
McMahon, Joseph
Toughman, Peter
Shanor, Henry

Pages 102-118.
ROLL OF CAPT. GEORGE GIBSON'S COMPANY (Probably from Ross County).

Served from December 31, 1814, until February 23, 1815.

Capt. George Gibson
Sergt. Mathew Mitchel
Sergt. George Watson
Corp. Richard Bradley

Privates.
Anderson, James
Benjamin, William
DeWitt, George
Edward, John
Francisco, Joseph
Hoselton, Jacob
Haverlow, William
Jones, Abel
Lock, John
Macklin, Thomas
Mason, James
McCoy, John
Richey, Andrew
Sweet, Stephen
Tway, John

Lieut. Mathew Littleton
Sergt. John Armstrong
Corp. Thomas Binton
Corp. William Seeds
Musician Thomas Littleton

Privates.
Argo, Abraham
Campbell, Hugh
Davidson, John
Fewel, John
Hamilton, James
Harrison, James
Igo, Daniel
King, Joshua
Lafferty, John
Morris, Richard
McCartney, Duke
McArthur, Duncan
Rodgers, Philemon
Swegert, Daniel
Wolf, Phillip

Ensign, Henry Gutches
Sergt. James McCollister
Corp. Thomas Richardson
Musician, Jacob Croghan

Privates.
Biviton, Basil
Culbertson, Robert
Elder, Thomas
Fullnig, Alexander
Heaston, Martin
Helsel, Daniel
Jaram, William
Ken, James
Martin, David
Mann, Reuben P.
McFadden, William
McCollum, Archibald
Stultz, Jacob
Simpson, Richard
Marshall, Thomas

Pages 103-104.
ROLL OF CAPT. WARREN BISSELL'S COMPANY
(Probably from Trumbull and Mahoning Counties).

Served from August 26, until November 30, 1812.

Capt. Warren Bissel
Ensign, Nicholas McConnel
Sergt. Asa Baldwin
Sergt. Parkis Woodruff
Sergt. Isaac Blackman
Corp. John Murphy

Privates.
Arrels, John
Beggs, Joseph
Brothers, John
Crawford, William
Cowden, Reynolds
Craft, Thomas
Dustman, Jacob
Dix, John
Fight, Jacob
Franks, Jacob
Gilbert, Henry
Gilbert, Samuel
Hardinger, Jacob
Hardy, John
Kline, Phillip
Love, Samuel
Love, William
Mears, Joseph
Maxwell, Robert
McCreary, William
McMullen, John
McGill, Joseph
McConnel, Richard
Noble, David
Reed, William
Stall, Andrew
Sell, John
Simons, Adam
Turner, Samuel
Potter, Samuel Y.
White, James
Whitezell, Jacob

Lieut. Caleb Baldwin
Ensign, Joseph Porter
Sergt. Simon Hall
Sergt. Philarmon Stilson
Corp. Abner Crossman
Corp. Henry Fitch

Privates.
Burgess, Robert
Buchanan, William
Beardsley, Josiah
Chaircher, David
Cunningham, James
Crooks, James
Diers, Jacob
Eckman, James
Fowler, John
Fankles, William
Graham, Jesse
Hamilton, Hugh
Hoyles John
Johnson, Abraham
Leonard, William
Liddle, John
Marchant, Joseph
Mokeman, George
McCombs, Thomas
McCreary, John
McGill, Robert
McConnel, Phillip
Onansweat, John
Rummage, Thomas
Spargo, George
Sharon, Hugh
Simons, Abraham
Turner, John
Upton, Benjamin
Walker, Josiah
White, James, Sr.

Lieut. Alexander Reany
Sergt. George A. Stilson
Sergt. John Dowlin
Sergt. Andrew Stull
Corp. William McCreary
Drummer, Michael Pelts

Privates.
Buchanan, John
Buchanan, Walter
Crossman, Abner
Cowden, John
Craze, Alexander
Denniston, David
Dawson, Aaron
Fitch, Henry
Foulk, Henry
Fish, Abner
Goucher, Robert
Hamilton, William
Hampton, John
Jack, James
Landon, Henry
Murphy, John
Malcom, Fall
Manchester, Benjamin
McMillen, Charles
McCombs, David
McGill, William
McCrary, Thomas
Rose, Robert
Rose, David
Spargo, George S.
Shields, William
Rose, John
Peterman, Jacob
Willey, Frederick
Wilson, Peter
Zedeker, John

ROSTER OF OHIO SOLDIERS IN WAR OF 1812   93

Page 105.   Vol. I.

ROLL OF CAPT. HARVEY MURRAY'S COMPANY.
(Probably from Cuyahoga County.)

Served from August 21, until November 30, 1812.

Rank and Name of Soldier.

Capt. Harvey Murray
Sergt. Ebenezer Green
Sergt. Thomas Hamilton
Corp. Asa Dille

Privates.

Burk, Aretas
Bishop, John
Beacher, Sylvester
Carlton, John
Dille, Samuel
Fish, Ebenezer
Judd, Daniel S.
Guy, Lee
McHuth, Thomas
Prentiss, Robert
Sumey, John
Thorp, Bazaleel
Vanduzen, Heartman
White, William

Rank and Name of Soldier.

Lieut. Lewis Dille
Sergt. Simion Moss
Corp. John Lauterman
Corp. Martin Shellhous
Drummer, Daniel Kielor

Privates.

Burk, Joseph
Bradley, Moses
Bills, James S.
Doyle, Anthony
Ewart, Samuel
Freeman, Zebulon R. S.
James, John
King, Stephen
McConkey, William
Ogden, Benjamin
Shadrick, Parker
Taylor, John
Williams, Joseph
Williamson, Mathew

Rank and Name of Soldier.

Ensign, Alfred Kelley
Sergt. Seth Doan
Corp. James Rost
Fifer, Adolphus Carlton

Privates.

Branden, Charles
Burk, Silas
Clark, Mason
Dille, Luther
Eldred, Moses
Harberson, Robert
James, Jackson
Mingus, Jacob
Noyes, Samuel
Read, David
Stearns, Luther
Thomas, Thomas
Wighteman, John

Page 106.

ROLL OF CAPT. JAMES HEZLEP'S COMPANY (County Unknown.)

Hezlep's Company served from January 1, until March 9, 1813.

Capt. James Hezlep
Sergt. Joseph McCombs
Sergt. Merriden Bixby
Corp. Adam Rallston

Privates.

Ague, George
Bissell, John
Castle, Joseph
Ellis, John
Foster, Ross
Graham, William
Lowry, Robert
Russell, James
Ray, Andrew
Truesdale, Hugh
Walters, James

Lieut. David Clendenin
Sergt. William H. Wright
Corp. Isaac McCombs
Corp. Johnson Lowry

Privates.

Andrews, Samuel
Baldwin, Bryan
Dean, Elijah
Foster, Henry
Fitch, Samuel
Jones, David
McFarland, William
Reed, John
Struthers, Alexander
Trusedale, James
Watson, William
Kyle, Joshua

Ensign, William Trusdale
Sergt. James Strain
Corp. Henry Mathews
Sergt. Joseph Applegate

Privates.

Brown, William
Bixby, Willis
Decker, Abraham
Foster, John
Garner, Hiram
Kirkpatrick, Andrew
McFarland, Andrew
Ragers, Reuben
Stephen, John F.
Trusedale, John
Strain, John

Pages 107-108-109.

ROLL OF CAPT. JOSEPH KRATZER'S COMPANY (County Unknown).

Served from July 29, until September 8, 1813.

Capt. Joseph Kratzer
Sergt. John Askren
Sergt. Robert Patton
Corp. Thomas Grogen
Corp. Caleb Shreve

Privates.

Boatman, Henry
Cowen, Levi
Crofford, William
Davidson, Daniel
Evans, Hugh
Fomb, Mathew
Gilgus, John
Johnson, James
John, Daniel
Kindall, James
Lucas, William
Miller, Hugh
Murphy, Thomas
Marshall, James
Pindal, John
Prichert, Jacob
Parish, Joshua
Record, Josiah
Springer, Uriah
Washburn, Isaac

Lieut. Barnett Ristine
Sergt. Benjamin Griffith
Sergt. Isaac Lucas
Corp. David McLaughlin
Corp. William Line

Privates.

Baty, David
Coulter, William Sr.
Cowen, Levi, Sr.
Denny, William
Ewing, Robert
Fenton, William
Howland, Levi
Jolley, Thomas
Kendall, Aaron
Long, Joseph
Lucas, Robison
Mortain, William
McKehon, Daniel
McIntire, Samuel
Pettijohn, Amos
Patin, John
Reeves, Thomas
Strane, Thomas
Stroaph, George
Walker, James
Whey, James

Ensign. Robert Breckenrige
Sergt. Thomas Shrow
Lieut. Benjamin Purdon
Corp. Uriah Higginbothom
Drummer, Simion Gardner

Privates.

Bonor, John
Coulter, William Jr.
Cross, James
Davis, Isaac
Forbs, Thomas
Glaze, Alexander
Higginbothom, John
John, William
Kinnett, Arthur
Lucas, John
Bare, William
Moore, William
McLaughlin, Patrick
Hains, Joseph
Phillips, Valentine
Pettijohn, Edward
Reed, William
Scott, Robert J.
Thomas, Rus
Wilson, David

Pages 110-111-112. Vol. I.

ROLL OF CAPT. DAVID HINE'S COMPANY (From Trumbull & Mahoning Cos.)

Served from August 23, until September 17, 1812.

Rank and Name of Soldier.

Capt. David Hine
Ensign, Thomas McCune
Sergt. Silas Johnston
Corp. Christopher Razon
Corp. Whitney, Smith

Lieut. Edmond P. Tanner
Ensign, Nicholas McConnel
Sergt. Daniel Fish
Corp. Joseph Bruce
Fifer, Jacob Osborn

Lieut. George Monteith
Sergt. Julius Fanner
Sergt. John Huston
Corp. Linus Tracy
Drummer, Zuah Cook

Privates.

Anderson, Arthur
Brunstetter, Henry
Chul, Henry
Carter, Joseph
Crays, Alexander
Fisher, Isaac
Godsped, Nathaniel
Hiter, George
Henry, Francis
Hayes, John
Kimmel, Phillip
Leonard, William
Leonard, Nicholas
Munns, William
McCreary, Robert
McConnaughy, James
McKinney, Henry
McKee, John
Noble, David
Pollock, James
Parker, John
Ripley, Harvey
Steel, William
Stephenson, Elijah
Smith, George
Taft, Aaron
White, John

Ague, Nathan
Bartholomew, Asahel
Calhoon, Samuel
Crumb, Henry
Condera, Ranels
Ford, Isaac
Guild, Jairus
Houck, Henry
Harting, John
Hoover, Abraham
Kerr, Robert
Leonard, George
Manchester, Benjamin
Marshall, William
McConnal, John
McCollon, John
McClane, Robert, Jr.
McLaughlin, John
Osborn, Conrad
Packert, Garret
Powers, Jacob
Roll, Benjamin
Saxton, John
Stump, Henry
Turner, John
Taylor, Simons
Young, John

Boyd, Henry
Camp, John
Carver, Seneca
Cummins, Thomas
Tharp, James H.
Green, Samuel
Hile, John
Hewey, Francis
Hull, Jacob
Jack, James
Landon, Henry
Lach, Abraham
Moore, James
McMullin, John
McCulley, John
McDonald, James
McKinney, William
Irwin, Thomas
Osborn, Joseph
Parker, Jacob
Parkhurst, Isaac
Shook, Jacob
Storm, Michael
Stewart, Daniel
Thomas, William
Venamor, Nicholas

Pages 113-114.

ROLL OF CAPT. JAMES KILGORE'S COMPANY (Probably from Ross Co.)

Served from October 1, until November 5, 1812.

Capt. James Kilgore
Sergt. John Galaspy
Sergt. Adam Stewart

Lieut. William Johnston
Sergt. James How
Corp. William Malone

Ensign, William Niblack
Sergt. Hugh Dolshon

Privates.

Arthers, Samuel
Beall, Phillip
Corkin, Thomas
Chenowoth, Joseph
Fields, Peter
Little, James
Moler, Jacob
Ridgeway, David
Thomas, Webster

Alexander, Francis
Butte, Thomas
Campbell, Jonothan
Dyer, Gasper
Hanson, Hollis
Lytle, Hugh
Poor, George
Reed, James
Vial, John

Alcutt, Israel
Cartright, Nathaniel
Chenowith, Elijah
Eckenbarger, Stephen
Kelley, Samuel
Miller, Watson
Rawles, Elijah
Stanholt, George
Wells, Absalom

Page 115.

ROLL OF CAPT. GEORGE KESLING'S COMPANY (Probably from Warren Co.)

Served from September 27, until October 20, 1812.

Capt. George Kesling
Sergt. William Ellis

Lieut. William Slaiback
Sergt. Stephen Minor

Lieut. John T. Ross
Sergt. John McCormac

Privates.

Aldridg, Joseph
Bilderback, Gabriel
Carvell, Jacob
Foley, William
Long, John
Montford, David
Mays, Samuel
Morgan, Jesse
McManis Robert
Noble, Joshua
Stires, Ralph
Trimble, Daniel
Watson, Robert

Blackford, John
Bordman, John
Cornell, Sylvanus
Hatfield, Clark
Lowen, James A.
Mullin, William
Mays, John
Moore, Nathan
McCann, Alexander
Richardson, Daniel
Steel, Joseph
West, Hugh
White, Thomas

Boosoe, Henry
Cassairt, Henry
Ellis, Isaac
Headley, William
Long, Minor
Mansfield, John
Morehead, John
McLean, Aaron
McCall, Robert S.
Ray, William
Stonebraker, Jacob
West, William

Pages 116-117. Vol. I.
ROLL OF CAPT. PHILLIP KISER'S COMPANY
(Probably from Champaign County).
Served from September 19, until October 19, 1812, and from August 12, until September 21, 1813.

Rank and Name of Soldier.	Rank and Name of Soldier.	Rank and Name of Soldier.
Capt. Phillip Kiser	Lieut. William Rumple	Lieut. John Rhodes
Lieut. James Toomer	Ensign, Daniel Kilbinger	Sergt. Patrick McKinley
Sergt. Peter Pence	Sergt. Benjamin Pence	Sergt. Nathan Dannall
Sergt. William Steel	Sergt. Colon, Moore	Sergt. John Fitch
Sergt. George Crosby	Corp. John Tofflenover	Corp. Edden Jenkins
Corp. John West	Corp. Nelson Lansdell	Corp. William Haltz
Corp. John Pyatt	Corp. Ebenezer Rhodes	Corp. Nathan Adamson
Drummer, Joseph Jones	Drummer, Edward Tarbutton	Fifer, Pressley Ross
	Fifer, Henry Armacush	
Privates.	**Privates.**	**Privates.**
Baker, Samuel	Baker, John	Boswell, George
Beatty, John	Beacon, William	Blue, John
Bags, William	Bozier, Isaac	Bacer, Isaac
Bradford, Charles	Barnes, William	Bates, John
Barnes, Horatio	Colbert, John	Crafton, Ambias
Cirkel, Abraham	Cowhick, Thomas	Chapman, Elijah
Cox, Joseph	Clark, Absalom	Cowen, Joseph S.
Davis, Andrew	Darnell, Roswell	Darnell, David
Diltz, Samuel	Dilton, William	Dawson, John
Dawson, James	Dudley, Jabez	Dudley, John
Edgar, Andrew	Elliott, Mills	Forman, William
Flemming, Henry	Foley, William	Godard, Jesse
Gray, David	Grafton, James	Hall, Joseph
Herd, Thomas	Huls, Henry	Howell, Joshua
Humble, Valentine	Hunter, James	Holler, John
Idol, Jacob	Jones, Stephen	Jones, David
Jones, Isaac	Jenkins, Russell	Jackson, Daniel
Kiblinger, Adam	Kelley, Sampson	Kirkpatrick, George
Kelley, Thomas	Largent, John	Lansdale, Nelson
Lansdale, Thomas	Loudeback, Daniel	Little, John
Maggert, John	Martin, Isaac	Moody, John
McBeth, Andrew	Nason, Daniel	Nelson, Thomas
Protsman, David	Prince, Adam	Pence, Daniel
Pence, Henry	Pence, Abraham	Pence, Samuel
Reid, John	Rouse, Levi	Rouse, John
Rose, John	Rector, Samuel	Smith, David
Smith, John	Sibert, Henry	Segar, David
Smith, David, Jr.	Swanger, John	Steele, Joseph
Snodgrass, James	Syns, Joseph	Stephens, Abraham
Smith, Peter	Stranbarger, John	Sills, Michael
Stepelton, John	Speace, Daniel	Shockey, Abraham
Taylor, John	Taber, Robert	Tunks, Phillip
Tarbutton, Eli	Wilson, Robert	West, Stukell
Welch, George	Wells, Thomas	West, Edmund
Walker, George W.	West, Thomas	West, John

Page 119.
ROLL OF SERGT. JAMES EAKINS' COMPANY (County Unknown).
Served from July 28, until August 13, 1813.

Sergt. James Eakins	Sergt. Jacob Cox	Corp. James Ferren
Corp. Jacob Newland		
Privates.	**Privates.**	**Privates.**
Brewer, Jacob	Beckman, Gabriel	Beaver, Mathias
Beaver, Michael	Chapman, Henry	Horn, James
Horn, Joseph	Herdman, John	Mershon, Solomon
Mershon, Daniel	Mershon, Timothy	Mershon, Henry
Smith, John	Smith, William	Thomas, Nathan
Thomas, Phillip	Thompson, Henry	Thoroman, Charles
	Williams, William	

Pages 120-121-122.
ROLL OF LIEUT. JOHN DEVAULT OR DEVALL'S COMPANY
(Probably from Washington County).
Served from January 31, until April 10, 1815.

Lieut. John Devault or Devall	Sergt. Isaac House	Sergt. Thomas Devault
Sergt. Levi Bevington	Corp. Gilbert Harley	Corp. Morris Baker
	Corp. James Plymell	
Privates.	**Privates.**	**Privates.**
Aye, Henry	Chad, George	Callender, John
Doty, Ephraim	Dyer, William	Doty, William
Dunkle, Jacob	George, Ephraim	Harrison, William
Hobaugh, Phillip	Harter, John	Hurley, William
Hayes, David	Harrison, Phillip	Holbough, John
Hotter, Benjamin	Long, Benjamin	Long, Robert
Mitchell, Robert	Moore, Samuel	Mitchell, Samuel
Moore, Benjamin	Neely, George	Neely, Benjamin
Rhodes, George	Rhodes, Richard	Roebuck, Benjamin
Sharoertz, Daniel	Shackles, Richard	Sanders, John
Sanders, Ezra	Kerr, William	Kile, Oliver
Chaver, Joseph	Roebuck, George	Travis, Ezra
Thompson, Davis	Wright, Caleb	Winder, Joseph
Yates, Maurice	Yates, Horace	

Page 123. Vol. I.

ROLL OF CAPT. DAVID DANIELS' COMPANY (County Unknown).

Served from July 28, until August 28, 1813.

Rank and Name of Soldier.

Capt. David Daniels
Sergt. James Buckman

Privates.

Bumgarner, John
Collison, Moses
Downing, William
Guthrie, George
Kelleson, John

Rank and Name of Soldier.

Lieut. Abraham Bonnet
Sergt. William Rea
Corp. Joseph Boiler

Privates.

Brown, William
Chinworth, Eli
Guthrie, John
Hotsenpiler, Jacob
Morrison, James
Pry, Jacob

Rank and Name of Soldier.

Ensign, Henry Slaven
Corp. David Miller

Privates.

Brown, John
Cheny, Isaac
Gallagher, Mansfield
Foster, Isaac
Nessel, George

Pages 124-125-126-127.

ROLL OF CAPT. ADAM BERRY'S COMPANY (From Pickaway & Ross Cos.)

Served from April 11, until May 12, 1813, and from April 11, until May 12, 1814.

Capt. Adam Berry
Ensign, John Thebus
Sergt. George Spangler
Sergt. Blain
Sergt. John Clark
Corp. Hugh Caul
Drummer, Jacob Smith

Privates.

Alcot, Israel
Beck, Alexander
Bellote, Walter
Barber, Edward
Cobb, Hugh
Coaley, James R.
Cheneworth, George
Dod, Adam
Evans, Aldridge
Graham, Joseph
Hurst, Thomas
Harbert, Richard
John, Thomas
Kimble, Jacob
Laurence, Henry
Linn, Jacob
Mathew, John
Myers, John
Moore, James
Nubegal, William
Newman, William
Odle, Stephen
Pervolt, Thomas
Ritchie, Andrew
Redden, Robert
Strawser, David
Snodgrass, John
Sodden, John
Timons, Henry
Timmers, Samuel
Winland, William
Waldron, Phillip

Lieut. Arthur McPhee or McKee
Sergt. John Beavens
Sergt. Thomas Powell
Sergt. George Fry
Sergt. John Shoup
Corp. John Knight
Fifer, George Shaugler

Privates.

Andrew, Thomas
Ballinger, Joseph
Ballard, Linsey S.
Bagley, Thomas
Cogley, Thomas
Chenworth, Thomas
Chambers, John
Dunn, Zephaniah
Fullen, Alexander
Grant, William
Hall, James
Haynes, Henry
Johnson, Jacob
Kinser, George
Lunback, Henry
Lewis, William
Marsh, Titus
Munday, John
McCord, Thomas
Nease, Abraham
Knight, John
Pertee, George
Peters, Jacob
Redden, Reuben
Southviord, Henry
Sewel, David
Steward, Stephen
Thomas, Andrew
Trulling, Abraham
Vangundie, John
White, Peter
Waldron, George
Wiggins, John

Ensign, John Thompson
Sergt. Jacob Smith
Sergt. John Spores
Sergt. Adam Zehrung
Corp. Phillip Least
Corp. Stephen Stewart

Privates.

Burben, Edward
Brown, Joshua
Blane, John
Clark, John
Crum, Thomas
Clark, Robert
Dungan, Titus
Erwin, William
Frye, George
Garratt, Russell
Harmon, Samuel H.
Harpster, Peter
Johnston, Joel
Kennison, Reuben
Lambart, Isaac
Miller, George
Mounts, Humphrey
Martz, George
McFadden, William
Noland, William
List, Phillip
Petty, Absalom
Reed, Samuel
Ratcliff, Charles
Sidenbender, John
Sowder, John
Suthard, Henry
Troy, Jacob
Turly, Andrew
Vestle, Nathan
Warren, Moses
Wykoff, John

Page 128.

ROLL OF CAPT. ALEXANDER BROWER'S COMPANY (County Unknown).

Served from February 12, until May 23, 1813.

Capt. Alexander Brower
Corp. William Aldridge

Privates.

Campbell, Joseph
Knatt, James
Harvey, Christopher
Rose, Ephraim
Smallwood, Richard

Ensign, Samuel Cresswell
Drummer, John Moore

Privates.

Eakin, John
Hurt, John
Hammond, David
Smith, Jacob
Stephenson, John

Sergt. Isaac West
Fifer, Samuel Coburn

Privates.

Figley, Simeon
Hoffmer, Daniel
Pugh, Aaron
Shiveley, Christopher
Yarnell, Abraham

Pages 129-130-131-132. Vol. I.

ROLL OF CAPT. ROBERT GILMORE'S COMPANY (County Unknown).

Served from August 24, until August 28, 1812, and from February 10, until August 15, 1813.

Rank and Name of Soldier.	Rank and Name of Soldier.	Rank and Name of Soldier.
Capt. Robert Gilmore	Lieut. John Reddin	Lieut. Frederick Harmon
Lieut. William Barkheimer	Ensign, William Ross	Sergt. Robert Young
Sergt. Horace Ladd	Sergt. Ephraim Rose	Sergt. John Sharard
Sergt. William Maxwell	Corp. John Smith	Corp. John Gardner
Corp. William Coburn	Corp. Thomas Greenfield	Corp. Samuel Whitney
Fifer, Thomas Thornbaugh	Drummer, Virgil Moore	

Privates.

Asburn, William	Augustine, George	Armstrong, Benjamin
Augustine, Henry	Bailey, Joshua	Bowlen, John
Belet, Mathew	Burns, Peter	Bricker, John
Bower, David	Bell, William	Burnes, Harvey
Burk, Gains	Baldwin, Amzi	Celkers, George
Cradds, Phillip	Craign, John	Clark, John
Coss, Nathaniel	Campbell, Samuel	Carter, John
Cross, Thomas	Carroll, Phillip	Doop, John
Dunlap, John	Denun, James	Dawson, William
Deigreis, John	Downard, James	Bennet, Conrad
Endsey, Andrew	Ewing, Samuel	Flemming Patrick
Freet, George	Gilmore, John	Gotthalls, Johann
Gotthalls, William	Gossage, Thomas	Golloway, James
Grier, David	Hoover, Jacob	Heany, Jacob
Hammond, Jacob	Hall, James	Hannon, John
Hopkins, Benjamin	Hart, Lewis	Holmes, Stephen
Haley, Joseph	Judd, Daniel S.	Kuntz, John
Knap, Caleb	Leech, Benjamin	Leaper, Samuel
Lee, Lemuel	Mapel, David	Mellinger, John H.
Merker, James	McComis, James	McKinley, James
McClelland, Thomas	McMillen, James	McClorg, Joseph
McKonkey, William	McLaughlin, George	McElwin, Robert
Pagle, Mordecai	Peterman, Jacob	Patton, John
Palmer, Jesse	Pond, Phineas	Pettibone, Henry S.
Pettibrook, Morton	Reed, Thomas	Rose, Asa
Ray, James	Rogers, Samuel	Rogers, Richard
Ranson, Abide	Robbins, Joseph	Ross, Adams
Stone, Jeremiah	Steele, Jacob	Smith, Adam
Saint, John	Steward, Samuel	Shull, Adam
Saint, Joseph	Switzer, John	Shultz, Henry
Spidle, John	Shenefelt, John	Seelye, Abner
Sike, Phillip	Shively, Christian	Smith, Zepheniah
Saint, Lewis	Stephens, John	Stewart, David
Sipe, Phillip	Stevens, Daniel	Taylor, George
Tulley, James	Underwood, Joseph	Van Horn, Peter
White, Ira	Wyant, Burget	Woods, George
Ward, Robert	Wall, Joseph	Warner, Chauncey
Watson, Robert	Woodward, Daniel	Williams, John
Williams, Charles	Young, Seth	Zuver, George

Pages 133-134-135.

ROLL OF CAPT. WILLIAM DOUGLAS' COMPANY
(Probably from Knox and Richland Counties).

Served from August 26, until October 10, 1812, and from May 4, until May 19, 1813.

Capt. William Douglas	Lieut. John Wheeler	Lieut. Daniel Ayres
Lieut. Samuel Everett	Sergt. Daniel Cooper	Sergt. John C. Gilkison
Sergt. Joseph Berry	Sergt. Henry Markley	Sergt. Cyrus Langworthy
Sergt. William McCartney	Sergt. Abel Cook	Corp. Thomas Axtell
Corp. Edward Wheeler	Corp. Levi Sutton	

Privates.

Ashley, Abel	Adams, James	Burns, Jabez
Bartlett, David	Barney, Charles	Bevans, William
Baptist, John	Cooper, Jacob	Cooper, Elias
Coe, Luther	Chambers, William	Casper, William
Durphy, Freeman	Durbin, Scott	Downs, William
Dowds, William	Corwin, Benjamin	Forsythe, James
Fishback, Richard	Gilkison, James M.	Giberson, Joseph
Hall, William	Irvin, James	Jackson, John
Kimble, Daniel	Johnston, Levi	Layland, John
May, Chison	Mazers, Peter	Mazers, John
Mazers, Nathan	Macaber, John	Loveridge, James
Ogle, Enoch	Peoples, David	Peoples, Robert
Rodgers, Joseph	Ridal, John	Spry, Perry
Smith, James	Shurr, William	Strong, Harley
Sawyer, John	Yeoman, Samuel	

Page 136. Vol. I.
ROLL OF LIEUT. ICHABOD NYE'S COMPANY (Probably from Knox County).
Served from October 27, until December 27, 1812, and from May 4, until May 19, 1813.

Rank and Name of Soldier.	Rank and Name of Soldier.	Rank and Name of Soldier.
Lieut. Ichabod, Nye, Sr.		
Privates.	**Privates.**	**Privates.**
Barrell, Joseph	Hinthorn, John, Sr.	Hinthorn, John, Jr.
Jackson, Zeba	Laylin, Charles	Miller, Andrew
McGoing, Charles	McCartney, William	Pierce, Lewis
Pool, John	Tegardson, George	

Page 138.
ROLL OF CAPT. THOMAS CLAUSON'S COMPANY (From Montgomery County).
Served from August 23, until September 17, 1812.

Capt. Thomas Clauson	Lieut. John Archer, Jr.	Ensign Benjamin Luce
	Sergt. William Blair	
Privates.	**Privates.**	**Privates.**
Allen, Jeremiah	Bigger, Thomas	Baltimore, Phillip
Codington, William	Clauson, Abraham	Clauson, Peter
Covolt, Ephraim	Day, William	Dill, William
Dunkin, John	Dunken, Peter	Ewing, Garner
Gerrard, John	Hatfield, Owen	Hufferd, John
Lunderland, Peter	Luce, Moses	Lee, Henry
Loy, Peter	Mills, James	Majors, James
Majors, David	McKinney, John	Shanks, Peter
Shanks, John	Snowden, James	Sanders, John
Watkins, Daniel	Watkins, John	

Page 139.
ROLL OF CAPT. ABNER AYRES' COMPANY (County Unknown).
Served from May 4, until May 19, 1813.

Capt. Abner Ayres	Ensign Amos A. Royce	Sergt. William Smith
Sergt. Jacob Mitchell	Sergt. John Trimble	Corp. Isaac Williams
Corp. George Ayres	Corp. John Brown	Drummer, John Haldemer
Privates.	**Privates.**	**Privates.**
Aker, Andrew	Brown, Thomas	Joseph, Bland
Boles, Thomas	Day, Josiah B.	Grant, Josiah
Johnston, Daniel	Light, Celeste	Manning, Alfred
McGown, James	McIntire, James	Pinkley, John
Roberts, William F.	Thompson, Andrew	

Page 140.
ROLL OF CAPT. GEORGE ZIEGLER'S COMPANY (County Unknown).
Served from May 6, until May 20, 1813.

Capt. George Ziegler	Lieut. John Donaldson	Ensign Abraham Pickering
Sergt. Charles McCormick	Sergt. Heck, John	Sergt. William McIntosh
Sergt. Henry Donaldson	Corp. David Crossin	Corp. Jacob Claws
Corp. Jacob Collars	Corp. Thomas Martin	
Privates.	**Privates.**	**Privates.**
Alexander, James	Allen, Jedediah	Rabb, Jonothan
Bugh, John	Cablien, Caleb	Donaldson, Aaron
Finck, George	Fickel, Daniel	Kitsmiller, Andrew
Lassley, Peter	Miller, James	Millholland, Thomas
McCollum, Samuel	Newel, John	Neysemauger, David
Overmire, Peter	Prickets, Clement G.	Peppus, John
Pence, Jacob	Reed, William	Ricketts, William
Raver, William	Styers, John	Smith, Hezekiah
Trout, John	Taylor, John	

Page 141.
ROLL OF CAPT. JOSEPH COLEMAN'S COMPANY (Probably from Miami Co.)
Served from May 4, until May 19, 1813.

Capt. Joseph Coleman	Lieut. Thomas McKee	Sergt. Thomas Erwin
Sergt. Jacob Martin	Corp. Nathan Mages	Corp. George Downs
Privates.	**Privates.**	**Privates.**
Asheraft, Jonothan	Lalin, John	Marquis, William
Spry, Perry	Smith, James	Thompson, Uriah
Wilson, John		

Pages 144-145. Vol. I.

ROLL OF CAPT. LEMUEL CONNELLY'S COMPANY (County Unknown).
Served from July 28, until September 5, 1813.

Rank and Name of Soldier.	Rank and Name of Soldier.	Rank and Name of Soldier.
Capt. Lemuel Connelly	Lieut. Joseph Paset, Sr.	Ensign John Parratt
Ensign Samuel Holladay	Sergt. Joseph Creamor	Sergt. James Sanderson
Sergt. William Blackmore	Sergt. William Young	Sergt. Daniel Saward
Corp. Samuel Wicke	Corp. Stephen Hunt	Corp. George Wilson
Corp. William Tracy	Corp. Abraham Workman	Musician, Robert Smith
	Musician, William Kift	
Privates.	**Privates.**	**Privates.**
Antus, John	Arnold, John	Baldwin, William
Bates, William	Bentley, Jonothan	Creamer, David
Day, Bazel	Devitt, George	Cochran, Barnabus
Garrison, Abner	Grady, James	Godfrey, Thomas
Hance, Lemuel	Howe, Jacob	Jones, Oliver
Kirkpatrick, James	Kilgore, Clark	Limes, William
Moon, William	Michael, Jacob	Miller, John
McKay, Jesse	McChandless, Hugh	McFarland, John
Pauley, David	Popejoy, William	Pool, Edward
Rankin, Hugh	Ruport, George	Rankan, Thomas
Sanderson, Alexander	Sawyer, George	Short, Henry
Studiman, William V.	Stanfar, Pierce	Somerville, John
Tracy, Solomon	Tracy, William	Tharp, William
Vann, John	Wilson, George	Wright, Hosea
Witty, William	Wright, David	Workman, John

Page 146.

ROLL OF CAPT. ZECHARIAH P. DEWITT'S COMPANY.
(Probably from Butler County).
Served from September 20, until November 19, 1814.

Capt. Zechariah P. DeWitt	Lieut. John Freeman	Ensign, Henry Watts
Sergt. Samuel Pressley	Sergt. Philip Wiggins	Sergt. John Garard
Sergt. George Kirkpatrick	Corp. Henry Riggs	Corp. Abraham Ansman
Corp. Clement Bostwick	Corp. William H. Lloyd	
Privates.	**Privates.**	**Privates.**
Albartson, William	Albertson, Nathaniel	Black, David
Bridgford, William, Sr.	Bridgford, William, Jr.	Bridgford John
Beedle, Simeon	Coe, Joseph	Cantwal, Hugh
Dollahan, John	Dunn, George F.	Devore, John
Ewing, Matthew	Fowler, James	Fowler, Jeremiah
Freeman, John	Hall, Peter	Hancock, James
Harper, Joseph	Jones, Jonas	Johnson, John
Morris, Enoch	Milan, John	Morris, William
Morris, Jacob	Sloan, Richard	Seward, Isaac
Tilson, Leonard	Jones, John	Taylor, Robert
Taylor, William	Truman, John	Whilavre, John

Page 147.

ROLL OF CAPT. JACOB BELL'S COMPANY (County Unknown).
Served from September 14, until October 14, 1812.

Capt. Jacob Bell	Lieut. William Kerr	Ensign, Thomas Powers
Sergt. James H. Martin	Sergt. John Brady	Sergt. Reuben Ryan
Sergt. John Clark	Corp. William Denman	Corp. Joseph Hand
Corp. William Curry	Corp. John Lingle	
Privates.	**Privates.**	**Privates.**
Allen, Jacob	Andrews, Isaac	Bryan, James
Brown, Aaron	Bell, Abel	Baird, John
Codington, William	Craig, Daniel	Edwards, Elijah
Griffin, David	Hand, Aaron	Kelly, William
Keeter, John	Morris, William	Miller, Elias
Morris, Enoch	Moxer, Ebenezer	Martin, William
Mott, John	Rowe, Joseph	Rowe, Abraham
Stogdon, William	Spencer, Joseph	Snyder, Samuel
Simpson, Allen	Vanblaugher, Peter	Vanmater, Abraham
Welsh, William	Weaver, Henry	Whittaker, Daniel

Page 148.

ROLL OF CAPT. JAMES BARNETT'S COMPANY. (County Unknown.)
Served from August 23, until September 19, 1812.

Capt. James Barnett	Lieut. James McEiven	Ensign, David Steel
Sergt. Henry Gagany	Sergt. William Patterson	Sergt. John Tucker, Jr.
Corp. Mathew M. Dodd	Corp. John Kelley	Corp. Robert Young
	Drummer, Cyrus Thartan	
Privates.	**Privates.**	**Privates.**
Allen, Moses	DuPriest, Charles	Gott, John
Hinner, John	Buckhannon, James	Jones, Isaac
Lowrey, Joseph	Musselman, John	McLucas, Samuel
McLucas, William	McGrew, William	Neff, Christopher
Osborn, David	Parson, Lewis	Robb, Johnson
Shepherd, Thomas	Tucker, John Sr.	VanSkogk, Joseph
Wilson, Samuel	Wolf, Conrad	Wade, James
Veale, Samuel	Wagner, Michael	York, Jeremiah

Page 149. Vol. I.

ROLL OF CAPT GEORGE BUCHANAN'S COMPANY (Probably from Miami Co.)

Served from May 5, until August 13, 1812.

Rank and Name of Soldier.	Rank and Name of Soldier.	Rank and Name of Soldier.
Capt. George Buchanan	Lieut. James C. Caldwell	Ensign, Gardner Bobo
Sergt. Andrew Tilford	Sergt. Joseph Hale	Sergt. Benjamin Saunders
Sergt. James Barnett	Sergt. David McClung	
Privates.	**Privates.**	**Privates.**
Allen, Nathan	Brown, James	Black, Jacob
Beedle, Abraham	Bimgardner, Jacob	Balbee, William
Blue, Michael	Beedle, Jacob	Beedle, Joseph
Duprey, Stephen	Freeman, Noah	Fulkirth, William
Fugate, Edward	Foster, Elijah	Garard, John
Hamer, George	Haney, Jacob	Hurley, Cornelius
Huston, Joseph	Hickman, David	Hurley, Zechariah
Johnson, Giles	Jenkins, George	Jackson, Jacob
Jackson, John	Knoop, John	Leonox, Richard
Lupton, John	Montgomery, Robert	Millhouse, John
Mackey, Samuel	McClary, John	McPhaddon, James
North, William	Prillaman, Christian	Prillman, Daniel
Potts, James	Polset, John E.	Shepherd, Elijah
Thompson, Andrew	Tullis, Aaron	Shoaf, George
Stetler, Abraham	Stedler, John	Shaw, Thomas

Pages 150-151-152.

ROLL OF CAPT. JOHN CLARK'S COMPANY (Probably from Green County).

Served from October 18, until November 20, 1812, and from August 10, until September 5, 1813.

Capt. John Clark	Lieut. John Blessing	Lieut. Samuel Jenkins
Ensign, Boston Hoblit	Ensign, Robert Breddy	Sergt. James Buckles
Sergt. William Knight	Sergt. John Long	Sergt. Edward Allen
Sergt. James Ross	Sergt. Isaachar Pepper	Sergt. John McElvey
Sergt. Perry Timmons	Corp. James Rowe	Corp. Robert Demis
Corp. Arthur Lavis	Corp. John Dysert	Corp. John Biddle
Corp. James Stephenson	Corp. Thomas Cason	Corp. Benjamin Allen
Privates.	**Privates.**	**Privates.**
Armstrong, John	Amos, Pleasant	Biddle, Henry
Buckles, David	Brown, William	Blue, Daniel
Brown, Zechariah	Cully, Thomas	Cramer, Solomon
Clark, William	Cully, Joseph	Carroll, Samuel
Caldhoon, John	Cook, James	Cox, John
Dureavida, Samuel	Dougherty, Samuel	Dunwida, John
Davis, James	Dennis, Mathias	Dennis, Jonothan
Dennis, Samuel	Ennis, Samuel	Earl, James
Flowers, Aaron	Griffith, Benjamin	Hibbs, Abner
Howard, Nicholas	Hamilton, William	Jones, Joshua
Jones, Lewis	Bucklrs, Henry	Lewis, Joel
Logue, John	Lewis. Jesse	Lackey, John
Meriman, Joshua	Miller, Charles	Mills, Constantine
Merriman, Aaron	Jones, Thomas	Miniar, Phillip
Miniar, Stephen	Meekins, John	McKnight, Robert
McKee, Joseph	McArthur, Duncan	Porter, James
Rice, Pitch	Rayburn, William	Rodgers, John
Ridley, James	Sackett, Joseph	Smith, Jacob
Sanders, Jesse	Smith, Thomas	Lanime, William
Thorn, Jacob	Whickear, Asa	Warfield, Richard
Worthington, John	Wiley, Jesse	Williams, Gammage
Worthington, Ephraim	Walker, Charles	

Page 153.

ROLL OF CAPT. SAMUEL CALDWELL'S COMPANY (Probably from Warren County).

Served from August 23, until September 18, 1812.

Capt. Samuel Caldwell	Lieut. John C. Death	Lieut. Thomas Covenhoven
Cornet, Robert Young	Sergt. Stephen Reeder	Sergt. Daniel Storms
Sergt. Joseph Crane	Sergt. James Death, Jr.	Q. M. Sergt. James W. Lanier
Corp. Samuel Campbell	Corp. William Harrison	Corp. Christian Petfish
	Corp. Joseph Parks, Jr.	
Privates.	**Privates.**	**Privates.**
Abbott, John	Allen, John	Bowersack, David
Baldwin, William	Bell, Benjamin	Barnett, John
Craig, Obediah	Death, Bazil	Death, James E.
Death, Samuel	Debrock, Alexander	Ferris, Joseph
Flinn, Daniel	Galbraith, Joseph	Gordon, George
Hammel, Joseph	Irwin, David	Jordan, John
Keslin, Peter	Lang, Charles	Miller, James
McFreen, John	McCord, John	McMeen, Josiah C.
McClure, Ezekial	Orr, Samuel	Perry, William
Potter, Hiram	Payen, Stephen	Robison, Robert
Ross, John	Squires, Timothy	Trimble, James
Vanott, Samuel	Wer, Alexander	Walker, Gracon
Ware, Phillip	Young, Jacob	Troxel, Joseph

Page 154. Vol. I.
ROLL OF CAPT. THOMAS WILLIAMS' COMPANY (County Unknown).

Served from August 29, until September 9, 1812.

Capt. Thomas Williams
Sergt. Samuel Rose

Lieut. Isaac Chambers
Sergt. Edward Haskney

Ensign, Aurelius Thrall

Privates.

Andrews, Isaac
Barret, Stephen
Collins, John
Dush, John
Faunbaker, John
George, John
Hannon, James
Lane, Dutton
Leach, Nehemiah
Moore, Cyrus
Mark, John
Mapes, Thomas
Potter, Jacob
Russell, Phillip
Simpson, Samuel L.
Tharp, Josiah
Warner, Lyman
Weikiger, Abraham

Privates.

Alexander, William
Bennett, Isaac
Collins, Woodgate
Duffey, Hugh
Gray, William
Hedley, Samuel
Hoover, John
Loran, John
Lane, Benjamin
Miller, William
Matson, William
Neselrode, Christopher
Priest, Levi
Spray, John W.
Tipton, Solomon
Thrailkield, Thomas
Walker, Daniel
Williamson, John

Privates.

Arnold, John
Cook, Alexander
Deaver, Walter
Funk, Jacob
Gray, Samuel
Hill, Pressley R.
Kidd, William
Longley, George
Morris, Jesse M.
Many, Michael
Mills, John
Norman, James
Russell, James
Sheldon, Thomas
Twitzer, John
Tharp, Joel
Woodward, William
Whitaker, Isaac

Pages 155-156-157.
ROLL OF CAPT. HENRY BRUSH'S COMPANY (Probably from Ross County).

Served from July 20, until October 4, 1812.

Captain Henry Brush
Ensign, William S. Hutt
Sergt. Robert Stockton
Sergt. Samuel Swearingen
Corp. Richard Snyder
Corp. John Buck

Lieut. William Beach
Ensign, John Stockton
Sergt. Craighead Ferguson
Sergt. Jacob Cryder
Corp. Henry May
Corp. Frederick Fisher
Corp. Matthew Simpson

Lieut. John Entricken
Sergt. William Robinson
Sergt. Henry L. Prentice
Sergt. William Armstrong
Corp. James McDougal
Corp. Joseph Cissna

Privates.

Armstrong, William
Buchanan, Henry
Brown, Peter
Baker, Henry
Cissna, James
Campbell, William
Dougherty, Levi
DuSouchel, Francis
Downs, William
Eastwood, Isaac
Frazer, Malilon
Ferguson, John
Huston, James
Hall, James
Immell, Israel
Johnston, David
Bayley, Thomas
Mitchell, John
Morris, Priestly
McArthur, Duncan
McRoberts, William
Peebles, John
Robinson, James
Shaffer, Jacob
Simpson, Oliver
Stockton, John
Tiffin, Joseph
Willett, Samuel
Watson, John
Williamson, Thomas

Privates.

Andrews, Hugh
Bailey, William
Brush, Edmond
Chew, Colby
Cissna, Stephen
Cunningham, Samuel
Davison, William
Davis, Samuel
Dribler, George
Devault, Lemuel
Fulton, William
Hoffman, Adam E.
Hoffman, John
Hughes, Alexander
Johnson, William
Leister, Peter
Langham, John S.
Mitchell, James S.
McGrim, William
McCann, John G.
Orr, Samuel
Pierce, Edward W.
Russell, James
Stewart, Archibald
Steel, John
Thompson, Nathan
Trewitt, Solomon
Watson, John
Williams, Samuel
Young, George

Privates.

Beyerly, Michael
Bready, Robert
Barber, Uriah
Cissna, Joseph
Creighton, William
Curry, James
Davis, Lewis
Dill, Robert
Evans, Horatio
Essex, Jesse
Finnemore, Ebenezer
Holmes, Robert
Hall, John
Hutcheson, Ezekial
Langham, Elias
Hutt, William S.
Miller, Joseph
Monroe, Jonothan
McCollough, Samuel
McGregor, Daniel
Petty, Ebenezer
Rust, George
Shaver, James
Smith, Adam
Sherlock, Edward
Taylor, Isaac
Thompson, John
Wallace, Cadwallader
Williams, Abraham

Page 158.
ROLL OF CAPT. DAVID KASEBEER'S COMPANY (County Unknown.)

Served from August 1, until October 31, 1812.

Capt. David Kasebeer
Sergt. George Stout

Lieut. Samuel Kniseley
Corp. Jacob Snyder

Ensign, John Hornish
Corp. John Stiflor

Privates.

Beavar, Jacob
Butt, Benjamin
Bickle, Thomas
Eakin, James
Fruckler, Henry
Gomer, David
Heaton, Joseph
Kollar, Adam

Privates.

Bess, Isaac
Butt, Joseph
Bickle, David
Flickenger, John
Foreman, David
Hurst, Samuel
Hubaugh, Frederick
Kasebeer, Samuel

Privates.

Baker, George
Baker, John
Cross, Isaac
Foreman, Philip
Gibbs, Isaac
Henney, Frederick
Jackson, Edward
Luninger, George

ROLL OF CAPT. DAVID KASEBEER'S COMPANY (Continued).

Rank and Name of Soldier.

Privates.
Long, Joseph
Neal, Andrew
Robnett, James
Shook, Valentine
Shanaman, Henry
Taylor, John
Willard, Ludwig

Pages 159-160.

Rank and Name of Soldier.

Privates.
Misor, John
Robinet, George
Shull, Frederick
Sodoris, Frederick
Snelbecker, John
Williams, Henry
Winkelock, Philip

Rank and Name of Soldier.

Privates.
Mills, Samuel
Roop, Jacob
Snyder, Adam
Sullivan, John
Sweeny, Jacob
Williams, Benjamin

ROLL OF CAPT. JAMES ANDREWS' COMPANY (County Unknown).
Served from September 4, until December 31, 1813, and From January 1, until March 2, 1814.

Capt. James Andrews
Sergt. William Vandervourt
Sergt. William B. Hamilton
Corp. Joseph Arthur

Privates.
Arthur, James
Badger, Daniel
Bull, Abraham
Boone, Bramfield
Brummingham, Elias
Collins, George
Cooper, James
Davis, Azariah
Degraft, Joseph
Edinger, Philip
Fisher, David
Hand, David
Hughes, Isaac
Knott, Joseph
Moore, Samuel
Morning, John
McAdams, Scutler
Porter, John
Robb, Peter
Stewart, Hall
Smith, Jacob
Thompson, Barnard
Vandervourt, John
Wiland, John

Pages 161-162-163-164.

Lieut. Ledowick Weller
Sergt. William Milspaugh
Corp. John Brown
Corp. William Drake

Privates.
Armstrong, William
Brown, Daniel
Buchanan, John
Brannon, John
Cooper, George
Clements, Greer
Conner, Hugh
Davis, William
Deuey, John
Fisher, John, Sr.
Galbreath, Samuel
Hewey, Joseph
Holladay, Joseph
Lewis, Walcut
Melott, Isaac
Marquith, John C.
McKee, William
Powers, Thomas
Roudibash, Daniel
Stouder, William
Shumard, Thomas
Thompson, James
Wood, Richard
Willis, Levi

Ensign, Henry Sly
Sergt. Joseph Gossett
Corp. Elias Porter
Fifer, Robert Ross

Privates.
Barkley, George
Brown, Michael
Bull, Walter
Bennet, Benjamin
Christy, John D.
Crichfield, Philip
Douglass, Oliver
Eberhardt, Andrew
Fisher, John Jr.
Hill, Knotley
Hand, Thomas
Hewitt, John
Morris, Clement
Melott, Richard
Miller, Burgher
Nash, John
Brindola, Jacob
Reeves, James
Strickland, William
Strickland, Henry
Tubb, Jesse
Willis, John

ROLL OF CAPT. SAMUEL ASHTON'S COMPANY (County Unknown.)
Served from February 21, until August 21, 1814.

Capt. Samuel Ashton
Sergt. William Cornell
Sergt. Bromfield Boone
Corp. Owen Davis

Privates.
Andrews, Robert
Arbaugh, Peter
Bates, Amos
Bradberry, James
Bingland, Joseph
Castaller, John
Chambers, Samuel
Campbell, John
Dungan, Joseph
Davis, Daniel
Davis, John
Elliott, John
Fisher, Jacob
Granden, Samuel
Harris, Joshua
Harland, Israel
Heaton, John
Kelly, John
Jackson, John
Martin, James
McStanus, Isaac
Noble, Anthony
Roseboom, Henry
Rairde, Jonothan
Sterbaugh, Peter
Stites, Stephen
Shields, Patrick
Shivy, George
Titsworth, William
Vanclef, Tunis
Wilcox, William H.

Lieut. John Burget
Sergt. Levi Walter
Corp. Joseph McGinniss
Corp. Elijah Deneen
Corp. Elijah Duncan

Privates.
Awwick, Christian
Bell, James
Bracken, Thomas
Bally, John
Boles, William
Carr, James, Jr.
Carr, James, Sr.
Carley, Justus
Dickey, James
Dickey, George
Denon, John M.
Elly, Joseph
Gray, William
Garrison, Jonothan
Howard, James
Hammer, Joseph
Harlin, Ishmael
Keyboone, Henry
Mann, Richard
Moore, Leban
McClure, William
Parker, Samuel
Richmond, Jonothan
Huntsman, George
Shields, John
Smith, Elias
Snider, John
Seward, Brian
Veal, Samuel
Vail, John C.
Whittesay, Joseph

Ensign, Azor Skillman
Sergt. John Morris
Corp. John Heaton
Corp. John Barton

Privates.
Abbott, Jeremiah
Bunker, John
Berry, Benjamin
Blackford, Laamon
Bailey, John
Chestnut, Thomas
Clark, James
Deneen, Samuel
Deneen, John M.
Dougherty, Nathan
Early, Justus
Frakes, Nathan
Gates, John
Gustin, Samuel C.
Howard, Aaron
Horr, James
James, John
Lane, Anlsney
Meeker, Peter
Mott, Jeremiah
McMannin, Isaac
Ringland, Joseph
Roseboom, Gilbert
Smith, Thomas
Spiny, George
Shoemaker, Michael
Smith, Thomas
Thomas, Cornelius
Vaughn, Garner
William, James
York, Abram

Pages 165-166. Vol. I.
ROLL OF CAPT. JOHN KELLEY'S COMPANY (Probably from Scioto County).
Served from July 28, until August 28, 1813.

Rank and Name of Soldier.	Rank and Name of Soldier.	Rank and Name of Soldier.
Capt. John Kelley	Lieut. Joseph Kell	Ensign, William Carpenter
Sergt. William Jones	Sergt. Christian Yingling	Sergt. Jonothan Lambert
Sergt. John Cannon	Fifer, Charles Kelley	Drummer, John Brown
Corp. William Wilson	Corp. George Baker	Corp. Pressley Gillilan
	Corp. Joel Church	
Privates.	**Privates.**	**Privates.**
Brown, Aaron	Bannagar, John	Barles, Frederick
Bell, Isaac	Clark, Cornelius	Cunningham, William
Drury, Lawson	Davison, Nathaniel	Furgeson, John
Furgeson, James	Gibruth, James	Halley, Andrew
Hewey, George	Henry, James	Henry, Samuel
Limbarger, Peter	Lambart, Isaac	Melville, Jonothan
Neal, Walker	Osborn, Morgan	Speary, James
Suitor, William	Stover, John	Yingling, Andrew

Pages 167-168.
ROLL OF CAPT. ISAAC MERIDITH'S COMPANY
(Probably from Coshocton County).
Served from August 26, 1814, until February, 1815.

Capt. Isaac Meridith	Lieut. Andrew Wharton	Ensign, Henry Kidner
Sergt. Samuel Stephens	Sergt. Elijah Collins	Sergt. Lemuel Steel
Corp. Thomas Allen	Corp. Samuel Elson	Corp. William Heburn
Corp. Ephraim Thayer	Musician, Jacob D. Brown	Musician, Edward DeLong
Privates.	**Privates.**	**Privates.**
Brown, Joseph	Brown, William	Benedict, Alvin
Bryant, William, Sr.	Bryant, William, Jr.	Bingit, William
Crazier, James	Culver, Levi	Cass, Ira
Cullins, John	Croy, Alexander	Corson, John
Cummings, James	Cosner, William	Caterman, Michael
Debarton, Thomas	Edwards, John	Gillum, Samuel
Jennings, Bailies	Greenfield, John	Gibson, John
Henry, George	Hardy, Thomas	Hyet, Moses
Johnson, George	Ketcham, Zepheniah	Kidner, John
Lane, Benjamin	Lane, Dutton	Lawrence, Thomas
Lefler, George	Long, Joseph	Moore, William
Mealman, John	Mathews, Noah	Meridith, Henry
Miller, Phillip	McClung, Thomas	McGiffin, John
McMallon, John	Newman, George	Phillips, Adam
Parker, Nathaniel	Ray, John	Stafford, Richard
Stephenson, Moses	Sanderson, Robert	Sanderson, William
Sugner, John	Thompson, David	Workman, Thomas
	White, Thomas	

Page 169.
ROLL OF CAPT. CHARLES F. MASTIN'S COMPANY
(Probably from Scioto County).
Served from July 28, until August 28, 1813.

Capt. Charles F. Mastin	Lieut. Samuel Darlington	Ensign, William McDonald
Sergt. David Murphy	Sergt. William Crull	Sergt. Jesse Cockrell
Corp. Richard Trimmer	Corp. James McAuley	Corp. James Clark
Corp. Henry Crull	Sergt. Abraham Barrett	
Privates.	**Privates.**	**Privates.**
Beauchamp, David	Peloat, George	Beloat, Walter
Blower, John	Armstrong, Aaron	Crull, John
Daniels, Samuel	Green, Charles	Glaze, Abraham
Johnson, Isaac	Reed, Samuel	Shoemaker, Jacob
Smith, Robert	Swamm, Linsey Z.	Scott, Joseph
Travice, Joseph		

Pages 170-171-172.
ROLL OF CAPT. SAMUEL ROSS' COMPANY (County Unknown).
Served from March 23, until August 23, 1814. Part served from February 17, until May 17, 1814.

Capt. Samuel Ross	Lieut. Hugh Ferguson	Ensign, Obediah Wimans
Sergt. William Holmes	Sergt. Robert Blair	Sergt. Benjamin McEvans
Sergt. Robert Bennet	Corp. James Lamb	Corp. Robert Doughty
Corp. Elijah Nichols	Corp. William Taylor	Musician, William Lane
	Musician, Andrew Smith	
Privates.	**Privates.**	**Privates.**
Allen, Nicholas	Bonner, Reuben	Bonner, Jacob
Cahill, Thomas	Couch, Isaiah	Doyall, Charles
Doughty, Hugh	Dunford, William	Dunham, Charles
Davidson, John	Doyle, John	Chalmers, William
Douthman, Daniel	Edmonds, Louis, Jr.	Evans, Lewis, Jr.
Edmonds, Louis, Sr.	Evans, Louis, Sr.	Field, Benjamin S.
Ferguson, Thomas	Fletcher, Jacob	Fried, Jacob

ROLL OF CAPT. SAMUEL ROSS' COMPANY (Continued).

Rank and Name of Soldier.

Privates.

Gibson, Alexander
Holton, Tilley
Lindsey, Elijah
Muir, John
McCall, Robert
Parker, James
Porter, Phillip
Quick, John
Rubarts, John
Smith, Jonothan
Stone, William
Taylor, John
Turner, James
Virden, Jedediah
Williams, Elijah
Wheeler, Benjamin

Guard, William
Henderson, Joseph
Lanham, Clement
Moore, Anthony
McMillan, James
Parker, Robert
Porter, George
Rounds, James
Rardin, Timothy
Smith, Jacob
Simon, Frederick
Tannyhill, Vivian
Taylor, William
Watson, Jacob
Ward, James
Westerfield, Samuel

Hunyval, Asa
Keithler, Joseph
Lyon, William
Miller, Lewis
Merchant, Joel
Parker, George
Orr, William
Richardson, William
Smith, George
Sigman, John
Simmerman, Frederick
Talliferro, Jones
Virden, Josiah
Whitaker, Henry
Walsur, Nicholas
Wrey, George

Page 173.
ROLL OF CAPT. JOSEPH WALKER'S COMPANY (Probably from Knox Co.)
Served from August 8, 1812, until June 10, 1813.

Capt. Joseph Walker
Sergt. John Beving
Sergt. Barney John
Corp. George Dickinson
Drummer, Henry Clemens

Lieut. Richard M. Brown
Sergt. Archibald Crafford or Crawford
Corp. Joliah Trimly
Fifer, Rowley Clark

Sergt. John Elliott
Sergt. Peter Kile
Corp. Samuel Evirt
Corp. Lewis Grinstaff

Privates.

Barton, Michael
Emmet, Abraham
Haun, Emmanuel
King, Joseph
Munsen, Alexander
Rogers, Isaac
Strong, Harley
Simpkins, Benjamin
Wolf, Jacob
Wood, James
Wallace, William

Davidson Robert
Enos, Alexander
Kile, Jacob
Linn, Adam
McConnell John
Ryan, John
Smith, John
Swigart, David
Walker, Phillip
Welker, Powell
Welker, Paul
Yoman, Samuel

Davy, Michael
Elwell, David
Kile, Nicholas
Mifford, John
Newel, Reverent
Sunderland, John
Stewart, Benjamin
Sprague, Perez
Welker, Andrew
Walker, Alexander
Welker, Andrew

Pages 174-175-176.
ROLL OF CAPT. JAMES RIGHTMIRE'S COMPANY
(Probably from Licking Co.)
Served from May 4, until May 19, 1813, and from September 8, 1814, until March 5, 1815.

Capt. James Rightmire
Sergt. John Wells
Sergt. Samuel Dunlap
Corp. William Starner
Corp. Elijah Harris
Musician, Valentine Dial

Lieut. George Hull
Sergt. Burwell
Sergt. Daniel Dial
Corp. John Harbert
Fifer, David Cox
Musician William Spig

Ensign, Wadly Smith
Sergt. Jonas Frye
Sergt. Thomas Merit
Corp. Joshua Downs
Drummer, Joseph Beckwith

Privates.

Alspaugh, Adam
Barlow, Abraham
Bigsby, Titus
Botton, John
Channel, Isom
Chapman, Timothy
Dison, Turner
Doty, Thrazey
Dial, Phillip
Goodrich, Stephen G.
Holt, James
Hull, Uriah
Harris, Jesse
Harrod, John
Miller, Henry
Mix, Justice
McGowan, James
McMillen, Robert
Potter, Nathan
Robinson, Joel
Night, William
Stitwell, Stephen
Stripe, Warner
Smith, James
Thompson, Rennold
Vansarsdol, Cornelius
Winsett, Joseph
Wills, William
Woodrow, William

Agg, Frederick
Bashford, Thomas
Baker, John
Brown, Ebenezer
Cunningham, Joseph
Culverson, Jeremiah
Damaval, Edward
Dial, George
Evans, Joshua
Green, John
Harris, Isaac
Howard, Charles S.
Harrod, Levi
Ireland, Nobel
Morris, William
Mains, William
McCrary, Benjamin
Nemerick, Jacob
Priest, Hankey
Rupp, Jacob
Shillinbarger, Isaac
Stotts, Daniel
Strobe, William
Spirgin, James
Trimbly, Josiah
Vance, Joseph
Wist, James
Wilkin, John

Boner, James
Brister, Jacob
Brown, Jeremiah
Claybough, William
Chapman, William
Drumple, Charles
Darrie, Ezziah
Davies, Nathaniel
Fortner, John
Hull, James
Hilman, Daniel
Harris, William
Harris, Enoch
Low, James
Merrit, John
McCormick, Moses
McMillen, Ephraim
Ogden, James
Pumpey, Joshua
Regah, John
Shump, William
Stephens, Chester
Strobe, James
Smith, Phillip
Thomas, William
Woodward, Ashel
Woodruff, Ogden
Walker, Robert

Page 177. Vol. I.
ROLL OF CAPT. WILLIAM M. BURK'S COMPANY (County Unknown).
Served from July 28, until August 28, 1813.

Rank and Name of Soldier.
Captain William M. Burk
Sergt. Thompson Sebring
Corp. William Conchlin

Privates.
Bentley, Joseph
Berry, James
Colegrove, William
Louderbach, Peter
Louderbach, Conrad
Osborn, James
Sikes, Edward
Sikes, Levi

Rank and Name of Soldier.
Lieut. George Salladay
Sergt. Matthew Curran
Corp. Jacob Woodring
Corp. George Bradshaw

Privates.
Barcus James
Bonsor, Joseph
Haes, James
Moore, Samuel
Louderbach, John
Patton, Samuel
Stockham, Aaron
Wate, James
Wolford, Frederick

Rank and Name of Soldier.
Sergt. John Cook
Sergt. John Sallada
Corp. Reuben Chaflin

Privates.
Brady, William
Bradshaw, Isaac
Hues, Henry
Moore, John
Nicholas, William
Patton, Thomas
Saladay, Daniel
Wickson, Barnabus

Page 178.
ROLL OF CAPT. ELIJAH COCKRELL'S COMPANY (Probably from Scioto Co.)
Served from July 28, until August 28, 1813.

Capt. Elijah Cockrell

Privates.
Millar, John W.
Barnes, John
Conway, Simon
Howard, Samuel
Mustard, William
Richmond, R. R.
Smith, William
Walls, Levin

Ensign James Delag

Privates.
Bowers, Solomon
Bumgainer, Reuben
Chinworth, Richard
Kenney, John
Mustard, Samuel
Slater, Ezekial
Vinson, Jesse
Walls, Joshua

Privates.
Black, John
Currie, Henderson
Howard, Amos
Lewis, Abraham
McAuley, Henry
Sailor, Jeremiah
Walls, James

Page 193.
ROLL OF CAPT. JOHN CAMPBELL'S COMPANY (Probably from Portage Co.)
Served from July 1, 1812, until June 30, 1813.

Capt. John Campbell
Sergt. Louis Day
Sergt.. Louis Ely
Corp. Daniel Burroughs

Privates.
Amadown, Abiscan
Campbell, Robert
Coleman, William
Harmon, Enos
Jones, David
Moore, David
McCartney, Edward
Pettibone, Henry
Reading, Richard
Redfield, Samuel
Tuthill, Samuel
Thornton, William
Williams, John

Lieut. Alva Day
Sergt. Ralph Buckland
Corp. Charles Chittenden
Corp. John Turner

Privates.
Allen, Miles
Carter, Charles
Caris, John
Harmon, Zacheus
Jacobs, John
Mayfield, William
McManus, John
Roos, Henry
Reading, George G.
Smith, John
Thompson, Job
Underwood, Joel
Williard, Phillip

Ensign Aaron Waston
Sergt. John Wright
Corp. John Harmon

Privates.
Buckley, Ebenezer
Cross, Nathan
Day, Seth
Hartle, Samuel
Moore, Mark
McGill, James
Newberry, Chaney
Ray, James, Jr.
Rowley, Thomas
Turrel, Peter
Thompson, Samuel
Ward, William

Page 194.
ROLL OF CAPT. DANIEL F. REEDER'S COMPANY (County Unknown).
Served from September 14, until October 14, 1812.

Capt. Daniel F. Reeder
Lieut. Bratton Crawford
Sergt. Nathaniel Fitchner

Privates.
Andrews, William
Cowen, James, Jr.
Coil, Samuel
Case, Thomas
Drake, Samuel
Gowdy, Alexander
Hayse, Caleb M.
Laurens, Jonothan
Maloy, James
McCall, James
Robinson, James H.
Spinning, Benjamin
Wickersham, John

Capt. Robert Hays
Ensign Henry Loziere
Sergt. John Galbraith

Privates.
Blackburn, Benjamin
Constant, Thomas
Case, Samuel
Clement, Isaac
Ewen, William
Hatfield, Franz
Dunbar, Joseph
Miller, George
Montford, Henry
Rawl, Mathew
Pope, William
Symonton, Cyrus

Lieut. Samuel Yeoman
Sergt. William Snook
Sergt. Richard Gimanton

Privates.
Bunnel, Henry
Crain, Daniel
Crawford, John
Colier, James
Gowdy, James
Hayse, Robert
Lamiston, Eleazor
Magan, Evan
McMann, James
Rawl, Week
Shawhaney, James
Van Pelt, Alexander

Pages 196-197. Vol. I.

ROLL OF CAPT. JOSEPH C. HAWKINS' COMPANY (County Unknown).

Served from September 30, 1813, until March 29, 1814.

Rank and Name of Soldier.	Rank and Name of Soldier.	Rank and Name of Soldier.
Capt. Joseph C. Hawkins	Lieut. John Saylor	Ensign Peter Painer
Sergt. Thomas Nubet	Sergt. William Stephens	Sergt. Ezekial DuWees
Sergt. John Quinn	Corp. Thomas Foster	Corp. William Curry
Corp. Joshua Cloyd	Corp. Jesse Smith	

Privates.

Aikins, Benjamin	Aply, John	Allen, James
Arby, Abraham	Alred, James	Black, Frederick
Biers, Isaac	Brannin, Samuel	Brown, John
Brummet, Spencer	Christman, Jacob	Clark, John
Coble, Eli	Cladwell, Train	Creeson, Isaac
Dickey, John	Davis, Robert	Davis, David
Dollyheid, Jesse	Ellis, John	Fox, John
Gamble, John	Gordon, Charles	Gordon, Samuel
Hopkins, Lemuel	Hawkins, Byrd	Harter, William
Hamilton, Alexander	Hayes, Robert	Housten, Thomas
Hel, John	Haworth, Jehu	Hawkins, John
Ireland, Peter	Kenut, Henry	Keilum, Joseph
Keek, Henry	Landers, Daniel	Lenar, Samuel
Lenen, Peter	Lincoln, Thomas	Listre, Elephas
Mash, William	McElvey, Alexander	McClure, John
Matney, Elias	Niekum, Michael	Niekum, John
Nelson, John	Quinn, James	Russle, Charles
Niekum, Peter	Shoemaker, Daniel	Stone, William
Rian, James	Smith, Thomas	Saxon, James
Stephens, David	Stephens, David	Sproule, John
Smith, Zadoc	Worle, Samuel	Smith, Thomas
Tharp, Hiram	Williams, Joseph	Wier, John
Williamson, John	York, Newberry	Wiley, Samuel

Pages 199-200.

ROLL OF CAPT. WILLIAM MILLER'S COMPANY (County Unknown).

Served from ———— 16, until March 16, 1814.

Capt. William Miller	Lieut. Owen T. Reeves	Ensign David Coon
Sergt. James Jackson	Sergt. John Stephens	Sergt. Jeremiah Shoppell
Sergt. Archibald Thompson	Corp. John Wilmouth	Corp. John Heckethorne
Corp. William Shaynefelt	Corp. Jacob Rush	Fifer, Daniel Bowsher

Privates.

Bowhan, Adam	Beck, James	Bishop, William
Beatty, Samuel	Cummins, William	Cox, William
Conner, Aaron	Cox, Benjamin	Davis, John
Davis, John	Defenbaugh, Joseph	Dukes, Jacob
Duvall, Mareen H.	Falkner, John	Greenho, Andrew
Grimm, George	Graham, Thomas	Haines, Peter
Harbut, George	Ice, George	Ice, William
Justice, John	Kennedy, James	Kanada, James
Kent, James	Kent, Daniel	Krider, George
Kirk, John	Molatt, John	Morris, Joseph
Miller, Hugh	McQuay, James	McCinna, Henry
Puntenney, Aquilla	Pontius, Solomon	Pomewell, John
Pomewell, Thomas	Parton, Andrew	Purtee, Joseph
Purtee, James	Rabourn, Hugh	Rodgers, Lewis R.
Reed, Jacob	Smith, Charles	Shepherd, Peter
Swaggart, Daniel	Spees, Mathias	Shambaugh, Phillip
Stayner, John	Trullinger, Phillip	Wright, Joseph
Williams, Enoch	Walker, Daniel	Walter, Jacob
Williams, Isaac	Young, Daniel	Zimmer, Phillip

Pages 216-217.

ROLL OF CAPT. REZIN SHELBY'S COMPANY (County Unknown).

Served from July 23, until September 6, 1813.

Capt. Rezin Shelby	Lieut. David Frazier	Ensign Jacob Frazier
Sergt. Enoch Ballak	Sergt. David Craig	Sergt. John Augustine
Sergt. Jacob Hellum	Corp. Dorman Cade	Corp. Thomas Wolverton
Corp. Moses Morris	Corp. John Cado	

Privates.

Albin, Samuel	Bashford, Francis, Sr.	Bashford, Francis, Jr.
Bending, James	Bradley, William	Creviston, John
Cruver, Christie	Caldwell, William	Coon, Jacob
Essex, Isaac	Essex, Milcay	Gibson, Robert
Huston, John	Harber, Richard	Hardie, Henry
Long, Andrew	Morris, James	Morris, Joseph
Myers, George	Morris, John	Metgar, John
Newhous, Abraham	Phillips, William	Richeson, John
Ryason, Samuel	Rogen, Jonothan	Smith, William
Sisco, Joseph	Stonecock, John	Silivan, James
Vinson, John	Yagar, John	

Pages 210-211-212-213-214-215. Vol. I.

ROLL OF CAPT. LUTHER SHEPHERD'S COMPANY (Probably from Ross Co.)

Served from February 16, until June 16, 1814, part served until August 16, 1814.

Rank and Name of Soldier.	Rank and Name of Soldier.	Rank and Name of Soldier.
Capt. Luther Shepherd	Lieut. John Mulligan	Lieut. William Kirker
Ensign Samuel Mansfield	Ensign Thomas Smith	Ensign Samuel Bliss
Sergt. James Bliss	Sergt. Nyel Nye	Sergt. John Dyer
Sergt. Thomas Compton	Sergt. Arthur McFarland	Ensign Henry Bayne
Sergt. Peter Daily	Sergt. Nathan Chany	Sergt. Moses Warren
Sergt. John Enismyer	Corp. John Ensminger	Corp. Thomas McCime
Corp. Caleb Cox	Corp. John Buck	Corp. John Dolbay
Corp. Abraham McGinnis	Corp. Archibald Raborn	Corp. Thomas McCline
Fifer, Varnum G. Wilson	Drummer, John McKinley	Drummer, Elijah Johnson

Privates.

Anway, George	Amos, Pleasant	Anderson, Cornelius
Barkley, Samuel	Barker, William	Bardman, Samuel
Brooks, Samuel	Barruk, John	Batey, Samuel
Baily, James	Blue, Frederick	Baker, John
Buck, John	Butt, Rignal	Buntin, Alexander
Baker, George	Boner, James	Buckley, Samuel
Chipp, John	Cokenour, John	Cox, John
Comer, Emanuel	Coon, Jacob	Clay, Mathews
Cormick, James	Cooper, John	Clearwaty, Thomas
Clay, Thomas	Cissna, Stephen	Cockmour, John
Conner, Emanuel	Dolbay, John	Device, Henry
Dayton, Spencer	DeWitt, George	Dorman, Jesse
Davis, Henson	Frost, Hemon	Frost, Marcus
Fremont, Luke	Fulen, William	Foster, John
Flinn, Thomas	Fuller, Alexander	Frazier, John
Fuller, William	Goff, Salithiel	Greenfield, John
Hatfield, Thomas	Hutchinson, William	Harper, James
Harper, Robert	Hoop, John	Hamilton, John
Herrin, Timothy	Henderson, John	Hixon, John
Herrold, Jesse	Hughey, Isaac	Jones, William
Jones, Thomas	Jones, Asa	Jack, Andrew
Keon, Jacob	Kirkpatrick, Andrew	Kendall, William
Kirk, Elisha	King, Charles	Landen, Lewis
Linscott, John	Lewis, James	Long, Thomas
Loverton, Daniel	Landin, Levin	Lewis, William
Mowers, Henry	Maddon, Dennis	Mershon, Timothy
Mahaffy, Robert	Mayse, Little Berry	Murray, Benjamin A.
McLain, Moses	McEntire, Robert	McNeal, Joseph
McKinley, John	McKee, John	Nash, Azor
Otinger, William	Parish, John	Phipps, David
Partlow, Amos	Pinkerman, John	Porter, Aquila
Pendell, Thomas	Puckett, Martin	Parker, William
Rowland, Samuel	Rice, Mordecai	Robertson, William
Redmond, Joseph	Ross, Isaiah	Ross, Samuel
Russell, Alexander	Stedman, Abel	Swigg, Jesse
Simmons, William	Smedley, George I.	Sawyer, George
Sanderson, William	Twigg, Jesse	Turner, John
Thompson, John	Thorn, Jacob	Vigus, Paul
Wallace, Austin	Wether, James	Wyckoff, Nicholas
Williams, Nathan	Waters, Jacob	White, John
Wyckoff, John	Walden, William	Wirt, James
	Williams, Thomas	

Page 218.

ROLL OF SERGT. JACOB SINN'S COMPANY (Probably from Ross County).

Served from August 22, 1814, until February 21, 1815.

Sergt. Jacob Sinn   Musician, Richard Price

Privates.

Dollarhide, Jesse	Downing, William	Bacon, Ira
Fort, Francis	Hammersley, George	Hews, Robert
Hammett, George	Krein, Adam	Kunn, James
Lowins, Hyatt	Lowman, Joseph	Liston, George
Miller, John	Markin, Thomas	Murray, Daniel
Smith, David	Smith, Thomas	Syphers, George
Sellers, Jacob	Slawson, James	Tuttle, Isaiah
Sissions, Benjamin	Vanmetre, Henry	Winn, William S.
Williams, Joseph		

Pages 221-222-223-224. Vol. I.

ROLL OF CAPT. CALEB HOSKINS' COMPANY (Probably from Ross County).

Served from July 28, until September 7, 1813, part served from January 3, until April 10, 1815.

Rank and Name of Soldier	Rank and Name of Soldier	Rank and Name of Soldier
Capt. Caleb Hoskins	Lieut. Seth Vanmater	Lieut. Aaron Foster
Ensign Andrew Smalley	Ensign Hugh Cook	Sergt. John Moore
Sergt. David Coblar	Sergt. Christopher Beekman	Sergt. Nathaniel Chapman
Sergt. William Hartell	Sergt. Joseph Ross	Sergt. John McCord
Corp. Morwin Williams	Corp. William Hanes	Corp. Simon Shumaker
Corp. John Pollard	Corp. John Highley	Corp. Levin Right
Corp. John Anderson	Corp. Isaac Rockhold	Musician, Henson David
	Musician, William Davis	

Privates.

Adams, William	Beekman, John	Beddle, George
Beekman, James	Burnes, Robert	Bamfield, John
Braley, James	Bodkins, George	Bowman, John
Burk, James	Carson, Joseph	Cloud, Thomas
Corn, Jonothan	Cross, James	Cross, Thomas
Carter, Samuel	Carter, Daniel	Cummins, Thomas
Cauchy, Samuel	Crouch, William	Cooper, John
Clines, George	Crow, David	Corkwell, Henry
David, James	Downing, John	Danes, Daniel
Davison, Benjamin	Dungen, William	Florow, Joshua
Freeland, Jacob	Guthridge, Thomas	Gilmore, John
Grogan, James	Hurdman Henry	Hurdman, Michael
Hamilton, Samuel	Hibbs, Jacob	Harmon, Henry
Hughes, Samuel	Izard, Eli	Ivans, John
Johnston, John	Kingery, Berry	Kimble, William
Kuder, George	Kees, Cane	Lockhart, Thomas
Lowderbeck, Zach	Mines, James	Mustard, Samuel
Markland, William	Myers, Jacob	Morrison, James
Miller, George	Michael, George	Mulford, Ezekial
McGarah, William	McGee, John	McDonald, James
McWhorter, Henry	Ouley, Nicholas	Porter, James
Pucket, Redman	Pike, Jarviss	Dickup, Frederick
Raller, Adam	Shard, Nathaniel	Satterfield, William
Spears, William	Strope, Harvey	Treber, Jacob
Thomas, Asia	Suderfield, Charles	Shelah, George
Suderfield, James	Taylor, William	Roads, Aden
Jackson, Jesse	Travis, Robert	Tansey, Eli
Towers, William	VanBuckerk, Thomas	Van Nule, Absalom
Watson, Loren	Wilson, John	Weak, George
	Wilson, James	

Pages 225-226.
ROLL OF CAPT. GEORGE BRYAN'S COMPANY (Probably from Ross County).

Served from July 28, until September 9, 1813.

Capt. George Bryan	Lieut. William Smith	Ensign Jesse Edwards
Sergt. John Haslip	Sergt. Samuel Edwards	Sergt. Jonothan Passmore
Sergt. Andrew Davidson	Corp. Elias Hatheney	Corp. Skinner Bloomfield
Corp. John Stephens	Corp. Jacob Edginton	Drummer, John Smith
	Fifer, Henry Malone	

Privates.

Bowman, William	Blake, James	Baird, Robertson
Cochran, William	Clark, James	Chips, John
Clark, Robert	Carroll, Robert	Cartright, William A.
Cheesman, John	Crawford, William	Edmondson, Samuel
Egington, Joshua	Edgington, Abraham	Edgington, Isaac
Gordon, Basil	Guthridge, Charles	Hurst, Abraham
Holmes, Thomas	Johnston, Elisha	King, Barlett
Leedom, John	Morford, Thomas	Matheney, Charles
Moore, Daniel	Moore, James	McGoony, Thomas
McClure, Ralph	McClanchan, William	McGin, Robert
McGin, Daniel	Noleman, Richard	Page, David
Preston, Luther	Paterson, John	Reynolds, James
Ralolson, Mathias	Paul, John	Viqus, Paul
Wade, John	Wine, John	

Page 227.
ROLL OF LIEUT. SETH VAN MATRE'S COMPANY. (County Unknown.)

Served from August 25, 1814, until January 24, 1815.

Lieut. Seth Van Matre	Sergt. Nathaniel Chapman	Sergt. Charles Beekman
Corp. John Russell	Corp. James Mines	

Privates.

Alexander, John	Gibson, James	Hayes, John
Harbaugh, Fred	Hill, Joseph	Jack, James
Jordan, John	Lewis, James	Lewitz, Curtis
Langweld, Robert	Mershore, Solomon	Mershore, Daniel
McLaughlin, ——	McFarland, James	Petty, John Richard
Park, Daniel	Paul, Benjamin	Rodes, Aden
Scott, John C.	Sharp, William T.	

Pages 228-229-230. Vol. I.

ROLL OF CAPT. JOHN VAN METER'S COMPANY (County Unknown).

Served from July 29, until August 17, 1813, part served from August 23, 1815, until February 22, 1816.

Rank and Name of Soldier.	Rank and Name of Soldier.	Rank and Name of Soldier.
Capt. John Van Meter	Lieut. Samuel Jones	Ensign Jacob Hickle
Ensign John Keys	Sergt. Aaron Jones	Sergt. James Dempsey
Sergt. Joseph Doty	Sergt. John May	Sergt. Aaron James
Sergt. George L. Crockett	Corp. Martin Doty	Corp. Humphrey Mounts
Corp. Peter Throckmorton	Corp. Peter Straser	Corp. John Russell
Corp. Nathan Hicks	Drummer, Richard Price	

Privates.

Austin, Thomas	Barcus, Jacob	Barcus, Joseph
Brown, Henry	Burdington, Aeneas	Creechbarme, George
Cade Robert	Cyphers, George	Dumm, Christian
Deresbach, Benjamin	Dresbach, Henry	Dresbach, Martin
Downs, Thomas	Ezra, Jonothan	Flinn, Joshua
Grafton, Ambrose	Hayes, Solomon	Harper, John
Hickle, Tevault	Hayes, John	Henry, James
Hill, Joseph	Jones, Jabez	Irwin, Andrew
Guthrie, William	Jones, Henry	Jones, Moses
Guess, Anthony	Keller, George	Kirk, John
Lyons, Morris	Malatt, John	DeMars, Thomas
Oliver, John	Pontius, Jacob	Plummer, Jacob
Pontious, John	Paull, Benjamin	Rogers, Lewis R.
Reedy, Conrad	Reedy, John	Reedy, Michael
Reid, John	Ross, Solomon	Strazer, Solomon
Straser, John	Sapeins, Gabriel	Sutton, John
Scott, John C.	St. Muels, Gabriel	Vallequette, Christopher
Throckmorton, John	Vinson, Cuthbert	
Weider, Henry	Webster, George	

Pages 231-232-233.

ROLL OF CAPT. SAMUEL DENISON'S COMPANY
(Probably from Trumbull and Mahoning Counties).

Served from August 26, untill November 16, 1812.

Captain Samuel Denison	Lieut. David Augustus Adams	Ensign William Swan
Sergt. Benjamin Armitage	Sergt. Amos Gray	Sergt. William Carlton
Sergt. David Dunwoodie	Sergt. Jesse Alderman	Sergt. Nathaniel Cook
Corp. James Walton	Corp. Robert Stewart	Corp. Matthew J. Scott
Corp. David Rauer	Drummer, William Moon	Fifer, Joseph McGill

Privates.

Armitage, Ephraim	Amiestein, Daniel	Anderson, James
Arrel, John	Boyd, Andrew	Baggs, Joseph, Sr.
Bredon, John	Bell, William	Beard, John
Brothers, John	Barsley, Josiah	Buchanan, William
Crawford, William	Carlton, Peter	Carr, John
Cowden, William	Cowden, Ranels	Crays, Alexander
Day, John	Dinwiddie, John	Dinwiddie, Thomas
Dawson, Aaron	Dickson, John	Eckman, James
Fight, Jacob	Fight, Jacob, Jr.	Ferguson, Samuel
Fowler, Thomas	Gwahe, Robert	Hits, George
Henry, Francis	Howard, William	Kays, David
Kimmel, Philip	Lyon, Isaac	Linn, James
Leonard, John	Liddle, John	Moore, John
Mann, Samuel	Moore, Sampson	Miller, Conrad
Moon, James	McClellan, David	McMurray, John
McMurray, William	McConnal, David	McKnit, William
McConnal, Philip	McGill, Robert	McConnal, John
McGill, William	McKinney, Henry	McDonald, James
McKinney, William	Nelson, John	Noble, David
Oswal, Jacob	Poyers, John	Poly, John
Rose, John	Rummel, Henry	Ripple, George
Stewart, David	Swazer, Isaac	Stephenson, Elijah
Storm, Michael	Stout, Jonothan	Tully, John
Walter, Robert	Wilson, Thomas	Wilson, David
Wilson, Edward	Yost, John	

Page 234.

ROLL OF LIEUT THOMAS C. NUTTER'S COMPANY.
(Probably from Ross County.)

Served from July 29, until August 17, 1813.

Lieut. Thomas C. Nutter	Sergt. Anthony Morton	

Privates.

Privates.	Privates.	Privates.
Dawson, David	Donnely, James	Crouch, Joseph
Goodman, Peter	Goule, George	Goodman, Samuel
Goodman, Daniel	Haynes, Andrew	Hall, William
Carshner, Daniel	Carshner, Jacob	Stein, George
Tents, Lawrence	Webster, Stewart	White, James

Pages 243-244. Vol. I.

ROLL OF CAPT. ELIHU MOSES' COMPANY (County Unknown).

Served from August 24, until September 5, 1812. Part served from September 19, 1814, until February 23, 1815.

Rank and Name of Soldier.	Rank and Name of Soldier.	Rank and Name of Soldier.
Capt. Elihu Moses	Lieut. Lewis Walcutt	Lieut. Hezekiah Hine
Ensign Robert Gault	Ensign Sheldon Osborn	Sergt. Levi Ormsbury
Sergt. Ephraim White	Sergt. David Curtis	Sergt. Levi Armsby
Sergt. Daniel Burroughs	Sergt. Lyman Hine	Sergt. Thomas Reed
Corp. George Barnes	Corp. Griswold Gillett	Corp. Conrad Turner
Corp. Rhoderick Norton	Corp. Asa Waldon	Corp. Willis I. Walcott
Corp. Smith Hurd	Fifer, Mark Oviatt	Drummer, Ezra Curtis
Drummer, Joy Hurd	Fifer, Comfort Hurd	

Privates.

Adams, Subel	Boyd Thomas	Bartholomew, Charles
Bartholomew, Jacob	Bronson, Elisha	Bradford, Joel
Bradford, William	Brockway, Romanty	Barklor, John
Bristol, Thomas	Carpenter, Lewis	Curtis, Sheldon
Cummings, John	Cummings, William	Cox, John
Curtis, Lewis	Dunlap, William	Daniel, James
Fausler, John	Fish, Abner	Higgins, Silas
Heart, Gad	Higley, Thompson	Krigler, Michael
King, Nathan	Koigler, Jacob	May, Charles
Martial, William	Marshall, James	Moore, Frederick
McCombs, Robert	Norton, George	Norton, Zacheus
Norton, Henry	Norton, John	Osborn, Gilbert
Reed, William	Rook, James	Stillman, John D.
Stacey, Mathew	Southwortt, Joseph	Turk, Ephraim
Trescott, Ira	Upton, Benjamin	Van Vey, Isaac
Walker, Jonothan	Wilson, Elijah	Walcott, Josiah
Walcott, Horace	Wilson, John	Witts, Zepheniah
Waid, Alexander	Williams, Allen	Bushnell, Alexander
Adkins, John	Buck, James	Bailey, David
Beebe, Samuel	Burk, Onin	Clow, Daniel
Crawford, Alexander	Curtis, Calvin	Hamilton, William
Clark, Elijah	Dickenson, Elijah	Hart, Alva
Harrington, Zenas	Hum, Samuel	Hutson, Andrew
Hunt, Ezra	Hutson, Mathew	Haney, James
Hutson, Thomas	Hofsteater, David	Knapp, Andrew
Harper, Archibald	Johnson, Chandler	Little, James
Linkin, William	Lary, Isaac H.	Phelps, Spencer
Murphy, James	McKnit, William	Reed, Benjamin
Quiggle, Peter	Ring, William W.	

Pages 245-246.

ROLL OF CAPT. RIAL McARTHUR'S COMPANY (County Unknown).

Served from August 22, until October 29, 1812. Part served from April 27, until May 22, 1813.

Capt. Rial McArthur	Lieut. Wiley Hamilton	Ensign Charles Powers
Sergt. Joshua King	Sergt. Alpha Wright	Sergt. David Kenny, Jr.
Sergt. Lunar Bishop	Sergt. Samuel Checney	Corp. Edmund Strong
Corp. Drake Fellows	Corp. Justice Barnes	Corp. Justin E. Frink
Drummer, Stephen W. Butler	Fifer, Ara Gritt	

Privates.

Adams, Philander	Allen, Samuel	Allen, Miles
Arthur, Aaron	Ayres, Asa	Atkins, Samuel, Jr.
Bierin, Henry	Bradley, James	Baldwin, Eliakin
Bissel, Orris	Blackman, Elijah, Sr.	Baldwin, James
Bellows, Ithamar	Bradley, Justice	Boosinger, John
Baird, Robert	Baird, William	Butler, Henry
Adams, Moses, Jr.	Cacklin, Christy	Campbell, John
Collins, John	Castle, John	Chapman, Titus
Chaney, Samuel	Cook, David	Darrow, Nathaniel
Decker, Aaron	Draper, Asa	Ellet, Thomas
Ellet, David	Eggleston, Moses	Ellet, George
Fogger, Samuel	Furgeson, Samuel	Granger, Horace
Gaylor, Stewart	Green, Abner	Hall, James
Heart, William	Heyns, Samuel	Haymaker, George
King, Henry	King, Charles	Kent, Zardus
Kent, Zeno	Kennedy, David	Lowrey, Shubal H.
Liverton, Dixon	Lindley, Jesse	Lappin, William
Lappin, John	Neal, Jesse	Norton, Peter
Nighman, George	Perkins, Elisha	Perkins, Stephen
Powers, David	Preston, Samuel	Preston, David, Jr.
Preston, John S.	Preston, Lott	Prior, William
Pease, Ebenezer	Perkins, Grant	Pelton, John
Powers, George	Prior, David	Russel, Samuel
Blair, Bohan	Ridlake, Daniel	Spicer, Amos, Jr.
Sacket, Norman	Singletary, John C.	Strong, David
Tousley, Joseph	Tupper, Hezekiah	Thompson, James
Vanhyning, Thomas	Wright, John, Jr.	Wilcox, David
Woolcott, Alfred	Williams, Barnabus	Woodward, Stephen
Wyatt, Ezra	Williams, John	Sacket, Leander

Page 247 Vol. I.

ROLL OF CAPT. WILLIAM N. HUDSON'S COMPANY
(From Geauga or Portage Counties.)
Served from August 24, until August 31, 1812.

Rank and Name of Soldier.
Capt. William N. Hudson
Privates.
Archer, William Sr.
Gilmore, Samuel
Lacey, Jaspar B.
Osborn, Alexander

Rank and Name of Soldier.
Ensign Erastus Creary
Privates.
Archer, William Jr.
Kent, Elihu L.
Minor, John
Singletary, Uriah I.
Sheffield, Alpheus

Rank and Name of Soldier.
Corp. Ashbel Gilmore
Privates.
Eames, Isaac
Lacey, George B.
McConnaughey, Porter D.
Sheffield, Leroy

Pages 248-249-250

ROLL OF CAPT. ROBERT McELWAIN'S COMPANY. (County Unknown.)
Served from September 28, until October 25, 1812, and from April 20, until July 16, 1813.

Capt. Robert McElwain
Sergt. Andrew Knox
Sergt. William Devlon
Sergt. John Hayes
Corp. David McElwain
Privates.
Applegate, William
Allen, George
Bell, Charles
Black, Samuel
Biram, William
Calliston, James
Funk, John
Gilner, William
Harper, Alexander
Harrison, L. B.
Jolyndll, James
Kerns, Samuel
March, David
McDonald, William
Odle, William
Rollins, Samuel
Reed, William
Runion, John
Redden, Edward
Smith, William

Lieut. Robert Tate
Sergt. John Jewett
Sergt. Aaron Archer
Corp. Benjamin Salmon
Corp. William Hays
Privates.
Allen, Jeremiah
Buck, John
Biggs, Joseph
Bragg, John
Carden, Armstrong
Chichester, Elias
Flick, William
Gunsol, Michael
Hurley, Zedick
Gone, David I.
Kennedy, Robert
Kent, Terren
Maxwell, Ephraim
McElvain, David
Plyman, James
Rankins, John
Roback, George
Rodgers, Henry
Reed, William
Stephenson, Thomas
Webster, James B.

Ensign Jacob Funk
Sergt. Andrew Richards
Sergt. John Funk
Corp. John Sowards
Privates.
Archer, John
Bell, Isaiah
Black, William
Baldwin, Uriah
Croze, John
Freeland, Luke
Gilbert, Henley
Gaskill, John
Harrison, Joseph
Ellis, Henry
Kerr, John
LoVally, Jacob
Mowberry, Reuben
McClure, William
Pendegrass, James
Rankins, William
Riddle, David
Redden, Mathew
Rodgers, Benjamin
Taylor, George

Page 252

ROLL OF CAPT. JOEL BEREMAN'S COMPANY (Probably from Highland Co.)
Served from March 28, until September 28, 1812.

Capt. Joel Bereman
Sergt. James Heslet
Corp. Jesse Williams
Corp. William Rion
Privates.
Beard, John R.
Cosby, Stith
Edgington, Joseph
Hoop, John
Haigh, Job
Kelso, Michael
Strain, William
Sturin, Thomas

Lieut. Hugh Rodgers
Sergt. William Black
Corp Robert Fitzpatrick
Corp. John Hoop
Privates.
Burns, James
Coe, Joseph
Eavans, Samuel
Hoffman, Phelix
Hilderbrand, David
McGowan, John
Steward, Willson
Watts, Thomas

Ensign Peter Cooley
Sergt. Nathan Roansevell
Corp. Jacob Metzgar

Privates.
Bryan, Jesse
Dick, Quintin
Gibson, Samuel
Fitzpatrick, John
Hix, Nathan
McRight, James
Shoomaker, Solomon

Page 253

ROLL OF CAPT. REUBEN WESTFALL'S COMPANY
(Probably from Miami County.)
Served from May 1, until May 15, 1812, and from October 24, until November 13, 1812.

Capt. Reuben Westfall
Sergt. Moses Garard
Privates.
Alexander, James
Brown, John
Coats, James
Edwards, James
Kern, John
McJimsey, Robert
Swailes, Rice
Trader, Tegal
Thomas, Adam
White, Robert
Robbins, Richard

Lieut. Amos Petite
Corp. Elias Garard
Privates.
Arnold, David
Ballinger, Even
Cothran, James
Hunter, William
Kyle, Samuel
McJimsey, William
Smith, Jonathan
Thomas, Samuel
Westfall, Levi
Orbison, John

Sergt. Jesse Miller

Privates.
Bennett, Benjamin
Ballenger, Daniel
Curtis, James
Kern, Henry
Layton, Joseph
North, Richard
Smith, Henry
Thornsburg, Uriah
Westfall, Joel
Richardson, John

ROSTER OF OHIO SOLDIERS IN WAR OF 1812

Pages 254-255 Vol. I.

ROLL OF CAPT. RICHARD SLOAN'S COMPANY (County Unknown).

Served from October 8, 1812, until April 7, 1813.

Rank and Name of Soldier.	Rank and Name of Soldier.	Rank and Name of Soldier.
Capt. Richard Sloan	Lieut. John Hawkins	Ensign John Harter
Sergt. William McCreary	Sergt. Charles Hole	Sergt. Simon Cassidy
Sergt. Michael Straw	Corp. William Hendricks	Corp. Andrew Spaight
Corp. Tetrach Fall	Corp. William Davis	Drummer, Thomas M. Dill
	Fifer, John Byers	
Privates.	**Privates.**	**Privates.**
Abbott, James	Abshire, James	Allen, William
Bloomfield, Samuel	Banfill, John	Bloomfield, Nathaniel
Bloomfield, John	Blackley, Littleberry	Bennet, James
Banfill, Enoch	Abshire, Isaac	Cox, James
Cloyd, Joshua	Faris, James	Faris, David
Foster, Thomas	Harris, Benjamin	Hopkins, Lemuel
Hollowell, Adam	Hamilton, Samuel	Harris, John
Huston, James	Hayes, William	Hill, Thomas
Hawkins, Joseph	Highlander, William	Killough, James
Loy, Jacob Jr.	Lyons, David	Martin, Andrew
Masee, James	Minigs, William	Morphew, James
Minigs, John	Mitchell, John	McNitt, John
McGano, James	Ozias, Jacob	Payton, John
Phillips, William	Worl, Joseph	Shoemaker, Christian
Small, James	Shetler, Jacob	Sidfen, Andrew
Smith, Samuel	Singer, Joseph	Shanks, Jacob
Sanders, Robert	Sutton, James	Sprowl, Robert
Stephens, David	Stone, Andrew	Strader, George
Swaney, James	Ramsey, Nathan	Riley, John
Thompson, George	Utt, John	Wolf, John
Woodward, Asahel	Woodward, Eli	Wright, William
	Wright, Levin	

Page 256

ROLL OF CAPT. ZECHARIAH FERGUSON'S COMPANY
(Probably from Green County).

Served from September 23, until October 30, 1812.

Capt. Zechariah Ferguson	Lieut. Peter Borden	Ensign, James Popenoe
Sergt. Samuel D. Kirkpatrick	Sergt. Andrew Hawker	Sergt. Isaac Morgan
Sergt. George Hittle	Corp. Peter Hoy	Corp. Jacob Cosler
Corp. Abraham Cosler	Corp. Samuel Bowen	
Privates.	**Privates.**	**Privates.**
Anderson, Seth	Ashby, Lawrence	Borders, George
Birely, William	Coy, Jacob	Coy, Adam
Cyphers, John	Davis, David	Engle, Isaac
Freeman, William	Gott, John	Givens, James
Gibson, Robert	Hill, James	Hames, Jacob
John, James	John, Joseph	Judy, John
John, Lemuel	Kiser, John	Kingerly, Martin
Key, George	Morgan, Joshua	Manning, Benjamin
Maxwell, William	Noble, Joshua	Owens, Thomas
McClure, William	Palmer, Joseph	Poag, William
Powell, Joseph	Russell, Adam	Swigerd, John
Rose, William	Steele, David D.	Shoe Phillip
Solinger, Adam	Tucker, John	
	Vance, Daniel	

Page 256.

ROLL OF CAPT. JOHN S. WALLACE'S COMPANY
(Probably from Hamilton Co.)

Served from August 23, until September 4, 1812.

Capt. John S. Wallace	Lieut. William Stanley	Ensign, George G. Terrence
Sergt. Joseph B. Robinson	Sergt. John Humes	Sergt. John Hilton
	Sergt. William Berry	
Privates.	**Privates.**	**Privates.**
Barker, Thomas	Biger, John	Bowl, Robert, Jr.
Boal, James	Blanchard, William	Bird, Richard
Bruin, Isaac	Clark, John	Cary, Chris
Chase, L. Homadine	Carr, Francis	Davison, Thomas
Eson, Alexander	Finice, John	Greenlie, Will
Gibson, John	Garner, Alexander	Gard, Seth
Horne, David	Horne, Ebenezer	Hall, Stephen
Henderson, Thomas	Hogan, Niles	Hardy, Richard
Irwin, William	Jessup, John	Kemper, Stephen
Karr, Robert	Levensworth, Seth M.	Lining, John
Layre, Samuel I.	Leward, Jacob	Meek, Edward
Malson, John	Pierce, Eli	Pancoast, Jonothan
Rodgers, William	Rogers, Samuel	Stone, Ethan
Sayre, Leonard	Snider, David	Sears, Benjamin
Stites, Thomas	Thompson, Thomas	Van Benkton, Daniel
Wilson, James	Woodworth, Daniel	Watson, John

Page 258.
ROLL OF CAPT. PETER BACUS' COMPANY (Probably from Scioto County).
Served from July 28, until August 28, 1813.

Rank and Name of Soldier.
Capt. Peter Bacus
Sergt. John Cutright
Corp. David Stumbough

Privates.
Abbott, Jeremiah
Bowin, William
Furst, Francis
Gillilan, William
Kindall, Booton
Link, Jacob
Osborn, William
Stewart, George

Rank and Name of Soldier.
Lieut. Peris Thompson
Sergt. Jonothan B. Hand
Drummer, William Burt

Privates.
Abbott, Eben
Blithe, Thomas
Fulson, Samuel
Humbough, Adam
Kimbol, William
Malone, Richard
Proebster, I. Adam
Woolf, Andrew

Rank and Name of Soldier.
Ensign, John Thompson
Sergt. Henry Sumner

Privates.
Bell, Benjamin
DeWitt, W.
Fetzer, John
Hall, John
Louis, William
Miller, Abraham
Powell, William

Pages 259 260.
ROLL OF CAPT. ANDREW HEMPHILL'S COMPANY (County Unknown).
Served from July 28, until September 5, 1813.

Capt. Andrew Hemphill
Sergt. James Latta
Sergt. George McCann
Sergt. Merit Jameson
Corp. Jacob Caylor

Privates.
Andrews, Gibson
Fisher, John
Gossom, William
Harris, Amos
Hoskins, John
Killough, William
Kor, Christian
Myers, John
McCracken, Isaac
Roads, George
Platt, Henry
Shoemaker, David
Turnipseed, Christian

Lieut. James McConnel
Lieut. Aaron Foster
Sergt. Robert Hurley
Corp. William Brown
Corp. Jacob Hire
Drummer, Moses McKensie

Privates.
Anderson, Samuel
Fruet, Gilly
Gossard, Jacob
Hire, Daniel
Johnston, William
Kerr, George
Michie, Mathew
Near, James
Rambo, Michael
Spikes, Francis
Shanor, Henry
Vanderman, Henry
Williams, Calvin

Ensign, Jacob Hare
Ensign, Gutham Anderson
Sergt. Conrad Vanderman
Corp. John Baird
Corp. Joshua Smithson

Privates.
Clark, James
Goldsberry, Jonothan
Grubb, Daniel
Hire, George
James, William
Lease, John
Mitchell, Frederick
Newlain, Jacob
Powell, Emery
Streebey, Peter
Turner, James B.
Vanderman, Mathias

Pages 261-262.
ROLL OF CAPT. ISAAC PANCAKE'S COMPANY (Probably from Ross County).
Served from July 28, until September 5, 1813.

Capt. Isaac Pancake
Sergt. John Down
Corp. George Seavers

Privates.
Adams, John
Brittenham, Mathias
Chamberlain, William
Goldsberry, Thomas
Gimmons, Amos
Lowery, Solomon
McQua, James
Parish, James
Roseboom, Abraham
Timmons, George

Ensign, Arthur McCarty
Sergt. Richard V. Hoddy
Corp. John Clossen
Musician, Amsted Carson

Privates.
Brown, Edward
Brown, Phillip
Cochran, James
Haggert, Daniel
Jones, Amos
Mahone, Joshua
Parish, John
Porter, Henry
Stothard, Septimus
Templain, John

Sergt. William Staggs
Corp. James Corey
Musician, Samuel Mark

Privates.
Brittenham, Aaron
Chamberlain, Jacob
Fields, William
Henderson, Daniel
Long, George
McCarty, James
Parish, William
Porter, William
Stumbe, Adam

Page 266.
ROLL OF CAPT. BENJAMIN GOLDSBERRY'S COMPANY (County Unknown).
Served from July 28, until August 15, 1813.

Capt. Benjamin Goldsberry
Sergt. Cornelius Johnston
Corp. John Hamilton

Privates.
Cunningham, Samuel
Denflinger, Cornelius
Gradless, William
Leigore, Joseph
Stookey, Abraham

Ensign, Henry Hester
Sergt. Michael Summerman
Corp. William Bell
Fifer, Samuel Edwards

Privates.
Davis, William
Essex, Jesse
Jamison, Samuel
Pick, William
Vanderman, Conrad

Sergt. John Ireland
Corp. Francis Tully
Corp. Joshua Smithson

Privates.
Devorse, Joseph
Gipson, Andrew
Jameson, Ment
Pereu, William
Wilson, Stephen

Page 278. Vol. I.
ROLL OF CAPT. NATHANIEL BEASLEY'S COMPANY (County Unknown).
Served from August 22, until October 22, 1812.

Rank and Name of Soldier.	Rank and Name of Soldier.	Rank and Name of Soldier.
Capt. Nathaniel Beasley	Lieut. William Russell	Ensign, Abraham Colven
Sergt. William Marsh	Sergt. Thomas Wright	Sergt. George Harrison
Sergt. Elijah Redmon	Corp. Andrew Davidson	Corp. Joseph Brownfield
Corp. Benjamin Griffith	Corp. John Reed	Fifer, George Ramsey
Privates.	**Privates.**	**Privates.**
Boatman, John	Boggess, William	Brooks, Adolphus
Cline, Daniel	Compton, John	Chambers, Elijah
Cole, Lewis	Criswell, David	Clark, Samuel
Duffey, William	Evans, Samuel	Evans, Thomas
Haynes, William	Killen, James	Lane, James
Munay, Joseph	Moore, John	Murphy, John
McKittrick, James	Osler, Charles	Peterson, Thomas
Pollard, Robert	Roads, Israel	Roads, Thomas
Stout, John	Sullivan, John	Storay, John
Shevalier, William	Sargent, James	Sroph, John
Smith, Walter	Smith, John	Shirely, Timothy
Stephenson, Ralph	Swisher, John	Thompson, John
Trotter, Elijah, C.	Woods, Tobias	Wilson, Gustavus

Pages 263-264-265.
ROLL OF CAPT. JOSEPH ROCKHOLD'S COMPANY (Probably from Ross Co.)
Served from July 28, until September 5, 1813.

Capt. Joseph Rockhold	Lieut. Abraham Pebble	Lieut. Joseph O'Brian
Ensign, Amaziah Morgan	Ensign, Joseph Heistand	Sergt. James Mahan
Sergt. Levi Wells	Sergt. Isaac Rockhold	Sergt. John Barton
Sergt. John Hendershot	Sergt. Iadeth Tully	Corp. Samuel Logan
Corp. Adam Gilfillen	Corp. Charles O'Brian	Corp. Benjamin Bromley
Privates.	**Privates.**	**Privates.**
Brakeman, William	Beekman, Abraham	Briant, Elijah
Briant, Peter	Beekman, Aaron	Blackstone, John
Black, Abraham	Benona, Christian	Bonner, Henry
Clay, William	Cochran, David	Chafford, Solomon
Cameron, Alexander	Demoss, James	Dunlap, Robert
Ewing, Samuel	Elliott, Burgiss	Eubanks, Mathew
Eubanks, David	Beekman, Christopher	Freshour, Daniel
Freshour, Abraham	Foster, Lawrence	Grove, Frederick
Goodman, James	Gant, Jacob	Hartley, John
Hartley, Obijah	Johnston, John	Gray, John
Layton, Asher	Lowman, Joseph	Layton, Elias
Mason, Samuel	Minna, Bonna	Marquis, Isaac
Merrman, Enoch	McDonald, John	Nicely, Henry
Nevan, Alexander	Ogle, Joseph	Pendrill, Gabriel
Patterson, John	Price, Robert	Pherron, Phillip
Rowley, Alpheus	Roberts, Asa	Reeves, John D.
Stockton, William	Stockton, Thomas	Sleter, Jeremiah
Slater, James	Shepley, Peter	Scartler, Alexander
Cowden, Samuel	Straton, Charles	Senter, George
Thompson, Joseph	Wheaton, Humphrey	Wyckoff, Isaac
Williams, Robert	Williamson, Charles	

Page 267.
ROLL OF CAPT. CLAYTON WEBB'S COMPANY
(Probably from Hamilton County).
Served from August 24, until September 20, 1812.

Capt. Clayton Webb	Lieut. John Armstrong	Ensign, Nathan Hatfield
Sergt. James Jones	Sergt. Peter Bell	Sergt. David Kelley
Sergt. James Armstrong	Corp. William Landen	Corp. Stephen Cobley
Privates.	**Privates.**	**Privates.**
Askron, Thomas	Burrows, Joseph	Black, Peter
Black, David	Burdsall, Josiah	Crichfield, Phillip
Clark, Ichabod	Cross, Ignatius	Crosson, Benjamin
Christ, George	Davis, William	Earhart, Samuel
Ferris, John	Gordon, James	Greenwood, Will
Huff, John	Hawkins, Reson	Hawkins, Richard
Hosbrook, Archibald	Johnson, Charles	Jenkins, Henry
Jones, John T.	Knopper, Jacob	Lee, Louis H.
Miller, Jacob J.	Keely, John	Martin, John
Mawhinny, James	Martin, William	Mack, Erastus
Moln, John	Mail, George	Nicely, Abraham
Orr, Andrew	Parker, Jacob	Robinson, Edward
Riggs, Henry	Welch, Robert	Schillinger, William

Page 279. Vol. I.

ROLL OF LIEUT. JOHN McARTHUR'S COMPANY (Probably from Ross Co.)
Served from July 28, until August 27, 1813.

Rank and Name of Soldier.	Rank and Name of Soldier.	Rank and Name of Soldier.
Lieut. John McArthur	Sergt. John Sample	Sergt. James Larkins
Sergt. James Riley	Corp. James Dean	Corp. Ezra Lucas
Corp. Robert Miler	Corp. Joseph Morton	
Privates.	**Privates.**	**Privates.**
Blane, Thomas	Brackney, Benjamin	Burkley, John
Blain, James	Cannon, Handy	Cunningham, Adam
Caldwell, James	Cassel, John	Clark, Daniel
DeVoss, Isaac	Kelley, Mathew	Kerr, Adam
Logan, John	Morton, John	Morrow, Richard
Milligan, Hugh	McClure, William	McCracken, Alexander
	Young, Silas	

Pages 275-276.

ROLL OF JACOB YOUNG'S COMPANY (From Knox and Richland Counties.)
Served from August 26, until October 31, 1812.

Capt. Jacob Young	Lieut. George Sapp	Lieut. Insly Johnston
Ensign, John Parcel	Ensign, Amos H. Royer	Ensign, Daniel Ayres
Sergt. Ziba Jackson	Sergt. Jesse Inlow	Sergt. Andrew Kirkpatric
Sergt. Peter Wolf	Sergt. John Logan	Sergt. Joseph Denman
Sergt. Henry George	Corp. William Evans	Corp. William Tucker
Corp. James Johnston	Corp. Peter Johnston	Corp. Daniel Conger
Corp. Noah Young	Drummer, John Halderman	Fifer, Mathew Merrit
Privates.	**Privates.**	**Privates.**
Austin, David	Austin, James	Arbuckle, Samuel
Brown, Benjamin	Barcus, James	Bryan, Eliab
Bal' Hiram	Bue, Samuel	Brown, John, Jr.
Beers, Jabez	Cremer, John	Conger, Thomas
Davis, Azaniah, Jr.	Day, Josiah D	Dalrymple, Israel
Denman, Uriah	Davis, David	Drake, William
Dickson, Miron	Fitting, Castar	Herrod, John
Herrod, William	Harris, Elijah	Holt, James
Huffmire, William	George, Richard	Inlow, Isaac
Irwin, James	Johnston, Samuel	Kimbel, Daniel
Knight, William	Lepley, George	Lewis, Samuel
Lyon, Benjamin	Lyon, Absalom	Lindley, John P.
Mirick, Higgins	Morrison, John	Mitchell, Nathaniel
Melick, David	McCreary, James	Nuffmore, Wilson
Ostin, James	Ogden, James	Pierce, George
Robinson, William	Rush, Peter	Spurgeon, James
Slater, John	Shaw, David	Sams, Andrew
Strong, Truman	Shur, Jacob	Peoples, David
Talmage, Joseph	Thomas, William	Welker, Solomon
Williams, Thomas	Woodruff, Stephen	Walker, Alexander
	Walker, John	

Pages 285-286.

ROLL OF CAPT. STEPHEN HORSEY'S COMPANY.
(Probably from Pickaway County.)
Served from July 28,, until August 26, 1813.

Capt. Stephen Horsey	Lieut. James Nevill	Ensign, Cornelius Mikel
Sergt. John Pancake	Sergt. Balitha Linch	Sergt. Daniel Justice
	Sergt. Pierce Atchison	
Privates.	**Privates.**	**Privates.**
Atchison, Fielding	Beavins, Josiah	Benedict, James
Campbell, Robert	Chipman, John	Dodd, Isaac
Diver, James	Dumond, Isaac	Devenport, Wesley
Foresman, Henry	Flemming, John	Galbraith, John
Hubbard, John	Henderson, David	Horsey, Edward
Henderson, James	Henderson, John	Hanaman, George
Johnson, Richard	Knight, Enos	King, William
Leonard, Charles	Lacount, James	Moore, James
Moore, Fergus	McGroos, Isaac	Nicholas Christian
Randle, Tibble	Romine, Abraham	Ridman, James
Rively, Daniel	Smith, Henry	Sullivan, Aaron
Seabourn, Doress	Shuff, Frederick	Shephard, William
Van Waggoner, John	Van Horn, Walter	Waples, Derixson
Wanaughmaker, Phillip	Whitsell, Daniel	

Pages 280-281-282-283-284.

ROLL OF CAPTAIN WILLIAM MUNN'S COMPANY (County Unknown).
Served from July 28, until August 28, 1813, and from February 16, until March 16, 1814.

Capt. William Munn	Lieut. Joseph Kelley	Lieut. Tapley White
Ensign, Abraham Stewart	Ensign, John Clemens	Sergt. Thomas Phillips
Sergt. Richard Johnson	Sergt. John Ruke	Sergt. John Bennet
Sergt. William G. Robinson	Sergt. James Gilbruth	Sergt. Briar Griffin
Sergt. John Cannon	Corp. Samuel Crull	Corp. John Bennet
Corp. Jesse Martin	Corp. Henry Crull	Corp. Eli Rogan
Corp. William Holland	Corp. Yoel Church	Drummer, Charles Bennet
Fifer, Elijah Jacobs		

ROLL OF CAPT. WILLIAM MUNN'S COMPANY (Continued).

Rank and Name of Soldier.

Privates.

Anderson, Jacob
Barret, Elijah
Buck, James
Crookham, George L.
Cline, George
Dener, John
Dawson, Othe
Farney, John
Graham, John
Gillilan, Hugh
Gilmore, William
Gunies, James
Hadley, George
Hubbell, Rowland
Graham, Joseph
Lewis, Abraham
Munroe, Charles
Monroe, Solomon
Mounts, Enoch
McKenney, William
Perry, Isaac
Runkle, George
Star, John
Shane, Daniel
Sherlock, John
Satherland, John
Utt, Adam
Waggoner, James

Anderson, Mark
Brewer, James
Bowser, Adam
Cox, William
Cartmell, Samuel
Duncan, John
Davis, Nathaniel
Fry, Joseph
Goodin, Daniel
Gunies, John
Gibson, John
Hill, John
Hollingshead, William
Johnson, James
Kuby, Nathan
Linton, William
Monroe, Barnabas
Martin, Hugh
Miller, William
McKenney, Theadore
Pemil, Enoch
Reynolds, James
Sierot, John
Seberell, Nicholas
Strange, William
Timmonds, John
Utt, Jacob
Walker, John
Wilson, Alexander

Alkin, John
Bonner, Abraham
Copias, John
Cross, Robert
Calhoun, William
Craig, Thomas
Fleming, Andrew
Finley, James
Grubb, Joseph
Gilmore, Robert
Gilsten, James
Haddox, William
Howard, Lewis
Jones, William
Kennedy, Robert
Linch, Samuel
Martin, John
Mercer, Levi
Morrison, Robert
Nelson, Jonothan R.
Radcliffe, Daniel
Sappington, Thomas
Stigalls, Frederick
Satterly, Isaac
Stewart, Jeremiah
Thomas, Jacob
Walker, John D.
Wells, Absalom

Pages 287-288.

ROLL OF CAPT. HENRY SLACK'S COMPANY (Probably from Delaware Co.)

Served from August 24, until September 25, 1812. Part served from July 26, until August 13, 1813.

Capt. Henry Slack
Sergt. Gilbert Carpenter
Corp. Daniel Alden
Corp. Henry Love
Corp. Sylvester Drake

Lieut. Gilbert Weeks
Sergt. Mathew Marvin
Corp. Benjamin Shoemaker
Corp. Robert Carpenter
Fifer, Mathias Vanloon

Lieut. Benjamin Carpenter
Sergt. Alexander Smith
Corp. Leonard Jones
Corp. James Carpenter

Privates.

Anway, George
Budd, John
Bonnet, Isaac
Day, Charles
Gregory, David
Hess, George
Heath, Samuel
Jones, David
Landon, David
Leonard, Samuel
Morehous, Philemon
Perfect, Truman
Phipps, William
Slack, John
Scoby, John
Shoemaker, Benjamin
Williams, William

Armstrong, David
Brown, John
Carpenter, Moses
Fairchild, Benjamin
Harris, Samuel
Hills, Louis
Jones, Richard
Keys, Isaac
Lewis, John
Longwell, Ralph
Munson, Mishael
Perfect, Thomas
Rosecrans, John
Skeels, Jonothan
Steward, Solomon
Patrick, Joseph
Young, John

Bishop, Daniel
Barr, Alva
Closson, Jacob
Ford, Augustus
Harper, James
Helt, Michael
Johns, Francis C.
Kepler, Samuel
Lane, Daniel
Manvill, George
Osterhout, Gideon
Phipps, John
Ross, John
Smith, William
Studevant, George
Waters, Nehemiah
Young, Andrew

Page 289.

ROLL OF CAPT. JAMES NISBET'S COMPANY (County Unknown.)

Served from April 28, until August 12, 1812.

Capt. James Nisbet
Sergt. Daniel Kenselo
Sergt. Isaac Harral
Corp. Peter Shidler

Lieut. Joseph Lower
Sergt. James W. Maxwell
Corp. Frederick Utt
Corp. Willis Copland
Fifer, William D. Williams

Ensign Henry Johnston
Sergt. Bestly M. Burris
Corp. James Taylor
Drummer, Jacob Parker

Privates.

Allen, John
Beard, Paul
Banfield, Thomas
Caster, William
Davis, Silas
Gard, Levi
Howard, Thomas
Kircheval, Samuel
Larsh, Paul
Michael, Frederick
McDowell, James

Aldred, Isaac
Bell, John
Bishop, William
Case, Samuel
Demoss, Charles
Gamble, Robert
Harton, Isaac
Kircheval, John
Lease, Daniel
McDaniel, John
Nelson, William

Ashby, Abraham
Butt, Phillip
Clap, Tobias
Dooley, Abner
Flemming, Mitchel
Grisom, George
Hendricks, William
Krieger, Jacob
Moore, Jesse
McKnutt, Alexander
Purviance, David P.

ROLL OF CAPT. JAMES NISBET'S COMPANY (Continued).

Rank and Name of Soldier.

Privates.
Penlan, Alexander
Russel, Charles
Stephens, David
Van Aarsdal, Peter

Rank and Name of Soldier.

Privates.
Pierce, Eros
Snider, Baltzer
Sprowl, Robert
Vanwickle, Daniel
Winich, Daniel

Rank and Name of Soldier.

Privates.
Reed, Adam
Smith, Charles
Shannon, James
West, Jeptha

Page 290.

ROLL OF CAPT. HUGH FLINN'S COMPANY (County Unknown).
Served from July 28, until August 13, 1813.

Capt. Hugh Flinn
Sergt. James Wheaton
Corp. Jacob Chenewith

Privates.
Chenewith, Isaac
Chenewith, Abraham
Burk, Michael
Keen, James
Sewell, David
Travis, Asa

Sergt. William Hackney
Corp. Henry Carter
Corp. Robert Montgomery
Musician, Uriah Chenewith

Privates.
Chenewith, John
Carter, Thomas
Davis, John F.
Moore, William
Tucker, Levi
Wiley, Thomas

Sergt. John Perril
Corp. Edwin H. Smith
Musician, Richard Chenewith

Privates.
Chenewith, Elijah
Chenewith, Joseph
Howard, Cornelius
Montgomery, John
Thomburgh, William

Page 291.

ROLL OF LIEUT. MARTIN NUNKEEPAR'S COMPANY.
(Probably from Ross County.)
Served from July 29, until August 7, 1813.

Lieut. Martin Nunkeepar
Sergt. Joshua Hall
Corp. Moses Wiggins

Privates.
Abanatha, John
Evet, John
Hall, James
Larrick, Isaac
Worley, Daniel

Ensign John O'Neal
Sergt. Zedekiah Dawson
Drummer, Joseph Polem

Privates.
Bensher, Jacob
Frye, Henry
Hartman, Philip
Ramy, Presley
Williams, Enoch

Sergt. Joseph Fermon
Corp. Joseph Porter

Privates.
Cremeon, John
Godfrey, Lewis
Halderman, David
Stanley, Thomas

Pages 292-293.

ROLL OF CAPT. ISAAC DAWSON'S COMPANY (Probably from Ross Cunty).
Served from August 22, until September 24, 1812, and from May 6, until May 18, 1813.

Capt. Isaac Dawson
Ensign, John McCoy
Sergt. James McCoy
Sergt. James Bunn

Privates.
Armstrong, Thomas
Cochran, John
Corbett, Joseph
Dunn, Peter
Eschine, Daniel
Goodin, John
Hicks, Willis
Justice, John
Lee, Parker
Massie, Thomas
Mullin, Joseph
McMahon, Robert
Perkins, John
Parish, Meredith
Enger, Mathias
Sommers, William
Smith, John
Timmons, John
Thimons, Edmon
Will, David, Sr.

Lieut. John Perkins
Ensign, John Caldwell
Sergt. John Rodgers
Sergt John Vanmeter

Privates.
Burnes, John
Corbett, David
Clarridge, Edmon
Dyor, William
Fisher, John
Guthrie, William
Hinton, Thomas
Kerr, William
Loveless, Joseph
Mace, John
Mounts, Humphrey
Niece, George
Perkins, John Sr.
Potts, Nathan
Rodgers, Benjamin
Stockton, George
Stone, Daniel
Thweeks, Elijah
Will, George
Williams, Isaac

Lieut. John McCollough
Sergt. Mathias Enge
Sergt. Oratio Walker

Privates.
Cochran, James
Collins, Samuel
Crouch, James
Dawns, James
Gibson, John
Green, Charles
Hanes, Peter
Kerr, John
Moreland, William
Morris, Jeremiah
McCafferty, David
Ogden, John
Phillips, William Jr.
Purtee, James
Rogers, Mathew
Stockton, William
Seath, William
Timmons, George
Will, David
Walker, Thomas

Page 294.

CAPT. JAMES DAVIS' COMPANY (Probably from Ross County).
Served from July 30, until August 30, 1813.

Capt. James Davis
Sergt. Prior Griffith

Privates.
Clark, Daniel
Goodwin, John
James, John
Mathews, Isaac
McMullen, John
Scott, Peter

Ensign, Abraham Stewart
Corp. Eli Ragoon

Privates.
Clark, James
Heath, Amos
Luzador, Thomas
Murphy, Andray
Longshow, James
Tenebaugh, Jacob

Sergt. Curtis Berry
Corp. Richard Heath

Privates.
Cordrey, Shepherd
Hibben, Samuel
Miller, Warrick
Martin, William
Summers, William
Wilson, Caleb

ROLL OF CAPT. DANIEL MUSSELMAN'S COMPANY
(Probably from Ross County).
Served from July 27, until August 18, 1813.

Rank and Name of Soldier.	Rank and Name of Soldier.	Rank and Name of Soldier.
Capt. Daniel Musselman	Lieut. Christopher Bickle	Ensign, Jacob Whitzel
Sergt. Valentine Engle	Sergt. Michael Heater	Sergt. Adam Bowhan
Sergt. Mensil Ellis	Corp. Jonas Marble	Corp. Robert Caldwell
Corp. Abraham Davis	Corp. John Wilson	

Privates.

Brink, Robert	Coon, Jacob	Chambers, John
Claypool, Isaac	Clayton, William	Engler, Jacob
Fink, Henry	Ferron, Daniel	Glover, William
Goodman, John	Hammersley, George	Hivley, Jacob
Holarstat, Jacob	Ingam, Isaiah	Johnson, George
Jones, Moses	Migers, Mathias	Myres, Abraham
Markle, John	Myers, Jacob	Mosey, Jacob
McKin, John	Nayhart, Peter	Piper, Phillip
Sipes, Mathias	Smith, Thomas	Shaw, Samuel
Tittle, Jacob	Whitsel, Samuel	Wiley, John
	Wright, Thomas	

ROLL OF CAPT. ARCHIBALD STEWART'S COMPANY (County Unknown).
Served from March 26, until April 26, 1813.

Capt. Archibald Stewart	Lieut. William Williams	Sergt. Daniel Downs
Sergt. William Stewart	Sergt. Alexander Numan	Sergt. Jeremiah Bowen
Corp. Samuel Morecraft	Corp. Isaac Hughes	Fifer, Hamilton Rogers

Privates.

Binley, James	Burton, Thomas	Brown, David
Boyd, George	Bousman, Nichodemus	Claypool, James
Davis, John	Fitzpatrick, Daniel	Gratridge, Joseph
Lee, Benjamin	Mason, Mathew	Norton, David
Martin, Archer	Norton, Giles	Mason, Isaac
Stephens, Robert	Stewart, Thomas	Spencer, Beverly
Tharp, Levi	Tharp, William	Tharp, Abner
Thomas, Joel	Taylor, William	Reed, John
Rutledge, William	Williams, Henry	Williams, James
	Walters, Levi	

ROLL OF CAPT. ABNER BARRETT'S COMPANY
(Probably from Champaign County).
Served from August 9, until September 9, 1813.

Capt. Abner Barrett	Lieut. Edward Jones	Sergt. John Kelley
Sergt. James Guthridge	Sergt. Jacob Hazel	Sergt. Allen Minturn
Corp. John B. Neal	Corp. Obediah Valentine	Corp. William Kelley
	Corp. Jesse Gutridge	

Privates.

Adams, John	Baker, Aaron	Bracken, Nathan
Britten, Evans E.	Beatty, Miles C.	Britten, Nathan
Binley, James	Chaney, Edward	Chaney, William
Cartmell, John	George, Richard D.	Cory, John
Crage, John	Burnside, William	Frankeberger, John
Gilpin, Elias	Cartmell, William	George, William M.
Hudson, Edward	Harbert, William	Hutson, Abraham
Hendrix, William	Hutsin, James	Hoover, Peter
Hall, Bradford	Jones, Daniel	Lafferty, John
Kain, John	Minturn, George	Jones, Justice
Long, David D.	Kelley, Gilbert	Minturn, Bunnel
Mathews, James	Neally, Mathew	Oppy, Abraham
Runyon, John	Piper, John	Price, William
Pierce, Andrew	Reese, Maurice	Rathburn, John
Runyon, John Jr.	Sitzer, Henry	Sayre, Thomas
Tucker, Isaac	Thompson, John	Thompson, Joshua
Tucker, Samuel	Rees, Jacob	Valentine, David
Vanse, Solomon	Ward, Obed	

ROLL OF CAPT. ENOCH GEST'S COMPANY (County Unknown).
Served from February 17, until March 17, 1813.

Capt. Enoch Gest	Lieut. Elijah Stout	Ensign, Richard Phillips
Sergt. James Moon	Sergt. James Winters	Sergt. Benjamin B. Cox
Sergt. Joseph Vanhat	Corp. Samuel Robertson	Corp. Jacob Jones
Corp. Joseph Ferris	Corp. Robert Bennet	

ROLL OF CAPT. ENOCH GEST'S COMPANY (Continued).

Privates.

Andrews, James
Burk, Elisha
Clark, Mathew
Compton, Abraham
Creglon, Christian
Davis, Thomas
Fridley, John
Gwrin, Silas
Gray, Martin
Harper, Mathew
Johnson, William
Kimble, Henry
Job, Archibald R.
Leonard, Cory
Moorehead, William
McGunnegle, John
Roney, James
Smith, Jacob
Simpson, Alexander
Tarrens, Samuel
Wing, Ebenezer
Wolverton, Daniel
Wing, Silas

Allison, Alexander
Boyer, William
Croyes, William
Cameron, William R.
Coplon, Willis
Dennis, Benjamin
Ferguson, James
Guerin, Elias R.
Huston, Joseph
Howard, Abner
Jones, Jonothan
Jackson, John
Lilly, John
Meeker, David
Northan, Walter B.
Ross, John
Shonian, Jacob
Tumbleson, John
Tucker, Ephraim
Watson, John
Wilkinson, John L.
Wheeler, Thaddeus
Johnson, William

Burrel, John
Connet, Henry
Campbell, Andrew
Carson, David
Coleman, Thomas B.
Earley, John
Ford, Elijah
Gorman, Hugh
Hill, James M.
Irwin, John
Jessup, Isaac
Kibby, Ephraim
Meeker, John
McGee, William W.
Nichols, Leicester
Riggle, Benjamin
Shots, John
Tousley, Amos
Vaneaton, Levi
Winters, John
Wade, John
Probus, Henry
Johnson Eleazar

Page 301.

ROLL OF CAPT. SAMUEL McCORMICK'S COMPANY
(Probably from Hamilton County).

Served from September 1, until September 30, 1813.

Capt. Samuel McCormick
Sergt. William G. Serviss
Sergt. Abner Garard
Corp. Calvin Ward

Lieut. John Hopkins
Sergt. Owen Todd
Corp. John Farquer
Corp. David Ayers

Ensign, John Knox
Sergt. William Dixon
Corp. Ephraim Munthan

Privates.

Baldwin, Thomas
Biddle, Solomon
Conner, Luke
Campbell, James
Eastwood, Benjamin
Fitzwater, Thomas
Hopkins, John
Hopkins, John Sr.
Johnson, John M.
Miller, William
McCollum, Thomas
Riley, Ely
Shaw, Daniel
Smith, James
Smith, Jacob
Ward, Luther
Watson, William

Burroughs, James
Cawer, William
Cunningham, Richard
Bostwick, Clement
Flinn, William Jr.
Fordeck, Christopher
Hudson, Shadrach
Hurley, Joel
Marsh, Isaac
Mounts, Providence
McCollister, Michael
Ramsey, George
Stewart, William
Sunderland, Die
Todd, Paxton
Ward, Ashbel
Westfall, William

Bush, Jacob
Cook, Thomas
Chambers, James N.
Depriest, Charles
Flinn, William Sr.
Havens, William
Havens, Benjamin
Gordon, John
Marsh, Joseph
McKinney, Anthony
McCollister, Frederick
Reeder, Benjamin
Shaw, Isaiah
Smith, Thomas
Vanscoyke, Joseph
Watson, Isaac
Wood, Robert

Page 305.

ROLL OF CAPT. WILLIAM LINDSEY'S COMPANY
(Probably from Hamilton County).

Served from August 25, until September 25, 1812.

Capt. William Lindsey
Sergt. James Robb
Sergt. Isaac Ferguson
Corp. Timothy Riddler

Lieut. John Shaw
Sergt. George Rinker
Corp. Elijah Lindsey
Corp. Isaac Ford

Ensign Isaiah Ferguson
Sergt. John Beltt
Corp. Robert Donham

Privates.

Beezley, William
Donham, Amos
Ferguson, Hugh
Gray, Andrew
Morris, Joseph
Rinker, George
Welsh, Thomas
White, David

Brown, Joshua
Donham, Abel
Gray, John
Moring, Redham
McCord, Richard
Rardin, Jacob
Wood, James

Conner, Timothy
Fitzpatrick, James
Gray, Neeley
Morris, Benjamin
Rardin, Timothy
Snyder, John
Williams, Samuel

ROLL OF CAPT. ROBERT McCLELLAND'S COMPANY
(Probably from Greene County).

Served from August 22, until September 22, 1812, and from May 25, until November 24, 1813.

Rank and Name of Soldier.

Capt. Robert McClelland
Ensign David Douglas
Sergt. Isaac Miller
Sergt. John Barnes
Corp. William Sutton
Corp. Jacob Beals
Fifer, Robert Snodgrass

Lieut. James McBride
Ensign William Erwin
Sergt. Jacob Hozier
Corp. Samuel Lawrence
Corp. John Alexander
Corp. William Constant
Musician, William Harrison

Lieut. Elisha Leslie
Sergt. Samuel Snodgrass
Sergt. John McDaniel
Corp. Henry Webb
Corp. John Hacker
Corp. Adam Wolf
Musician, Daniel DeWitt

Privates.

Alexander, Francis
Benitt, James
Benham, John
Buchanon, James
Campbell, William
Cain, Joseph
Cruson, Cornelius
Cottrell, John
Devore, John
DeWitt, Isaac
Fallows, Isaac
Gott, John
Hamilton, William
Hoop, John
Huse, John
Junkins, James
Kune, Hugh
Kendall, William
Martin, Samuel
Moreland, John
Murphy, John
McCoy, John
Nimerick, John
Perry, Allen
Paige, William
Reed, William
Sutton, William G.
Saunders, Aaron
Smith, John
Smith, William
Vance, James
Vaughn, Thomas
Whicker, John
Watson, James

Allen, William
Bias, Isaac
Benjamin, Thomas
Babcock, Thomas
Currie, Robert
Casebolt, Robert
Cox, Israel
Dean, Robert
Douglas, James
Eatton, Joseph
Follist, John
Griffith, Benjamin
Holmes, John
Hibbs, Abner
Haddox, Nimrod
Johnson, William
Knight, Samuel
Mitchell, James
Murphy, John
Meninghall, William
McFarlin, John
McDaniel, Demesy
Noble, Joshua
Poage, William
Russell, Moses
Snodgrass, William
Sparks, Thomas
Sheley, Benjamin
Smith, Spencer
Shoe, Phillip
Vaughn, William
Vance, John
Wilson, Joseph
Wolff, Jacob
Weaver, Christian

Burney, Thomas
Bowen, Ephraim
Benjamin, Lewis
Collier, Moses
Cain, Samuel
Concleton, David
Cunningham, John
Dickensheets, William
Downey, William
Edge, George D.
Griffy, Daniel
Glenn, William
Hufford, John
Hutchison, George
Jones, Benjamin
Knight, William
Laird, Benjamin
Miller, William Poog
Moore, William C.
Mitchell, Jesse
McKaig, Benjamin
Neely, James
Page, James
Rich, Jacob
Reagon, Reason
Snodgrass, James
Smith, Thomas
Shelinger, George
Snodgrass, Robert
Todd, John B.
Vaneaten, John
Vance, Joseph C.
Wilson, David
White, William

Page 306.
ROLL OF LIEUT. GARNER BOBO'S COMPANY (Probably from Miami Co.)
Served from September 26, 1812, until March 26, 1813.

Lieut. Garner Bobo

Sergt. Jonothan Couch
Corp. Thomas Green

Corp. David Knight

Privates.

Adams, Joseph
Dickson, Nicholas
French, Ezekial
Mellinger, John
Mann, John
Shaver, Simon
Vaneman, James

Ballinger, James
Dye, Samuel
Harrison, Richard
Mason, Peter
Redinger, Andrew
Statler, Christopher
Woodruff, Hampton

Bedle, Daniel
Baker, Peter
Mann, Barnabus
McConnoughey, David
Simons, Adam
Stranbarger, Joseph

Page 307.
ROLL OF CAPT. EZEKIAL KIRTLEY'S COMPANY (County Unknown).
Served from May 27, until November 27, 1813.

Capt. Ezekial Kirtley
Corp. Barnabus Blue

Sergt. Samuel Reed
Corp. Samuel Williams

Sergt. Sampson Coats

Privates.

Brown, William
Folkerth, William
Haney, Jonas
Jenkins, Isachor
Mendenhall, William
Overfield, Benjamin
Stockstill, Thomas
Sharp, David

Carson, David
Goble, Daniel
Hudson, John
Lowery, Fielding
Moore, Samuel
Price, John
Saunders, George
Woodbourne, Robert

Childers, John
Goble, John
Ingle, John
Miller, Joseph
Dye, John B.
Stewart, Joseph
Stinchcomb, David

ROSTER OF OHIO SOLDIERS IN WAR OF 1812

Pages 308-309. Vol. I.

ROLL OF CAPT. HENRY ZUMALT'S COMPANY (From Hamilton County).
Served from August 22, until September 30, 1812.

Rank and Name of Soldier.	Rank and Name of Soldier.	Rank and Name of Soldier.
Capt. Henry Zumalt	Lieut. Henry Chapman	Ensign Thomas Connel
Sergt. John Ross	Sergt. William Pangburn	Sergt. Samuel Ross
Sergt. Robert Allen	Corp. Robert Davidson	Corp. William W. Daniel
Corp. Chinley Mitchell	Corp. Noah Ellis	Fifer, John Allen
Privates.	**Privates.**	**Privates.**
Archer, Johnson	Alexander, Benjamin	Blair, John
Burget, Abraham	Burget, Valentine	Brunden, Andrew
Burget, Aaron	Bingerman, Frederick	Criss, Frederick
Calvin, James	Currey, William	Durand, Nicholas
Davis, Thomas	Ellis, Abraham	Evans, Duncan
Fee, Elisha	Gibson, James	Gibson, Andrew
Grogan, James	Hill, John	Hesler, George
Hall, Charles	Gould, William	Hillman, Joseph
Hall, Edward	Hicks, Robert	Jennings, Thomas
Jolley, Samuel	Jennings, Israel	Kerchival, Daniel
King, Victor	Landson, George	Lindsey, John
Lucas, Jacob	Leming, William	Leming, Samuel
Leming, Abraham	Little, George	Moore, Andrew
Mackland, John	Minor, Ephraim	Myers, Francis
McCurdy, Robert	Parker, James	Pangburn, Lype
Preston, Daniel	Reynolds, Daniel	Rees, Abel
Ross, William	Springer, Job	Shingle, George
Sellars, Peter	Stapleton, Joseph	Smith, James
Skedman, Ralph	Shick, John	Thompson, George S.
Thompson, Samuel	Woodruff, John	Woodruff, Jacob
Woodruff, William	Woodruff, William, Jr.	Wolars, Samuel
Williams, Isaac	Wright, George	Wood, James

Page 311.

ROLL OF CAPT. WILLIAM B. JONES' COMPANY (County Unknown).
Served from September 14, until October 14, 1812.

Capt. William B. Jones	Lieut. Simon Phillips	Ensign Abraham R. Caldwell
Sergt. John Elliott	Sergt. John Drybread	Sergt. William Morris
Corp. Alexander Grant	Corp. Samuel Hardin	Corp. David Bell
	Corp. Perry Orndorf	
Privates.	**Privates.**	**Privates.**
Bett, Henry	Bears, John	Barnfield, Thomas
Blackburn, William	Campbell, Samuel	Cooper, Justice
Evans, David	Howard, James	Howard, Stephen
House, Andrew	Hardin, Charles	Jones, William
Montgomery, Hugh	Montford, Aaron	Montgomery, Thomas
Montgomery, William	Montgomery, Henry	Price, Michael
Pottinger, Dennis	Pickle, Thomas	Pickett, Joseph
Ralph, Louis	Stokes, Joseph	Sallee, William
Shaw, Knowles	Sallee, Samuel	Thompson, John
	Wyne, James	

Page 312.

ROLL OF CAPT. GARVIN JOHNSTON'S COMPANY (County Unknown).
Served from August 23, until September 18, 1812.

Capt. Garvin Johnston	Lieut. James Norris	Ensign Thomas Barber
Sergt. James Brown	Sergt. William Gillespie	Sergt. James Johnston
Sergt. Jonothan Baldwin	Fifer, William Williamson	Drummer, Isaac Covenhover
Privates.	**Privates.**	**Privates.**
Brown, William	Caldwell, Joseph	Elliott, Robert
Fossett, Thomas	Gillis, John	Gillis, Reuben
Griffies, John	Harrison, Isaac	Holinshade, James
Johnston, William	Johnston, Alexander	Lowery, Abraham
Linning, Michael	McCord, James	McCord, Robert
Phillips, Lemuel	Ratcliffe, Daniel	Russell, Findley
Ross, John	Ross, David	Trowsdale, Samuel
Williams, Lewis	Woodruff, Hempton	Ward, Daniel W.

Page 313.

ROLL OF CAPT. DANIEL KAIN'S COMPANY (County Unknown).
Served from August 24, until September 24, 1812.

Capt. Daniel Kain	Lieut. Samuel Irwin	Ensign William Sloan
Sergt. James Perrine	Sergt. Oliver Lindsey	Sergt. Rodger W. Waring
Sergt. Benjamin Tingley	Corp. William South	Corp. John Boyd
	Corp. G. S. Bryan	
Privates.	**Privates.**	**Privates.**
Arthurs, James	Blair, John	Blair, Robert
Beck, Levi	Beck, Samuel	Boyd, William
Cran, Davis	Cade, Thomas	Dole, Joshua

ROLL OF CAPT. DANIEL KAIN'S COMPANY (Continued.)

Rank and Name of Soldier.

Privates.
Dole, Joseph
Ellis, Benjamin
Fountain, Mathew
Fletcher, William
Gould, Jesse
Hall, John
Knott, William
Laaghlin, James
Morris, Thomas
McCollum, Hugh
Prickett, Josiah
Stephens, Jesse
Sanders, Isaac
Thornburgh, Thomas
Vanosdole, James
Williams, William

Rank and Name of Soldier.

Privates.
Danberry, Spencer
Earhart, John
Flitcher, Jesse
Foot, Thomas S.
Glancy, William
James, Isaac
Knott, Joseph
Moorehead, John
McClure, Richard
Nuber, Jacob
Reeves, John
Schroder, John F.
Snider, Adam
Townsley, William
Vanosdole, Robert
Wilson, Peter

Rank and Name of Soldier.

Privates.
Dunn, Robert
Ellison, Jackson
Foster, Israel
Frambus, Joseph
Huling, Isaac
Jinkings, Zephaniah
Leeds, Robert
Lattermore, John
McKnight, John
Osborn, John
Rust, Thomas
South, Isaac
Smith, Joseph
Shotwell, John
Wagaman, John
Wood, Vincen

Page 314.

ROLL OF CAPT. JOSEPH LUCAS' COMPANY (Probably from Green County).

Served from January 20, until March 2, 1813.

Capt. Joseph Lucas

Sergt. Isaac Garard
Corp. Abraham Lucas

Sergt. Henry Bone

Privates.
Brewin, William H.
Beales, Jacob
Downey, John
Foster, Samuel
Price, William
Shillinger, George
Thornbury, George

Privates.
Bales, John
Beason, Thomas
Ellis, Jacob
Harris, Steward
Price, George
Turner, Joseph
Thornbury, James

Privates.
Beales, Jonothan
Copeland, William
Murphy, David
Fair, Thomas
Ross, John
Townsend, Zepheniah

Page 316.

ROLL OF LIEUT. CRAIGHEAD FERGUSON'S COMPANY (County Unknown).

Served from April 19, until October 18, 1813.

Lieut. Craighead Ferguson
Sergt. Jacob Shaffer
Corp. Benjamin Short

Ensign Alexander Gray
Sergt. John Myers
Corp. Thomas Johns

Sergt. James T. Hutton
Corp. Benjamin Hoff
Corp. Thomas H. Colivet

Privates.
Abraham, Israel
Butler, John E.
Conner, Aaron
Dalson, Peter
Kent, Davis
McDonald, Enoch
Slawson, James H.
Wright, Moses

Privates.
Bagley, Thomas
Baker, James
Cisna, Stephen
Ferree, Henry
King, Charles
Sibral, Nicholas
Sands, Joseph
Williamson, Thomas

Privates.
Buck, William
Craighton, William
Dayton, Spencer
Hall, James
Lindsey, Andrew
Slaughter, William
Stuick, Peter

Page 317.

ROLL OF CAPT. JOHN PATTERSON'S COMPANY (Probably from Warren Co.)

Served from July 6, until July 23, 1814.

Capt. John Patterson
Sergt. Alexander Johnston
Corp. John Gillis

Ensign William S. Crain
Sergt Thomas Phillips
Corp. Henry Williamson
Fifer, Isaac Conover

Sergt. William Gillespie
Sergt James Johnston
Drummer, Henry Catick

Privates.
Conner, John
Dawson, John
Griffis, John
Johnston, William
Moore, John
Oiter, Phillip
Phillips, John
Sutton, Absalom

Privates.
Chambers, John
Forough, Robert
Gillespie, John
Kennedy, Robert
McCord, Robert
Phillips, Samuel
Sawyer, John
Ross, David

Privates.
Crane, George
Commin, Martin
Hormel, John
Landon, John
Norton, Joseph
Pates, Michael
Shephard, Joseph

Pages 318-319.

ROLL OF CAPT. DAVID OLIVER'S COMPANY (County Unknown).

Served from July 5, until August 18, 1814.

Capt. David Oliver
Sergt. Andy Dripes
Sergt. John Dunsath
Corp. Peter Trout
Fifer, Henry Reisingson

Lieut. James Wilmoth
Sergt William T. Starkes
Corp. Peter Stull
Corp. John Smith

Ensign Nathaniel Williams
Sergt James Mansfield
Corp Freeman Rittenhouse
Drummer, Christian Oblinger

ROLL OF CAPT. DAVID OLIVER'S COMPANY (Continued).

Rank and Name of Soldier.

Privates.

Adams, James
Brightwell, William
Cornwell, John
Ewing, John
Gannon, Abner
Graham, Thomas D.
Harris, Elisha
Hindes, John
Jackson, Samuel
Lord, John P.
Millen, Anthony
McCowen, George
Nelson, Thomas W.
Oldham, Thomas
Provost, Joseph
Richey, Stephen
Smith, John J.
Laberto, John
Sutton, Tingley
Stotten, John
Salman, Daniel
McConnell, Jeremiah
Teetley, Joseph
Templeton, John
Vanhook, William B.
Wallace, William
West, James

Rank and Name of Soldier.

Privates.

Bailey, Barzilla
Clark, Lemuel
Eaverson, George
Force, Whitfield
Gillis, William
Gant, John
Horn, Ellis
Hantin, Arthur
Legg, John
Moore, William
Moore, William, Jr.
McDonald, Joseph
Nevis, Tillman
O'Neele, James
Patt, Lemuel
Radley, John
Stephens, Moses
Strong, Zebulen
Sloop, John
Stewart, William
Salman, James
Eve, Tillman
Teetley, James
Templeton, David
Wise, Solomon
White, Alexander
Wallin, Edward

Rank and Name of Soldier.

Privates.

Bildenbeck, Daniel
Clark, Thompson
Evans, Robert
Greene, Alevicious
Gannon, William
Gaunt, Robert
Hanley, John
Irwin, John
Lockhart, John
Milton, Benjamin
Miller, John
McOnde, Jeremiah
Nevis, Daniel
Oldham, Nathaniel
Ponder, Jesse
Richey, John
Steele, John
Sellers, Peter
Smith, Daniel
Sale, Clayton
Sutton, English
McReynolds, Joseph
Tweedy, Robert
Taylor, George W.
Wilmouth, Warren
Wheeler, William
Woodcock, John

Pages 320-321.

ROLL OF CAPT. JOHN SPENCER'S COMPANY, OHIO SPIES
(Probably from Licking County).

Served from August 27, until September 25, 1812, and from September 4, 1813, until March 4, 1814.

Capt. John Spencer
Cornet, Jacob Mann
Sergt. John Peck
Sergt. John C. Spencer
Sergt. Isaac Dougherty
Corp. Enoch Smith

Lieut. Abraham Bennet
Ensign John Benham
Sergt. Jesse Sutton
Sergt. Robert B. Covert
Corp. Enoch Wilkin
Corp. James Patten
Musician, Richard Baker

Lieut. Henry Goode
Sergt. Daniel Eaton
Sergt. Martin Robinson
Sergt. Abner Meek
Corp. Isaac Good
Musician, Daniel Crane

Privates.

Anderson, William
Blackburn, James
Brewin, Thomas
Carnal, Silvanus
Cul, Joel
Codington, Isaac
Colter, William
Deane, John
Clyne, George
Fox, David
Garner, Job
Hogan, James
Hinkston, Benjamin
Jackson, Samuel G.
Linsey, John
Lassee, John
Lynn, Samuel
Mills, John
Mullin, James
McCray, Daniel
Morrow, Lewis
Payne, Absalom
Rycraft, Joseph
Sheafe, George
Spragg, James
Whitmore, Miles

Privates.

Allen, John
Blackford, J. K.
Blackford, William
Cahill, Daniel
Cline, John
Copeland, Joseph
Cawthorn, William S.
Daugherty, William
Evans, David
Freeman, James
Griffin, James
Holmes, John
Gill, John
Kirkpatrick, William
Swailes, Rue
Lawrence, George
Linsey, Leonard
Morton, Benjamin
Mills, Daniel
McDaniel, William
McDowell, Demsy
Parkhill, John
Ruble, Samuel
Silsby, David
Thompson, James
Wallace, John

Privates.

Alexander, John
Bedunnah, Ebenezer
Conklin, William
Cahill, Isaac
Codington, Freeman
Clark, Abraham
Cummins, Andrew
Death, George
Elliott, Wright
Garner, Henry
Hamilton, Isaac
Hoblet, David
Fugus, Clement
Kennear, James
Lee, John
Lyttle, John
Meek, Abner
Murphey, John
Mossburgh, Henry
Newkirk, Jacob
Ogler, John
Patterson, John
Sawyer, John
Scott, Joseph
Whitaker, John
Young, John

Pages 322-323.

ROLL OF CAPT. JOHN WILLIAMS' COMPANY (County Unknown).

Served from October 6, until October 26, 1812, and from August 25, 1813, until January 4, 1814.

Capt. John Williams
Sergt. William Hickman
Sergt. Phillip S. Williams
Corp. James Harvey
Corp. Peter Price
Musician, William Kennedy

Lieut. Jesse Edward
Sergt. John Shidaker
Sergt. Daniel Rowzer
Corp. Stephen Davis
Corp. John Shell
Musician, Abraham Myers

Ensign Samuel Clappen
Sergt. John Johnston
Sergt. Adkinson, Henry
Corp. Zebulan Wallace
Corp. Israel Price

ROLL OF CAPT. JOHN WILLIAMS' COMPANY (Continued).

Rank and Name of Soldier.	Rank and Name of Soldier.	Rank and Name of Soldier.
Privates.	**Privates.**	**Privates.**
Cramer, Abraham	Clingan, James	Clingan, Edward
Corey, John	Croy, Peter	Davis, Stephen
Euhart, Jacob	Fritz, Christian	Fraze, James
Harvey, James	Helvie, John	Helvie, Adam
Hickman, William	Johnston, John	Lowthain, George
Lennon, James	Lowthain, Absalom	Madden, William
Mitchell, William	Myers, Lewis	Mann, Isaac
Manson, David	Cory, Daniel W.	Price, Jeremiah
Price, Michael	Price, Israel	Rouzer, Daniel
Rouzer, John	Sunderland, Francis	Sunderland, Peter
Stafford, Joseph	Stafford, Ralph	Shell, James
Sailor, Philip	Shell, Christian	Songer, Adam
Stafford, James	Woodburn, Joseph	Wallace, John
Saunders, William	Wisehart, Benjamin	

Pages 324-325.

ROLL OF CAPT. HIRAM RUSSELL'S COMPANY (County Unknown).

Served from February 8, until May 23, 1813.

Capt. Hiram Russell	Sergt. Thomas Star	Sergt. O. C. Dickinson
	Corp. Lewis Hoyt	
Privates.	**Privates.**	**Privates.**
Andrews, Richard	Andrews, Sherman	Alderman, Eber
Arnold, William	Baker, Hubbard	Bailey, Iddo
Buell, Ezra	Burnham, Joshua	Ballad, Ezekial
Caughey, Joseph	Doyle, Anthony	Dickinson, Elisha
Findley, John	Fowler, Chester	Ferguson, Hans
Galloway, James	Graham, Jesse	Henning, Jacob
Hough, Henry	John, James	Laughlin, Robert
Lafferty, William	Mapes, Henry	McKonkey, William
McKnight, Robert, Jr.	McFarland, William	Newton, Lemuel
Nelson, Hugh	Queen, John	Ray, James
Russell, Job	Rodgers, Richard, Jr.	Sweet, Amos
Shaler, John	Scoville, Reuben	Sessions, James
Stephens, Daniel	Smith, James	Spitstone, Adam
Pond, Phineas	Tuttle, Samuel	Turner, Conrad
Warner, Chancy	Willetts, John	Woodworth, Albigence
Waldorff, Phillip		

Page 326.

ROLL OF CAPT. JOHN DAVIS' COMPANY (Probably from Green Co.)

Served from May 3, until May 20, 1813.

Capt. John Davis	Lieut. David M. Laughead	Lieut. Stephen Commwell
Cornet, Henry Barnes	Sergt. John B. Todd	Sergt. Adam Shigley
Sergt. David Hanes	Sergt. John John	
Privates.	**Privates.**	**Privates.**
Blue, Davis	Black, Peter	Barker, Joseph
Clifford, Thomas	Devone, John	Elam, John
Gibson, John	Glum, Thomas	Gill, Hugh
Lamm, Josiah	Mitchell, James	Munthoud, Ephraim
McFarland, John	Shaw, Amos	Talbert, Josiah G.
Shanks, Thomas	Taylor, John A.	Vance, John
Watson, James	West, William	White, John

Page 327.

ROLL OF CAPT. ROBERT GOWDY'S COMPANY (Probably from Green Co.)

Served from August 23, until September 21, 1813.

Capt. Robert Gowdy	Lieut. Thomas Constant	Sergt. Samuel Gray
Sergt. William Sutton	Sergt. Joel Hixon	Sergt. James Fire
Corp. William Sterrett	Corp. John Loid	Corp. William Simpson
Corp. David Conkelon	Drummer, William Allen	Fifer, Samuel Simpson
Privates.	**Privates.**	**Privates.**
Aldreedezr, Littleberry	Barber, John	Beales, Jonothan
Bruce, James	Barnes, Alexander	Bell, Daniel
Conkelon, Samuel	Curtis, Wiley	Gibson, John
Gawley, Ryan	Gill, John	Hough, Joseph
Hummer, Peter	Hoop, Andrew	Gibson, Thomas
Joiner, Charles	Jones, Jacob	John, William
Larew, Abraham	Moore, James	Maxey, Martin
Maxey, Stephen	Oemm, Samuel	Sutton, William G.
Seaman, Peter	Salsberry, James	Townsley, George
Thornberry, George	Thornberry, John	Turner, Henry
Vanard, Francis	Wright, Josiah	

Pages 328-329. Vol. I.
ROLL OF CAPT. SAMUEL HERROD'S COMPANY (County Unknown).
Served from September 15, until October 15, 1812, and from August 1, until August 16, 1813.

Rank and Name of Soldier.

Capt. Samuel Herrod
Ensign Thomas Constant
Sergt. David Lawhead
Sergt. David Garrison
Sergt. Reuben Johnson
Corp. Thomas Watson

Privates.

Andrews, Hugh
Bromagem, James
Beason, Thomas
Cuswell, James
Cutright, Peter
Durraugh, John
Frazier, James
Galloway, James
Hanna, Robert
Husted, John N.
Johnston, Isaac
Jenkins, William
Ladd, John
Lamme, James
Maxwell, William
Moore, Charles A.
Mitchell, Forgis
McFarland, John
McClellan, William
Norris, Nathan
Paullin, Joseph
Buckles, Robert
Donaldson, Alexander
Radgsdale, Alexander
Sutton, Jesse
Shaw, Amos
Stout, Bonem
Stout, Isaac
Townsley, Thomas
Thompson, James
Watson, Thomas
Wright, John

Rank and Name of Soldier.

Lieut Robert Gowdy
Ensign Samuel Musick
Sergt. William Andrews
Sergt. Anthony Cannon
Sergt. Andrew Douglas
Corp. James Andrews

Privates.

Ash, Adam
Bransen, Eli
Bromagem, Samuel
Collier, James
Callander, William
Edgar, William
Ferguson, Zechariah
Guin, Amos
Hornback, Samuel
Henderson, Joseph
Johnson, Aaron
Johnson, Reuben
Ladd, Christopher
Lamme, David
Mendenhall, John
Miller, John
McFarland, Arthur
McFarland, Robert
McCulley, John
Ogden, William
Hoop, Andrew
Paullin, Jacob
Kain, Thomas
Rodgers, William
Sterett, Joseph
Sutton, Garner
Sharp, William
Shanks, Thomas
Turner, John
Thomas, Indian
Wright, Hugh
Wolf, John

Rank and Name of Soldier.

Lieut. Christopher L. Sroupe
Sergt. William Buckles
Sergt. William Campbell
Sergt. Evan Brock
Sergt. Thomas Kelso
Corp. James Bouls

Privates.

Adams, Samuel
Best, Elias
Borders, George
Campbell, John
Duley, Samuel
Feris, James
Goff, John F.
Gawen, Johnson
Hartman, Peter
Jenkins, Lancelot
Johton, Benjamin
Kent, James
Long, Thomas
Long, John
Morton, John
Mullen, Charles
McCoy, William
McBride, Henry
McCoy, William
Palmer, Joseph
Parris, Joseph
Pickering, Henry
King, Richard
Reed, John
Sutton, John
Selvey, James
Sroupe, David
Turner, Robert
Turner, Allen
Thornberry, John
Watson, John
Wilson, Joseph

Page 330.
ROLL OF CAPT. JOHN HUMES' COMPANY (Probably from Clermont Co.)
Served from January 30, until April 10, 1814, and from January 11, until April 10, 1815.

Capt. John Humes
Sergt. John Steel
Sergt. John Meeks
Corp. Edward Gandy

Privates.

Arthur, William
Bunald, John
Bell, William
Bigg, Isaac
Crosson, William
Coleman, Isaac
Davis, Noah
Fossett, William
Gates, Uriah
Higbee, Amasa
Kirgen, David
Little, David
McKee, Thomas
Shull, Phillip
Smith, Burris
Shaw, Solomon
Test, William

Lieut. James Turner
Sergt. Thomas Holland
Corp. Joseph Anderson
Corp. Robert Evans
Fifer, William Lane

Privates.

Ayers, Henry
Boreland, James
Burg, Richard
Cutright, Aaron
Couch, Isaiah
Carroll, John
Debruler, Reason
Frambes, Peter
Gibb, John
Hamel, Thomas
King, Leonard
Moore, John
Powers, Isaac
Sellers, Peter
Tillatson, Luther
Void, Henry
Wheeler, Benjamin

Ensign Levi Moore
Sergt. Charles Troy
Corp. William Congar
Drummer, George Smith

Privates.

Burke, James
Beam, David
Bushman, David
Coleman, Leroy
Clinton, Archibald
Chance, John
Floro, Thomas
Griffin, Ebenezer
Gard, William
Hinde, John
Leonard, John
Mallott, Zedekiah
Stalo, John L.
Storey, Washington
Thomas, Ephraim
Washburn, Josiah

Page 331.
ROLL OF CAPT. ALEXANDER BLACK'S COMPANY (County Unknown).
Served from August 18, until August 26, 1812.

Capt. Alexander Black
Sergt. Samuel Wilson
Sergt. Eli Wilson

Lieut. Alexander Snoddy
Sergt. Robert Clark

Ensign John Moore
Sergt. John Tites

ROLL OF CAPT. ALEXANDER BLACK'S COMPANY (Continued.)

Rank and Name of Soldier.

Privates.
- Alexander, Joseph
- Crow, Joseph
- Elliott, John
- Lockridge, James
- Martin, Job
- McIlvain, Moses, Sr.
- Newell, Hugh
- Petty, Ezekial
- Smith, Henry
- Tipton, John

Rank and Name of Soldier.

Privates.
- Baird, John
- Clark, Thomas
- Gunn, John
- Moore, Samuel
- Moviele, Batiece
- McIlvain, Moses, Jr.
- Newell, Thomas
- Smith, Joel
- Simes, John
- Wace, Stephen
- Workman, John

Rank and Name of Soldier.

Privates.
- Boyd, William
- Dunn, John
- Kirkwood, William
- Moore, Raphael
- McCloud, William
- McDonald, Ebenezer
- Newell, William
- Shields, David
- Server, Jacob
- Wall, John

Page 332.

ROLL OF CAPT. JAMES CAMPBELL'S COMPANY (County Unknown).
Served from October 20, 1812, until April 20, 1813.

- Capt. James Campbell
- Sergt. David Henderson
- Sergt. Richard Copeland
- Corp. Thomas Dille

- Lieut. John Nichols
- Sergt. Thomas Thompson
- Corp. John H. Smith
- Corp. Jeremiah Russell

- Ensign Zepheniah Bell
- Sergt. Isaac Coleman
- Corp. Joshua Russell

Privates.
- Archer, John
- Bundy, Joseph
- Coleman, Nathaniel
- Crampton, Henry
- Evans, Garrett
- Goness, David
- Hunter, Joseph
- Hisket, Benjamin
- Lewis, Samuel
- Moore, Daniel
- McConnell, James
- Pool, John
- Shekan, Joshua
- Swart, Jacob
- Stoner, Henry
- Tipton, Thomas
- Workman, William
- Workman, Amos

Privates.
- Beatty, William
- Barton, Michael
- Coleman, Samuel
- Diven, John
- Ferguson, James
- Gorley, John
- Harris, Simon
- Kirk, Joseph
- Lewis, Stephen
- McKittrick, John
- Price, William
- Pearce, George
- Stephens, Benjamin
- Smith, Bazel
- Swanny, George
- Tagert, Isaac
- Wilkins, Thomas
- Wheeler, William

Privates.
- Burvit, Benjamin
- Conner, Robert M.
- Clark, Jacob
- Elrue, Burned
- Fonda, Lawrence
- Gant, Reuben
- Hopny, Samuel
- Kincaid, Joseph
- Martian, John
- McConnell, Robert
- Porter, Reason
- Roberts, Jacob
- Slater, John
- Stackhous, Jacob
- Stephenson, John
- Vanwey, Burrus
- Wilkins, Andrew

Page 333.

ROLL OF CAPT. NICHOLAS DAVIS' COMPANY (County Unknown).
Served from August 18, 1814, until February 25, 1815.

- Capt. Nicholas Davis
- Sergt. David Mulligan
- Sergt. John Mulligan
- Corp. John Humphrey

- Lieut. Abraham Layfert
- Sergt. John Rankin
- Corp. George Duffield
- Corp. Silas Roose

- Sergt. Robert Gooke
- Sergt. William Boyles
- Corp. William Guttery

Privates.
- Bell, Adam
- Bunyon, Henry
- Freete, George
- Gullinger, Martin
- Muney, James
- Niles, Sanford
- Patrick, Robert
- Russell, Joseph
- Smith, David
- Wilson, David

Privates.
- Bashford, Joseph
- Buram, William
- Force, Thomas
- Kling, John
- Maynard, Ezra
- Ogel, Mordecai
- Roberson, Walter
- Smith, Andrew
- Springer, William
- West, Thomas

Privates.
- Buneyer, Daniel
- Clinton, Charles
- Gurwell, William
- Lockerd, Eleben
- Maides, William
- Pool, Conrad
- Rerigh, Andrew
- Sample, James
- Sanderlin, Thomas

Page 334.

ROLL OF CAPT. JAMES FLAGG'S COMPANY (Probably from Washington County).
Served from October 20, 1812, until January 11, 1813.

- Capt. James Flagg
- Sergt. Lary Ford
- Sergt. Peletiah White
- Corp. Joseph Witten

- Lieut. Benedie Hutchinson
- Sergt. John Greenman
- Corp. Jacob Lane
- Corp. John G. Askell

- Ensign, Nathaniel Olney
- Sergt. David Trobridge
- Corp. Charles Thomas

Privates.
- Alpha, Daniel
- Anderson, James
- Baker, John
- Coalman, Daniel
- Cady, Philip
- Dennis, Thomas
- Emerson, Asa
- Goodwin, James
- Hutchinson, James
- Ingles, John
- Morris, Nehemiah
- Priest, Richard D.
- Witten, James

Privates.
- Abbott, George
- Burbank, Seth D.
- Burchet, Jonah
- Castle, George
- Chapman, Simon
- Dougherty, George
- Ewing, James
- Gosset, John
- Harris, George
- Kidd, John
- Olds, Gilbert
- Starke, Pardon

Privates.
- Adams, James
- Britton, Nathan
- Barrett, John
- Coverton, Henry
- Cline, William
- Donahue, Daniel
- Fordice, Stanton
- Hutchins, James
- Heinman, Curtis
- Knight, James
- Mallary, Elisha
- Walker, James B.

Page 335. Vol. I.
ROLL OF CAPT. JEREMIAH SIMMS COMPANY (County Unknown).
Served from February 20, until March 20, 1813.

Rank and Name of Soldier.	Rank and Name of Soldier.	Rank and Name of Soldier.
Capt. Jeremiah Simms	Lieut. William Buckley	Ensign, Joseph Clevinger
Sergt. James McIntire	Sergt. Abner Martin	Sergt. Arthur Collison
Sergt. James Morris	Corp. John A. Swearinger	Corp. Alexander Hayes
Corp. Andrew Sparks	Corp. Jacob Smith	

Privates.

Bailey, Michael L.	Bailey, Amos	Callison, John, Sr.
Callison, John, Jr.	Elliott, William	Elliott, Thomas
Frantz, Jacob	Hallin, Joseph	Kellar, John
Ludlow, Cooper	Lintz, Peter	Minnick, John
Mesate, James	Morris, Richard	Morris, Benjamin
Martin, Jacob	Martin, Isaac	Miller, Martin
Olinger, Philip	Olinger, Jacob	Overpeck, William
Palmer, Elias	Seffel, Samuel	Stewart, Stephen
Thompson, Francis	Tamplin, John	Wickerly, William
	Waggoner, John	

Page 336.
ROLL OF CAPT. JOSEPH EVANS' COMPANY (Probably from Ross County).
Served from February 24, until March 24, 1813.

Capt. Joseph Evans	Lieut. Joseph Stokes	Ensign, Samuel Haines
Sergt. William Green	Sergt. Thomas Segar	Sergt. Job Sharp, Jr.
Sergt. Thomas Marshel	Sergt. Benjamin Smith	Musician, David Henly
	Musician Thomas Atha	

Privates.

Branson, Robert	Brown, John	Bishop, William
Curl, Samuel	Downs, Joseph	Garwood, Lott
Green, John	Haines, Thomas	Haines, William
Inskup, Lewis	Pope, Nathaniel	Painter, Abraham
Marmon, Richmon	Reams, Caleb	Reams, Jeremiah
Pickerell, Nicholas	Sharp, Allen	Sharp, William
Rea, John	Sharp, Jesse	Warner, Jack

Pages 337-338-339.
ROLL OF CAPT. WILLIAM WILSON'S COMPANY (Probably from Ross Co.)
Served from March 3, until August 15, 1814.

Capt. William Wilson	Lieut. Cornelius Stringer	Ensign, William Miller
Sergt. Samuel Lamberson	Sergt. Stephen Mahaffey	Sergt. John Oslin
Sergt. Benjamin Stephenson	Corp. Joseph Watson	Corp. James Armstrong
Corp. Thomas Owens	Corp. James Tulk	Fifer, Thomas Mathews

Privates.

Allfather, Adam	Anderson, Mark	Bronkart, Louis
Bowen, Constant	Babb, Bell	Beyner, George
Beamer, Adam	Black, Joseph	Beers, Thomas
Coss, David	Cline, Phillip	Carr, Peter
Cockrill, Joseph	Dunkin, James	Davis, John H.
Dowl, John	Bontsong, Jonothan	Daugherty, David
Foreman, David	Fareare, John	Gibbs, Isaac
Gardner, Isaac	Henell, Christopher	Hall, John
Barbaugh, Samuel	Holmes, Thomas	Harding, Israel
Hilhouse, John	Jefferrs, Thomas	James, David
Kasebeer, Samuel	Kruger, John	Long, William
Longley, George	Morris, George	Maple, David
Mathews, James	McHutens, James	McHenry, David
McKee, John	Nixon, Andrew	Norris, Charles
Prewith, William	Parr, William	Parr, Thomas
Romine, Abraham	Sreak, Jacob	Sickman, Luke
Smith, George	Stent, George	Swyer, George
Sly, John	Sullaven, George	Summers, Isaac
Turel, John	Taylor, Samuel	Wilson, James
Williams, James	Woodward, William	Waggoner, David
	Watson, Robert	

Page 340.
ROLL OF CAPT. FRANCIS PATTERSON'S COMPANY (County Unknown).
Served from October 17, 1812, until December 22, 1813.

Capt. Francis Patterson	Lieut. David Scott	Ensign, James Merris
Sergt. William Patterson	Sergt. George Bradford	Sergt. Michael Lennon
Sergt. Archibald Campbell	Corp. Eliza Griffith	Corp. Jacob John
Corp. Daniel Houser	Corp. Robert Kiddle	

Privates.

Blue, Frederick	Bedele, Calvin	Christian, John
Clark, Solomon	Beard, John	Croy, Peter
Culbertson, Robert	Dye, Andrew	Duncan, Robert
Frane, William	Greer, John	Garard, Isaac

ROLL OF CAPT. FRANCIS PATTERSON'S COMPANY (Continued.)

Rank and Name of Soldier.

Privates.
Guthrie, James
Hosier, Isaac
Kiser, John
Meeker, John
Maloy, James
Perry, Orin
Shover, Jacob
Tanner, Edward
Vinyard, Rezin
Weaver, Peter

Rank and Name of Soldier.

Privates.
Hurley, Robert
Hannah, Thomas
Kirby, John
Moyer, Isaac
Neff, Lewis
Shaffer, John
Shephard, Thomas
Rogel, Jacob
Woolfe, Conrad
Wollaston, George

Rank and Name of Soldier.

Privates.
Haines, Ephraim
Jackson, Jesse
Lehman, Henry
Morgan, Cornelius
Newman, William
Seth, George
Sprague, Stephen
Underwood, John
Wilson, Samuel

Page 341.

ROLL OF CAPT. JAMES STEELE'S COMPANY (Probably from Fayette Co.)

Served from August 22, until September 30, 1812.

Capt. James Steele
Sergt. Maj. Joseph H. Crane
Sergt. John Strain
Corp. Alexander Grimes

Lieut. George Grove
Sergt. John Folkirth
Sergt. James Henderson
Corp. George Harris

Ensign, James McClure
Sergt. Ralph Wilson
Corp. Matt Patton
Corp. David Henderson

Privates.
Brier, James
Bay, William
Enoch, John
Guy, Alexander
Jennings, Henry
Lowe, John
McCain, James
McCarter, Simpson
McCabe, John
Petticrew, James
Rowan, John
Sunderland, Daniel
Worley, Caleb
Wallaston, George

Privates.
Brier, David
Collins, Jeremiah
Fryback, William
Holderman, John
King, Samuel M.
Montgomery, William
McNair, Moses
McCleary, Robert
Newcom, George
Robinson, Andrew
Smith, Ira
Vanscoys, William
Ward, George

Privates.
Bay, James
Devor, John
Gordon, Lewis
Hatfield, Moses
Green, Joshua
Miller, James
McCormick, William
Maybroll, Jonothan
Newcom, John
Riffle, David
Smith, Abraham
Vanasdel, William
Watton, Samuel

Page 342.

ROLL OF CAPT. THOMAS STRETCH'S COMPANY
(Probably from Champaign County).

Served from November 27, until December 27, 1812.

Capt. Thomas Stretch
Sergt. James McLaughlin
Sergt. Frederick Stonebager

Lieut. Ezekial Arrowsmith
Sergt. George Faulkner
Corp. Joseph Hill

Ensign, Walker Johnston
Sergt. William Sargent
Corp. John Long, Sr.

Privates.
Comer, David
Clark, Reuben
Humphries, Robert
Harber, Elisha
Longfeller, Joseph
Metz, Emanuel
Maggeat, Adam
Mitchell, John
McIntyre, Thomas
Stephens, Christian
Whiteman, John

Privates.
Comer, Peter
Colbert, Jesse
Hufman, Jeremiah
Kite, Benjamin
Lyon, John
Monroe, James
Mitts, Samuel
Megill, John
Smith, James
Runkle, Peter
Wilson, William

Privates.
Clark, Marcus
Dils, Samuel
Hanback, Lewis
Kite, Samuel
Long, John, Jr.
Moody, John
Mitchell, James
McAlexander, James
Slegle, Jacob
Stephens, John

Pages 343-344-345.

ROLL OF CAPT. WILLIAM STEPHENSON'S COMPANY
(Probably from Green County).

Served from October 24, until December 22, 1812, and from Sept. 20, 1813, until March 20, 1814

Capt. William Stephenson
Lieut. Edward Jones
Sergt. Thomas Sleeth
Sergt. William Kelley
Corp. James McKaig
Corp. William Price
Fifer, Henry Steenbarger

Lieut. Samuel Stites
Ensign, Daniel Kebbinger
Sergt. Moses McNair
Sergt. William Harper
Corp. William Wilson
Corp. Elias Gilkin
Drummer, John Gillelan

Ensign, John McCally
Sergt. Alexander Ireland
Sergt. Peter Pence
Corp. Peter Stephenson
Corp. Nelson Lansdell
Fifer, Jonothan Claton
Drummer, Joseph Jones

Privates.
Adams, John
Bradley, John
Black, John
Benson, Thomas
Cleton, William
Davis, Zebe
Davis, Noah
Ellis, William

Privates.
Babcock, Simon
Beeth, James
Bates, John
Browder, Wesley
Campbell, John
Dunn, Simon
Dittz, John
Forbes, George

Privates.
Benet, Francis
Bennett, George
Babcock, William
Casad, John
Criswell, David
Carpenter, Joseph
Evans, George
Follis, Isaac

ROLL OF CAPT. WILLIAM STEPHENSON'S COMPANY (Continued.)

Privates.

Garlough, Adam
Gregory, Daniel
Hussey, Christopher
Hopkins, Richard
Hodge, John
Hale, Bradford
Jones, Thomas
Kiser, John
Loomon, Joseph
Myers, George
Meed, Daniel
Miles, Christian
McManime, William
Oppy, David
Roberts, John
Smith, William
Skilliland, Lewis
Stephenson, John
Thomas, John
Waggoner, George
Wilson, John

Grose, William
Hardman, Henry
Hussey, Nathan
Hustide, Aaron
Harstock, William
James, Thomas
Kendle, John
Loomon, Ralph
Miller, Charles
Martin, Jacob, Sr.
McAuly, William
Norman, Jacob
Read, William
Steeth, James
Snip, Abraham
Strain, John
Tatman, Edward
Turner, James
Wilson, James
Walbourne, Robert
Ward, Obediah

Gibson, Monteleon
Harker, John
Harris, Stewart
Hammell, Valentine
Ivens, Richard
Krigler, Jacob
Lippingcot, Obediah
Lambert, John
Moody, James
Mills, Lewis
McKaig, John
Olinger, Jacob
Rose, William
Smith, Caleb
Stephenson, James
Spuce, Daniel
Thomas, Abraham
Vaughn, William
Winget, Caleb
Winget, Hugh
Wolf, Jacob

Pages 346-347.

ROLL OF CAPT. AARON STRONG'S COMPANY (County Unknown).
Served from October 7, until December 15, 1812.

Capt. Aaron Strong
Sergt. Bulkey Comstock
Sergt. Ira Wilcox
Corp. Samuel Hayden

Lieut. Chaney Barker
Sergt. Roswell Tuller
Corp. Joseph Heath
Corp. Norman Case
Fifer, Mathias Vanloon

Ensign, Aaron Welsh
Sergt. Nahum King
Corp. Isaac Harrison
Drummer, Sylvester Drake

Privates.

Benjamin, Daniel
Barker, William N.
Carpenter, Nathan
Calkins, Lovewell
Dickey, John
Dunham, Walter
Evans, Edward
Fischar, Josiah
Fisher, George
Foust, Abraham
Gale, Jesse
Hilt, Daniel
Hare, John
Lewis, John
Main, Cloyer
Mitchell, Samuel
McCutcheon, Robert
Napp, Thomas D.
Patterson, John
Rath, Nathan
Reed, Daniel
Strong, Daniel
Silbee, David
Slate, Valentine
Teedell, Joseph
Olds, Ezra, Jr.
Welsh, Orora
Welsh, Samuel
Young, Andrew

Bardsley, Darius
Bety, Francis
Case, Orlando
Cooper, John
Denton, Justice
Davis, John D.
Filge, Daniel
Foltner, Joshua N.
Fancher, Henry
George, Thomas
Hall, William
Hilt, Jacob
Judd, Liman
Maxfield, Amos
Manville, John
Mitchell, Moses
McGinnis, Samuel
Nelson, Robert
Perry, Samuel
Royee, Nijad
Robinson, Thomas
Sharp, Gant
Stark, James
Scribner, John
Tylor, Richard
Van Loon, Jacob
Wallace, Heman
Wallis, Solomon
Zimmerman, Henry

Bixby, Appleton
Brown, Thomas
Case, Nathan
Davis, Elezer
Dixon, Myron
Dunlebarger, Frederick
Foose, William
Foust, Henry
Fancher, William
Griswold, Isaac
Humphrey, Lemuel
Helt, John
Keyes, Tolman
Millington, Peter
Manville, Flemming
Milliken, John
McCumber, Jeremiah
Pultney, Aquila
Phillips, John
Reed, Samuel
Scott, Asa
Simmers, Ephraim
Kent, Daniel
Tuttle, Rosswell, Jr.
Tarboss, John
Watson, William
White, James H.
Wyatt, Nathaniel

Page 348.

ROLL OF CAPT. ROBERT RUSSELL'S COMPANY (Probably from Scioto Co.)
Served from July 28, until August 22, 1813.

Capt. Robert Russell
Sergt. William Cole
Corp. Andrew Beles

Lieut. William Russell
Sergt. Joseph McKee
Corp. Thomas Clerk

Sergt. John Eakins
Sergt. William Murpny

Privates.

Beles, Peter
Green, Nathaniel
Lard, John S.
Ralston, Robert
Stout, Isaac

Colvin, George
Killin, John
Marvin, Silas
Roberts, Lewis
Stout, Jesse

Colvin, Jacob
Kinyon, Jonothan
McCall, William
Severingham, Duke
Stitts, William

Pages 349-350. Vol. I.

ROLL OF CAPT. JOSEPH CURTIS' COMPANY (County Unknown).

Served from February 23, until March 28, 1814.

Rank and Name of Soldier.	Rank and Name of Soldier.	Rank and Name of Soldier.
Capt. Joseph Curtis	Lieut. Isaac Clements	Ensign Joash Edwards
Sergt. Henry Shuey	Sergt. William P. Andrews	Sergt. David Hayes
Sergt. John Mathias	Corp. John Sedgwick	Corp. Stephenus Clark
Corp. John Woods	Corp. Hugh Stephenson	Drummer, Joseph Stephenson

Privates.	Privates.	Privates.
Aughe, William	Bryan, Ebenezer	Brandenburgh, Jacob
Brian, George S.	Bearnheart, Benjamin	Carter, Joshua
Clevenger, Samuel	Cox, John	Cattlan, Harris
Cornell, Hell	Clements, John	Cummins, Robert
Crosson, Columbia	Cox, William	Death, Aaron
Dunkin, William	Duterrow, Jacob	Elberhart, Samuel
Fendley, William	Fox, Frederick	Griffith, Benjamin
Gustin, Samuel N.	Gray, Amos	Holley, Daniel
Hathaway, Samuel	Hines, John	Hester, Jacob
Herner, Jacob	Hayes, Caleb W.	Kelsey, Daniel
Lesenea, Samuel	Long, Robert	Long, Joseph
Laird, David	Montgomery, Elisha	Merrit, Abraham
Merrit, Joseph	McDonald, James	McReynolds, William
Potter, Hiram	Penticost, Simfon	Reed, Ezra
Reed, John	Reed, Leonard	Rase, Benjamin
Ree, Charles	Reagin, Daniel	Reagin, Reason
Shank, Jacob	Sweeney, William	Snyder, Henry
Sentmire, George	Stephenson, Thomas	Smith, Obediah
Seamon, Jaconiah	Sutpir, John	Thorn, Eli
Benard, Jesse	Benard, Stephen	Wells, Benedict
Willias, William	Wilkins, William	Wilson, Peter A.
	Young, Jacob	

Page 251.

ROLL OF CAPT. SIMON PHILLIPS' COMPANY (County Unknown).

Served from July 22, 1813, until January 25, 1814.

Capt. Simon Phillips	Lieut. Wear Cassady	Ensign, Patrick McGriff
Sergt. Ethelred Delk	Sergt. James Hole	Sergt. Jacob Miller
Sergt. John Huit	Corp. George Miller	Corp. Christian Frederick
Corp. William Douglas	Corp. Thomas Pickle	Musician, Anthony Atchison
	Musician, John Wenn	

Privates.	Privates.	Privates.
Atkins, John	Biers, John	Cassady, Thomas
Cassady, William	Griffin, John	Guntle, Jacob
Gift, Peter	Garrett, William	Hill, Jacob
Harter, Philip	Kerrie, Dennis	Michael, Jacob
Moss, Jacob	Moss, John	McGriff, John Sr.
McGriff, John, Jr.	Phillips, Daniel	Phillips, Hezekiah
Pickle, Henry	Phillips, Lewis	Pickle, Tobias
Phillips, Valentine	Ross, Benjamin	Rape, Lewis
Scott, Thomas C.	Shelton, Joel	Tanner, James
Webb, Adron	Whitsel, George	Winegardner, John

Page 352.

ROLL OF CAPT. SAMUEL BRIER'S COMPANY (County Unknown).

Served from April 12, until October 11, 1813.

Capt. Samuel Brier	Lieut. Jacob Lighty	Ensign, Daniel Hearton
Sergt. William Miller	Sergt. Cornelius Ganasdol	Sergt. Samuel Arnold
Sergt. Joseph R. John	Corp. Mathew M. Dodds	Corp. Joseph Blair
Corp. David Heaston	Corp. Daniel Hatch	Musician, Conrad Slagle
	Drummer, Isaac Walker	

Privates.	Privates.	Privates.
Arnte, George	Bay, William	Blair, James S.
Branburg, George	Bucken, Michael	Cofman, Jacob
Cox, William	Crull, Daniel	Casdy, Simon
Cronn, Daniel	Cox, William	Deiterick, Peter
Dice, Paul	Enoch, John	Edomes, Edmond
Coblentz, Jacob	Gelelant, Emanuel	Heister, George
Henry, George	Harshman, Jacob	Jones, Price
Kader, Phillip	Kelsen, Daniel	Lawrose, John
Lechlider, George	Haman, Solomon	McDonald, Archibald
McCreary, Nathan	Overholser, Jacob	Phillips, Thomas
Pettit, James	Phweyn, Charles	Pickles, Simon
Reed, William	Rickey, John	Shelly, Jacob
Studebaker, John	Statler, William	Parks, Joseph
Swart, John	Shively, Isaac	Talburt, James
Wood, Ashbury	Wolf, Jacob	Westfall, John
Wood, Samuel	Woodhouse, Henry	

ROSTER OF OHIO SOLDIERS IN WAR OF 1812

Pages 353-354. Vol. I.

ROLL OF CAPT. WILLIAM McCONNELL'S COMPANY (County Unknown).
Served from April 5, until July 26, 1813.

Rank and Name of Soldier.
Capt. William McConnell
Sergt. John Handle
Sergt. Benjamin Walters
Corp. Lawrence Wisecamere

Privates.
Bowers, Jacob
Bice, John
Degarmore, William
Gaumer, Daniel
Justice, James
Keeler, James
Moore, John
McCully, Patrick
Rough, Peter
Stots, Jacob
Varnon, Samuel
Woods, Thomas

Rank and Name of Soldier.
Lieut. Jacob Wisecamere
Sergt. Robert Wilson
Corp. John Bowers
Corp. John Schelberry
Drummer, Mathew Robins

Privates.
Boggs, Robert
Cooksey, Josiah
Finkbone, John
Haire, John H.
Kenney, Thomas
Kirk, Jesse
Mace, Daniel
McKune, William
Robison, David
Stump, Abraham
Walters, John

Rank and Name of Soldier.
Ensign, John Brown
Sergt. Joseph McConnell
Corp. Robert Hawk
Fifer, George Slack

Privates.
Barret, Henson
Courts, Thomas
Fickle, Benjamin
Hart, David
Kain, John
Moore, Robert
Mires, Charles
Over, Jacob
Slack, Jacob
Varnon, Joseph
Watson, John

Pages 355-356.

ROLL OF CAPT. WILLIAM MORROW'S COMPANY (County Unknown).
Served from April 29, until August 7, 1813.

Capt. William Morrow
Sergt. Alexander Harper
Corp. John Hollyday

Privates.
Blair, Benjamin
Blair, John
Callamber, Richard
Finch, Joseph
Harper, Benjamin
Huffman, Henry
Keanier, Adam
King, Reuben
Montgomery, Humphrey
McMann, William
Peterson, Jacob
Roberts, Moses
Shannon, Thomas

Lieut. James Harper
Sergt. Daniel Hare
Corp. Samuel W. McConnell
Corp. John Harper

Privates.
Bellinger, Joshua
Carr, Thomas
Davis, Jacob
Frame, George
Hemphill, John
Irwin, William
Kirkendall, Jeremiah
Miller, Ferdinand
McConnell, John
McConnell, William
Ramsey, Lyle
Stookey, Samuel
Taylor, William

Ensign, Daniel Robins
Sergt. Joseph Boggs
Corp. Henry Pittenger

Privates.
Blair, William C.
Cowler, John
Dear, John
Griffith, Evan
Hemphill, Mathew
Jones, Abner
Kennedy, Robert
Miller, Stephen
McMann, Samuel
Pummel, James
Robbins, Phillip
Stephenson, Thomas
Wilson, James

Page 357.

ROLL OF CAPT. DAVID EWING'S COMPANY (From Fairfield County).
Served from April 8, until July 16, 1813.

Capt. David Ewing
Sergt. Nathaniel Reed
Sergt. John Abrams
Corp. George Rodabough

Privates.
Culps, Jacob
Foster, Frederick F.
Hume, John
Mentzer, David
Shiang, William
Smither, George
Trumph, John

Lieut. Thomas Ewing
Sergt. William Springer
Corp. George Hollenback
Corp. Jacob Eversol

Privates.
Cunningham, Daniel
Gunder, Henry
James, Kirke
Post, Russell E.
Smither, John
Smither, Daniel
Weaver, Jacob

Ensign, John Burton
Sergt. George Carpenter
Corp. John Rees
Drummer, John Beaver

Privates.
Connkle, Adam
Hollenback, John
Kirby, John
Rodabough, Jacob
Stewart, James
Tripe, William

Page 358.

ROLL OF CAPT. ANDERSON SPENCER'S COMPANY (County Unknown).
Served from June 4, until December 5, 1813.

Capt. Anderson Spencer
Sergt. Patrick Cassiday
Sergt. Jonothan Pierson
Corp. Ephraim Elkins

Privates.
Alston, Benjamin
Clifton, Nathan
Davis, John
Hesley, Henry
Mahan, John
Martin, Robert
McDonald, William
Simons, John
Smith, James
Vinadge, David

Lieut. Ephraim Cattlen
Sergt. John Wells
Corp. Joel Drake
Corp. David Alexander
Musician, Harris Cattleton

Privates.
Bradberry, Hezekiah
Davis, Richard D.
Freeman, Elijah F.
Knox, William
Mitchell, Parker
Martin, William
McDaniel, Joshua
Sanders, John
Stine, Christian
Woodruff, Jesse

Ensign, Benjamin D. Davis
Sergt. David Line
Corp. John Hunter
Musician, William Sheley

Privates.
Bramon, Henry
Davis, Daniel
Gordon, Ross
Line, Moses
Murphy, Edward
Miller, Daniel
Spivey, John
Seward, Caleb
Thompson, John
Whitaker, Daniel

ROLL OF CAPT. JOSEPH JENKINSON'S COMPANY
(Probably from Hamilton County.)
Served from August 11, 1812, ———

Rank and Name of Soldier.	Rank and Name of Soldier.	Rank and Name of Soldier.
Capt. Joseph Jenkinson	Lieut. Stephen Gano	Lieut. Alexander Gibson
Sergt. William Kerr	Sergt. John Cox	Sergt. John Craven
Sergt. John S. Ludlow	Corp. Sampson Mooney	Corp. Joseph Weekley
Privates.	**Privates.**	**Privates.**
Ayres, John	Avery, Coleman	Baum, Jonas
Blooker, Samuel	Bonnel, Samuel	Corn, Peter
Clark, John S.	Crow, Thomas S.	Coppin, Joseph
Clark, William	Donnell, James	Drips, Andrew
Engle, Phillip	Evens, Robert	Hanley, John
Gardner, Robert	Garret, Curtis	McDonald, James
Leadam, Jacob	McMaster, William	Pike, Richard M.
Nelson, Robert	Norris, Richard	Smith, Thomas B.
Pots, Charles	Satterly, Isaac	Wheeler, Alvin
Smith, John H.	Shunk, John	Whiteside, William
White, Joseph	White, John	Zains, Adam

ROLL OF CAPT. WILLIAM LUCE'S COMPANY (Probably from Miami Co.)
Served from August 23, 1812, until February 22, 1813.

Capt. William Luce	Lieut. John McClary	Ensign John Dodds
Sergt. Edward Dyer	Sergt. Benjamin John	Sergt. John Brown
Sergt. Robert McElhaney	Corp. Robert Elliott	Corp. Jeremiah Collins
Corp. Abraham Corrall	Corp. Peter Rodebaugh	Rrummer, Samuel Buck
	Fifer, Peter Musselman	
Privates.	**Privates.**	**Privates.**
Bull, Amos	Bowman, Gilbert	Boles, John
Brown, John	Blair, William	Creviston, Henry
Coleman, George	Catro, Charles	Clark, Andrew
Cofman, Jacob	Cofman, Henry	Cook, John
Deem, John	Fall, Hanteter	Green, John
Houser, John	Hannason, Samuel	Long, Jesse
More, Samuel	McGraw, James	McGrew, Samuel
McGrew, Archibald	Rial, Jaq	Robbins, John
Scott, David	Stitter, Daniel	Tinckle, Nicholas
Westfall, Job	Wead, John	

ROLL OF CAPT. WILLIAM RAMSEY'S COMPANY (Probably from Preble Co.)
Served from October 11, 1813, until April 7, 1814.

Capt. William Ramsey	Sergt. James Newton	Corp. Samuel Douglas
Drummer, William Dailey	Fifer, Henry Newton	
Privates.	**Privates.**	**Privates.**
Bobebrake, John	Beeson, James	Baley, Gough
Clawson, Josiah	Dougherty, Thomas	Dougherty, Edward
Dailey, Dennis	Green, David	Harlin, John
Hammon, Philip	Hammon, William	Hamilton, Andrew
Kester, Paul	Kays, John	Killough, John
Kirkham, Mikel	Lambert, Jonothan	Lesh, Henry
Morris, William	McGaw, Moses	Pressley, John
Pressley, Joseph	Pressley, Robert	Stephen, Richard
Stephen, William	Smith, Robert	Smith, Phillip
Wead, Andrew	Wright, John	White, Johab

ROLL OF CAPT. JOSEPH EWING'S COMPANY (County Unknown).
Served from August 9, 1813, until February 8, 1814.

Capt. Joseph Ewing	Lieut. John Archer	Ensign Truman Munger
Sergt. Joshua Burk	Sergt. John Windslow	Sergt. Ezra Kellog
Sergt. Daniel Watkins	Corp. Samuel Ewing	Corp. Lewis Lorris
Corp. John Garrard	Corp. Joseph Hancock	Drummer, Henry King
	Fifer, Thomas Hatfield	
Privates.	**Privates.**	**Privates.**
Bonta, Henry	Brown, Conrad	Brooks, Jacob
Baldwin, Ezekiel	Butt, Henry	Butt, John
Brown, William	Branblossom, Abraham	Cox, Elijah
Cortner, John	Cortney, William	Cunningham, William
Coffman, Henry	Delop, William	Douglas, Robert
Gallahan, Jonas	Graham, George	Gilbert, Thomas
Holtzklaw, James	Houston, Edward	Haines, Ephraim
Ifert, Jacob	John, Lemuel	Kizer, Rannab
Luce, Benjamin		

ROLL OF CAPT. JOSEPH EWING'S COMPANY (Continued).

Rank and Name of Soldier.

Privates.
Loveless, Sylvanus
Middal, John G.
Overholster, John
Predy, William
Rodes, Jacob
Scott, Alexander
Scott, William
Thompson, John
Wood, Aquila
Wood, Joshua
Warner, Jacob

Rank and Name of Soldier.

Privates.
Muzzleman, Peter
Mill, George
Pool, George
Quinn, James
Riffle, Jacob
Scribner, Azor
Shell, Joseph
Tennent, Alexander
Whitsell, Henry
Whitaker, John
Webb, John
Zeazel, John

Rank and Name of Soldier.

Privates.
Majors, William
Messenger, Nicholas
Peck, John
Rittenhous, Peter
Rittenhouse, Obediah
Sumption, Charles
Scott, Moses
Van Skike, John
Westfall, Job
Warts, Israel
York, Aaron

Page 365

ROLL OF CAPT. THOMAS MICKEY'S COMPANY (Probably from Franklin Co.)
Served from August 25 until October 10, 1812.

Capt. Thomas Mickey

Privates.
Armstrong, John
Carter, Joseph
Hopkins, James
McElvain, John

Privates.
Brickle, John
Driver, John
Jones, Richard
Newcome, Christopher

Privates.
Congell, Joseph
Fuller, William
Morehead, Thomas
Sells, Peter

Page 370

ROLL OF CAPT. SAMUEL BLACK'S COMPANY (County Unknown).
Served from August 24, 1812, until February 24, 1813.

Capt. Samuel Black
Sergt. John Black
Sergt. James Bruce
Corp. Isaac Ellis

Lieut. James McBride
Sergt. William Smith
Corp. Henry Wil!iams
Corp. William Beason
Fifer, William Harrison

Ensign George Price
Sergt. Myers, John
Corp. Francis Kelley
Drummer, Roswell W. Smith

Privates.
Albin, John
Black, Peter
Bigger, John
Casey, Jacob
Evans, Benjamin
Goble, Daniel
Hushaw, Peter
Hall, Abner
Hamilton, James
Kennedy, John
Loofberrard, Jacob
Minick, Peter
Moore, John H.
McIntire, Joseph
McFarland, John
Price, John.
Richard, Conrad
Shirely, Samuel
Venard, Francis
Wood, Zedock
Wood, John

Privates.
Black, James
Buchanon, James
Concklin, John
Dill, William
Elliott, John
Gilliland, Thomas
Hook, Hugh
Hayes, James
Hayes, John
Kelley, Abner
Melvin, Ebenezer
Miller, George
Murphy, Thomas
McClure, James
McWhalen, Hugh
Russell, Robert
Snodgrass, Robert
Smith, Samuel
Vance, Joseph
Williams, Levi
Williams, William

Privates.
Birt, William
Blaney, Robert
Confer, Jacob
Dickensheets, Henry
Elliott, Alexander
Hide, John
Hobbs, Littleton
Gaff, John
Ivers, Richard
Loofberrard, David
Miller, John
Murphy, Oratio
Morris, Henry
McBride, Jesse
Palmer, Layton
Ross, Alexander E.
Sutton, Jesse
Smith, Robert
Whalon, John
Willey, Hugh N.

Page 372

ROLL OF CAPT. SOLOMON BENTLEY'S COMPANY (Probably from Belmont County)
Served from August 22 until October 22, 1812.

Capt. Solomon Bentley
Sergt. Joseph Grimes
Sergt. James Kyle
Corp. Dennis Forrest

Lieut. Joseph Kirkwood
Sergt. James Nixon
Corp. David Dille
Corp. John Vroyd

Ensign George Love
Sergt. Hugh Brown
Corp. William McCoy
Musician Evan Rodgers

Privates.
Adeidler, Caleb
Dallis, John
Day, Israel
Erskine, Thomas
Gilliland, Thomas
Harriman, David
Kyzer, Thomas
Marques, William
Powel, Joseph
Robinson, John
Simeson, James
Wright, Coleman H.

Privates.
Armstrong, Travis
Carrington, Nicholas
Devore, John
Grimes, John
Gilliland, Morgan
Irvin, George
Long, Adam
McMahan, Dennis
Rankin, Joseph
Shepherd, Arnold
Starr, James
Watson, Robert

Privates.
Cluney, Alexander
Dillon, Samuel
Ditzler, John
Goeshorn, Leonard
Herd, William
Howel, William
Lashley, Hezekiah
Park, James
Rider, Obed
Shepherd, Isaiah
Tarrier, John

Page 373 Vol. I.

ROLL OF CAPT. PETER BACUS' COMPANY (County Unknown).
Served from August 19 until September 18, 1812.

Rank and Name of Soldier.	Rank and Name of Soldier.	Rank and Name of Soldier.
Capt. Peter Bacus	Lieut. Levin Willoughby	Sergt. John Conrad
Sergt. Adam Brinter	Sergt. Nicholas Sibral	Sergt. Thompson Sebring
Corp. Seaburn Hinton	Corp. Thomas Phillips	Corp. George Chad
Corp. William Dean	Drummer, John Stall	

Privates.

Byers, William	Barker, Joseph	Black, John
Cutright, Henry	Cassill, Abraham	Curts, John
Dever, John	Extine, Daniel	Fultz, Jacob
Fulk, Henry	Francis, Joseph	Hull, Isaac
Hines, Adam	Husk, John	Harley, Carter
Ice, Jacob	Hornback, John	Knox, Benjamin
Linton, William	Murphy, Redmond	McHenry, Aaron
Overly, Jacob	Overly, David	Rusk, Moses
Ray, William	Rush, George	Rush, Josiah
Shoote, Richard	Strucy, Michael	Swaggert, Daniel
Shane, Henry	Sullivan, William	Smith, Samuel
Sullerback, John	Stewart, James	Strevey, Daniel
Smith, William	Taylor, Nimrod	Vezey, William
Vanmetre, Henry	Wech, John	

Page 374

ROLL OF CAPT. ANDREW DILL'S COMPANY (County Unknown).
Served from May 1, 1812, until May 1, 1813.

Capt. Andrew Dill	Lieut. William Weatherington	Ensign John H. DeLorshmuts
Sergt. Andrew McMahan	Sergt. Robert McElvain	Sergt. Josiah Williams
Sergt. William Mickey	Corp. Jonathan Piper	Corp Joseph Morgan
Corp. Samuel C. Rayl	Corp. Barnabus McMahan	Musician, Roswell W. Smith

Privates.

Abbott Armstrong D.	Bogard, Joseph	Burk, Joseph
Buck, William	Braden, James	Breckinridge, Joseph
Conner, John	Carns, John	Davies, William
Denny, John	Culbertson, Samuel	Dyer, Samuel
Ford, Benjamin	Harrison, James	Hamler, Jacob
Ice, George	Hott, Peter	Lewin, John
Lynn, Lewis	Leonard, John	Martin, Daniel
Mettel, Abel	Monel, Jesse	McNutt, James
Nicherson, Uzziah	Nicherson, Isachar	Parkinson, John H.
Robinson, Daniel	Right, George	Richtes, John
Reid, Charles	Stiers, Henry	Sordan, Jonathan
Shafer, Frederick	Wolf, Charles	Whiteman, James
Williams, Matthew	Walling, Asa	Wyant, John

Page 375

ROLL OF CAPT. GABRIEL COX'S COMPANY (Probably from Champaign Co.)
Served from September 14 until October 16, 1812.

Capt. Gabriel Cox	Lieut. Nicholas Sturm	Ensign Nicholas Van Densan
Sergt. Ezekiel Rice	Sergt. Walker Aldridge	Sergt. James Herd
Sergt. William B. Craghill	Corp. John Reid	Corp. John Bowman
Fifer, Newton Burroughs	Drummer, William Hull	

Privates.

Blair, William	Beacon, David	Bendure, William
Blackford, John	Brooks, Thomas	Carter, Israel
Dotson, Thomas	Dean, Barzilla	Dillon, William
Davidson, Stephen	Dillon, Richard	Gerard, Jacob
Green, John	Goodfellow, Moore	Griffith, Azel
Gandy, Abijah	Herd, Thomas	Hutchinson, Thomas
Hunt, John	Heaton, Jonah	Haney, James
Hopkins, Richard	Hanna, David	Jones, Stephen
Jones, David	Keyser, Benjamin	Kennedy, Samuel
Moss, Jacob	Price, John	Patrick, Johnson
Parks, James	Perry, James	Rudesilly, Jacob
Smith, David	Smith, John	Sturm, Mathias
Spencer, Aaron	Simpson, Alexander	Turner, Robert
White, Benjamin	Williams, Zechariah	White, Joseph

Pages 378-379

ROLL OF CAPT. JEHIEL GREGORY'S COMPANY (Probably from Ross Co.)
Served from July 28 until September 3, 1813.

Capt. Jehiel Gregory	Lieut. Jacob Dunbaugh	Ensign Thomas Ewing
Sergt. Montgomery Perry	Sergt. Andrew Gregory	Sergt. John Bell
Sergt. Elijah Pilcher	Corp. John Cox	Corp. William Rines
Corp. John Jackson	Corp. Edward Pilcher	

Vol. I.
ROLL OF CAPT. JEHIEL GREGORY'S COMPANY (Continued.)

Rank and Name of Soldier.	Rank and Name of Soldier.	Rank and Name of Soldier.
Privates.	**Privates.**	**Privates.**
Ackley, Henry	Abbott, John	Bananes, George
Bananes, Jacob	Davis, Samuel	Goodridge, Timothy
Graham, William	Howtell, Hiram	Kenney, John
Polk, Ciphus	Polk, Eber	Ranul, Daniel
Rabonet, Ezekiel	Rewis, George	Rabb, Johnson
Reynolds, Justice	Richardson, Abraham	Spence, Abraham
Speed, George	Stroud, Joel	Simonton, Jacob
Stedman, Abel	Seloy, Gabriel	Tucker, John
True, Josiah	Wright, John	Waters, Josiah

Page 380
ROLL OF ENSIGN JACOB HOOVER OR HOOBER'S COMPANY
(Probably from Ross County.)
Served from July 28 until August 18, 1813.

Ensign Jacob Hoover or Hoober	Sergt. George Corwine	Sergt. William McKonkle
Sergt. William Stewart	Corp. Michael Robinson	
Privates.	**Privates.**	**Privates.**
Bowman, Daniel	Bowman, Benjamin	Corwine, Samuel
Chenworth, Thomas	Fewell, John	Graham, Robert
Hultz, William	Harrel, Daniel	Jordan, Jones
Mounts, Eli	McMullin, Alexander Jr.	Rhidemeer, Frederick
Stewart, George	Stegall, Frederick	Thomas, Ormes
Vineyard, James	Wilson, George	Wood, Jonothan
Williams, Amos	Wilson, James	Warren, James
Warren, Greenbury	Wells, Peter	Wells, Isaac

Page 381
ROLL OF CAPT. TIMOTHY BUELL'S COMPANY
(Probably from Washington County).
Served from August 1 until September 7, 1813.

Capt. Timothy Buell	Lieut. Peter White	Lieut. Salvanus Olney
Ensign James Leget	Sergt. Nathaniel Hamilton	Sergt. George Nixon
Sergt. Jabez Palmer	Sergt. S. D. Buell	Corp. Samuel Nott
Corp. Edward Corner	Corp. John Barrough	Corp. Nicholas Chapman
Privates.	**Privates.**	**Privates.**
Blackmer, Timothy	Coleman, Daniel	Corns, John
Clark, John C.	Coleman, Elisha	Cuddington, Zechanah
DeLong, Henry	Dunbar, Thomas	Demont, Richard
Dennis, Thomas	Ellis, Benjamin	Gates, Timothy, Jr.
Gates, Stephen	William F.	Havens, Henry
Jennings, Zebulum	Kimball, Titus	Lawrence, R., Jr.
Liget, Robert	Laughey, John	Laughey, William
Miller, Jacob	McGee, Robert	Miller, Samuel
McCoy, Alexander	McConnel, John	Nulton, Jacob
Palmer, Benjamin F.	Perry, John	Porter, John R.
Pruant, William	Quigley, Horace	Rair, Dennis
Ray, James	Scott, John	Smith, Nathaniel
Taylor, John	Wilson, Jonothan	Whitney, Jonothan
Wood, Paulus E.	Zuthinger, Clark	

Pages 382-383
ROLL OF CAPT. JOHN RAMSEY'S COMPANY (County Unknown).
Served from December 1, 1812, until March 9, 1813.

Capt. John Ramsey	Lieut. James Anderson	Ensign, Lindsey Cannon
Sergt. Thomas Roseburg	Sergt. James Craighead	Sergt. James Rainsey
Sergt. Samuel Zolly	Corp. John Hunter	Corp. Phillip Fout
Corp. Joseph Fife	Corp. William Hamilton.	
Privates.	**Privates.**	**Privates.**
Augustine, Henry	Anderson, James	Beer, James
Brown, Joseph	Bennet, James	Craig, Robert
Cannon, Thomas	Daugherty, James	Daugherty, Samuel
Earley, James	Earley, David	Fife, James
Fife, Samuel	Frank, Adam	Furney, John
Farmer, Thomas	Graham, John	Guthery, William
Guthery, Samuel	Goss, Mathias	Gardner, Jacob
Geddes, James	Hamilton, Jonothan	Hunter, Samuel
Hayes, David	Hickman, Nicholas	Haggart, William
Hurney, Adam	Jackson, John	Kees, Russell
Lamburn, Josiah	Figgins, Samuel	Campbell, John
Carnes, George	Craig, William	Meek, Samuel
Meek, Robert	Meek, William	McLaughlin, Robert
McLaughlin, William	McDonald, Duncan	McAlily, Samuel
McCullough, James	McCready, William	Opdyke, Albert
Prince, William	Paul, Benjamin	Paul, Henry
Pollock, William	Grimm, Jacob	Robinson, Jonah
Rupert, Jacob	Smith, Sampson	Sheets, Jacob
Sheets, John	Simcock, Michael	Thompson, John L.
Walls, Richard	Wright, Gilbert	Shirts, Peter
Whitmore, John	Shiver, Samuel	

Pages 384-385 Vol. I.

ROLL OF CAPT. JAMES DOWNING'S COMPANY (County Unknown).

Served from January 1 until March 9, 1813.

Rank and Name of Soldier.	Rank and Name of Soldier.	Rank and Name of Soldier.
Capt. James Downing	Lieut. Peter Johnston	Ensign, Thomas Smith
Sergt. John Forsythe	Sergt. John Barke	Sergt. Michael McGowin
Sergt. Samuel Richards	Corp. Abraham Bair	Corp. Benjamin Atkinson
Corp. John Warden	Corp. Joseph Bashford	Fifer, Jesse Ellis
Privates.	Privates.	Privates.
Burke, John	Bower, Henry	Bair, John
Bair, David	Barber, Henry	Baird, Andrew
Bower, John	Boyle, Richard	Crites, William
Camp, Henry	Dixon, John	Forsythe, Andrew
Funk, Samuel	Gruble, John	Holtz, John
Fulks, George	Henning, Jacob	Hartner, Jacob
Howman, Isaac	Hiser, Peter	Kinney, Peter
Heffner, David	Kepler, Andrew	Leatherman, Peter
Knap, Caleb	Mills, Eli	Murry, Patrick
Mills, Abraham	Morrison, James	McCaughey, Joseph
Mathews, Isaac	Nelson, William	Patten, Mathew
Nedeck, Samuel	Perkins, James	Painter, Jacob
Powel, John	Parker, Thomas	Parkerson, Jacob
Pinckney, Adam	Rodgers, Levi	Rodgers, John
Richards, Daniel	Ryla, Elijah	Strickland, Edward
Reed, Adam	Smith, Jacob	Stover, Samuel
Stephens, Daniel	Thompson, John	Vaughn, Richard
Smetts, John	Voyt, James	Worley, Thomas
Vaughn, Jonothan	Winis, Barnabas	White, Samuel
Wike, George	Williams, John	

Pages 386-387

ROLL OF CAPT. WILLIAM BLACKBURN'S COMPANY (County Unknown).

Served from December 1, 1812, until March 9, 1813.

Capt. William Blackburn	Lieut. Samuel Ferguson	Ensign, George Grimes
Sergt. Benjamin Holm	Sergt. William Milner	Sergt. Samuel Swoy
Sergt. George Wiseman	Corp. Andrew Gilson	Corp. Phillip Branderberry
Corp. Daniel Cross	Corp. Joseph Earl	Fifer, Daniel McCaskey
	Drummer, Frederick Blecher	
Privates.	Privates.	Privates.
Armstrong, Thomas	Anderson, Andrew	Booker, Isaiah
Brown, Joseph	Bootz, George	Branderberry, Conrad
Betz, Frederick	Britton, Archibald	Bell, William
Bishop, Joseph	Bradfield, Joseph	Bashan, Ezekial
Brinker, Peter	Brown, William	Canehey, Joseph
Curl, Charles	Foulks, Charles	Fishel, Frederick
Grimes, John	Gibson, David	Gibson, John
Harwood, Peter	Hahn, Caleb	Helmick, Adam
Jumper, Joseph	Jones, Nicholas	Kuntz, John
Kuntz, Emanuel	Moody, Joseph	Miller, Stephen
Mannon, William	Moss, Phillip	Myers, John
Night, Robert	Panner, Jesse	Patterson, Joseph
Queen, Samuel	Queen, John	Redmond, Jacob
Rodger, George	Robinson, John	Rossell, Job
Sheets, George	Stephens, Benjamin	Sooy, Samuel
Shanke, Jacob	Swardley, John	Skelton, John
Turnipseed, John	Wolf, John	Wolf, Phillip
Wolf, George	Wollem, Jacob	Welker, William
Willitts, John	Woolam, Henry	

Pages 388-389

ROLL OF CAPT. JOSEPH K. McCUNE'S COMPANY (County Unknown).

Served from February 12 until August 12, 1813.

Capt. Joseph K. McCune	Lieut. Thomas Kirkpatrick	Ensign, John Day
Sergt. Abraham Pollock	Sergt. Jonothan Eddington	Sergt. Alexander D. Tucker
Sergt. John McFarson	Corp. William C. Slaughter	Corp. Moses Powell
Privates.	Privates.	Privates.
Bailey, James	Baird, Robert	Bingham, David
Briggs, James	Burch, Zebulum	Barnard, William
Corningham, Edward	Chandler, Daniel	Deans, George
DeLong, Isaac	Dawson, Henry	Cummings, William
Deaver, Walter P.	Feroson, Robert	Gibson, George
Griffith, William	Heaton, Joseph	Holt, James
Hibner, John	Haddon, William	Hutchison, George
Lane, Dutton	Mingus, William	Moss, Nehemiah
McFarland, Samuel	Parker, Henry	Parscale, Cornelius
Patterson, Obediah	Ross, John	Shepardson, Jared
Rattle, James	Switzer, John	Snider, Jacob
Spry, Elijah	Welsh, William	Waggoner, Mathias
Swank, Philip		

Page 390. Vol. I.

ROLL OF CAPT. WILLIAM GILL'S COMPANY. (County Unknown.)

Served from April 16, 1812, until April 17, 1813.

Rank and Name of Soldier.	Rank and Name of Soldier.	Rank and Name of Soldier.
Capt. William Gill	Lieut. Wynekoop Warner	Ensign Jacob Witt
Sergt. Alexander McBratney	Sergt. Thomas Riddle	Sergt. Titus Shotwell
Sergt. John Gorden	Corp. Parry Hulse	Corp. James Bigley
Corp. Ezekial Boggs	Corp. Asaph Butler	Fifer, John Robinson
	Drummer, Archibald Lafferton	

Privates.	Privates.	Privates.
Browny, John	Bryan, Aaron	Butler, Eli
Bright, Nicholas	Boyd, William	Berry, Joseph
Colter, Archibald, Sr.	Crooks, James	Colman, Samuel
Coulter, Archibald, Jr.	Edwards, Walter	Edy, Job
Fairhurst, William	Gassaway, Benjamin	Gardner, John
Hamilton, John	Hardesty, Lewis	Hardesty, John
Holmes, Thomas	Harred, Samuel	Hammerly, Joseph
Lansdown, William	Lamson, John	Mitchell, Henry
Martin, Robert	Montgomery, Robert	Miller, John
McMahon, John	McWilliams, Alexander	Neff, Henry
Piper, Tristan	Porterfield, Robert	Paitens, Christian
Ritchie, William	Ritchie, Robert	Rankin, John
Rouse, George	Fisher, John	Scott, William
Stowden, Jacob	Stewart, James	Stephenson, Arthur
Scott, Joseph	Scott, John	Spurgeon, Nathan
Smith, Robert	Skinner, William	Taylor, James
Willis, William	Wood, George	Watkins, Thomas .

Page 391.

ROLL OF CAPT. BENJAMIN MAPEL'S COMPANY.
(Probably from Belmont County.)

Served from February 7 until March 7, 1815.

Capt. Benjamin Mapel	Lieut. Jacob Winnings	Ensign Augustine Andrew
Sergt. James Swindler	Sergt. James Bashford	Corp. James Jobes
Corp. John Sprangler	Drummer, John Marshall	

Privates.	Privates.	Privates.
Abrams, Anthony	Alexander, James	Augustine, George
Burk, Moses	Boyles, Nurman	Bennet, Thomas
Bassett, Ebenezer	Brenner, Jacob W.	Cole, Ezekial
Collear, Joseph	Fowler, John	Franks, Michael
Grove, William	Lyle, William	Lewis, Thomas B.
Miller, Samuel	Pinewell, Elias	Russell, Joshua
Russell, David	Rukeson, Jacob	Spedle, William
Swinehart, Daniel	Taylor, Abner	Welsh, John
West, Adam	Welday, Abraham	Yeckne, Charles
Lutchlenwatter, Jacob		

Page 392.

ROLL OF CAPT. JOHN McELROY'S COMPANY.
(Probably from Belmont County.)

Served from October 20, 1812, until January 11, 1813.

Capt. John McElroy	Lieut. Anthony Welzer	Ensign David Rook
Sergt. Alexander Smiley	Sergt. Thomas Gourley	

Privates.	Privates.	Privates.
Ault, Peter	Baker, Charles	Burkirk, Isaac
Cucklen, Samuel	Dean, Daniel	Dean, Aaron
Dean, Benjamin	Duff, David	Duff, John
Graham, William	Grubb, Jacob	Hardesty, Robert
Hardesty, Samuel	Hughs, James	Logan, John
Markes, Samuel	McClelland, David	Nillane, James
Renneson, John	Renneson, William	Robertson, Robert
Smith, Anthony	Shipman, Stephen	Tharp, John
Vanwy, Charles	Work, Alexander	Wilson, George
Word, Morcer	Taggert, James	

Page 393.

ROLL OF CAPT. VENE STONE'S COMPANY.
(Probably from Geauga County.)

Served from August 23, until August 30, 1812.

Capt. Vene Stone	Lieut. Eli Fowler	Ensign Gunyon Moss
Sergt. Theadore Royer	Sergt. Stephen H. Worthington	Sergt. John Charter
Sergt. Simon Burroughs	Corp. Solomon Charter	Corp. Simon Speng
Corp. Solomon Harks	Drummer, Jacob Burton	Fifer, Adolphus Coulton

Privates.	Privates.	Privates.
Andrews, Amos	Andrews, Leman G.	Brooks, Jonothan
Brooks, Ichabod	Bradley, Bildad	Bradley, Moses
Bradley, Selah	Bradley, Gomer	

Pages 395-396.   Vol. I.

ROLL OF CAPT. WILLIAM T. CULLUM'S COMPANY. (County Unknown.)

Served from September 4, 1813, until March 2, 1814.

Rank and Name of Soldier.
Capt. William T. Cullum
Sergt. Purnell I. Reddish
Sergt. Solomon Slayback
Corp. John Miller
Drummer, Thomas Ogdon

Privates.
Argadine, Edward
Brewner, Jacob
Cary, Benajah
Collins, John
Carr, Samuel, Sr.
Clark, Thomas
Falkner, James
Goldthwaite, Nathaniel
Hope, David C.
Huffman, Jonas
Hageman, Simon, Sr.
Isrig, Daniel
Oslin, John
Murphy, Albert
Miller, Samuel
Moore, William
McKee, Anthony
McBride, Samuel
Noble, Henry
Packer, Barnabus
Park, Israel
Pack, Samuel D.
Simson, Alexander
Shadley, James
Speere, James
Shaddak, Shank
Taylor, Robert

Rank and Name of Soldier.
Lieut. William Misner
Sergt. Peter Carle
Corp. James Nicholson
Corp. William Frazee
Fifer, Joseph Broughard

Privates.
Broughman, Joseph
Bash, William
Cameron, Daniel
Congar, James
Carr, Samuel, Jr.
Collier, Hazel
Flint, John
Gray, William
Hubard, Vivdate
Hunter, James
Hageman, Simon, Jr.
Irwin, William
Osgood, Nathan
Miller, John
Moore, Samuel
Masters, William
McKee, James
McFeally, Thomas
Noble, John
Potts, Charles
Pherris, Joseph
Robertson, Cuthbert
Sands, Daniel
Stell, John
Shiffer, Lambert
Thomas, David
West, John

Rank and Name of Soldier.
Ensign Francis Cullum
Sergt. William Williamson
Corp. Morgan Huff
Corp. Ephraim Earle

Privates.
Brooks, John
Brook, Stephen
Conklin, Joseph C.
Cathers, Robert
Carr, William
Cramer, John
Farmer, Tatley
Harrison, Charles
Henderson, John
Harrison, Merines
Hufner, Thomas
Jessup, Walter
Kain, Richard
Miller, James
Miller, Silas
Mockridge, Samuel
McFerin, Samuel
McKee, William
Nicholas, Jonothan
Pack, Enos
Pack, Nathan T.
Russell, Moses
Swim, Ezra S.
Skull, John
Shed, Silas
Trisler, Peter

Page 397.

ROLL OF CAPT. GEORGE SHEMMELL'S COMPANY. (County Unknown.)

Served from August 7, 1813, ―――――.

Capt. George Shemmell

Lieut. John Guard
Sergt. Cornelius Hand

Ensign George Sluthrin

Privates.
Andreas, Peter
Blickensturfer, Jacob
Baker, Peter
Bales, Abraham
Carson, John
Danner, Jacob
Flitkinger, John
Gibson, George
Hill, Charles
Haverstock, Conrad
Johnston, Lemuel
Miller, Jacob
Purcussele, Christian
Ridgeway, Thomas
Shark, Valentine
Thompson, Jacob
Walton, Esse
Williams, Levi

Privates.
Alwood, Christopher
Burnet, Richard
Butt, William
Clum, John
Corpman, John
Eakin, Daniel
Forney, Abraham
Hill, Jesse
Hogland, William
Jackson, Francis
Minick, Phillip
Rutter, Jolly
Shane, Abraham
Study, George
Uhrick, Michael
Walgamurth, Joseph
Walters, Samuel
Wetty, John

Privates.
Biddinger, Henry
Baker, George
Balsly, Jacob
Cline, Henry
Deardorf, Isaac
Foster, Jesse
Gossage, Benjamin
Harbaugh, Isaac
Hill, William
Most, Joseph
Price, Thomas
Rippeth, William
Sharp, John Jacob
Stocker, Trumbow, John
Vail, George
Williams, Thomas
Walters, Jacob
Young, Jacob

Page 398.

ROLL OF JOHN AUGUSTINE'S COMPANY. (County Unknown.)

Served from September 6 until November 24, 1814.

Capt. John Augustine
Sergt. David Kemp
Sergt. Phillip Shou
Corp. Michael C. Homan

Lieut. Peter Conkel
Sergt. Samuel Crawford
Corp. James Gaff
Drummer, Jacob Bash
Fifer, Thomas Tidball

Ensign, Augustine Bushong
Sergt. John Augustine
Corp. Joseph B. Sedball
Drummer, Jesse Ellis

Privates.
Allenton, James
Conley, James
Geddis, James
Lester, Christopher
McPherson, James
Palmer, James
Rosberry, William

Privates.
Arnold, John
Carrington, John
Harriman, William
Lewis, Francis
McConnell, Wilson
Risher, Daniel
Swinehart, Samuel

Privates.
Bryan, Daniel
French, Samuel
Hall, James
McConnichy, Hugh
Palmer, John
Robinson, Jonothan
VanArsteen, Frederick

ROSTER OF OHIO SOLDIERS IN WAR OF 1812

ROLL OF CAPT. JOHN NIMMON'S COMPANY. (County Unknown.)
(Incomplete.)

Served from October 1, 1812, until March 31, 1813.

Rank and Name of Soldier.	Rank and Name of Soldier.	Rank and Name of Soldier.
Capt. John Nimmon	Lieut. Anthony Loustenhiser	Ensign, Felty Shoop
Sergt. John Warden	Sergt. Seldon Woster	Corp. George Almonds
	Musician, John Kuntz	

ROLL OF MARTIN SITTLER'S COMPANY.
(Probably from Columbiana County. Incomplete.)

Served from August 25 until November 5, 1812.

Capt. Martin Sittler	Lieut. Conrad Yarian	Sergt. John Roose
Sergt. Albert Opdyke	Sergt. James Watson	Sergt. Mathias Yearian
Corp. John Forney	Corp. Peter Forney	Corp. Adam Forney
	Private, George Lowfure	

ROLL OF CAPT. SAMUEL WATSON'S COMPANY. (County Unknown.)

Served from September 18 until October 18, 1812.

Capt. Samuel Watson   Sergt. Daniel McMichael

Privates.	Privates.	Privates.
Coon, Jacob	Coon, John	Coon, George
Eldfield, Jonothan	Goss, William	McClure, Samuel
McClure, Thomas	McClure, James	McClure, James Jr.
Robbins, Elisha	Riddle, William	Speir, Duncan
Stout, Jacob	Sent, Jacob	Sent, John
Sent, John Jr.	Sent, Daniel	Weyrick, John
Weyrick, Peter	Watson, Amaziah	

ROLL OF CAPT. JOHN GREER'S COMPANY.
(Probably from Knox County.)

Served from August 26 until October 10, 1812.

Capt. John Greer	Lieut. Carey Cooper	Ensign, John Cook
Sergt. John Wells	Sergt. George Low	Sergt. Smith Hadley
Sergt. David Brown	Drummer, Daniel Dial	Fifer, Stephen Butler

Privates.	Privates.	Privates.
Arnold, John	Ayres, Ashel	Ackre, Adam
Atherton, Francis	Baker, John	Baughman, Jacob
Brown, Jeremiah	Blakeney, Francis	Boyle, John
Brown, Samuel	Carnes, Abraham	Chapman, Timothy
Doty, Frazer	Davis, Alexander	Earlewine, Adam
Craig, Jonothan	Dodd, Judathan	Guinn, John
Garrison, John	Green, John	Harris, Jesse
Harrod, James	Harris, James	Holt, Even
Humphreys, John	Hoglin, George	Harrod, Lerue
Johnston, Samuel	Lepley, Joseph	Lewis, Samuel
Martin, James	McBride, Robert	McBride, Thomas
McKee, Alexander	Pool, John	Pinkley, John
Pumphrey, Joshua	Nail, Henry	Shafer, Benjamin
Spurgeon, George	Shop, Benjamin	Swore, Jesse
Strange, James	Smith, William	Smith, George
Sapp, William	Tallmage, Joseph	Thompson, Andrew
Truax, William	Tawnyhill, Charles	Vanosdoll, Charles
Young, John Jr.	Young, Aaron	Welker, Jacob
Zimmerman, John	Zinn, George	

ROLL OF CAPT. GEORGE HOSHER'S COMPANY. (County Unknown.)

Served from February 16 until April 16, 1814. Part served until August 16, 1814.

Capt. George Hosher	Lieut. Michael Walter	Ensign, William Evens
Sergt. Henry Bonoteel	Sergt. Enekial Joseph	Sergt. John Livingston
Sergt. John Miller	Corp. Massy Climer	Corp. Joshua Evens
Corp. Michael Hively	Corp. Daniel Spohn	Corp. John Hiles
Sergt. William McIntosh	Drummer, William Boan	

Privates.	Privates.	Privates.
Baker, Joseph	Bold, Henry	Bryan, William
Bixter, Christian	Courson, John	Chambers, James
Chester, George	Clem, Henry	Davis, Aquila
Daniel, John	Demas, Thomas	Fisher, Jacob
Friend, William	Farmer, Samuel	Futhy, Isaac
Friend, George	Gibbs, Daniel	Green, Jacob
Guin, Hezekiah	Green, Robert	Hills, John
Houts, Christian	Hoy, Phillip	Helm, John

ROLL OF CAPT. GEORGE HOSHER'S COMPANY (Continued.)

Rank and Name of Soldier.

Privates.
- Hiland, Edward
- Hively, Michael
- Looker, Jonothan
- Lair, Andrew
- Lott, George
- Lappwine, Gabriel
- Miller, Phillip
- Meeker, Aaron
- Moyer, John
- Morris, William
- McClung, Thomas
- Nutt, David
- Parish, John
- Ray, Abraham
- Shaffer, William
- Stephens, Justice
- Stevens, Chester
- Vandermark, John
- Webster, Jacob

Rank and Name of Soldier.

Privates.
- Hawey, James
- Jenkins, Evan
- Love, James
- Lobdell, Samuel
- Lineburg, Peter
- Martin, Joseph
- Miller, John
- Moore, Thomas
- Miller, Othias
- Moredeck, William
- McCormick, James
- Pair, Thomas
- Ricketts, John
- Ridenour, Martin
- Stouter, John
- Sutton, John
- Thrush, Michael
- Westfall, Harvey
- Westfall, Henry

Rank and Name of Soldier.

Privates.
- Humbarger, Peter
- King, Jacob
- Limbaugh, George
- Larimore, Joseph
- Lineburg, William
- Meeker, Moses
- Messmore, George
- Meek, John
- Mercer, Robert
- McWilliams, Alexander
- Nogle, Isaac
- Pressler, John
- Russell, William
- Spicer, John
- Sinbary, William
- Signer, George
- Turner, Benjamin
- Williams, William

Pages 404-405-406-407-408-409-410-439.

ROLL OF CAPT. WILLIAM KILGORE'S COMPANY. (County Unknown.)

Served from February 16 until April 16, 1814. Part served until August 16, 1816.

- Capt. William Kilgore
- Lieut. Aaron Foster
- Sergt. Richard Berry
- Sergt. William T. Ricords
- Sergt. Thomas Nichols
- Corp. James Dean
- Corp. Charles Green
- Corp. Morgan Osburn
- Corp. Daniel Relley
- Corp. Samuel Arnold

Privates.
- Arman, George
- Bowen, Shadrack
- Bradon, Robert
- Bennett, Isaac
- Cooper, William
- Clarke, Simon
- Cremead, Smith
- Cooper, William
- Corey, Abraham
- Davis, Lewis
- Devorss, John
- Emery, James
- Foulkeson, John
- Gray, James G.
- Gooden, Daniel
- Grimes, John
- Hood, Edward
- Harris, Amos
- Hasselton, David
- Hannon, John
- Kirkpatrick, David
- Laslin, John
- Moots, Jacob
- Miller, George M.
- Mason, Owen
- Mathews, Samuel
- McCord, John
- McCartney, Duke
- Pool, Edward
- Powers, Michael
- Russell, James
- Russell, Bazil
- Razell, Barzilla
- Scroggs, Alexander
- Shane, Daniel
- Seabrell, Nicholas
- Todhunter, Thomas
- Williams, Ezekial
- Wood, Conley
- Webb, William
- Wells, Squire
- Walker, John
- Bush, Daniel
- Coil, Thomas
- Grady, John
- King, John

- Lieut. James Krusen
- Ensign, Charles Wells
- Sergt. George Kerr
- Sergt. Martin Peterson
- Sergt. James Gilruth
- Corp. Mathew Young
- Corp. Samuel White
- Corp. Thomas E. Johnson
- Corp. Handy Cannon
- Corp. Shadrack Bowen

Privates.
- Arnold, Samuel
- Bradley, Owen
- Boots, Jacob
- Barker, John
- Carey, Abraham
- Clark, Thomas
- Christy, Joel
- Crull, Henry
- Dearborn, Nathan
- Depew, George
- Davis, John
- Finimore, John
- Green, Samuel
- Gragg, William
- Gilmore, William
- Gilliland, Hugh
- Hasselton, Daniel
- Holt, William
- Headley, George
- Hoffman, Leonard
- Logue, John
- Ledmore, Clement
- Mathias, Samuel
- Mathews, Thomas
- Mounts, Joseph
- McCandless, Nathaniel
- McCandless, Hugh
- O'Brien, Charles
- Painter, Elias
- Prior, Griffith
- Relley, Nathan
- Robison, James
- Swinney, John
- Stingley, Leonard
- Swanzy, John
- Timmons, Eli
- Vandamen, Conrad
- Williams, Calvin
- West, James
- Wright, John
- Woodall, Cosby
- Blair, Thomas
- DeWitt, George
- Hayes, Andrew
- Lane, William

- Ensign, William Holloway
- Sergt. James McArthur
- Sergt. Samuel Johnson
- Sergt. John Haner
- Sergt. William Robinson
- Corp. Clement Ledman
- Corp. John Hoddey
- Corp. Nathan Relley
- Corp. George Armon
- Corp. Charles Benett

Privates.
- Anderson, John
- Bowen, Gardner
- Brunt, Jonothan
- Brewer, James
- Coder, Simeon
- Campbell, William
- Clark, James
- Church, Joel
- Dooley, Samuel
- Davis, Benjamin
- Day, Overton
- Frye, Joseph
- Groves, John
- Green, Charles
- Gilmore, Robert
- Hopkins, David
- Hair, Daniel
- Hison, Daniel
- Holland, William
- Jacobs, Elijah
- Lafton, John
- Moses, Thomas
- Mark, John
- Mains, William
- Mounts, Enoch
- McClure, Michael
- McLaughlin, William
- Peacock, Ezekial
- Patterson, John
- Ryan, Messack
- Rinely, Daniel
- Roe, John
- Selden, Spencer
- Spencer, Seldon
- Swine, John
- Taylor, Nehemiah
- Windall, Joseph
- Ware, Daniel
- Webb, Jehiel
- Wonstaff, Daniel
- Webb, John
- Corey, John
- Fergans, Daniel
- Jameson, Jacob
- Roi, Zechariah

Pages 414-415-416. Vol. I.
ROLL OF CAPT. MICAH WOOD'S COMPANY. (County Unknown)
Served from February 16 until August 15, 1814.

Rank and Name of Soldier.
Capt. Micah Woods
Ensign, William Newel
Sergt. Isaac Henderson
Corp. Thomas Mays

Privates.
Adams, William
Buzzard, Robert
Bell, Andrew
Baldwin, John R.
Borer, Abraham
Branson, Isaac
Camp, Richard
Cummings, William
Dunlap, William
Dawson, Othy
Earl, David
Groom, Thomas
Gibson, John
Hobaugh, George
Holman, Jesse
Hill, John
Jolly, William
Kessinger, John
Mears, Samuel
Moore, Elijah
Nicely, David
Parker, Joseph
Qirrey, John
Shields, John
Statelar, Joseph
Summer, Isaac
Stigall, Frederick
Talbot, Rhodney
Titus, Peter

Rank and Name of Soldier.
Lieut. Samuel Pope
Sergt. Benjamin Naylor
Corp. John Cruzan
Corp. Adam Shaffer

Privates.
Andrews, John
Bever, Christian
Boatman, George
Bill, Charles
Brown, William
Cummings, Robert
Coffee, Mitchell
Dutcher, John
Duncan, Alexander
Davis, Nathaniel
Earl, Isaac
Grady, Thomas
Gibson, James
Henry, John
Hilderbrand, Phillip
Howard, Lewis
Knox, John L.
Laycock, Peter
Marshall, James
Miller, Rush P.
McLaughlin, George
Paige, David
Robbins, Joseph
Shoemaker, Frederick
Shepherd, John
Sanbach, John
Satterlee, Isaac
Thormar, Jacob
Taylor, William

Rank and Name of Soldier.
Ensign, Archabel Beckwith
Sergt. August Richards
Corp. Alexander Campbell

Privates.
Alkire, John
Blaze, John
Bishop, Samuel
Borer, Adam
Blair, Daniel
Creed, David C.
Covin, John
Derby, Stephen
Dennis, John
Evans, Thomas
Frye, John
Grub, Joseph
Hill, Joseph
Hair, William
Hubble, Rowland
Johnston, John
Kinsely, David
Lucas, James
Montgomery, Andrew
Miller, Gilbert
Paine, Thomas
Peny, Isaac
Reynolds, James
Smith, Jacob
Smith, Jeremiah
Starr, John
Shaffer, Adam
Timmins, John
Venoy, William

Pages 417-418.
ROLL OF ABSALOM VANMATRE'S COMPANY. (Probably from Ross County.)
Served from September 28 until October 25, 1812, and from July 29 until August 18, 1813.

Capt. Absalom Vanmatre
Sergt. Joseph Vanmatre Jr.
Sergt. Samuel Jones

Privates.
Burger, Christian
Bowers, Jacob
Clevanger, Abraham
Gallispie, Jonothan
Jones, Isaac
Lane, Peter
Marsh, Peter
McCulloch, Samuel
Noble, Benjamin
Rush, James
VanMatre, Abner
VanMater, Samuel
White, Absalom
White, Isaac

Lieut. Joseph Vanmatre
Sergt. William Clavanger
Sergt. Pierce Vanmatre
Ensign, David Johnson

Privates.
Braskny, Hudson
Clevenger, Samuel
Gillispy, Hugh
Hammer, William
Jones, Daniel
Miller, Isaac
Marsh, George
McDonald, Robert
Noble, William
Stroup, Anthony
Shockley, Benjamin
Walton, Henry
Walton, Nathaniel
Walton, Aaron

Ensign, John Seaman
Sergt. George Fedrick
Sergt. John Shockley

Privates.
Bowers, David
Cox, William
Gillispy, Thomas
Jones, Oliver
Gainer, Enoch
Miller, John
Massee, James
McKilbeans, John
Pitson, Mathias
Ross, David
Vanmater, Isaac
White, Jason
White, William

Page 426.
ROLL OF CAPT. CALVIN HOADLY'S COMPANY. (County Unknown.)
Served from August 27 until November 1, 1812.

Capt. Calvin Hoadly
Sergt. Silas Wilmot
Sergt. David Beebe
Corp. Ephraim Vaughn

Privates.
Adams, Benoni
Culver, Martial
Frost, Lyman I.
Fowls, Ephraim
Hickcox, Earl
Hill, John W.
Morgan, Sylvester
Pardy, Samuel
Tyler, Seymour
Terrell, Wyllys
Vaughn, Jonothan

Lieut. Lathrop Seymour
Sergt. Elias Frost
Corp. Richard Vaughn
Corp. Roswell Scoville

Privates.
Bunnel, Daniel
Doam, Timothy
Fowls, Abraham
Geer, James
Hickcox, Jared
Morgan, Ira B.
Osborn, Thomas
Pritchard, Beard
Terrell, Iryah S.
Terrell, Tillotson
Wilmot, Ebenezer

Ensign, Daniel Bronson
Sergt. Samuel Y. Potter
Corp. Noah Warner

Privates.
Beeb, Loman C.
Eddy, David
Fowls, John
Hoadly, Clark
Hickcox, Samuel
Morgan, Asa
Potter, Zaphna
Robinson, Asath
Terrell, Oliver
Tunell, Philander
Wooster, Sheldon

Page 427. Vol. I.

ROLL OF CAPT. TIMOTHY BISHOP'S COMRANY. (County Unknown.)

Served from August 22 until October 2, 1812.

Rank and Name of Soldier.	Rank and Name of Soldier.	Rank and Name of Soldier.
Capt. Timothy Bishop	Lieut. John Cunningham	Ensign, Abraham Ozman
Sergt. Isaac Ozman	Sergt. Aaron Miller	Sergt. Moses Decker
Corp. Henry Post	Corp. Pliny Brown	Corp. John Galloway

Privates.	Privates.	Privates.
Bawn, Isaac	Brown, Daniel	Brown, Samuel Jr.
Carter, William	Eddings, Henry	Farran, Leman
Johnston, Andrew	Jordon, James	Maze, John
Mallet, Henry	Matlin, Alexander	Miller, Samuel
Miller, Alexander	Miller, Isaac	Ozman, Israel
Robinson, Abner	Stanford, James	Spaulding, Jesse
Spillman, Charles	Walcott, Alfred	

Pages 428-429.

ROLL OF CAPT. AMOS LUSK'S COMPANY. (County Unknown.)

Served from August 22 until November 30, 1812, and from January 1, until March 9, 1813.

Capt. Amos Lusk	Lieut. George W. Holcomb	Lieut. John Caris
Ensign, Hiram King	Sergt. Charles Miles	Sergt. William Chamberlings
Sergt. Comfort Raney	Sergt. Nathaniel Stone	Sergt. Henry Post
Sergt. Roswell Scoville	Sergt. Alexander Hall	Sergt. Jonothan B. Bissell
Sergt. Moses Jordon	Corp. Amos Chamberlain	Corp. John Gaylor
Corp. Milo L. Hudson	Corp. Myron Huttinson	Corp. Ami Baldwin
Corp. Timothy Holcomb	Corp. Daniel Brown	Corp. Joseph Baird
Corp. Moses Jordon	Drummer, Joseph B. Bishop	Drummer, Asa Rose
	Fifer, Henry Wood	

Privates.	Privates.	Privates.
Auter, Claron	Allen, Jesse	Allen, Nathaniel
Bostwick, Adna H.	Brown, Daniel	Baird, Joseph
Baird, James	Burdick, James	Ballford, Moses
Baldwin, Caleb	Beach, David	Brian, Robert
Brine, Henry C.	Bishop, David	Croy, Richard
Cackler, John	Chamberlain, Joseph	Cain, Gabriel
Carpenter, Richard	Cannon, George	Cochran, William
Cook, James	Draper, Asa	Drake, Francis B.
Dillingham, John	Ellsworth, Elijah	Fisher, Joseph
Gardner, David	Hall, John	Hill, John
Johnson, Daniel H.	Jordon, James	Johnston, Samuel
Lindley, Abia	Lindley, Jesse	Lindley, Ichabod
Metcalf, Jonothan	Muttin, Alexander	Messenger, Nathaniel H.
Mallet, John	McConoughy, Jarvis	Newton, John
Nye, Joshua	Norton, Lebbeus	Owen, Thomas
Oviatt, John	Oviatt, Herman	Oviatt, Benjamin
Pond, David	Prior, Warden	Pease, George
Pease, Ebenezer	Post, Lina	Richardson, Micaiah
Riley, Julius, Jr.	Robinson, Abner	Spilman, James
Sacket, Harvey	Sweet, Amos	Spaulding, Jesse
Spellman, Charles	Shaw, John	Steel, Alexander
Sutliff, Jesse	Tickner, David	Vauhining, Thomas
Vail, Samuel	Wilcox, David	Walker, James
Walker, Robert	Walker, George	Whitaker, William
Willys, Martin	Whorton, James	Wilson, James
Wills, John	White, Joel	Williams, Jonothan
	Wilcox, Isaac	

Page 431.

ROLL OF CAPT. THOMAS RICE'S COMPANY. (County Unknown)

Served from August 22 until October 3, 1812.

Capt. Thomas Rice	Lieut. Thomas Vallhyning	Sergt. Abel Woodward
Sergt. Theodore Hammon	Sergt. Henry Clark	Sergt. Jonothan Gaylord, Jr.
Corp. Samuel Osman	Corp. Gibson Gates	Corp. William Lappin
Drummer, Zenas Kelsey	Fifer, Thomas Gaylord	

Privates.	Privates.	Privates.
Baker, Samuel	Cackler, Abraham	Gaylord, Stewart
Haymaker, John	Haymaker, George	Johnston, Nathan
Latta, Moses	Lappin, John	Nighman, George
Owen, Thomas	Powers, George	Rodgers, Constant
Strong, David	Turner, Samuel	Turner, John
Vaner, Abel	Wyatt, Ezra	Wells, John
Woodward, Stephen		

ROSTER OF OHIO SOLDIERS IN WAR OF 1812 143

Page 432. Vol. I.

ROLL OF CAPT. SAMUEL HALE'S COMPANY. (County Unknown)
Served from August 22 until October 3, 1812.

Rank and Name of Soldier.	Rank and Name of Soldier.	Rank and Name of Soldier.
Capt. Samuel Hale	Lieut. William Honson	Ensign, Jamin Hulbert
Sergt. Charles Crittenden	Sergt. Ira Hulbert	Sergt. Alexander Hall
Sergt. Martin Kemp, Jr.	Corp. Daniel Culver	Corp. Johan Blakely
Corp. Barnabus Williams	Corp. William Johnson	Drummer, Bradford Waldo
Privates.	**Privates.**	**Privates.**
Adams, Moses Jr.	Allen, Nathaniel	Allen, Jesse
Baird, Joseph	Baird, William	Beach, James
Buzzard, Henry	Baird, James	Bradford, Moses
Boosinger, George	Boosinger, John	Bellows, Ithmar
Bradley, Ariel	Bradley, Justice	Baird, Robert
Cook, David	Cunningham, Amzi	Chamberlain, Luther
Dunlap, Thomas	DeHaven, Nathaniel	Elliott, George
Fretih John	Hall, David	Hall, James
Hall, John	Hale, John	Hale, Thomas
Hart, William	Holcomb, Timothy	Haines, Samuel
Haines, Benjamin	Haines, John	Kent, James
Moore, Lee	Minard, Daniel	Martin, John
McCormick, James	Norton, Peter	Pelton, John
Spicer, Minard	Sackett, Harvey	Sackett, Leander
Simcock, George	Smith, Robert	Tickner, David
Tickner, John	Tupper, Ezekial	Tupper, Reuben
Upson, Reuben	Upson, Stephen	Van Garden, James
Way, David	Whittlesey, Harvey	Willis, Martin

Page 433

ROLL OF CAPT. EBENEZER HARMON'S COMPANY. (County Unknown.)
Served from August 22 until October 7, 1812.

Capt. Ebenezer Harmon	Lieut. Joseph Eggleston	Ensign, Eber Kennedy
Sergt. Chauncey Eggleston	Sergt. Brainard Spencer	Corp. Jonothan B. Russell
Corp. Eli Cannon	Corp. Warren Squire	Corp. Justice Parrish
	Fifer, Isaac D. Faxon	
Privates.	**Privates.**	**Privates.**
Ayres, Asa	Blackman, John H.	Bidlake, Daniel
Baldwin, Eliakim	Blair, Behan	Baldwin, James
Blackman, Elijah, Jr.	Blair, James	Baldwin, Sanford
Baldwin, Henry	Baldwin, Caleb	Cannon, George
Cannon, Stephen	Bissell, Orris	Crooks, William
Eggleston, Moses	Ferguson, Samuel H.	Granger, Horace
Eggleston, Martin	Herrick, James W.	Kent, Zeno
Kent, Zardis	Messenger, Ebenezer	Norton, Lebbeus
Kennedy, Zebno	Norton, Selden	Norton, Eber
McConnekey, Jarvis	McHerdry, James	Plum, James
Perkins, Grant	Peese, Jem	Riley, Julius, Jr.
Richardson, Micaiah	Russell, Samuel	Riley, Eppy
Squire, Aaron	Singletary, John C.	Spencer, George
Sweet, Amos	Sheldon, Gershon	Webb, Lyman
Wheeler, Oliver	White, Joel	

Page 434.

ROLL OF CAPT. PHILLIP McNEME'S COMPANY. (County Unknown.)
Served from August 14 until October 14, 1812.

Capt. Phillip McNeme	Lieut. John Jackson	Ensign, D. Hoffman
Sergt. John Clark	Sergt. Jonothan Corbell	Sergt. Charles Shukley
Sergt. Jacob Crabil	Corp. John Dillman	Corp. Isaac Temple
Corp. John Cook	Corp. William D. Baily	Drummer, John Botts
	Fifer, Noah Downs	
Privates.	**Privates.**	**Privates.**
Ater, Jacob	Ater, George	Brown, Joseph
Bready, James	Briggs, Walter	Clark, Stephen
Champ, Alexander	Davis, Jeremiah	Davis, Benjamin
Gordy, Thomas	Hammon, William	Hines, Jacob
Leonard, Alexander	McRea, Alexander	Nolin, Thomas
Nier, Jacob	Nolan, Edward	Redman, James
Smith, Jonas	Stothard, Joseph	Shanton, Charles
Thompson, O.	Thompson, Igantius	Timins, Stephen
Watson, Robert		

Page 435.

ROLL OF CAPT. CHARLES WOLVERTON'S COMPANY.
(Probably from Miami County.)
Served from August 24 until September 23, 1812.

Capt. Charles Wolverton	Lieut. James Blue	Ensign, Reuben Westfall
Sergt. Samuel Kyle	Sergt. Ezekial Kirtley	Sergt. James Morrow
Sergt. James Brown	Corp. John Pelford	Corp. John McClary
Corp. James Marshall	Corp. Nathaniel Garard	

ROLL OF CAPT. CHARLES WOLVERTON'S COMPANY (Continued.)

Rank and Name of Soldier.

Privates.

Bedle, Solomon
Bull, Thomas
Campbell, John
Dumont, Peter
Garard, James
Gibson, Andrew
Hunt, George
Martin, Corbly
Junkins, Lancelot
Leland, Simon
Marshall, Joseph
McFarland, William
Stephenson, Robert
Westfall, Levi

Rank and Name of Soldier.

Privates.

Bedle, Samuel
Bedle, Abraham
Crossley, Joseph
Dye, William
Garard, Henry
Hay, James
Howell, Samuel
Ingerson, Benjamin
Jackson, James
Lloyd, David
McCoy, James
Pollock, John
Stephenson, William
White, Robert

Rank and Name of Soldier.

Privates.

Barnes, Robert
Bull, John
Crowder, William
Frost, William
Garard, Abner
Hamil, Hugh
Hayes, James
Junkin, George
Linvill, John
Layton, Joseph
McGallaway, James
Rodgers, Thomas Jr
Thompson, James

Pages 39-40.

ROLL OF CAPT. JAMES GATES' COMPANY.
(Probably from Champaign County.)

Served from August 18 until September 23, 1812, and from July 30 until August 13, 1813.

Capt. James Gates
Sergt. John Boyce
Sergt. Jacob Flemming
Sergt. William Boyce
Corp. Aaron Shall

Lieut. James Munire
Sergt. Aquila Ellsworth
Sergt. James Haney
Corp. Joel Thomas
Fifer, Newton Burroughs

Ensign, John Best
Sergt. Thaddeus Tuttle
Sergt. Samuel Carey
Corp. Henry Harris
Drummer, William Green

Privates.

Bulderach, Gabriel
Boyce, William
Carter, Benjamin
Dugan, John
Ellsworth, Moses
Gable, Thomas
Gates, Henry
Hall, John
Judy, Benjamin
Lockart, John
Morris, Richard
Osborn, Edward
Plummer, James
Reswin, Joseph
Sturd, James W.
Shell, Aaron
Tarbutton, Eli

Privates.

Bright, Edward
Brooks, Thomas
Collins, James
Dillon, Isaac
Fee, Lewis
Gable, Robert
Goble, Hiram
Haines, Absalom
Kenton, William
Lewis, Zebulum
McClintock, William
Osborn, James
Richards, Saul
Reagan, William B.
Smith, John
Shaffer, Peter
Wallingford, Benjamin

Privates.

Beizly, Joseph
Carter, Lewis
Caldwell, John
Dimit, James
Goodfellow, Moor
Gates, John
Garwin, William
Judy, John
Kilt, George
Moore, John
Nelson, Thomas
Plummer, Greenbe
Richards, Silas
Shell, Jonah
Sergent, Ezekial
Tuttle, John

Pages 335-336

ROLL OF CAPT. TIMOTHY TITUS' COMPANY.
(Probably from Miami County.)

Served from September 4, 1813, until March 14, 1814.

Capt. Timothy Titus
Sergt. Severs Hudson
Sergt. George Whitmore
Corp. John Devors

Lieut. Daniel West
Sergt. Daniel Mills
Corp. John Fate
Corp. Job Severs
Fifer, William McKee

Ensign, Adam Milmon
Sergt. Philip Everman
Corp. Michael Tiernan
Drummer, Ashbel Crane

Privates

Baldwin, Daniel
Bushels, Henry
Bunnel, Noah
Crook, John
Crosin, Edward
Dill, Solomon
Garwood, Willliam
Goodpaster, John
Horner, Samuel
Irvin, Eli
Kriteser, Henry
Lofort, Lewis
Myers, Jacob H.
McDonald, John
Reynard, John
Shight, Peter
Sidels, Israel
Surface, Henry
Van Skike, John
Winnings, Lewis
Yillock, Charles

Privates

Buchels, David C.
Burrows, John
Bunnel, John
Cast, John
Davis, George
Dollison, Rezing
Gray, Thomas
Gaskil, Samuel
Hurst, William
Jones, Joshua
Lacey, John
Linley, Francis
Mills, Michael
Orchey, Job
Stites, John F.
Smith, Obediah
Stipo, George
Settlemyre, William
Vineyard, John
Wells, Abraham

Privates

Baird, George
Buckles, David B.
Boner, Patrick
Cast, Archibald
Downs, David
Emmet, John
Garwood, Hosea
Hilt, William
Hayes, William D.
Kelow, Samuel
Lacey, William
Meed, Isaac N.
McLaughlin, Darby
Phillips, Thomas
Stilley, Elisha
Surface, Andrew
Stanford, Philip
Tittle, John
Waggoner, Michael
Watson, Moses

ROSTER OF OHIO SOLDIERS IN WAR OF 1812

Pages 136-137. Vol. I.

ROLL OF CAPT. ICHABOD NYE'S COMPANY (CAVALRY).
(Probably from Knox County.)
Served from August 26, until October 4, 1812.

Rank and Name of Soldier.
Capt. Ichabod Nye
Sergt. William Bartlet
Corp. Jonothan Hunt
Farrier, Michael Coliass
Privates.
Ash, David
Bonnet, Isaac
Dunlap, John
Harrod, James
Harrod, Samuel
Inlow, Jesse
Leonard, Amos
Middlemer, John
Morton, Stephen D.
Smelt, Samuel H.
Smith, George
Woodruff, Johab

Rank and Name of Soldier.
Lieut. James Craig
Sergt. Isaac Beam
Corp. Stephen D. Minton
Farrier, Michael Cleck
Privates.
Ayres, James
Berrit, David
Dickinson, George
Holmes, Nicholas
Howard, Samuel
Layton, John
Lyberger, George
Minton, Stephen
Smith, Samuel H.
Smith, James
Walker, James
Walker, Joseph
Walker, John

Rank and Name of Soldier.
Cornet, John Barney
Sergt. Solomon Giller
Trumpeter, John Kizer
Privates.
Adams, Elijah
Davidson, George
Garrison, John
Hunt, Jonothan
Irwin, John
Long, Hughes
Mills, John
Mills, Michael
Stilly, John
Selley, William H.
Waggoner, Ferall
Watson, Noah

Page 361.
ROLL OF CAPT. HENRY COONROD'S COMPANY (CAVALRY).
(Probably from Pickaway County.)
Served from May 9, until May 24, 1813.

Capt. Henry Coonrod
Sergt. Thomas R. Duncan
Sergt. Hane Harrelton
Corp. Jacob Stingly
Privates.
Adamson, Isaac
Grim, George
Johnson, James
Laundry, Simeon
Milison, Bernard

Lieut. William Nicol
Sergt. James Stanley
Corp. David Martin
Corp. Peter Augistean
Privates.
Baum, Jonas
Grim, David
Keller, George
Moore, Isaac
Nevill, Robert

Cornet, Joseph Maurice
Sergt. Thomas Harbert
Corp. Robert Johnston
Privates.
Baum, Jacob
Hossleton, Samuel
Lulby, John
Myer, William
Nichols, John

Page 367.
ROLL OF CAPT. BENONI PEARCE'S COMPANY (LIGHT DRAGOONS.)
(County Unknown.)
Served from November 1, 1812, until January 25, 1813, and part from Aug. 8 until Oct. 8, 1812.

Capt. Benoni Pearce
Sergt. James Bell
Corp. George W. Reynolds
Privates.
Alexander, William
Chandler, Samuel
Evans, David
Frazier, Mahlon
Heap, George
Mercer, Jacob
Meiers, Solomon
Prior, John

Lieut. John Lee
Sergt. Martin Chandler
Corp. Solomon Mayers
Privates.
Betz, John
Carpenter, John C.
Frazier, William
Granstaff, William
Ireland, Thomas
Marshall, Andrew
McLain, Daniel
Prior, Isaac
Woodward, William

Cornet, James Warden
Corp. John Harvey
Trumpeter, George Green
Privates.
Best, Valentine
Bowermaster, Peter
Funk, Jacob
Hawey, John
Mercer, George
Morrow, William
Parkinson, John
Scott, Samuel

Pages 368-369.
ROLL OF CAPT. JOSEPH VANCE'S COMPANY (DRAGOONS.)
(Probably from Franklin County.)
Served from August 24, until October 14, 1812. Part served from August 1, until Sept. 4, 1813.

Capt. Joseph Vance
Lieut. Jacob Keller
Sergt. Benjamin Steward
Corp. Daniel McFarland

Privates
Boggs, John
Beasley, Isaac
Dyer, Robert
Davison, Andrew
Edgar, John
Hunter, John
Hereoff, William
King, Samuel
Mark, William
McElvain, James
Parrish, Orris
Reed, Alexander
Shannon, Samuel
Smart, Isaac
Stumpbough, John
Upson, Alfred
Wing, Oliver

Lieut. Joseph Grate
Cornet, Francis Stewart
Sergt. John M. White
Corp. Adam Reed
Trumpeter, Andrew McElvain
Privates
Barr, John
Courtney, Richard
Dillingham, Ajalon
DeLashmutt, Van B.
House, Richard
Hunter, Joseph
Hill, Willard
Kile, John
McKensey, James
McElvain, John
Pinkard, William
Rennick, Asahel
Shron, Joseph
Starr, Joseph
Sullivan, Lucas
Watts, John
Winsel, John

Lieut. Jacob Read
Sergt. Daniel Liggert
Corp. Henry Weston
Corp. William Hunter

Privates
Brown, Henry
Culbertson, Samuel
Dickey, Michael
DeLashmutt, John K.
Goetschins, Nicholas
Hilsel, John
Kean, John
Kern, John
McGowan, John
McElvain, William
Power, Luther
Shannon, John
Simpkins, John
Strain, John M.
Swam, Gustavus
White, Alexander

Page 394 Vol. 1.

ROLL OF CAPT. JAMES DOUD'S COMPANY (CAVALRY.)
(County Unknown)

Served from August 22, to November 30, 1812, and from January to March, 1813.

Rank and Name of Soldier.
Capt. James Doud
Cornet, Joseph Colt
Corp. Russell, Starr
Corp. Comfort Starr

Privates
Brainard, Ira
Brainard, John
Chidester, Philo
Loveland, John
Mann, William D.
Osborn, Elias R.
Stilson, George A.
Haydon, Samuel M.
Warner, Elisha

Rank and Name of Soldier.
Lieut. Zalman Fitch
Sergt. William Fitch
Corp. Comfort Migatt
Musician, Hugh Baird

Privates
Benedict, Billy
Chidester, Hezekiah
Davidson, Samuel
Logan, William
Miles, Daniel
Pinder, Austin
Sprague, William
Turner, Conrad
Wetmore, Josiah

Rank and Name of Soldier.
Lieut. Ensign Church
Sergt. Linus Brainard
Corp. Abijah Peck
Musician Daniel Miles

Privates
Bostwick, Adna H.
Case, Ariel
Fitch, Cook
Miles, Samuel
Michaels, Moses
Ramsey, Hugh S.
Turner, Samuel
Taft, Aaron

Vol. 2, Page 394.

ROLL OF CAPT. SAMUEL McCORD'S COMPANY (CAVALRY.)
(County Unknown.)

Served from August 16, until September 18, 1812.

Capt. Samuel McCord
Cornet, James Shipman
Sergt. Sampson Hubbell
Corp. David Taylor

Privates.
Armstrong, Thomas
Clifford, John
Foley, William
Green, John
Harvey, John
Haines, William
McCoy, John
Neihle, Lawrence
Vanmeter, Jacob

Lieut. Thomas Vance
Sergt. James Roberts
Sergt. Conrad Goodlove
Trumpeter, William Eals

Privates.
Anderson, James
Dawson, John
Gibbes, Samuel
Hopkins, Richard
Hunter, George
Konklin, John
Morris, Thomas
Smallwood, Walter
Welsh, James
Ward, Robert

Lieut. James Foley
Sergt. William McKinnon
Corp. Jeremiah Curl

Privates.
Benson, George
Frazure, Benjamin
Blend, John
Harr, Daniel
Hodge, William
McDonald, James
McGrew, Mathew
Thompson, John
Ward, John B.

Pages 395-396.

ROLL OF CAPT. ELIAS MURRAY'S COMPANY (CAVALRY.)
(Probably from Delaware County.)

Served from September 20, to November 19, 1814.

Capt. Elias Murray
Cornet, Robert Jameson
Sergt. Joseph Prince
Sergt. David Dix
Sergt. Sylvester Root
Corp. Solomon Steward
Corp. Ezra Steward
Saddler, Abner Root

Privates.
Adams, Elias
Arnold, Calvin
Bush, John
Conklin, Jacob
Creamer, John
Cunningham, Joseph
Dixon, Miran
Friley, Martin
Gabriel, William
Hardin, John
Hughes, Joseph S.
Kent, William
Loofbourow, John
Munroe, Lemuel F.
Pufut, James
Riley, Henry
Slack, John
Thompson, John
Werley, Henry

Lieut. Daniel Prince
Cornet, Roswell Tulles
Sergt. Forest Meeker
Sergt. William Patton
Sergt. Aaron Welch
Corp. Nathaniel Ulyatt
Corp. Adam Shover
Farrier, James Harper

Privates.
Agord, James S.
Basker, Orlando H.
Carpenter, Alfred
Cowgill, Morris
Crown, Thomas
Davis, Eleazor
Dunn, Andrew
Foust, David
Helt, Daniel
Harper, James
Hinton, Levi
Kent, Daniel
Longwell, Ralph
Olds, Benjamin
Phelps, Levi
Root, Azariah
Smith, William
Trindle, James
Vose, Rupert

Lieut. James M. Crawford
Sergt. Cyrus Hubbard
Sergt. William Riley
Sergt. George Manvill
Sergt. James Nugent
Corp. James Carpenter
Trumpeter, William Lother

Privates.
Appleton, Bixbe
Beebe, Chauncy
Cherry, John
Crawford, David
Crunkeltin, Joseph
Dixon, Abel
Eaton, Stephen S.
Ford, Augustus
Helt, George
Hillman, Benjamin
Jones, Leonard
Kent, James
Lewis, Joseph
Meeker, Forest
Pelton, Johnson
Robinson, Mellen
Thomas, David
Wilson, John
Williamson, John

Vol.2. Page 398.

ROLL OF CAPT. CHARLES DEVOL'S COMPANY (CAVALRY.)
(Probably from Washington County.)

Served from October 20, to December 18, 1812.

Rank and Name of Soldier.	Rank and Name of Soldier.	Rank and Name of Soldier.
Capt. Charles Devol	Lieut. Isaiah Scott	Lieut. Washington Olney
Sergt. James White	Sergt. William White	Corp. John Clark
Corp. Pardon Cook	Corp. Samuel Reid	
Privates.	**Privates.**	**Privates.**
Brown, Solomon	Browning, Thomas	Finch, Maurice
Olney, Gilbert	Pixley, Argelus	Quigley, John
Shuttleworth, Joseph	Tucker, Joshua	Whittle, Samuel
	Wood, Paulus E.	

Page 399.

ROLL OF CAPT. JOHN McNEAL'S COMPANY (CAVALRY.)
County Unknown.)

Served from August 23, until October 14, 1812.

Capt. John McNeal	Lieut. William Nicols	Lieut. Jacob Markle
Cornet, George Keller	Sergt. Thomas K. Duncan	Sergt. Samuel E. Barr
Sergt. Thomas Harcell	Corp. Robert Hill	Corp. Abraham Stingley
Corp. Thomas Waddle	Corp. John Fonman	Musician, John Williams
Saddler, Charles Coveleer	Farrier, Adam Pence	
Privates.	**Privates.**	**Privates.**
Augustine Peter	Baum, Jonas	Conrad, Adam
Crane, James	Conrad, Henry	Chambers, James
Dolby, John	Ferguson, John	Ferguson, William
Grimm, George	Grimm, David	Graham, James
Hill, Eli	Hahn, Phillip	Johnson, James
Johnson, Robert	Kile, Abraham	Milliser, Barney
Martin, David	Moore, Isaac	McCort, John
Nash, Chester	Rodgers, James	Stanley, James
Stingley, Jacob	Vandorn, Hezekiah	Weaver, Anthony
Welly, John	Wilson, Andrew	Wolf, George
	Wolf, John	

Page 266

ROLL OF LIEUT. EZEKIEL BLUE'S DETACHMENT.
(Probably from Ross County.)

Served from July 28, until August 28, 1813.

Lieut. Ezekial Blue	Ensign Hugh Cook	Sergt. John Beauchant
	Corp. Isaac Johnston	
Privates	**Privates**	**Privates**
Briggs, Robert	Chamberlain, Wyatt	Funk Jacob
Surrals, Mathew	White, Daniel	White, John
	Young, John	

Page 381

ROLL OF CAPT. MOSES PATTERSON'S MOUNTED COMPANY.
(Probably from Highland County.)

Served from September 14, until October 14, 1812.

Capt. Moses Patterson	Lieut. David Strain	Ensign Samuel Evans
Sergt. Augustus Richards	Sergt. James Rodgers	Sergt. Joseph Patterson
Sergt. John McConnel	Corp. John Thornton	Corp. Price Evans
Corp. James Jolly	Corp. Samuel McConnel	
Privates	**Privates**	**Privates**
Adair, George	Buckham, Thomas	Blair, John
Connell, John	Davies, Jacob	Evans, Dan
Flinn, Joshua	Finch, Josiah	Frame, George
Harper, James	Hinton, Evans	Hedd, Bigges
Jolly, David	Keys, William	Lamb, Maxwell
Midseker, David	Monn, William	Morrow, William
McMunn, William	McConnel, James	Pittenger, Nicholas
Rapp, David	Riddick, Samuel D.	Strain, John R.
Smalley, Joseph	Swartz, Sebastian	Swartz, Henry
Tayler, William	Templin, Peter	Wilson, John

Page 393 Vol. I.

ROLL OF CAPT. G. W. BARRERE'S COMPANY (CAVALRY.)
(Probably from Highland County.)

Served from April 30, 1812, until May 6, 1813.

Rank and Name of Soldier.	Rank and Name of Soldier.	Rank and Name of Soldier.
Capt. G. W. Barrere	Lieut. John Davidson	Ensign John Elliott
Sergt. Sovereign Brown	Sergt. Peter Hoop	Sergt. Robert Hunter
Sergt. Benjamin Eakins	Corp. Henry Addison	Corp. David N. Gardner
Corp. Gideon Jackson	Corp. William Davidson	Bugler, Wm. Stockton

Privates.

Bond, Henry	Badgley, Robert	Barnes, Jacob
Boatman, Elias	Barden, George	Bowman, John
Borden, John	Barngrover, George	Borden, David
Borden, Jacob	Charles, Andrew	Campton, William
Colvin, John	Campton, Robert	Duckwall, John
Davidson, John	Eakins, St. Clear	Gibler, John
Gibler, Phillip	Grisley, Levi	Hill, William
Hough, Paton	Hoffman, Jacob	Hair, John
Jackson, James	Losier, John	Morrow, Robert, Sr.
Morrow, Robert, Jr.	Malcom, James	Malcom, Samuel
Moury, Samuel	McKinley, Robert	McQuinty, William
Nelson, William	Nesbit, Robert	Osborn, Enoch
Parkison, George	Robison, William	Robison, George
Roberts, Joshua	Ross, John	Swaim, Joseph
Sanderson, William	Welkins, Abraham	

Page 397 Vol. 2.

ROLL OF CAPT. WILLIAM KENDALL'S COMPANY (CAVALRY.)
(Probably from Scioto County.)

Served from July 28, until August 28, 1813.

Capt. William Kendall	Lieut. George Clengman	Lieut. Allen Moore
Cornet, William Jones	Sergt. Nathan Glover	Sergt. James Collins
Sergt. Samuel G. Jones	Sergt. Joseph Boynton	Corp. Charles C. Boynton
Corp. Samuel Nichols	Corp. John Clengman	Corp. Thomas Brown
Musician, William Lowery	Farrier, Lloyd Johnstin	

Privates

Adams, Francis	Brady, Samuel	Brown, John
Burley, Daniel	Burkles, William	Bennet, Thomas
Barger, Jacob	Byerly, Michael	Conner, Cornelius
Clark, Jonothan	Curtis, Joseph	Fuert, Benjamin
Gunn, Howell	Glover, Elijah	Gharkey, David
Huff, Jesse	Huff, Caleb	Hall, Samuel A.
James, John	King, John	Lock, Benjamin
Margrove, Abner	Munn, James	Moore, Lewis
McKinney, Solomon	Prather, John	Phillips, James
Robey, William	Richert, Henry	Robison, William
Sheley, Henry	Shangler, Jacob	Sappinger, Thomas
Slack, Abraham	Taylor, Nimrod	Welch, Abraham
White, Uriah	Young, Samuel	

Page 400.

ROLL OF CAPT. ALEXANDER GIBSON'S COMPANY (ARTILLERY.)
(Probably from Butler County.)

Served from September 11, until November 30, 1812.

Capt. Alexander Gibson	Lieut. William Karr	Sergt. Andrew Drips
Sergt. John Cox	Sergt. John S. Ludlow	Sergt. Joseph Winkley
Corp. Sampson Mooney	Corp. Richard McPike	Drummer Alvin Wheeler
	Fifer, Samuel Bonnet	

Privates

Ayers, John	Ayers, Isaac	Baun, Jonas
Clark, William	Cask, John S.	Craven, John
Coleman, Avery	Crow, Thomas S.	Coppin, Joseph
Donald, James	Engle, Philip	Evans, Robert
Fotherzole, Geo. W.	Garret, Curtis	Gardner, Robert
Handley, John	Looker, Samuel B.	Love, Peter
McDonald, James	McMaster, William	Nelson, Robert
Norris, Richard	Satterly, Isaac	Potts, Charles
Smith, Thomas B.	Sedan, Jacob	Smith, John
Shank, John	White, John	White, Thomas
Whiteside, William		

ROSTER OF OHIO SOLDIERS IN WAR OF 1812

Page 382. Vol. 2.

ROLL OF CAPT. JACOB FUDGE'S MOUNTED COMPANY.
(Probably from Warren County.)

Served from September 27, until October 20, 1812.

Rank and Name of Soldier.	Rank and Name of Soldier.	Rank and Name of Soldier.
Capt. Jacob Fudge	Lieut. Joseph Stephens	Ensign William Campbell
Sergt. John Fiester	Sergt. Robert Morris	Sergt. Jacob Woots
Privates.	**Privates.**	**Privates.**
Ayers, Michael	Button, James	Bonta, Peter A.
Chambers, John	Crow, William	Cox, Joshua
Forquer, Thomas	Haynes, David	Harbsell, Abraham
Hartter, George	Jamison, John	Kitchen, Stephen
Lee, Henry	Myers, George	Mills, Joseph
McMahon, Joseph	Newton, Henry	Payon, Jacob
Ridenour, Samuel	Ridenour, Jonothan	Ridenour, Peter
Rabourne, Joseph	Stinson, Alexander	Sellers, John
Toler, William	Trinkle, John	Thompson, James
Welsh, John	Vanest, John	

Page 383

ROLL OF CAPT. JOHN ELLIS' MOUNTED COMPANY.
(Probably from Adams County.)

Served from September 28, until October 28, 1812.

Capt. John Ellis	Lieut. Elijah Martin	Ensign William Dunlap
Sergt. John Evans	Sergt. Peter Wiles	Sergt. Adam McPherson
Privates.	**Privates.**	**Privates.**
Austin, Nelson	Alexander, John	Bland, Micajah
Cutler, Benjamin	Cormick, James	Ellis, Samuel
Fetters, Charles	Flaugher, Jacob	Henry, John
McKenny, Hezekiah	McPherson, David	Reeves, Ila
Reeves, Daniel	Riggs, Zach	Wiles, Christian
	Yates, William	

Page 384.

ROLL OF CAPT. DANIEL COLLIER'S MOUNTED COMPANY.
(County Unknown.)

Served from September 30, until October 28, 1812.

Capt. Daniel Collier	Lieut. Seth Vanmatre	Ensign Isaac Earles
Sergt. Peter Lewis	Sergt. Jonothan Horne	
Privates.	**Privates.**	**Privates.**
Boyd, Jonothan	Biddle, George	Cox, Jacob
Clay, Mathew	Chapman, Nathaniel	Cobbler, David
Davis, William	Downing, Meshach	Killen, John
Metz, Jacob	Mines, James	Mershon, Daniel
Newland, Jacob	Porter, James	Taylor, William
Thompson, James	Wikoff, Samuel	

Page 385.

ROLL OF CAPT. SAMUEL DAVIS' MOUNTED COMPANY.
(Probably from Ross County.)

Served from September 28, until October 28, 1812.

Capt. Samuel Davis	Lieut. Daniel Robbins	Ensign George Teter
Sergt. Daniel Hare	Sergt. Philip Hare	Sergt. Thomas McDonald
	Sergt. Hugh Cochran	
Privates.	**Privates.**	**Privates.**
Boye, George	Boye, Francis	Boggs, Joseph
Blair, William	Canida, Robert	Core, Henry
Canley, John	Clover, Peter	Dean, James
Davis, Asa	Edmiston, John	Gradless, William
Hester, Henry	Hopkins, Moses	Hare, Jacob
Huston, Joseph	McDonald, Thomas	Pummel, James
Riley, James	Rockhold, Joseph	Robbins, Moses
Shirlock, Edward	Shannon, Thomas	Smithson, Joseph
Waugh, Lemon	Yaren, Adam	

Page 386.

ROLL OF CAPT. THOMAS LEWIS' MOUNTED COMPANY.
(Probably from Ross County.)

Served from September 28, until October 28, 1812.

Capt. Thomas Lewis	Sergt. John Hayslip	Sergt. Peter Shults
Privates.	**Privates.**	**Privates.**
Bayless, John	Bayless, Nathan	Blake, Samuel
Casseldine, John	Campbell, John	Campbell, Samuel
Cain, James	Cain, Jesse	Cormick, James
Earley, George	Earley, Michael	Morehead, Mathew
McBride, James	Saunders, Francis	Scott, Joseph
Redman, George	Washburn, Nathaniel	Wilson, Benoni

Pages 179-180 Vol. I.

ROLL OF CAPT. WILLIAM HUSTON'S MOUNTED COMPANY
(Probably from Scioto County.)

Served from October 1, until November 1, 1812.

Rank and Name of Soldier.

Capt. William Huston
Sergt. Nathan Glover

Privates

Applegate, Charles
Boynton, Joseph E.
Dollarhead, William
Chamberlain, Anson
Curany, Mathew
Darlington, Samuel
Gunn, Zina
Jones, David
Kelby, John
Moore, Phillip, Jr.
Power, William
Robey, William
Salada, John
Turner, John R.
Wheeler, Amos

Rank and Name of Soldier.

Lieut. Allen Moore
Sergt. Samuel G. Jones
Sergt. Ezra Osborn

Privates

Bartow, Kimber
Burk, William M.
Davison, Nathaniel
Chamberlain, Hyatt
Carpenter, William
Fuqua, Moses M.
Grant, William
Jones, William
Loyd, Johnson
McKenney, Solomon
Perry, Samuel
Smith, John
Tomlison, John
Thompson, James
Wilson, Braden

Rank and Name of Soldier.

Cornet, Uriah White
Sergt. James Collins

Privates

Brown, John, Jr.
David, Elnathan
Barkels, Frederick
Chappen, Reuben
Cannon, John
Glover, Asa
Hammett, John
Johnston, John
Musgrove, Abner
Pain, Olney
Rankin, William
Swords, William
Thompson, Robert
Wheeler, Nathaniel

Pages 181-182

ROLL OF LIEUT. JOHN HAYSLIP'S MOUNTED COMPANY.
(County Unknown.)

Served from September 13, until December 9, 1814.

Lieut. John Hayslip
Sergt. Thomas Lockhart

Privates

Bayless, Daniel
Briggs, Thomas
Carey, Isaac
Galloway, James
Harris, Thomas
Murphy, Recompense
McCollum, Isaac
Paul, John
Rader, John
Strict, Joseph
Warren, Peter

Lieut. Isaac Foster
Sergt. James Hayslip

Privates

Browning, Edman
Collins, Elijah
Dining, Daniel
Hubanks, Foster
Lambert, Joseph
Mannan, William
Pemberton, Fountain
Pollard, John
Sparks, George
Sutton, William G.
Woods, Simon

Ensign John Moore
Sergt. William Rowland

Privates

Baird, Robert
Crawford, George
Ellison, Andrew
Hempleman, Jacob
Moore, John
McHenry, Alexander
Paul, James
Pennington, Obediah
Stephenson, John
Walker, Joseph
Walling, William

Pages 183-184

ROLL OF CAPT. JOHN FOSTER'S MOUNTED COMPANY.
(Probably from Ross County.)

Served from September 14, until October 14, 1812.

Capt. John Foster
Sergt. David Lyons
Sergt. William Slaughter
Corp. Samuel Corwin

Privates

Burke, Paul
Bogart, Cornelius
Hodges, Daniel
Henson, Harrod
Jacks, Gardner
Leads, Absalom
Mount, Eli
Stewart, William
Wells, Peter

Lieut. John Woods
Sergt. Corwin George
Corp. Abraham Stewart
Corp. Thomas Graham

Privates

Bevens, Philip
Carter, Henry
Hoover, Jacob
Heath, Richard
Loney, John
Longshore, James
Pancake, John
Switzer, Peter
Wilson, George

Ensign Richard Tomlinson
Sergt. John Heath
Corp. William McCorkle
Corp. Caleb Wilson

Privates

Bishong, John
Debruler, Jacob
Hampton, Dudley
Hamson, John
Hulse, William
Lockhart, Elijah
Scott, Peter
Wood, Jonathan

Page 185.

ROLL OF CAPT. WILLIAM LEEDOM'S MOUNTED COMPANY.
(Probably from Ross County.)

Served from September 28, until October 28, 1812.

Capt. William Leedom

Privates.

Baird, Robinson
Ellison, James
Marcus, Jacob

Lieut. George Bryan
Sergt. Robert Baird

Privates.

Edgington, Isaac
Gutridge, Charles
Naylor, George

Sergt. William Smith

Privates.

Edgington, Joshua
Hoslip, John
Waldran, Henry

Pages 186-187. Vol. I.

ROLL OF CAPT. JAMES DUNLAP'S MOUNTED COMPANY.
(Probably from Ross County.)

Served from July 28, until August 17, 1813.

Rank and Name of Soldier.	Rank and Name of Soldier.	Rank and Name of Soldier.
Capt. James Dunlap	Lieut. James McCoy	Ensign John Rodgers
Privates.	**Privates.**	**Privates.**
Benedick, James	Benedick, George	Barton, Jesse
Beal, Philip	Blue, John M.	Blue, John
Boyd, Francis	Brown, James	Corbet, Joseph
Corbett, David	Coon, Henry	Coon, Adam
Clark, James	Dawnard, James	Dyer, William
Currey, William	Dines, James	Gatt, Jacob
Gilfillen, John	Grady, John	Gamble, John
Heness, William	Henderson, David	Innis, William
Jamison, Charles	Johnson, Thomas	Kirkbride, John
Lisney, John	Latta, Moses	May, Henry
Miller, James	Mitchell, John	Miskinens, William
Mace, John	McCoy, Dickson	McCoy, Alexander
McNeal, John	McCafferty, Richard	McKee, Mathew
McCluer, James	McLaughlin, William	McCoy, John
Newman, George	James, Adam	Parrish, Meredith
Parker, Jesse	Reaves, John	Rinley, Daniel
Rosaboom, John	Rayburn, John	Robinson, William
Stone, Daniel	Stanton, Abraham	Shoemaker, Peter
Thompson, Wheeler	Timmens, John W.	Wilcut, John
	Walker, William	

Page 188.

ROLL OF CAPT. JOHN BOGGS' MOUNTED COMPANY.
(Probably from Ross County.)

Served from September 27 until October 14, 1812.

Capt. John Boggs	Lieut. William Miller	Ensign Daniel Musselman
Sergt. Henry David	Sergt. James Roberts	Sergt. Jacob Frazer
	Sergt. Valentine Angel	
Privates.	**Privates.**	**Privates.**
Abbott, Elijah	Baum, Jacob	Campbell, William
Bunsey, John	Ernheart, Jacob	Evans, David
Forsman, Robert	Galbraith, John	Jones, John
Johnston, James	Kooder, John	Kieler, James
Levengood, Jacob	Lobaugh, Daniel	McKinnon, William H.
McKinnon, Daniel	Newhouse, Anthony	Price, James
Pollard, John D.	Phillips, James	Rennels, John
Rooder, Peter	Reid, William	Rowe, George
Simms, William	Smith, John	Willenmyer, Jacob

Pages 189-190.

ROLL OF CAPT. WILLIAM RUTLEDGE'S MOUNTED COMPANY.
(Probably from Ross County.)

Served from May 7, until May 20, 1813.

Capt. William Rutledge	Lieut. William Lamb	Ensign James Reyborn
Sergt. Nathaniel Spencer	Sergt. Daniel Kerr	Sergt. Garnet Lauman
Sergt. John Watson	Corp. John Gilfillan	Corp. James Bramble
Corp. William Baley	Corp. James McCallister	
Privates.	**Privates.**	**Privates.**
Anderson, Levi	Anderson, John	Arrington, David
Brown, Edmond	Brown, Peter	Baitman, William
Clifford, James	Clark, John	Chestnut, William
Crampton, John	Clark, William	Curtis, Drayton N.
Edwards, Edward	Fortimer, Richard	Frye, Joseph
Fultz, Conder	Fortney, Peter	Gibbs, James
Green, George	Hume, George	James, Adam
Kelley, Jonothan	Leister, Peter	Lownes, George
Lacey, John	Mills, Levin	Millar, William
Mayhigh, Levin	McCormick, Samuel	McCollister, Henry
McCollister, Daniel	Onley, Charles	Phillips, James
Pickens, John	Prentice, Henry L.	Reese, Ludwick
Romine, Elias	Romine, Amos	Stoll, Frederick
Smith, Amos	Smith, George	Smith, Green
Snyder, John	Scott, James	Thompson, Abraham
Tucker, John	Tiffin, Clayton	Thompson, William
Thompson, Joseph	Utt, Adam	Utt, Jacob
Walker, John	Williams, William	White, Thornely L.
Wright, Moses H.		

Pages 191-192. Vol. 2.

ROLL OF CAPT. JOHN CAMPBELL'S MOUNTED COMPANY.
(Probably from Ross County.)
Served from September 13, until December 9, 1814.

Rank and Name of Soldier.

Capt. John Campbell
Lieut. John Evans
Sergt. Jonothan Wisner

Privates.

Bishop, Peter
Copple, Daniel
Dunlap, Alexander
Edwards, George
Greenley, William
Glendenning, John
Knox, John
Middleton, William
Pricherd, James
Payn, Benjamin
Runnels, Henry
Stewart, William M.
Shreve, Caleb
Shaw, James
Wills, William

Rank and Name of Soldier.

Lieut. Samuel Ellis
Sergt. David Lawwill
Sergt. Charles Larsh
Musician, James Lawwill

Privates.

Cooper, Thomas
Canley, Thomas
Ellis, Jeremiah
Elsey, Lewis
Gardner, Simon
Hewitt, Richard
Key, Samuel M.
McPherson, Samuel
Parker, William
Reid, Traves
Rains, John
Stewart, William
Stivers, James
Prickett, William
Wisby, Joseph
Wills, James

Rank and Name of Soldier.

Lieut. Peter Shaw
Sergt. Joseph Runnels
Sergt. James Brownfield

Privates.

Conn, Robert
Davison, William
Ellis, Jesse
Elaney, Moses
Grimes, William
Kratzer, Joseph
Mahaffey, William
Newlen, James
Pritchard, Jacob
Rains, Alexander
Springer, Job
Scott, John
Shaw, Russle
Turner, John
Wherry, James

Page 198.

ROLL OF CAPT. WILLIAM MILLER'S MOUNTED COMPANY.
(Probably from Pickaway County.)
Served from May 8, until May 20, 1813, and from February 16, until March 16, 1814.

Capt. William Miller
Sergt. Joshua Miller
Corp. Thomas Spillman

Privates.

Bowsher, Anthony
Bawton, Adam
Colter, Charles
Dickson, George
Graham, Robert
House, John
Hobbs, Richards
Hannady, William
Meyres, Jacob
Reister, George
Spicer, Jonothan
Shaw, Samuel
Stoder, Christopher
Wollenton, Thomas

Lieut. Peter Rou
Sergt. Henry Wise
Corp. Benjamin Reynals

Privates.

Blair, William
Brown, Robert
Cade, Dorman
Funk, Henry
Gibson, Robert
Hively, Jacob
Justice, Jesse
Kenser, Peter
Rush, Josiah
Richardson, John
Swaggart, Daniel
Sullivant, James
Neff, Adam
Walton, Jacob
Wintin, William

Ensign Jacon Frazier
Sergt. George Hoffman

Privates.

Bryner, John
Bothin, George
Craig, David
Ferrin, Daniel
Hannan, Samuel
Hardesty, Richard
Johnston, Henry
Loofborrow, Peter
Ross, Jacob D.
Stoke, Jacob
Strouse, Philip
Streevy, Joseph
Wolfly, Coonrad
Whitsel, Samuel

Pages 204-205.

ROLL OF CAPT. WILLIAM KENDALL'S MOUNTED COMPANY.
(Probably from Ross County.)
Served from September 13, until September 20, 1814.

Capt. William Kendall
Sergt. Nathan Glover
Sergt. John Knox

Privates.

Andrews, John
Brady, Samuel
Brown, John
Culp, Jacob
Culp, Cornelius
Emmons, Case
Funk, Jacob
Greaves, George
Hitchcock, James
Huston, William
Hice, Phillip
Long, Joel
McDowell, John
Normon, James
Payton, William
Rankins, William
Spangler, Jacob
Triggs, Thomas
Wheeler, Isaac
Wood, Daniel

Lieut. George W. Clingman
Sergt. Samuel G. Jones
Saddler, James Beacham
Musician, William Lowery

Privates.

Abbot, James
Barber, Isaac
Brickles, William
Codot, Lemuel
Dawson, Abijah
Ferguson, John
Feurt, Gabriel
Gee, Joseph
Hewet, Thomas
Hull, Isaac
Kirkendall, David
Moore, Philip
McAuley, Henry
Noel, John, Jr.
Patten, James
Ritter, Frederick
Sheets, John
Vincen, Jesse
Wilson, James
White, Copley

Ensign, Allen Moore
Sergt. Charles C. Boynton
Farrier, Johnston Loyd

Privates.

Armstrong, Jeremiah
Bonsor, Samuel
Bonner, Cornelius
Collins, John
Davison, Nathaniel
Flanders, Ezekiel
Feurt, Thomas
Hice, Andrew
Horley, Andrew
Headley, William
Lowderback, Zechariah
Moore, Lucius
Noel, John
Obourn, James
Price, Joseph
Sapington, Stephen
Timmons, John
Wilson, Barnabas
Williams, Robert

ROSTER OF OHIO SOLDIERS IN WAR OF 1812 153

Page 219. Vol. I.
ROLL OF CAPT. NATHANIEL MASSIE'S MOUNTED COMPANY.
(Probably from Ross County.)
Served from May 1, until May 19, 1813.

Rank and Name of Soldier.	Rank and Name of Soldier.	Rank and Name of Soldier.
Capt. Nathaniel Massie	Lieut. James Menary	Ensign Samuel Wilson
Sergt. Alexander Menary	Sergt. John McDonald	Sergt. Gustavus Wilson
Corp. Henry Kiewsley	Corp. Meredith Parish	Corp. John Dunlap
Privates.	**Privates.**	**Privates.**
Armstrong, John	Bukman, Abraham	Blackstone, John
Brown, George	Beckman, William	Bryan, George
Cummins, Hermandez	Cary, Isaac	Cochran, James
Camble, William	Camble, Dunning	Cochran, David H.
Clawson, John	Dunlap, James	Dyer, Robert
Edwards, James	Elliott, David	Ford, William
Gunston, Thomas	Gray, James G.	Goth, Jacob
Hedges, Enoch	Hamilton, John	Hemphill, Andrew
Jank, John	Jenkins, Samuel	Kilgore, William
Kent, William	Loyan, Samuel	Ludlow, William
Morris, John	Mathews, Alexander	Morgan, Amaziah
Montgomery, Hugh	McCraken, Isaac	McArthur, Duncan
McCullough, John	McCoy, Dixon	McLain, Alexander
Parker, William	Porter, George	Russell, Reuben
Rockhold, Joseph	Reeves, Samuel	Rider, Jacob
Storm, John	Shaffer, Menary	Stockton, George
Shields, John	Showden, Samuel	Turner, James B.
Taylor, Joseph	Wilcox, William	Ward, John
Walsh, Joseph	Watts, Hamey	

Page 220.
ROLL OF CAPT. JAMES RENICK'S MOUNTED COMPANY.
(County Unknown.)
Served from May 7, until May 18, 1813.

Capt. James Renick	Ensign Daniel Hoffman	Sergt. John Stephenson
Sergt. James McKinsey	Sergt. David Marsh	Sergt. David Thomas
Privates.	**Privates.**	**Privates.**
Alkire, John	Brown, Zechariah	Burbridge, Benjamin
Barnes, William	Cochran, Alexander	Casler, James
Campbell, Joseph	Crippin, Joseph	Driver, James
Dyer, Robert	Dodd, Isaac	Graham, William
Heath, Asahel	Hollings, George	Hayse, Maurice
Leavell, John	Messick, Nathan	Madden, John
Martin, John	McGroves, Isaac	McKinney, Henry
Renick, Asahel	Stephenson, David	Willetts, John
Ward, Absalom	Wischart, Henry	Yates, David

Pages 235-236-237-238.
ROLL OF CAPT. JOHN ROADANNOUR'S MOUNTED COMPANY.
(From Gallia County.)
Served from August 1, to September 4, 1813.

	Lieut. Luther Shepherd	Ensign Nathan Nuson
Capt. John Roadannour	Lieut. Luther Shepherd	Ensign Nathan Nuson
Ensign John Kerr	Ensign John Ellison	Sergt. Anthony R. Magnet
Sergt. Alvan Rathburn	Sergt. Frederick Kerns	Corp. William T. Graves
Corp John Vandenbender	Corp William Chandler	Musician, Jonah Powell
Privates.	**Privates.**	**Privates.**
Aleshire, John	Arthur, Benjamin	Aleshire, Peter
Aleshire, Abraham	Arthur, Amos	Arthur, Nimrod
Aleshire, David	Archer, Earl P.	Brown, James Ellison
Bucher, John	Bailey, David	Bailey, John
Blagg, Samuel W.	Byers, George	Burris, George
Benedick, E. H.	Cating, John	Calhoun, Robert V.
Cooper, Charles	Durst, Daniel	Denham, Daniel
Ewings, William	Enstminger, John	Fletcher, Joseph
Farr, George	Fuller, Alfred T.	Gaston, Jonah
Glasburn, George	Gillasple, Moses	Holcomb, Samuel P.
Hubbel, Abijah	Hale, John	Hackett, Jeremiah
Highley, Cyrus	Holcomb, Stephen	Hank, Isaac, Jr.
Hughes, Silas	Hughes, Jonothan	Hysel, Frances
Humphrey, William	Hill, Jacob	Howell, William
Huston, Joseph	Heeten, David	Hawk, Isaac, Sr.
Hysell, Leonard	Hubbell, Jesse	Hoppis, George
Jones, Phillip	Jones, Thomas	Keeten, George
Kelley, Isom	Keeten, William	Lyman, Samuel
Lotz, Abraham	Lawless, Pressley	Long, Elisha
Long, Benjamin	Maples, Fanny	Mathews, James
Miller, Joseph	Miller, Isaac	Mosbarger, Joseph
Moore, Elijah	Mennehan, Edward	Moler, John
Miller, Charles	Moler, Daniel	Montgomery, David
McCoy, Joseph	McCarty, David	Pinkerton, John
Putnam, William	Parsons, Horris	Reese, Patrick
Rhay, Martin	Russell, William	Stone, Erastus
Shasteen, John	Smith, William	Scott, Charles
Saxton, John	Sharp, John	Swim, John
Shaw, Cushing	Scurloch, Hugh	Simonne, Francis
Thomas, Jason	VanShultz, Alexander	Wooten, Thomas
Wooten, Samuel	Wells, Zimri	Williams, Jonothan

Pages 239-240. Vol. I.

ROLL OF CAPT. DAVID SHELBY'S MOUNTED COMPANY.
(Probably from Ross County.)
Served from September 4, until October 14, 1812.

Rank and Name of Soldier.	Rank and Name of Soldier.	Rank and Name of Soldier.
Capt. David Shelby	Lieut. John Barnes	Ensign Jonothan Clark
Sergt. Samuel Jones	Sergt. Joseph Martin	Sergt. James Delay
Sergt. Moses Coleston	Corp. Elias Reed	Corp. Arthur Chenewith
Corp. James Ruckman	Corp. Henry Morris	
Privates.	**Privates.**	**Privates.**
Brown, William	Chenewith, Isaac	Chenewith, Thomas
Carter, Henry	Chenewith, John	Chenewith, Jacob
C———, Thomas	C———, Abner	Davies, William H.
Evans, John	Evans, Lewis	Frazier, David
Frazier, James	Gutheny, John, Jr.	Groves, Lewis
Glass, Joseph	Guthery, Joseph	Guthery, John, Sr.
Guthrie, William	Hamilton, William	Hopkins, William
Huston, James	Hotsenbiller, Jacob	Hatton, William
Howard, Joseph	Justice, John	Jenkins, James
Jenkins, Baldwin	Heaverlo, James	King, David
Kerr, Thomas	Krug, John	Manary, Hugh
Myers, Samuel	Perrell, John	Rawlings, Nathan
Rodgers, Hezekiah	Rodgers, Lewis	Stalcup, John
Shelby, Joseph	Stipp, Abraham	Swan, Thomas
Smith, Edward H.	Verden, William	Williams, Joseph
	Williams, Nathan	

Pages 272-273.

ROLL OF CAPT. JOHN LOGAN'S MOUNTED COMPANY.
(Probably from Ross County.)
Served from September 14, until December 9, 1814.

Capt. John Logan	Lieut. Francis Thompson	Ensign James Wells
Sergt. William Tangber	Sergt. James Gutherie	Sergt. Donty Utter
Sergt. Samuel Bennett	Sergt. Richard Johnson	Corp. Joseph Gossett
Privates.	**Privates.**	**Privates.**
Arthur, James	Barber, James	Calvin, Luther
Calvin, James	Corathers, Irwin	Cochran, John
Downing, Timothy	Emerson, John	Florer, James
Frazier, John	Henderson, James	Hizer, Andrew
Hedges, William	Justice, Jesse	Jenkins, Zepheniah
Latimore, Samuel	Latimore, John	Minor, Ephraim
Meranda, Samuel	Mathews, Nehemiah	McClure, Jonothan
McClean, Richard	Moore, Moses	Norris, James
Osburn, Benjamin	Parker, Jacob	Plicard, Henry
Perry, Joseph	Ross, Thomas	Prewin, Robert
Riley, Elexious	Shaw, Hugh	Swearingen, Van B.
Slider, Elijah	South, David	Smith, Johab
Suran, David	Sampson, Isaac	Sargent, Rezin
Taylor, Aaron	Wall, James	Williams, Eli
Watson, Jacob	West, Hugh	West, George

Page 274.

ROLL OF LIEUT. ANDREW GUTTERY'S MOUNTED COMPANY.
(Probably from Warren County.)
Served from September 20, to November 19, 1814.

Lieut. Andrew Guttery	Sergt. Benjamin Baldwin	Sergt. John Ulrey
Privates.	**Privates.**	**Privates.**
Coburn, Francis	Crosson, Barnwell	Cox, Richard
Cru, Robert	Feaster, Richard	Hale, Stephen
Leggett, Henry	Little, David	Miller, John
Nutt, Moses	Paxton, Samuel	Parker, George
Robertson, John	Sutton, Eli	Sibbitt, Richard
Stout, Edward	Sergeant, David	Varner, Jacob

Page 310

ROLL OF CAPT. ROBERT HAINES' MOUNTED COMPANY.
(Probably from Hamilton County.)
Served from July 29, until August 13, 1813.

Capt. Robert Haines	Lieut. Hugh Ferguson	Ensign Jonathan Donahm
Sergt. James Robb	Sergt. Hezekiah Lindsay	Sergt. Isaac Ferguson
Sergt. James Arthur	Corp. Thomas Littleton	Corp. Nathan Sutton
Corp. William Donham	Corp. Thomas Welsh	

Vol. I.
ROLL OF CAPT. ROBERT HAINES' MOUNTED COMPANY (Continued.)

Rank and Name of Soldier.	Rank and Name of Soldier.	Rank and Name of Soldier.
Privates	**Privates**	**Privates**
Apple, Daniel	Bell, William	Bittle, Josiah
Bollinger, Peter	Cuppy, Henry	Chapman, Robert
Chapman, Earnest	Clift, Horatio	Dial, John C.
Dillman, John	Frura, Michael	Ferguson, Francis
Fitzpatrick, James	Hymer, Levi B.	Hyrner, John B.
Kinsey, Jacob	Lewis, George	Loyd, Reuben
Long, Samuel	Lacock, Nathan	Mourning, Benjamin
Miller, Hamilton	Mourning, John	Mattox, Elijah
Mattox, John	McCone, Aquila	Nichols, William
Nichols, Philip	Pricket, Isaiah	Pricket, Nicholas
Roberts, Edward	Rardin, David	Rhymor, Martin
Renker, Levi	Short, Jacob	Snyder, Daniel
Whitaker, John	White, David	

Page 366
ROLL OF CAPT. THOMAS HINKSON'S MOUNTED SPIES.
(County Unknown.)
Served from February 14, 1812, until May 5, 1813

Capt. Thomas Hinkson	Lieut. Archibald Dowden	Lieut. Hugh Young
Sergt. William King	Sergt. Joseph Baker	
Privates	**Privates**	**Privates**
Bradshaw, Robert	Baker, Jacob	Carter, John
Carter, Samuel	Davis, Ezekial	Davis, Benjamin
Devne, William	Good, Isham	Graham, David
Hayes, Jacob	Hinkson, John	Inman, John
Jenkins, John	Moore, William	Mosher, Philip
McGrew, John	Redmon, Elijah	Robb, Andrew
Spencer, William	Scroufe, John	Steele, Jacob
Spencer, James	Taylor, Pierce	Tipton, William
Thornton, James	Venard, William	Venard, Francis
Walverton, Daniel	Workman, Daniel M.	

ROLL OF CAPT. DANIEL WOMELDORF'S MOUNTED COMPANY.
(From Gallia County.)
Page 376-377
Served from August 1, until August 18, 1813.

Capt. Daniel Womeldorf	Lieut. Nathaniel Gates	Lieut. James Bing
Corp. John Cocomore	Sergt. Tousaint Schouman	Sergt. James Wilson
Cornet, John Graham	Corp. Isaac Butler	Corp. John B. Noland
Sergt. Jacob Moler	Corp. Amos Chitwood	Trumpeter James Van Sent
Saddler, Peter Chapdu	Farrier, John Campbell	
Privates	**Privates**	**Privates**
Adkins, Philip	Brown, Jeremiah	Buck, William
Bing, William	Boggs, Ezekial	Cushing, Henry
Collison, William	Donally, William	Dowel, Robert
Donally, Andrew	Donally, John	Ewing, Andrew
Beck, John	Fletcher, Joseph, Jr.	Forgey, Hugh
Hickle, George	Irvin, David	Lasby, Jonothan
Martindits, John	Marvin, Calvin	Mathews, Thomas
McCarley, John	Nox, Nehemiah	Potter, Pelig
Rickabough, John	Rickabough, Adam	Rickabough, John, Jr.
Reed, William K.	Ridgeway, David	Robinson, James
Symnes, Butler	Tyler, George	Tharp, James
	Wilkes, James	

Pages 387-388. Vol. 2.
ROLL OF CAPT. JAMES WILSON'S MOUNTED COMPANY.
(Probably from Ross County.)
Served from September 28, until October 5, 1812.

Capt. James Wilson	Capt. Allen Trimble	Lieut. James Wilson
Ensign Joseph McClain	Lieut. Joseph McClain	Ensign James Odell
Sergt. William Head	Sergt. Samuel Keys	Sergt. David Mitchell
	Sergt. Joseph Davidson	
Privates.	**Privates.**	**Privates.**
Blunt, Eli	Blunt, Solomon	Boyd, Samuel
Bryam, Edward	Boatman, George	Crawford, Alexander
Chapman, Isaac	Chenney, Nathan	Chaney, Benjamin
Combs, Job	Dunham, Samuel	Davidson, John
Evans, Isaac	Greenfield, John	Grady, James
Hulet, William	Hindman, John	Hinton, Benjamin
Hinton, William	Hare, William	Hougham, Isaac
Keys, John	King, William	Lantz, Henry
Mushow, Solomon	Moyes, Littleberry	May, James
McConnel, David	Nichols, George	Odell, James
Odell, Thomas	Parmer, John	Patton, William
Rockhold, John	Swearingen, Duke	Sharp, Andrew
Stafford, James	Swadley, Jacob	Stutts, Jacob
Shelts, Peter	Strain, Samuel B.	Smallic, Isaac
Smith, Jeremiah	Trop, Jacob	West, Hiram
White, William	Wilson, James	Wilson, Thomas

Pages 400, 401, 402 Vol. 2.

ROLL OF CAPT. GEORGE SANDERSON'S COMPANY.
27th United States Infantry.
(From Fairfield, Franklin, and Delaware Counties, and part of Western Reserve.)

Served in 1813 and 1814.

Rank and Name of Soldier.	Rank and Name of Soldier.	Rank and Name of Soldier.
Capt. George Sanderson	Lieut. Abner P. Risney or Pinney	Lieut. John H. Mifford
Lieut. Arora or Andory Butler	Lieut. Andrew Bushnell	Ensign William Hall
Lieut. Abraham Fisk	Lieut. Ira Morse	Sergt. Chaney Case
Sergt. Maj. Linus Williams	Sergt. John Vanmeter	Sergt. John Nelbling
Sergt. Chauncey Miller	Sergt. Robert Sanderson	Corp. Peter Cary or Gary
Sergt. Joshua Pierce	Sergt. Luther Edson	Corp. Smith Headley
Corp. John Dugan	Corp. John Collings	
Corp. Daniel T. Bartholomew	Drummer John C. Sharp or Jonathan C. Shupe	
	Fifer Adam Leeds or Abraham Deeds	

Privates

Anderson, William	Anderson, Joseph	Atkins, John
Alloways, Joseph	Boyl, Thomas	Bartholomew, John
Berryman, John	Bixler, Henry	Bartholomew, Abraham
Bartholomew, Samuel	Braden, James	Beebee, Sheldon
Brown, James	Beaty, John	Brady, Eli
Burdinoo, Charles	Battiese, John	Baker, Daniel
Busley or Bussey, John	Billings, Thomas	Benjamin, Daniel
Case, Henry	Clark, Joseph	Cassy, Archibald
Clay, Joseph	Collins, Holden R.	Cremens, Blades
Cady, William	Case, Nathan	Cabe or Cole, Chester P.
Clark, Chaney	Cady, Samuel	Carlton, Almon
Cook, Stephen	Crosby, David	Canely, Peter
Canway, Lewis	Canway, Jacob	Davis, Jesse
Draper, Asa	Dunham, Walter	Daugherty, George
Devore, Enos	Daily, Benjamin	Evans, John
Ellinger, Joseph	Fulk, Peter	Forsythe, John
Filkall, Daniel	Faid, John	Grimes, Ephraim
Gregory, Elenathan	Gibson, Joseph	Gates, William L.
Gause, Samuel	Hunt, John	Haggarty, James
Hinkley, Josiah	Hall, John	Hartman, Frederick
Hughes, David	Holcomb, Perlin	Harter, John
Headley, Jacob	Harberson, John	Icas, John
Jee, John	Jackson, James	Jones, James
Johnson, John	Joice, Ambrose	Johnson, John L.
Kisler, John	Kissinger, George	Kincaid, James or Jonas
Kitzmiller, Jonothan	Kinisman, Samuel	Larimore, or Larimon, Joseph
Lief, Henry	Leonard, Amos	Leathers or Lathere, Fred'k
Miller, Peter	Merrill, Hosea	Mullen or Mellow, Joshua
Leonard or Loveland, Merinas W.	Lanther, or Luther, William	Mains, Henry
Moore, or Mose, James	Mapes, Thomas	McGarvey, Maurice
Miller, Andrew	McElwayne, John	McConkey or McCarkey, John
McClung, Joseph	McClung, John	McClair, or McClain, William
McCloud, Frances	McBride, John	Nickerson, Isacher
McConnell, John	McCord, Alexander	Pratt, Lemuel or Samuel
Naper, William	Osborn, George	Palmer, Luther
Parks, George	Paine, Powell or Roswell	Parkhurst or Burkhardt, Ben
Pierce, Arzell	Ray, John	Raphy, George
Ridenour, David	Reed, William	Shadley, Henry
Rogers, Elijah	Rose, Asa	Straller or Stratler, Joseph
Spry, Perry	Severs, David	Shypower, or Shyhawk, Christian
Severs, John	Smith, Christian B.	Summers, Ephraim
Sunderland, John	Shears, Mynder	Shoup, or Shroup, Jacob
Smith, Charles	Strait, Hendy C.	Skolls or Skills, Henry
Smith, John	Senor, or Siner Adam	Sheanar, Solomon
Serdan, Jonothan	Sharp, Thomas	Trevinger, Jacob
Shadwick, George	Taylor, David S.	Tucker, Frederick
Tesler, Frederick	Thorp, Benjamin	Tyler, Seymoor
Thorp, John I.	Twadle, Joseph	Vanney, L.
Vanney, I.	Vancleaf, P.	Weaver, James
White, Ansel	Walker, Alexander	Walters, David
Wright, Joseph	Wheatley, Thomas	Wolffly, Coonrod
Wheeler, Jacob	Welshaus, John	Wilson, Archibald
Williams, Flavel	Wallace, William	Wilson, Joseph
Woodsworth, D.	Watson, William	Zeigler or Zipler, Daniel
Young, J.	Zimmerman, Henry	

ROLL OF CAPT. GROVE CASE'S COMPANY 27th U. S. INFANTRY.
(Probably from Licking County.)
Served from May 5, until May 18, 1813.

Rank and Name of Soldier.	Rank and Name of Soldier.	Rank and Name of Soldier.
Capt. Grove Case	Lieut. Alexander Holmes	Ensign William Stedman
Sergt. Silas Winchel	Sergt. William Holmes	Corp. Lester Case
	Corp. James White	
Privates.	**Privates.**	**Privates.**
Bancroft, Ethan	Case, Frederick	Case, Timothy
Critton, Gabriel	Critchet, Mathew H.	Comwell, Archibold
Carpenter, Benjamin	Colman, Julius	Every, Simeon
Elliott, Cornelius	Gillman, Elisha S.	Graves, Josiah
Holmes, Joseph	Knox, Titus	Kandol, Caleb
Messenger, Campbell	Mays, John	Munson, Jesse
Phelps, Levi	Pratt, Worthy	Phillips, John H.
Parker, John	Rose, Hilon	Rose, Samuel, Jr.
Stephen, Justice	Sennel, John	Wells, John
West, Joseph	Wilson, Amos	

Page 421.
ROLL OF CAPT. SAMUEL SWEARINGEN (26th U. S. INFANTRY NOT GIVEN.)
(Probably from Ross County.)
Served from January 1, until April 8, 1814.

Capt. Samuel Swearingen

Page 422.
ROLL OF CAPT. RICHARD GRAHAM (19th U. S. INFANTRY NOT GIVEN.)
(County Unknown.)
Served from April 1, until May 15, 1813.

Capt. Richard Graham   Lieut. John D. Reeves

Page 423.
ROLL OF CAPT. COLLINS (19th U. S. INFANTRY NOT GIVEN.)
(Probably from Ross County.)
Served from March 16, 1814, until March 6, 1816.

Capt. Collins   Private Levin Fisher

SURNAME INDEX

This index includes the names of counties from which the military companies were drawn.

ABANATHA, 117
ABAT, 19
ABBOT, 29 46 135 152
ABBOTT, 10 38-40 54 61 89 100 102 112 113
   126 134 151
ABDERSON, 42
ABEL, 6 88
ABLE, 58
ABONATHER, 47
ABOT, 76
ABRAHAM, 29 38 50 90 122 156
ABRAMS, 131 137
ABSALOM, 69
ABSHIRE, 112
ACHISON, 56
ACHMAND, 66
ACKER, 66
ACKLEY, 135
ACKLIN, 66
ACKRE, 139
ACTON, 22 53 75
ADAIR, 25 32 147
ADAM, 61
ADAMS, 4-6 8 11 12 24 26 32 37 44 51 56 73
   75 76 78-81 85 88 89 97 108-110 113 118
   120 123 125 126 128 141 143 145 146
   148
ADAMS CO, 21 24 25 68 71 74 75 81 149
ADAMSON, 95 145
ADDER, 54

ADDISON, 148
ADDY, 69
ADEIDLER, 133
ADGATE, 50
ADKINS, 66 89 110 155
ADKINSON, 85 88
ADLINDEL, 41
ADORD, 146
ADREWS, 77
ADY, 14
AGER, 41
AGG, 104
AGLER, 8
AGUE, 77 93 94
AID, 47 48
AIKINS, 106
AINSWORTH, 65
AIVATTS, 67
AKER, 98
AKINS, 67 88
ALANOON, 55
ALBAN, 41 68 68
ALBARTSON, 99
ALBERT, 9
ALBIN, 43 106 133
ALBOGAST, 91
ALBON, 60
ALBRIGHT, 45
ALCOT, 96
ALCUTT, 94

ALDEN, 78 116
ALDERMAN, 50 81 85 88 89 109 124
ALDRED, 116
ALDREEDEZR, 124
ALDRID, 26
ALDRIDE, 87
ALDRIDG, 94
ALDRIDGE, 60 96 134
ALDWICK, 46
ALESHIRE, 74 153
ALEXANDER, 5 6 11 16 20 24 43 47 49 62 66 70 73 77 85 94 98 101 108 111 120 121 123 126 131 137 145 149
ALEXANER, 28
ALEY, 13
ALFERD, 56
ALFRED, 56
ALHED, 65
ALKIN, 116
ALKIRE, 54 141 153
ALKUE, 54
ALL, 82
ALLBERRY, 29
ALLEN, 6 14 17 25 27 29 36 37 66-68 73 76 80 83-86 89 90 98-100 103 105 106 110-112 116 120 121 123 124 142 143
ALLENTON, 138
ALLFATHER, 127
ALLISON, 32 35 50 63 119
ALLOWAYS, 156
ALLSPAUGH, 14
ALLVED, 85
ALMONDS, 139
ALPHA, 14 126
ALRED, 85 106
ALSBACK, 28
ALSPACH, 29
ALSPAUGH, 104
ALSTON, 131
ALTBAUGH, 8
ALTEN, 41
ALTMAN, 31 67
ALWOOD, 138
AMADOWN, 105

AMASA, 54
AMBROSE, 57
AMEN, 74
AMIESTEIN, 109
AMMACH, 66
AMMON, 73
AMOS, 100 107
AMS, 49
AMSPACH, 66
ANDERSIN, 23
ANDERSON, 5 7 11 17 18 21 22 24 28 33 36 37 38 42 44 51 54 59 63-65 69 71 72 75 82 85 88 92 94 107-109 112 113 116 123 125-127 135 136 140 146 151 156
ANDREAS, 138
ANDRES, 77
ANDREW, 37 47 48 59 87 96 98 137
ANDREWS, 5 9 14 33 37 42 47 56 62 63 68 76 79 81 85 86 88 90 93 99 101 102 105 113 119 124 125 130 137 141 152
ANGEL, 151
ANGO, 11
ANKENEY, 13
ANKERMAN, 49
ANSER, 60
ANSMAN, 99
ANSPAUGH, 68
ANTHONY, 40
ANTIS, 75
ANTONIDES, 11
ANTRICKS, 27
ANTRINK, 29
ANTUS, 99
ANWAY, 107 116
APLY, 106
APPLE, 155
APPLEGATE, 37 39 80 93 111 150
APPLETON, 146
ARBAUGH, 102
ARBOE, 53
ARBOGAST, 91
ARBUCKLE, 115
ARBUTE, 12
ARBY, 106

ARCHBOD, 9
ARCHER, 14 40 41 76 80 98 111 121 126 132 153
ARENDT, 19 24
ARGADINE, 138
ARGEBUTE, 47
ARGO, 8 11 53 70 92
ARICK, 41
ARINGTON, 48
ARMACUSH, 95
ARMAN, 140
ARMITAGE, 109
ARMON, 53 140
ARMSBY, 110
ARMSTRONG, 7 9 10 16 23 35 36 39 46 48 49 51 60 63 70 72 74 78 82 90 92 97 100-103 114 116 117 127 133 136 146 152 153
ARNEL, 71
ARNES, 76
ARNESWORTH, 52
ARNOLD, 7 26 39 50 51 76 81 82 99 101 111 124 130 138-140 146
ARNTE, 130
ARREL, 109
ARRELS, 92
ARRINGTON, 151
ARROWSMITH, 128
ARTEMAR, 56
ARTHERS, 94
ARTHUR, 57 59 76 102 110 125 153 154
ARTHURS, 42 43 121
ASBAUGH, 27
ASBURN, 97
ASH, 125 145
ASHBAUGH, 27 55
ASHBROOK, 59
ASHBY, 22 37 112 116
ASHER, 6 7
ASHERAFT, 98
ASHIRAFT, 15
ASHLEY, 29 53 97
ASHTON, 17 102
ASKELL, 126
ASKIN, 38
ASKREN, 93
ASKRIN, 22
ASKRON, 114
ASKSEN, 72
ATCHESON, 52
ATCHISON, 115 130
ATER, 52 143
ATERS, 47
ATHA, 14 127
ATHEL, 37
ATHERTON, 139
ATKIN, 78 84
ATKINS, 24 110 130 156
ATKINSON, 69 74 85 136
ATWATER, 56
AUBURN, 45
AUDRICK, 91
AUGHE, 130
AUGISTEAN, 145
AUGUSTINE, 62 63 97 106 135 137 138 147
AULT, 6 41 49 137
AURS, 41
AUSBACH, 28
AUSPACH, 28
AUSTAIN, 23
AUSTIN, 4 57 84 89 109 115
AUSTON, 149
AUTER, 43 58 142
AVERY, 5 6 10 70 132
AWWICK, 102
AXTELL, 97
AYE, 83 95
AYERS, 6 9 11 31 36 76 115 119 125 132 148 149
AYRES, 12 75 97 98 110 139 143 145
AYUBRIGHT, 64
BABB, 24 67 98 127
BABBET, 43
BABBIT, 58 81
BABCOCK, 55 56 85 120 128
BACCUS, 46
BACER, 95
BACHAN, 25
BACHMAN, 84
BACHUS, 23

BACON, 60 76 107
BACUS, 113 134
BADEN, 51
BADENE, 61
BADGER, 4 65 91 102
BADGLEY, 44 148
BADGLY, 72
BADKIN, 33
BADRIDGE, 68
BAGBY, 16
BAGEA, 91
BAGGEASS, 21
BAGGS, 109
BAGLEY, 96 122
BAGS, 95
BAICHET, 14
BAIGLE, 53
BAIGS, 68
BAIL, 9
BAILER, 14
BAILES, 14
BAILEY, 11 20 34 39 40 45 74 81 85 97 101 102 110 123 124 127 136 153
BAILISS, 8
BAILLE, 65
BAILS, 75
BAILY, 89 107 127 143
BAIN, 25
BAINDAN, 61
BAIR, 8 20 61 136
BAIRD, 8 33 35 61 75 99 108 110 113 126 136 142-144 146 150
BAIRED, 61
BAITMAN, 151
BAKER, 9 11 14 17-19 27 29 31 36 37 40 43 45-48 50 52-54 58 66 68 71 73-76 78 95 101 103 104 107 118 120 122-124 126 137-139 142 155 156
BAL, 115
BALA, 61
BALBEE, 100
BALDIN, 27
BALDRIDGE, 20 68 75
BALDWIN, 17 18 40 44 49 54 56 74-76 82 87-89 91-93 97 99 100 110 111 119 132

BALDWIN (continued) 141-144 154
BALENGER, 55
BALES, 89 122 138
BALEY, 28 57 57 132 151
BALL, 13 57 61 82
BALLAD, 124
BALLAK, 106
BALLARD, 21 25 32 40 46 81 85 96
BALLENGER, 111
BALLFORD, 142
BALLINGER, 75 80 96 111 120
BALLY, 102
BALSFORE, 61
BALSLY, 138
BALTIMORE, 41 51 98
BALY, 87
BAMFIELD, 108
BAMHILL, 8
BANANES, 135
BANCROFT, 56 157
BANE, 36 72 91
BANES, 91
BANFIELD, 116
BANFILL, 68 112
BANING, 22
BANIT, 36
BANNAGER, 103
BANNANES, 135
BANNETT, 59
BANNING, 67 88
BANNON, 38 59
BANSCROFT, 72
BANT, 61
BANTHAN, 14
BAPTIST, 97
BARBAUGH, 127
BARBER, 19 33 46 47 57 61 96 101 124 136 152 154
BARBURT, 72
BARBY, 64
BARCUS, 7 105 109 115
BARDEN, 148
BARDMAN, 107
BARDSLEY, 79 82 129

BARE, 69 93
BARGER, 148
BARK, 105
BARKARD, 13
BARKDOLL, 59
BARKE, 136
BARKELOV, 23
BARKELS, 150
BARKER, 11 28 32 47 64 66 76 79 84 107 112 124 129 134 140
BARKES, 14
BARKEY, 14
BARKHEIMER, 97
BARKLEY, 88 102 107
BARKLOR, 110
BARKS, 7
BARLEN, 61
BARLER, 14
BARLES, 103
BARLEY, 31 81
BARLON, 41
BARLOW, 12 29 65 84 104
BARNARD, 136
BARNES, 6 8 9 11 31 41 55 57 60 70 73 85 87 88 95 105 110 120 124 144 148 153 154
BARNETT, 9 41 62 99 100
BARNEY, 97 145
BARNFIELD, 121
BARNGROOVER, 20
BARNGROVER, 148
BARNHART, 31 82
BARNHILL, 68
BARR, 5 6 27 28 31 68 116 145 147
BARRACK, 16
BARRELL, 98
BARREN, 70
BARRERE, 148
BARRET, 15 56 101 116 131
BARRETT, 15 36 41 75 103 118 126
BARRON, 60
BARROUGH, 135
BARRUK, 107
BARRY, 40 73
BARSLEY, 109

BARTAN, 34
BARTHOLOMEW, 29 50 73 82 84 88 89 94 110 156
BARTLESON, 12
BARTLET, 145
BARTLETT, 85 97
BARTLEY, 5
BARTON, 10 13 39 41 70 102 104 114 126 151
BARTRAM, 81
BARTWO, 150
BARUCH, 67
BASCHE, 11
BASCULOE, 39
BASH, 54 138
BASHAM, 63
BASHAN, 136
BASHFORD, 9 104 106 126 136 137
BASHNELL, 88
BASHORD, 106
BASKER, 146
BASSETT, 137
BATCHELDER, 43
BATCHER, 45
BATCHLOR, 22
BATEMAN, 11 48
BATES, 17 40 41 49 59 64 66 70 76 77 83 85 88 95 99 102 128
BATEY, 107
BATTIESE, 156
BATTRICK, 11
BATTROLL, 65
BATY, 46 93
BAUGHER, 29
BAUGHMAN, 15 26 79 139
BAUM, 52 132 145 147 151
BAUMGARDENER, 27
BAUMGARDNER, 27
BAUMONT, 29
BAUN, 148
BAVINGTON, 80
BAVIS, 39
BAWERS, 5
BAWHAN, 23
BAWICK, 27

BAWN, 10 26 61 142
BAWSHER, 10
BAWTON, 152
BAXTER, 58
BAY, 4-6 9 14 15 17 69 128 130
BAYLER, 58
BAYLES, 45 49
BAYLESS, 149 150
BAYLEY, 22 101
BAYMAN, 65
BAYN, 22
BAYNE, 23 66 107
BEA, 29
BEACH, 39 70 79 82 101 142 143
BEACHAM, 152
BEACHER, 93
BEACHT, 6
BEACON, 95 134
BEAHAM, 70
BEAKER, 36
BEAL, 13 151
BEALES, 122 124
BEALL, 4 94
BEALS, 120
BEAM, 29 125 145
BEAMER, 8-10 14 127
BEAR, 29 32
BEARD, 9 12 24 28 35 50 58 69 87 88 109 111 116 127
BEARDSLEY, 32 92
BEARNHEART, 130
BEARS, 121
BEARY, 14
BEASLEY, 23 42 60 68 86 114 145
BEASON, 25 49 122 125 128 133
BEATTY, 4 15 22 69 87 95 106 118 126
BEATY, 156
BEAUCHAMP, 103
BEAVAR, 101
BEAVENS, 96
BEAVER, 27 95 131
BEAVERS, 53
BEAVINS, 115
BEBOUT, 10
BECHS, 45

BECHT, 62
BECK, 96 106 121 155
BECKER, 27 28
BECKET, 34
BECKETT, 53
BECKMAN, 34 95 153
BECKWER, 49
BECKWITH, 104 141
BEDDLE, 108
BEDELE, 127
BEDLE, 120
BEDLER, 65
BEDLS, 144
BEDUNNAH, 123
BEEB, 44 141
BEEBE, 42 83 110 141 146
BEEBEE, 156
BEECH, 79 86
BEEDLE, 99 100
BEEKMAN, 108 114
BEELER, 17
BEEM, 73
BEEMAN, 55
BEEMER, 6
BEER, 54 55 58 63 135
BEERS, 72 115 127
BEESON, 132
BEETH, 128
BEEZLEY, 119
BEEZLY, 91
BEGGS, 92
BEIZLY, 144
BELAIR, 82
BELCH, 7
BELDING, 56
BELES, 129
BELET, 97
BELKNAP, 9 10
BELL, 8 10 12-14 16 18 20 25 33 36 42 44 46 48 49 50 56 58 63 68 69 74 88 91 97 99 100 102 103 109 111 113 114 116 121 124-126 134 136 141 145 155
BELLAIRE, 27
BELLAR, 74
BELLINGER, 131

BELLOTE, 96
BELLOWS, 110 143
BELMONT CO, 13 16 20 41 66 69 133 137
BELOAT, 103
BELSER, 18
BELTT, 119
BELVILLE, 41
BENARD, 130
BENDING, 106
BENDURE, 134
BENEDICK, 72 151 153
BENEDICT, 50 84 103 115 146
BENET, 128
BENETT, 140
BENHAM, 59 120 123
BENHIEMER, 28
BENITT, 120
BENJAMIN, 11 25 82 83 92 120 129 156
BENNER, 29
BENNET, 18 23 29 31-33 40 45 47 55 63 68 75 79 97 102 103 112 115 118 123 135 137 148
BENNETT, 5 9 14 38 39 64 101 111 128 140 154
BENNIS, 51
BENONA, 114
BENSHER, 117
BENSLEY, 61
BENSON, 23 33 146
BENTLEY, 69 74 81 99 105 133
BENTON, 44 65
BEREMAN, 20 111
BERER, 46
BERGIS, 26
BERKALOR, 34
BERNARD, 16
BERNHART, 14
BERRAUGH, 54
BERRIT, 145
BERRY, 5 13 26 32 34 37 42 45 51 69 74 96 97 102 105 112 117 137 140
BERRYHILL, 41
BERRYMAN, 31 156
BERTHAM, 86
BERTHE, 50

BERTRAM, 84
BESHONG, 45
BESS, 101
BEST, 125 144 145
BETCHMAN, 35
BETSER, 10
BETT, 121
BETTS, 39 51
BETY, 129
BETZ, 8 62 68 136 145
BEUL, 27
BEVANS, 97
BEVARD, 16
BEVENS, 150
BEVENTON, 32
BEVER, 141
BEVERS, 53
BEVING, 104
BEVINGTON, 75 95
BEVINS, 26
BEWEN, 85
BEYELY, 46
BEYERLY, 101
BEYMER, 69 74
BEYNER, 70 82 127
BIACCUS, 23
BIAS, 120
BIBER, 23
BICE, 131
BICKELL, 73
BICKLE, 101 118
BIDDINGER, 17 138
BIDDLE, 100 119 149
BIDENGER, 62
BIDLAKE, 143
BIDWELL, 81
BIEDWELL, 81
BIERIN, 110
BIERS, 68 106 130
BIGAM, 38
BIGER, 112
BIGG, 125
BIGGER, 98 133
BIGGS, 22 40 66 73 80 111
BIGLEY, 20 137

BIGNEL, 85
BIGNELL, 86
BIGNOL, 88
BIGSBY, 104
BILBEE, 20
BILBERT, 85
BILDENBECK, 123
BILDERBACK, 14 94
BILL, 141
BILLINGS, 156
BILLMAN, 66
BILLS, 93
BILSLEY, 46
BILZER, 49
BIMBECK, 71
BIMGARDNER, 100
BINCKELY, 67
BINCKLEY, 66
BING, 18 155 155
BINGAMAN, 59
BINGERMAN, 121
BINGHAM, 136
BINGIT, 103
BINGLAND, 102
BINLEY, 118
BINTER, 15
BINTON, 92
BIRAM, 111
BIRD, 14 36 45 112
BIRDRALL, 12
BIRELY, 112
BIRT, 133
BIRTSILL, 38
BIRTTEL, 7
BISETT, 79
BISHONG, 150
BISHOP, 12 15 33 35 37 53 63 66 78 79 84 87
    93 106 110 116 127 136 141 142 152
BISLAND, 33
BISON, 80
BISSEL, 92 110
BISSELL, 92 93 142 143
BISSHIP, 20
BISSILA, 6
BIST, 36

BITTENGER, 63
BITTLE, 155
BITZER, 26 49
BIVITON, 92
BIXBY, 93 129
BIXLER, 156
BIXTER, 139
BLACK, 8 10 14 20 24 29 32-35 38 45 46 62
    66 68 71 72 80 87 99 100 105 106 111
    114 124-128 133 134
BLACKBURN, 6 22 43 50 62 63 105 121 123
    136
BLACKFORD, 11 94 102 123 134
BLACKLEY, 112
BLACKMAN, 77 92 110 143
BLACKMER, 83 135
BLACKMORE, 99
BLACKSTON, 114
BLACKSTONE, 153
BLAGG, 153
BLAIN, 96 115
BLAIR, 32 54 56 75 76 80 98 103 110 121
    130-132 134 140 141 143 147 149 152
BLAKE, 18 45 59 60 62 70 108 149
BLAKELY, 79 143
BLAKER, 63
BLANCHARD, 112
BLAND, 60 70 149
BLANE, 25 37 96 115
BLANEY, 133
BLANKENEY, 139
BLATNER, 28
BLAUGHER, 37
BLAYLOCK, 41
BLAZE, 21 50 141
BLE, 37
BLECHER, 136
BLEND, 146
BLESSING, 100
BLEW, 73
BLICKENSTURFER, 138
BLINN, 89
BLISS, 36 107
BLISSARD, 51
BLITHE, 113

BLOCKSON, 39
BLOO, 27
BLOOKER, 132
BLOOMFIELD, 108 112
BLOSS, 82
BLOTZLEY, 73
BLOUNT, 31
BLOWER, 103
BLUE, 15 38 52 54 57 65 75 77 95 100 107 120 124 127 143 147 151
BLUNT, 31 60 70 155
BLY, 18
BOAKLEY, 47
BOAL, 11 112
BOAN, 139
BOARDMAN, 79
BOATMAN, 6 44 93 114 141 148 155
BOBBENMYER, 27
BOBEBRAKE, 132
BOBENMOYER, 28
BOBLITS, 47
BOBO, 100 120
BOCHARD, 73
BOCHERT, 13
BODDER, 11
BODKINS, 108
BOEN, 28
BOERSTLER, 42
BOGARD, 134
BOGART, 150
BOGGESS, 114
BOGGS, 6 36 54 57 66 131 137 145 149 151 155
BOID, 139
BOILER, 96
BOILS, 8 44
BOKER, 41
BOLABOB, 12
BOLAND, 11
BOLDMAN, 75
BOLER, 41
BOLES, 98 102 132
BOLIN, 68
BOLLINGER, 155
BOLLS, 44

BOLNER, 20
BOLSER, 20
BOLTHARD, 42
BOMBGARDEN, 91
BONAR, 20
BONBRAKE, 38
BOND, 4 48 85 87 90 148
BONE, 17 40
BONEBRAKE, 38
BONEHAM, 13
BONEHAN, 16
BONER, 104 107 144
BONESTEEL, 66
BONHAM, 34 69 73
BONN, 14
BONNEL, 5 12 132
BONNER, 18 26 48 103 114 116 152
BONNET, 96 116 145 148
BONNY, 35
BONOR, 41 93
BONSER, 33
BONSLATER, 29
BONSOR, 152
BONSTEEL, 139
BONTA, 132 149
BONTSONG, 127
BOOK, 110
BOOKER, 58 62 136
BOONCUTTER, 26
BOONE, 102
BOOSE, 139
BOOSINGER, 110 143
BOOSOE, 94
BOOTLE, 52
BOOTOM, 86
BOOTS, 16 18 47 49 64 140
BOOTZ, 136
BORAFF, 20
BORAN, 20
BORCIN, 26
BORDEN, 77 91 112 148
BORDER, 36
BORDERS, 112
BORDMAN, 94
BORELAND, 125

BOREN, 48
BORER, 91 141
BORLAND, 75
BORRER, 47
BORROW, 27
BORT, 29
BORTH, 14
BOSTON, 74
BOSTWICK, 56 99 119 142 146
BOSWELL, 95
BOSWICK, 54
BOTHIN, 152
BOTKIN, 60 91
BOTTON, 104
BOTTS, 143
BOTZLEY, 74
BOUCHER, 27 50
BOULER, 66
BOULS, 125
BOUR, 44
BOURNE, 86
BOURON, 39
BOURROUGHS, 91
BOUSMAN, 118
BOUT, 48
BOVEL, 20
BOVIKER, 34
BOW, 22
BOWAN, 82
BOWDLE, 52
BOWEN, 11 19 23 40 89 112 118 120 127 140
BOWER, 36 97 136
BOWERLY, 20
BOWERMASTER, 145
BOWERS, 5 18 19 44 47 48 59 69 105 131 141
BOWERSACK, 100
BOWGHMAN, 65
BOWHAN, 106 118
BOWIN, 113
BOWL, 112
BOWLAND, 66
BOWLEN, 97
BOWLIN, 63

BOWMAN, 8 20 28 29 37 39 43 44 48 51 72 81 108 132 134 135 148
BOWSER, 58 116
BOWSHER, 10 23 106 152
BOY, 5 13
BOYARD, 32
BOYCE, 60 144
BOYD, 16 18 31 48 49 51 58 66 68 74 77 80 82 85 94 109 110 118 121 126 137 149 151 155
BOYE, 149
BOYER, 28 32 37 39 50 91 119
BOYL, 156
BOYLAND, 61
BOYLE, 14 136 139
BOYLES, 5 45 66 73 126 137
BOYNTON, 148 150 152
BOYS, 12 17
BOZIER, 95
BRACKEN, 57 102 118
BRACKIN, 85
BRACKNEY, 44 57 115
BRADBERRY, 102 131
BRADBURY, 39
BRADBY, 76
BRADEN, 88 134 156
BRADFIELD, 6 26 63 67 136
BRADFORD, 58 68 77 95 110 127 143
BRADING, 32
BRADLEY, 10 32 51 53 54 60 73 76 88 92 93 106 110 128 137 140 143
BRADON, 77 81 140
BRADSHAW, 39 54 105 155
BRADWAY, 18 59
BRADWELL, 20
BRADY, 8 13 51 73 99 105 148 152 156
BRAGG, 34 80 111
BRAIDY, 18
BRAINARD, 85 146
BRAKEMAN, 114
BRAKIN, 85
BRALEY, 108
BRAMBLE, 46 64 151
BRAME, 28
BRAMHALL, 13

BRAMON, 131
BRANABERRY, 63
BRANBLOSSOM, 132
BRANBURG, 130
BRAND, 12
BRANDEBERRY, 7 8
BRANDEBURG, 45
BRANDEN, 93
BRANDENBURGH, 130
BRANDERBERRY, 62 136
BRANDHEVER, 28
BRANNAN, 70
BRANNIN, 106
BRANNON, 102
BRANSEN, 125
BRANSON, 127 141
BRANSTETTER, 18
BRANT, 75
BRASKNY, 141
BRATELL, 8
BRATTEN, 21
BRATTON, 68
BRATZ, 27
BRAY, 74
BRE, 95
BREADY, 101 143
BRECKENRIDGE, 55
BRECKENRIGE, 65 93
BRECKINRIDGE, 134
BREDDY, 51 100
BREDEN, 85
BREDON, 109
BREECE, 61
BREEDLOVE, 52
BREES, 57
BREM, 13
BRENNEN, 50
BRENNER, 137
BRENNEY, 19
BRENT, 28
BREOME, 24
BRESON, 66
BRESSLEE, 27
BRESSLER, 28
BRETZ, 19 24

BREVARD, 41
BREWER, 22 25 26 37 91 116 140
BREWIN, 122 123
BREWNER, 138
BREXCUNT, 12
BRIAM, 40
BRIAN, 27 130 142
BRIANT, 18 34 38 75 114
BRICE, 44
BRICKER, 97
BRICKLE, 55 133
BRICKLES, 152
BRICKLOW, 10
BRIDGE, 61 84
BRIDGER, 38
BRIDGES, 39
BRIDGFORD, 99
BRIDING, 19
BRIENT, 33 84
BRIER, 128 130
BRIGGS, 7 18 36 52 81 136 143 147 150
BRIGHT, 13 56 65 137 144
BRIGHTWELL, 123
BRIGINTINE, 68
BRIKAN, 24
BRILL, 41 74
BRINDOLA, 102
BRINE, 27 142
BRINEMAN, 6
BRINER, 33
BRINEY, 40
BRINK, 118
BRINKER, 33 63 136
BRINTER, 134
BRINY, 40
BRISTER, 104
BRISTOL, 79
BRISTON, 110
BRISTOW, 38
BRITTEN, 118
BRITTENHAM, 51 113
BRITTON, 63 126 136
BRITZ, 62
BROADBURY, 17
BROADWAY, 55

BROADWELL, 20 39 67 85
BROCAW, 7 58
BROCK, 54 125
BROCKAR, 8
BROCKWAY, 77 85 110
BRODERICK, 61
BRODERS, 125
BROKAN, 10
BROKAW, 9
BROKES, 82
BROMAGEN, 125
BROMBACH, 27
BROMLEY, 114
BRONCE, 44
BRONER, 46
BRONKAR, 72
BRONKART, 127
BRONSON, 110 141
BROOGHER, 58
BROOK, 138
BROOKAN, 7
BROOKE, 13
BROOKHART, 27
BROOKS, 5 12 22 29 35 46 56 67 75 76 82 83
    89 90 107 114 132 134 137 138 144
BROOMERSHINE, 58
BROSURE, 40
BROTELL, 7
BROTHER, 92
BROTHERLAN, 33
BROTHERS, 109
BROTON, 31 69
BROUGHARD, 138
BROUGHER, 52
BROUGHMAN, 138
BROUSE, 62
BROUSMAN, 15
BROWBAKER, 74
BROWDER, 128
BROWER, 20 96
BROWERN, 8
BROWERS, 8
BROWN, 4 6-8 11 12 14 16 17 19 20 22-24 26
    27 29 31-33 35 36 38-43 45-55 57 58 60
    62-65 68-70 72 74 75 78-80 82-86 88-90

BROWN (continued)
    92 93 96 98-104 106 109 111 113 115 116
    118-120 127 129 131-133 135 136 139
    141-143 145 147 148 150-156
BROWN CO, 22
BROWNER, 8 11
BROWNFIELD, 52 114 152
BROWNING, 14 65 67 72 147 150
BROWNY, 137
BRUBECK, 71
BRUCE, 9 94 124 133
BRUDE, 38
BRUIN, 112
BRUK, 68
BRUKEBILL, 14
BRUMBACK, 18
BRUMMET, 106
BRUMMINGHAM, 102
BRUNDAGE, 78 79 83
BRUNDEN, 121
BRUNDON, 60
BRUNER, 27 59
BRUNHED, 75
BRUNK, 42
BRUNSTETER, 77
BRUNSTETTER, 94
BRUNT, 140
BRUSE, 38
BRUSH, 60 101
BRUVER, 66
BRYAM, 155
BRYAN, 16 17 19 26-28 49 66 69 72 80 99
    108 111 115 121 130 137 138 150 153
BRYANN, 139
BRYANT, 39 103
BRYNER, 152
BRYON, 38
BUCHAMAN, 42
BUCHANAN, 61 64 67 77 88 92 100-102 109
BUCHANON, 60 76 120 133
BUCHELS, 144
BUCHER, 153
BUCK, 8 24 54 61 81 101 107 110 111 116
    122 132 134 155
BUCKEN, 130

BUCKET, 66
BUCKHAM, 147
BUCKHANNON, 99
BUCKLAND, 105
BUCKLES, 22 36 100 125 144
BUCKLEY, 8 11 105 107 127
BUCKMAN, 96 153
BUCKSLEY, 56
BUCKSON, 66
BUDD, 79 116
BUDENOT, 74
BUE, 115
BUEL, 4 85
BUELL, 50 82 87 124 135
BUGH, 98
BUKER, 13
BULDERACH, 144
BULGAR, 47
BULGER, 8 47 91
BULL, 87 102 132 144
BULVERSON, 104
BUMGAINER, 105
BUMGARNER, 96
BUMGAVANCE, 70
BUMP, 46
BUMTRAGER, 17 85
BUN, 13 26
BUNALD, 125
BUNCH, 84
BUNDY, 13 16 56 126
BUNEYER, 126
BUNKER, 102
BUNN, 26 47 49 117
BUNNEL, 59 105 141 144
BUNSEY, 151
BUNTEN, 18
BUNTER, 17
BUNTIN, 107
BUNYON, 126
BURBACK, 8
BURBANK, 126
BURBEN, 96
BURBRIDGE, 54 153
BURCAW, 26
BURCH, 136

BURCHET, 126
BURCHFIELD, 6 9
BURDET, 76
BURDETT, 72
BURDICK, 142
BURDINGTON, 109
BURDINOO, 156
BURDSALL, 114
BUREL, 50
BURG, 125
BURGE, 82
BURGER, 141
BURGES, 17
BURGESS, 68 76 88 92
BURGET, 102 121
BURGETT, 33
BURIS, 10
BURK, 8 13 33 43 45 93 97 105 108 110 117 119 132 134 137 150
BURKDALE, 7
BURKE, 73 76 125 136 150
BURKELLOW, 86
BURKETT, 25
BURKHARDT, 156
BURKIRK, 137
BURKIS, 11
BURKITT, 71
BURKLES, 148
BURKLEY, 115
BURKUM, 126
BURLEY, 148
BURMAN, 12 29
BURN, 29 87
BURNAN, 67
BURNES, 37 41 45 52 62 75 85 88 97 108 117
BURNET, 76 80 138
BURNETT, 20 38 39 64 81 88
BURNEY, 10 13 36 120
BURNHAM, 85 86 124
BURNS, 12 20 24 40 61 97 111
BURNSIDE, 118
BURNUM, 84
BURR, 40
BURREL, 36 119

BURRES, 13
BURRIS, 6 17 39 49 116 153
BURROUGH, 81
BURROUGHS, 74 105 110 119 134 137 144
BURROW, 29 50
BURROWS, 13 114 144
BURT, 59 69 113
BURTLE, 39
BURTON, 11 33 38 118 131 137
BURVIT, 126
BURWELL, 81 85 104
BURY, 14
BURYS, 69
BUSBEE, 90
BUSBEY, 31
BUSBY, 60
BUSH, 19 26 35 40 60 75 90 119 140 146
BUSHELS, 144
BUSHMAN, 125
BUSHNELL, 77 86 110 156
BUSHONG, 68 138
BUSICK, 80
BUSKIRK, 91
BUSLEY, 156
BUSSEL, 36
BUSSEY, 156
BUSY, 9
BUTCHER, 60
BUTH, 21
BUTLER, 4 39 41 43 50 59 60 66 70 73 78 79 82 110 122 137 139 155 156
BUTLER CO. 12 17 19 20 40 57 59 99 148
BUTLINGER, 33
BUTT, 41 101 107 116 132 138
BUTTE, 94
BUTTERBAUGH, 13
BUTTLES, 5
BUTTON, 76 149
BUTTS, 13
BUTZ, 67
BUXTON, 65
BUZZARD, 25 73 141 143
BYARS, 90
BYEL, 64
BYERLY, 4 148

BYERS, 25 39 72 112 134 153
BYFIELD, 20
BYLES, 44
BYRN, 38
C-------, 154
CABE, 156
CABLIEN, 98
CACHEART, 70
CACKLER, 142
CACKLIN, 110
CADE, 23 84 106 109 121 152
CADOW, 33
CADWICK, 16
CADY, 58 126 156
CAGY, 19
CAHAMMON, 6
CAHILL, 7 59 103 123
CAHOON, 56 84 89
CAIDE, 54
CAILEY, 38
CAIN, 24 40 72 75 120 142 149
CAIRNS, 60 70 71
CALDHOON, 100
CALDWELL, 10 23 26 66 85 86 89 100 106 115 117 118 121 144
CALE, 89
CALEY, 31
CALHOON, 64 94
CALHOUN, 51 76 77 116 153
CALIHAN, 6
CALING, 49
CALKINS, 129
CALL, 5
CALLAHAN, 62
CALLAMBER, 131
CALLANDER, 125
CALLENDER, 95
CALLIHAN, 39
CALLING, 47
CALLISON, 50 80 127
CALLISTON, 111
CALRIL, 19
CALVIN, 31 85 88 121 154
CALWELL, 34
CAMBEL, 63

CAMBELL, 24 126
CAMBLE, 16 153
CAMBO, 19
CAMELL, 22
CAMERON, 26 62 72 90 114 119 138
CAMLER, 11
CAMP, 8 94 136 141
CAMPBELL, 4-6 10 11 17 22-24 27 29 36 39
  42 44 53 57 63 65 66 74 75 80 89 91 92
  94 96 97 100-102 105 110 115 119-121
  125-128 135 140 141 144 149 151-153
  155
CAMPLIN, 40
CAMPTON, 148
CAMRON, 19
CAMUN, 34 35
CANADY, 23
CANE, 25 39
CANEHEY, 136
CANEL, 27
CANELY, 156
CANFIELD, 90
CANIDA, 149
CANLEY, 149 152
CANN, 6 10
CANNELL, 4
CANNON, 7 24 50 63 87 103 115 123 135
  140 142 143 150
CANNOR, 26
CANTER, 20
CANTRELL, 54 57
CANTWAL, 99
CANTWELL, 9 60 71 73
CANWAY, 156
CAPHART, 36
CAPLES, 85
CAPLIN, 44
CAPS, 44
CARBERT, 15
CARD, 20 29
CARDEN, 111
CARDER, 54 80
CARDRE, 48
CARE, 43
CARES, 71

CAREY, 26 140 144 150
CARGEY, 29
CARHART, 60
CARIS, 56 105 142
CARLE, 58 138
CARLEY, 102
CARLISLE, 22 27 40 73 89 90
CARLS, 56
CARLTON, 5 56 76 77 85 93 109 156
CARMAN, 22
CARNAL, 123
CARNES, 63 69 135 139
CARNEY, 41 58
CARNIAN, 18
CARNIHAN, 57
CARNOHAN, 55
CARNS, 134
CARO, 68
CAROTHERS, 9
CARPASS, 36
CARPENTER, 7 11 16 29 41 43 46 47 54 56
  74 75 78 82 83 103 110 116 128 129 131
  142 145 146 150 157
CARPER, 17 62
CARR, 17 18 23 33 38 68 73 80 102 109 112
  127 131 138
CARRAMAN, 36
CARREL, 22 37
CARRIN, 78
CARRINGTON, 74 133 138
CARROL, 73
CARROLL, 35 51 69 97 100 108 125
CARSEY, 34
CARSHNER, 109
CARSON, 6 57 67 73 74 108 113 119 120 138
CARTER, 6 21 22 23 39 55 56 64 77 80 88 94
  97 105 108 117 130 133 134 142 144 150
  154 155
CARTMELL, 91 116 118
CARTMILE, 26
CARTMILL, 23
CARTREE, 60
CARTRIGHT, 54 94 108
CARTWAL, 54
CARTWRIGHT, 18 40

CARUTHERS, 13 68
CARVELL, 94
CARVER, 78 94
CARVIN, 59
CARY, 21 65 112 138 153 156
CASAD, 128
CASDELE, 87
CASDY, 130
CASE, 22 56 59 70 79 82 84 86 88 105 116 129 146 156 157
CASEBEAR, 17
CASEBOLT, 120
CASEY, 16 31 39 65 133
CASHNER, 32
CASK, 148
CASKER, 17
CASKEY, 20
CASKY, 63
CASLER, 153
CASLET, 19 58
CASON, 100
CASPER, 97
CASPERSON, 75
CASS, 60 70 73 86 103
CASSADY, 130
CASSAIRT, 94
CASSEL, 115
CASSELDINE, 149
CASSELMAN, 5
CASSIDAY, 112 131
CASSILL, 134
CASSMAN, 82
CASSY, 156
CAST, 40 144
CASTALLER, 102
CASTER, 57 116
CASTLE, 65 66 81 93 110 126
CASTNER, 47
CASTO, 54
CASTOR, 56
CATERLIN, 6 61
CATERMAN, 103
CATHERS, 138
CATICK, 122
CATING, 16 153
CATLIN, 45
CATRO, 132
CATT, 6 62
CATTERLINE, 14
CATTIM, 46
CATTLAN, 130
CATTLEN, 131
CATTLETON, 131
CAUCHY, 108
CAUGHEY, 6 8 62 124
CAUL, 96
CAVES, 14
CAVET, 23
CAVETT, 25
CAVIN, 11 74 75 86
CAW, 44
CAWER, 77 119
CAWTHORN, 123
CAYLOR, 76 113
CEASSON, 8
CELIX, 36
CELL, 16
CELLAR, 79
CELLERS, 97
CHAD, 47 95 134
CHADWICK, 16 44
CHAFFIN, 7
CHAFFORD, 114
CHAFLIN, 105
CHAILES, 31
CHAINA, 73
CHAINEY, 73
CHAIRCHER, 92
CHAISMAN, 39
CHALFIN, 17
CHALFINT, 67
CHALMERS, 103
CHAMBER, 15 149
CHAMBERLAIN, 62 113 142 143 147 150
CHAMBERLINGS, 142
CHAMBERS, 9 13 15 36 40 42 67 71 72 87 96 97 101 102 114 118 119 122 139 147
CHAMERLAIN, 142

CHAMP, 32 33 52 53 143
CHAMPAIGN CO, 15 43 72 90 91 95 118
    128 134 144
CHANCE, 70 91 125
CHANDLER, 35 76 136 145 153
CHANEY, 7 25 31 44 65 110 118 155
CHANNEL, 27 50 104
CHANY, 107
CHAPDU, 155
CHAPLIN, 35
CHAPMAN, 5 14 20 29 32 44 56 61 75 82 84
    85 95 104 108 110 121 126 135 139 149
    155
CHAPPELL, 51
CHAPPEN, 150
CHARING, 7
CHARLES, 148
CHARTER, 137
CHARWEATER, 44
CHASE, 8 76 81 89 112
CHATFIELD, 88
CHAVER, 95
CHAW, 79
CHEDD, 52
CHEENEY, 110
CHEESMAN, 108
CHEMITH, 46
CHENEWITH, 117 154
CHENEWORTH, 96
CHENNEY, 155
CHENOWETH, 15
CHENOWITH, 94
CHENOWOTH, 94
CHENWORTH, 96 135
CHENY, 96
CHERRY, 17 31 32 37 54 146
CHERRYHOHNEY, 17
CHESNUT, 45
CHESREY, 88
CHEST, 37
CHESTER, 139
CHESTNUT, 45 73 102 151
CHEVERGAR, 65
CHEW, 64 88 101
CHICHESTER, 111

CHICK, 121
CHIDESTER, 80 146
CHILBEY, 72
CHILBY, 72
CHILDER, 84
CHILDERS, 12 18 50 60 120
CHILDS, 33
CHILL, 34 75
CHINOWITH, 55
CHINWORTH, 45 96 105
CHION, 10
CHIPMAN, 115
CHIPP, 107
CHIPS, 108
CHISIMORE, 62
CHITTENDEN, 105
CHITTENDON, 56
CHITWOOD, 74 155
CHIVILIER, 11
CHOCKLEY, 141
CHONAY, 25
CHONNER, 30
CHORN, 80
CHRIST, 11 20 28 36 114
CHRISTIAN, 18 127
CHRISTIE, 18 27
CHRISTMAN, 66 106
CHRISTY, 8 9 11 27 85 102 140
CHRYS, 9
CHUB, 88
CHUL, 94
CHURCH, 103 115 140 146
CHURIN, 22
CIRCKEL, 95
CISNA, 34 122
CISSNA, 48 101 107
CLADWELL, 39 106
CLAP, 116
CLAPP, 76
CLAPPEN, 123
CLARE, 6
CLARK, 10 12 14-16 18-20 26 29 31 33 36-40
    43 45-48 50-53 55 57 59 61 63-65 68-70
    72 74 79 81 86 88 90 91 93 95-97 99 100
    102-104 106 108 110 112-115 117 119

CLARK (continued)
    123 125-128 130 132 135 138 140 142
    143 147 148 151 154 156
CLARK CO, 45
CLARKE, 140
CLARKSON, 51 52
CLARRIDGE, 117
CLARTON, 14
CLARY, 6
CLASPELL, 40
CLATON, 128
CLAUS, 28
CLAUSON, 98
CLAWS, 98
CLAWSON, 85 91 132 153
CLAY, 34 45 107 114 149 156
CLAYBOUGH, 29 104
CLAYPOOL, 26 118
CLAYTON, 14 23 27 118
CLEARWATY, 107
CLEAVENGER, 77
CLEAVER, 85
CLEBINGER, 40
CLECK, 145
CLEM, 139
CLEMANS, 45
CLEMENS, 46 70 87 104 115
CLEMENT, 105
CLEMENTS, 102 130
CLEMMINGS, 91
CLEMONS, 54
CLENDENIN, 43 93
CLENGMAN, 148
CLERK, 33 129
CLERMONT CO, 19 42 125
CLESS, 58
CLETON, 128
CLEUD, 69
CLEVANGER, 141
CLEVE, 41
CLEVELAND, 82 91
CLEVENGER, 25 34 130 141
CLEVER, 81
CLEVINGER, 53 127
CLIEVELAND, 89

CLIFFORD, 9 13 16 34 74 124 146 151
CLIFT, 155
CLIFTON, 34 35 51 57 131
CLIMER, 139
CLINE, 14 24 33 37 41 46 65 90 114 116 123
    126 127 138
CLINES, 28 108
CLINGAN, 124
CLINGER, 62
CLINGMAN, 152
CLINTON, 19 85 88 125 126
CLINTON CO, 35
CLLINS, 43
CLOAR, 31
CLOE, 50
CLOSE, 6
CLOSSEN, 113
CLOSSON, 34 116
CLOUD, 14 108
CLOUGHBURG, 90
CLOUSER, 18
CLOVER, 34 35 53 149
CLOW, 110
CLOYD, 106 112
CLOYDE, 66
CLUM, 138
CLUMM, 17
CLUNE, 33
CLUNEY, 133
CLUNY, 74
CLYMER, 65
CLYNE, 58 123
CMKEE, 139
COALBY, 61
COALEY, 96
COALMAN, 126
COATS, 60 70 111 120
COBB, 96
COBBLER, 149
COBERLEY, 33
COBERLY, 26
COBLAR, 108
COBLE, 106
COBLENTZ, 58 130
COBLEY, 37 114

COBMAN, 41
COBORN, 71
COBURN, 38 96 97 154
COCCLON, 27
COCHERAN, 83
COCHERN, 54
COCHRAIN, 33
COCHRAN, 20 22 26 34 35 43 46 51 53 54 61 69 75 81 99 108 113 114 117 142 149 153 154
COCHRANE, 84
COCHRIN, 79
COCK, 33 66
COCKERLL, 105
COCKMOUR, 107
COCKRELL, 103 105
COCKRILL, 127
COCOMORE, 155
COCRAN, 20
CODDINGTON, 72
CODER, 140
CODINGTON, 41 65 91 98 99 123
CODOT, 152
COE, 21 23 44 45 56 97 99 111
COFFEE, 141
COFFEN, 57
COFFEY, 25 44 50 58 91
COFFIELD, 41
COFFMAN, 29 44 65 132
COFMAN, 130 132
COGILL, 49
COGLE, 69
COGLEY, 96
COGSWELL, 43
COHAGEN, 87
COHALL, 46
COIL, 105 140
COIT, 146
COKENOUR, 107
COKLE, 29
COLBERT, 95 128
COLBRAITH, 89
COLBY, 40
COLDWELL, 61
COLE, 29 33 43 55-57 68 75 90 114 129 137 156
COLEGROVE, 46 105
COLEMAN, 4 38 40 76 81 86 98 105 119 125 126 132 135 148
COLEMAND, 135
COLEMUEL, 12
COLES, 74 83
COLESTON, 154
COLGAN, 21
COLGREAVE, 69
COLHOUN, 84
COLIASS, 145
COLIER, 105
COLIVET, 122
COLLAR, 69
COLLARD, 43
COLLARS, 98
COLLEAR, 137
COLLIER, 4 25 26 71 86 120 125 138 149
COLLIERS, 87
COLLINGS, 156
COLLINS, 17 20 22-24 26 32 36 44 51 56 68 69 71 75 91 101-103 110 117 128 132 138 144 148 150 152 156 157
COLLIS, 17
COLLISON, 12 91 96 127 155
COLLISTER, 59
COLLUMBER, 47
COLLY, 60 70
COLMAN, 137 157
COLSTIN, 54
COLTER, 123 137 152
COLTHARD, 42
COLUMBER, 33
COLUMBIANA CO, 62-64 67 139
COLVEN, 114
COLVIN, 24 129 148
COLWELL, 4 46
COMBS, 25 155
COMER, 107 128
COMHWAST, 37
COMMIN, 122
COMPTON, 42 77 107 114 119

COMS, 49
COMSTOCK, 84 89 129
COMWELL, 157
CONCHLIN, 105
CONCKLIN, 133
CONCLETON, 120
CONDERA, 94
CONDON, 6
CONDRON, 69
CONE, 81
CONET, 56
CONFER, 11 87 133
CONGAR, 125 138
CONGELL, 133
CONGER, 115
CONKEL, 15 138
CONKELON, 124
CONKLIN, 16 123 138 146
CONLEY, 38 138
CONN, 9 15 24 26 152
CONNAL, 92
CONNAWAY, 10
CONNEL, 47 121
CONNELL, 4 75 87 147
CONNELLY, 99
CONNER, 6 16 27 35 45 47 61 69 73 83 106 107 119 122 126 134 148
CONNET, 14 119
CONNOR, 25
CONOVER, 122
CONOWAY, 9
CONRAD, 27 46 134 147
CONROY, 42 57
CONSOLVER, 41
CONSOR, 105
CONSTANT, 105 120 124 125
CONUKLE, 131
CONWAY, 105
COOK, 6 8 24 35 39 50-52 55 60-62 64 70 83-85 88 94 97 100 101 105 108-110 119 132 139 142 143 147 156
COOKNS, 38
COOKSEY, 36 131
COOL, 27 29
COOLEY, 14 29 70 81 111

COON, 10 11 15 38 46 53 61 82 106 107 118 139 151
COONARD, 33
COONRAD, 31
COONROD, 145
COONS, 10 18
COONTS, 66
COOPER, 14 22 40 49 52 53 55 58 68 77 79 83 84 97 102 107 108 121 129 139 140 152 153
COPAS, 25
COPAZ, 75
COPELAND, 14 122 123 126
COPES, 48
COPIAS, 116
COPLAND, 116
COPLINGER, 49
COPLON, 119
COPPEL, 20 22
COPPIN, 132 148
COPPLE, 26 152
COPSEY, 53
CORATHERS, 154
CORBELL, 143
CORBERRY, 70
CORBET, 14 51 151
CORBETT, 117 151
CORBIT, 6
CORDEN, 50
CORDRAY, 60
CORDREY, 117
CORE, 149
COREY, 113 124 140
CORKIN, 94
CORKWELL, 52 108
CORMAC, 43
CORMICK, 67 107 149
CORN, 75 108 132
CORNELISON, 37
CORNELIUS, 73
CORNELL, 29 94 102 130
CORNER, 135
CORNETT, 12
CORNING, 63
CORNINGHAM, 136

CORNS, 135
CORNWELL, 123
CORPMAN, 138
CORPUS, 65
CORRALL, 132
CORRELL, 48
CORREY, 75
CORSON, 103
CORTNER, 132
CORTNEY, 132
CORWIN, 12 34 97 150
CORWINE, 135
CORY, 34 118 124
COSAN, 15
COSBEY, 12
COSBY, 111
COSHOCTON CO, 73 103
COSLER, 112
COSS, 13 66 74 97 127
COSSIT, 85
COSSNER, 103
COSTER, 13
COTERAL, 19
COTEREL, 15
COTGREAVE, 4 42
COTHRAN, 111
COTHREN, 79
COTRELL, 19
COTTERAL, 19
COTTON, 77 78
COTTRELL, 13 120
COUCH, 39 103 120 125
COUGHLIN, 40
COULTER, 50 93 137
COULTON, 137
COUNTRYMAN, 18 49
COUR, 47
COURESSEN, 29
COURSON, 139
COURTNEY, 145
COURTRIGHT, 73
COURTS, 131
COVALT, 39
COVE, 35
COVELEER, 147

COVENHOVEN, 100
COVENTON, 91
COVERT, 123
COVERTON, 126
COVIN, 141
COVOLT, 98
COWAN, 15 40 79
COWDEN, 35 77 92 109 114
COWEN, 91 93 95 105
COWGER, 49
COWGILL, 146
COWHICK, 95
COWLER, 131
COWLES, 84
COWLEY, 84
COWTHERS, 9
COX, 8 14 22 26 39 41 47 51 57 58 61 64 65
    73 95 100 104 106 107 110 112 116 118
    120 130 132 134 141 148 149 154
COXWELL, 51
COY, 11 112
COZA, 26
COZAD, 26
CRABB, 34 52
CRABIL, 143
CRABILL, 52
CRABLE, 54
CRADDS, 97
CRADLE, 77
CRAFFORD, 104
CRAFT, 54 73 76 77 92
CRAFTON, 95
CRAGE, 118
CRAGHILL, 134
CRAHILL, 91
CRAIG, 20 23 40 60 63 67 70 82 99 100 106
    116 135 139 145 152
CRAIGE, 89
CRAIGHEAD, 63 135
CRAIGHTON, 31 32 122
CRAIGN, 97
CRAIN, 71 105 122
CRAMER, 8 19 29 32 65 100 124 138
CRAMPTON, 126 151
CRAN, 121

CRANDALLS, 36
CRANE, 17 22 36 64 100 122 123 128 144 147
CRANK, 39
CRANNY, 76
CRANTRALL, 91
CRARY, 58
CRATEN, 41
CRATH, 54
CRATON, 41
CRAVEN, 132 148
CRAVISTONE, 52
CRAW, 76
CRAWFORD, 5 9 11 13 19 34 38 54 65-67 72 76 81 85 88 92 104 105 108-110 138 146 150 155
CRAYS, 94 109
CRAZE, 92
CRAZIER, 103
CREAMER, 65 99 146
CREARY, 111
CRECY, 62
CREDMER, 8
CREECHBARME, 109
CREED, 22 25 141
CREEK, 25
CREESON, 106
CREGLON, 119
CREIG, 14
CREIGH, 52
CREIGHTON, 64 101
CREMEAD, 140
CREMEENS, 12
CREMENS, 156
CREMEON, 117
CREMER, 115
CREMWELL, 13
CRESSON, 62
CRESSWELL, 58 96
CREVAN, 87
CREVISTON, 106 132
CRIBS, 62 69
CRICHFIELD, 102 114
CRICHOR, 58
CRICKET, 49

CRIDER, 58
CRIDLEY, 33
CRIMINIE, 18
CRIPPEN, 44 84
CRIPPIN, 84 153
CRIPPS, 8
CRISPIN, 51
CRISS, 121
CRISTLER, 85
CRISWELL, 87 114 128
CRITCHE, 29
CRITCHET, 157
CRITES, 43 61 136
CRITTEN, 27 29
CRITTENDEN, 143
CRITTON, 157
CRITZ, 82
CROBET, 82
CROCKER, 76
CROCKETT, 109
CROFFAD, 27
CROFFORD, 6 93
CROFT, 67
CROGHAN, 92
CROMBY, 90
CRONE, 72
CRONINGER, 62
CRONNAN, 88
CROOK, 144
CROOKHAM, 116
CROOKS, 5 35 47 67 69 76 89 92 137 143
CROOSE, 14
CROSBY, 32 55 66 82-84 88 89 95 156
CROSE, 54
CROSIN, 144
CROSLEY, 11
CROSLY, 91
CROSS, 8 20 44 46 55 58 62 88 93 97 101 105 108 114 116 136
CROSSIN, 98
CROSSLEY, 53 91 144
CROSSMAN, 76 92
CROSSON, 114 125 130 154
CROTHER, 81

CROTHERS, 9 66 80
CROUCH, 12 14 26 29 49 108 109 117
CROUSE, 7 12 63
CROW, 41 50 108 126 132 148 149
CROWDER, 144
CROWE, 4
CROWEL, 58 84
CROWELL, 89
CROWFORD, 13
CROWL, 8
CROWLEY, 18
CROWN, 146
CROY, 17 35 65 91 103 124 127 142
CROYES, 119
CROZE, 111
CRU, 154
CRUCA, 45
CRULL, 23 28 46 103 115 130 140
CRUM, 77 96
CRUMB, 11 94
CRUMHIEN, 53
CRUMLEY, 90
CRUMPTON, 64
CRUNKELTIN, 146
CRUSAN, 21 75
CRUSON, 120
CRUST, 20
CRUTERS, 12
CRUVER, 106
CRUZAN, 141
CRYDER, 47 101
CUBBERLY, 54
CUCKLEN, 137
CUDDINGTON, 135
CUGY, 27
CUL, 123
CULBAGES, 58
CULBERTSON, 11 36 92 127 134 145
CULLEMBER, 48
CULLEN, 57
CULLINS, 103
CULLISON, 44
CULLUM, 138
CULLY, 100
CULP, 5 23 31 39 152

CULPS, 131
CULVER, 36 55 103 141 143
CUMBERLAND, 23
CUMMIN, 40 59
CUMMINGS, 20 23 51 77 103 110 136 141
CUMMINS, 12 18 19 22 40 60 72 74 94 106 108 123 130 153
CUMONT, 144
CUNNINGHAM, 16 22 27 29 34 50 59 71 75 81 84 92 101 103 104 113 115 119 120 131 132 142 143 146
CUP, 33
CUPP, 9
CUPPIN, 57
CUPPS, 44
CUPPY, 155
CUPT, 33
CURANY, 150
CURL, 15 60 91 127 136 146
CURLS, 62
CURRAN, 105
CURREY, 44 121 151
CURRIE, 87 105 120
CURRY, 11 39 46 99 101 106
CURTIN, 77
CURTIS, 4 14 42 46 50 55 60 72 79 82 83 110 111 124 130 148 151
CURTS, 134
CURTZ, 10
CUSHING, 155
CUSSACK, 35
CUSTARD, 89
CUSTER, 57
CUSTIN, 84
CUSWELL, 125
CUTLER, 11 149
CUTRIGHT, 33 46 47 113 125 134
CUTRITE, 33
CUTTHALL, 62
CUTTLER, 33
CUYAHOGA CO, 89 93
CYPHERS, 109 112
CYRUS, 69
DAGEN, 71
DAILEY, 132

DAILY, 39 107 156
DAINE, 82
DAINS, 44 72
DALLAS, 74
DALLIS, 133
DALRYMPLE, 115
DALSON, 122
DALY, 64 85
DAMANS, 73
DAMAVAL, 104
DAN, 38
DANBERRY, 122
DANES, 12 108
DANFORD, 12 20 58
DANFORTH, 61
DANHAN, 40
DANIEL, 21 39 72 110 121 139
DANIELS, 4 19 46 50 71 87 96 103
DANNER, 138
DARBY, 49
DAREUTH, 51
DARK, 74
DARLIN, 35 53
DARLING, 14
DARLINGTON, 26 33 103 150
DARMER, 36
DARNELL, 71 95
DARRIE, 104
DARRILL, 71
DARROW, 5 43 69 110
DART, 54
DAUBERT, 90
DAUGHERTY, 60 63 123 127 135 156
DAUGHTER, 81
DAVENPORT, 53
DAVID, 23 108 150 151
DAVIDSON, 9 11 14 16 23-25 31 54 89 92 93 103 104 108 114 121 134 145 146 148 155
DAVIES, 32 45 104 134 147 154
DAVIS, 6 8 9 13 15 16 19 22 23 25 29 33 34 37 39-42 44 45 48-50 52 54 57 60 61 66 68-72 74 75 78-85 91 93 95 100-102 106-108 112-119 121-129 131 135 139-141 143 144 146 149 155 156

DAVISON, 19 61 89 101 103 108 112 145 150 152
DAVY, 104
DAWITT, 53
DAWNARD, 151
DAWNS, 117
DAWSON, 4 15 46 54 57 65 86 88 91 92 95 97 109 116 117 122 136 141 146 152
DAY, 15 18 22 23 35 53 56 61 64 66 74 75 78 80 98 99 105 109 115 116 133 136 140
DAYTON, 52 107 122
DEAFENBAUGH, 14
DEAL, 31 32 66
DEALLE, 46
DEAN, 9 18 41 76 87 93 115 120 134 137 140 149
DEANE, 40 123
DEANS, 136
DEAR, 131
DEARBORN, 140
DEARDORD, 18
DEARDORF, 69 138
DEATH, 29 90 100 123 130
DEAVER, 101 136
DEBARTON, 103
DEBATNON, 69
DEBOTT, 29
DEBROCK, 100
DEBRUBAR, 38
DEBRULER, 125 150
DECAMP, 17
DECAMPS, 25
DECAVER, 35
DECKER, 11 13 16 27 75 93 110 142
DECKEY, 61
DECKLE, 36
DECKRON, 79
DECORSEY, 89
DEEM, 132
DEEN, 89
DEENS, 59
DEFENBAUGH, 106
DEFREE, 85
DEGAR, 9
DEGARMORE, 131

DEGOIN, 6
DEGRAFT, 102
DEHAVEN, 26 49 143
DEITERICK, 130
DELAG, 105
DELANO, 64
DELASHMUTT, 145
DELAWARE CO, 33 78 79 82 83 116 146 156
DELAY, 154
DELK, 130
DELONG, 5 17 27 41 59 85 103 135 136
DELONGHART, 70
DELOP, 132
DELORSHMUTS, 134
DELSEVER, 79
DELSHAVER, 27 90
DEMARS, 109
DEMAS, 139
DEMEL, 77
DEMING, 88
DEMON, 102
DEMONT, 135
DEMOSS, 68 114 116
DEMPSEY, 109
DENCEN, 17
DENEEN, 88 102
DENER, 116
DENFLINGER, 113
DENHAM, 42 153
DENIKE, 38
DENISON, 109
DENMAN, 12 27 50 99 115
DENNEN, 82 102
DENNEY, 40 82
DENNIS, 42 51 60 71 100 119 126 135 141
DENNISON, 54 67 76 88 92
DENNY, 5 6 12 28 32 46 52 74 93 134
DENSON, 47
DENT, 86
DENTON, 79 129
DENUN, 97
DEPBACH, 23
DEPEW, 140
DEPRIEST, 11 119

DEPSON, 83
DEPUE, 75
DERAA, 88
DERBY, 141
DERESBACH, 109
DERICKSON, 84
DERMITT, 87
DERRICKSON, 84
DERRY, 8 9
DERVEES, 66
DETZLER, 27
DEUEY, 102
DEVAL, 11
DEVALL, 41 66 95
DEVALT, 36
DEVAULT, 95 101
DEVE, 26
DEVEDAUGH, 36
DEVENPORT, 115
DEVENS, 56
DEVER, 58 134
DEVICE, 107
DEVINE, 155
DEVION, 80
DEVITT, 99
DEVLON, 111
DEVOL, 147
DEVONE, 124
DEVOR, 128
DEVORE, 8 9 41 73 74 99 133 156
DEVORS, 144
DEVORSE, 113
DEVORSS, 35 140
DEVOSS, 53 115
DEVOUR, 16
DEWALT, 10 62
DEWEES, 50 73
DEWEESE, 27
DEWELL, 9
DEWEY, 83
DEWITT, 11 16 37 55 75 92 99 113 120 140
DEWITTT, 107
DEWOLF, 42 88
DEXAN, 25
DIAL, 104 139 155

DIAM, 32
DIBBLE, 84
DIBERT, 29
DICE, 130
DICK, 8 111
DICKARD, 17
DICKENS, 4
DICKENSHEETS, 120 133
DICKENSON, 55 110
DICKERSON, 67 88
DICKESON, 50 91
DICKEY, 8 9 40 61 83 102 106 129 145
DICKINS, 23
DICKINSON, 33 55 72 75 80 85 88 104 124 145
DICKISON, 54 80
DICKSON, 36 80 109 115 120 152
DICKUP, 108
DIDELL, 84
DIDMERTY, 46
DIDZLER, 74
DIERS, 92
DIGBEE, 42
DIGBY, 37
DIGREIS, 97
DILAWTER, 23
DILDEN, 79
DILE, 35
DILL, 19 31 35 40 59 60 69 85 98 101 112 133 134 144
DILLCOE, 17
DILLE, 65 74 93 126 133
DILLINGHAM, 76 142 145
DILLMAN, 155
DILLON, 26 41 74 75 77 85 95 133 134 144
DILLY, 66 70
DILS, 128
DILSHAVER, 27
DILTZ, 95
DILWORTH, 25
DIMES, 51
DIMINCK, 83
DIMIT, 144
DINES, 75 151
DINFORD, 41

DINGMAN, 85
DINING, 150
DINWIDDIE, 109
DINWIDDLE, 88
DISBERRY, 19
DISHERTY, 27
DISON, 104
DITTO, 27
DITTOE, 28
DITTZ, 128
DIVAULT, 51
DIVEN, 126
DIVER, 115
DIX, 92 146
DIXON, 22 27 29 47 54 56 64 67 82 89 119 129 136 146
DIXSON, 51 57
DOAM, 141
DOAN, 93
DOD, 96
DODD, 99 115 139 153
DODDS, 130 132
DODGE, 85
DODSON, 39
DOHARTY, 85
DOHERTY, 41
DOLAHAN, 47
DOLBAY, 107
DOLBEE, 52
DOLBY, 39 147
DOLE, 121 122
DOLL, 16 49
DOLLAHAN, 99
DOLLARHEAD, 150
DOLLARHIDE, 107
DOLLERHIDE, 39
DOLLISON, 144
DOLLMAN, 143
DOLLY, 53
DOLLYHEID, 106
DOLSEN, 25
DOLSHON, 94
DOMAN, 68
DOMLY, 74
DONAHAM, 154

DONAHUE, 126
DONALD, 148
DONALDSON, 56 74 81 98 125
DONALLY, 155
DONELSON, 32
DONEMIRE, 34
DONHAM, 119
DONHYAM, 154
DONNELL, 132
DONNELY, 29 109
DONNLY, 12
DONNOLLY, 74
DONOUER, 69
DOOLEY, 38 116 140
DOOP, 97
DOREN, 48
DORENHOUR, 28
DORMAN, 107
DORMIN, 51
DORN, 73
DORREL, 60
DOTSON, 134
DOTY, 23 27 58 61 74 82 95 104 109 139
DOUD, 146
DOUGHER, 41
DOUGHERTY, 19 22 39 43 45 63 70 91 100-102 123 126 132
DOUGHMAN, 50
DOUGHTON, 81
DOUGHTY, 20 70 103
DOUGLAS, 5 17 22 32 41 48 84 90 97 120 130 132
DOUGLASS, 102
DOULT, 73
DOUTHMAN, 103
DOVE, 43
DOVER, 26
DOWDEN, 9 39 57 72 155
DOWDS, 97
DOWEL, 155
DOWELL, 60 71
DOWL, 127
DOWLEY, 48
DOWLIN, 92
DOWN, 113

DOWNARD, 76 97
DOWNEY, 13 120 122
DOWNHOUER, 66
DOWNING, 26 32 33 45 54 61 72 96 107 108 136 149 154
DOWNS, 47 51 97 98 101 104 109 118 127 143 144
DOYALL, 103
DOYELL, 6
DOYLE, 25 85 93 103 124
DOZZARD, 49
DRAKE, 4 12 13 29 37 40 45 78 81 83 102 105 115 116 129 131 142
DRAPER, 80 110 142 156
DRENAN, 24
DRENNEN, 83
DRESBACH, 10 23 109
DRESBACK, 109
DRIBLER, 101
DRIGGS, 44
DRIPES, 122
DRIPS, 132 148
DRIVER, 78 79 83 133 153
DRODDY, 55
DRUCHMILLER, 8
DRUM, 16
DRUMMOND, 47
DRUMPLE, 104
DRURY, 103
DRYBREAD, 121
DRYDEN, 23 24 25 45
DUBLER, 67
DUC, 77
DUCK, 56 62
DUCKWALL, 148
DUDDLE, 74
DUDDLESON, 90
DUDLEY, 95
DUEKNALL, 44
DUER, 81
DUFER, 59
DUFF, 55 137
DUFFEY, 101 114
DUFFIELD, 126
DUGAN, 42 71 77 144 156

DUGGIN, 38
DUKE, 5 27 29 68
DUKES, 106
DULEY, 125
DULGAIN, 51
DULL, 64 89
DUM, 91
DUMFORD, 59
DUMM, 109
DUMOND, 115
DUMONT, 39
DUNAHAM, 40
DUNBAR, 82 105 135
DUNBAUGH, 134
DUNCAN, 44 46 48 57 65 83 88 102 116 127 141 145
DUNDEY, 56
DUNDLEBERGER, 83
DUNFIELD, 41
DUNFORD, 103
DUNGAN, 96 102
DUNGELBARGER, 75
DUNGEN, 108
DUNHAM, 49 83 103 129 155 156
DUNKEL, 31
DUNKEN, 98
DUNKIN, 72 98 127 130 147
DUNKLE, 95
DUNLAP, 10 20 23 34 47 51 97 104 110 114 141 143 145 149 151-153
DUNLARY, 12
DUNLEBARGER, 129
DUNN, 16 23 27 47 65 76 83 96 99 117 122 126 128 146
DUNNAVAN, 29
DUNSATH, 122
DUNSETH, 38 58
DUNWIDA, 100
DUNWOODIE, 109
DUPLETE, 27
DUPRET, 27
DUPREY, 100
DUPRIEST, 99
DURALL, 6
DURAND, 121

DURBIN, 97
DUREAVIDA, 100
DURHAM, 19
DURMP, 53
DUROGEN, 36
DURPHY, 97
DURRAUGH, 125
DURRIS, 90
DURST, 74 153
DUSH, 101
DUSOUCHEL, 101
DUST, 12
DUSTIN, 90
DUSTMAN, 76 88 92
DUTCHER, 141
DUTERROW, 130
DUTTON, 49
DUVALL, 106
DUWEES, 106
DUWITT, 17
DYAL, 61
DYE, 47 57 61 70 120 127 144
DYER, 94 95 107 117 132 134 145 151 153
DYERS, 64
DYSART, 26
DYSER, 23
DYSERT, 52 100
DYTON, 56
EACRET, 19
EAGIN, 60
EAKIN, 46 74 96 101
EAKING, 138
EAKINS, 31 95 129 148
EALS, 146
EAMES, 111
EARHART, 114 122
EARL, 51 89 91 100 136 141
EARLE, 62 138
EARLES, 149
EARLEY, 26 119 135 149
EARLEYWINE, 139
EARLICK, 47
EARLS, 18 53
EARLY, 32 63 102
EARMMAND, 90

EARNEST, 52
EASLEY, 72
EASLINGER, 66
EASON, 70
EASTBURN, 75
EASTON, 19
EASTWOOD, 19 101 119
EATON, 6 24 123 146
EATTON, 120
EAVANS, 111
EAVERSON, 123
EBERHARDT, 102
ECHBURY, 36
ECHELBERGER, 47
ECKENBARGER, 94
ECKERT, 12
ECKLEBERNE, 47
ECKLEY, 9
ECKMAN, 76 92 109
ECLEBERRY, 36
EDDINGS, 142
EDDINGTON, 60 71 136
EDDY, 12 141
EDGAR, 95 125 145
EDGE, 120
EDGELL, 35
EDGERTON, 75
EDGIN, 29
EDGINGTON, 108 111 150
EDGINTON, 20 75 108
EDGOL, 73
EDINGER, 102
EDINGTON, 7
EDLINGER, 39
EDMIND, 71
EDMISTON, 34 149
EDMONDS, 47 103
EDMONDSON, 108
EDMONS, 47
EDOMES, 130
EDSON, 32 156
EDWARD, 14 92 123
EDWARDS, 4 11 16 20 21 33 42 43 58 59 69
    99 103 108 111 113 130 137 151-153
EDWIN, 43
EDY, 137
EGBERT, 73
EGGLESTON, 110 143
EGINTON, 20 108
EGNON, 57
EHUMAN, 28
EIKELBERN, 48
EISLEY, 25
EISTER, 6
ELAM, 36
ELANEY, 152
ELBERHART, 130
ELDER, 11 26 62 92
ELDFIELD, 139
ELDRED, 93
ELI, 13 92
ELKINS, 131
ELLAM, 124
ELLER, 65
ELLET, 110
ELLINGER, 156
ELLIO, 29
ELLIOT, 7 24 29 35
ELLIOTT, 13 18 20 27 32 59 65 67 68 75 85
    90 95 102 104 114 121 123 126 127 132
    133 143 148 153 157
ELLIS, 11 26 32 72 77 93 94 106 111 118 121
    122 128 133 135 136 138 149 152
ELLISON, 6 8 11 24 25 35 50 74 75 122 150
ELLITON, 87
ELLSION, 16 153
ELLSWORTH, 142 144
ELLY, 102
ELLZROTH, 41
ELM, 48
ELROD, 9
ELRUE, 126
ELSEY, 48 152
ELSON, 103
ELSTON, 19
ELSWORTH, 56 91
ELWELL, 71 90 104
ELWOOD, 25
ELY, 82 83 105
ELZA, 46

EMALING, 8
EMBERRY, 25
EMBRICK, 35
EMERICK, 37
EMERSON, 14 40 46 58 126 154
EMERY, 9 31 140
EMMET, 33 104 144
EMMINS, 33
EMMONS, 152
EMONS, 53
EMRY, 9
ENDSEY, 97
ENGE, 117
ENGER, 117
ENGERSTEM, 6
ENGLAND, 14 25 28 48 55
ENGLE, 13 25 39 82 85 112 118 132 148
ENGLER, 118
ENGLIS, 72
ENISMYER, 107
ENLIT, 39
ENNIS, 60 72 100
ENOCH, 41 128 130
ENOS, 82 104
ENSBY, 22
ENSEY, 11
ENSIGN, 83 89
ENSLOW, 82
ENSMINGER, 107
ENSTMINGER, 153
ENTEL, 38
ENTREKIN, 47
ENTRICKEN, 101
ENTRIKIN, 47
ENTRINGER, 74
ERAY, 25
ERICK, 68
ERMABRINGER, 11
ERNHEART, 151
ERSKINE, 74 133
ERWIN, 22 39 41 59 83 96 98 120
ESCHINE, 117
ESCOL, 73
ESENY, 47
ESON, 112

ESPICH, 69
ESSEX, 46 101 106 113
ESSIG, 62
ESTEL, 19
ESTEP, 6 62
ESTIL, 58
EUBANKS, 114
EUHART, 124
EVANS, 4 5 16 20-22 26 27 29 31 33 34 47
    48 56 70 73 83 87 90 93 96 101 103 104
    114 115 121 123 125-129 133 141 145
    147-149 151 152 154-156
EVE, 123
EVENS, 132 139
EVERETT, 70 74 75 85 97
EVERHART, 17 20 22
EVERLY, 72
EVERMAN, 27 144
EVERSOL, 131
EVERTS, 34
EVERY, 157
EVET, 117
EVINS, 79
EVIRT, 104
EWART, 93
EWEN, 105
EWIN, 84
EWING, 4 15 32 34 37 65 93 97-99 114 123
    126 131-134 155
EWINGS, 70 153
EXLINE, 23 26
EXTINE, 134
EYLER, 20
EYMON, 75
EZRA, 109
FAIBR, 62
FAID, 156
FAIKBONE, 71
FAILY, 26
FAIR, 122
FAIRCHILD, 79 116
FAIRCHILDS, 79
FAIRFIELD CO, 18 66 71 73 90 131 156
FAIRHURST, 137
FALK, 49

FALKNER, 29 106 138
FALL, 68 112 132
FALLMAN, 57
FALLOWS, 120
FALSONE, 81
FAMILIAR, 34
FANAGH, 88
FANATA, 34
FANCH, 56
FANCHER, 129
FANKELBERGER, 15
FANKIE, 78
FANKLES, 92
FANNAH, 67
FANNER, 77 94
FAPPEN, 4
FARBAR, 68
FARDEN, 19
FAREARE, 127
FARGNER, 38
FARIS, 112
FARMER, 19 27 29 39 50 63 135 138 139
FARN, 16
FARNEY, 116
FARNON, 13
FARQUER, 6 119
FARR, 153
FARRAN, 142
FARRELL, 27
FARROW, 81 85
FATE, 14 144
FAUCHER, 79 79
FAULKNER, 84 90 128
FAUNBAKER, 101
FAUSLER, 110
FAUSNAUGHT, 27
FAVORITE, 65
FAXON, 143
FAYETTE CO, 77 80 128
FEAGANZE, 76
FEASTER, 40 154
FEATHERINGILL, 75
FEATHERKILLE, 24
FEDEROLPH, 23
FEDRICK, 141

FEE, 60 121 144
FEGLEY, 63
FELER, 7
FELLOWS, 110
FELTCH, 44
FENDLEY, 130
FENNEMORE, 18
FENNYMORE, 75
FENTON, 24 39 93
FEORU, 48
FERGANS, 140
FERGENS, 63
FERGESSON, 61
FERGUSON, 4 7 8 11 15 26 31 46-48 53 62
   66 83 101 103 109 112 119 122 126 136
   143 147 152 154 155
FERIS, 125
FERLER, 41
FERMON, 117
FERNAN, 34
FEROSON, 136
FERREE, 122
FERREN, 95
FERRIER, 16
FERRIN, 23 152
FERRIS, 12 56 59 70 100 114 118
FERRON, 118
FETHERCILE, 45
FETHERS, 24
FETICUCK, 69
FETTERS, 23 24 81 149
FETZER, 113
FEUIT, 26
FEURT, 152
FEWEL, 92
FEWELL, 135
FIBE, 63
FIBERT, 79
FICKEL, 98
FICKLE, 60 71 131
FIDDLER, 29
FIELD, 31 44 76 103
FIELDS, 11 32 61 94 113
FIESTER, 149
FIFE, 63

FIFER, 63 86
FIGGINS, 75 135
FIGHT, 76 92 109
FIGLEY, 96
FILES, 35
FILEY, 53
FILGE, 129
FILKALL, 156
FILSON, 32
FINCH, 131 147
FINCK, 98
FINDLAY, 10 20 42 70 85
FINDLEY, 4 13 16 20 22 124
FINICE, 112
FINIMORE, 140
FINK, 10 70 118
FINKBONE, 131
FINLAY, 56
FINLEY, 4 23 86 116
FINLONG, 19
FINMORE, 48
FINNEMORE, 26 53 101
FINNEY, 20 57 80
FIRE, 124
FIRESTONE, 12
FISCHAR, 129
FISCHER, 92
FISH, 8 50 56 89 92-94 110
FISHALL, 64
FISHBACK, 97
FISHEL, 136
FISHELL, 6
FISHER, 5-9 11 12 17-19 21-23 28 38 45 46 48 51 52 54 59 60 62 68 73 77 78 84 85 88 91 94 101 102 113 117 129 137 139 142 157
FISK, 156
FISKEL, 63
FISTER, 40
FITAP, 58
FITCH, 76 88 92 93 95 146
FITCHNER, 105
FITE, 42
FITSORT, 37
FITTING, 115

FITZGERALD, 27 59 91
FITZGEREL, 18
FITZGIRL, 59
FITZPATRICK, 71 90 111 118 119 155
FITZPPATRICK, 111
FITZWATER, 20 119
FIVECOAT, 6
FIVECOATS, 10 67
FLAGG, 126
FLAGLE, 19
FLAMING, 59
FLANDERS, 152
FLASHMAN, 66
FLAUGHER, 22 149
FLAUGHTER, 22
FLAUGLAR, 22
FLEAK, 59
FLECKER, 6
FLEEK, 39
FLEMIN, 53
FLEMING, 61 84 85 116
FLEMMIN, 55
FLEMMING, 18 40 48 52 53 65 66 95 97 115 116 144
FLESHAMAN, 66
FLESHER, 34 75 76
FLETCHER, 9 10 15 29 90 103 122 153 155
FLICK, 66 80 111
FLICKENGER, 62 101
FLINN, 20 31 100 107 109 117 119 147
FLINT, 138
FLITCHER, 122
FLITKINGER, 138
FLOOD, 15
FLORA, 38 39
FLORER, 154
FLORO, 125
FLOROW, 108
FLOWER, 37 89
FLOWERS, 35 37 77 100
FLOYD, 13 41
FLUHARTY, 34 35
FOAGEY, 45
FOBES, 81 85
FOGES, 76

FOGGER, 110
FOGLE, 13
FOGLER, 31
FOGT, 67
FOLCK, 13
FOLEY, 94 95 146
FOLKERTH, 120
FOLKIRTH, 128
FOLLIS, 128
FOLLIST, 120
FOLSOM, 85
FOLSOME, 81
FOLTNER, 129
FOMB, 93
FOMBLE, 43
FONCHER, 38
FONDA, 126
FONGY, 45
FONMAN, 147
FOOR, 61
FOORE, 60
FOOS, 77 78 79
FOOSE, 129
FOOT, 81 85 88 122
FOOTNEY, 48
FORAKER, 69
FORBENS, 13
FORBER, 62
FORBES, 85 128
FORBS, 93
FORBUS, 22
FORCE, 123 126
FORD, 7 39 41 55 62 70 85 90 94 116 119 126 134 146 153
FORDECK, 119
FORDICE, 40 126
FORDYCE, 40
FOREACRE, 35
FOREMAN, 82 101 127
FORESMAN, 115
FOREST, 41 66 74
FORGASON, 15
FORGEY, 155
FORMAN, 74 95 101
FORNEY, 63 138 139

FOROUGH, 122
FORQUER, 149
FORREST, 13 36 133
FORSBURG, 55
FORSMAN, 151
FORSYTHE, 61 97 136 156
FORT, 107
FORTIMER, 151
FORTNER, 33 47 104
FORTNEY, 151
FORY, 29
FOSS, 85
FOSSETT, 125
FOST, 15
FOSTER, 5 7 10 14 20 24 25 34 42 44 45 46 53-55 61 65 67 68 73 76 81 86 92 93 96 100 106-108 112-114 122 131 138 140 150
FOTHERZOLE, 148
FOULER, 27
FOULK, 7 8 88 92
FOULKESON, 140
FOULKS, 136
FOULS, 61
FOULT, 63
FOUND, 14
FOUNTAIN, 122
FOUST, 37 73 78 79 83 91 129 146
FOUT, 135
FOWLER, 22 32 66 76 85 88 92 99 109 124 137
FOWLS, 141
FOX, 6 15 59 70 72 83 106 123 130
FOY, 48
FRAKES, 11 102
FRAMBES, 125
FRAMBUS, 122
FRAME, 11 131 147
FRANAS, 8
FRANCE, 5 48
FRANCES, 64 134
FRANCIS, 10 37 47 48
FRANCISCO, 11 92
FRANE, 127
FRANK, 42 63 68 76 88 135

FRANKEBERGER, 118
FRANKLIN, 47 48
FRANKLIN CO, 10 31 55 65 79 84 90 133 145 156
FRANKS, 92 137
FRANTZ, 127
FRASER, 40
FRASIER, 39
FRASY, 50
FRAZE, 124
FRAZEE, 138
FRAZER, 19 20 32 39 42 72 101 151
FRAZIER, 75 86 89 106 107 125 145 152 154
FRAZURE, 146
FREDERICK, 5 7 8 17 31 39 43 49 56 63 85 130
FREDERICKS, 5
FREDRICK, 26
FREE, 39
FREED, 22
FREEDLY, 39
FREELAND, 25 71 108 111
FREEMAN, 54 57 61 62 73 89 93 99 100 112 123 131
FREEMONT, 107
FREET, 6 68 97
FREETE, 126
FRENCH, 32 58 84 89 120 138
FRERWODE, 15
FRERWODS, 15
FRESHOUR, 35 114
FRESSMAN, 52
FRETIH, 143
FREYHART, 52
FRIDLEY, 119
FRIED, 103
FRIEND, 139
FRIEZE, 19
FRILEY, 146
FRINK, 110
FRITZ, 124
FROST, 12 39 45 65 69 91 107 141 144
FROURDALE, 19
FRUCKLER, 101
FRUNK, 24

FRURA, 155
FRY, 25 96 116
FRYAR, 16 49
FRYATT, 6
FRYBACK, 65 128
FRYE, 23 29 32 60 70 96 104 117 140 141 151
FRYMAN, 74
FUDGE, 149
FUERT, 148
FUGATE, 15 26 100
FUGUS, 123
FUIK, 67
FUILINGER, 126
FULEN, 107
FULK, 14 72 134 156
FULKIRTH, 100
FULKS, 63 136
FULLEN, 96
FULLER, 11 17 29 45 53 55 72 82 86 107 133 153
FULLNIG, 92
FULSON, 57 113
FULTON, 8 9 12 22 44 45 47 50 53 58 74 101
FULTZ, 33 48 77 134 151
FUNK, 27 46 61 101 111 136 145 147 152
FUNSTON, 53
FUQUA, 150
FURBUSH, 58
FURET, 113
FURGESON, 85 103 110
FURNACE, 46
FURNEY, 135
FURROW, 51
FURRY, 16
FURST, 113
FURTHY, 60
FUSSEL, 82
FUTHEY, 71
FUTHY, 139
GABLE, 11 144
GABRIEL, 82 146
GADBERRY, 52
GAFF, 62 133 138
GAGANY, 99

GAGE, 82
GAINER, 141
GAITS, 47
GALASPY, 20 94
GALBRAITH, 68 100 105 115 151
GALBREATH, 102
GALBRITH, 53
GALE, 129
GALL, 18
GALLAGER, 64
GALLAGHER, 96
GALLAHAN, 132
GALLANT, 79 83
GALLBRAITH, 25
GALLESPIE, 87
GALLIA CO, 153 155
GALLISPIE, 141
GALLOWAY, 6 40 85 87 142 150
GALLOWEAY, 124 125
GALOR, 29
GAMBLE, 5 11 43 58 68 91 106 116 151
GAMBRIEL, 21
GAMER, 25
GAMES, 23
GANARD, 21 38
GANASDOL, 130
GANDY, 125 134
GANER, 12
GANNON, 123
GANO, 4 54 61 132
GANSEL, 80
GANSOY, 45
GANT, 47 87 114 123
GANY, 126
GANYARD, 77
GANYUM, 74
GARARD, 99 100 111 119 122 127 143 144
GARD, 17 37 40 58 60 73 112 116 125
GARDENER, 28
GARDINER, 34
GARDNER, 11 34-36 56 59 63 74 93 97 127 132 135 137 142 148 152
GARLOUGH, 129
GARNER, 93 112 123
GARNET, 17
GARRARD, 132
GARRATT, 96
GARRET, 25 44 48 132 148
GARRETT, 25 130
GARRINGE, 7
GARRINGER, 62
GARRISON, 16 18 40 59 81 99 102 125 139 145
GARRIT, 29
GARRYSON, 57
GARVER, 17 78
GARWIN, 144
GARWOOD, 18 127 144
GARY, 156
GASKIL, 144
GASKILL, 62 80 111
GASSAWAY, 137
GASSET, 31
GASSWAY, 16
GASTER, 27 57
GASTIN, 67
GASTON, 39 74 153
GATE, 56 144
GATES, 17 48 54 67 69 102 125 135 142 144 155 156
GATEWOOD, 32
GATT, 151
GATTON, 43
GAUL, 34
GAULT, 110
GAUMER, 131
GAUNT, 123
GAUSE, 156
GAVIN, 45
GAVIT, 50 70
GAWEN, 125
GAWLEY, 124
GAY, 39 54 84
GAYLOR, 110 142
GAYLORD, 84 89 142
GAYNE, 91
GEARHART, 85
GEARY, 72
GEAUGA CO, 76 90 111 137
GEBHART, 37

GEDDES, 63 135
GEDDIS, 138
GEE, 33 37 83 152
GEER, 36 141
GEIGER, 27
GELELANT, 130
GENDER, 48
GENTLE, 59
GENTREE, 21
GEORGE, 6 11 33 83 95 101 115 118 129 150
GEPPHART, 37
GERARD, 134
GERGUSON, 125
GERMAN, 35
GERODELLE, 88
GEROME, 11
GERRARD, 98
GERRON, 82
GERSHON, 56
GESSEL, 90
GESSELE, 73
GESSELL, 14
GEST, 118 119
GHARKEY, 148
GHITTLESSEY, 56
GIBB, 125
GIBBES, 146
GIBBON, 36
GIBBONS, 70
GIBBS, 39 44 45 64 74 82 88 101 127 139 151
GIBERSON, 97
GIBLEN, 31
GIBLER, 44 148
GIBRUTH, 103
GIBSON, 6 8-12 16 17 22 27 33 42 50 51 54 60 62 63 68 69 72-74 82 87-89 92 103 104 106 108 111 112 116 117 121 124 129 132 136 138 144 148 152 156
GIDDINGS, 85
GIFT, 130
GIGER, 19
GILASPIE, 53
GILBERT, 6 7 21 54 65 75 76 78 88 92 111 132

GILBREATH, 39
GILBRUTH, 115
GILCHRIST, 58
GILDERSLEIVER, 81
GILFILLAN, 35 151
GILFILLEN, 114 151
GILGUS, 93
GILHAM, 13
GILKERSON, 71
GILKEY, 37
GILKIN, 128
GILKINSON, 60
GILKISON, 97
GILL, 123 124 137
GILLASPEY, 72
GILLASPIE, 52 57 153
GILLELAN, 128
GILLELAND, 33
GILLER, 145
GILLESPIE, 121 122
GILLET, 56
GILLETT, 110
GILLIAN, 36
GILLIES, 79
GILLILAN, 103 113 116
GILLILAND, 8 41 46 74 133 140
GILLIS, 22 38 43 121-123
GILLISPY, 141
GILLMAN, 39 81 157
GILLSPY, 141
GILLUM, 73 103
GILMAN, 59 70 86
GILMON, 19
GILMOR, 29
GILMORE, 7 15 16 27 45 47-50 67 80 97 111 116 140
GILMRE, 108
GILNER, 111
GILPIN, 7 15 118
GILRUTH, 46 140
GILSON, 62 63 136
GILSTEN, 116
GIMANTON, 105
GIMM, 32
GIMMONS, 113

GINNING, 29
GINSEL, 34
GIPSON, 113
GISSARION, 57
GIVEN, 92
GIVENS, 33 87 112
GLADDEN, 68
GLADMAN, 27
GLADMORE, 10
GLANEY, 122
GLASBURN, 153
GLASBY, 84
GLASCOCK, 53
GLASCOW, 45
GLASGON, 24
GLASGOW, 75
GLASS, 7 91 154
GLAZE, 26 93 103
GLEASON, 88
GLEEZE, 57
GLEN, 120
GLENDANING, 21
GLENDENNING, 152
GLENN, 5 11 64 68 120
GLEZE, 20
GLICK, 73 90
GLODMAN, 6
GLOSSON, 8
GLOVER, 23 118 148 150 152
GLUM, 124
GOBLE, 57 63 91 120 133 144
GOBLIN, 59
GODARD, 95
GODDARD, 75 91
GODDEN, 51
GODFREY, 22 83 99 117
GODMAN, 90
GODSPED, 94
GOESHORN, 133
GOETIERY, 10
GOETSCHINS, 145
GOFF, 60 84 107 125
GOFLER, 31
GOHAN, 12
GOLDALHY, 39

GOLDBERRY, 113
GOLDSBERRY, 51 113
GOLDSBY, 87
GOLDSMITH, 55 72 76 85
GOLDTHWAITE, 138
GOLLOWAY, 97
GOMER, 101
GOMLY, 21
GONCHER, 67
GONE, 111
GONESS, 126
GOOD, 27 35 52 123 155
GOODALE, 5
GOODE, 22 65 123
GOODEN, 35 68 140
GOODENOUGH, 23 87
GOODFELLOW, 134 144
GOODIN, 38 39 116 117
GOODLOVE, 146
GOODMAN, 109 114 118
GOODPASTER, 144
GOODPASTURE, 19
GOODPOSTER, 59
GOODRICH, 29 79 85 104
GOODRIDGE, 135
GOODSPEED, 72 78 86
GOODWIN, 39 53 86 87 117 126
GOODY, 24
GOOKE, 126
GOOLEY, 52 75
GOOMON, 66
GOOSEHORN, 74
GORBY, 81
GORDAN, 38
GORDON, 9 20 31 32 37 52 65 68 82 100 106 108 114 119 128 131 137
GORDY, 143
GORLEY, 126
GORMAN, 85 119
GORMOR, 72
GORTON, 65
GOSLEE, 46
GOSS, 19 55 63 135 139
GOSSAGE, 97 138
GOSSARD, 76 113

GOSSELT, 31
GOSSET, 59 126
GOSSETT, 44 102 154
GOSSOM, 113
GOST, 19
GOTH, 153
GOTLIFFE, 22
GOTT, 99 112 120
GOTTHALLS, 97
GOUCHER, 92
GOULD, 4 42 82 121 122
GOULE, 109
GOURLEY, 137
GOW, 80
GOWDY, 36 87 105 124 125
GOWER, 17
GOWINGE, 54
GRABB, 66
GRACE, 8
GRAD, 44
GRADEN, 6
GRADLESS, 113 149
GRADY, 99 140 141 151 155
GRAFTER, 15
GRAFTON, 46 95 109
GRAGG, 77 140
GRAHAM, 8 12 19 21 33 36 38 51 52 54 57 63 64 74 85 91-93 96 106 116 123 124 132 135 137 147 150 152 153 155 157
GRAN, 15
GRANDEN, 102
GRANGER, 36 56 70 76 90 110 143
GRANSTAFF, 145
GRANT, 21 25 37 52 83 96 98 121 150
GRAPER, 35
GRATE, 145
GRATRIDGE, 118
GRAVES, 15 29 47 48 70 153 157
GRAY, 10 13 17 26 29 34 38 48 53 95 101 102 109 114 119 122 130 138 140 144 153
GRAYBILL, 29
GRAYHAM, 59
GRAYTES, 25
GRAYUM, 74

GREAVES, 152
GREEN, 8 12 15 27 29 36 43 46 48 50 51 59 65 71 73 74 80 82 85 88 91 93 94 103 104 110 117 120 127-129 132 134 139 140 144-146 151
GREEN CO, 100 112 122 124 128
GREENE, 46 47 123
GREENE CO, 13 63 87 120
GREENFIELD, 15 97 103 107 155
GREENHO, 106
GREENLE, 6
GREENLEE, 8 11
GREENLEY, 26 152
GREENLIE, 112
GREENMAN, 25 126
GREENOH, 10
GREENWOOD, 64 114
GREER, 14 65 127 139
GREGG, 18 54 57
GREGOR, 29
GREGORY, 40 43-45 57 78 84 86 116 129 134 135 156
GRELLE, 67
GREY, 39 59 71
GREYBILL, 90
GRIBBY, 31
GRIBNER, 8
GRIER, 41 97
GRIFFIN, 21 38 45 74 82 89 91 92 99 115 123 125 130
GRIFFIS, 122
GRIFFITH, 12 21 85 93 100 114 117 120 127 130 131 134 136
GRIFFY, 120
GRIGGS, 61 83
GRILTT, 110
GRIM, 6 10 145
GRIMES, 13 41 58 62 74 133 136 140 152 156
GRIMM, 8 64 106 135 147
GRIMMINGS, 26
GRIN, 63
GRINS, 46
GRINSTAFF, 104
GRISLEY, 148

GRISOM, 116
GRISWOLD, 84 129
GROGAN, 108 121
GROGEN, 93
GROMES, 128
GRONINGER, 26
GRONN, 130
GROOG, 68
GROOM, 11 141
GROOMER, 26
GROOMS, 25
GROON, 11
GROSCOSS, 88
GROSCOST, 81
GROSE, 15 129
GROSS, 73
GROTON, 65
GROU, 8
GROVE, 10 16 34 48 114 128 137
GROVER, 5 20 25 34
GROVES, 5 34 37 45 54 60 64 71 140 154
GROWEL, 29
GRUB, 141
GRUBB, 11 35 46 61 65 77 113 116 137
GRUBBS, 61
GRUBLE, 136
GRUNDY, 31
GRUNER, 8
GRY, 124
GUARD, 82 104 138
GUBBELL, 74
GUERIN, 119
GUERLEY, 56
GUERNSEY CO, 69 70
GUESBACH, 74
GUESS, 65 109
GUFEY, 64
GUILD, 50 94
GUIN, 125 139
GUINN, 139
GULLIFER, 22
GUMP, 26
GUN, 76
GUNCKEL, 37
GUNDER, 131

GUNDEY, 47
GUNIES, 116
GUNLES, 116
GUNN, 76 89 126 148 150
GUNSOL, 111
GUNSTON, 153
GUNTLE, 130
GURWELL, 126
GUSHWA, 37
GUSTIN, 102 130
GUTCHES, 92
GUTHENY, 154
GUTHERIE, 154
GUTHERY, 135 154
GUTHRIDGE, 108 118
GUTHRIE, 46 58 63 96 109 117 128 154
GUTHROP, 33
GUTRIDGE, 60 75 118 150
GUTSHALL, 8 9
GUTTERY, 7-9 126 154
GUVONER, 56
GUY, 65 78 93 128
GWAHE, 109
GWINNE, 32
GWRIN, 119
HACK, 58
HACKER, 120
HACKET, 56
HACKETT, 153
HACKNEY, 117
HADDIX, 13
HADDON, 136
HADDOX, 116 120
HADESTY, 15
HADIX, 47
HADLEY, 46 116 139
HAES, 105
HAFRER, 72
HAGEMAN, 138
HAGER, 41 52
HAGERFIELD, 67
HAGERMAN, 7 33
HAGGARD, 75
HAGGART, 135
HAGGARTY, 156

HAGGERT, 34 113
HAGGERTY, 21
HAGLEY, 47
HAHAN, 38 62
HAHN, 27 57 62 67 73 136 147
HAIDESTY, 15 22
HAIGH, 111
HAIL, 9 118
HAINES, 17 29 36 57 58 65 91 106 127 128 132 143 144 146 154 155
HAINS, 93
HAIR, 6 31 140 141 148
HAIRACT, 28
HAIRE, 131
HAKILL, 22
HALDEMER, 98
HALDERMAN, 115 117
HALE, 36 84 90 100 129 143 153 154
HALES, 5
HALEY, 44 46 56 64 97
HALFHILL, 82
HALL, 12 14 16 17 23 27 32 41 42 46 48 53 57 60 61 66 67 76 79 82 89 92 95-97 99 101 109 110 112 113 117 121 122 127 129 133 138 142-144 148 156
HALLE, 57
HALLER, 6 49
HALLEY, 103
HALLIN, 127
HALLINGER, 14
HALTZ, 95
HAMAN, 130
HAMBERGER, 28
HAMBLEN, 59
HAMEL, 125
HAMER, 100
HAMES, 112
HAMIL, 30 144
HAMILL, 43
HAMILTON, 9 11 18 19 20 35 36 39 40 51 55 58 63 66 76 78 90 92 93 100 102 106-108 110 112 113 120 123 132 133 135 137 153 154
HAMILTON CO, 43 72 112 114 119 121 132 154

HAMLER, 134
HAMMEL, 100
HAMMELL, 33 35 129
HAMMER, 141
HAMMERLY, 137
HAMMERSLEY, 107 118
HAMMET, 69
HAMMETT, 107 150
HAMMON, 27 132 142 143
HAMMOND, 19 24 66 72 96 97
HAMMUT, 48
HAMON, 41
HAMPTON, 46 89 92 150
HAMSON, 150
HANAMAN, 115
HANBACK, 128
HANCE, 65 99
HANCHELL, 90
HANCOCK, 99 132
HAND, 18 38 54 59 74 81 99 102 113 138
HANDCOCK, 58
HANDERSHOT, 114
HANDLE, 36 131
HANDLEY, 148
HANENAN, 8
HANER, 140
HANES, 108 117 124
HANET, 59
HANEY, 12 44 45 50 65 100 110 120 134 144
HANIEL, 30
HANIMAN, 74
HANING, 6
HANINGTON, 82
HANIS, 54
HANK, 153
HANKINS, 42 75
HANKS, 16 49 56 81
HANLEY, 8 123 132
HANLON, 8
HANNA, 5 12 61 68 70 125 134
HANNADY, 152
HANNAH, 14 63 67 81 85 128
HANNAMAN, 80
HANNAN, 152
HANNASON, 132

HANNER, 35
HANNING, 44
HANNON, 97 101 140
HANOVER, 23
HANSON, 16 47 48 94
HANTIN, 123
HANY, 38 88
HAPNER, 84
HAPPIS, 80
HARBAUGH, 22 63 108 138
HARBER, 35 106 128
HARBERSON, 85 93 156
HARBERT, 96 104 118 145
HARBISON, 38
HARBSELL, 149
HARBUT, 106
HARCELL, 147
HARCOURT, 39
HARD, 46
HARDEBROOK, 6
HARDEM, 36
HARDEN, 36
HARDENBROOKS, 68
HARDESTY, 13 33 36 60 137 152
HARDEY, 51
HARDIE, 106
HARDIN, 24 28 40 73 82 121 146
HARDING, 27 65 76 83 127
HARDINGER, 92
HARDISTY, 37
HARDMAN, 60 129
HARDY, 19 51 58 71 85 90 92 103 112
HARE, 31 35 60 71 113 129 131 149 155
HARFIELD, 114
HARGADINE, 91
HARITZ, 28
HARKER, 129
HARKS, 137
HARLAND, 11 102
HARLEY, 53 95 134
HARLIN, 57 102 132
HARMAN, 10 90
HARMON, 10 41 42 56 82 89 96 97 105 108 143
HARNAN, 32

HARNEL, 27
HARNESS, 34
HARNETT, 91
HARNISH, 7
HARNUM, 9
HAROD, 19
HARPER, 4 7 16 17 18 23 40 46 67 75 76 78 80 81 84 86 99 107 109-111 116 119 128 131 146 147
HARPSTER, 10 96
HARR, 39 146
HARRAL, 116
HARRED, 137
HARREL, 135
HARRELTON, 145
HARRIMAN, 6 7 13 32 54 133 138
HARRING, 83
HARRINGTON, 16 53 55 83 110
HARRIS, 15 16 18 20 21 24 26-31 36 38 40-42 48 50 54 55 60 71 73 81 87 102 104 112 113 115 116 122 123 126 128 129 139 140 144 150
HARRISON, 4 5 11 25 29 39 48 54 57 59 63 64 80 84 90 92 95 100 111 114 120 121 129 133 134 138
HARRISON CO, 9 11 67
HARRIT, 41
HARROD, 80 104 139 145
HARSH, 50
HARSHALL, 48
HARSHMAN, 12 71 130
HARSON, 81
HARSTOCK, 129
HART, 16 18 36 38 39 51 58 81 88 89 97 110 131 143
HARTEIL, 108
HARTEN, 12
HARTER, 57 65 95 106 112 130 156
HARTING, 94
HARTINGER, 89
HARTLE, 105
HARTLEY, 15 34 41 60 71 114
HARTMAN, 5 8 18 39 61 117 125 156
HARTNER, 136
HARTON, 116

HARTSELL, 35 56
HARTSHORN, 9
HARTSOCK, 73
HARTTER, 149
HARTWELL, 84
HARTZ, 28
HARTZEL, 37
HARTZELL, 56
HARVEY, 18 31 41 51 71 76 78 80 96 123 124 145 146
HARWOOD, 62 136
HASELTON, 75
HASHBARGER, 27
HASHER, 90
HASHPARGER, 15
HASKNEY, 101
HASLETON, 33
HASLIP, 108
HASSELTON, 140
HASTINGS, 18
HATCH, 44 45 72 78 79 83 130
HATFIELD, 21 37 38 65 72 94 98 105 107 128 132
HATHAW, 39
HATHAWAY, 18 23 40 41 43 60 130
HATHENEY, 108
HATHORN, 38
HATTEN, 33
HATTER, 31 49
HATTICKS, 46
HATTON, 48 154
HAU, 71
HAUGHEY, 8
HAUGHMAN, 7
HAUN, 104
HAVENS, 69 119 135
HAVERFIELD, 6 10 67
HAVERLOW, 11 92
HAVERSBACK, 74
HAVERSTOCK, 138
HAWEY, 89 140 145
HAWK, 22 67 80 131 153
HAWKER, 15 112
HAWKINS, 15 37 38 70 72 76 106 112 114
HAWLEY, 4 86

HAWMAN, 10 61
HAWN, 6
HAWORTH, 106
HAWTHORN, 10
HAWTHORNE, 7
HAWWRICK, 71
HAY, 144
HAYDEN, 89 129
HAYDON, 29 146
HAYES, 8 19 24 26 29 33 34 49 54 57 58 63 76-78 80 81 85 86 88 90 94 95 106 108 109 111 112 127 130 133 135 140 144 155
HAYMAKER, 110 142
HAYMAN, 15 21
HAYNES, 23 40 52 61 96 109 114 149
HAYS, 26 37 105 111
HAYSE, 105 153
HAYSLIP, 24 75 149 150
HAYWOOD, 74
HAZEL, 118
HAZELTINE, 58
HAZLETT, 59
HAZZARD, 54
HEAD, 155
HEADLEY, 52 94 140 152 156
HEADMAN, 31
HEAGE, 70
HEALY, 82
HEANEY, 16
HEANY, 97
HEAP, 145
HEARSOFF, 55
HEART, 110
HEARTON, 130
HEASTON, 11 92 130
HEATER, 52 118
HEATH, 8 17 25 48 52 57 64 78 116 117 129 150 153
HEATHMAN, 90
HEATON, 4 11 19 37 40 57 58 101 102 134 136
HEAVER, 78
HEAVERLO, 154
HEAVILORS, 83

HEBURN, 103
HECK, 28
HECKCOX, 88
HECKETHORNE, 106
HECKINTHORN, 62
HECKWELLER, 58
HECOX, 44 87
HEDD, 147
HEDDINGS, 8
HEDGES, 10 14 17 32 33 153 154
HEDINGTON, 23
HEDLEY, 101
HEEK, 63
HEEMTHORN, 7
HEETEN, 153
HEFFNER, 136
HEFNER, 61
HEIFKIN, 32
HEIGHEY, 27
HEIGHWAY, 72
HEINARY, 10
HEINLY, 23
HEINMAN, 126
HEINTZ, 28
HEISTAND, 114
HEISTER, 130
HEIZER, 59
HEL, 106
HELLENBACH, 46
HELLER, 31
HELLUM, 106
HELM, 139
HELMER, 25
HELMES, 73
HELMICK, 15 63 136
HELMS, 15 85
HELPHREY, 50
HELSEL, 92
HELSER, 14
HELT, 78 116 129 146
HELTERBRAND, 25 71
HELVIE, 124
HELWICK, 7
HEMMING, 89
HEMPHILL, 26 57 92 113 131 153

HEMPLEMAN, 25 150
HENANY, 23
HENDERSHOT, 34 66
HENDERSON, 5 6 8 20 22 24 28 41 45 50 53
    61 69 73 80 81 91 104 107 112 113 115
    125 126 128 138 141 151 154
HENDRICHS, 79
HENDRICK, 35 38 50
HENDRICKS, 38 47 49 112 116
HENDRICKSON, 22 56
HENDRIX, 15 118
HENESS, 66 151
HENHAM, 83
HENKINS, 14
HENLAND, 23
HENLEY, 38
HENLMAIN, 84
HENLY, 127
HENNELL, 127
HENNEY, 101
HENNING, 61 124 136
HENNIS, 51
HENRY, 7 8 13 16 23 27 33 39-41 57 66 72
    78 85 94 103 109 123 130 141 149
HENSETE, 87
HENSLEY, 15
HENSON, 39 150
HENTHORN, 41
HEPLER, 46
HEPNER, 63
HEPSEN, 15
HERCULES, 19 59
HERD, 74 95 133 134
HERDMAN, 95
HEREOFF, 145
HERNER, 130
HEROD, 24
HEROFF, 56
HERON, 38
HERRICK, 82 143
HERRIN, 38 39 107
HERRINGTON, 76
HERROD, 115 125
HERROLD, 107
HERRON, 36 73

HERSHBERGER, 19
HERSTATER, 52
HERTAND, 12
HESBR, 18
HESKE, 13
HESLER, 121
HESLET, 81 111
HESLEY, 131
HESS, 55 116
HESTER, 7 59 113 130 149
HETH, 45
HETSEL, 11
HETZER, 20
HEUSTON, 66
HEVELY, 7
HEWET, 152
HEWEY, 94 102 103
HEWINS, 84
HEWIT, 84
HEWITT, 21 44 46 51 85 102 152
HEWS, 107
HEWSON, 4
HEYNS, 110
HEZLEP, 93
HIACON, 45
HIALT, 27
HIBBEN, 117
HIBBER, 22
HIBBS, 40 100 108 120
HIBNER, 136
HICE, 152
HICKCOX, 141
HICKLE, 109 155
HICKMAN, 6 55 63 89 100 123 124 135
HICKS, 8 31 43 44 109 117 121
HICKSON, 25 48 91
HICSON, 47
HIDE, 133
HIDRICK, 48
HIESTAND, 24
HIGBEE, 125
HIGGENBOTHAM, 26
HIGGINBOTHAM, 46
HIGGINBOTHOM, 87 93
HIGGINS, 7 9 22 23 48 62 66 78 82 110

HIGH, 27 52
HIGHBANS, 26
HIGHES, 23
HIGHLAND, 90
HIGHLAND CO, 17 23 31 44 111 147 148
HIGHLANDER, 112
HIGHLEY, 108 153
HIGHLY, 84
HIGHMAN, 71
HIGHT, 18
HIGLEY, 56 110
HIGON, 61
HIL, 31 88
HILAND, 27 33 140
HILDERBRAND, 111 141
HILE, 94
HILES, 71 139
HILL, 6 10 15 27 33 38 43 51-53 56 59-61 64
    65 70 72 74-76 80 84 85 87 89 91 101 102
    108 109 112 116 119 121 128 130 138
    141 142 145 147 148 153
HILLARD, 45
HILLARY, 32
HILLENBOHKER, 87
HILLHOUSE, 66 127
HILLIARD, 44 65
HILLMAN, 4 69 121 146
HILLS, 79 83 84 116 139
HILMAN, 104
HILSEL, 145
HILSER, 136
HILSON, 140
HILT, 129 144
HILTEBRAND, 31
HILTON, 88 112
HIME, 54
HIMES, 47
HINCKLE, 12 80
HINCKLEY, 43
HINDE, 125
HINDES, 123
HINDMAN, 43 60 155
HINE, 54 94 110
HINEMAN, 23
HINES, 45 47 48 71 82 130 134 143

HINKLE, 75
HINKLEY, 156
HINKSON, 155
HINKSTON, 123
HINMAN, 89
HINNER, 99
HINTHORN, 98
HINTO, 29
HINTON, 23 31 32 117 134 146 147 155
HINZY, 9
HIPKINS, 74
HIRD, 91
HIRE, 75 113
HIRES, 65
HIRTH, 8
HIS, 20
HISER, 10 52
HISKET, 126
HISLEY, 81
HITCHCOCK, 6 10 56 82 87 152
HITCHINS, 39
HITCHOCK, 67
HITE, 27
HITER, 94
HITS, 109
HITTLE, 112
HIVELY, 46 139 140 152
HIVLEY, 118
HIVLING, 87
HIX, 111
HIXON, 60 107 124
HIXSON, 59
HIZER, 154
HOADLY, 141
HOAG, 68
HOBAUGH, 95 141
HOBBS, 46 133 152
HOBLET, 123
HOBLIT, 100
HOBOUGH, 33 48 54
HOBSON, 15
HOCK, 23
HOCKS, 36
HODDEY, 140
HODDY, 18 34 35 51 75 113

HODGE, 91 129 146
HODGES, 21 45 90 150
HOEL, 76
HOFF, 122
HOFFINES, 33
HOFFMAN, 27 55 62 63 84 101 111 140 143 148 152 153
HOFFMER, 96
HOFSTEATER, 110
HOFT, 68
HOGAN, 112 123
HOGE, 15
HOGES, 19
HOGLAND, 73 138
HOGLIN, 139
HOHN, 7
HOHNE, 62
HOISLIT, 50
HOKE, 27
HOKMER, 37
HOLARSTAT, 118
HOLBOUGH, 95
HOLBS, 32
HOLCOMB, 50 59 142 143 153 156
HOLCOMBE, 18
HOLDEN, 12 73
HOLDER, 29
HOLDERMAN, 65 84 128
HOLE, 58 84 112 130
HOLES, 8
HOLINSHADE, 121
HOLLADAY, 99 102
HOLLAN, 26
HOLLAND, 23 115 125 140
HOLLANDBACK, 60
HOLLENBACK, 73 131
HOLLER, 58 95
HOLLEY, 130
HOLLIDAY, 66
HOLLINBACK, 70
HOLLINGER, 13
HOLLINGS, 153
HOLLINGSHEAD, 116
HOLLORY, 32
HOLLOWAY, 51-53 75 80 140

HOLLOWELL, 112
HOLLY, 10 56
HOLLYDAY, 131
HOLM, 136
HOLMAN, 141
HOLMES, 7 8 13 16 32 38 41 50 67 97 101 103 108 120 123 127 145 157
HOLMSTED, 79
HOLSON, 10
HOLT, 4 104 115 136 139 140
HOLTON, 104
HOLTS, 61
HOLTZ, 136
HOLTZKLAW, 132
HOLVERSTAT, 13
HOLVERSTOTT, 23
HOMAN, 138
HOMDEL, 13
HOMERO, 85
HOMES, 137
HONE, 84
HONEY, 80
HONK, 36
HONNEL, 16
HONSON, 64 143
HOOD, 29 51 67 90 91 140
HOOFMAN, 42
HOOK, 46 50 133
HOOKER, 90
HOOLE, 19
HOOP, 107 111 120 124 125 148
HOOPER, 14 65
HOOTE, 134
HOOTON, 76
HOOVER, 11 13 21 25 27 32 36 42 48 50 55 59 81 94 97 101 118 150
HOPE, 138
HOPHY, 126
HOPKINS, 23 33 35 38 75 76 78 81 85 90 91 97 106 112 119 129 133 134 140 146 149 154
HOPPER, 65
HOPPIS, 153
HOPSON, 48
HOR, 32

HORDEN, 28
HORLEY, 152
HORMEL, 122
HORN, 48 95 123
HORNBACK, 125 134
HORNBECK, 54
HORNE, 14 112 149
HORNER, 59 144
HORNEY, 80
HORNISH, 101
HORR, 102
HORSBERRY, 26
HORSEY, 73 115
HORTMAN, 49
HORTON, 73
HOSACK, 17
HOSBEN, 9
HOSBROOK, 39 114
HOSELTON, 92
HOSEY, 54
HOSHER, 139 140
HOSHLER, 139
HOSIER, 28 128
HOSKENSON, 44
HOSKINS, 32 70 76 79 83 108 113
HOSLIP, 150
HOSS, 33
HOSSELTON, 52
HOSSIER, 65
HOSSLETON, 145
HOSSMAN, 10
HOST, 5
HOSTER, 61
HOSTETTER, 10 64
HOTEN, 44
HOTSENPILLER, 96
HOTSENVILLER, 154
HOTT, 32 134
HOTTER, 95
HOTTICKS, 48
HOTZENBECKLAR, 33
HOUCK, 85 94
HOUGH, 20 81 85 124 148
HOUGHAM, 37 155
HOUGHAN, 31

HOUGHMAN, 31
HOUGHTON, 82 84
HOUSE, 46 95 121 145 152
HOUSEHOLDER, 5 28 64
HOUSER, 58 65 127 132
HOUSET, 33
HOUSH, 21
HOUSMAN, 49
HOUSMOND, 25
HOUSTEN, 106
HOUSTON, 132
HOUTS, 139
HOUTY, 67
HOVER, 36 75 78
HOVEY, 67
HOW, 45 87 94
HOWARD, 14 17 23 39 46 48 52 100 102 104 105 109 116 117 119 121 141 145 154
HOWE, 16 17 35 49 81 99
HOWEL, 16 43 133
HOWELL, 41 45 72 74 95 144 153
HOWEY, 60
HOWITT, 73
HOWLAND, 21 22 93
HOWMAN, 136
HOWTELL, 135
HOY, 17 64 112 139
HOYE, 6
HOYLES, 92
HOYLS, 89
HOYT, 4 69 87 124
HOZIER, 120
HOZLER, 58
HUBANKS, 150
HUBARD, 138
HUBAUGH, 101
HUBBARD, 54 56 82 115 146
HUBBEL, 153
HUBBELL, 45 74 116 146
HUBBERT, 52
HUBBLE, 18 141
HUBBS, 41
HUBER, 29 90
HUBERT, 33
HUDDLE, 64
HUDDLESTON, 19
HUDGALL, 57
HUDGILL, 61
HUDLOW, 84
HUDSON, 32 51 71 76 111 118-120 142 144
HUES, 105
HUEY, 22
HUFF, 11 50 81 91 114 138 148
HUFFER, 27
HUFFERD, 28 98
HUFFHINDS, 11
HUFFMAN, 7 9 14 15 18 28 37 40 66 71 131 138
HUFFMIRE, 115
HUFFORD, 24 120
HUFMAN, 128
HUFNER, 138
HUGGMAN, 53
HUGHEL, 43
HUGHES, 7 19 22 24 33 49 50 59 60 72 81 88 101 102 108 118 146 153 156
HUGHEY, 25 32 60 107
HUGHS, 16 17 19 22 46 137
HUISTAR, 28
HUIT, 130
HUKELL, 6
HUL, 29
HULBART, 81
HULBERT, 43 143
HULET, 155
HULIT, 49
HULK, 89
HULL, 8 9 29 35 52-54 64 73 77 78 81 86 88 94 104 134 152
HULLENBURGER, 28
HULLING, 122
HULS, 95
HULSE, 42 137 150
HULTZ, 135
HUM, 110
HUMASON, 88
HUMBARGER, 140
HUMBEL, 63
HUMBERGER, 28
HUMBLE, 95

HUMBOUGH, 113
HUME, 131 151
HUMES, 39 112 125
HUMISON, 88
HUMMER, 124
HUMPHREY, 12 18 59 76 90 129 153
HUMPHREYS, 91 139
HUMPHRIES, 128
HUMPREY, 89
HUNGERFORD, 85 88 89
HUNSBACH, 24
HUNSIKER, 38
HUNT, 22 42 44 52 63 73 88 91 99 110 134 144 145 156
HUNTER, 8 9 12 14 27-31 36 39 40 48 50 61 63 64 91 95 111 126 131 135 138 145 146 148
HUNTEROCK, 12
HUNTLEY, 83
HUNTSMAN, 102
HUNYVAL, 104
HUPP, 16
HURD, 25 110
HURDIN, 64
HURDMAN, 108
HURLESS, 67
HURLEY, 11 75 95 100 111 113 119 128
HURNEY, 135
HURST, 37 52 75 96 101 108 144
HURT, 26 96
HUSBAN, 22
HUSE, 47 120
HUSEY, 44
HUSHAW, 47 133
HUSHOW, 79
HUSK, 134
HUSSETER, 11
HUSSEY, 129
HUSTED, 43 125
HUSTIDE, 129
HUSTLER, 21
HUSTON, 7 8 47 48 56 71 85 88 91 94 100 101 106 112 119 149 150 152-154
HUTCHESON, 101
HUTCHIN, 88

HUTCHINS, 69 85 88 126
HUTCHINSON, 17 19 24 25 41 56 58-60 107 126 134
HUTCHISON, 4 54 69 85 120 136
HUTHOE, 19
HUTSENPELLER, 44
HUTSIN, 118
HUTSMAN, 67
HUTSON, 24 53 71 89 110 118
HUTT, 101
HUTTINSON, 142
HUTTON, 14 122
HUTTS, 47
HUWS, 39
HYATT, 88
HYDE, 18 45 47 59
HYDER, 17
HYER, 80
HYERS, 13
HYETT, 27 103
HYLAND, 28
HYMER, 155
HYRNER, 155
HYSEL, 153
HYSELL, 153
HYTES, 5
IBERS, 87
ICAS, 156
ICE, 32 106 134
IDDINGS, 8
IDOL, 95
IFERT, 58 132
IGGS, 11
IGO, 92
ILES, 76
IMMEL, 47
IMMELL, 101
IMMICK, 40
IMPSON, 84
ING, 33
INGALLS, 72
INGAM, 118
INGENON, 41
INGERSOL, 39 69
INGERSOLL, 4

INGERSOM, 85
INGERSON, 144
INGHAM, 23 79
INGLE, 65 120
INGLEHAG, 70
INGLES, 126
INGMAN, 14
INGMAND, 14
INLOW, 115 145
INMAN, 81 155
INNIS, 151
INNMAN, 36
INSCHO, 29
INSCO, 50
INSKUP, 127
INSTICE, 65
IRELAND, 39 66 68 84 104 106 113 128 145
IRONS, 34
IRVEN, 73
IRVIN, 97 133 144 155
IRWIN, 13 25 35 39 40 47 66 74 78 82 84 91 94 100 109 112 115 119 121 123 131 138 145
IRWING, 77
IRWN, 34
ISAACS, 17
ISAHART, 37
ISENOGEL, 41
ISENOGLE, 65
ISRAEL, 59 69
ISRIG, 138
ISTRY, 37
IVANS, 108
IVENS, 129
IVERS, 133
IZARD, 108
IZZARD, 24
JACK, 9 10 19 25 58 77 92 94 107 108
JACKMAN, 6 42 59
JACKOSN, 106
JACKS, 150
JACKSON, 11 17 24 28 52 56 58 60 63 65 83-85 88 95 97 98 100-102 108 115 119 123 128 134 135 138 143 144 148 156
JACOBS, 16 21-23 39 105 115 140

JACOBY, 23
JAMES, 6 21 26 29 36 49 52 65 66 76 77 79 90 93 102 109 113 117 122 127 129 131 148 151
JAMESON, 76 113 140 146
JAMISON, 29 46 67 91 113 149 151
JANEGAN, 49
JANIKEN, 49
JANINGS, 72
JANK, 153
JANUARY, 75
JAQUES, 74
JARAM, 92
JARDIN, 50
JAY, 72
JEE, 156
JEFFERRS, 127
JEFFERS, 60
JEFFERSON, 53 60
JEFFERSON CO 5-11 22 61 62
JEFFRIES, 19 35 59 71 73
JELLAND, 32
JELLEY, 8
JENKINS, 26 39 41 53 66 71 72 79 95 100 114 120 125 140 153-155
JENKINSON, 5 58 71 132
JENNINGS, 17 19 26 58 59 103 121 128 135
JESSE, 82
JESSUP, 49 58 112 119 138
JESTER, 19 40 59
JETT, 35 36
JEWELL, 54
JEWETT, 53 111
JEWITT, 42
JIMMISON, 54
JINKINGS, 122
JINNINGS, 6
JOB, 39 119
JOBES, 137
JOHN, 41 43 50 58 65 75 77 82 93 96 98 104 112 124 127 130 132
JOHNS, 116 122
JOHNSON, 5 9 10 20 27 29 32 33 35 37-40 43 44 48 50 56 58 61 64 65 67 71 73 74 77-79 81 82 84 85 88 89 93 96 99 100 101

JOHNSON (continued)
  103 107 110 114-116 118-120 125 140-
  143 145 147 151 154 156
JOHNSTIN, 148
JOHNSTON, 5-10 14 16 22 25 26 28-30 32-
  34 41 46-48 50 52-55 58 64 66 69-71 73
  75 84 85 87 90 94 96-98 101 108 113-116
  119 121-125 128 136 138 139 141 142
  145 147 150-152
JOHNSTONE, 60
JOHON, 37
JOHTON, 125
JOICE, 156
JOINER, 124
JOLLEY, 15 63 93 121
JOLLY, 25 36 68 87 141 147
JOLYMILL, 111
JONES, 8 11 12 16-19 21-23 25 26 29 34 38
  43-56 58-61 63 66 68 71 74-78 80 81 83-
  88 91-93 95 99 100 103 105 107 109 113
  114 116 118-121 124 128-131 133 134
  136 141 144 146 148 150-154 156
JONIKIN, 18
JONSOJIN, 49
JONSON, 64 92
JONSTON, 53 115
JORDAN, 25 100 108 135
JORDEN, 21
JORDON, 40 64 142
JOSEPH, 9 36 87 98 139
JOSLEN, 59
JOSLIN, 25 82
JOVIN, 91
JOWLES, 65
JOY, 41
JOYQUES, 16
JUDD, 93 97 129
JUDEY, 31
JUDSON, 56
JUDY, 32 112 144
JULIAN, 52
JULIN, 46 65
JUMP, 62
JUMPER, 62 136
JUNK, 51 53

JUNKEN, 87
JUNKIN, 144
JUNKINS, 120 144
JURDON, 48
JUSTICE, 10 31 46 47 55 106 115 117 131
  152 154
JUSTINE, 23
KADER, 130
KAIN, 42 118 121 122 125 131 138
KALE, 74
KALEP, 62
KAMELE, 14
KAMP, 64
KANADA, 106
KANDOL, 157
KANE, 54
KANET, 21
KANNALL, 95
KARN, 37
KARR, 112 148
KASEBEER, 101 102 127
KATTERMAN, 37
KAUG, 37
KAUTZ, 72
KAYS, 109 132
KAZEE, 65
KEAN, 6 145
KEANIER, 131
KEARNS, 57
KEASNOR, 55
KEASTON, 84
KEBBINGER, 128
KEEK, 106
KEELER, 85 131
KEELY, 114
KEEN, 74 117
KEENIN, 40
KEENOR, 92
KEERNS, 60
KEES, 8 63 108 135
KEETEN, 153
KEETER, 99
KEFFER, 6
KEGGINS, 65
KEIGHLER, 104

KEIGLER, 13
KEIKENEDALL, 52
KEISER, 15
KEISINGER, 64
KEITH, 86
KEIZE, 29
KELBY, 150
KELL, 29 103
KELLAR, 17 127
KELLENGER, 46
KELLER, 39 61 66 109 145 147
KELLESON, 96
KELLEY, 7 15 16 38 43 45 47 49 59 64 70 72
    84 93 94 95 99 103 114 115 118 128 133
    151 153
KELLIP, 80
KELLISON, 46
KELLOG, 90 132
KELLOUGH, 49
KELLUM, 106
KELLY, 7 8 59 62 64 99 102 133
KELOUGH, 66
KELOW, 144
KELSE, 49
KELSEL, 55
KELSEY, 12 130 142
KELSO, 89 111 125
KEMP, 24 41 62 85 138 143
KEMPER, 42 112
KEMPFT, 28
KEMPT, 26
KEMPTON, 56
KEN, 92
KENDAL, 80
KENDALL, 7 87 93 107 120 148 152
KENDLE, 129
KENISTRICK, 82
KENNARD, 24
KENNEAR, 123
KENNEDY, 11 12 36 40 42 87 106 110 111
    116 122 123 131 133 134 143
KENNEL, 7
KENNEY, 105 131 135
KENNISON, 96
KENNNELS, 25

KENNY, 110
KENSELO, 116
KENSER, 152
KENSOR, 37
KENT, 34 80 82 106 110 111 122 125 129
    143 146 153
KENTON, 38 42 144
KENUT, 106
KEON, 107
KEPLER, 61 78 79 83 116 136
KEPNOE, 77
KEPPNER, 88
KEPSHART, 37
KERCHIVAL, 121
KERLEY, 71
KERN, 111 145
KERNAHAN, 22
KERNE, 80
KERNS, 7 21 25 111 153
KERR, 6 7 11 17 25 35 54 59 60 62 76 78 80
    81 86 88 94 95 99 111 113 115 117 132
    140 151 153 154
KERRIE, 130
KESLIN, 100
KESLING, 94
KESLINGER, 94
KESSINGER, 141
KESSLER, 28
KESTER, 37 132
KETCHAM, 103
KETCHUM, 38 39
KEY, 4 58 112 152
KEYBOONE, 102
KEYES, 129
KEYON, 24
KEYS, 4 23 25 78 82 83 109 116 147 155
KEYSER, 134
KEYT, 38
KIBBY, 119
KIBLINGER, 95
KIDD, 15 35 67 101 126
KIDDLE, 127
KIDDY, 52
KIDNER, 103
KIELOR, 93

KIEWSLEY, 153
KIFT, 99
KIGAR, 14
KIGER, 40 61
KIKABIAUGH, 12
KILBINGER, 95
KILBOURN, 64 84
KILE, 10 32 64 95 104 145 147
KILGAR, 14
KILGORE, 44 76 80 94 99 140 153
KILLEN, 74 114 149
KILLIN, 129
KILLING, 71
KILLOUGH, 112 113 132
KILPATRICK, 24 61
KILT, 144
KILTON, 63
KILWELL, 33
KIMANNON, 16
KIMBALL, 135
KIMBEL, 115
KIMBLE, 32 65 81 96 97 108 119
KIMBOL, 113
KIMES, 44
KIMMEL, 46 94 109
KINCADE, 86
KINCAID, 24 34 38 67 126 156
KINDALL, 52 93 113
KINDELSPEAKER, 59
KINDER, 5 85
KINDESPEKER, 18
KINDLE, 61
KING, 4 11 23 25 26 28 33 34 36 40 41 43 44 51 52 54 55 61 65-67 76 82 83 85 86 89-93 104 107 108 110 115 121 122 125 128 129 131 132 140 142 145 148 154 155
KINGAN, 21
KINGERLY, 112
KINGERY, 31 33 44 108
KINGSBURY, 4
KINGSEY, 54
KINGSLEY, 84
KINISMAN, 156
KINKAID, 21
KINKEAD, 13 41

KINNARD, 14
KINNETT, 21 93
KINNEY, 36 77 81 86 88 136
KINNON, 67
KINNY, 62
KINSEL, 32
KINSELY, 141
KINSEN, 76
KINSER, 14 55 96
KINSEY, 5 155
KINSON, 61
KINTZELL, 10
KINYON, 129
KINZAN, 9
KIOUS, 80
KIRBY, 71 128 131
KIRCHEVAL, 116
KIRGEN, 125
KIRK, 14 49 66 73 84 106 107 109 126 131
KIRKBRIDGE, 51 151
KIRKENDALL, 46 131 152
KIRKER, 37 107
KIRKHAM, 132
KIRKLAND, 14 66
KIRKPATRIC, 115
KIRKPATRICK, 4 17 21 24 49-51 58 61 62 64 69 75 91 93 95 99 107 112 123 136 140
KIRKWOOD, 13 74 126 133
KIRTLEY, 120 143
KISER, 57 58 65 95 112 128 129
KISLER, 156
KISNER, 27
KISOR, 13
KISSINGER, 50 156
KITCEL, 21
KITCHEL, 19 40
KITCHELL, 59
KITCHEN, 149
KITE, 50 128
KITSMILLER, 98
KITZ, 41
KITZMILLER, 28 156
KIZEN, 9
KIZER, 15 50 60 132 145

KLELER, 151
KLEVER, 50
KLEY, 7
KLIEVER, 73
KLINE, 17 31 50 73 92
KLING, 126
KNADLER, 81
KNAP, 61 84 97 136
KNAPP, 84 110
KNATT, 96
KNEAR, 66
KNEE, 65
KNEFF, 23
KNIFE, 23
KNIGHT, 35 38 46 57 63 76 84 85 96 100 115 120 126
KNIS, 55
KNISELEY, 101
KNODDLE, 66
KNOLES, 54
KNOOP, 100
KNOP, 85
KNOPP, 77
KNOPPER, 114
KNOTT, 39 102 122
KNOWLS, 54 69
KNOWLTON, 55 89
KNOX, 35 50 54 71 111 119 131 134 141 152 157
KNOX CO, 97 98 104 115 139 145
KNOYER, 29
KOIGLER, 110
KOLLAR, 101
KONKLIN, 91 146
KOODER, 151
KOOGLAR, 13
KOOGLER, 60
KOON, 17
KOONS, 31
KOR, 113
KORN, 21
KOUE, 58
KOUNTZ, 57
KRANIAC, 14
KRATZER, 6 21 93 152

KREIN, 91 107
KREPPS, 62
KRIDER, 106
KRIEGER, 116
KRIGLER, 110 129
KRISE, 65
KRITESER, 144
KROFT, 62
KRUG, 154
KRUGER, 127
KRUPP, 64
KRUSEN, 140
KRUTZER, 17
KRUZEN, 20
KUBY, 116
KUDER, 108
KUHN, 58
KULKENDALL, 33
KULTZ, 26
KUMP, 27
KUNE, 120
KUNN, 107
KUNTZ, 62 63 97 136 139
KURTZ, 63
KUTZ, 62
KYL, 8
KYLE, 41 59 68 74 79 87 93 111 133 143
KYRK, 79
KYTE, 61
KYZER, 133
KYZOR, 74
LAAGHLIN, 122
LABERTO, 123
LACEY, 74 111 144 151
LACH, 94
LACKEY, 51 60 71 100
LACLEAR, 61
LACOCK, 11 155
LACOUNT, 115
LAD, 35
LADD, 53 56 97 125
LAEFLAND, 71
LAFERY, 18
LAFFER, 69
LAFFERTON, 137

LAFFERTY, 74 86 88 92 118 124
LAFFORD, 54 80
LAFTON, 140
LAIR, 140
LAIRD, 39 120 130
LAKE, 25 81 86 87
LALIN, 98
LALLERN, 33
LAMB, 4 14 15 19 27 74 103 147 151
LAMBART, 96 103
LAMBERSON, 127
LAMBERT, 66 70 103 129 132 150
LAMBERTON, 82
LAMBOON, 63
LAMBRIGHT, 27
LAMBURN, 135
LAMINGS, 49
LAMISTON, 105
LAMKINS, 33
LAMM, 11 124
LAMMA, 45
LAMME, 36 125
LAMONT, 82
LAMPHEIR, 37
LAMPHER, 27
LAMSON, 137
LANCASTER, 39 67
LANCING, 70
LANDEN, 107 114
LANDERS, 66 68 106
LANDFER, 67
LANDLIN, 107
LANDON, 21 39 57 77 78 92 94 116 122
LANDOR, 39
LANDRY, 65
LANDSALE, 95
LANDSON, 121
LANE, 6 7 14 15 26 29 32 34 44 60 67 71 76
    79 101-103 114 116 125 126 136 140 141
LANEY, 21
LANG, 21 23 100
LANGDON, 72
LANGHAM, 101
LANGLEY, 59 65 86
LANGLY, 88

LANGWELD, 108
LANGWORTHY, 97
LANHAM, 16 61 104
LANIER, 4 87 100
LANIME, 100
LANING, 7
LANK, 53
LANMAN, 74
LANSDALE, 95
LANSDELL, 95 128
LANSDOWN, 137
LANTHER, 156
LANTZ, 44 155
LAPE, 33
LAPPIN, 110 142
LAPPWINE, 140
LARD, 129
LARDE, 70
LAREN, 40
LAREW, 124
LARGENT, 90 95
LARIMER, 71
LARIMON, 156
LARIMORE, 140 156
LARINER, 24
LARKIN, 31
LARKINS, 115
LARNE, 12 29 36
LARRENCE, 51
LARRICK, 117
LARRIMER, 71
LARRY, 110
LARSH, 38 116 152
LASBOROUGH, 46
LASBY, 155
LASEY, 18
LASHLEY, 41 74 133
LASHLY, 24
LASLIN, 140
LASSEE, 123
LASSLEY, 98
LAST, 42
LATHEN, 22
LATHERE, 156
LATIMORE, 15 41 154

LATIN, 34
LATTA, 8 9 92 113 142 151
LATTERMORE, 122
LATTIMORE, 66
LATY, 58
LAUGHEAD, 124
LAUGHEY, 135
LAUGHLIN, 5 43 56 85 86 124
LAUGHTON, 82
LAUMAN, 151
LAUNDRY, 145
LAUNTZ, 70
LAURANCE, 58
LAURENCE, 10 96
LAURENS, 105
LAURY, 52
LAUTERMAN, 93
LAUTHERS, 8
LAVERTY, 11 31 32 53
LAVIS, 100
LAW, 41
LAWHEAD, 125
LAWLESS, 153
LAWMAN, 43
LAWRENCE, 5 7 36 62 72 75 103 120 123 135
LAWROSE, 130
LAWSON, 33 46 60 71
LAWWILL, 152
LAWYER, 53
LAYCOCK, 26 141
LAYFERT, 126
LAYLAND, 97
LAYLIN, 98
LAYMAN, 31 48
LAYRE, 112
LAYTON, 25 34 43 111 114 144 145
LEACH, 7 78 101
LEACHMAN, 22 41
LEADAM, 132
LEADS, 150
LEAPER, 97
LEAR, 31
LEASE, 96 113 116
LEASON, 38

LEATHER, 8
LEATHERMAN, 62 136
LEATHERS, 156
LEAVELL, 153
LEAVERTON, 18 44
LEAVITT, 42 83
LECHLIDER, 130
LECK, 11
LECKEY, 71
LEDMAN, 140
LEDMORE, 140
LEDOI, 58
LEDRUELL, 84
LEE, 13 18 32 45 46 47 59 79 80 84 91 97 98 114 117 118 123 145 149
LEECH, 24 97
LEED, 62
LEEDOM, 108 150
LEEDS, 122
LEELAND, 56
LEEPER, 15
LEES, 6 10
LEETH, 34
LEFFINGWELL, 86
LEFLER, 69 103
LEFORGAH, 26
LEGET, 135
LEGG, 54 123
LEGGETT, 154
LEHMAN, 128
LEHUGH, 36
LEIDY, 66
LEIGORE, 113
LEISTER, 64 101 151
LELAND, 144
LEMASTEN, 8
LEMEN, 58
LEMERT, 73
LEMING, 121
LEMMON, 27 91
LEMMONT, 61
LEMON, 72 83 90
LEMONS, 50
LENAR, 106
LENAWRED, 12

LENDSEY, 53
LENEN, 106
LENET, 19
LENNING, 19
LENNON, 124 127
LENNOX, 85
LEOMAN, 19
LEONARD, 20 21 52 77 78 83 92 94 109 115
    116 119 125 134 143 145 156
LEONOX, 100
LEPLEY, 115 139
LESENEA, 130
LESH, 132
LESLIE, 4 8 37 120
LESSLER, 28
LESTER, 86 138
LETHERS, 27
LETTERS, 21
LEUSEY, 61
LEVAILY, 111
LEVALLEY, 80
LEVAN, 57
LEVENGOOD, 151
LEVENSTON, 27
LEVENSWORTH, 112
LEVERTON, 25
LEVI, 12 31 70
LEWALLEN, 84
LEWARD, 112
LEWBARGER, 46
LEWIN, 32 134
LEWIS, 4 14 23 35 37 46 48 51 53 54 57 67
    68 72 78 79 83 86 88 91 96 98 100 102
    105 107 108 115 116 126 129 137-139
    144 146 149 155
LEWITZ, 108
LEWMAN, 61
LEYON, 84
LIANBURGER, 73
LICKING CO, 27 82 104 123 157
LIDDLE, 92 109
LIDEY, 28
LIEF, 156
LIGET, 20 135
LIGGERT, 145

LIGHT, 98
LIGHTBURN, 67
LIGHTY, 130
LIGINBOTHAM, 22
LIKMAN, 17
LILE, 88
LILLE, 88
LILLEY, 53
LILLIE, 86
LILLY, 88 119
LIM, 32
LIMBARGER, 103
LIMBAUGH, 140
LIMES, 99
LIMLEY, 41
LINART, 52
LINBACK, 73
LINCH, 11 115 116
LINCOLN, 106
LINDER, 40
LINDLEY, 110 115 142
LINDREYD, 8
LINDSAY, 25 52 154
LINDSEY, 23 38 56 61 104 119 121 122
LINDSLEY, 85
LINE, 12 93 131
LINEBURG, 140
LINEN, 65
LINES, 81
LINGINSTON, 139
LINGLE, 91 99
LINGO, 89
LINING, 19 112
LINK, 46 113
LINKIN, 110
LINKSWILER, 47
LINLEY, 144
LINLY, 41
LINN, 22 36 72 96 104 109
LINNEL, 70
LINNELL, 70
LINNET, 29
LINNING, 39 121
LINNINGER, 48
LINSCOTT, 107

LINSEY, 42 123
LINSLEY, 88
LINTEN, 49
LINTNER, 17
LINTON, 16 17 49 57 116 134
LINTZ, 127
LINVILL, 144
LINZE, 14
LIONS, 21
LIPENGEIT, 30
LIPLEY, 6
LIPPENCOCK, 38
LIPPINCOT, 129
LISH, 48
LISLE, 6 8 9 11
LISNEY, 151
LIST, 10 28 73 96
LISTER, 52
LISTERSEN, 51
LISTON, 46 107
LISTRE, 106
LITTELL, 15 65
LITTLE, 16 18 19 21 23 27 40 42 47 50 68 83 92 94 95 110 121 125 154
LITTLETON, 10 51 74 92 154
LIVERTON, 110
LIVINGOOD, 65
LIVINGSTON, 6 13 27 30 38 62 73
LLEWELLAN, 38
LLEWELLYN, 70
LLOYD, 5 10 13 16 25 45 53 64 91 99 144
LOAR, 60
LOARE, 71
LOBAUGH, 151
LOBDELL, 140
LOCK, 76 79 92 148
LOCKARD, 16
LOCKART, 24 144
LOCKERD, 126
LOCKHART, 14 26 49 68 108 123 150
LOCKRIDGE, 126
LODER, 43
LOEFLER, 28
LOFER, 33
LOFFBARROW, 33

LOFFLAND, 71
LOFORT, 144
LOGAN, 7 13 61 87 114 115 137 146 154
LOGN, 128
LOGUE, 6 51 52 100 140
LOID, 124
LOIS, 32
LOKE, 45
LONBACH, 32
LONEY, 46 150
LONG, 7 11 12 18 19 23 29 34 35 37 45 48 50 51 59 60 65 73 74 78 86 90 93-95 100 102 103 106 107 113 118 125 127 128 130 132 133 145 152 153 155
LONGBRAKE, 12
LONGFELLER, 128
LONGFELLOW, 39
LONGLEY, 101 127
LONGS, 29
LONGSHORE, 48 150
LONGSHOW, 117
LONGSTRETH, 13
LONGWELL, 35 78 116 146
LONNER, 16
LONSDALE, 15
LOOFBARROW, 33
LOOFBERRARD, 133
LOOFBORROW, 152
LOOFBOUROW, 146
LOOKER, 42 60 64 140 148
LOOKINGBELL, 78
LOOKINGELL, 83
LOOKS, 58
LOOLESS, 48
LOOMIS, 50 55
LOOMON, 129
LOOSBOROUGH, 68
LORAN, 101
LORD, 43 67 123
LOREL, 61
LORNMY, 66
LORRIS, 132
LOSIER, 7
LOSLER, 148
LOTHER, 146

LOTT, 140
LOTZ, 153
LOUDEBACK, 95
LOUDERBACH, 46 105
LOUGHER, 32
LOUIS, 113
LOURY, 8 16 52 54 57 65 69 88
LOUSTENHISER, 139
LOUTHER, 31
LOVE, 32 33 43 58 74 77 81 89 92 116 133 140 148
LOVEJOY, 75
LOVEL, 39 59
LOVELAND, 146 156
LOVELESS, 34 65 89 117 133
LOVERIDGE, 97
LOVERTON, 107
LOW, 13 58 90 104 139
LOWDEN, 5
LOWDERBACK, 152
LOWDERBECK, 108
LOWE, 128
LOWEN, 94
LOWER, 7 116
LOWERY, 5 11 88 89 113 120 121 148 152
LOWFURE, 139
LOWILL, 21
LOWINS, 107
LOWMAN, 34 53 107 114
LOWNES, 151
LOWREY, 99 110
LOWRY, 93
LOWTHAIN, 124
LOY, 98 112
LOYAN, 153
LOYD, 150 152 155
LOYE, 37
LOYEAR, 53
LOZIER, 105
LUCAS, 4 22 26 33 49 93 115 121 122 141
LUCE, 98 132
LUDLOW, 127 132 148 153
LUFTON, 60
LUIBY, 145
LUMAN, 89

LUMIS, 89
LUMPHIAN, 65
LUNAY, 11
LUNBACK, 48 96
LUNDERLAND, 98
LUNINGER, 101
LUPTON, 100
LUSAC, 33
LUSK, 142
LUTCHLENWATTER, 137
LUTHER, 156
LUTS, 78
LUTSER, 90
LUTZ, 9 31 46 52 73
LUZADOR, 117
LYBERGER, 145
LYBRAND, 31
LYLE, 7 137
LYMAN, 81 84 153
LYNCH, 18 52 72
LYNE, 32
LYNES, 26
LYNN, 15 70 123 134
LYON, 8 43 45 72 78 86 104 109 115 128
LYONS, 5 6 9 13 50 78 109 112 150
LYPCAP, 11
LYSE, 6
LYTLE, 4 57 74 94
LYTTLE, 123
MABLISE, 34
MACABER, 97
MACDONNELL, 4
MACE, 51 117 131 151
MACHAMAN, 7
MACHIN, 11
MACK, 59 114
MACKELHENY, 48
MACKERAL, 28
MACKEY, 56 67 69 100
MACKLAND, 121
MACKLIN, 92
MACKRELL, 14
MACOMBO, 56
MACY, 19
MADARIS, 21

MADARY, 48
MADDEN, 7 57 72 124 153
MADDON, 107
MADDOX, 54 75
MADEN, 26
MAGAN, 105
MAGEE, 14
MAGES, 98
MAGGARD, 72
MAGGEAT, 128
MAGGERT, 95
MAGILL, 33
MAGNET, 153
MAHAFFEY, 22 75 127 152
MAHAFFY, 107
MAHALA, 38
MAHAN, 35 114 131
MAHONE, 113
MAHONING CO, 77 92 94 109
MAIDES, 126
MAIERS, 85
MAIL, 114
MAILATT, 20
MAIN, 6 78 129
MAINES, 24
MAINS, 104 140 156
MAISH, 12
MAJORS, 98 133
MAKENSON, 72
MAKER, 83
MALATT, 109
MALCOLM, 31 92
MALCOM, 148
MALEN, 6
MALL, 7
MALLARY, 126
MALLET, 142
MALLON, 18
MALLORY, 29
MALLOTT, 59 125
MALONE, 16 17 49 94 108 113
MALONEY, 34
MALOOT, 42
MALORY, 26
MALOT, 19

MALOY, 105 128
MALSON, 112
MALTBIE, 36
MANAGAN, 61
MANARY, 154
MANCHESTER, 92 94
MANDY, 32
MANLOVE, 66
MANLY, 52 56 59
MANN, 9 11 36 43 54 57 63 72 78 82 85 92 102 109 120 123 124 146
MANNAN, 150
MANNAY, 74
MANNING, 19 35 55 63 65 69 98 112
MANNON, 14 49 136
MANPENY, 59
MANSFIELD, 11 12 17 50 72 94 107 122
MANSION, 64
MANSON, 124
MANTIAL, 11
MANVIL, 78
MANVILL, 146
MANVILLE, 116 129
MANY, 101
MAPEL, 97 137
MAPES, 86 124 156
MAPLE, 70 127
MAPLES, 101 153
MARAINVILLE, 83
MARANVIL, 82
MARBLE, 118
MARCH, 8 32 111
MARCHANT, 92
MARCKEL, 32
MARCUS, 150
MARFOOT, 16
MARGROVE, 148
MARIATY, 15
MARING, 13
MARK, 34 37 53 101 113 140 145
MARKEL, 23 31
MARKES, 137
MARKEY, 87
MARKIE, 118
MARKIN, 107

MARKLAND, 39 68 74 75 108
MARKLE, 147
MARKLEY, 97
MARKS, 38 79 83
MARLATT, 77
MARLEY, 18
MARLING, 17
MARLOW, 41
MARMON, 127
MARON, 25
MARQUES, 133
MARQUIS, 34 57 74 98 114
MARQUITH, 102
MARRIS, 15 91
MARSH, 8 55 57 59 91 96 114 119 141 153
MARSHALL, 4 8 15 23 24 36 39 55 60 68 69 71-73 89 92-94 110 137 141 143-145
MARSHAM, 85
MARSHAWN, 49
MARSHEL, 127
MARTAIN, 69
MARTIAL, 110
MARTIAN, 126
MARTIN, 8-12 17-19 21-24 34-38 40 42 46 52 54 55 57-61 63 65 68-71 74 82 87 92 95 98 99 102 112 114-118 120 126 127 129 131 134 137 139 140 143-145 147 149 153 154
MARTINDITS, 155
MARTS, 31 32
MARTZ, 96
MARVIN, 79 116 129 155
MASEY, 58
MASH, 106
MASON, 11 28 42 56 92 114 118 120 140
MASSEE, 112 141
MASSIE, 117 153
MAST, 14
MASTER, 58
MASTERS, 23 41 61 74 138
MASTERSON, 61
MASTIN, 103
MATCH, 8
MATHENY, 76 108
MATHER, 23

MATHERS, 5 12 21
MATHEW, 37 96
MATHEWS, 5 13 15 21 31 32 38 39 44 46 50 55 63 65 74 85 86 93 103 117 118 127 136 140 153-155
MATHIAS, 32 49 130 140
MATHIEAS, 51
MATLIN, 142
MATNEY, 106
MATSON, 101
MATTOON, 56
MATTOX, 34 45 58 155
MATTS, 58
MAUGHMEN, 51
MAUNDEY, 85
MAURICE, 145
MAWHINNY, 114
MAWYERS, 24
MAXEY, 124
MAXFIELD, 84 88 129
MAXUM, 77
MAXWELL, 7 8 50 58 61 78 80 85 92 97 111 112 116 125
MAY, 13 43 52 97 101 109 110 151 155
MAYBROLL, 128
MAYER, 13
MAYERS, 145
MAYFIELD, 15 105
MAYHAN, 53
MAYHIGH, 151
MAYNARD, 79 84 126
MAYS, 6 30 94 141 157
MAYSE, 13 107
MAZE, 142
MAZERS, 97
MCADAMS, 9 38 57 102
MCAFFERTY, 51 52
MCALEXANDER, 128
MCALISTER, 10 46 54 64
MCALLISTER, 51 64
MCALLITY, 135
MCARTHUR, 5 11 25 51-53 77 91 92 100 101 110 115 140 153
MCAULEY, 33 103 105 152
MCAULLEY, 43

MCAULY, 129
MCBERY, 60
MCBETH, 91 95
MCBRATNEY, 137
MCBRIDE, 7 34 64 69 120 125 133 138 139 149
MCBROOM, 32
MCCABE, 4 18 19 71 128
MCCAFFERTY, 76 80 117 151
MCCAGUE, 75
MCCAIN, 21 40 128
MCCALISTER, 51
MCCALL, 25 26 34 46 59 94 104 105 129
MCCALLA, 38 73
MCCALLE, 63
MCCALLEY, 6
MCCALLISTER, 34 151
MCCALLY, 10 37 128
MCCAMMON, 58
MCCAN, 76
MCCANDLESS, 32 140
MCCANLESS, 32
MCCANLY, 46
MCCANN, 46 46 64 94 101 113
MCCARKEY, 156
MCCARLEY, 155
MCCARROL, 34
MCCARTER, 60 61 128
MCCARTHEN, 87
MCCARTHY, 90
MCCARTNEY, 11 18 91 92 97 98 105 140
MCCARTY, 74 113 153
MCCASKEY, 6 136
MCCATCHEN, 9
MCCAUGHEY, 62 136
MCCAWN, 16
MCCAYNE, 75
MCCELGIN, 21
MCCHANDLESS, 99
MCCHENEY, 24
MCCIME, 107
MCCINNA, 106
MCCLAIN, 14 155 156
MCCLAIR, 156
MCCLANE, 41 94
MCCLANEHAN, 108
MCCLAREN, 24
MCCLARKIN, 66
MCCLARY, 9 10 58 62 100 132 143
MCCLAY, 7
MCCLEAIN, 15
MCCLEAN, 23 154
MCCLEARY, 8 9 41 128
MCCLELLAN, 12 62 78 109 125
MCCLELLAND, 6-8 12 22 45 62 75 97 120 137
MCCLENAHAN, 75
MCCLENNAHAN, 75
MCCLERG, 6 86
MCCLERY, 7
MCCLEVAR, 80
MCCLINTICK, 7
MCCLINTOCK, 5-7 16 48 49 52 53 144
MCCLONG, 88
MCCLORG, 97
MCCLOSKEY, 40
MCCLOUD, 6 56 77 126 156
MCCLUER, 151
MCCLUNG, 7 24 38 71 100 103 140 156
MCCLURE, 4 20 25 34 47 62 100 102 106 108 111 112 115 122 128 133 139 140 154
MCCOHN, 11 21
MCCOLGAN, 20
MCCOLIN, 8
MCCOLISTER, 48 92
MCCOLLAN, 11
MCCOLLESTER, 26
MCCOLLEY, 8
MCCOLLISTER, 19 25 38 51 59 67 119 151
MCCOLLOM, 78
MCCOLLON, 20 94
MCCOLLOUGH, 101 117
MCCOLLUM, 19 92 98 119 122 150
MCCOLLUN, 42
MCCOLPEN, 20
MCCOLUM, 25
MCCOMB, 85 89
MCCOMBS, 8 9 20 77 92 93 110
MCCOMIS, 97

MCCONE, 155
MCCONIKEY, 8
MCCONKEY, 7 9 67 93 156
MCCONLEY, 71
MCCONN, 60
MCCONNAL, 78 94 109
MCCONNAUGHEY, 111
MCCONNAUGHY, 94
MCCONNEKEY, 143
MCCONNEL, 17 18 31 32 38 67 92 94 113 131 135 147 155
MCCONNELL, 4 8 13 36 60 61 70 104 123 126 131 138 156
MCCONNICHY, 138
MCCONNOUGHEY, 120
MCCONOUGHY, 142
MCCORD, 11 90 96 100 108 119 121 122 140 146 156
MCCORKLE, 150
MCCORMAC, 13 94
MCCORMACK, 10 13 14
MCCORMICK, 28 38 45 48 71 75 98 104 119 128 140 143 151
MCCORT, 147
MCCOWEN, 123
MCCOWN, 21
MCCOY, 8 11 18 23 25 34 38 41 44 46 51 66 74 81 85 87 92 117 120 125 133 135 144 146 151 153
MCCRACKEN, 35 64 113 115
MCCRADY, 25
MCCRAGHILL, 13
MCCRAKEN, 153
MCCRARY, 28 92 104
MCCRAY, 46 123
MCCREADY, 8 135
MCCREARY, 77 89 92 94 112 115 130
MCCREDY, 63
MCCREERY, 49 78
MCCRISTEY, 40
MCCRISTY, 19
MCCRORG, 24
MCCULLEY, 72 87 94 125
MCCULLISTER, 19
MCCULLOCH, 11 45 58 75 141

MCCULLOH, 72
MCCULLOUGH, 4 7 8 38 46 63 67 68 72 86 87 135 153
MCCULLY, 7 131
MCCULOCH, 64
MCCUMBER, 129
MCCUN, 41
MCCUNE, 41 94 136
MCCURDY, 121
MCCUTCHAN, 84
MCCUTCHEON, 36 129
MCDANIEL, 19 32 42 50 54 58 72 73 116 120 123 131
MCDERMIT, 25
MCDERMOTT, 68
MCDILL, 52
MCDONALD, 4 5 7 8 13 31 34 36 38 46 53 60 63 66 71 76 77 80 94 103 108 109 111 114 122 123 126 130-132 135 141 144 146 148 149 153
MCDONNOUGH, 19
MCDONOUGH, 43 85
MCDOUGAL, 26 101
MCDOWELL, 23 61 116 123 152
MCDUGAL, 26
MCEDWARDS, 19
MCEIVEN, 99
MCELHANEY, 132
MCELHENY, 48
MCELHINEY, 41 69
MCELHINY, 41 75
MCELROY, 7 26 53 137
MCELVAIN, 111 133 134 145
MCELVEY, 53 73 100 106
MCELVY, 82
MCELWAIN, 4 80 111
MCELWAYNE, 156
MCELWIN, 97
MCENERY, 78
MCENTIRE, 9 107
MCEOWN, 61
MCEVAIN, 38
MCEVANS, 103
MCFADDEN, 7 8 10 11 13 16 60 71 75 92 96
MCFALL, 8 89

MCFARLAND, 29 33 34 45-48 72 75 77 86 87 90 91 93 99 107 108 124 125 133 136 144 145
MCFARLIN, 120
MCFARSON, 136
MCFEALLY, 138
MCFERIN, 138
MCFERRON, 22
MCFERSTON, 14
MCFILLY, 83
MCFREEN, 100
MCGALLAWAY, 144
MCGANO, 112
MCGARAH, 108
MCGARVEY, 74 156
MCGAUGHEY, 41
MCGAW, 132
MCGEE, 11 20 21 73 108 119 135
MCGEHRON, 24
MCGIFFIN, 70 103
MCGILL, 59 92 105 109
MCGIN, 108
MCGINLEY, 29
MCGINNIS, 76 107 129
MCGINNISS, 102
MCGLONE, 24
MCGOING, 98
MCGONEGAL, 9
MCGONIGLE, 10
MCGONIGRE, 8
MCGOONY, 108
MCGOUGGAL, 57
MCGOWAN, 37 70 80 104 111 145
MCGOWEN, 61
MCGOWIN, 136
MCGOWN, 98
MCGRAW, 49 132
MCGREGOR, 101
MCGREW, 41 57 99 132 146 155
MCGRIFF, 130
MCGRIM, 101
MCGROOS, 115
MCGROVES, 153
MCGUNNEGLE, 119
MCHAN, 91

MCHARM, 42
MCHENRY, 32 68 82 127 134 150
MCHERDRY, 143
MCHUTENS, 127
MCHUTH, 93
MCILVAIN, 126
MCINA, 34
MCINTIRE, 9 24 45 53 71 93 98 127 133
MCINTOF, 43
MCINTOSH, 8 56 91 98 139
MCINTYRE, 57 128
MCIVAIN, 126
MCJIMSEY, 111
MCKAIG, 120 128 129
MCKAIN, 10
MCKANNA, 26
MCKAY, 8 99
MCKEAN, 48
MCKEE, 8 11 13 20 47 49 59 61 64 69 72 88 94 96 98 100 102 107 125 127 129 138 144 151
MCKEECHAN, 43
MCKEEHAM, 4
MCKEEL, 58
MCKEHON, 93
MCKELVEY, 54
MCKELVY, 89
MCKENNEY, 23 116 119 150
MCKENNY, 149
MCKENSEY, 64 145
MCKENSIE, 113
MCKENZIE, 34 89
MCKEW, 16
MCKEWN, 22
MCKEY, 86
MCKIBBEN, 55
MCKILBEANS, 141
MCKILKRICK, 21
MCKIN, 118
MCKINLEY, 43 50 60 64 95 97 107 148
MCKINNER, 9
MCKINNEY, 15 23 26 45 56 57 61 94 98 109 148 153
MCKINNON, 7 91 146 151
MCKINSEA, 9

MCKINSEY, 22 63 153
MCKINSTRY, 17 44
MCKINTORPE, 62
MCKINTRY, 44 45
MCKITTERICK, 29
MCKITTRICK, 114 126
MCKNIGHT, 12 56 64 100 122 124
MCKNIT, 109 110
MCKNUTT, 116
MCKONKEY, 89 91 97 124
MCKUNE, 76 131
MCLAIN, 33 41 46 107 145 153
MCLAINE, 29
MCLANE, 32 72 73
MCLARKIN, 66
MCLAUGHLIN, 8 31 38 55 59 63 64 75 78 80 86 93 94 97 108 128 135 140 141 144 151
MCLEAN, 12 36 47 94
MCLEE, 58
MCLILLY, 63
MCLINLY, 67
MCLOELAND, 83
MCLONG, 12
MCLOUD, 50
MCLUCAS, 99
MCMACHTEN, 27
MCMAHAN, 35 74 133 134
MCMAHON, 37 38 78 92 117 137
MCMAIN, 19
MCMAINES, 19
MCMAINS, 19
MCMAKEN, 17
MCMALHON, 149
MCMALLON, 103
MCMAMES, 6
MCMANIME, 129
MCMANIS, 94
MCMANN, 105 131
MCMANNIN, 102
MCMANUS, 17 105
MCMARROW, 81
MCMASTER, 132 148
MCMEAN, 19
MCMEEN, 100

MCMICHAEL, 139
MCMILLAN, 7 8 42 104
MCMILLEN, 8 41 44 77 92 97 104
MCMILLER, 67
MCMILLES, 50
MCMILLIGAN, 68
MCMILLIN, 74
MCMINS, 53
MCMULLEN, 66 72 77 85 92 117
MCMULLIN, 17 39 46 77 89 94 135
MCMUNN, 147
MCMURRAY, 109
MCNAGHTEN, 28
MCNAIR, 128
MCNAMES, 27
MCNEAL, 17 20 31 34 35 48 53 58 60 61 71 76 107 147 151
MCNEALL, 43
MCNEAR, 83
MCNEEL, 92
MCNEELEY, 20
MCNEELY, 59
MCNEILLY, 39
MCNEME, 143
MCNIGHT, 66
MCNILES, 6
MCNITT, 112
MCNOWN, 21
MCNUTT, 32 65 134
MCONDE, 123
MCPAKE, 22
MCPHADDON, 100
MCPHEE, 96
MCPHERSON, 4 13 138 149 152
MCPIKE, 148
MCPORSON, 45
MCQUA, 113
MCQUAY, 106
MCQUEA, 53
MCQUELKIN, 72
MCQUINTY, 148
MCRANKEY, 8
MCREA, 143
MCREYNOLDS, 65 123 130
MCRICKEN, 5

MCRIGHT, 75 111
MCROBERTS, 47 57 101
MCSTANUS, 102
MCSTRAIN, 20
MCVAY, 43 49 90
MCVILAN, 25
MCWHALEN, 133
MCWHORTEN, 12
MCWHORTER, 108
MCWILLIAMS, 70 137 140
MCWRIGHT, 45
MEACH, 9
MEAKRE, 47 48
MEAL, 46
MEALMAN, 70 103
MEANAUGH, 76
MEARS, 89 92 141
MEASOMORE, 90
MECHAN, 67
MECKER, 146
MEDELRA, 47
MEDFORD, 65
MEDILL, 66
MEDLY, 16
MEED, 70 129 144
MEEDER, 140
MEEK, 7 11 58 62 63 69 74 112 123 135 140
MEEKER, 7 37 86 88 102 119 128 140 146
MEEKINS, 100
MEEKLE, 58
MEEKS, 8 125
MEENACH, 91
MEENY, 81
MEESE, 63
MEET, 33
MEGILL, 128
MEGONGLE, 17
MEGRUE, 19
MEHAFEY, 20
MEIERS, 145
MEIR, 49
MELAND, 12
MELICK, 115
MELLEN, 20
MELLING, 84

MELLINGER, 97 120
MELLOW, 71 75 156
MELONE, 8 16 39
MELOTT, 102
MELVILLE, 103
MELVIN, 46 133
MENARY, 4 43 53 153
MENDENHALL, 120 125
MENEL, 39
MENICE, 15
MENINGHALL, 120
MENNEHAN, 153
MENSER, 29
MENSHALL, 11
MENSON, 54
MENTEENTH, 71
MENTERLY, 32
MENTZER, 131
MEPENGER, 16
MEPER, 11
MERANDA, 154
MERCER, 52 116 140 145
MERCHANT, 14 15 104
MEREDITH, 14 61
MERGRUE, 19
MERIDITH, 103
MERIMAN, 100
MERIT, 104
MERKER, 97
MERRELS, 89
MERRILL, 156
MERRIMAN, 55 100
MERRIS, 127
MERRIT, 19 70 104 115 130
MERRITT, 82
MERRMAN, 114
MERSHON, 95 107 149
MERSHORE, 108
MERWIN, 36
MESATE, 127
MESSENGER, 56 70 133 142 143 157
MESSER, 8 13 33 36 53 55
MESSICK, 33 153
MESSMORE, 140
METADOW, 5

METCALF, 43 68 142
METGAR, 106
METTEL, 134
METTS, 54 86
METTZ, 62
METZ, 7 128 149
METZGAR, 111
MEYARS, 23
MEYER, 49 59
MEYERS, 37
MEYGUILT, 52
MEYRES, 152
MIAMI CO, 65 98 100 111 120 132 143 144
MICHAEL, 52 53 61 65 66 76 84 99 108 116 130
MICHEALS, 146
MICHEL, 35
MICHIE, 113
MICKENS, 51
MICKEY, 133 134
MICKSELL, 37
MICKSON, 79
MIDDAL, 133
MIDDAUGH, 66
MIDDLEMER, 145
MIDDLESWORTH, 22 90
MIDDLETON, 152
MIDDLETOWN, 22
MIDDOGH, 65
MIDKIFF, 16
MIDSEKER, 147
MIDSKER, 31
MIERS, 41 73 82
MIETT, 62
MIFFORD, 104 156
MIGATT, 146
MIGERS, 118
MIKEL, 115
MIKESEL, 58
MIKSELL, 14
MILAN, 99
MILAR, 16
MILES, 62 129 142 146
MILEY, 37 38
MILISON, 145

MILL, 133
MILLAR, 105 151
MILLARD, 60
MILLAWY, 41
MILLEN, 123
MILLER, 4 6-11 13 14 16-20 23 26-29 31-34 36 37 39-41 43 44 46-51 53 55 57-62 65-71 74-77 82-85 87 89 90 93 94 96 98-109 111 113-117 119 120 123 125 127-131 133 135-142 151-156
MILLFORD, 15
MILLHISER, 82
MILLHOLLAND, 39 43 98
MILLHOUSE, 100
MILLIGAN, 44 78 115
MILLIGEN, 45
MILLIGIN, 68 75
MILLIKEN, 129
MILLINGER, 64
MILLINGTON, 79 129
MILLISER, 147
MILLISON, 90
MILLPOLLAND, 60
MILLS, 4 6 8 27 35 37 42 50 56 61 98 100-102 123 129 136 144 145 149 151
MILMON, 144
MILNER, 68 69 136
MILNOR, 62
MILRICK, 115
MILSLAGEL, 17
MILSPAUGH, 102
MILTER, 6
MILTON, 58 90 123
MINARD, 143
MINAY, 68
MINEAR, 51
MINER, 13
MINES, 108 149
MINGUS, 93 136
MINIAR, 100
MINICH, 43
MINICK, 133 138
MINIGS, 112
MINNA, 114
MINNICH, 58

MINNICK, 58 127
MINNIEAR, 13
MINNIS, 7
MINOR, 25 77 91 94 111 121 154
MINSHAL, 23
MINSHALL, 25 72
MINTER, 83
MINTIER, 10
MINTIRE, 20
MINTON, 8 62 145
MINTURN, 118
MIRANVILLE, 83
MIRES, 28 37 53 131
MIRUR, 62
MISER, 8
MISKGIMENS, 71
MISKIMINS, 51
MISKINNENS, 151
MISNER, 57 138
MISOR, 102
MISSAMORE, 33
MISSIMORE, 91
MISSMORE, 73
MISSNER, 4 61
MITCHEL, 37 39 49 51 92
MITCHELL, 7 10 13 20 25 36 45 47 48 70 79
 81 84 87 95 98 101 112 113 115 120 121
 124 125 128 129 131 137 151 155
MITTS, 54 128
MIX, 104
MIZER, 17
MIZNER, 39 81
MIZZICK, 52
MOARY, 67
MOATS, 29
MOCK, 28 36
MOCKRIDGE, 138
MOFFETT, 25
MOFFIT, 10
MOHOLEN, 26
MOIN, 114
MOKEMAN, 92
MOLATT, 106
MOLER, 94 153 155
MOLES, 78

MONCRIEF, 12
MONDOR, 21
MONEL, 134
MONINGER, 85
MONLOYNE, 61
MONMAR, 15
MONN, 147
MONNETT, 23 32
MONOHAN, 37
MONROE, 18 36 46 62 71 83 101 116 128
MONTEIGH, 94
MONTEITH, 71 77
MONTFORD, 94 105 121
MONTGOMERY, 6 9 22 24 27 45 52 54 75
 81 82 84 100 117 121 128 130 131 137
 141 153
MONTGOMERY CO, 11 98
MONTIER, 8
MONTONEY, 72
MONZER, 62
MOODIE, 87
MOODY, 6 15 27 50 62 65 72 95 128 129 136
MOON, 32 36 38 81 99 109 118
MOONEY, 47 48 132 148
MOOR, 70 78
MOORE, 4 7-9 15 20-27 29 32 33 36-41 44 46
 48 53 54 56 59-63 66 68-73 75-78 83-87
 90 93-97 101-105 108-110 114-117 120-
 126 131 133 138 140 141 143-145 147
 148 150 152-156
MOOREHEAD, 17 119 122
MOORHEAD, 40
MOORMAN, 12
MOOSE, 41
MOOTS, 72 76 140
MORBET, 67
MORE, 89 132
MORECRAFT, 118
MOREDECK, 140
MOREHART, 28 29 90
MOREHEAD, 6 55 94 133 149
MOREHOUS, 52
MOREHOUSE, 116
MORELAND, 117 120
MORETON, 74

MOREY, 86
MORFORD, 108
MORGAN, 25 35 36 46 82 94 112 114 128
    134 141 153
MORING, 119
MORKIER, 56
MORLANA, 53
MORLEY, 77
MORNING, 102
MORNINGSTAR, 13
MORPHEW, 66 112
MORPHEY, 29 66
MORRIS, 11-13 15 20 23 28 33 34 37 38 44
    46 48 53-55 63 73 78 85 92 99 101 102
    104 106 117 119 121 122 126 127 132
    133 140 144 146 149 153 154
MORRISON, 5 8 9 20 21 38 39 45 47 60 68
    76 79 81 84 86 88 96 108 115 116 136
MORROW, 4 21 25 42 44 87 115 123 131 143
    145 147 148
MORSE, 12 56 86 156
MORTAIN, 93
MORTON, 43 58 61 89 115 123 125 145
MOSBARGER, 153
MOSBRY, 19
MOSE, 156
MOSES, 23 34 86 88 110 140
MOSEY, 118
MOSH, 32
MOSHER, 55 155
MOSS, 23 37 86 91 93 130 134 136 137
MOSSBURGH, 123
MOST, 138
MOSTELLER, 17
MOTHERSPAW, 73
MOTINGER, 67
MOTSINER, 19
MOTT, 4 56 99 102
MOUNT, 150
MOUNTS, 23 32 46 96 109 116 117 119 135
    140
MOURNING, 155
MOURY, 31 148
MOUTEIGH, 71
MOVIELE, 126

MOWBERRY, 80 111
MOWEN, 7
MOWER, 43
MOWERS, 107
MOWERY, 88
MOXER, 99
MOYER, 37 67 128 140
MOYES, 155
MUCE, 8
MUCHLIN, 36
MUIR, 104
MUIZEL, 41
MULFORD, 108
MULIN, 21 59
MULL, 72
MULLEN, 18 69 125 156
MULLENOWE, 37
MULLER, 11
MULLIGAN, 107 126
MULLIN, 12 19 59 94 117 123
MULLOTT, 23
MUMS, 60
MUNAY, 114
MUNDAY, 96
MUNDEL, 59
MUNEY, 39 45 126
MUNGER, 4 132
MUNIRE, 144
MUNN, 115 116 148
MUNNS, 78 94
MUNROE, 58 79 116 146
MUNSEN, 104
MUNSON, 5 78 86 116 157
MUNTHAN, 119
MUNTHOUD, 124
MUNTIER, 9
MURDOCK, 12 13 70
MURFIN, 25
MURFOOT, 27
MURPHEY, 12 16 123
MURPHY, 13 14 16 18 24-26 28 33 34 36 40
    57-59 65 72 77 91-93 103 110 114 117
    120 122 129 131 133 134 138 150
MURRAY, 8 14 22 28 46 61 64 93 107 146
MURREY, 31

MURRY, 136
MUSGROVE, 150
MUSHOW, 155
MUSICK, 125
MUSSELMAN, 41 47 99 118 132 151
MUSSER, 7 19 43 43
MUSSETT, 80
MUSSLEMAN, 48
MUSSTER, 67
MUSTARD, 26 34 53 105 108
MUSTART, 105
MUSTER, 69
MUTHERBAUGH, 16
MUTTIN, 142
MUZZLEMAN, 133
MYER, 77 145
MYERS, 4-7 10 16 19 21 23 28 29 31 32 35
    60 62 63 75 76 80 96 106 108 113 118
    121-124 129 133 136 144 149 154
MYNES, 57
MYON, 6
MYRES, 118
MYSETT, 80
NAGAL, 82
NAIL, 45 139
NANCE, 69
NAPER, 82 156
NAPIER, 82
NAPP, 129
NARMAN, 36
NASH, 21 24 102 107 147
NASON, 12 95
NAUFOSSEN, 13
NAULOON, 78
NAVE, 13
NAYHART, 118
NAYLOR, 42 74 141 150
NAYS, 20
NEACE, 52
NEADSTAY, 11
NEAL, 17 23 76 102 103 110 118
NEALLY, 66 90 118
NEAR, 113
NEARSON, 59
NEASE, 96

NEAVIS, 43
NEBB, 52
NEDECK, 136
NEEDLES, 65
NEEL, 5 11
NEELY, 39 62 95 120
NEEVER, 61
NEFF, 10 27 41 42 47 48 66 73 99 128 137
    152
NEGLEY, 65
NEIBLING, 156
NEIGHDICK, 62
NEIHLE, 146
NELEY, 34
NELSON, 13 18 20 23 25 26 57 62 67 71 85
    86 95 106 109 116 123 124 129 132 136
    144 148
NEMERICK, 104
NESBIT, 148
NESELRODE, 101
NESSEL, 96
NEVAN, 114
NEVELS, 72
NEVILL, 115 145
NEVILLE, 12 15 39
NEVIS, 123
NEWBEN, 41
NEWBERRY, 56 105
NEWCOM, 128
NEWCOMB, 57
NEWCOME, 133
NEWCUM, 61
NEWEL, 15 98 104 141
NEWELL, 21 22 126
NEWHOUS, 106
NEWHOUSE, 151
NEWKIRK, 17 58 123
NEWLAIN, 113
NEWLAND, 21 76 95 149
NEWLEN, 152
NEWMAN, 14 18 25 36 50 75-77 96 103 128
    151
NEWPORT, 40
NEWSON, 74
NEWSTETLER, 68

NEWTON, 72 77 86 124 132 142 149
NEYSEMAUGER, 98
NIBLACK, 22 94
NICASON, 29
NICE, 33 59
NICELY, 18 114 141
NICHERSON, 134
NICHLASS, 46
NICHOL, 57
NICHOLAS, 26 27 67 105 115 138
NICHOLS, 12 13 16 43 47 53 58 64 103 119 126 140 145 148 155
NICHOLSON, 18 58 76 88 91 138
NICKERSON, 156
NICKLOW, 72
NICKUM, 66 68
NICLES, 15
NICOL, 145
NICOLS, 26 147
NIECE, 23 46 117
NIEKUM, 106
NIER, 143
NIGH, 27 33 90
NIGHMAN, 110 142
NIGHT, 104 136
NILES, 83 126
NILLANE, 137
NILSON, 21
NIMERICK, 120
NIMMON, 139
NINEMYOR, 49
NISBET, 116 117
NISELEY, 49
NIXON, 9 24 46 60 70 72 74 127 133 135
NOAH, 84
NOBLE, 41 53 55 56 83 92 94 102 109 112 120 138 141
NOBLES, 89
NOCKS, 36
NOEL, 4 26 152
NOGLE, 65 140
NOISWENTER, 32
NOLAN, 71 143
NOLAND, 45 53 96 155
NOLEMAN, 108

NOLEN, 28
NOLIN, 52 143
NOLLAND, 46
NOOL, 64
NOONEY, 56
NORLAN, 39
NORMAN, 101 129
NORMON, 152
NORRIS, 14 36 39 52 56 121 125 127 132 148 154
NORTH, 32 50 78 100 111
NORTHAN, 119
NORTHROP, 86
NORTON, 77 82 83 89 110 118 122 142 143
NOTEMAN, 32
NOTESTINE, 67
NOTRUGE, 19
NOTT, 135
NOTTINGHAM, 46
NOUELMAN, 75
NOWELS, 73
NOWLAND, 53
NOX, 155
NOYES, 82 84 93
NOYS, 33 86
NUBEGAL, 96
NUBER, 122
NUBET, 106
NUERKER, 67
NUFFMORE, 115
NUGENT, 146
NUGIN, 39
NULAND, 75
NULTON, 135
NUMAN, 118
NUNENGAN, 15
NUNER, 48
NUNKEEPAR, 117
NUSON, 153
NUTT, 140 154
NUTTER, 109
NUTTLER, 109
NUTTS, 37
NYE, 4 42 52 77 86 88 90 98 107 142 145
O'BRIAN, 114

O'BRIEN, 53 140
O'DONALD, 73
O'HARA, 23
O'NEAL, 117
O'NEELE, 123
O'NEIL, 55
O'NIEL, 53
OAKMAN, 42
OAKWOOD, 73
OBED, 52
OBLINGER, 122
OBORN, 71
OBOURN, 152
ODBERT, 8
ODE, 111
ODELL, 20 26 74 155
ODLE, 16 32 47-49 96
OEMM, 124
OFFNER, 33
OFNEAR, 53
OGDEN, 38 45 51 61 86 93 104 115 117
OGDON, 138
OGEL, 126
OGEN, 125
OGG, 46 87
OGLE, 8 69 97 114
OGLER, 123
OGLESBY, 15
OILER, 19
OITER, 122
OLCOTT, 47
OLDEN, 74
OLDHAM, 17 47 123
OLDRID, 24
OLDS, 56 76-78 83 126 129 146
OLENDORF, 39
OLINGER, 80 127 129
OLIVE, 29 30
OLIVER, 60 109 122 123
OLMSTED, 84
OLNEY, 126 135 147
ONANSWEAT, 92
ONARWERT, 89
ONLEY, 151
OPDYCHE, 63

OPDYKE, 135 139
OPPY, 118 129
ORAHOOD, 18
ORBISON, 111
ORCHEY, 144
ORMSBURY, 110
ORMSBY, 89
ORN, 19
ORNDORF, 121
ORR, 9 38 48 59 76 80 100 101 104 114
ORSON, 61
ORTMAN, 47
ORWIG, 29
OSBORN, 4 6 7 40 50 78 89 94 99 103 105 110 111 113 122 141 144 146 148 150 156
OSBORNE, 79
OSBURN, 140 154
OSGOOD, 138
OSLER, 7 114
OSLIN, 127 138
OSMAN, 25 26 142
OSMUN, 71
OSTERHOUT, 32 78 116
OSTIN, 115
OSWAL, 109
OTINGER, 107
OTIS, 68
OTT, 48
OTTER, 25
OTTWELL, 46
OUNSBURY, 77
OUTLEY, 108
OVER, 131
OVERDEER, 65
OVERFIELD, 120
OVERHOLSER, 130
OVERHOLSTER, 133
OVERLY, 47 134
OVERMIEIR, 10
OVERMIRE, 28 66 98
OVERPECK, 127
OVERSTEEL, 13
OVIATT, 110 142
OWEN, 15 27 55 142

OWENS, 17 36 66 70 72 112 127
OWINGS, 87
OXFORD, 54
OZIAS, 112
OZMAN, 142
PACE, 82
PACK, 70 138
PACKERT, 94
PACKMAN, 6
PAGE, 22 26 75 80 108 120
PAGLE, 97
PAIER, 73
PAIGE, 120 141
PAIN, 32 34 58 77 82 84 150
PAINE, 76 87 141 156
PAINER, 106
PAINTER, 5 7 18 39 47 71 80 127 136 140
PAIR, 140
PAIRS, 7
PAKCER, 138
PALLMAN, 77
PALMER, 6-9 31 32 43 49 62 79 84 88 97 112 125 127 133 135 138 156
PANCAKE, 54 113 115 150
PANCOAST, 80 112
PANGBURN, 121
PANMITRE, 22
PANNER, 22 136
PARAMORE, 9
PARCEL, 115
PARCELS, 13
PARDE, 13
PARDO, 82
PARDY, 141
PARET, 69
PARIS, 16 24 77
PARISH, 17 37 55 93 107 113 117 140 153
PARK, 13 40 45 77 88 108 133 138
PARKER, 11 20 22 23 26 34 35 38 51 56 60 69 71-73 76 77 80 82 83-85 94 102-104 107 114 116 121 136 141 151-154 157
PARKERSON, 34 136
PARKHILL, 123
PARKHURST, 78 94 156
PARKINSON, 72 134 145

PARKISON, 148
PARKS, 7 19 45 47 50 100 130 134 156
PARMENTO, 79
PARMER, 155
PARMESTER, 37
PARR, 16 28 30 73 127
PARRATT, 99
PARRIS, 125
PARRISH, 13 67 143 145 151
PARROTT, 68
PARSCALE, 136
PARSON, 10 99 153
PARSONS, 46 61 77
PARTHER, 148
PARTLOW, 107
PARTON, 106
PASET, 99
PASMORE, 58
PASSMORE, 108
PATCHEL, 18
PATCHIN, 87
PATERSON, 108
PATES, 122
PATIN, 93
PATMAN, 89
PATON, 36
PATRICK, 78 79 81 86 88 90 91 116 126 134
PATT, 123
PATTEN, 18 22 23 25 31 37 38 62 91 123 136 152
PATTENS, 137
PATTER, 73
PATTERSON, 5 8 10 17 18 21 25 31 34 38 39 41 43 58 62 68 77 78 82 99 114 122 123 127-129 136 140 147
PATTON, 20 45 54 59 74 75 81 82 88 93 97 105 128 146 155
PAUGBURN, 11
PAUL, 33 63 108 135 150
PAULEY, 99
PAULL, 44 68 109
PAULLIN, 125
PAXTON, 60 77 154
PAY, 64
PAYEN, 100

PAYN, 29 37 152
PAYNE, 66 123
PAYON, 149
PAYQUES, 13
PAYTON, 112 152
PEACOCK, 140
PEAK, 57
PEALMAN, 48
PEARCE, 16 126 145
PEARE, 90
PEARGRIN, 69
PEARS, 90
PEARSON, 22 66
PEARSONS, 83
PEASE, 4 43 110 142
PEASLEY, 26
PEATT, 60
PEAUGH, 14
PEBBLE, 114
PECK, 9 12 66 83 123 133 146
PEEBLES, 101
PEEK, 59
PEESE, 143
PEGG, 50
PELFORD, 143
PELLY, 14
PELSON, 24
PELTON, 79 86 110 143 146
PELTS, 92
PELTZ, 89
PEMBERTON, 26 47 68 150
PEMIL, 116
PENCE, 50 95 98 128 147
PENDELL, 107
PENDERGRASS, 111
PENDRILL, 114
PENIX, 65
PENLAN, 117
PENNECOLT, 75
PENNEWITT, 24
PENNINGTON, 68 150
PENNIWIT, 24
PENNY, 50 83
PENO, 15
PENSE, 57 67

PENTICOST, 82 130
PENTY, 32
PENTZ, 60
PENY, 78 79 83 141
PEOPLES, 97 115
PEPPER, 51 100
PEPPUS, 98
PEREU, 113
PERFECT, 116
PERKEY, 66
PERKINS, 4 16 44 62 86 88 110 117 136 143
PERRELL, 154
PERRIL, 117
PERRINE, 121
PERRO, 40
PERRY, 8 12 13 21 23 38 56 60 78 79 100
  116 120 128 129 134 135 150 154
PERRY CO, 66
PERSON, 40 81
PERTEE, 96
PERVOLT, 96
PESSY, 10
PETERBAUGH, 13
PETERMAN, 77 89 92 97
PETERS, 27 32 46 52 96
PETERSON, 5 6 8 9 14 25 71 114 131 140
PETFISH, 100
PETITE, 35 111
PETITT, 60
PETMAN, 41
PETTIBONE, 97 105
PETTIBROOK, 97
PETTICORD, 64
PETTICREW, 58 128
PETTIEND, 15
PETTIJOHN, 20 21 50 93
PETTIT, 130
PETTITT, 71
PETTY, 15 28 53 57 96 101 108 126
PEVISE, 60
PEW, 76
PHEBUS, 52 54
PHELPH, 24
PHELPS, 13 19 51 63 79 84 87 110 146 157
PHERRIS, 138

PHERRON, 114
PHIBIS, 54
PHILIPS, 157
PHILLIP, 57 78 130
PHILLIPS, 8 12 14 17 34 46 58 64 74 83 87
    93 103 106 112 115 117 118 121 122 129
    130 134 144 148 151
PHILLIS, 36
PHIPPS, 78 107 116
PHLWEYN, 130
PHONTS, 77
PIATT, 71
PICK, 113
PICKAWAY CO, 52 57 96 115 145 152
PICKENS, 35 48 151
PICKERELL, 127
PICKERING, 16 98 125
PICKET, 13
PICKETT, 121
PICKLE, 37 121 130
PICKLES, 130
PIERCE, 32 35 36 40 47 49 53 57 63 71 72 82
    101 112 115 117 118 156
PIERSON, 12 22 65 131
PIGMAN, 60 70
PIKE, 108 132
PILCHER, 134
PILE, 25
PILLERS, 34
PILSON, 17 68 85
PIMCIONS, 27
PINCE, 28
PINCKNEY, 8 136
PINDAL, 93
PINDER, 146
PINE, 17 39
PINEWELL, 137
PINKARD, 145
PINKERMAN, 107
PINKERTON, 153
PINKLEY, 98 139
PINKSTATH, 14
PINNEL, 61
PINNEY, 32 156
PIPENGER, 8

PIPER, 67 118 134 137
PITKIN, 56
PITMAN, 13 16
PITSON, 141
PITTEGER, 5
PITTENGER, 10 31 46 131 147
PITTINGER, 5 10
PITTY, 26
PITZER, 4 43 86
PIXLEY, 43 147
PLACE, 57 61
PLATT, 72 113
PLATTER, 35
PLEASANT, 52
PLEISSIS, 5
PLICARD, 39 154
PLOTNER, 73
PLOTT, 18
PLOW, 39
PLOWMAN, 26
PLUM, 78 79 143
PLUMB, 23
PLUMER, 28
PLUMMER, 23 37 109 144
PLYMAN, 80 111
PLYMELL, 95
POAG, 112
POAGE, 120
POBST, 19
POE, 8 64
POFFINBERGER, 39
POGNE, 30
POKE, 72
POLEN, 60 117
POLING, 28
POLK, 44 45 135
POLLACK, 60
POLLAND, 49
POLLARD, 24 33 48 108 114 150 151
POLLOCK, 7 59 63 69 72 94 135 136 144
POLLY, 19
POLSEN, 59
POLSET, 100
POLSTEN, 53
POLSTIN, 53

POLY, 109
POMEROY, 90
POMEWELL, 106
POMROY, 90
PONCE, 14
PONCOTT, 41
POND, 56 97 142
PONDER, 123
PONENMYER, 14
PONTIOUS, 109
PONTIUS, 6 32 106 109
POOL, 8 53 76 77 80 98 99 126 133 139 140
POOR, 50 94
POPE, 19 58 105 127 141
POPEJOY, 18 57 80 99
POPENOE, 112
POPHAM, 7
PORK, 6
PORTAGE CO, 54-56 105 111
PORTER, 7 10 19 21 36 40 51 52 60 88 89 92 100 102 104 107 108 113 117 126 135 149 153
PORTERFIELD, 137
POST, 71 131 142
POSTLER, 55
POSY, 39
POTS, 132
POTSTON, 55
POTTER, 13 14 23 44 54 61 77 86 92 100 101 104 130 141 155
POTTERF, 38
POTTINGER, 121
POTTS, 7 8 40 57 62 100 117 138 148
POUCH, 62
POUND, 41
POWEL, 133 136
POWELL, 19 33 35 46 50 54 59 62 67 84 90 96 112 113 136 153 156
POWELSON, 34
POWER, 39 145 150
POWERMASTER, 49
POWERS, 5 34 54 57 69 78 82 94 99 102 110 125 140 142
POYENS, 78
POYERS, 109

PRATHER, 20
PRATT, 29 60 70 77 79 156 157
PREBLE CO, 132
PREDY, 133
PRENTICE, 77 101 151
PRENTISS, 89 93
PRESCOTT, 89
PRESSLER, 140
PRESSLEY, 99 132
PRESTON, 7 43 58 108 110 121
PREWIN, 154
PREWITH, 127
PRIBBLE, 66
PRICE, 4 13 17 19-21 34 40 41 43 62 66 80 83 86 109 114 118 120-124 126 128 133 134 138 151 152
PRICHARD, 8
PRICHERD, 152
PRICHERT, 93
PRICKET, 155
PRICKETS, 98
PRICKETT, 34 91 122 152
PRIDDY, 57 80
PRIEST, 23 73 101 104 126
PRILLAMAN, 100
PRILLMAN, 100
PRIMMER, 14
PRIMROSE, 65
PRINCE, 13 95 135 146
PRINGLE, 60
PRIOR, 88 110 140 142 145
PRITCHARD, 5 141 152
PROBUS, 119
PROCTOR, 82
PROEBSTER, 113
PROPECK, 90
PROSE, 50
PROTSMAN, 95
PROTZMAN, 37
PROUDFOOT, 66 73
PROVATT, 32
PROVOLT, 72
PROVOST, 123
PROVOTT, 45 46
PRUANT, 135

PRUDDEN, 78
PRY, 46 96
PRYER, 15
PTIMAN, 16
PUCKET, 26 74 108
PUCKETT, 107
PUDLE, 49
PUFUT, 146
PUGH, 6 29 79 96
PULLEN, 73
PULLY, 41
PULTNEY, 129
PUMMEL, 131 149
PUMPEY, 104
PUMPHREY, 9 139
PUNCHER, 10
PUNCHES, 33
PUNCHOS, 73
PUNN, 80
PUNTENNEY, 106
PUNTIUS, 10
PUNTNEY, 84
PURCELL, 11
PURCUSSELE, 138
PURDON, 21 93
PURDY, 13
PURSEL, 5 52 53
PURSELL, 65 75
PURTEE, 106 117
PURVIANCE, 84 116
PUTNAM, 153
PUTTHORF, 5
PYATT, 13 71 95
PYATTE, 16
PYKE, 24
PYLES, 23
QIRREY, 141
QUEEN, 16 49 124 136
QUICK, 104
QUIER, 56
QUIGGLE, 81 110
QUIGLE, 77
QUIGLEY, 4 13 135 147
QUILLEN, 6 9
QUILLIN, 11

QUIN, 6 63
QUINN, 8 68 87 106 133
QULN, 63
RABB, 135
RABER, 90
RABONET, 135
RABORN, 107
RABOURN, 106
RABOURNE, 149
RACE, 23
RADCLIFF, 53
RADCLIFFE, 52 55 116
RADER, 29 86 150
RADGSDALE, 125
RADISH, 91
RADLEY, 123
RADON, 14
RAGAN, 32
RAGER, 33
RAGERS, 93
RAGGER, 39
RAGISON, 9
RAGOON, 117
RAIDER, 75
RAILSBACK, 84
RAINEY, 7 70 72
RAINS, 48 152
RAINSE, 48
RAINSEY, 135
RAINY, 17
RAIR, 135
RAIRDE, 102
RALINGS, 154
RALL, 58
RALLER, 108
RALLSTON, 93
RALOLSON, 108
RALPH, 121
RALSTON, 6 9 61 129
RAMAGE, 78
RAMBO, 113
RAMER, 47
RAMMAGE, 13
RAMSEY, 7 10 15 18-21 36 47 51 56 63 65-67 112 114 119 131 132 135 146

RAMY, 117
RANDALL, 56 81 83 85 86
RANDAN, 26
RANDLE, 115
RANDOLPH, 7 8
RANER, 109
RANEY, 36 142
RANKAN, 99
RANKIN, 34 43 74 80 91 99 126 133 137 150
RANKINS, 26 111 152
RANKLE, 28
RANNELS, 67
RANSON, 97
RANUL, 135
RAPE, 130
RAPER, 42
RAPHY, 156
RAPP, 147
RARDIN, 26 104 119 155
RAREDON, 28
RARGER, 50
RASE, 130
RASEY, 47
RASH, 66
RATCLIFF, 48 64 96
RATCLIFFE, 121
RATH, 129
RATHBONE, 70 77
RATHBURN, 118 153
RATTLE, 136
RAULSTON, 68
RAVER, 98
RAVERS, 64
RAWL, 105
RAWLES, 94
RAWLEY, 89
RAWLINGS, 53
RAWLINS, 77
RAY, 6 31 37 38 43 47 56 58 64 71 74 93 94 97 103 105 124 134 135 140 156
RAYBOURN, 32
RAYBURN, 100 151
RAYDOR, 50
RAYEN, 69

RAYL, 134
RAYNOLDS, 9 60
RAZELL, 140
RAZIER, 49
REA, 96 127
READ, 16 48 93 129 145
READER, 18 34 80
READING, 6 105
REAGAN, 22 144
REAGEL, 37
REAGIN, 43 130
REAGLEN, 18
REAGON, 47 120
REAM, 58
REAMER, 17
REAMEY, 69
REAMS, 127
REAN, 27
REANY, 92
REASE, 48
REASONER, 69
REAT, 90
REAVES, 151
REBSTOCK, 85
RECOB, 35
RECORD, 93
RECTOR, 15 95
REDDEN, 56 80 96 111
REDDIN, 97
REDDING, 59
REDDISH, 138
REDENBAUGH, 12 58
REDER, 22
REDFERN, 48
REDFIELD, 105
REDICK, 63
REDING, 12
REDINGBAN, 12
REDINGER, 120
REDINOUR, 28
REDMAN, 24 143 149
REDMON, 86 114 155
REDMOND, 26 107 136
REE, 130

REECE, 44 61
REED, 8-11 13-15 18-20 26 28 33 38 41-43
    49 56 57 60 61 64 66 68 70 73 77 80-82
    89-94 96-98 103 106 110 111 114 117
    118 120 125 129-131 136 145 154-156
REEDER, 12 21 80 100 105 119
REEDS, 130
REEDY, 23 109
REEKARD, 71
REELS, 7
REES, 15 18 35 49 70 79 82 118 121 131
REESE, 8 64 118 151 153
REESLEY, 84
REEVE, 86
REEVES, 13 17 19 36 44 46 54 70 81 88 93
    102 106 114 122 149 153 157
REGAH, 104
REGAN, 47
REICKELDARFER, 32
REID, 21 23 33 57 66 91 95 109 134 147 151
    152
REIFER, 43
REILEY, 140
REILY, 140
REISLINGSON, 122
REISTER, 152
REIVES, 45
REIVS, 45
RELY, 28
REMINGTON, 89
RENESON, 66
RENICK, 42 52 57 153
RENKER, 155
RENNELS, 151
RENNESON, 137 137
RENNICK, 145
REPNER, 32
REPROGLE, 61
RERIGH, 126
RESENER, 72
RESLINGER, 49
RESON, 37
RESS, 59
RESWIN, 144
RETHN, 13

RETTER, 46
RETTINHOUSE, 59
REVENAUGH, 8 11
REVENOUGH, 11
REWES, 23
REWIS, 135
REX, 66 66
REYBORN, 151
REYBURN, 45
REYNALS, 152
REYNARD, 144
REYNOLD, 121
REYNOLDS, 6 11 14 16 21 24 28 39 40 42 44
    45 61 65 69 86 91 108 116 135 141 145
REYPHOLE, 49
RHAY, 153
RHEA, 45
RHIDEMEER, 135
RHIDENOUR, 49
RHOADES, 60
RHODES, 49 87 90 95
RHYMOR, 155
RHYNEARSON, 19
RIAL, 132
RIAN, 12 106
RICE, 13 14 44 45 50 62 85 100 107 134 142
RICH, 59 120
RICHARD, 67 133
RICHARDS, 9 22 31 51 57 60-62 66 71 80 91
    111 136 141 144 147
RICHARDSON, 4 6 10 12 17 26 33 40 41 44
    51 56 61 64 66 69 85 92 94 104 111 135
    142 143 152
RICHE, 67
RICHELDAIFER, 31
RICHERT, 148
RICHESON, 106
RICHEY, 7 12 15 92 123
RICHIE, 64
RICHISON, 11 67
RICHLAND CO, 97 115
RICHMOND, 35 102 105
RICHTER, 33
RICHTES, 134
RICHY, 62

RICKABAUGH, 50 50
RICKABOUGH, 155
RICKETTS, 98 140
RICKEY, 6 10 12 52 83 130
RICKNER, 73
RICORDS, 140
RIDAL, 97
RIDDEL, 9
RIDDICK, 147
RIDDLE, 4 11 62 64 68 111 137 139
RIDDLER, 119
RIDENHOUR, 14 90
RIDENOUR, 11 27 140 149 156
RIDER, 10 58 84 133 153
RIDGEWAY, 78 94 138 155
RIDGLEY, 50
RIDLAKE, 110
RIDLEN, 59
RIDLER, 12
RIDLEY, 51 100
RIDMAN, 115
RIDNOUR, 46
RIFFE, 133
RIFFLE, 128
RIGDON, 57
RIGGAN, 27
RIGGLE, 119
RIGGS, 22 24 37 38 81 99 114 149
RIGHT, 9 108 134
RIGHTLEY, 14
RIGHTMIRE, 104
RIGLEY, 29
RIKER, 12
RILEY, 8 10 15 22 25 29 38 55 58 68 112 115
    119 142 143 146 149 154
RIMION, 38
RINEAR, 10
RINEDSON, 59
RINEHART, 17
RINELY, 26 140
RINES, 134
RING, 110
RINGEN, 84
RINGER, 68
RINGLAND, 102
RINKER, 119
RINKIN, 32
RINLEY, 151
RION, 111
RIPE, 15
RIPLEY, 94
RIPPETH, 138
RIPPEY, 8
RIPPLE, 109
RIPROGLE, 61
RISHER, 138
RISK, 58
RISLEY, 90
RISNER, 40
RISNEY, 156
RISONER, 36
RISTEIN, 22
RISTINE, 93
RITCHEY, 8
RITCHHART, 53
RITCHIE, 96 137
RITCHY, 11
RITHARD, 45
RITTEN, 26 64
RITTENGER, 22
RITTENHOUS, 133
RITTENHOUSE, 122 133
RITTER, 6 8 9 11 13 49 152
RIVELY, 115
ROACH, 7
ROAD, 27
ROADAMOUR, 42 86
ROADANNOUR, 153
ROADARMOUR, 74
ROADENS, 18
ROADS, 18 48 49 108 113 114
ROANSEVELL, 111
ROBACK, 111
ROBB, 8 10 17 59 81 99 102 119 154 155
ROBBE, 18 58
ROBBEN, 87
ROBBINS, 21 24-26 44 66 67 84 97 111 131
    132 139 141 149
ROBBONS, 7
ROBBY, 57

ROBE, 27
ROBERSON, 126
ROBERT, 17 89
ROBERTS, 11 14 19 20 26 28 31 49 76 79 86 91 98 114 126 129 131 146 148 151 155
ROBERTSON, 7 10 12 40 65 72 90 107 118 137 138 154
ROBEY, 148 150
ROBINET, 102
ROBINS, 63 77 131
ROBINSON, 4 8 13 15 19 20 22 26 29 36 39 43 48 50-53 57 63 72 74 79 80 86 91 101 104 105 112 114 115 123 128 129 133-138 140-142 146 151 155
ROBINSTON, 75
ROBISON, 56 61 64 100 131 140 148
ROBNETT, 102
ROBY, 57
ROCE, 142
ROCHEFITER, 19
ROCK, 7 67
ROCKHOLD, 49 108 114 149 153 155
ROCKWELL, 82 83
RODABOUGH, 131
RODEBAUGH, 132
RODERICK, 79
RODES, 11 15 108 133
RODGER, 136
RODGERS, 20 25 43 49-51 55 69 80 92 97 100 106 111 112 117 124 125 133 136 142 144 147 151 154
RODWICK, 15
ROE, 16 75 140
ROEBUCK, 25 75 95
ROFF, 7 67
ROGAN, 40 48 115
ROGEL, 128
ROGEN, 106
ROGERS, 7 11 14 17 20 31 34 41 42 55 62 67 68 72 74-76 79 97 104 109 112 117 118 156
ROI, 140
ROIS, 89
ROLBUCK, 47
ROLINS, 82
ROLL, 78 94
ROLLER, 7 42
ROLLEUR, 9
ROLLINS, 23 51 111
ROLLSTON, 64
ROLSTON, 32 67 82
ROMAN, 59
ROMBO, 69
ROMINE, 51 55 64 115 127 151
RONEY, 119
ROODER, 151
ROODS, 28
ROOF, 34 36 41 58
ROOK, 33 89
ROOKER, 66
ROOP, 17 26 102
ROOS, 105
ROOSA, 20 21
ROOSE, 62 126
ROOT, 4 29 75 83 146
ROSABOOM, 151
ROSAL, 76
ROSBERRY, 138
ROSE, 29 37 41 66 68-70 76 77 89 92 95-97 101 109 112 129 142 156 157
ROSEBAUGH, 63
ROSEBERRY, 54
ROSEBOOM, 34 35 102 113
ROSEBROUGH, 18
ROSEBURG, 135
ROSECRANS, 79 116
ROSS, 7 9 11-13 16 19 20 23 35 39 41 44 45 48 49 50 52 54 58 60 65 66 69 72 74 94 95 97 100 102-104 107-109 116 119 121 122 130 133 136 141 148 152 154
ROSS CO, 12 16 18 21-23 34 35 40 44-49 51-54 64 75 80 87 91 92 94 96 101 107-109 113-115 117 118 127 134 135 141 147 149-155 157
ROSSEL, 63
ROSSELL, 136
ROST, 93
ROSWELL, 84 156
ROTH, 78
ROTHBURN, 81

ROU, 152
ROUDIBASH, 102
ROUGH, 7 62 131
ROUGHTON, 51
ROULES, 48
ROUNDS, 104
ROUNDY, 42
ROUNSAVELL, 81
ROUSE, 9 31 95 137
ROUSH, 31 75
ROUSON, 73
ROUT, 45 87
ROUTZEN, 7
ROUZER, 124
ROW, 10 13 15 53 80
ROWAN, 54 128
ROWE, 50 83 99 100 151
ROWELL, 15 44
ROWL, 32
ROWLAND, 62 64 68 107 150
ROWLESS, 47
ROWLEY, 105 114
ROWZER, 123
ROYCE, 98
ROYEE, 129
ROYER, 115 137
ROYES, 76
ROYSELL, 6
ROYSHER, 85
ROYSTON, 13
ROZELL, 80
RUBART, 13
RUBARTS, 104
RUBB, 18
RUBLE, 18 41 123
RUCK, 36 62
RUCKMAN, 154
RUDD, 83
RUDDICK, 48 64
RUDE, 21
RUDESELL, 47
RUDESILLY, 134
RUDINAN, 62
RUDOLPH, 28
RUDWILL, 7

RUE, 13
RUFFNER, 14
RUGG, 79 84
RUGHERFORD, 74
RUKE, 115
RUKESON, 137
RULEY, 9
RULY, 9
RUMAGE, 77
RUMMAGE, 92
RUMMEL, 17 109
RUMPLE, 95
RUNCLE, 46
RUNION, 12 111
RUNK, 74
RUNKIN, 80
RUNKLE, 28 116 128
RUNNELDS, 33
RUNNELS, 152
RUNYON, 15 91 118
RUPARD, 76
RUPE, 15
RUPERT, 135
RUPORT, 99
RUPP, 104
RUPPORD, 63
RUSAGE, 77
RUSE, 26
RUSER, 12
RUSH, 12 13 19 31 37 52 106 115 134 141 152
RUSK, 134
RUSSEL, 11 47 85 110 117
RUSSELL, 6 8 15 24 32 34 35 37 40 43 46 50 52 56 66 68 73 74 76 77 83 90 91 93 101 107 109 112 114 120 121 124 126 129 133 137 138 140 143 153
RUSSLE, 29 106
RUST, 101 122
RUTAN, 67
RUTHERFORD, 72 74
RUTLEDGE, 4 6 17 85 88 118 151
RUTTER, 41 72 138
RYAN, 12 58 82 92 99 104
RYASON, 106

RYCRAFT, 123
RYDER, 35 74
RYNEARSON, 40
RZON, 94
SABIN, 55
SABINE, 55
SACKET, 89 110 142
SACKETT, 17 100 143
SACKHOUSE, 59
SACKWOOD, 59
SADDLER, 53
SADLER, 35
SAFFORD, 4 42 86
SAGE, 44
SAILOR, 105 124
SAIMNONS, 9
SAIN, 29 67
SAINT, 8 97
SAINTCLAIR, 53
SAINTCLEAR, 14
SAINTJOHN, 19
SAINTMUELS, 109
SALADA, 46 150
SALADAY, 105
SALARTS, 10
SALE, 123
SALISBURY, 46
SALLADA, 105
SALLADAY, 105
SALLADY, 46
SALLEE, 68 121
SALLSBURY, 23
SALMAN, 123
SALMON, 17 80 111
SALOR, 70
SALSBERRY, 124
SALTERS, 52
SALTINGSTALL, 15
SALTMAN, 5
SALTS, 16 47 49
SALTSGIVER, 70
SALTSMAN, 5
SALTZMAN, 5
SAMCOCK, 63
SAMES, 21

SAMPLE, 35 68 80 115 126
SAMPLES, 33
SAMPSON, 12 33 40 91 154
SAMS, 115
SAMSON, 19
SANBACH, 141
SANBURN, 59
SANDERLIN, 10 126
SANDERS, 12 36 68 95 98 100 112 122 131
SANDERSON, 31 71 99 103 107 148 156
SANDS, 25 122 138
SANER, 62
SANFOSS, 10
SANKEY, 7
SANOR, 7
SANTEE, 34
SAPEINS, 109
SAPINGTON, 152
SAPP, 5 115 139
SAPPINGER, 148
SAPPINGTON, 116
SARGENT, 15 20 22 40 57 61 114 128 154
SARSH, 38
SARTMAN, 14
SATERFIELD, 70
SATHERLAND, 116
SATHREN, 41
SATTERFIELD, 108
SATTERLEE, 141
SATTERLY, 116 132 148
SAUFT, 28
SAUL, 11
SAUNDERS, 34 80 100 120 124 149
SAVAGE, 22 31 55
SAWARD, 54 99
SAWTELL, 56 83
SAWYER, 36 58 71 72 97 99 107 122 123
SAXON, 106
SAXTON, 78 94 153
SAYLOR, 32 106
SAYRE, 58 72 112 118
SCADAN, 69
SCAMAN, 48
SCAMEHORN, 38
SCARTLER, 114

SCHELBERRY, 131
SCHENCK, 37 42
SCHILLINGER, 114
SCHOLES, 7 9 10
SCHOOLER, 72
SCHOOLEY, 61
SCHOOMOVER, 11
SCHOUMAN, 155
SCHOVEY, 79
SCHRODER, 122
SCHULTZ, 7 62
SCIOTO CO, 23 26 30 33 46 103 105 113 129 148 150
SCISCO, 43
SCOBY, 76 116
SCOFIELD, 50
SCOGGANS, 41
SCOGIN, 40
SCOT, 29
SCOTT, 9 11 16 17 21 23 24 29 36 38 41 45 48 50 52 54 58 60 61 63 67-69 76 80 86 87 89 93 103 108 109 117 123 127 129 130 132 133 135 137 145 147 149-153
SCOVIL, 88
SCOVILL, 83 86
SCOVILLE, 124 141 142
SCRIBNER, 15 82 83 129 133
SCROGGS, 10 140
SCROUFE, 155
SCUDDER, 57 59
SCUDER, 40
SCURLOCH, 153
SEABOURN, 115
SEABRELL, 140
SEABRING, 71
SEAMAN, 21 59 124 141
SEAMON, 130
SEAMORE, 53
SEARFAS, 32
SEARS, 55 112
SEATH, 117
SEATON, 17
SEAVERS, 113
SEBASTIAN, 77
SEBERELL, 116
SEBERN, 76
SEBRET, 24
SEBRING, 15 79 105 134
SECHRIST, 19
SEDAN, 148
SEDBALL, 138
SEDGWICK, 39 130
SEEDS, 55 92
SEELYE, 97
SEFFEL, 127
SEGAR, 91 95 127
SEGERT, 26
SELBY, 81
SELDEN, 140
SELEY, 56
SELL, 49 73 77 89 92
SELLARS, 121
SELLER, 21
SELLERS, 30 107 123 125 149
SELLEY, 145
SELLS, 55 72 85 133
SELLWOOD, 59
SELOY, 135
SELVEY, 125
SENFF, 47
SENIOR, 19
SENNEL, 157
SENOR, 156
SENT, 139
SENTER, 114
SENTMIRE, 130
SERDAN, 156
SERGANT, 87 91
SERGEANT, 46 87 154
SERGENT, 144
SERVER, 126
SERVISS, 119
SESSIONS, 124
SETH, 128
SETON, 38
SETTLEMYRE, 144
SEVERELL, 47
SEVERINGHAM, 129
SEVERS, 51 53 144 156
SEWARD, 12 17 18 35 59 60 99 102 131

SEWEL, 96
SEWELL, 46 117
SEWILL, 39
SEWISON, 9
SEY, 61
SEYBRING, 60
SEYLOR, 80
SEYMORE, 16 50
SEYMOUR, 16 49 55 141
SHACKELFORD, 85
SHACKLES, 95
SHACKLY, 60
SHADDAK, 138
SHADDOCK, 16
SHADLEY, 58 60 71 73 138 156
SHADRICK, 93
SHADWICK, 27 156
SHAFER, 6 31 134 139
SHAFFER, 6 9 21 37 58 101 122 128 140 141 144 153
SHAGLEY, 48
SHALE, 10
SHALER, 124
SHALL, 91 144
SHAMBAUGH, 106
SHANAMAN, 102
SHANE, 69 116 134 138 140
SHANEMAN, 17
SHANG, 64
SHANGLER, 148
SHANK, 54 130 148
SHANKE, 136
SHANKS, 68 91 98 112 124 125
SHANNON, 40 41 74 83 117 131 145 149
SHANOR, 92 113
SHANTON, 52 143
SHANTZ, 66
SHAPARD, 15
SHAPPELL, 61
SHARARD, 97
SHARD, 108
SHARK, 138
SHAROERTZ, 95
SHAROHAN, 19
SHARON, 92

SHARP, 22 26 44 52 63 71 72 78 84 86 108 120 125 127 129 138 153 155 156
SHASTEEN, 153
SHATTO, 69
SHATTS, 78
SHAUGLER, 96
SHAUL, 91
SHAVER, 31 48 101 120
SHAW, 6 18 19 21 22 24 27 35 37 40 49 54 58 61 63 72 74 82 83 100 115 118 119 121 124 125 142 152-154
SHAWBER, 6
SHAWBRAD, 57
SHAWHAN, 59 73
SHAWHANEY, 105
SHAYLOR, 56
SHAYNEFELT, 106
SHEAFE, 123
SHEAFFER, 14
SHEAFOR, 40
SHEANAR, 156
SHEANIKS, 58
SHEARER, 58
SHEARS, 156
SHED, 138
SHEDERLY, 39
SHEDMICK, 50
SHEEBR, 9
SHEEHAN, 8 63
SHEET, 19
SHEETS, 58 59 62 63 67 135 136 152
SHEFER, 31 37
SHEFFIELD, 111
SHEILDS, 52
SHEINBARGER, 62
SHEKAN, 126
SHELAH, 108
SHELBY, 6 28 106 154
SHELDON, 88 101 143
SHELEY, 120 131 148
SHELL, 123 124 133 144
SHELLHOUS, 93
SHELLINGER, 120
SHELLY, 130
SHELPMAN, 26

SHELTON, 23 130
SHELTS, 155
SHEMMELL, 138
SHENARD, 60
SHENEFELT, 97
SHENKLE, 38
SHENTAFFER, 52
SHEPARD, 17 27 41 52 53
SHEPARDSON, 136
SHEPHARD, 41 70 74 86 115 122 128
SHEPHERD, 6 9 21 23 34 35 41 42 45 61 75 82 99 100 106 107 133 141 153
SHEPLER, 40
SHEPLEY, 114
SHERARD, 37 73
SHERICK, 17
SHERLEY, 53
SHERLOCK, 101 116
SHERMAN, 70
SHERRARD, 71
SHERRY, 60
SHERWIN, 40
SHERWOOD, 37
SHETLER, 112
SHEVALIER, 114
SHEVEL, 70
SHEW, 82
SHEWALD, 39
SHEWMAKER, 25 49
SHIANG, 131
SHICK, 59
SHIDAKER, 123
SHIDELER, 37
SHIDELES, 44
SHIDLER, 44 66 116
SHIELDS, 17 19 38 49 54 62 78 92 102 126 141 153
SHIERS, 66
SHIEVER, 42
SHIFELTON, 89
SHIFFER, 138
SHIGHT, 144
SHILLINBARGER, 104
SHILLING, 36 39
SHILLINGER, 122

SHILTON, 22
SHINER, 24
SHINGLE, 121
SHINGLEDECKER, 13
SHINGLER, 39 72
SHINN, 25 39
SHIPLEY, 69 70
SHIPMAN, 16 41 55 137 146
SHIRELY, 23 114 133
SHIRER, 28
SHIRLEY, 53 64
SHIRLOCK, 149
SHIRTS, 63 135
SHISLER, 24 31
SHISSON, 62
SHIVEL, 69
SHIVELEY, 11 96
SHIVELY, 97 130
SHIVER, 135
SHIVERS, 63
SHIVY, 102
SHOAF, 100
SHOAT, 37 57
SHOCKEY, 95
SHOCKLEY, 141
SHODE, 14
SHOE, 112 120
SHOEMAKE, 52
SHOEMAKER, 6 14 18 51 52 78 86 102 103 106 112 113 116 141 151
SHOLENBERGER, 27
SHOMAN, 119
SHOOK, 62 63 83 94
SHOOL, 102
SHOOMAKER, 111
SHOOP, 27 68 139
SHOP, 139
SHOPE, 14 23 23
SHOPPELL, 106
SHOPWELL, 42
SHORB, 62
SHORT, 51 57 62 67 71 99 122 155
SHOTS, 119
SHOTWELL, 73 122 137
SHOU, 138

SHOUP, 71 73 78 96 156
SHOUPE, 23
SHOURD, 59
SHOUTS, 53
SHOVE, 70
SHOVER, 79 128 146
SHOW, 66 79
SHOWDEN, 153
SHRAYER, 82
SHREEVES, 57
SHREVE, 93 152
SHREVES, 55
SHRIEKENGUST, 47
SHRIMP, 71
SHRIVER, 48
SHROFE, 91
SHROKLEY, 53
SHRON, 145
SHROUP, 156
SHROW, 93
SHROYER, 81
SHRUH, 26
SHRYOCK, 73
SHUCKMAN, 40
SHUEY, 11 12 130
SHUFELTON, 89
SHUFF, 115
SHUKEY, 44
SHUKLEY, 143
SHULL, 66 77 86 90 97 102 125
SHULTS, 68 149
SHULTZ, 62 68 97
SHUMAKER, 108
SHUMAN, 69
SHUMANION, 61
SHUMARD, 102
SHUMP, 104
SHUNK, 67 132
SHUNKWEILER, 23
SHUPE, 40 156
SHUR, 115
SHURR, 97
SHURRAN, 61
SHURTZ, 73
SHUTE, 46

SHUTTLEWORTH, 147
SHYHAWK, 156
SHYPOWER, 156
SIBART, 15
SIBBIT, 154
SIBERT, 95
SIBRAL, 122 134
SICKMAN, 70 127
SIDELS, 144
SIDENBENDER, 47 48 96
SIDFEN, 112
SIDNEY, 76
SIEROT, 116
SIGLER, 49
SIGMAN, 104
SIGNAR, 28
SIGNER, 23 35 140
SIKE, 97
SIKES, 23 105
SILAMAN, 88
SILBEE, 129
SILERS, 27
SILEY, 59
SILLIVAN, 106
SILLMAN, 21
SILLS, 15 95
SILSBY, 123
SILVER, 38
SILVERS, 41 73
SILVERTHORN, 82
SILVIS, 16
SIMCOCK, 135 143
SIMEN, 61
SIMES, 26 45 126
SIMESON, 133
SIMKINS, 32
SIMMERMAN, 38 104
SIMMERS, 129
SIMMINS, 43
SIMMONS, 6 9-11 16 32 37 65 107
SIMMS, 51 127 151
SIMON, 89 104
SIMONNE, 153
SIMONS, 7 24 71 77 78 92 120 131
SIMONTON, 38 66 135

SIMPKINS, 104 145
SIMPSON, 11 17 27 37 53 76 85 92 99 101
    119 124 134
SIMSON, 138
SIN, 39
SINBARY, 140
SINGER, 38 85 112
SINGLETARY, 110 111 143
SINKIN, 60
SINN, 25 107
SINNARD, 12 19
SINNORS, 17
SINOR, 156
SIPE, 12 13 97
SIPES, 118
SIPLE, 28
SIRK, 90
SISCO, 58 106
SISERSAN, 57
SISK, 34
SISSIONS, 6 107
SITTLER, 139
SITZER, 118
SKEDMAN, 121
SKEELS, 10 32 82 84 116
SKELTON, 6 136
SKIDMORE, 7 38 55
SKILINGE, 87
SKILLILAND, 129
SKILLMAN, 102
SKILLS, 156
SKINNER, 12 21 35 39 42 55 56 72 76 84 137
SKIPTON, 15
SKOLLS, 156
SKOUTEN, 34
SKULL, 138
SLACK, 78 79 116 131 146 148
SLAGLE, 42 72 130
SLAIBACK, 94
SLANE, 45
SLATE, 129
SLATER, 35 70 105 114 115 126
SLAUGHTER, 15 18 21 46 53 122 136 150
SLAVEN, 96
SLAWSON, 107 122

SLAYBACK, 138
SLAYBOCK, 58
SLAYBROOK, 4
SLEETH, 128
SLEGLE, 128
SLETER, 114
SLIDER, 154
SLIEZEMAN, 72
SLOAN, 44 99 112 121
SLOO, 72
SLOOP, 123
SLOPER, 79
SLOSSEN, 64
SLOVER, 88
SLUTHOWER, 73
SLUTHRIN, 138
SLY, 102 127
SMALEY, 63
SMALL, 20 112
SMALLEY, 20 57 108 147
SMALLIE, 155
SMALLWOOD, 68 96 146
SMALLY, 20
SMALWOOD, 42
SMART, 145
SMEDLEY, 107
SMEED, 47
SMELT, 145
SMELTZER, 36
SMETTS, 136
SMILEY, 17 45 75 137
SMITH, 6-17 20 21 23-26 28 29 31-35 37-44
    46 48-56 58-68 70-86 88-91 94-108 111
    112 114-137 139 141 143-146 148 150
    151 153-156
SMITHER, 131
SMITHSON, 31 113 149
SMITTEL, 20
SMOLLY, 75
SMOOT, 8 19 59
SMOTHER, 73
SMTIH, 72 95
SMUTHERS, 79
SNEDAKER, 21
SNEDAKERGER, 21

SNEDECOR, 23
SNELBEKER, 82
SNELL, 38
SNELLING, 13
SNIDER, 7 9 67 76 102 112 117 122 136
SNIDIKER, 13
SNIFF, 35
SNILLBECKER, 102
SNIP, 129
SNODDY, 125
SNODGRASS, 36 42 96 120 133
SNOOK, 40 59 105
SNOOKE, 19
SNOOP, 59
SNOW, 56
SNOWDEN, 98
SNUFF, 19 59
SNYDER, 21-23 38 48 49 67 73 89 99 101 102 119 130 151 155
SOCKRIDER, 33
SODDEN, 96
SODORIS, 102
SODOURS, 74
SOEY, 62
SOLEDY, 28
SOLINGER, 112
SOLOMON, 9
SOLSEL, 20
SOMEN, 43
SOMERVILLE, 99
SOMMERS, 117
SOMS, 26
SONAB, 37
SONGER, 124
SOOY, 136
SORDAN, 134
SOUP, 33
SOUTH, 39 121 122 154
SOUTHARD, 37 76
SOUTHVIORD, 96
SOUTHWORTH, 56
SOUTHWORTT, 110
SOWARDS, 80 111
SOWDER, 96
SOWERS, 90

SPACHT, 8
SPAIGHT, 112
SPANGLER, 27 32 36 72 96 152
SPANGLEY, 68
SPARGO, 77 89 92
SPARKES, 22
SPARKS, 85 87 120 127 150
SPARR, 28 69
SPARROW, 91
SPARY, 46
SPAULDING, 142
SPEACE, 95
SPEAKER, 7
SPEAKMAN, 64
SPEARE, 42
SPEARS, 108
SPEARTH, 8
SPEARY, 103
SPEDLE, 137
SPEED, 6 135
SPEEDY, 10
SPEER, 70
SPEERE, 138
SPEES, 106
SPEIR, 139
SPELLMAN, 50 56 142
SPELMAN, 10 16
SPENCE, 38 44 135
SPENCER, 16 18 38 40 42 50 54 58 60 61 77 82-84 90 99 118 123 131 134 140 143 155
SPENDER, 151
SPENG, 137
SPICER, 110 140 143 152
SPIDEL, 10
SPIDLE, 64 97
SPIDY, 10
SPIEDLE, 27
SPIELLE, 68
SPIERS, 26
SPIES, 28
SPIG, 104
SPIKEN, 9
SPIKER, 9 10 85
SPIKES, 113
SPILLHOUSE, 86

SPILLMAN, 70 142 152
SPILMAN, 142
SPINNING, 61 105
SPINY, 102
SPIRGIN, 104
SPIRLING, 40
SPITLER, 19
SPITSTONE, 124
SPIVEY, 131
SPLITSTENE, 86
SPOHN, 28 67 139
SPONG, 23 47 64
SPONGE, 25
SPOONER, 43 82 83
SPOONY, 89
SPORES, 96
SPPONER, 56
SPRADER, 90
SPRAGG, 123
SPRAGS, 41
SPRAGUE, 67 104 128 146
SPRANGLER, 137
SPRAY, 101
SPREY, 15
SPRINGER, 28 32 54 61 93 121 126 131 152
SPROOT, 57
SPROUL, 59 66
SPROULE, 106
SPROWL, 112 117
SPRY, 91 97 98 136 156
SPUCE, 129
SPURGEON, 45 115 137 139
SPURGIN, 36
SQUIRE, 40 143
SQUIRES, 56 84 100
SRAIN, 69
SRANFR, 11
SREAK, 127
SROPH, 114
SROUF, 87
SROUPE, 87 125
STACEY, 110
STACKHOUS, 126
STAFFORD, 31 45 76 103 124 155
STAGG, 76

STAGGS, 113
STAGLE, 37
STAGNER, 35
STAIMATES, 24
STAIN, 5
STAKE, 43 78
STALCUP, 154
STALL, 27 32 48 77 92 134
STALLY, 14
STALO, 125
STANBERRY, 18 26 50 84
STANBROUGH, 18
STANBURY, 17
STANBY, 44
STANFAR, 99
STANFORD, 15 142 144
STANHOLT, 94
STANHOPE, 47
STANLEY, 15 33 56 69 89 112 117 145 147
STANTON, 40 151
STAPLETON, 45 121
STAR, 116 124
STARETT, 36
STARK, 17 78 129
STARK CO, 62
STARKE, 126
STARKER, 36
STARKES, 122
STARKEY, 15
STARKHAM, 46
STARN, 5
STARNER, 104
STARNS, 59
STARR, 38 43 44 48 74 76 133 141 145 146
STATE, 89
STATELAR, 50 141
STATELU, 16
STATEN, 11
STATLER, 120 130
STATLOE, 73
STATON, 22
STAYNER, 106
STEADY, 80
STEARNES, 40
STEARNS, 19 93

STEART, 13
STEDLER, 100
STEDMAN, 44 107 135 157
STEEL, 22 26 27 59 66 67 73 94 95 99 101 103 125 142
STEELE, 17 41 58 87 95 97 112 123 128 155
STEELY, 52
STEEN, 53
STEENBARGER, 128
STEENROD, 72
STEER, 10
STEETH, 129
STEGALL, 135
STEIN, 109
STEINS, 17
STEIR, 28
STEIRS, 61
STELL, 17 138
STELLA, 16
STELLAR, 16
STENER, 67
STENT, 127
STEP, 55
STEPELTON, 95
STEPHEN, 17 93 106 132 157
STEPHENS, 4 11 17 22 29 36 39 41 42 47 49 57 60 61 62 63 67 72 73 79 89 95 97 103 104 106 108 112 117 118 122-124 126 128 136 140 149
STEPHENSON, 4 13 14 17 24 26 29 42 55 70 75 86 87 94 96 100 103 109 111 114 126-131 137 144 150 153
STERBAUGH, 102
STERETT, 125
STERLING, 12
STERNS, 58
STERRETT, 87 124
STERWART, 13
STETHERN, 24
STETLER, 100
STETS, 59
STEUDEVANT, 78 79
STEVEN, 6
STEVENS, 7 9 10 60 97 140
STEVENSON, 32

STEVERS, 21
STEVESON, 65
STEWARD, 13 16 26 78 96 97 111 116 145 146
STEWART, 4 6 7 13 16 19 22 26 29 39-41 44 45 49 54 60 61 68 73 82 87 90 92 94 96 97 101 102 104 109 113 115-120 123 127 131 134 135 137 145 150 152
STIARWOLT, 55
STICKLER, 24
STIDGER, 62
STIERS, 69 70 134
STIFLOR, 101
STIGALL, 141
STIGALLS, 116
STILES, 19 58 59
STILL, 18 44
STILLEY, 144
STILLMAN, 31 89 110
STILLY, 6 145
STILSON, 92 146
STILT, 45
STILWELL, 13 72 77
STIMMEL, 32
STINCHCOMB, 120
STINE, 40 61 131
STINGLEY, 18 140 147
STINGLY, 145
STINSON, 45 47 64 69 149
STIPO, 144
STIPP, 154
STIPS, 36
STIRES, 94
STIRWOLT, 55
STITES, 70 102 112 128 144
STITTER, 132
STITTS, 129
STITWELL, 104
STIVERS, 26
STIVESON, 57
STOAKES, 9 10
STOAKS, 9
STOCKARD, 68
STOCKER, 138
STOCKHAM, 105

STOCKSTILL, 120
STOCKTON, 34 51 54 101 114 117 148 153
STOCKWELL, 13 24 82
STODER, 152
STOGDON, 99
STOKE, 152
STOKER, 58
STOKES, 6 121 127
STOLL, 151
STOLTZ, 28
STONE, 40 54 66 68 82 84 89 97 104 106 112 117 137 142 151 153
STONEBAGER, 128
STONEBAKER, 40
STONEBRAKE, 17
STONEBRAKER, 94
STONEBRING, 27
STONECOCK, 106
STONER, 15 62 64 66 69 126
STONES, 89
STOOKEY, 18 113 131
STOOT, 44
STORAY, 114
STORER, 24
STOREY, 25 89 125
STORM, 15 78 94 109 153
STORMS, 24 100
STOTHARD, 113 143
STOTS, 131
STOTTEN, 123
STOTTS, 30 39 73 90 104
STOUDER, 102
STOUT, 24 36 40 66 68 76 80 82 89 91 101 109 114 118 125 129 139 154
STOUTEN, 34
STOUTER, 140
STOVER, 9 10 36 46 62 69 103 136
STOW, 50 56 89
STOWDEN, 137
STRADER, 18 38 112
STRADLEY, 15
STRAIN, 9 10 17 18 20 23 25 32 53 93 111 128 129 145 147 155
STRAIT, 156
STRALL, 7

STRALLER, 156
STRANBARGER, 95 120
STRANBAUGH, 40
STRAND, 45
STRANE, 93
STRANGE, 116 139
STRASER, 109
STRATHER, 87
STRATLER, 156
STRATON, 114
STRATTAN, 34
STRATTON, 56 76
STRAW, 23 49 112
STRAWSER, 96
STRAZER, 109
STREATOR, 56
STREET, 61 68
STREEVEY, 113
STREEVY, 152
STRETCH, 128
STREVEY, 134
STRICKLAND, 39 62 83 102 136
STRICT, 150
STRINGER, 127
STRIPE, 104
STRIPER, 14
STRIPES, 73
STROAPH, 93
STROBE, 104
STROMAN, 19
STRON, 56 66
STRONG, 28 42 82 87 89 97 104 110 115 123 129 142
STRONIE, 19
STROPE, 108
STROSSER, 23 23
STROTHERD, 51
STROUD, 44 135
STROUFVER, 23
STROUP, 49 141
STROUSE, 152
STRUBEL, 81
STRUCY, 134
STRUTHERS, 93
STRWY, 35

STUART, 4 38
STUCE, 25 71
STUCKMAN, 46
STUDEBAKER, 130
STUDEVANT, 116
STUDIBAKER, 85
STUDILAKER, 65
STUDIMAN, 99
STUDY, 138
STUICK, 122
STULL, 92 122
STULT, 27
STULTZ, 27 33 49 92
STULZ, 49
STUMBLE, 113
STUMBOUGH, 113
STUMP, 31 37 94 131
STUMPBOUGH, 145
STUNTZ, 83
STUPE, 28
STURD, 144
STURGEON, 28 47 50 74
STURLIN, 111
STURN, 134
STUSE, 10
STUTCH, 80
STUTHARD, 34
STUTTERBACH, 23
STUTTS, 155
STUTZ, 11
STYERS, 98
STYPMAN, 13
SUDDICK, 65
SUDERFIELD, 108
SUGNER, 103
SUITER, 46
SUITOR, 103
SULLAVEN, 127
SULLERBACK, 134
SULLIVAN, 7 9 17 46 61 67 68 102 114 115 134 145
SULLIVANT, 152
SULY, 42
SUMALT, 43
SUMEY, 93

SUMMER, 19 141
SUMMERMAN, 113
SUMMERS, 46 84 117 127 156
SUMMERSET, 45 47 52
SUMNER, 18 113
SUMPTION, 85 133
SUMTER, 13
SUNDERLAND, 37 65 66 104 119 124 128 156
SUPER, 44
SURAN, 154
SURFACE, 144
SURRALS, 147
SUTEN, 59
SUTHARD, 27 96
SUTHERLAND, 23 89
SUTLIFF, 56 86 142
SUTPIR, 130
SUTTERFIELD, 75
SUTTON, 4 6 17 19 36 37 40 41 43 50 59-61 71 73 84 86 97 109 112 120 122-125 133 140 150 154
SUZART, 37
SWACKHAMNAR, 69
SWADLEY, 18 155
SWAGER, 78 88 89
SWAGGART, 11 106 152
SWAGGERT, 10 134
SWAILES, 111 123
SWAIM, 148
SWAIN, 43 48
SWALLOW, 12
SWAM, 9 145
SWAMBY, 9
SWAMM, 103
SWAN, 109 154
SWANE, 49
SWANEY, 112
SWANGER, 95
SWANGLE, 6
SWANK, 38 57 72 136
SWANNY, 53 126
SWANZY, 140
SWARD, 13
SWARDLEY, 136

SWARING, 65
SWART, 126 130
SWARTS, 24
SWARTWOOD, 42 66
SWARTWORD, 85
SWARTZ, 19 31 147
SWATSWELER, 81
SWATSWELLER, 88
SWAZER, 109
SWEARENGEN, 31
SWEARINGEN, 101 155 157
SWEARINGER, 127
SWEARINIGEN, 63
SWEENEY, 18 59 130
SWEENY, 102
SWEET, 11 15 82 92 124 142 143
SWEETT, 74
SWEGART, 39
SWEGERT, 92
SWERINGEN, 154
SWETLAND, 79
SWICKARD, 5
SWIFT, 82
SWIGAR, 68
SWIGART, 10 62 104
SWIGERD, 112
SWIGG, 107
SWIHSER, 65
SWILER, 71
SWILES, 14
SWIM, 8 38 138 153
SWIN, 7 58
SWINDLER, 137
SWINE, 140
SWINEHART, 67 137 138
SWING, 39
SWINNEY, 140
SWISHER, 15 18 33 84 114
SWITER, 71
SWITZER, 7 46 62 67 97 136 150
SWORDS, 150
SWORE, 139
SWOY, 136
SWYER, 127
SYMNES, 155
SYMONDS, 37
SYMONTON, 105
SYMS, 95
SYPHERS, 107
TABER, 57 90 95
TAFT, 94 146
TAGART, 63
TAGERT, 126
TAGGART, 43
TAGGERT, 137
TALBERT, 69 124
TALBOT, 69 83 141
TALBURT, 139
TALLIFERRO, 104
TALLMAGE, 139
TALMAGE, 115
TALOR, 13 60
TAMER, 67
TAMPLIN, 127
TANGANARY, 52
TANGBER, 154
TANGNARY, 53
TANNER, 35 55 94 128 130
TANNYHILL, 104
TANQUARY, 48
TANSEY, 108
TAPLIN, 40
TAPPEN, 82
TARBOSS, 129
TARBUTTON, 60 95 144
TARNILL, 88
TARRANCE, 28
TARRBUTTON, 60
TARRENS, 119
TARRIER, 74 133
TASELMAN, 21
TATE, 35 111
TATMAN, 38 129
TAWEY, 46
TAWNYHILL, 139
TAYLER, 147
TAYLOR, 4 6 9 15 17 36 38 40 45 49 50 53 56-59 61 64 65 67-69 72 78-80 86 90 91

TAYLOR (continued)
    93-95 97-99 101-104 108 111 116 118
    123 124 127 131 134 135 137 138 140
    141 146 148 149 153-156
TEABOULT, 40
TEAGARDEN, 11 33
TEARMAN, 58
TEEDELL, 129
TEETER, 35
TEETERS, 6
TEETLEY, 123
TEETS, 26
TEGARDSON, 98
TEMPLAIN, 113
TEMPLAR, 37
TEMPLE, 143
TEMPLETON, 59 123
TEMPLIN, 15 147
TEND, 67
TENEBAUGH, 117
TENET, 10
TENNANT, 66
TENNENT, 133
TENNET, 42
TENTS, 109
TERAL, 53
TERREL, 56 72
TERRELL, 141
TERRENCE, 112
TERRET, 53
TERRIS, 56
TERRY, 35 40
TERWILLEGAR, 20
TESLER, 156
TEST, 125
TETER, 149
TETRICK, 70
TEVIS, 38
TEWELL, 45
THARP, 9 15 57 90 91 94 99 101 106 118 137
    155
THARTAN, 99
THARTP, 118
THATCHER, 19 24 58 75
THAYER, 103

THEBUS, 46 96
THERMAN, 18
THERMON, 20
THILLYER, 70
THIMONS, 117
THIRBY, 18
THIRMAN, 53
THMPSON, 13
THOMAS, 12 18 20 21 26 29 32 34 39 40 55
    57 59 62 67 70 76 77 80-82 90 93-96 102
    104 108 111 115 116 118 125 126 129
    135 138 144 146 153
THOMBURGH, 117
THOMPSON, 4 6 7 9 10 12 14 15 17-24 31-
    34 37-41 47 48 51 53-55 57 59 62-64 67
    70-77 79-81 84-86 90 95 96 98 100-107
    110 112-114 118 121 123 125-127 131
    133 135 136 138 139 143 144 146 149-
    151 154
THORMAR, 141
THORN, 51 78 100 107 130
THORNBAUGH, 97
THORNBERRY, 44 124 125
THORNBILL, 12
THORNBURGH, 122
THORNBURY, 122
THORNE, 7
THORNILEY, 14
THORNLEY, 14 15
THORNLY, 43
THORNSBURG, 111
THORNTON, 18 25 60 105 147 155
THOROMAN, 95
THORP, 41 46 56 84 93 156
THORRINGTON, 81
THRAILKIELD, 101
THRALL, 50 70 101
THRASH, 29
THROCKMORTON, 10 109
THROERT, 35
THROGMORTON, 23 32
THURMAN, 25
THURSH, 140
THWEEKS, 117
TIBBS, 66

TIBELGHEIN, 39
TICKNER, 142 143
TIDBALL, 138
TIDD, 26 72 86
TIERMAN, 144
TIFFIN, 86 101 151
TIGARD, 17
TIGLE, 58
TILFORD, 100
TILL, 10
TILLATSON, 125
TILSON, 99
TIMINS, 143
TIMMARDS, 37
TIMMENS, 151
TIMMERS, 96
TIMMINS, 141
TIMMONDS, 116
TIMMONS, 51 54 68 75 76 80 100 113 117 140 152
TIMONS, 48 51 76 96
TIMOTHY, 12
TIMPLIN, 51
TINCKLE, 132
TINDLES, 59
TINGEL, 59
TINGLEY, 9 13 121
TINKER, 83 86
TINKEYS, 58
TINNIS, 72
TIPMAN, 12
TIPTON, 7 9 11 15 53 68 101 126 155
TISE, 14
TISON, 15
TITES, 125
TITSWORTH, 102
TITTLE, 118 144
TITUS, 9 141 144
TIVEL, 11
TIVERS, 152
TOBIN, 5
TODD, 13 32 87 119 120 124
TODHUNTER, 140
TOFFLENOYER, 95
TOFT, 50

TOLBAT, 69
TOLBERT, 14 58
TOLBIT, 66
TOLER, 149
TOLLAND, 84
TOLLAR, 40
TOLLIA, 42
TOLLMAN, 33
TOMLEY, 39
TOMLIN, 25
TOMLINSON, 33 47 150
TOMLISON, 150
TOMPSON, 49 53
TOMTIZ, 36
TON, 63
TONG, 72
TONLINSON, 48
TOOHINDER, 18
TOOMER, 95
TOOTLE, 51
TOOTS, 52 53
TOPPE, 9
TOPPEN, 64
TOPPIN, 84
TORBET, 14 52
TORRANCE, 73
TORRENCE, 36 40 82
TOTTEN, 37
TOUGHMAN, 92
TOUSLEY, 110 119
TOWELL, 36
TOWERS, 108
TOWNSEND, 12 122
TOWNSLEY, 12 77 87 90 91 124 125
TRACEY, 50 81
TRACY, 94 99
TRADER, 111
TRALL, 89
TRANEN, 10
TRASEY, 7
TRAVICE, 103
TRAVIS, 33 95 108 117
TRAXIER, 23
TREBER, 108
TREGO, 45 47

TREHERAN, 54
TRELAND, 18
TRESCOTT, 89 110
TREVINGER, 156
TREWITT, 101
TREY, 33
TRIBEY, 81
TRICKER, 19
TRIFORD, 77
TRIGGS, 152
TRIMBLE, 4 5 19 43 58 59 94 98 100 155
TRIMBLY, 104
TRIMLY, 104
TRIMMER, 103
TRINDLE, 78 146
TRINKLE, 149
TRION, 37
TRIPE, 131
TRIPPY, 63
TRISLER, 138
TRIVET, 49
TROBRIDGE, 71 126
TROOVINGER, 28
TROP, 44 155
TROTH, 49
TROTTER, 71 114
TROUPE, 25
TROUT, 14 24 29 98 122
TROUTWINE, 43
TROVINGER, 27
TROWBRIDGE, 54
TROWSDALE, 121
TROXEL, 100
TROXELL, 54
TROY, 96 125
TRUAX, 16 38 139
TRUBEE, 13
TRUBER, 34
TRUBY, 13
TRUCKMILLER, 9
TRUDLE, 19
TRUE, 135
TRUESDALE, 93
TRUEX, 13
TRUKLE, 39

TRULINGER, 106
TRULLING, 96
TRUMAN, 99
TRUMBLE, 17
TRUMBULL CO, 77 92 94 109
TRUMP, 19 59
TRUMPH, 131
TRUNKEY, 88
TRUSDALE, 93
TRUSDILL, 88
TRUSEDALE, 56 86 93
TRUSNER, 24
TRYBACK, 33
TUBB, 102
TUBBS, 83
TUBLE, 42
TUBOSS, 83
TUCHBONE, 71
TUCKER, 24 32 36 37 43 58 75 91 99 112
    115 117-119 135 136 147 151 156
TULBE, 72
TULK, 36 127
TULLASS, 50
TULLER, 76 82 129
TULLES, 146
TULLEY, 97
TULLINGER, 84
TULLIS, 32 40 100
TULLY, 53 109 113 114
TUMBLESON, 119
TUMMAN, 52
TUNDERBURG, 43
TUNELL, 141
TUNKS, 91 95
TUNTTIGER, 21
TUPPER, 4 110 143
TURBEE, 84
TUREL, 127
TURK, 110
TURLY, 71 96
TURMAN, 19
TURNER, 33 56 57 69 77 89 92 94 104 105
    107 110 113 122 124 125 129 134 140
    142 146 150 152 153
TURNEY, 84

TURNIPSEED, 9 92 113 136
TURREL, 105
TURRELL, 34
TUTHILL, 34 85 105
TUTLER, 19
TUTTLE, 13 19 40 45 47 48 54 58 58 72 74
  76 86 89 91 107 124 129 144
TWADDLE, 58
TWADEL, 79
TWADLE, 156
TWAY, 92
TWEED, 38
TWEEDY, 123
TWEET, 48
TWIG, 29
TWIGG, 107
TWIMPSEED, 62
TWITZER, 101
TYAN, 140
TYFFE, 57
TYLA, 136
TYLER, 34 60 61 79 141 155 156
TYLERS, 82
TYLOR, 129
TYRELL, 86
UARTZ, 10
UHRICK, 138
ULM, 47
ULN, 47 48
ULNEY, 26
ULOOLLEY, 43
ULP, 81
ULYATT, 146
UMMPHREYS, 50
UNDERWOOD, 26 97 105 128
UNGREN, 37
UPDEGRAF, 9
UPDEGRAFF, 58 64
UPDEGRAFT, 10
UPP, 60 71
UPSON, 55 143 145
UPTON, 77 89 92 110
USHER, 71
UTT, 23 66 112 116 151
UTTER, 154

VAIL, 38 58 102 138 142
VAINUM, 36
VALE, 52
VALENTINE, 118
VALLEQUETTE, 109
VALLHYNING, 142
VALTERS, 8
VAMOY, 41
VAN, 45
VANA, 55
VANAARSDAL, 117
VANALLA, 14
VANAMBURGH, 91
VANAMON, 74
VANANDE, 74
VANARD, 124
VANARTSTEEN, 138
VANASDEL, 128
VANASDOL, 42
VANBENKTON, 112
VANBIBBEN, 7
VANBLARECOM, 23
VANBLAUGHER, 99
VANBUCKERK, 108
VANCATON, 87
VANCE, 36 40 41 50 52 54 57 85 104 112
  120 124 133 145 146
VANCHORCK, 58
VANCLEAF, 156
VANCLEF, 102
VANCLEVE, 41 42
VANCULTZ, 91
VANCURIN, 59
VANDAMARK, 90
VANDAMEN, 140
VANDEMARK, 13 29
VANDENBENDER, 153
VANDENBENEN, 74
VANDENSAN, 134
VANDERMAN, 28 113
VANDERMARK, 140
VANDERMART, 14
VANDERVOURT, 102
VANDERWOLT, 34 35
VANDERWORT, 38

VANDEY, 27
VANDINE, 74
VANDORN, 10 147
VANDUZEN, 93
VANEATEN, 120
VANEATON, 119
VANEMAN, 120
VANEMBAUGH, 16
VANER, 142
VANEST, 149
VANETER, 41
VANFOSSEN, 16 16
VANGARDEN, 143
VANGEMBEY, 48
VANGUNDIE, 96
VANHAT, 118
VANHINING, 142
VANHOENE, 5
VANHOOK, 123
VANHOOT, 26
VANHORN, 7 42 68-70 97 115
VANHORNE, 5 60
VANHYNING, 110
VANLEER, 61
VANLOON, 116 129
VANMATER, 31 99 108 141
VANMATRE, 108 141 149
VANMETER, 91 109 117 146 156
VANMETRE, 71 107 134
VANN, 99
VANNATA, 28
VANNATTATE, 28
VANNEY, 156
VANNIETER, 53
VANNORMAN, 77
VANNOTT, 58
VANNULE, 108
VANOSDOLE, 122
VANOSDOLL, 139
VANOTT, 100
VANPELL, 70
VANPELT, 24 75 105
VANRINORT, 33
VANSARSDOL, 104
VANSATTA, 28

VANSCOYK, 66
VANSCOYKE, 119
VANSCOYOE, 57
VANSCOYS, 128
VANSE, 118
VANSENT, 155
VANSHULTZ, 153
VANSICKLE, 40 60
VANSKIKE, 19 133 144
VANSKOGK, 99
VANSKOY, 48
VANTILBURGH, 6
VANTINE, 46
VANVEAL, 34
VANVEY, 110
VANVICKEL, 32
VANWAGGONER, 115
VANWEY, 126
VANWICKLE, 117
VANWIKLE, 15
VANWINCK, 71
VANWINKLE, 39
VANWY, 137
VANWYE, 89
VANZANT, 25
VARNER, 44 45 154
VARNON, 131
VASER, 33
VAUGHAN, 15 44
VAUGHN, 9 45 76 81 102 120 129 136 141
VEACH, 40
VEAIL, 32
VEAL, 102
VEALE, 99
VELIOGALL, 32
VENAMOR, 94
VENARD, 133 155
VENCAMP, 65
VENEMAN, 78
VENOY, 141
VENSON, 34
VEOGE, 32
VERDEN, 154
VERDIAR, 45

VERDIN, 53 71
VERDON, 33
VERNAM, 36
VERNARD, 18
VERNON, 38
VESTAL, 76
VESTLE, 96
VEZEY, 134
VIAL, 94
VIDITE, 82
VIGUS, 107
VINADGE, 131
VINAGE, 40
VINCEN, 152
VINEY, 90
VINEYARD, 135 144
VINGARD, 59
VINING, 79
VINNING, 82
VINSON, 45 106 109
VINTON, 83
VINYARD, 128
VIQUS, 108
VIRDEN, 60 104
VIRGIN, 57
VISTEL, 53
VOGLE, 13
VOID, 125
VOLAND, 28
VOLNS, 32
VONTORER, 33
VOORHEES, 21
VOORHINS, 40
VOORHIS, 12 19
VORHEES, 61
VORHES, 59
VORHIS, 59
VOSE, 146
VOWEN, 59
VOX, 83
VOYT, 136
VROYD, 133
VUBS, 9
VULGEHOTT, 15
WABLETON, 19

WACE, 126
WADDELL, 16
WADDLE, 16 68 69 76 80 147
WADE, 26 38 45 57 72 75 99 108 119
WADSWORTH, 4
WAGAMAN, 122
WAGAMEN, 58
WAGG, 28
WAGGAMON, 57
WAGGNER, 66
WAGGONER, 21 25 26 33 58 73 85 116 127 129 136 144 145
WAGGONNER, 39
WAGNER, 27 58 99
WAGONER, 11 13-16
WAIBT, 27
WAID, 86 86 110
WAIDLAW, 42
WAITE, 55 73
WAITES, 42
WAITS, 42
WAKELAND, 19
WAKEMAN, 86
WAKINS, 74
WALBOURNE, 129
WALCOTT, 110 142
WALCUTT, 110
WALDEN, 40 56 78 107
WALDER, 89
WALDO, 143
WALDON, 110
WALDORF, 22 81 86
WALDORFF, 124
WALDRAN, 150
WALDREN, 16
WALDRER, 49
WALDRON, 75 96
WALFORT, 55
WALGAMURTH, 138
WALKER, 8 10 15 16 20 38 42 51 54 88 91-93 95 100 101 104 106 110 115-117 126 130 140 142 145 150 151 156
WALKLY, 82 89
WALL, 25 63 72 97 126 154

WALLACE, 9 10 19 22 23 35 40 43 45 47 48
    61 71 72 79 90 91 101 104 107 112 123
    124 129 156
WALLACH, 59
WALLARD, 14
WALLASTON, 128
WALLEN, 82
WALLER, 17
WALLIN, 123
WALLING, 47 134 150
WALLINGFORD, 144
WALLIS, 24 40 129
WALLS, 35 69 105 135
WALRAVEN, 67
WALSH, 153
WALSUR, 104
WALT, 44
WALTBURN, 87
WALTER, 31 67 102 106 109 139
WALTERS, 14 36 36 41 42 83 93 118 131
    138 156
WALTON, 10 109 138 141 152
WALTZ, 15
WALVERTON, 155
WANAUGHMAKER, 115
WANICH, 70
WANWEY, 14
WAPLES, 115
WARBINGTON, 39
WARD, 4 17 18 21 27 29 41 48 50 52 55-57
    61 66 69 72 73 76 84 87 91 97 104 105
    118 119 121 128 129 146 153
WARDEN, 43 48 61 139 145
WARDER, 136
WARE, 16 59 100 140
WARFIELD, 100
WARING, 72 121
WARLINE, 23
WARNE, 70
WARNER, 5 14 33 54 56 67 68 83 97 101 124
    127 133 137 141 146
WARNOCH, 34
WARPENBAY, 67
WARRELL, 66

WARREN, 13 59 78 80 96 107 135 150
WARREN CO, 94 100 122 149 154
WARSON, 71
WARTS, 18 133
WARWICK, 80
WASHBORN, 24
WASHBURN, 11 20 26 49 61 93 125 149
WASHINGTON CO, 14 71 95 126 135 147
WASLEY, 75
WASON, 20
WASSIN, 60
WASSON, 38
WASTON, 105
WATE, 105
WATERFIELD, 61
WATERMAN, 44
WATERS, 17 19 44 107 116 135
WATERSON, 72
WATKIN, 84
WATKINS, 7 33 41 45 59 98 132 137
WATROUS, 82
WATS, 34
WATSON, 6 10 17 19 28 33 36 38 48 51 54
    60 61 63 64 74 82 85 87 88 91-94 97 101
    104 108 112 119 120 124 125 127 129
    131 133 139 143-145 151 154 156
WATT, 46
WATTENS, 36
WATTON, 128
WATTS, 53 69 99 111 145 153
WAUGH, 13 50 149
WAY, 8 69 143
WAYMAN, 30
WAYNE, 87
WAYY, 45
WEAD, 47 65 132
WEAIN, 19
WEAK, 108
WEAL, 15
WEAR, 19
WEARE, 58
WEATHERHEAD, 65
WEATHERINGTON, 55 134
WEAVER, 10 19 28 57-59 60 61 66 71 74 84

WEAVER (continued)
   99 120 128 131 147 156
WEBB, 13 34 36 54 58 62 65 85 88 114 120
   130 133 140 143
WEBER, 67 85
WEBSTER, 19 26 48 68 77 83 84 90 109 111
   140
WECH, 134
WECKHAM, 44
WEDMORE, 49
WEEDEN, 16
WEEKLEY, 132
WEEKS, 37 40 59 76 78 79 116
WEER, 40
WEESE, 35
WEETART, 48
WEEVER, 15
WEIDER, 23 46 47 109
WEIKIGER, 101
WEILY, 147
WEIR, 39 40 44
WEISER, 32
WEIZER, 137
WELCH, 8 10 15 37 38 53 83 95 114 146 148
WELDAY, 9 11 67 137
WELIT, 78
WELKER, 63 67 104 115 136 139
WELKIN, 10
WELKINS, 148
WELLER, 69 102
WELLS, 5 15 18 27 30 35 40 67 69 70 90 94
   95 104 114 116 130 131 135 139 140 142
   150 153 154 157
WELSH, 6 37 48 60 61 71 79 83 99 119 129
   136 137 146 149 154
WELSHAUS, 156
WELSHHOUS, 73
WER, 100
WERELEY, 146
WERNER, 43
WESCOTT, 32
WESH, 29
WESHAMER, 27
WESLEY, 64
WESLING, 37

WEST, 5 7 10 13 15 16 21 25 46 53 94-96 117
   123 124 126 137 138 140 144 154 155
   157
WESTBAY, 86
WESTBROOK, 24
WESTENBAEGAR, 14
WESTERFIELD, 39 104
WESTERN, Reserve 156
WESTFALL, 4 13 41 42 57 58 76 80 111 119
   130 132 133 140 143 144
WESTHOFER, 85
WESTLAKE, 41
WESTON, 145
WETHER, 107
WETMER, 28
WETMORE, 146
WETTY, 138
WEVER, 44 79
WEYER, 5
WEYRICK, 139
WHALEY, 24
WHALON, 133
WHAN, 82
WHARTON, 38 103
WHEALER, 27
WHEATLEY, 75 156
WHEATON, 34 114 117
WHEDOM, 43
WHEELAN, 39
WHEELAND, 47
WHEELER, 5 6 15 27 46 50 56 79 81 84 88
   97 97 104 119 123 125 126 132 143 148
   150 152 156
WHEITZELL, 31
WHERRY, 41 152
WHETMORE, 82
WHETSEL, 32 118
WHETSON, 71 80
WHETSTONE, 18 59
WHEY, 93
WHICKEAR, 22 100
WHICKER, 36 120
WHILAVRE, 99
WHISLER, 32
WHITACRE, 37 63

WHITAKER, 10 90 101 104 123 131 133 142
WHITCOMB, 21
WHITE, 7 9-12 14 20 23-25 32 34 38-40 43
    49 50 52 55 59 61 64 68 69 71-73 76-78
    80-82 84 86 87 89 90 92-94 96 97 103
    107 109-111 115 119 120 123 124 126
    129 132 134-136 140-145 147 148 150
    151 152 155-157
WHITECALE, 64
WHITEHOUS, 90
WHITEHOUSE, 29
WHITELEATHER, 7
WHITELOCK, 13
WHITEMAN, 21 128 134
WHITEN, 65
WHITERIDE, 21
WHITERS, 79
WHITERSELL, 58
WHITESEL, 91
WHITESELL, 31 38
WHITESIDE, 132 148
WHITEZELL, 92
WHITFORD, 32 79
WHITLEY, 20 20
WHITMORE, 8 63 123 135 144
WHITNELL, 65
WHITNEY, 65 97 135
WHITSEL, 130 152
WHITSELL, 21 89 115 133
WHITSEN, 71
WHITSIDE, 21
WHITTAKER, 99 155
WHITTEN, 50
WHITTENGER, 79
WHITTERSBEY, 78
WHITTESAY, 102
WHITTLE, 147
WHITTLESEY, 4 57 143
WHITZEL, 118
WHITZELL, 31
WHORTON, 142
WIAND, 27
WIBRIGHT, 80
WICK, 77
WICKART, 17

WICKE, 99
WICKERLY, 127
WICKERSHAM, 7 62 105
WICKERT, 7
WICKLE, 66
WICKMAN, 45
WICKOFF, 25
WICKS, 80
WICKSON, 105
WIDER, 82
WIDNER, 39 48 82 83
WIELAND, 85
WIER, 106
WIGGINS, 82 96 99 117
WIGHTEMAN, 93
WIKE, 136
WIKKEL, 19
WIKOFF, 75 149
WILAND, 13 102
WILCOCK, 34
WILCOX, 12 53 56 76 77 79 83 84 90 102
    110 129 142 153
WILCOXEN, 26 71
WILCUT, 151
WILDBAN, 31
WILDICK, 67
WILES, 12 149
WILEVER, 17
WILEY, 14 40 41 52 53 57 64 80 100 106 117
    118
WILFONG, 47
WILKEN, 31
WILKERSON, 17
WILKES, 20 155
WILKIN, 10 20 31 104 123
WILKINS, 9 10 30 48 67 70 126 130
WILKINSON, 31 38 40 47 58 59 68 72 119
WILKISSON, 48
WILL, 33 117
WILLARD, 84 102
WILLCOCKS, 34
WILLCOXEN, 26
WILLENMEYER, 33
WILLENMYER, 151
WILLER, 21

WILLETS, 31
WILLETT, 101
WILLETTS, 32 43 124 153
WILLEY, 40 89 92 133
WILLFONG, 64
WILLIAM, 10 27 34 36 37 40 53 70 79 80 135
WILLIAMS, 11-13 16 18 19 22 25 26 29 33-37 41-44 46 48-51 53 55 57 58 60 64 66 69 71 72 74-76 79 82 84 85 87 89 90 91 93 95 97 98 100-102 104-108 110 111 113-123 127 133-136 138 140 142 143 147 151-154 156
WILLIAMSON, 5 20 24 26 29 32 59 68 72 93 101 106 114 121 122 138 146
WILLIARD, 105
WILLIAS, 29 130
WILLIBEY, 63
WILLIBY, 9
WILLIMAN, 85
WILLIMAS, 124
WILLINGTON, 64 67
WILLIS, 15 30 39 51 57 59 61 91 102 137 143
WILLITS, 6 31 63 73
WILLITTS, 136
WILLOUGHBY, 47 134
WILLS, 24 38 104 142 144 152
WILLSBY, 9
WILLYARD, 56
WILMOT, 56 141
WILMOTH, 122
WILMOTT, 56
WILMOUTH, 106 123
WILRICK, 37 69 70
WILSON, 4 12 13 15 17 20-23 25 27 28 32 34 36 38 40 41 43 44 46 48-50 53 54 59-61 63-65 67-71 73 76 78 79 81 84 87 89-93 95 98 99 103 107-110 112-114 116-118 120 122 125-131 135 137 142 146 147 149 150 152 153 155-157
WILYS, 142
WIMANS, 103
WIMP, 69
WINANS, 65 78

WINAS, 67
WINCHEL, 157
WINCHIT, 29
WINDALL, 140
WINDER, 25 95
WINDERS, 90
WINDLE, 76 89
WINDPAN, 16
WINDRYER, 22
WINDSLOW, 132
WINDSOR, 56
WINE, 70 108
WINEGARDNER, 130
WINFAUGH, 47
WING, 119 145
WINGATE, 4
WINGET, 87 129
WINGETT, 33
WINGFIELD, 10
WINICH, 117
WINIMS, 31
WININS, 89
WINIS, 32 136
WINKELOCK, 102
WINKLEY, 148
WINLAND, 96
WINLIN, 10
WINN, 40 107
WINNER, 39 60 66 71
WINNINGS, 57 137 144
WINNISON, 12
WINSED, 37
WINSEL, 145
WINSET, 55
WINSETT, 76 104
WINSON, 105
WINSOUGH, 48
WINTER, 19 20 50 71
WINTERMATE, 77
WINTERS, 15 28 47 118 119
WINTERSLAM, 73
WINTERSTEIN, 33
WINTHROP, 58
WINTIN, 152
WINTRINGER, 22

WIRACK, 70
WIRE, 45
WIRGENT, 38
WIRICK, 69
WIRT, 107
WIRTZ, 63
WISBER, 47
WISBEY, 44
WISBY, 152
WISE, 123 152
WISECAMERE, 131
WISECARVER, 36
WISECAWERE, 4
WISECOOP, 49
WISEHART, 124 153
WISELY, 13
WISEMAN, 62 69 136
WISHART, 53
WISNER, 152
WIST, 104
WISTBAY, 25
WITHCUTT, 64
WITHERSELL, 58
WITHROW, 68 83
WITMOER, 32
WITT, 137
WITTEN, 126
WITTERS, 42
WITTS, 110
WITTY, 99
WIZE, 10
WLLS, 38
WOISTELL, 9
WOLARS, 121
WOLCOTT, 36 89
WOLD, 48
WOLF, 11 12 14 19 24 26 32 37-39 42 47 48
    52 62 79 86 92 99 104 112 115 120 125
    129 130 134 136 147
WOLFF, 11 60 120
WOLFFLY, 156
WOLFLY, 152
WOLFORD, 18 46 69 82 105
WOLLAM, 63
WOLLASTON, 128

WOLLEN, 136
WOLLENTON, 152
WOLLOUGHBY, 47
WOLMS, 8
WOLVERTON, 4 72 106 119 143 144
WOMACKS, 21
WOMELDORF, 4 155
WONSOY, 18
WONSTAFF, 140
WOOD, 5 11 24 42-45 48 60 64-67 70 75-77
    82 84 86 102 104 119 121 122 130 133
    135 137 140-142 147 150 152
WOODALL, 140
WOODBICK, 70
WOODBOURNE, 120
WOODBRIDGE, 69
WOODBURN, 57 124
WOODCOCK, 123
WOODEN, 83
WOODFIN, 17
WOODHOUSE, 130
WOODMAN, 42
WOODRING, 105
WOODROW, 104
WOODRUFF, 37 38 43 61 88 92 103 115 120
    121 131 145
WOODS, 5 9 17 21 23 97 114 130 131 141
    150
WOODSWORTH, 54 156
WOODWARD, 36 55 85 87 89 97 101 104
    110 112 127 142 145
WOODWORTH, 39 86 112 124
WOOLAM, 136
WOOLCOTT, 110
WOOLCUT, 35 78
WOOLEY, 39
WOOLF, 18 62 113
WOOLFE, 128
WOOLFORD, 77
WOOLSEY, 47
WOOSTER, 141
WOOTEN, 153
WOOTERS, 12
WOOTS, 149
WORK, 38 69 71 137

WORKMAN, 6 41 72 76 99 103 126 155
WORLE, 66 85 106
WORLEY, 9 45 117 128 136
WORLINE, 32
WORSHEN, 38
WORSON, 25
WORSTELL, 11 22
WORTERS, 86
WORTHINGTON, 52 76 100 137
WORTMAN, 21
WORTZ, 58
WOSTER, 139
WOTRING, 29 90
WOVERSTON, 143
WREN, 91
WRENCH, 83
WREY, 104
WRIGHT, 5 16 18 20-23 25 26 29 31 33 38-
    40 43 44 46 54 58 59 63 64 68-74 76 77
    79 82 84 89-91 93 95 99 105 106 110 112
    114 118 121 122 124 125 132 133 135
    140 151 156
WRIST, 67
WRITTER, 33
WROTEN, 51
WYANT, 97 134
WYATT, 65 78 83 110 129 142
WYCKOFF, 21 34 64 114
WYCOFF, 85
WYEKOFF, 107
WYER, 52
WYKOFF, 43 96
WYLAND, 13
WYNE, 121
YAGER, 106
YAREN, 149
YARLAN, 139
YARNAL, 81
YARNELL, 64 96
YATES, 6 13 22 50 53 54 74 82 95 149 153
YAZEL, 12
YEAGER, 57
YEAKEY, 47 48
YEAKY, 47
YEALDHALL, 7

YEANIN, 63
YEAR, 8
YEARIAN, 139
YECKNE, 137
YELMAN, 86
YEOMAN, 97 105
YERDEN, 81
YERIAN, 13 16
YETMAN, 88
YIELHALL, 10
YILLOCK, 144
YINGLING, 46 103
YOAKIN, 4
YOCUM, 53
YODER, 36
YOKE, 41
YOKEY, 45
YOMAN, 104
YONEL, 84
YONTES, 65
YOOBS, 7
YORGER, 49
YORK, 40 84 99 102 106 133
YOST, 13 109
YOUNG, 5 11 14-16 18 20 24 25 28 34 37 52
    54 56 57 59 61 67 75 77 78 89 90 94 97
    99 100 101 106 115 116 123 129 130 138-
    140 147 148 156
YOUNGER, 38
YUTSLER, 15
ZAINS, 132
ZANE, 15 72
ZARBIT, 13
ZEANER, 63
ZEAR, 8
ZEARING, 31
ZEAZEL, 133
ZEDECKER, 92
ZEDERCHAI, 78
ZEHRUNG, 96
ZEIGLAR, 17
ZEIGLER, 16 156
ZEISTER, 52
ZELLER, 37
ZERIL, 88

ZERING, 32
ZIEGLER, 98
ZIGNEN, 28
ZIMMER, 106
ZIMMERMAN, 32 59 62 68 82 129 139 156
ZINN, 139
ZIPLER, 156

ZOLLY, 135
ZOOTMAN, 28
ZOPS, 52
ZUMALT, 121
ZUTHINGER, 135
ZUVER, 97
ZWERNER, 58

www.ingramcontent.com/pod-product-compliance
Lightning Source LLC
Chambersburg PA
CBHW062007220426
43662CB00010B/1264